Footp
North

Dave Winter
1st edition

The mountain-side is simply a stone wall standing up 10,000 feet. Below is a river called Sint u-ho [Indus]... We proceed by a hanging rope bridge and cross the river".

Fa-Hien, 5th century AD Chinese traveller.

Northern Pakistan Highlights

See colour maps at back of book

1 Islamabad
Islamabad's magnificent Faisal Masjid is one of the world's largest mosques

2 Rawalpindi
Have a real South Asian shopping experience in the Rajah Bazaar

3 Peshawar
Visit the Old City for a genuine frontier-town feeling

4 The Khyber Pass
Take a romantic steam train journey to this legendary mountain pass

5 The Hindu Kush
Delight in the unique trekking opportunities at the heart of this exhilarating range

6 The Shandur Pass
Watch the sport of kings, polo, as it was always meant to be played

7 Phandur and Khalti Lake
Visit some of Pakistan's most jaw-dropping scenery

8 Chilas
Get a sense of history by viewing the stunning rock art

9 Nanga Parbat
The world's ninth highest mountain

10 Baltoro Glacier
One of the best trekking routes in the world takes you to Concordia and K2

11 Deosai Plateau
Landscape is on a massive scale in this uniquely beautiful area

12 Shigar and Khapulu
These picturesque villages showcase centuries-old mosques and Khanquahs

13 Minapin
Sit pool-side in a flower-filled garden in Minapin, and gaze up at the mighty Rakaposhi

14 Rakaposhi Base Camp Trek
One of Pakistan's easiest treks to see the great mountain Rakaposhi up close

15 Baltit Fort
Superbly renovated and with stunning views across the valley

16 Ganesh
Enjoy a little bit of living history and culture at the restored heart of the village

17 Hussaini Bridge
Experience heart-stopping moments crossing the 'Indiana Jones'-like bridge

18 Kara Kuli Lake
One of the KKH's most beautiful spots

19 Kashgar
A great introduction to Central Asia at this town's famous Sunday market

Contents

Introducing
Northern Pakistan 9

Essentials
Planning your trip 12
Where to go 12
When to go 14
Language 15
Finding out more 15
Before you travel 17
Visas 17
Money 26
Touching down 27
Getting around 31
Sleeping 36
Food and drink 37
Entertainment 39
Festivals and events 39
Shopping 43
Sport and activities 44
Trekking 45
Health 55
Common problems 56
Further information 61
Keeping in touch 62

Guide

Islamabad and Rawalpindi
Ins and outs 68
Islamabad 70
Listings 74
Rawalpindi 83
Listings 85
Rawalpindi/Islamabad to Peshawar 92
Listings 94

Peshawar Valley and Chitral Valley
Peshawar and around 99
Listings 109
Peshawar to Chitral 117
Listings 121
Chitral Valley 123
Listings 138
Kalash Valleys 132
Listings 138
Upper Chitral 140
Listings 147
Chitral to Gilgit 148
Listings 160

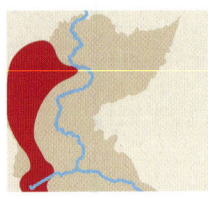

The Karakoram Highway: Hazara to Gilgit
Hazara 166
The start of the Karakoram Highway 167
Listings 172
Kaghan Valley 175
Listings 181
Indus Kohistan 184
Listings 190
Diamar District 192
Listings 205
Gilgit District 208
Listings 221

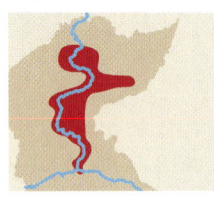

Baltistan
Skardu 235
Listings 239
The Deosai plateau 244
Shigar River Valley 248
Listings 254
Khapulu 255
Listings 258
Hushe Valley 259
Listings 264

The Karakoram Highway: Lower Hunza to Gojal
Lower Hunza and Nagar 2 268
Listings 277
Central Hunza 279
Listings 281
Karimabad 282
Listings 285
Around Karimabad 290
Listings 298
Nagar 1 300
Listings 304
Gojal (Upper Hunza) 305
Listings 313
Shimshal Valley 315
Listings 319
Chapursan Valley 319
Listings 324

Once off the main road, you may find that the narrow, rocky gorge that seems to go nowhere suddenly opens out into a broad, inhabited valley, such as 'hidden' Shimshal. See page 315.

The Karakoram Highway: Sust to Kashgar

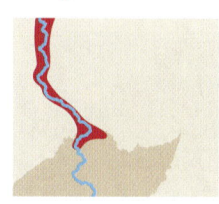

Sust and the Khunjerab Pass	328
Listings	334
Into China	336
Listings	343
Kashgar and beyond	345
Listings	352

Background

History	358
Culture	368
Land and environment	374
Books	378

Footnotes

Useful words and phrases	382
Urdu	382
Burushaski	385
Wakhi	385
Shina	386
Balti	386
Khowar	387
Kalasha	387
Food glossary	388
Index	390
Map index	394
Map symbols	395
Complete title listing	396
Credits	398
Acknowledgements	399

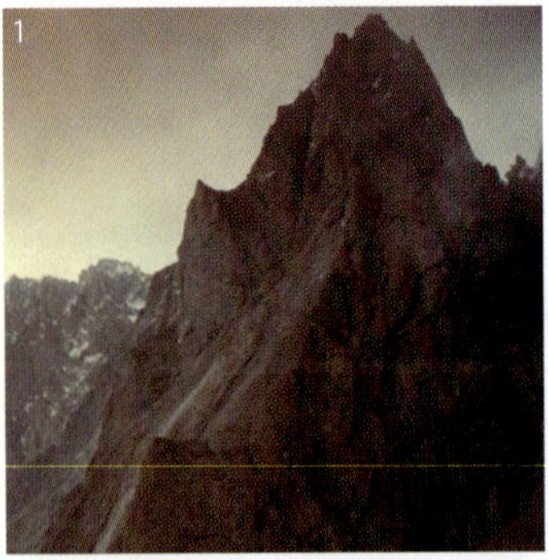
1

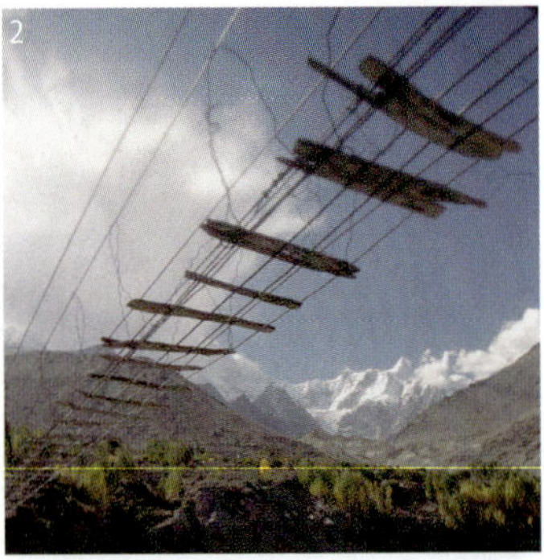
2

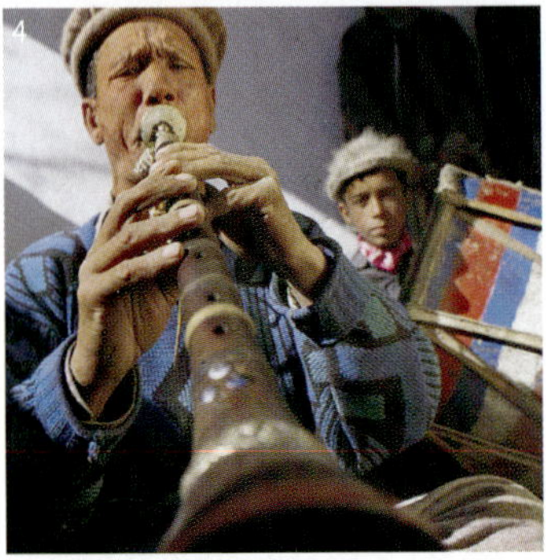
4

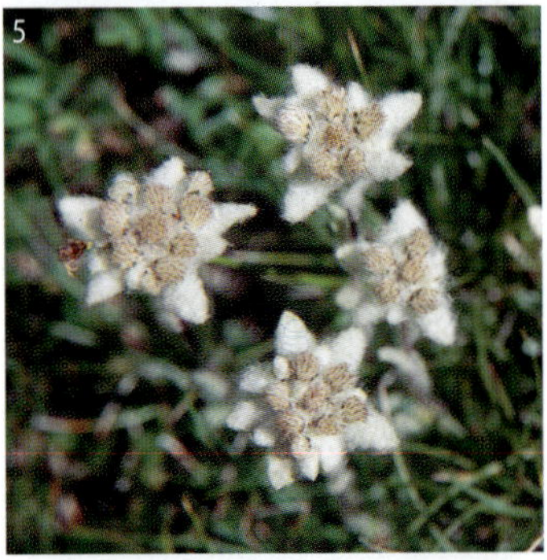
5

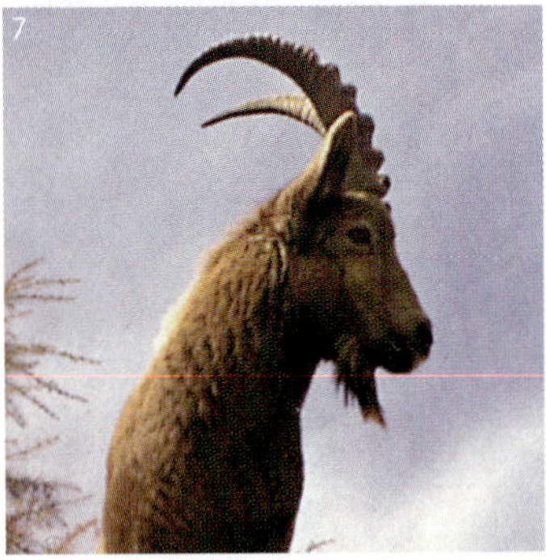
7

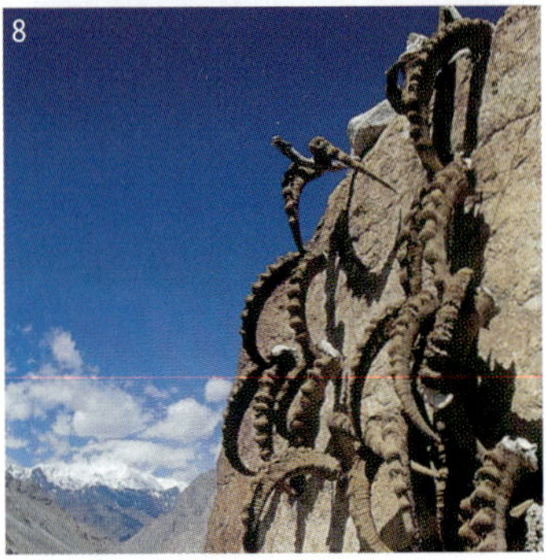
8

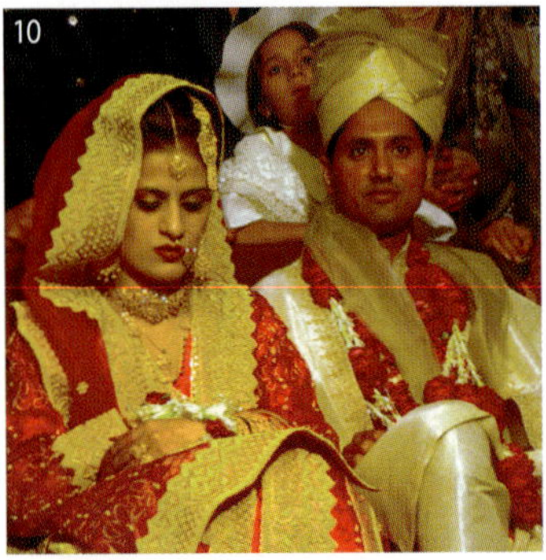
10

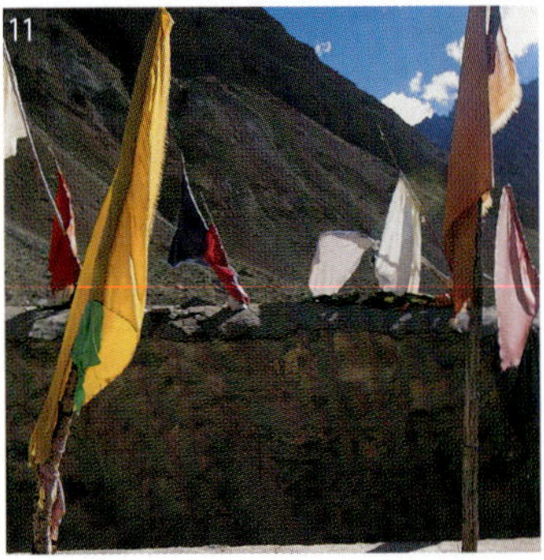
11

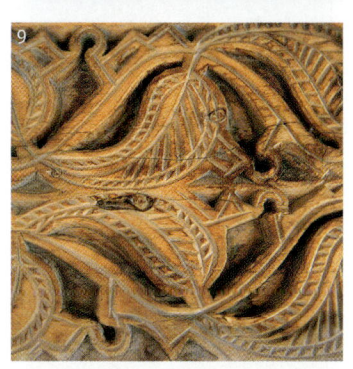

1 *Northern Pakistan has some of the world's best, and most challenging, trekking routes, such as those through the glorious Hushe Valley.* ▸▸ *See page 259.*

2 *It may look like the set of an Indiana Jones movie, but such bridges are a part of everyday life.* ▸▸ *See page 306.*

3 *Trekking with a local guide can give you a valuable insight into the landscape and culture of the region.* ▸▸ *See page 45.*

4 *The rugged and boisterous version of polo in this part of the world is played with a musical accompaniment.* ▸▸ *See page 149.*

5 *There are around 5,700 different plant species in Pakistan, 500 of which are listed as endangered.* ▸▸ *See page 377.*

6 *Many of the older buildings in northern Pakistan, such as Baltit Fort in Hunza, show a Tibetan influence.* ▸▸ *See page 283.*

7 *The ibex is one of the many mammals, including snow leopard and bears seen all over the region.* ▸▸ *See page 376.*

8 *Villagers like to decorate their homes and shrines with the horns of the mountain ibex. In some valleys, sustainable wildlife conservation projects revolve around controlled trophy hunting.* ▸▸ *See page 377.*

9 *Many of the four to five hundred year old shrines and places of worship are being lovingly restored, such as this in Gircha* ▸▸ *See page 319.*

10 *Each valley and side valley in the north of Pakistan has its own distict cultural traditions, and visitors are often invited to participate.* ▸▸ *See page 368.*

11 *The Chapursan Valley is the next new thing waiting to be 'discovered'. Many of the shrines here mark miracles performed by the valley's revered saint, Baba Ghundi.* ▸▸ *See page 319.*

12 *Nearly every meal in Pakistan is accompaigned by nan or the humble chapati.* ▸▸ *See page 37.*

Soaring high
Northern Pakistan is home to 12 of the world's top 30 peaks, with five over 8,000 m, 25 over 7,500 m and some of the longest glaciers outside of the polar regions. Short hikes from the Karakoram Highway can bring you to awesome viewpoints such as this, at Borit Sar near Passu. See page 307.

North West Frontier Province

This guide includes the highlights of Pakistan's fascinating North West Frontier Province (NWFP) as well as the Karakoram Highway (KKH). Peshawar is one of those mad, compelling frontier towns, where wild-looking Pathan tribesmen do their shopping in the Old City's crowded bazaars. It is also an excellent base from which to visit the famous gun factories at Darra, or the legendary Khyber Pass. Further north at the gateway to the Hindu Kush, is the Chitral Valley, offering sublime mountain scenery and trekking options, and a veritable mix of peoples including the non-Muslim Kalash, Ismaili Muslims, Sunni Pathans and semi-nomadic Wakhis. There is also the opportunity to head east from Chitral over the Shandur Pass to Gilgit, on one of the country's most appealing journeys through some of its best scenery.

Rawalpindi/Islamabad to Gilgit

There are two main highlights on a trip along the Karakoram Highway between Rawalpindi/Islamabad and Gilgit, the first being the actual road trip itself. Here you can wonder at this marvel of engineering, a road that for much of its route has been blasted out of the rock. You can also gets to grips with a mountainside that drops sharply away from the road, in some places for up to 300 m right down to the boiling Indus below. If you prefer to look up rather than down, then be prepared for another daunting sight, this time the massive bulk of Nanga Parbat towering above you, the world's ninth highest mountain. Not only does the KKH have to detour to go around this colossal block of rock, ice and snow, so does the Indus itself.

Baltistan

If you like to walk, then Baltistan is the place for you. One of the world's most famous, and demanding, treks follows the Baltoro glacier to the very heart of the Karakorams at Concordia, from where some of the world's highest peaks (including K2) dominate the skyline. Away from the snow and ice, the vast Deosai plateau, 4,000 m above sea-level, becomes a carpet of brightly-coloured flowers in summer and may offer you the chance to spot a rare Himalayan brown bear. Alternatively, spend time amongst the hardy and welcoming Balti people, who populate the villages that dot the valleys of Baltistan.

Hunza, Nagar and Gojal

The Hunza Valley is the most sought-after destination in the north of Pakistan, yet it remains far from overcrowded or touristy. Centred on the charming village of Karimabad, with its scaled-down neighbour Altit, it's the ideal place to unwind or undertake a couple of short one- to two- day hikes. Across the river from Hunza is Nagar, a slower-paced, less-visited alternative. Gojal, sometimes referred to as Upper Hunza, offers some of the most accessible trekking opportunities for the first-time hiker, as well as challenging routes for more experienced mountain walkers. The tiny villages of Passu and Gulmit are bases for a series of rewarding day-hikes, serving as a good initiation for those planning something a little more ambitious. Those with a pioneering spirit may care to head for the Chapursan Valley, where it is possible to get to the base of the world's ninth highest mountain, Nanga Parbat, in little more than a two- to three-hour walk.

And on to China

This guide doesn't stop when the Karakoram Highway reaches Pakistan's border with China; it continues all the way to the Central Asian town of Kashgar, with its famous Sunday Market, taking in the breathtakingly beautiful lake at Kara Kuli along the way.

A foot in the door

Famously, it was Pakistan that England cricket legend Ian Botham was talking about when he said "I wouldn't even send my mother-in-law there". Unfair or not, Pakistan has found itself labouring under an image problem. In fact, most of the foreign news coverage of this country seems to feature that strange period after midday prayers on a Friday, when a few hotheads leave the mosque to chant anti-US slogans.

If truth be told, the people of Pakistan are amongst the friendliest and most hospitable that you are ever likely to come across. Indeed, the consensus among those who have visited both countries is that it has the same diversity, exotica and chaos as India, but without the hustlers and hassles.

Pakistan certainly doesn't receive its fair share of visitors, which seems a little bewildering given the impressive attractions of the country. The truthful reason is that each time Pakistan threatens to take off as the next big adventure travel destination, some event, often beyond its control, seems to put the mockers on it. War in Afghanistan, nuclear testing, military coups, border skirmishes with India and global recession, have all scuppered Pakistan's oft-predicted tourism boom at some time or other. Next year is surely Pakistan's year; in the meantime, its underexposure is an attraction in itself.

Travellers not daunted by sensationalist reports are slowly returning to Pakistan, and are finding a safe, unspoilt adventure playground and one of the world's last true wildernesses. Pakistan remains a remarkably affordable country in which to travel. Luxury comes cheap, and cheap comes dirt cheap. Sending your mother-in-law here these days would certainly be a treat, not a banishment.

Essentials

Planning your trip	12
Where to go	12
When to go	14
Tours and tour operators	14
Finding out more	15
Language	15
Disabled travellers	15
Gay and lesbian travellers	16
Student travellers	16
Travelling with children	16
Women travellers	16
Before you travel	17
Visas	17
Permits for 'Restricted Areas'	19
Duty free allowance	20
What to take	21
Money	22
Currency	22
Changing money	23
Cost of travelling	24
Getting there	24
Air	24
Overland	26
Touching down	28
Rules, customs and etiquette	28
Safety	29
Getting around	31
Air	31
Train	31
Road	32
Maps	35
Sleeping	36
Food and drink	37
Food	37
Drink	38
Entertainment	39
Festivals and events	39
National public holidays	40
Islamic holy days	41
Shopping	43
Sport and activities	44
Trekking	45
Types of trek	46
Classification of treks	47
Organizing a trek	50
Health	55
Before travelling	55
Common problems	56
Other afflictions	60
Further information	61
Keeping in touch	62
Media	63

● Footprint features..

Touching down	29
How big is your footprint?	30
The hazards of road travel in Pakistan	32

Planning your trip

Where to go

Which route
Although an end-to-end journey along the Karakoram Highway (KKH) may seem the most logical way to explore this beautiful region, there are a number of factors to consider if you wish to get the most out of a visit to Northern Pakistan. Much can depend on your mode of transport: take your pick from public bus and jeep services, tour buses, bicycle or your own two feet. Itineraries vary according to length of trip, interest and area and terrain that you are prepared to cover. If you have a Chinese visa, you may wish to continue to Kashgar and probe deeper into China, the Central Asian republics of Kyrghizstan, Uzbekistan and the like. There are many side valleys off the KKH to explore, and numerous trekking possibilities. The famous North West Frontier Province (NWFP), Peshawar, Chitral and the Kalash Valleys can all fit in to a journey along the KKH with some preparation.

Suggested itineraries → *See also the colour map at the end of the book.*
As noted in the introduction, there are a number of factors to bear in mind when planning your route. Key among these are a) time available; b) having a visa for China, since they are not available on the border; c) choosing the highlights; and d) avoiding the dangerous or less interesting areas. If we start with this last point first, there is a case for missing out the whole section of the KKH between Rawalpindi/Islamabad and Chilas during your travels through the north of Pakistan. There are two reasons for this. Although there is some dramatic scenery along this route, notably where the KKH is perched on a narrow cliff edge above the thundering Indus River below, there are comparitively few interesting spots along this stretch of the highway. Secondly, the people of Kohistan and Diamar Districts are not the most welcoming hosts in Pakistan. Your presence in their settlements along the KKH will be tolerated, rather than welcomed, and although there is negligible threat to your personal safety, there are many reports of cyclists having stones thrown at them by the region's kids. Women should certainly not cycle here alone. The side valleys off the KKH in Kohistan and Diamar are another matter entirely. With a few exceptions, excursions up these valleys should not be attempted (unless you're on official business and accompanied by armed guards). There are some itineraries below that allow travellers to avoid much or all of the Kohistan and Diamar Districts. But don't despair: there are plenty of accessible diversions further up the KKH.

This guide provides extensive information for those planning on stopping en route along the KKH, with particular notes on distances and places to stay and eat. It also provides varied and detailed information on the rest of Northern Pakistan. Obviously the more time you spend, the greater the rewards will be: you could complete the Rawalpindi/Islamabad to Kashgar trip in five days, but what fun would that be?

The grand route (clockwise)
From **Rawalpindi/Islamabad**, head west to **Peshawar**, perhaps visiting **Taxila** on the way (1). After exploring Peshawar, with excursions to **Khyber Pass**, **Darra Adam Khel** and some Gandharan Buddhist sites in the Peshawar Valley (3-4), head north via the Lowari Pass to **Chitral** (2). After exploring Chitral and surrounding area (2), including perhaps some time spent in the **Kalash Valleys** (3), head east over the **Shandur Pass** towards **Gilgit** (3, but 6-7 days are better to appreciate the fabulous

spots in between). From Gilgit, before tackling the KKH, you could head east to Baltistan, most notably the settlements of Skardu and Khapulu, plus the Shigar and Hushe valleys (7, but 14 days would allow greater exploration). Alternatively, head down to Fairy Meadows for a few days (4). Having returned to Gilgit, head north along the KKH. Most travellers go directly to Karimabad (3 hours), although there are welcoming diversions to Chaprot Valley or Rakaposhi base camp via Minapin (4). Having relaxed in Karimabad, Altit and Duikar (4) in Central Hunza, follow the KKH north to Gulmit and Passu in Gojal, two small villages that are starting points for a whole host of popular day-hikes (3-4). If you're feeling adventurous, spend some time in the Chapursan Valley (4). After a night in Sust (1), take the bus across the Chinese border to Tashkurgan (1), and on the next day to Kashgar (1, but you may like to spend several days at the stunning Kara Kuli lake between these two towns). From Kashgar (3), the world is your lobster, with the choice of heading east into Tibet (very hard, technically illegal), north and then east into the rest of China, northwest into Kyrghistan and Central Asia, or you could return to Pakistan.

> *Figures in brackets are the very minimum number of days required to complete these routes by public transport.*

The grand route (anticlockwise)

Before heading north from Rawalpindi/Islamabad along the KKH, you may wish to first head west to Peshawar, perhaps visiting Taxila on the way (1). After exploring Peshawar, with excursions to Khyber Pass, Darra Adam Khel and some Gandharan Buddhist sites in the Peshawar Valley (3-4), return to Rawalpindi/Islamabad. The leg of the KKH between Rawalpindi/Islamabad and Gilgit can be completed in 14-18 hours by bus, or 3-4 days if you stop at points in between (although only Fairy Meadows could really be labelled a highlight). Having explored the area around Gilgit (2-4), there are several choices to be made. You could head east to Baltistan, most notably the settlements of Skardu and Khapulu, plus the Shigar and Hushe valleys (7, but 14 days would allow greater exploration), before returning to Gilgit. You could also explore the area between Gilgit and Chitral (3-7), although if you want to go to Chitral itself, it may be an idea to follow this route once you've seen the areas further north along the KKH. The route north from Gilgit to Hunza, Gojal on to China is described in the clockwise route above. If, after reaching either Sust or Kashgar, you turn round and return to Gilgit, you can then complete the anticlockwise circuit by heading west to Chitral (3-7), exploring the Chitral and Kalash Valleys (3-5), before returning south via the Lowari Pass to Peshawar (2).

> *Cyclists with limited time may like to put their bikes on a bus between Rawalpindi/Islamabad and Gilgit, allowing more time for exploring remote areas further north.*

North via the Swat Valley

This route effectively misses out the section of the KKH between Rawalpindi/Islamabad and Besham. From Peshawar you head up the Swat Valley (3-7), before heading over the Shangla Pass from Khwazakhela to Besham on the KKH (4 hours). From here, refer to the anticlockwise route above. This section can also be taken from north to south, bypassing the lower stretches of the KKH, as part of the clockwise route.

North via the Kaghan Valley

This route bypasses the section of the KKH between Mansehra and Chilas, although it's not necessarily a simple journey. After reaching Mansehra from Rawalpindi/Islamabad (4 hours), head northeast up the attractive Kaghan Valley on public transport as far as Naran (1). From there, you can either hire a private jeep to head north over the 4,175-m Babusar Pass to Chilas (1), or you can walk (3-6). Note that this is a fairly lawless area.

Flying into the north

There are three different spectacular flights that take you into the heart of Pakistan's mountainous north, although all are heavily oversubscribed with frequent cancellations due to poor weather. These are the folowing: **Peshawar-Chitral** (the only route in during winter), **Islamabad-Gilgit** and **Islamabad-Skardu**. Consult individual towns for further information.

When to go

The best time to visit the north of Pakistan is during the spring, summer and autumn months (**March-November**). Flowering and fruiting trees in spring and autumn make the Hunza region in particular a delightful sight, with cooler summer temperatures than on the hot plains of the rest of Pakistan, although temperatures in summer can be extremely unpleasant the length of the Indus gorge and in Gilgit. The main trekking season in the Northern Areas and NWFP extends from June to September. Heavy rainfall around September often leads to land-slides blocking the KKH. During the winter months, much of the north is snowbound (Chitral is only accessible by air or via Afghanistan during this period), and most of the accommodation on the KKH north of Karimabad closes between December and February (although you will certainly always manage to find something). The Khunjerab Pass between Pakistan and China is only open to foreigners between 1 May and 31 December, but it may open later and close earlier if the weather is poor. For details and further information about holidays and festivals, see page 39, and for specific information on travelling during Ramadan, see page 41.

Tours and tour operators

In Pakistan

In many parts of the north of Pakistan (but notably Gilgit, Hunza, Baltistan and Chitral), every second person you meet either claims to be a guide or has his own tour company. Some of them hold government licences, but this is not always the badge of quality that it should be. Those guides and tour companies listed in this guide are those that the writers have personal knowledge of, or have been highly recommended to Footprint by more than one source. Word of mouth can also be a good indication of who and who not to use and of general reputations. Tour companies are listed in the city/town that they operate from (many also have branch offices); so, look first under Islamabad, Rawalpindi, Gilgit, Skardu, Karimabad, Peshawar and Chitral.

Abroad

Most of the major international adventure and 'exotic' tour operators offer trips to northern Pakistan, although most only include it as part of a 'Silk Road' tour, with the Pakistan leg being no more than five days of a 14-day tour, for example. Most of the international companies sub-contract actual handling arrangements to a Pakistan-based tour company.

A small selection of tour operators in the UK include: **Encounter Overland**, 2002 Camp Green, Debenham, Stowmarket, Suffolk, IP14 6LA, T0870-4994478, www.encounter.co.uk; **Explore Worldwide**, 1 Frederick Street, Aldershot, GU11 1LQ, T01252-760000, www.exploreworldwide.com; **Himalayan Kingdoms**, Old Crown House, 18 Market Street, Wotton-under-Edge, Gloucs, GL12 7AE, T01453-844400, www.himalayankingdoms.com. In France there is also **Nouvelles Frontieres**, T+33 (0)825000747, www.nouvelles-frontieres.fr.

Finding out more

Tourist offices

The tour operators and other organizations mentioned in the text are best placed to give further information on organized tours and specialist interest travel in Pakistan. On a more general level, the government-run **Pakistan Tourism Development Corporation** (PTDC) has a number of information centres abroad, but on the whole they are of little help ⓘ *Head office: Pakistan Sports Complex ('Jinnah Stadium' on some maps), just off Shahrah-e-Kashmir, to the southeast of the Tourist Campsite, T9204556, www.tourism.gov.pk, Mon-Thu 0900-1600, Fri 0800-1230.* The various branches of PTDC within the country, and their provincial offshoots are likely to be of more help, although their usefulness varies.

Internet

The problem with listing websites providing information on Pakistan is that such resources tend to come and go, arriving in a blaze of glory then failing to be updated before disappearing entirely. One constant is the government-run site, www.pak.gov.pk, which provides the official line on most things you could wish to know, but be aware that these government-run websites in Pakistan are frequently hacked and go off-line for long periods. The official website of the Northern Areas is also worth a look: www.northernareas.org.pk.

Language

Although there is a complex language pattern in the areas covered by this handbook (see Background, page 382, for full details), anyone with a reasonable grasp of English should find communication fairly easy. If you're going to learn one language for travel in this region, then learn Urdu. Whilst travelling in northern Pakistan you will come across numerous other languages and dialects, but it is rare not to find someone who can speak at least some English, and rarer still to find a non-Urdu speaker. However, it is always good to be able to address someone in their own language, and some basic words and phrases are listed on page 382.

Disabled travellers

Pakistan makes no specific considerations for disabled travellers, and travel here (particularly on public transport) would be extremely demanding. If you are disabled you should contact the travel officer of your national support organization. They can provide literature or put you in touch with travel agents specializing in tours for the disabled. **The Royal Association for Disability and Rehabilitation** (RADAR), Unit 12, City Forum, 250 City Road, London, EC1V 8AF, T020-72503222, www.radar.org.uk, is a good source of advice and information in the UK.

Further information on options for disabled travellers is can be found by contacting the following organizations, although they currently have nothing specific concerning Pakistan: **Mobility International**, PO Box 10767, Eugene, OR 97440, USA, info@miusa.org; www.atlholidays.com, which specializes in organizing holidays for disabled travellers, or **Access-Able Travel Source**, www.access-able.com.

Some travel companies are beginning to specialize in exciting holidays, tailor-made for individuals depending on their level of disability. For those who have access to the internet there is a Global Access - Disabled Travel Network Site that you can visit, www.geocities.com/Paris/1502. It is dedicated to providing information for 'disabled adventurers' and includes a number of reviews and tips from members of the public. You might want to read *Nothing Ventured* edited by Alison Walsh (Harper Collins), which gives personal accounts of worldwide journeys by disabled travellers, plus advice and listings.

Gay and lesbian travellers

Homosexuality is illegal in Pakistan, although few cases ever seem to be brought to court and the harsh punishments are rarely enforced. Many visitors are surprised by the common sight of young Pakistani men holding hands, or being physically intimate in public (seeing two policemen or soldiers walking down the street hand in hand remains an extraordinary sight). Generally, this is just a sign of friendship, and does not mean that they are gay. However, a number of commentators are now beginning to bring up the previously taboo subject of pre-marriage homosexuality. Foreign visitors are advised to avoid all public displays of physical affection.

Student travellers

Anyone in full-time education is entitled to an International Student Identity Card (ISIC). These are issued by student travel offices and travel agencies around the world. In Pakistan they entitle you to a 50 % discount on rail tickets and may get you a discount on NATCO buses. Head Office: ISIC Association, Box 9048, 1000 Copenhagen, Denmark, T45-33939303.

Travelling with children

The few parents travelling with younger children that you meet in the places covered by this handbook speak of the life-enriching experience, although all seem to agree that it is fairly hard work. Foreign children are well received by Pakistanis, and will be royally entertained, but there is no escaping the fact that there are some long journeys in this part of the world and public transport tends to be slow, cramped and not particularly child-friendly.

Items such as disposable nappies (diapers) can only really be found in Rawalpindi, Islamabad and Peshawar, and even then it may not be the brand/size that you are used to. Health issues, such as vaccinations and avoiding dehydration (a common problem for children) are dealt with in the health section on page 55.

Women travellers

Travelling in Muslim countries is undoubtedly harder for women than for men, and more so for women travelling alone. Even when travelling with a male companion or in a group, women need to be particularly aware of the cultural context. Most Pakistani women never travel alone, and outside of the main cities they are rarely seen in public. This in itself can make travelling around hard work. Certain more remote and tribal areas are not safe for women on their own; specific warnings are given in the relevant sections. The widely held perception of Western women is based on the images in Western magazines, films and satellite TV, which portray them as having loose sexual morals. This, along with the fact that in their rigidly segregated society many young Pakistani males openly admit to feeling sexually frustrated, can lead to problems of sexual harassment. Cases of violent sexual assault are, however, extremely rare and a firm, unambiguous response will deal with most situations. In public, the best approach is to make a scene. Any form of impropriety towards women is a gross violation of the tenets of Islam and someone is bound to come to your aid; the perpetrator meanwhile will quickly vanish in a cloud of shame. It is worth remembering that a good Muslim would consider it improper to be alone with a female in private, so any attempt to contrive such a situation should set alarm bells ringing.

Many female travellers in Pakistan strongly advise adopting the local dress of *shalwar kameez* (baggy trousers and long over shirt which comes down to the knees) and *dupatta* (scarf) to cover the head in more conservative areas. This is a matter of choice. The important thing is to wear baggy, loose-fitting clothes that do not highlight the lines of your body, and not to expose anything more than head, hands and feet. A scarf is always useful for covering up further if you begin to feel exposed or uncomfortable in a given situation; it is also very good protection against the sun. Some women argue that it makes absolutely no difference to a determined male what you are wearing. However, given that actual harassment is relatively rare, the main object of dressing modestly is to show respect for Islamic values and not cause offence.

If you are put off the idea of visiting Pakistan by the above, don't be. Plenty of women travel around Pakistan and the majority are very enthusiastic about the country. While it can be very demanding, there are also distinct advantages. In the vast majority of situations women are treated with great respect. Seasoned female travellers in Pakistan argue that they get the best of both worlds. As a foreigner they are generally accorded the status of 'honorary males' in public, while in private they have access to female society, from which men are excluded. Pakistani women, although largely invisible in public life, are a dominant force in family life at home. When invited to a Pakistani household, male guests are usually confined to the guest room while women are whisked away behind the scenes into the 'real' household, where they can meet wives, mothers, sisters and other members of the extended family. Other advantages include the best seats at the front of buses and in special women's compartments on trains, and going straight to the front of lengthy queues.

Social etiquette regarding Pakistani women varies enormously, and is perhaps most visible in the areas covered by this handbook. In Islamabad, for example, you will meet upper and middle-class women who are free to move around as they please, often well educated and highly westernized. In remote, rural and tribal areas women are rarely seen at all and only go out in public with a full burqa, while there are parts where female literacy is an unknown concept entirely. In most circumstances women do not shake hands with men and offering your hand is likely to cause confusion and embarrassment. Men should never take photographs of women without their consent, or more importantly that of their male escort. Female tourists are more likely to be given permission to take photos of women but should never take it for granted.

Before you travel

Visas → *For latest visa information go to www.pak.gov.pk.*

Regulations regarding visas are subject to change, so it is essential to check the current situation with the issuing embassy. **All foreign nationals require a valid visa** or 'landing permit' for visiting Pakistan, with a few exceptions. Tourist visas are valid for a period of 60 or 90 days (although some embassies, eg Beijing, sometimes only issue 30-day visas). Single and double entry visas are available and both types must be used within six months of the date of issue. In the case of double entry visas, each visit is restricted to a period of 90 days. If you are travelling up to Kashgar (China), and then returning to Pakistan, it makes things easier if you obtain a double entry visa in advance. See pages 26 and 81 for details of visas for China.

In 2000, in a drive to promote tourism, most nationalities could obtain a **free 30-day landing permit upon arrival**. In theory, these landing permits can be extended into 90-day tourist visas by paying the appropriate fee (with the 90 days starting from the date of entry), although some people have experienced problems doing this. Foreigners' registration was also discontinued as part of this promotion. NB This system was suspended in October 2001 following the terrorist attacks on the USA and subsequent action in Afghanistan. Foreigners' registration was also reintroduced. It is to be hoped that the original arrangements will be put back into effect soon, as tourism in Pakistan struggles once again to find its feet. At time of going to press in 2004, however, foreign nationals were required to obtain a visa in advance.

> For details of Pakistani embassies' websites and email addresses go to www.pak.gov.pk and click on 'Information Desk'. For details of foreign embassies in Pakistan, see Islamabad, page 81.

You are strongly advised to carry your passport with you at all times; you may be required to produce your documents at check posts, particularly when crossing between provinces, entering tribal or restricted areas, and travelling along the KKH. For details of foreigners' registration and other permits, see page 83.

Visa costs

Visa fees vary according to your nationality (reciprocal arrangement) and are subject to frequent changes. These are the prices of a single-entry tourist visa when applied for in your country of residence in 2004: UK £49; Ireland €38; USA US$94; France €32; Germany €38; Australia AUS$76. Note that foreign nationals may have to provide proof of residency if applying in a country other than their own, or provide a 'letter of recommendation' from their own embassy. NB Israelis are not given visas.

Transit visas

With the introduction of a 30-day landing permit upon arrival for most nationalities, transit visas should have become history. However, those arriving by land may still only be given transit visas (and even then these remain at the discretion of immigration officials). Transit visas are usually only valid for 72 hours, but you may get seven days. Converting a transit visa into a full tourist visa is time consuming, and is best done in Islamabad (see page 83). Visitors are strongly advised to **obtain a full visa beforehand** if at all possible.

Visa extensions

It is easiest to extend a visa (and convert a landing permit into a tourist visa) in Islamabad, although the Deputy Commissioners in Gilgit, Peshawar and Skardu are now authorized to do this. One 90-day double entry extension is usually the best you can get, but this arrangement varies. At the time of going to press, most DCs were referring visitors to Islamabad for visa extensions.

Foreigners' registration

This formality is the source of much confusion in Pakistan, seemingly among officials as well as tourists. It was formally abandoned in 2000, but was reintroduced following the September 2001 attacks on the USA and subsequent war in Afghanistan; hopefully this is just a temporary measure, although at time of going to press, foreigners' registration is still in force.

The requirements are as follows: nationals of Britain, Australia and the UAE are not required to register. All other foreigners visiting Pakistan for more than 30 days are required to formally register their presence as a 'resident' in the country before the 30 days are up. This can be done in most towns and cities through the Foreigners' Registration Office or Senior Superintendent of Police (SSP). Bring two passport photos and you will be issued with a Certificate of Registration and Residential Permit. Before leaving Pakistan you must then apply for an exit permit from the last town you stay in; take your Certificate of Registration and Residential Permit to the Foreigners' Registration/SSP office and you will be issued with it. **NB** There have been instances where travellers have been told that they must obtain their exit permit from the same office as they originally registered at. This is not the case. If this happens to you, enlist the help of the nearest PTDC office.

Pakistani embassies around the world

Australia, PO Box 648, 4 Timbarra Crescent, O'Malley Act-2606, Mawson, 2607 Canberra, T2901676. Consulates: Sydney T2677250, Melbourne T6087153. **Austria**, Hofzeile 13, A 1190, Vienna, T367381. **Bangladesh**, NE (C) 2, Road 71, Gulshan, Dhaka, T885387. **Belgium**, Avenue Delleur 57, Brussels 1170, T6738007. **Canada**, Burnside Building, 151 Slater Avenue, Suite 608, Ottowa, Ontario K1P 5H3, T2387881, F2387296. Consulates: Toronto T2501255, Montreal, T8452297. **China**, 1 Dong Zhi Men, Wai Da Jie, San Li Tun, Beijing 100600, T5321217. Consulate: Hong Kong T28270681. **Denmark**, Valeursvej 17, 2900 Hellerup, Copenhagen, T31621693. **France**, 18 Rue Lord Byron, Paris 75008, T01-45622332. **Germany**, Rheinallee 24, 53173 Bonn, T95530. **India**, 2/50-G Shantipath, Chanakyapuri, New Delhi 110021, T600603. Generally only issues 1-month, single-entry visas, need 1 application form plus photo, bank draft (currently Indian Rs2,700) payable to the High Commission for Pakistan (issued at bank inside Ashoka Hotel, 5 mins' away), and a letter of recommendation from your own embassy (but only if you cannot prove you haven't previously visited Pakistan), visa issued same day. **Iran**, Koocha-e-Ahmed, Eatmadzadeh, Block 1, Jamshedabad Shomali, Tehran, T394330. Consulates: Mashad T29845, Zahedan T23666. **Italy**, Via Della, Camillucia 682, 00135 Rome, T36301775. Consulates: Genoa T3628554, Naples T7532865. **Japan**, 2-14-9 Moto Azabu, 2 Chome, Miato-Ku, Tokyo, T34544861. Consulate: Osaka T2262483. **Kazakhstan**, 25 Tulebayeua, Alma Ata, T331502. **Nepal**, PO Box 202, Panipokhari, Kathmandu, T418446. **Netherlands**, Amaliastraat-8, 2514 JC, The Hague, T3648948. **New Zealand** (Consulate) 251 Kapa Road, Kohimarama, Auckland 5 N-2, Auckland, T3072238. **Norway**, Eckersbergsgata 20, 02244 Oslo, T555197. **Russia**, 17 Ul Sadova Kudrinskaya, Moscow, T2503991. **Spain**, Avda Pio XII 11, 28016 Madrid, T3459138. Consulates: Barcelona T2574230, Bilbao T4320845, Seville T228921. **Sweden**, Sergels Tong 12, 14 TR11-57, Stockholm, T203300. Consulate: Gothenburg T812124. **Switzerland**, Bernastrasse 47, Ch-3005, Berne, T3525063. **Tajikistan**, Tajikistan Hotel, Dushanbe, T275153. **UK**, Visa section, 34 Lowndes Square, London SW1X 9JN, T020-7664-9200 (recorded visa info T0891-880880), F020-7664-9224. Consulates: Bradford T661114, Birmingham T2334123, Glasgow T4295335, Manchester T2881349. **USA**, 2315 Massachusetts Avenue NW, Washington DC 20008, T9396200, F3870484. Consulates: New York T8795800, Los Angeles T4410167, Boston T2675555, Chigago T8537630, San Francisco T7780677. **Uzbekistan**, Tchilanzar Street 25, Tashkent, T771003.

Working in Pakistan

The opportunities for paid work in Northern Pakistan are virtually non-existent, although teachers of English may be able to find some (usually unpaid) work.

Permits for 'Restricted Areas'

Sensitive or unstable areas in Pakistan are often designated 'Restricted Areas' and can only be visited with a permit (usually called a 'No Objection Certificate', or NOC) issued by the relevant authority. Such 'Restricted Areas' include the Federally

Administered Tribal Areas, parts of NWFP, parts of the Northern Areas and most of AJ&K. Permits are usually obtained in the regional capital, and full details of procedures for applying are given in the the travelling text. Trekkers and mountaineers also require permits for certain areas (see page 45). Warnings about specifically dangerous places are given in the relevant pages of the travelling text.

Vaccination requirements

There are a number of health-related matters which must be tackled up to a month before arriving in Pakistan (notably vaccinations and malaria-prevention measures). See the Health section on page 55 for full details. Officially you must have a Yellow Fever vaccination certificate if arriving from a country where the disease is endemic. In practice this is rarely enforced. All foreigners coming to Pakistan for more than one year are required to produce a certificate confirming that they do not have HIV/AIDS (but this is also rarely enforced).

Duty free allowance

The official list of items which can be imported free of duty by foreign tourists makes amusing reading ('one electric smoothing iron, one portable electric hot plate, one hairdryer for lady tourists only'). Basically all items which may be reasonably required can be brought in. Alcohol is forbidden; if found it is usually 'confiscated' by customs officials against a receipt which in theory allows you to reclaim it on leaving, but don't count on it. With a little gentle persuasion they sometimes relax the rules; try saying that it is a gift for Christian friends. The official limit on tobacco is 200 cigarettes or 50 cigars or 1lb of tobacco. Officially, gifts should not exceed Rs1,000 in value. Cameras and camcorders can be imported free of duty. However, these and other valuable items or professional equipment, including jewellery, laptop computers etc, should be declared to customs and recorded in your passport, and must be brought out again personally.

Duty free shopping
Islamabad's duty free shop is not worth speaking of. If you fly via Dubai, Bahrain or Abu Dhabi, you will also have access to a bewildering range of electrical and other goods. There are duty free shops in Islamabad, but they have a very limited selection of goods.

Currency regulations
There are no restrictions on the amount of foreign currency, either cash or travellers' cheques, that tourists can bring in to Pakistan, or take out with them when they leave the country. However, a limit has been set of just Rs100 of local currency that can be brought in or taken out.

Export restrictions
The export of antiquities is prohibited. Jewellery up to the value of Rs25,000 that has been bought in Pakistan, provided it is not made wholly or mainly of gold, can be exported free of duty, but you must be able to produce foreign exchange encashment receipts up to the value of the jewellery. Other items, including carpets, can be exported up to the value of Rs75,000 provided you obtain an Export Permit. This is a time-consuming process; ask for help from the dealer you bought the goods from, or from PTDC officials. You will need the sales receipt, encashment receipts up to the value of the goods and photocopies of these and the relevant pages of your passport.

Departure tax

Note that an airport departure tax is charged on all international departures. In early 2004, this was Rs600 for first-class passengers and Rs400 for economy (when you reconfirm your flight, check to see whether this is included in the initial ticket price). A Foreign Travel Tax of Rs500 is charged on all international tickets purchased in Pakistan. An airport tax of Rs100 is also charged on domestic flights (usually included in the price of the ticket). There are no departure taxes for land crossings, although a sizeable 'tax' is incorporated into your bus ticket fare for the trip from Sust across the Khunjerab Pass into China.

What to take

This is not a comprehensive list of what to take, but here are a few points worth bearing in mind. **Appropriate clothing** depends on the season and area in which you will be travelling. In summer, light, loose-fitting cottons are a must. A shalwar kameez (baggy pants and long, loose-fitting overshirt) can be bought very cheaply in Pakistan, off the peg or tailor-made, and is ideal in hot, humid weather (although if you're arriving from China they're hard to find until you get to Gilgit). It also helps you to blend in a little and draws a warm response from Pakistanis to see you wearing their national dress. Footwear should likewise be as airy as possible for hot weather; comfortable sandals or light canvas trainers are a good bet. If you plan to trek, don't forget to bring suitable footwear with you (trainers/light walking boots are fine if you're not attempting anything too ambitious). In the mountains, warm clothing is essential. It is important for both men and women to dress modestly; shorts, singlets etc are likely to cause offence. For women, a scarf to cover their heads where necessary is very useful. See also the advice for women travellers above.

If you are on **medication**, bring sufficient supplies. It is probably readily available, but brand names may differ and stocks may be out of date. Some medicines deteriorate rapidly in hot conditions. Contact lens cleaning equipment is available only in Islamabad/Rawalpindi and Peshawar. Likewise for tampons and contraceptives, although sanitary towels can be found in Chitral and Gilgit. **Insect repellents** are generally less effective than the stronger Western varieties, although good mosquito coils are readily available. Strong **sunscreen** can be difficult to find.

Spare **passport photos** are very useful for any bureaucratic dealings. Take **photocopies** of all important documents in case of loss or theft (also leave a set with friends at home or, ideally, in Pakistan, and perhaps email yourself with details of your passport and travellers' cheques etc). Photos of family and home are an excellent way of bridging the cultural gap and always generate great interest.

Budget travellers should bring their own **padlock** to use in cheaper hotels where doors are often secured by a padlockable bolt. A **cotton sheet sleeping bag** is also very useful for when the available sheets are dirty. A secure **money belt** is the best way to carry money and documents.

It is highly recommended that you bring all your **film** and **batteries** from home (APS is particularly hard to find, and most other film is not stored well). Fuji in Rawalpindi has the freshest film stock (see Rawalpindi shopping, page 88). Islamabad and Kashgar are possibly the only places where you can download digital photos. For details of digital image storage, see http://adrianwarren.com/faq/ontheroad.shtml#storing.

Some **trekking equipment** (second-hand tents, mats, sleeping bags, stoves) can be bought or rented in Gilgit and Skardu, but quality is highly variable.

Insurance

Always take out travel insurance before you set off and read the small print carefully. Check that the policy covers the activities you intend or may end up doing. Also check exactly what your medical cover includes, ie ambulance, helicopter rescue or emergency flights home. Also check the payment protocol. You may have to cough up first (literally) before the insurance company reimburses you. It is always best to dig out all the receipts for expensive personal effects like jewellery or cameras. Take photos of these items and note down all serial numbers.

You are advised to shop around. STA Travel and other reputable student travel organizations offer good value policies. Young travellers from North America can try the **International Student Insurance Service** (ISIS), www.internationalstudent.com/insurance. Other recommended travel insurance companies in North America are: **Access America**, T1-866-8073982, www.accessamerica.com; **STA Travel**, T1-800-777 0112, www.sta-travel.com; **Travel Assistance International**, T1-800-8212828, www.travelassistance.com; **Travel Guard**, T1-800-8264919, www.travelguard.com, and **Travel Insurance Services**, T1-800-9371387, www.travelinsure.com.

Older travellers should note that some companies will not cover people over 65 years old, or may charge higher premiums. The best policies for older travellers (UK) are offered by **Age Concern**, T0845-601234, www.ageconcern.org.uk, and **Saga**, T0800-0565464, www.saga.co.uk/travel.

Money

Currency

The Pakistani currency is the Pakistani rupee (usually just referred to as the 'rupee' and written as 'Rs'). Notes come in denominations of Rs1,000, 500, 100, 50, 10, 5, 2 and 1. The rupee is divided into 100 paise, although the coins of 50, 25, 20, 10 and 5 paise are gradually disappearing. The lower denomination notes are slowly being replaced with coins. Unlike in India, currency notes are usually accepted whatever their condition, unless they have been seriously damaged or defaced. Obtaining change for larger currency notes can be difficult in remoter areas; it is well worth accumulating a good supply of smaller notes. For details of the cost of travelling in Pakistan, see page 24.

How to take your money

It is worth giving some advance thought to the way in which you will carry your travelling funds. The US dollar is the most widely accepted currency, followed by the pound sterling. The euro can generally only be changed in Rawalpindi/Islamabad, Peshawar, Gilgit and Kashgar, but this should slowly change as banks adapt. A secure money-belt worn beneath your clothing is the best way to carry your documents and travelling funds, although it is worth having a few other 'stashes' in case of emergencies (eg some money hidden in your day-pack, some in your luggage etc).

❗ *Current exchange rates (Summer 2004) are £1: Rs105.8, €: Rs68.64, US$1: Rs59.5. See also www.oanda.com for up to date exchange rates.*

Cash

It is unwise to carry all your travelling funds in the form of cash. However, it is advisable to have some hard currency cash for use in emergencies (or when banks are shut). A good mix of high and low denomination (recently issued) US$ bills is the best bet.

Travellers' cheques

This is the best way to carry the bulk of your travelling funds since they can be replaced if lost/stolen. Note, however, that even the well-known brands of travellers' cheques rarely live up to their advertising when it comes to replacing lost cheques in Pakistan. US dollars and pound sterling are the two most widely accepted currencies, with other currencies only really being convertible in the state capital cities, although Euro travellers' cheques are becoming more widely accepted. Like cash, you tend to get marginally better rates on larger denominations. **American Express** travellers' cheques are probably the best bet, largely because, with an office in Islamabad, replacing lost travellers' cheques should (in theory) be more straightforward. Make sure that you keep your travellers' cheques purchase receipts separate from the cheques themselves. When buying your travellers' cheques, whenever possible go to the offices of the company issuing the cheques (eg for American Express cheques go to an Amex office) rather than an agency (eg a travel agent or building society that also sells Amex travellers' cheques); this will speed things up if you need them replaced.

Credit cards

Outside of Rawalpindi/Islamabad, Peshawar and Kashgar you'll find few places to use a credit card. American Express card holders can use their cards to buy travellers' cheques at Amex offices, or to cash personal cheques there, while Visa and Mastercard holders can obtain (rupee) cash advances on their cards at the international banks in these cities (this is a time-consuming process, and can involve a hefty commission fee). ATMs are popping up in the major cities which can be used for withdrawing cash against credit cards (eg Muslim Commercial Bank ATMs work with MasterCard and Visa Electron). Note that ATMs discharge used notes, and their poor condition can make the machines rather erratic; if possible, only use ATMs during bank opening hours in case you need to report a malfunction.

Changing money

Banks

A number of domestic banks in Pakistan and China are authorized to change foreign currency and travellers' cheques, as are foreign banks. Commission rates vary from bank to bank so it is worth shopping around. Note that outside of the main towns, Pakistani banks must obtain current exchange rates from their head offices; these usually don't arrive until late morning, leaving little time to conduct any transactions. It should also be noted that the further you move away from a large city, the poorer the rate you are likely to get. For example, if you are travelling up the KKH, the rate in Rawalpindi will be better than the rate in Gilgit, which will be better than the rate in Karimabad, which in turn will be better than the rate in Sust. Changing money (and especially travellers' cheques) can be a tediously time-consuming process.

Licensed money changers

These are to be found in most towns and cities, and at border crossing points. They are perfectly legal and provide a much quicker service for changing cash and travellers' cheques. NB At the time of research, there was a significant difference between the official bank exchange rates and the open market (or so-called 'kerbside') rates being offered by licensed money changers. This is a reflection of the dire state of the Pakistani economy and the lack of confidence in the rupee; if and when the situation improves, the gap between the official bank rate and the 'kerbside' rate is likely to narrow.

Hotels

Many of the larger hotels will also change foreign currency, and in some cases travellers' cheques, but generally at slightly lower rates than the banks.

Black market
Unlicensed money changers generally offer identical rates to their licensed counterparts, but will not issue you with currency-exchange receipts. Those who approach you in the bazaars are likely to be working on a commission basis; they are often not the most trustworthy of characters and are best avoided.

Currency-exchange receipts
You will receive a currency-exchange receipt when changing money through a bank or authorized dealer. You may be required to produce such receipts if you wish to reconvert rupees upon departure, or when buying international air tickets inside Pakistan.

Transferring money to Pakistan
American Express and ANZ Grindlays can make instant money transfers to their banks in Pakistan, but charge a high fee. National Bank of Pakistan and Habib Bank branches abroad charge less, but can take two to three days. The cheapest option is to have a bank draft posted out to you personally by priority mail.

Reconverting rupees on departure
Banks at the airports and land crossing points will be able to reconvert rupees upon your departure, although they generally only have US dollars in cash. You will have to show currency-exchange receipts to the value of the amount you wish to reconvert.

Cost of travelling

Eating, sleeping and travelling costs in Pakistan are extremely cheap by Western standards, and are probably better value in the north than in the rest of the country. By staying in the cheapest (but still clean and well-run) hotels, eating at 'local' restaurants, and by relying on public transport, budget travellers can still get by on as little as US$10 per day (sometimes less!). By increasing your budget to around US$20 a day you will be able to experience a significant improvement in the standard of accommodation, as well as allowing you to travel on a more luxurious form of transport (eg buses with reserved seats, private jeeps etc). Sleeping, eating and transport options are available in Pakistan for all budgets, whether travelling with a backpack or a suit bag.

Getting there

Air

Pakistan is easily accessible by air from just about any part of the world (London nine hours, New York 17 hours, Bangkok six hours), and is served by both rock-bottom discount airlines and more upmarket companies. A flight bought from a discount ('bucket') shop in London will cost around £330 return (London-Karachi-London), while a return to Islamabad costs from £500 (London-Islamabad-London), although it pays to shop around. If money (and not time) is your key consideration, you can fly to Karachi and then travel overland to Islamabad. Alternatively, internal flights are very cheap when bought in Pakistan.

If you intend spending all your time in the regions covered by this handbook, it makes a lot of sense to fly in to Islamabad (page 70). Fewer companies fly to

Discount flight agents

UK and Ireland
STA Travel, 86 Old Brompton Rd, London, SW7 3LH, T020-74376262, www.statravel.co.uk They have other branches in London, as well as in Brighton, Bristol, Cambridge, Leeds, Manchester, Newcastle-Upon-Tyne and Oxford and on many university campuses. Specialists in low-cost student/youth flights and tours, also good for student IDs and insurance.
Trailfinders, 194 Kensington High Street, London, W8 7RG, T020-79383939.

North America
Air Brokers International, 323 Geary St, Suite 411, San Francisco, CA94102, T01-800-883 3273, www.airbrokers.com Consolidator and specialist on RTW and Circle Pacific tickets.
STA Travel, 5900 Wilshire Blvd, Suite 2110, Los Angeles, CA 90036, T1-800-777 0112, www.sta-travel.com Also branches in New York, San Francisco, Boston, Miami, Chicago, Seattle and Washington DC.
Travel CUTS, 187 College St, Toronto, ON, M5T 1P7, T1-800-667 2887, www.travelcuts.com Specialist in student discount fares, Ids and other travel services. Branches in other Canadian cities.

Australia and New Zealand
Flight Centres, 82 Elizabeth St, Sydney, T13-1600; 205 Queen St, Auckland, T09-309 6171. Also branches in other towns and cities. www.flightcentres.com.au
STA Travel, T1300-360960, www.statravelaus.com.au; 702 Harris St, Ultimo, Sydney, and 256 Flinders St, Melbourne. In NZ: 10 High St, Auckland, T09-366 6673. Also in major towns and university campuses.
Travel.com.au, 80 Clarence St, Sydney, T02-929 01500.

Islamabad than the main international gateway of Karachi, but this is gradually changing and fares are coming down.

Islamabad International Airport

Arrival/departure formalities Upon arrival you will be required to fill out a disembarkation card, and occasionally a health card also. The disembarkation card is collected at passport control. At times when 'landing permits' are being issued to most nationalities (obviating the need for a visa, see page 17), just join the normal queue for passport control. Having collected your baggage, pass through customs (foreigners are rarely stopped, although airport security may check to see if your luggage tags match).

Upon departure, note that you are theoretically only allowed inside the terminal building three hours before your flight leaves (this rule may be waived for foreigners). You must pass through security (including baggage x-ray) before you can check in. Check-in clerks will collect the departure tax (Rs400 economy, Rs600 club/first class, check with your airline to see if this has been included within your ticket price). Fill in the embarkation card which is collected by passport control, and then proceed to the departure lounge. There is a further security check (x-ray and body search) before embarkation; you may even be required to identify your luggage before it is loaded on the plane.

Domestic flights PIA, Aero Asia, Bhoja Air and Shaheen Air all have offices just outside the arrivals terminal where you can buy tickets for onward domestic flights. Note that these are considerably cheaper when bought in Pakistan rather than when bought abroad.

Services Banks at the airport are open 24 hours (cash and travellers' cheques); rates are marginally inferior to those available in town. There are branches of the **National Bank of Pakistan** and **Habib Bank** in the baggage collection hall. Outside the building there are more foreign exchange counters, as well as touts for money changers. Also outside is the **Tourist Information** counter (24 hours), as well as offices for some of the luxury hotels (the **Marriott, Holiday Inn, Pearl Continental, Serena** and **Shalimar**). Left luggage facilities are not available at the airport. Duty free is available to passengers arriving and departing. Alcohol is not available, but cigarettes are incredibly cheap (US$8 for 200), although most of what's on display is not particularly exciting (nappies, hairspray etc). Once you have checked-in for departure, there are four very fast internet terminals in the waiting area (Rs60 per hour). Porters are available and should have the correct fee displayed on a badge. There is a café/snack bar outside and another in the terminal, but both are basic and overpriced. ▶▶ *See also page 68 for information on Islamabad airport.*

Overland

Pakistan has land border crossing points with China, India, Iran and Afghanistan.

To/from China and Central Asia

For those travelling on the KKH, the most important land border is with China. If travelling to China, it is essential to **obtain a visa in advance** since they are not available on the border. The Chinese embassy in Islamabad issues visas in one to three days (see page 81). It is not permitted to take private vehicles into China unless prior arrangements have been made (this can take months, and also works out to be very expensive). In theory this restriction also applies to bicycles (the visa application form may state that a special permit is required). This border crossing is officially open from May 1- December 31, but is weather dependent so may open later and close earlier.

Pakistani border formalities are completed at Sust ('Afiyatabad'), while Chinese formalities are completed at Tashkurgan. For those arriving in Pakistan from China without a visa, the situation can be unpredictable, but it is generally possible to get a seven-day transit visa on the border (extendable in Islamabad, but this involves unwanted hassle so you should get your visa in advance if possible). The only Pakistani embassy in China is in Beijing, some 4,000 km from the Pak-China border, and they have a tendency to only issue one-month, as opposed to three-month, visas. For further details on crossing the border between Pakistan and China, see page 338.

From the Chinese city of Kashgar it is possible to travel on to Kyrghizstan via the Tourgat Pass, although you will need a Kyrghiz visa in advance (available in Islamabad) and a permit to cross the pass (which can be arranged in Kashgar). It is also possible to travel on from Kashgar to Urumqi, and then from there to Kazakhstan (visas in Islamabad). A seldom undertaken, but much talked about, option from Kashgar is to travel to Lhasa in Tibet via Mount Kailash. Since permits for this gruelling trip are not available in Kashgar, this journey is technically illegal, although a number of travellers continue to attempt it.

To/from India

Despite their long frontier, there is currently only one recognized border crossing between Pakistan and India, located between Lahore and Amritsar. The border towns are Wagah (23 km from Lahore) on the Pakistani side, and Attari (39 km from Amritsar) on the Indian side. The border should be open every day of the year, although it is worth enquiring locally about holiday arrangements. Use the bus/foot combination to cross here since the train takes forever.

It is worth getting your visas in advance (they are extremely difficult to obtain on the border). Indian visas are only available in Islamabad (see page 81), while Pakistani visas are only available in New Delhi. For further details about India, consult *Footprint India*.

To/from Iran

The only official border crossing point between Pakistan and Iran is at Taftan, 84 km from the Iranian city of Zahedan and over 600 km from Quetta in Baluchistan (Pakistan). Trains run between Zahedan and Quetta (you usually have to change at the border town of Taftan, 24 hours from Quetta, however), although they are very slow (minimum 32 hours), or you can make the journey by bus which is much quicker (around 15 hours) but less comfortable. *Footprint Pakistan* has unrivalled coverage of Baluchistan.

There is an Iranian embassy in Islamabad, and consulates in Peshawar, Lahore, Karachi and Quetta, but getting a visa is very much a hit or miss affair. At the time of researching, the Iranian consulate in Quetta claimed that it was issuing transit visas (usually valid for seven days and extendable by a further week once inside Iran) to tourists within 10 days. Some readers have also written to say that the Iranian consulate in Lahore is issuing visas without too much hassle. Islamabad remains a bad place to apply for a visa. Bear in mind, however, that the situation is liable to change without warning. The Pakistani embassy is located in Tehran, with consulates in Mashad and Zahedan, but you are strongly advised to obtain your Pakistani visa before leaving home (especially given the limited time available on an Iranian transit visa).

To/from Afghanistan

During the Taliban's reign, visas for individual travellers were at times remarkably easy to come by at the consulates in Quetta and Peshawar. However, the Pakistanis refused to issue permits for the recognized land crossings between the two countries, and so unless you could hitch a lift in on an NGO flight, the only way to enter Afghanistan was to be smuggled in illegally (with all the inherent risks that involved). How things stand after the fall of the Taliban is not entirely clear, but it should be generally assumed that it is not safe for foreigners to visit; apart from the very real risk of getting caught up in fighting, there is the added danger from several million landmines remaining in the country. At the time of going to press, visas for Afghanistan were only being issued to accredited journalists and aid workers.

The two main border crossings are at Torkham, on the Khyber Pass between Peshawar and Jalalabad, and at Chaman, between Quetta and Kandahar. Most of Pakistan's border with Afghanistan is, however, extremely porous. If you are keen to find out about the current situation in Afghanistan, Peshawar is the best place to get up-to-date information. There are over a hundred NGOs still based there, working with Afghan refugees in Pakistan and across the border in Afghanistan itself. **ACBAR** (Agency Co-ordinating Body for Afghan Refugees) and **ARIC** (ACBAR Resource and Information Centre) share premises in Peshawar's University Town (see page 116).

At time of going to press, the Foreign and Commonwealth Office no longer dissuades against travellers visiting Pakistan, but advises against all non-essential travel to northern and western Baluchistan, western North-West Frontier Province, rural Sindh and border areas. For further updated information, consult www.fco.gov.uk

Touching down

Rules, customs and etiquette

Pakistan is an extremely hospitable country where visitors are generally treated with great respect. It is important to reciprocate that respect and to show sensitivity towards cultural norms in order to avoid giving offence.

Conduct
You will be judged to a large extent by the way you dress; a neat and clean appearance will command more respect and get a better response in any situation. Scanty or tight-fitting clothes cause great offence to Muslims. For their own safety and wellbeing, women need to take particular care over this, although it applies just as much to men. Open displays of affection between couples also cause offence and are not acceptable in public. It is common, however, to see young Pakistani men walking around hand in hand.

Courtesy
It never pays to be rude or discourteous in Pakistan; doing so will invariably make things more difficult than they might otherwise be. Likewise, direct confrontation is never a good idea and is the surest way of eliminating any hope of achieving your aims in a particular situation. Unfortunately bureaucracy can be a major headache in Pakistan, with reams of red tape surrounding even the simplest of tasks. Bureaucrats are a law unto themselves and can be rude, obstructive and unhelpful. The only way to deal with this is to be patient, polite and firm. Open displays of anger or frustration only serve to delight them.

Visiting mosques and shrines
Non-Muslims are welcome in most mosques and shrines, but there are exceptions. Always remove your shoes before entering. A thick pair of socks are useful for walking across baking hot floors. It is particularly important to dress modestly, not exposing anything more than head, hands and feet. Women should also cover their heads. Never walk directly in front of someone who is praying.

Hands
The left hand is considered unclean in Pakistan and should never be used for eating. More accurately, the rule is that the left hand should not be raised to the mouth, or dipped into a communal dish during a meal. It is perfectly acceptable to hold your roti in the left hand and tear bits off with the right. Avoid offering or accepting things with the left hand.

Begging
Beggars are less common in Pakistan than in India. The standard advice is that it is better to give to a recognized charity working with the poor than to make largely ineffectual handouts (although this is really a matter of personal judgement). In parts of Hunza you may be plagued by children asking for pens etc.

Tipping
Tipping is generally expected in more expensive restaurants, although many also have a service charge. Offering 10% is considered generous; 5% or rounding off with loose change is perfectly acceptable. Use your discretion. Beware of nodding at

Touching down

Emergency services Police T15, Fire T16, Ambulance T115
Directory enquiries T17 (in major towns only)
Official time Pakistan is five hours ahead of Greenwich Mean Time
Official languages Urdu, English and a host of regional languages
Business hours There is considerable regional variation in business hours. Timings often differ for winter and summer. Note that during Ramadam most offices and businesses are only open from 0800/0900-1200/1300. The weekly public holiday has now been shifted from Friday to Sunday. This means that Friday has virtually become a half-day (with most businesses closing at 1200 for Friday prayers and many not reopening during the afternoon), while Saturday has also in many cases become a de facto half-day (with many government offices closing mid-afternoon). Generally, the following hours apply:
Banks: Mon-Thu 0900-1200, 1400-1600, Fri 0900-1130, Sat 0900-1200, Sun closed.
Government offices: Mon-Thu 0900-1200, 1400-1600, Fri 0900-1130, Sat 0900-1200, Sun closed. **Museums**: Usually 0900-1700 in summer (1600 winter), closed Wed. **Post offices**: Mon-Thu 0900-1500 (some later), Fri 0900-1130, Sat 0900-1200, Sun closed. **Shops**: Mon-Sat 0900-1900, closed Sun (and closed for prayers 1200-1400 on Fri). **Telephone offices**: usually open 24 hours in larger towns.
Voltage 220/240 volts, 50/60 cycles AC. Most plug sockets are two-pin. Power cuts or 'load-shedding' are common, particularly in remoter areas. Power surges can be a problem; delicate equipment such as laptops should be protected by a surge adaptor.
Weights and measures Officially, metric. However, miles are sometimes quoted on older distance markers and by the older generation. Cloth merchants and tailors still work in yards. Locally used weights include the tola (around 12 g) and the seer (just under 1 kg).

waiters as they bring you your change; they are liable to interpret this as an indication that they can pocket the money as a tip. Rounding up room service bills generally ensures friendly and continuing attentiveness.

Photography

Photography of military installations, airports, railway stations, bridges and dams is prohibited. Do not take photos of women without permission.

Safety

With some notable exceptions, Pakistan is probably one of the safest countries in South Asia for foreign tourists. Basic common sense is the key to ensuring your safety and security in the majority of situations. Certain areas of Pakistan are dangerous for foreigners to travel in or visit. In the context of this guide, such areas include most of the side valleys off the KKH between Besham and Gilgit, the very upper reaches of the Kaghan Valley, plus many of the tribal areas of NWFP. Such areas are highlighted in the text. However, situations can change rapidly so it is always essential to check with tourism officials and/or the police regarding the current situation. Take heed of

How big is your footprint?

1 Where possible choose a destination, tour operator or hotel with a proven ethical and environmental commitment, and if in doubt ask.
2 Spend money on locally produced (rather than imported) goods and services and use common sense when bargaining – your few dollars saved may be a week's salary to others.
3 Consider staying in local, rather than foreign-owned, accommodation – the economic benefits for host communities are far greater – and there are far greater opportunities to learn about local culture.
4 Use water and electricity carefully – travellers may receive preferential supply while the needs of local communities are overlooked.
5 Don't give money or sweets to children – it encourages begging – instead give to a recognized project, charity or school.
6 Learn about local etiquette and culture – consider local norms and behaviour – and dress appropriately for local cultures and situations.
7 Protect wildlife and other natural resources – don't buy souvenirs or goods made from wildlife unless they are clearly sustainably produced and are not protected under CITES legislation.
8 Always ask before taking photographs or videos of people.

advice given by locals. When travelling in remoter areas, it is always a good idea to register your presence with the local police and/or the Deputy/Assistant Commissioner. The latter are generally well informed, helpful and speak good English. Women should not travel alone in remoter areas.

Specific information on travelling in Pakistan can be obtained from the following government advisory bodies, although their advice tends to be on the pessimistic/safe side: **US State Department's Bureau of Consular Affairs**, Overseas Citizens Services, Room 4800, Department of State, Washington, DC 20520-4818, USA, T202-6474000, http://travel.state.gov/travel_warnings.html. **British Foreign & Commonwealth Office**, King Charles Street, London, Sw1A 2AH,UK, T0870-6060290, www.fco.gov.uk. **Australian Department of Foreign Affairs**, Canberra, Australia, T02-62613305, www.dfat.gov.au/travel.

Theft

Never leave valuables and important documents in your hotel room (including more expensive hotels). If the room is secured by a padlockable bolt, use your own padlock, not the one supplied by the hotel. Take particular care in cheaper hotels and in crowded bus or railway stations where it is easy for someone to slip away with your bags. When on the move it is a good idea to secure any zips on your bags with a padlock.

Confidence tricksters are far rarer than in other countries of South and Southeast Asia. If someone offers to help you out or show you round, they are unlikely to be after something in return. However, you must still be on your guard, particularly in larger cities. Lahore has a bad reputation for confidence tricksters.

Police

The police are something of an unknown quantity in Pakistan. In larger centres they are generally helpful, but in remoter areas they sometimes do not speak any English. Wherever you are, they can be corrupt. If you do have anything stolen, report it immediately to the police and be sure to get a copy of the police report if you intend to claim against your insurance. It is a good idea to enlist the help of someone who speaks good English. If you run into problems with corrupt police in remoter areas, insist on being taken to the nearest Deputy Commissioner or Assistant Commissioner.

Drugs

Hashish, or charas, is readily available throughout Pakistan, with the exception of the Northern Areas. In many places, including Islamabad, there are profuse quantities of low grade cannabis growing wild. The authorities periodically get embarrassed by this and have it cut down and destroyed by burning it in huge bonfires around the city! In many communities it forms an integral part of the social fabric, particularly amongst the Pathans of NWFP. However, it is also illegal and foreigners should be extremely careful. There is no guarantee that someone offering to sell you hashish will not then go and inform the police. Penalties are stiff and, for larger quantities, generally involve a lengthy prison sentence. If you are intent on smoking, avoid actually buying it; most Pakistanis who indulge in the habit will be happy to share a smoke with you. Some travellers report instances of hashish being planted on them by corrupt police. If your bags are searched, try to ensure that this is done publicly and keep a close eye on what is going on. Such occurrences are thankfully rare. Don't even consider trying to smuggle drugs out of the country; Pakistan is recognized as a major drug producing country on the international scene and customs officials are generally on the alert.

Getting around

Air

Pakistan has an extensive air network, linking all the key cities and major district centres (see map of PIA's domestic air network). It is worth noting that internal flights are considerably cheaper when bought in Pakistan, rather than when booked and paid for abroad. Security on internal flights is tight, with even hand luggage often having to pass through two or three x-ray machines. You may even be requested to remove batteries from cameras and place them in the aircraft hold.

However, there are only three key routes that serve the mountainous north: Peshawar-Chitral; Islamabad-Gilgit; Islamabad-Skardu. All these flights are subject to weather conditions, needing clear visibility along the entire flightpath in order to operate. For full details consult the ins and outs sections of the relevant cities.

Train

Pakistan has an extensive network of railways that can provide a relatively comfortable and reasonably fast way of covering large distances, in addition to offering the opportunity to see the countryside and experience a slice of Pakistani society on the move. The main backbone of the system runs in a broad arc north-south between Peshawar and Karachi, via Rawalpindi and Lahore, with an important branch line to Quetta, and various other branches throughout Punjab, Sind and parts of Baluchistan and NWFP. However, little of this is relevant to travellers in the mountainous north, and even the Rawalpindi-Peshawar route is more conveniently tackled by road.

There are three categories of trains in Pakistan (Express, Mail, Passenger), and six classes of ticket, and foreign tourists should note that they are entitled to a 25%

The hazards of road travel in Pakistan

In theory, vehicles in Pakistan drive on the left. If you drive yourself, or are cycling, take great care. Pedestrians, cattle and a wide range of other animals roam at will. It can be particularly dangerous when driving after dark because few vehicles are ever lit. The general rule of night-driving in Pakistan seems to be to kill your lights as you approach an on-coming vehicle, and then hit them with the full beam just before you pass! Similarly, use of the indicator lights does not necessarily mean 'I am turning right/left'; it can also be read as 'Please overtake me to the left/right'!

There is next to no training for would be drivers, and the test is a farce. Licences are invariably obtained through bribery, and as a result there are real dangers from poor judgement and suicidal overtaking manoeuvres. The general rule on Pakistan's roads is 'might is right'. These dangers apply to both visitors with their own vehicles, and those travelling on buses and other forms of public transport. Pakistani newspapers are full of stories of buses 'turning turtle', followed invariably by the lines 'driver absconding'.

Accidents often produce large and angry crowds, so if you have an accident it is best to leave the scene and report it to the police as quickly as possible thereafter. It is probably also worth informing your own embassy.

---

discount (ISIC students 50%) by completing some time-consuming paperwork at the Commercial Department of Pakistan Railways in each city they wish to purchase a ticket. This means that you can travel, for example, the 1,260 km between Karachi and Lahore for around US$5, or for US$15 in the luxury of an air-conditioned berth.

Road

Bus

The principal means of getting around the mountainous north of Pakistan is by road, with jeeps running to the places that buses cannot reach. Buses in Pakistan come in all shapes and sizes, with varying degrees of speed and comfort/discomfort. There are both government-run and privately operated, 'express' and 'regular', services. The degree of comfort is nominally indicated by a prefix such as 'de luxe' or 'super de luxe'. Any bus without this prefix, or referred to in this handbook as a 'local bus', is likely to have unreserved seating, will carry more people inside (and possibly on the roof also) than you would think possible, will crawl along at 20 km per hour, have little legroom, and will be an extremely uncomfortable (but cheap) way to travel. Most of the government-run services fall into this category.

The government-run **Northern Areas Transport Company** (NATCO) operates services on the following routes: Rawalpindi-Gilgit; Gilgit-Chitral; Gilgit-Skardu; Skardu-Khapulu; Skardu-Shigar; Gilgit-Sust; Sust-Tashkurgan (China). ISIC cardholders can sometimes obtain a 50% discount, but not on de luxe services. The bulk of this workload falls upon the fleet of Bedford buses; a joy to look at, but not to travel on. In general, with the exception of the Gilgit-Chitral and Sust-Tashkurgan routes, private operators offer a more comfortable service on their so-called 'Flying Coaches'. These are generally slightly more expensive, but are quicker, more comfortable (sometimes with air conditioning) and usually have the assurance of a reserved seat. Booking in advance means that you are more likely to get a 'good' seat, although it is difficult to reach that happy compromise between comfort (seats near the front) and safety (seats away from the front). Next step down from the 'Flying Coaches' are the coasters, which can be comfortable if their 18 seat maximum number of passengers is respected. Minibuses are also used and are referred to by a number of manufacturers' names (eg Hiace).

Jeeps

Minibuses run on routes that they are blatantly not designed for, but when the track is deemed to be too rough (and that's very rough), jeeps take over. Cargo jeeps run on a number of routes, notably: Gilgit-Mastuj/Chitral; Chitral-Mastuj; Chitral-Kalash Valleys; Chilas-Babusar; Gilgit-Astor; Gilgit-Naltar; Gilgit-Bagrot Valley; Skardu-Shigar-Askole; Skardu-Deosai-Astor; Skardu-Khapulu-Hushe. Such cargo jeeps can either be 4WD vehicles, or converted Datsun pick-up trucks (especially in Indus Kohistan). Many of these services are demand-driven, but on many routes these vehicles are perilously over-crowded and extremely uncomfortable.

Alternatively, the most comfortable way to travel is on a private-hire jeep. Compared with public transport this is an expensive way to travel, although the cost can be shared by a number of passengers, making it very competitive on certain routes. It also has the advantage of comfort, plus being able to stop when and where you want. The cheapest way to hire a jeep is usually through a backpacker guesthouse manager, although there are more or less set prices on many routes and it probably won't be any cheaper than going through a reputable travel agency. Note that you often need to hire a jeep just to reach a trekking trail-head. Fuel and jeep maintenance costs have soared in recent years, although the sheer number of vehicles (and hence the resulting competition for business) in many parts of the Northern Areas means that this rise in costs has not yet been fully passed on to customers hiring jeeps.

Car hire

Self-drive car hire is virtually unknown in Pakistan; it usually involves car and driver. Larger hotels generally have a car and driver hire desk, as have most travel agents, with typical fees being around Rs500-800 per day plus a per kilometre charge (Rs8 per km on sealed roads and Rs10 per km on unmade roads). Jeep hire is more relevant in the mountainous north (see above).

Cycling

Those cycling the KKH may not quite be the pioneers of 15 or so years ago, but it still represents a great way to explore the mountainous north of Pakistan. Not only can cyclists enjoy that sense of freedom denied to bus travellers, but with a few notable exceptions, gradients are not particularly steep. However, some advance thought on how you are going to tackle the route is essential. For example, being able to say that you cycled the entire length of the KKH from Rawalpindi/Islamabad to Kashgar (or to Sust, at least) may be important to some riders, but this may not be the best use of your time and effort (also note that your daily distance covered may be up to 50% less than your normal rate back home). Many bike riders are now skipping the whole hot and unwelcoming section between Rawalpindi/Islamabad and Gilgit, and using that cycling time to explore other areas, such as the Gilgit-Chitral route, or the Baltistan area. Almost all buses in Pakistan, including those that make the journey across the border into China, are happy to take cycles on the roof. Make sure that your cycle is properly secured; it will probably sustain more damage being rattled around on the roof than through using it. Expect to pay 50-100 % extra on the fare. There still remains some confusion about cycling in China; see page 330 for some (hopefully temporary) bad news on the subject of cycling into China.

Although the KKH is sealed for its entire length, some parts are better maintained than others, and with land-slides (large and small) part and parcel of the travel experience, a mountain bike is probably preferable to a touring bike (and pretty much essential for the Gilgit-Chitral and Baltistan trips). Some degree of maintenance competence is required, particularly if you have problems in more remote areas. A tool kit and spares should be carried, especially by those with imported cycles, although local cycle repair shops are extremely resourceful and able to carry out the most unlikely of improvisations. Practise puncture repair before you set off too, and make sure your saddle is broken in before undertaking this trip. Those wanting to buy a bike in Pakistan will find Taiwanese mountain bikes on sale in Islamabad's Blue Area for around Rs5,000. The cast-iron framed, one-geared Pakistani and Chinese bikes are not suitable for the KKH (difficult to get going but plenty of momentum once you do!). Respect for the Islamic sense of decorum should be maintained, and lycra cycling shorts should not be worn, and certainly not by women.

Foreigners on imported cycles still attract a lot of attention, particularly in more remote areas. Keep an eye on your bike during meal and drink stops; adults and children alike are prone to fiddle with gear levers and brakes, and the occasional small hand may find its way into your paniers. Children also have a habit of applying your brakes as you trundle along! Warnings about specific danger-spots are given at the relevant point in the text, although it is worth emphasizing here that female cyclists (including those in women-only groups) are not recommended to tackle stretches such as Thakot Bridge to Chilas (Kohistan-Diamar) alone. Note that the kids in Kohistan no longer throw stones at cyclists – they all have sling-shots now! One suggested way of reducing the stone-throwing threat is to wave to everybody as soon as you see them; the tendency is to wave back, rather than fire off stones!

This guide contains very detailed 'routes' information (distances, food and rest stops etc) that will be of use to cyclists who need to stop at points between all the main settlements and sites. In many of the more popular backpacker hotels it is likely that you will meet other cyclists with whom you can exchange information. Look out also for the 'rumour books' at many of these hotels; they often have detailed information written by other cyclists. There are numerous websites with information on cycling the KKH, such as www.kiwisonbikes.com or www.pedalglobal.net, and the **Cyclists' Touring Club**, www.ctc.org.uk, access for members only.

Hitchhiking

Because public transport is so cheap in Pakistan, the concept of hitchhiking is virtually unknown. One exception is along the Central Hunza to Gojal section of the KKH. The Western 'thumbs-up' sign is unknown; just flag the vehicle down. Some drivers will expect at least the equivalent bus fare for giving you a lift. It is not advisable for women to hitchhike alone.

Private vehicles

If bringing your own motor vehicle, a Carnet de Passage (carnet) is essential. These are usually obtained from a motoring organization in your own country. Pakistan will accept both AIT and FIA carnets, although if you are continuing on to India (and Nepal) you will need an AIT carnet. Most carnets now feature both logos. If in doubt, contact the **AA** ① *155 Chenab Block, Iqbal Town, Lahore, T042-445320.* It is currently not possible to take a vehicle into China without prior arrangement, an expensive and time-consuming business. Both petrol and diesel are widely available in Pakistan, although the latter is much cheaper. Petrol is rarely above 92 octane and tends to be particularly 'dirty'.

Local transport

Auto-rickshaws
Cheaper than taxis, auto-rickshaws are the most convenient way of getting around many towns, although visitors should note that the variety found in Pakistan are even smaller than those found in India, and it is quite a squeeze to fit in two adults with backpacks. Very few have working meters so it is essential to agree the fare in advance. Note that in heavy city traffic you are much more vulnerable in a rickshaw than in a taxi.

Local buses
If you are staying in larger towns and cities for only a short time it is unlikely that you will get to grips with the local bus system. Routes are difficult to understand, the buses are often impossibly crowded, and it can be very brutal getting on and off the still moving bus. However, if you are determined, you will generally find someone who will ensure that you are on the right bus.

Minibuses
Many towns have minibus or Suzuki services which operate on a fixed route, but pick up and drop passengers on request (often referred to as 'wagons'). They are quicker than local buses, but equally crowded. In some rural areas, converted pick-ups are used for public transport (frequently referred to as Datsuns, whatever the make).

Taxis
Pakistan's taxi drivers are generally less money-grasping than those in India, and overcharging is less frequent. Nevertheless, it is always advisable to fix the price in advance. Do not be afraid to bargain, although you should be realistic; it is unlikely that you will pay the same as a local person. An exception to this general pattern of honesty is to be found at Islamabad Airport, where you may be asked for 10 times the correct fare. In many of the larger towns, there are numerous brand-new, comfortable, yellow taxis, many of which have working meters that the drivers are prepared to use.

Tongas
Horse-drawn carts, or tongas, are still found in many cities, operating on fixed routes, and pulled by mangy beasts usually revealing their entire rib cage.

Maps

Getting good maps in Pakistan is next to impossible and the best advice is to buy your maps in advance from a specialist seller before travel. For details of trekking maps, see page 49.

Stanfords ① *12-14 Long Acre, Covent Garden, London, WC2E 9LP, T020-7836-1321, www.stanfords.co.uk*, with over 80 well-travelled staff and 40,000 titles in stock, is the world's largest map and travel bookshop. It also has branches at 29 Corn Street, Bristol, BS1, and at 39 Spring Gardens, Manchester, M2.

Maps available from the **Survey of Pakistan** ① *Murree Rd, Faisabad, Rawalpindi, T450808, Sun-Thu 0900-1700*, make good wall posters (some are 2 m by 2 m) but are grossly out of date (the 'Northern Areas' map doesn't even show the KKH). You must select the maps blind from a catalogue, and they will then be brought down to you. Keep the receipt to show customs.

Sleeping

Hotels and guesthouses

Outside the main cities featured in this handbook (Rawalpindi/Islamabad, Peshawar, Kashgar), you will find few international-class hotels. However, if anything, hotels and guesthouses in the north of Pakistan tend to be better value and better run than elsewhere in the country. Those travelling in the mid to budget range are spoilt for choice, with plenty of extremely comfortable rooms in the C-D price category, and some very well-run backpacker haunts in the E-H price range.

Almost without exception, even the cheapest hotels have attached bath and toilet facilities. There are exceptions to this rule, and some hotels offer cheaper rooms where such facilities are shared. If contemplating such a deal, check both the room and the bathroom before committing yourself. In most hotels, toilets tend to be of the Asian 'squat' variety, rather than the Western WC. They are easy to adapt to and usually more hygienic. Many toilets in Pakistan are unable to cope with toilet paper so a separate waste-paper basket is provided. With the exception of hotels in the L and A categories, the word 'bath' is used to denote 'bathroom' as opposed to a 'bathtub'. Most bathrooms are equipped with either a shower or some sort of tap/bucket/scoop combination. In many hotels, hot water is only available during certain times of the day. If your bathroom has a bucket it is recommended that you keep it full at all times so that it is still possible to flush the toilet during water cuts. Few sinks have plugs, and towels, soap and toilet paper are rarely provided in budget hotels. NB It should be assumed that tap water, even in expensive hotels in big cities, is not safe for drinking or cleaning teeth. Many parts of Pakistan experience power cuts, or 'load-shedding' as it is euphemistically termed. It is worthwhile having a good torch handy. Many mid-price hotels have their own generators, although they tend to be unpleasantly noisy.

Only the more expensive hotels have central air conditioning (a/c); elsewhere rooms are cooled by individual units and occasionally 'air-coolers'. Many hotels in the D and E category will have a number of identical rooms, but with air conditioning, and priced in the C category. If you are paying extra for air conditioning, make sure that the unit is working properly. Almost all rooms, even in the cheapest hotels and dormitories, have a fan. In addition, most hotels can arrange laundry services very cheaply.

In cheaper hotels you may well be sharing your room and bathroom with a whole host of animal life, notably cockroaches, ants and geckos (harmless house lizards). Poisonous or dangerous animals are extremely rare, although bed bugs are far more common (and should be dealt with by changing room/hotel). Very few hotels have mosquito nets or effective mosquito screens.

Resthouses and inspection bungalows

In many remote areas of the Northern Areas and NWFP, the only accommodation available is in the form of government-run 'resthouses' and 'inspection bungalows'. These tend to be two- to three-bedroom bungalows that are used by travelling officials. In theory, you can stay in one if you obtain a booking chit from the department's regional headquarters, although at some it is possible to just turn up and request a room without doing this. Note, however, that visiting officials always have priority over tourists, even those who have a booking chit. Such resthouses are generally well furnished, clean and remarkably good value (usually in the hotel category E-G), but naturally, the best-located ones tend to be permanently full. They are usually cared for by a *chowkidar* (watchman/caretaker) who may be able to provide basic meals on request.

Hostels

There are a number of youth hostels in Pakistan run by the **Pakistan Youth Hostel Association** ⓘ *National Office, G-6/4, Garden Road, Aabpara, Islamabad, T826899*, but they are extremely variable, often inconveniently located, while the best ones seem permanently full. A cheap hotel is a better option.

Camping

Officially designated campsites are few and far between, although those trekking in the north will find almost unlimited camping options. Many hotels will allow you to pitch a tent in their grounds for a modest fee.

Eating

Food

At its very best, Pakistani food can be superb, at its worst, bland and uninspiring; meat-eaters are particularly well served. Travellers arriving from India may find the variety of dishes on offer in Pakistan less appealing. Vegetarians and vegans are not well catered for, although some of the backpacker haunts along the KKH offer good-value communal vegetarian meals (a little repetitive if you stay too long). In certain areas, vegetarians may have to redraw their own ethical boundaries, with many 'vegetable' meals cooked or served with meat stock and even plain rice sometimes containing unspecified 'crispy bits'. Although dishes of spinach, potatoes, okra, peas and the ubiquitous dhal (lentils) can be excellent when well prepared, all too often they are simply overcooked mush. In many areas, particularly transport stops, all that is on offer is dhal and chapati, okra ('bhindi/ladyfingers') and chapati, or poor quality mutton and chapati (see Health for tips on eating healthily). Although rice is available, wheat is the staple so most meals are eaten with either chapatis or nan. There is a food and eating out glossary at the end of the guide. For details on food in the Chinese towns covered in this guide, see page 337.

All the main cities have restaurants offering reasonable imitations of Chinese food. Western 'fast food' is becoming increasingly common across the country. In fact, among the middle classes the words 'fast food' are seen more as a style of cuisine than as a derogatory term describing nutritionally poor food. KFC, Pizza Hut and now McDonalds have, or are in the process of opening, branches in all the major cities.

Western-style breakfasts are generally available, with the emphasis on fried eggs, boiled eggs or omelette. Porridge and inferior cornflakes can also be found, but those seeking an egg, bacon and sausage fry-up are likely to be disappointed. Reasonable-quality Western confectionery is becoming more commonplace, but cheese fans are recommended to bring their own.

Eating out

Almost all hotels, whatever their status or category, have either a restaurant or dining hall, and they can often be very good value. Eating out in Pakistan is far cheaper than in the West, even at the top-end restaurants.

Most restaurants in Pakistan have 'family rooms'; sometimes a separate room, or simply an area partitioned off by a curtain or screen. Pakistani families almost always use this facility, so any travelling couples or females who want to avoid unwarranted attention are recommended to follow suit. Note that children are extremely welcome in even the most expensive restaurants and staff invariably go to great lengths to accommodate them.

In some smaller towns the choice of restaurant and cuisine may be limited to 'meat and chapati' places, where various parts of recently dead animals are hung up outside to tempt you in. In such circumstances it is generally best to follow the example of the local people and select the busiest one. There are also numerous roadside snack-sellers, offering tempting samosas, pakora etc. Obviously, health risks may well be increased, so it is wise to only eat things that you have seen freshly cooked.

Drink

Drinking water

Public water supplies, even in large cities, are nearly always polluted and unsafe to drink. This applies to both tap water in your hotel room and water served in a jug at the dining table. Bottled mineral water is widely available, although not all bottled water is mineral water; some is simply purified water from an urban supply. Check the seal of the bottle when buying and reject any that appears to have been resealed or tampered with. Many people begrudge spending one or two dollars a day on bottled water, but if it reduces the likelihood of illness it must surely be worth it. Note, however, that disposal of these plastic bottles is becoming a major environmental concern; perhaps investing in your own water purifyer is a greener solution.

Beverages and soft drinks

Tea, or chai, is the universal drink of Pakistan. It is generally made by throwing equal handfuls of tea and sugar into a pot, adding equal parts of UHT (long-life) milk and water, and bringing the whole thing to the boil. It is very sweet, but remarkably refreshing. Ask for chai, or 'Pakistani tea'. If you do not want sugar (*chini*) or milk (*dudh*), you should say so when ordering. Many places offer 'separate tea' or 'English tea', with a pot of tea, milk and sugar served separately. Chinese-style green tea (*khawa*) is available in many areas. Coffee is rarely found outside the bigger hotels, and even then it is generally instant coffee.

Bottled, carbonated drinks, such as Pepsi, Coca-Cola, 7-Up and Fanta are found almost everywhere, although prices rise as you move away from the main cities (eg Rs8 in Islamabad, Rs15 in Gilgit, or Rs25 in a five-star hotel). Cartons of fruit juice, most notably mango, are also widely available. In season, fresh mango, orange and banana shakes are common. NB Ice cubes should be considered unsafe because the water source is likely to be contaminated.

Alcohol

Pakistan is officially a dry country. Non-Muslim foreigners are, however, permitted to purchase locally produced beers and spirits on production of a special permit. Obtaining the permit does require a certain degree of persistence. The permits are available from the Excise and Tax Department in major cities, although they are only valid for the city or district within which they are issued. You will require your passport, photocopies of the relevant pages and some passport size photographs. Although the fee for the permit is small (Rs200), it can often only be paid at a certain bank on the other side of town from the permit office. The current allowance is nine litres per month, which can usually be bought from the more expensive hotels. Some top-end hotels have special bars where guests (and sometimes non-guests) can buy and consume alcohol. Murree Beer (advertised as being glycerine free!) can be remarkably good, although you do come across the odd rogue bottle. Varieties of whisky, gin, rum and vodka are also available. It is not permitted to bring alcohol into the country, although customs officers generally turn a blind eye to reasonable quantities, or 'confiscate' it against a receipt. Reasonable beer is extremely cheap in China. NB No permit required for non-Muslims at the Pearl Continental, Peshawar; simply show your passport.

Entertainment

Nightclubs and bars
Pakistan is the wrong country if you are seeking nightclubs and bars. In cities such as Islamabad and Peshawar which have large expatriate communities, there are thriving social scenes but they are difficult to penetrate for the casual, short-term visitor.

Cinemas
Far more accessible is the key local entertainment centre, the cinema, but they are only really available in the larger towns and cities. Like their Indian counterparts (which are hugely popular here), Pakistani films tend to be a combination of high-octane, non-stop violence, with sloppy love songs and coy love scenes intermittently interspersed. Many cinemas show Western films of the 'action' variety (Arnie, Stallone, Bruce Lee, James Bond etc). Western women (including those accompanied) often feel extremely uncomfortable on visits to the cinema.

Festivals and events

The following is a list of national public holidays and Islamic holy days (usually public holidays). Note that the precise timing of Islamic holy days is linked to the sighting of the new crescent moon (at Mecca), although there is sometimes a discrepancy in the formal sighting between different sects of Islam. Islamic holy days are unfortunately often a time of sectarian tension (and even violence) between Sunnis and Shias. There are also a number of unofficial regional holidays and festivals celebrated in the north of Pakistan. For a full calendar see www.holidayfestival.com.

Public/religious holidays and festivals, 2004-2007

2004
1 Jul Bank holiday
11 Jul Taqt Nashina (Ismaili areas)
End Jul Shandur Pass Polo
14 Aug Independence Day
Mid-Aug Utjao (Kalash Valleys)
6 Sep Defence of Pakistan Day
11 Sep Urs of Mohammad Ali Jinnah
12 Sep Leilat al-Meiraj
End Sep Phool (Birir Valley, Kalash)
15 Oct Ramadan starts
23 Oct Hunza Didar Sal Gira (Hunza)
1 Nov Jashan-e-Gilgit (Gilgit)
9 Nov Mohammad (Allama) Iqbal Day
14 Nov Eid el-Fitr
18 Nov Gojal Didar Sal Gira (Gojal)
13 Dec Birthday Sal Gira
Mid-Dec Chaomos (Kalash Valleys)
21 Dec Tumishiling (Hunza, Nagar)
25 Dec Birthday of Mohammad Ali Jinnah
31 Dec Bank holiday

2005
21 Jan Eid el-Adha
10 Feb Ras as-Sana
19 Feb Ashoura
End Feb Kitdit (Gojal), **Bo Pho/Taghun** (Hunza, Nagar, Gojal)
21 Mar Nauroz (NA and NWFP)
23 Mar Pakistan Day
End Mar Basant (Lahore)
21 Apr Moulid an-Nabi
1 May International Labour Day
Mid-May Joshi (Kalash Valleys)
End Jun Ginani/Chinir (Hunza, Nagar, Gojal)
1 Jul Bank holiday
11 Jul Taqt Nashina (Ismaili areas)
End Jul Shandur Pass Polo
14 Aug Independence Day
Mid-Aug Utjao (Kalash Valleys)
1 Sep Leilat al-Meiraj
6 Sep Defence of Pakistan Day
11 Sep Urs of Mohammad Ali Jinnah
End Sep Phool (Birir Valley, Kalash)
5 Oct Ramadan starts
23 Oct Hunza Didar Sal Gira (Hunza)

1 Nov Jashan-e-Gilgit (Gilgit)
4 Nov Eid el-Fitr
9 Nov Mohammad (Allama) Iqbal Day
18 Nov Gojal Didar Sal Gira (Gojal)
13 Dec Birthday Sal Gira
Mid-Dec Chaomos (Kalash Valleys)
21 Dec Tumishiling (Hunza, Nagar)
25 Dec Birthday of Mohammad Ali Jinnah
31 Dec Bank holiday

2006
10 Jan Eid el-Adha
31 Jan Ras as-Sana
9 Feb Ashoura
End Feb Kitdit (Gojal), Bo Pho/Taghun (Hunza, Nagar, Gojal)
21 Mar Nauroz (NA and NWFP)
23 Mar Pakistan Day
End Mar Basant (Lahore)
11 Apr Moulid an-Nabi
1 May International Labour Day
Mid-May Joshi (Kalash Valleys)
End Jun Ginani/Chinir (Hunza, Nagar, Gojal)
1 Jul Bank holiday
11 Jul Taqt Nashina (Ismaili areas)
End Jul Shandur Pass Polo
14 Aug Independence Day
Mid-Aug Utjao (Kalash Valleys)
22 Aug Leilat al-Meiraj
6 Sep Defence of Pakistan Day
11 Sep Urs of Mohammad Ali Jinnah
24 Sep Ramadan starts
End Sep Phool (Birir Valley, Kalash)
23 Oct Hunza Didar Sal Gira (Hunza)
24 Oct Eid el-Fitr
1 Nov Jashan-e-Gilgit (Gilgit)
9 Nov Mohammad (Allama) Iqbal Day
18 Nov Gojal Didar Sal Gira (Gojal)
13 Dec Birthday Sal Gira
Mid-Dec Chaomos (Kalash Valleys)
21 Dec Tumishiling (Hunza, Nagar)
25 Dec Birthday of Mohammad Ali Jinnah
31 Dec Bank holiday and Eid el-Adha

2007
20 Jan Ras as-Sana
29 Jan Ashoura
End Feb Kitdit (Gojal) and Bo Pho/Taghun (Hunza, Nagar, Gojal)
21 Mar Nauroz (NA and NWFP)
23 Mar Pakistan Day
End Mar Basant (Lahore)
31 Mar Moulid an-Nabi
1 May International Labour Day
Mid-May Joshi (Kalash Valleys)
End Jun Ginani/Chinir (Hunza, Nagar, Gojal)
1 Jul Bank holiday
11 Jul Taqt Nashina (Ismaili areas)
End Jul Shandur Pass Polo
11 Aug Leilat al-Meiraj
14 Aug Independence Day
Mid-Aug Utjao (Kalash Valleys)
6 Sep Defence of Pakistan Day
11 Sep Urs of Mohammad Ali Jinnah
13 Sep Ramadan starts
End Sep Phool (Birir Valley, Kalash)
13 Oct Eid el-Fitr
23 Oct Hunza Didar Sal Gira (Hunza)
1 Nov Jashan-e-Gilgit (Gilgit)
9 Nov Mohammad (Allama) Iqbal Day
18 Nov Gojal Didar Sal Gira (Gojal)
13 Dec Birthday Sal Gira
Mid-Dec Chaomos (Kalash Valleys)
20 Dec Eid el-Adha
21 Dec Tumishiling (Hunza, Nagar)
25 Dec Birthday of Mohammad Ali Jinnah
31 Dec Bank holiday

National public holidays

Pakistan Day (23 March), marks the 1956 resolution proclaiming the Republic of Pakistan. **International Labour Day** (1 May). **July Bank Holiday** (1 July), although most businesses and government offices remain open. **Independence Day** (14 August), celebrates the founding of Pakistan in 1947, and is marked by a grand military parade in Islamabad and the opportunity to buy Pakistani flags and patriotic badges (including missile-shaped ones bearing the motto 'crush India'). **Defence of Pakistan Day** (6 September), commemorates the Pak-India war of 1965, and features a military parade in Islamabad and numerous column inches in the newspapers dedicated to this great 'victory'. **Urs of Mohammad Ali Jinnah** (11 September), death anniversary of the founder of the nation. **Mohammad (Allama) Iqbal Day** (9 November), the birth anniversary of the great Urdu poet, who in 1930 proposed a separate state for the Muslims of South Asia. **Birthday of Mohammad Ali Jinnah** (25 December). **Bank Holiday** (31 December), although many businesses and government offices remain open.

Islamic holy days

The Islamic Calendar begins on 16 July, AD 622, the date of the Hijra ('flight' or 'migration') of the Prophet Mohammad from Mecca to Medina in modern Saudi Arabia, which is denoted as 1 AH (Anno Hegirae or year of the Hegira). The Islamic or Hijri calendar is lunar rather than solar, each year having 354 or 355 days, meaning that annual festivals do not occur on the same day each year according to the Gregorian calendar.

The 12 lunar months of the Islamic calendar, alternating between 29 and 30 days, are: Muharram, Safar, Rabi-ul-Awwal, Rabi-ul-Sani, Jumada-ul-Awwal, Jumada-ul-Sani, Rajab, Shaban, Ramadan, Shawwal, Ziquad and Zilhaj.

Ras as-Sana (Islamic New Year) 1st Muharram. The first 10 days of the year are regarded as holy, especially the 10th.

Ashoura 9th and 10th Muharram. Anniversary of the killing of Hussain, grandson of the Prophet Mohammad, commemorated by Shia Muslims. The Ashoura procession, with men beating and flagellating themselves, is a moving sight, although the possibility of Sunni-Shia tension at this time means that foreign tourists are usually kept well away. If you are in Gilgit or Baltistan, you may be confined to your hotel. In Rawalpindi, however, you may be encouraged to observe the proceedings close up. Ashoura also celebrates the meeting of Adam and Eve after leaving Paradise, and the end of the Flood.

Moulid an-Nabi (Birth of the Prophet Mohammad) 12th Rabi-ul-Awwal.

Leilat al-Meiraj Ascension of Mohammad from the Haram al-Sharif in Jerusalem. 27th Rajab.

Ramadan The holiest Islamic month, when Muslims observe a complete fast during daylight hours (sometimes referred to as 'Ramazan' in Pakistan). Businesses and Muslim sites operate on reduced hours during Ramadan. 21st Ramadan is the Shab-e-Qadr or 'Night of Prayer'.

Eid el-Fitr Literally 'the small feast', 3 days of celebrations, beginning 1st Shawwal, to mark the end of Ramadan.

Eid el-Adha Literally 'the great feast' or 'feast of the sacrifice', 4 days beginning on 10th Zilhaj. The principal Islamic festival commemorates Abraham's sacrifice of his son Ismail, and coincides with the pilgrimage to Mecca. Marked by the sacrifice of a sheep, feasting and donations to the poor.

Travelling during Ramadan

The holy month of Ramadan is the most important in the Islamic calendar, and certainly the one period of the year when everyday life is most dramatically affected. All Muslims are required to observe a total fast (which includes liquids and also smoking) between the hours of sunset and sunrise. Exceptions are made for the sick (or very elderly), pregnant women, travellers and young children.

From the point of view of the tourist travelling in Pakistan it is important to bear in mind the implications of this. Some people advise against visiting Pakistan during Ramadan. Such advice is really overstating the case (although if you are coming specifically for business it may be worth avoiding, since offices generally close by midday and significantly less gets done). To begin with, for the next 10 years or so, Ramadan falls during the winter months when days are shorter and

● *As a very general rule, Islamic holy days move 10 or 11 days earlier each year according to the Gregorian (solar) calendar.*

cooler, making it much less of an ordeal. In the main cities, it is always possible to obtain food at any time of day from the larger hotels and restaurants (Chinese restaurants are usually a good bet). Even in smaller towns, many restaurants are happy to serve non-Muslims, who are after all exempt, usually discreetly at the back of the dining hall. Bear in mind, however, that in remote areas smaller hotels sometimes close during Ramadan. Many bus and railway stations provide special facilities in deference to the exemption of travellers. It is always possible to buy fruit from the markets, and biscuits, cakes and so on from bakeries to take back to your hotel room.

Although it can certainly be more demanding travelling in Pakistan during Ramadan, there are also advantages. For non-smokers, bus and train journeys suddenly become far more pleasant. While tempers can sometimes begin to fray towards the end of the day, the actual breaking of the fast after sunset, which is marked by a snack called *Iftar* (several large meals follow on) is always a warm and friendly moment, with people invariably inviting you to share in their food. Likewise, the end of Ramadan, marked by Eidel-Fitr, is an occasion for huge celebrations and feasting characterized by outpourings of generosity and goodwill. Such moments are what a visit to Pakistan is all about. In fact, Ramadan can be one of the most rewarding times to visit the country. Furthermore, if you are spending most of your time in Ismaili areas, such as Hunza and Gojal, you are unlikely to encounter many difficulties during Ramadan.

Regional holidays and festivals

The following are just a selection of some of the regional holidays and festivals. Check locally for exact dates. For the date of *Urs* (death anniversaries) at specific shrines and tombs, see the relevant section of the travelling text.

Late Feb Kitdit A 'coming of spring' festival celebrated in Gojal.
Late Feb/early Mar Bo Pho/Taghun Celebrated in Hunza, Nagar and Gojal, and commemmorates the first ploughing/sowing of the year (wheat).
Spring, usually late Mar Basant A grand kite-flying festival held in Lahore, heralding the arrival of spring.
21 Mar Nauroz Celebrated in parts of the Northern Areas and NWFP, and marks the pre-Islamic vernal equinox (arrival of spring).
Mid-Apr Baisakhi Sikh holy day centred on the Panja Sahib Gurudwara in Hasan Abdal.
Late Jul/early Aug Shandur Pass Polo A spectacularly situated polo tournament (see further details on page 149), although it suffers from the fact that the date is often set on a whim.

Late Jun/early Jul Ginani/Chinir is celebrated in Hunza, Nagar and Gojal to mark the first wheat harvest of the year.
11 Jul Taqt Nashina Fervently celebrated in all Ismaili areas to mark the ascension of the present Aga Khan to the position of leader of the Ismaili community.
23 Oct Hunza Didar Sal Gira Commemorates the Aga Khan's first visit to Hunza, in 1960.
1 Nov Jashan-e-Gilgit Also known as the 'Gilgit Uprising', is commemmorated in the town by a week-long polo tournament.
18 Nov Gojal Didar Sal Gira Commemorates the Aga Khan's 1st visit to Gojal, in 1987.
13 Dec Birthday Sal Gira Celebrates the Aga Khan's birthday in Ismaili areas.
21 Dec Tumishiling A festival held in Hunza and Nagar to celebrate the death of Shri Badat of Gilgit.

One of the best times to visit the Chapursan Valley (see page 319) is during the autumn, to coincide with its many celebrations, including polo festivals, the autumn harvest festivals and weddings, which take place between October and December each year.

Shopping

Since the areas of Pakistan covered by this guide are the most popular with foreign visitors, the shopping options here are arguably better. Shops specifically aimed at foreign tourists are a good place to start since they often have an excellent range of goods all brought together under one roof and although prices tend to be higher, the quality of the goods is often considerably better than in the markets.

The most exciting places to hunt for goods are the traditional bazaars of the old quarters of towns and cities. There is an enormous variety of souvenirs, handicrafts, tribal jewellery, clothing, precious and semi-precious stones and other goods available in Pakistan, reflecting the country's rich resources and diversity of cultural traditions.

Bargaining is very much a part of everyday life in Pakistan, particularly in the bazaars and in tourist shops. There are exceptions to the rule, but on the whole the initial price you are quoted will be much more than the seller is actually prepared to accept. Some people find this off-putting, or fear that they are constantly being 'ripped-off', but the whole bargaining process can be enormously enjoyable if entered into in the right spirit. It's important to keep thing in perspective; most things in Pakistan are after all very cheap by Western standards. If you have set your heart on something, ask yourself what it is worth to you and use that as a benchmark.

Carpets

This is a major industry in Pakistan, making a significant contribution to export earnings. They are generally hand-woven and hand-knotted and made of wool, silk or a mixture of the two. The main centre of carpet making covered by this handbook is Peshawar, although there are several carpet-making schemes aimed at providing income for women that are up and running in Hunza, Nagar and Gojal. There is a huge variety of indigenous tribal designs, many of them very striking. The majority of the other designs are borrowed and adapted from other major carpet producing countries, such as Iran, Afghanistan and Turkey. Peshawar and Islamabad are perhaps the best places to shop for carpets, particularly ones brought over from Afghanistan. Kilims (flat-woven carpets) are significantly cheaper (and lighter) than knotted carpets, making them a practical and good-value option.

Embroidery

This has developed to a fine art, with distinctive regional designs and patterns, although the best examples often come from regions outside the scope of this handbook. In the north, the *chunghas* (loose cloaks) of Patti cloth found in Swat, Gilgit and Chitral are often beautifully embroidered around the collars, lapels and cuffs.

Jewellery

Gold and silversmiths and jewellers constitute one of the largest communities of craftsmen in Pakistan. Most distinctive is the chunky silver tribal jewellery of NWFP. Much of the gold and silver jewellery made and sold in the cities, however, is intricately fashioned and very delicate. Peshawar's Andarshah bazaar is perhaps the most dazzling place to look for jewellery, although even the smallest towns will have a jeweller where one can see work in progress. In NWFP and the Northern Areas it is possible to find beautiful items of lapis lazuli jewellery, much of it originating from Afghanistan.

Leatherwork

Leatherwork is an important craft in Pakistan. Traditionally perhaps the most important product was the leather *mashk* or water bag. Today the main products include items such as jackets, handbags, belts, shoes and sandals. Shoes and sandals are widely available, with each province having its own distinctive designs.

Metalwork
Peshawar is famous for its hammered brass and copper metalwork, with a huge range of items including plates, trays, boxes, vessels etc.

Textiles
Textiles are found throughout the country and display a huge variety of designs and techniques. *Khaddar* is the simplest cotton weave, used mostly in the traditional shalwar kameez. The *Lungi* is a draped cloth used in NWFP as a turban. The standard pattern is the *charkhana*, made up of small squares. *Patti* is a thick woollen cloth usually in a trill or herring-bone weave, typically found in the Swat, Chitral and Gilgit areas.

Woodwork
The Swat Valley is perhaps the most famous for its intricately carved architectural woodwork and furniture, although woodcarving is common throughout the mountainous north. In Swat, where the craft was undoubtedly most developed, it no longer seems to be practised, with most items offered for sale having been removed from old houses in the valley.

Sport and activities

The only real organized sport that you will see in the north of Pakistan is polo, although those used to the Prince Charles and Windsor Great Park version of the game may argue that there's nothing 'organized' about polo that you see here! Fast, dangerous and wild – perhaps the way it is meant to be played. The most spectacular polo event in Pakistan, arguably the world, is the annual tournament held at the 3,735-m-high Shandur Pass (see page 149 for further details). This event is generally held in July, but it is unwise to plan your whole trip around the tournament since the dates have an annoying habit of changing at the last minute. In many areas, young boys aspire not to be Imran Khan or Wasim Akram, but to be polo players.

If you are in Peshawar during the winter months you may be able to attend a game of *bushkazi*, an even more crazy Afghan version of polo, using a dead calf or goat as the object rather than a ball. Polo sticks are discarded as are the rules and it is a definite must-see.

Pakistan's national sport is cricket, with international matches being played in Rawalpindi and Peshawar (as well as other cities not covered in this book, but described in detail in *Footprint Pakistan*). This is a good country to see the sport played at the highest level since tickets are cheap (under £1 for Test matches!) and readily available. The following teams are due to tour Pakistan: October 2004, Zimbabwe; February 2005, India; March 2005, Sri Lanka; November 2005, England; October 2006, Zimbabwe; December 2006, West Indies; October 2007, South Africa.

The Adventure Foundation, which has offices at the Adventure Inn in Islamabad can organize horseriding, ballooning and paragliding. One of Pakistan's greatest attractions is the opportunities it offers for trekking and climbing. A selection of the main treks (and shorter walks) are covered in the travelling text (described at the point of departure), and there is also a section providing detailed practical information for anyone planning a trek (see page 45). Long stretches of the Indus are navigable and a couple of the tour operators offer boating trips on this formidable river. Although many of the rivers in NWFP and the Northern Areas have great potential for whitewater-rafting, this activity is still in its infancy here. There is a book on the subject: *Paddling the Frontier: a Guide to Pakistan's Whitewater*, by Wickliffe Walker.

Although Pakistan has enormous potential for skiing, facilities are poorly developed and you will have to bring all your own equipment. The Austrian-built chairlift at Malam Jabba in Swat, where there are several good slopes, was finally operational in 2001. Check with PTDC in Islamabad or Peshawar for the latest situation. The Adventure Foundation can also provide information and help you with organizing a skiing expedition in Pakistan.

Wildlife and protected areas

Pakistan's wildlife resources, particularly its many endangered species, are coming under increasing pressure, notably in the north. The demand for new agricultural land, deforestation, expansion of the tourism sector as well as military activity, means that many of the protected areas in the north of the country exist on paper only. Anyone planning to visit the national parks, wildlife sanctuaries or game reserves should first call upon the local administrative offices of the individual protected area; you will generally find knowledgable, dedicated staff who will facilitate your visit. Details of who to contact are included in the relevant section of the text. Few of the established tour companies advertise specific wildlife tours, although they can generally arrange one to suit your requirements. One exception is **Full Moon Night Trekking** (www.fmntrekking.com.pk or shafqathussain@hotmail.com), which is run by a former wildlife officer with the IUCN. Listed on page 377 are the various protected areas (some of which have yet to be accorded legal status) included within the scope of this guide, while page 376 has fuller details of the flora and fauna found in northern Pakistan.

Trekking

Northern Pakistan offers some of the best trekking in the world. The Karakoram, Himalaya and Hindu Kush ranges which dominate the Northern Areas and NWFP are truly spectacular, and offer a range of hiking and trekking opportunities to cover all tastes and inclinations, with everything from easy day-walks to demanding treks of up to three weeks or more.

Yet the potential of this region remains for the most part undiscovered. With the exception of one or two areas (the trek to the base camp of K2 in particular is far and away the most popular in Pakistan, and experiences many of the problems found in the Everest region of Nepal), trekking in Pakistan is generally completely free of crowds and pollution. The days when European explorers set out to fill in the 'blanks on the map' may be past, but this region remains one of the least comprehensively mapped in the world and is still full of adventure and excitement.

Aside from the natural beauty of the mountains and the peaceful, unspoilt solitude they offer, perhaps the most rewarding aspect of trekking in Pakistan is the contact it brings with the peoples who inhabit this beautiful and yet harsh environment. With one or two notable exceptions (see below), the peoples of northern Pakistan are friendly, hospitable and open in a way which seems to be characteristic of mountain people throughout the world. In Pakistan this is complemented by a fascinating variety of cultures; moving from one valley to the next, it is often possible to witness a complete change in the traditions, lifestyle, language and ethnic origins of the people.

General points

Trekking in Pakistan is more demanding than in countries like Nepal and even India, where facilities are so far developed that luxuries such as 'tea-shop trekking' are an option. In Pakistan this is not the case. Any trek involves having all the supplies and equipment, as well as the physical stamina, to be completely self-sufficient if need be. Most treks, if crossing a pass, rise to a minimum of 4,000 m and can reach anywhere up to 5,500 m. The terrain can be very demanding, crossing glaciers, glacial moraine, scree slopes and fast-flowing rivers, and involving numerous steep ascents and descents in the course of even a gradual overall climb. In this context, physical fitness, proper acclimatization and careful planning are crucial to your enjoyment and safety on a trek.

This section aims to provide detailed practical information on how to plan and organize a trek. The notes on specific treks which appear in the main travelling text aim only to give a general insight into what to expect.

We believe that any step-by-step descriptions of trekking in Pakistan should be treated with a healthy degree of scepticism. Mountain topography changes rapidly; avalanches, land-slides, glacial action, flooding and erosion all conspire to make a mockery of the concept of a fixed route. Bridges may be destroyed, paths washed away and re-routed along the opposite sides of valleys, or rendered completely impassable; glaciers inevitably shift, and with them the best routes across them. Other variables, such as the season, specific weather conditions and even the time of the day, can make the difference between the route across a pass being easily followed or waist-deep in snow, and rivers being easily fordable or impassable raging torrents.

> The list of restricted zone treks is liable to change, so you should check for yourself before setting off on a trek.

There is simply no substitute for up-to-the-minute, first-hand information about a particular area or route. Local tour operators are often a good source of information and can be very helpful. Talk to other trekkers and climbers; in Chitral, Gilgit and Skardu they are easily found, often congregating in specific hotels. Talk to local people, although the concept of 'local' also needs to be treated carefully; specific information, unless given by an experienced guide, is only likely to be accurate if the person giving it is actually from the particular valley.

Types of trek

Organized treks

There are a large number of foreign and local 'adventure travel' tour operators offering specialized trekking services in Pakistan. Foreign tour operators are the most expensive. Their main advantage is that everything is done for you – pay your money and you will be looked after from the airport until you return, with everything in between, short of actually walking, taken care of. If you can afford it and have limited time, this is undoubtedly the best way of avoiding the inevitably time-consuming process of planning and organizing a trek. Reputable foreign companies generally offer an excellent service, with carefully planned treks and experienced overseas staff and local guides combining to minimize the possibility of a hitch.

Many local tour operators are extremely competent and easily able to match the services of foreign companies, for less money. They are also generally very flexible, allowing you to plan your own itinerary and change it if necessary. However, liaising with local companies from abroad can occasionally be more difficult. If going through a smaller company it is essential to ensure that all the details regarding jeeps, guides and porters etc are clear beforehand. It is worth shopping around between the various companies to find the best deal.

For a list of major overseas and Pakistani tour operators offering trekking services, see page 14 and under individual towns and cities throughout the guide. Smaller local trekking agencies are included in the Directory sections of Chitral, Gilgit and Skardu.

Self-organized treks

By choosing to join an organized trek, all the responsibility for hiring porters and guides, buying supplies, arranging transport etc, is passed to the tour operator. The second option is to undertake all these aspects of the planning and preparation yourself. The main advantage of this is that it generally works out cheaper. The main disadvantage is that the planning and preparation is a time-consuming process and ultimately you will have to deal with any problems which may arise yourself. Be prepared to invest a few days at least organizing your trek. Read the information below on organizing a trek.

Independent trekking

The third option is the simplest and by far the cheapest. Hiring porters and guides is an expensive business. For two people for anything more than a few days, you soon encounter the logistical realities of having to hire porters to carry food for the porters, and enter a steep spiral of costs. If you are travelling on a budget, trekking independently is likely to be the only option. It is essential, however, that you have at least some experience of trekking, as it involves carrying all your own equipment and supplies, and finding your own way along the route. Trekking alone is not advisable. Many trekking areas in Pakistan are extremely remote and isolated, sparsely populated and without any reliable system of rescue; if you sustain an injury or get lost, you are on your own. The main disadvantage of this form of trekking is that, since you must be completely self-sufficient, your range is greatly limited. Assuming a maximum load of around 20 kg (which is a hefty weight to lug around at high altitude), you are likely to be able to trek for no more than five days at a time. The great advantage is that you do not have a retinue of porters following you around everywhere, and are free to camp where you choose, as oppose to being tied to the porters' recognized overnight stops.

One approach is to aim for a compromise which may either involve hiring a freelance guide to accompany you, carrying an equal load, or to hire one or two porters en route. If you hire porters in the area in which you are trekking, they will have a good knowledge of routes and their condition, and extend your range considerably. Hiring on an informal basis is easily done; it is often possible to set out without any porters or guides and then simply hire a local farmer or shepherd for a section of the trek, to get you across a difficult pass for example.

Classification of treks

A 'trek' is officially defined as any route which does not exceed 6,000 m in altitude. Treks are classified into 'open', 'restricted' or 'closed' zones. In the context of this handbook, trips that don't involve a night spent sleeping out are referred to as 'hikes' (becoming 'treks' if overnighting is required).

Open zone

The majority of treks fall into the open zone category, meaning that you are free to undertake the trek without a guide and without first gaining any official permission.

Restricted zone

Treks in restricted zones require that you obtain an official trekking permit for the particular trek you wish to undertake (see below) and that you employ a government-registered guide. Restricted areas include a 48-km zone approaching any of Pakistan's international borders (16 km in Azad Kashmir), parts of Chitral and the most popular treks in Baltistan (for example the Baltoro Glacier trek to Concordia and the base camp of K2). A full list of government-approved treks in restricted zones is given in the booklet *Trekking Rules and Regulations* (1996 edition), available from the PTDC head office in Islamabad. Restricted zone treks included in this guide are identified as such in the trek notes.

Closed zone

These areas are generally the most sensitive in political and military terms, for example the Siachen area close to the disputed Line of Control with India. They are off-limits to trekkers unless they are able to obtain special permission, which is very rarely granted. If you wish to trek in a closed zone you really need to have contacts in high places. Alternatively, try applying through one of the major local trekking agencies, which is more likely to have the relevant contacts and so give your application at least some chance of success.

Mountaineering

Venturing above 6,000 m is classified as 'mountaineering', for which a separate permit is needed. Mountaineering expeditions must pay a 'royalty' according to the altitude of the peak they are attempting and must be accompanied by a government-appointed liaison officer. Expeditions are governed by a series of rules and regulations as laid down by the Tourism Division of the Ministry of Culture, Tourism. They are outlined in a booklet entitled *Mountaineering Rules and Regulations* (1996 edition), available from the PTDC head office in Islamabad. Royalty fees for peaks over 6,500 m were slashed by 50% for the calender year 2004, something that may become more common as Pakistan attempts to increase visitor numbers.

Choosing a trek

Choosing the right trek is extremely important. Most obviously, the trek you undertake should match your level of fitness; unless you are fairly fit, setting off on a long, hard trek is likely to be an exhausting experience and so not particularly enjoyable. Likewise, if you have flown directly to Chitral, Gilgit or Skardu, it is essential that you acclimatize properly before undertaking any strenuous treks. If you have the time, the best approach is to do one or two shorter, easier treks first, before attempting anything more strenuous. It is well worth undertaking a programme of physical fitness training before you go. Bear in mind also that some treks do involve a certain level of technical difficulty, be it traversing glaciers, walking on snow, or fording rivers, which can be dangerous unless you (or your guide) have the experience and equipment to deal with the conditions. Note that if you wish to trek independently, you must trek in an open zone where a permit and registered guide are not required.

'Dangerous' areas

A number of areas in northern Pakistan, despite being in open zones, are inherently dangerous. These are invariably 'tribal' areas where banditry has been the norm for centuries, and remains so even today. The main areas where this is the case are Indus Kohistan (which includes all the side valleys leading off from the KKH in the area; the Jalkot, Tangir, Kandia, Darel and Thor valleys, as well as the route between Chilas and Babusar Pass), Daimar District (the approaches to the north side of Nanga Parbat from the KKH, also inhabited by Kohistanis), Swat Kohistan (the valleys north of Kalam leading over into the Gilgit river valley) and Dir Kohistan (the routes leading east from around Dir into Swat).

This does not mean that trekking is not possible in these areas, but that you need to take extra care. It is strongly advised (and in some cases officially required) that you trek with a reliable local guide and first inform the local authorities of your intended itinerary. The Deputy or Assistant Commissioners of each of these areas are the best people to turn to; they will be able to vet your guide, or help find one, and also advise you as to whether a particular area is safe at a given time.

Female trekkers

Women are advised not to trek alone in Pakistan. Even in the areas which are otherwise safe for women travellers, the spectacle of a woman walking through the mountains on her own may lead to misunderstandings and problems. News of your presence would certainly spread like wildfire and be likely to attract more than just idle curiosity from local people.

The only real option for solo women travellers is either to link up with other groups, or to hire a reliable guide to accompany you. In the latter case, going through a recognized company with a reputation to uphold is the best way to ensure your safety. Alternatively, make sure that a competent authority is informed as to the trek you are undertaking, and the identity of your guide (make sure the guide is aware of this also).

Health

Read the Health section (see page 55) for detailed information on staying healthy. Pay particular attention to the sections on acclimatization, altitude sickness and hypothermia. The golden rule is to allow plenty of time for acclimatization and to descend carefully to a lower altitude if the symptoms of altitude sickness manifest themselves. Avoiding hypothermia is largely a question of being properly equipped and observing basic common sense.

Getting sick is unpleasant at the best of times; while trekking it can also be dangerous in that you might be several days' walk from the nearest medical facilities, which are likely to be fairly basic anyway. The most common problems are diarrhoea and stomach upsets due to contaminated food and water. The best insurance against any form of diarrhoea is to take meticulous care over personal hygiene and the preparation of food, and to purify any water which has not been collected directly at source from a spring. If you have hired a cook, it is essential that he understands the importance of hygiene and proper food preparation; most locals have a far higher tolerance than foreigners, so it is usually necessary to directly supervise their cooking, initially at least.

The other main risk while trekking is of injury. Trekkers are strongly advised to learn about the basics of first aid. All trekking groups in restricted areas are officially required to have at least one member with some knowledge of first aid.

Trekking maps

Maps of northern Pakistan are fairly limited and vary greatly in their accuracy and reliability. Even the best available trekking maps are really only reliable on the main trekking routes. Within Pakistan there is little or nothing which is of any use to trekkers, so it is essential to obtain all your maps before leaving home.

The US Army Map Service (AMS) U502 series covers most of northern Pakistan at a scale of 1:250,000 in a series of eight sheets (two further sheets covering the border with Afghanistan are restricted). Published in the 1950s and 60s, most existing roads and jeep tracks are not shown (including the KKH), while village names are woefully inaccurate. However, they do on the whole give accurate information as to the topography and are useful in planning a trek (NB each map has a 'reliability' diagram dividing the map into poor/fair/good areas). Published in colour, they are also the most detailed in terms of contour information. International boundaries are not marked.

A book entitled *Mountaineering Maps of the World; Karakoram, Hindu Kush, Pamir and Tien Shan*, published in Japan in 1978 at a scale of 1:200,000 also covers most of northern Pakistan. Although the text is in Japanese, the maps themselves are labelled in Roman script. They are on the whole reasonably accurate. The main disadvantage is that this hefty volume is very expensive and quite difficult to find.

For the Karakoram range, the **Swiss Foundation for Alpine Research** 'orographical sketch map' in two sheets at a scale of 1:250,000, or the 'trekking map' in three sheets at a scale of 1:200,000 are the best available. Published in 1990, they are generally the most accurate, at least in terms of village names, trails and mountain topography (newer jeep tracks are often not marked). International boundaries with India and China are not marked. Leomann also publishes a set of four trekking maps of Gilgit, Hunza and Baltistan at a scale of 1:200,000.

There are also several more detailed maps. The excellent **Deutsche Himalaya Expedition** 1:50,000 maps in two sheets, one covering Nanga Parbat and the other Minapin Glacier, were published in 1934 but updated in 1980. The Chinese Institute of Glaciology, Cryopedology and Desert Research, **Acedemia Sinica**, published an excellent map of the Batura Glacier at a scale of 1:60,000 in 1978. There is also a Japanese map of the Baltoro Glacier at a scale of 1:100,000, published on the basis of the 1977 Japan-Pakistan K2 Expedition.

Buying maps

Most of the maps mentioned above can be obtained from the following places:

Cordee Books, 3A De Montford Street, Leicester LE1 7HD, UK, T0116-2543579.
Geo Buch Verlag, Rosental 6, D-800, Munchen 2, Germany.
ILH Geo Center, Schockenriestrasse 40A, Postfach 800830, D-700 Stuttgarte 80, Germany.
Libreria Alpina, Via C Coronedi-Berti 4, 40137 Bologna, Zona 3705, Italy.
Maplink, 25 East Mason Street, Santa Barbara, CA 93101, USA.

Michael Chessler Books, PO Box 2436, Evergreen, CO 80439, USA, T800-6548502.
Stanfords, 12-14 Long Acre, London WC2E 9LP, UK, T0207-8361321; 29 Corn St, Bristol, BS1; 39 Spring Gardens, Manchester, M2, www.stanfords.com.
Travel Bookshop, Rindermarkt 20, 8001 Zurich, Switzerland.
US Library of Congress; Geography and Map Division, 101 Independence Avenue, Washington, DC 20540, USA.

Organizing a trek

Permits

Permits for treks in restricted zones have to be applied for through a government-registered tour operator. Applications must be made in Islamabad, at the Ministry of Tourism, Pakistan Sports Complex ('Jinnah Stadium' on some maps), just off Shahrah-e-Kashmir (to the southeast of the Tourist Campsite), T051-9204556; this is a new location. Applications (in duplicate) must identify the relevant trek, give exact dates and a list of all people going on the trek, including passport details and two photos per person. A fee of US$20 per head is charged. Insurance must also be provided for all porters and guides. If the trek is one of those listed in the *Trekking Rules and Regulations* booklet, permits are generally issued within 24 hours (if not, the procedure takes a minimum of 15 days and you are required to take a Liaison Officer with you as well as a registered guide). Although the tour operator will deal with all the paperwork, the guide and group leader must present themselves at the offices of the Tourism Division in Islamabad for a briefing beforehand. The above information was correct at the time of research. However, there are concerted efforts to reduce the bureaucratic red tape associated with trekking in Pakistan; hopefully there will be constructive changes to the rules in the near future.

Guides

The guide is undoubtedly the most important component of any organized trek, and can make the difference between a trek being a highly enjoyable and rewarding success, or a complete disaster. The best guides will have experience of organizing and leading treks, and an understanding of the peculiarities of foreigners; particularly with respect to health, hygiene and fitness, but also in terms of their interest and motivation towards trekking (for example wanting time to enjoy and camp in the most picturesque spots). They will also have detailed knowledge of the particular trek you are setting off on.

It is crucial that you are able to communicate satisfactorily with your guide; in most circumstances this is determined by their grasp of English. Hiring a guide who is from the specific area in which you are going to trek is an enormous advantage. As well as being very familiar with the trek itself, he will be in a position to introduce you to local people (particularly family, friends or relations) along the way. This can make a trek infinitely more rewarding and open up a whole new world which would otherwise be far more difficult to connect with. The best guides will also take responsibility for hiring porters, ideally dealing with people with whom they are already familiar. This can be a great help when it comes to dealing with any disputes which may arise concerning porters.

Given the profitability of the profession it is not surprising that there is no shortage of people offering their services as guides. The main distinction is between government-registered guides, who are officially permitted to lead trekking groups, and unofficial guides. Government-registered guides are generally either working for one or more of the foreign/local trekking companies, or on a freelance basis, or, as is commonly the case, a combination of the two. They are generally reliable, although there is a great deal of variation in their level of competence. All will have a certificate confirming their status as registered guides (if someone is unable to produce one they are probably not registered). With unofficial guides, there is a much greater element of chance.

Both registered and unofficial guides, if they are any good, will have built up a collection of letters of recommendation from previous clients. This is invariably the most revealing indicator of their competence. Ultimately, however, and particularly in remoter areas, choosing a guide is largely a matter of intuition; at the least, you should get a sense of whether you feel comfortable putting yourself in that person's hands, and whether you are prepared to spend the duration of your trek with them. Local trekking companies will have their own register of guides; if you explain that you wish to organize your own trek they are usually willing to recommend an available guide.

It is usual practice to pay guides on a daily basis, as opposed to by stages (see below). Rates vary a great deal between different areas and according to the experience/competence of the guide, whether they are registered and the difficulty of the trek to be undertaken. The daily wages for guides generally range from around Rs500 up to Rs1,000. As a rule it is worth paying more for a guide with a proven reputation and experience; often it can end up saving a great deal more in the long run.

Porters

The terms and conditions on which porters are hired are the most frequent source of disputes and misunderstandings. If you have a good guide they will hopefully be able to foresee and avoid such difficulties. But however good your guide, it is crucially important that you involve yourself with the hiring of porters and are able to satisfy yourself that all the terms and conditions of their employment have been discussed, understood and agreed.

Porters are traditionally paid by the stage. Stages are more or less established, again according to tradition, along each particular route. Most disputes arise out of the fact that an average day's trek will usually cover at least two porter's stages, meaning that the rate of payment you agree with your porters is not per day, but per stage. At lower altitudes this can end up being very expensive; over flat terrain, a porter's stage may be no more than a couple of hours' walk. Make sure that it is crystal clear as to whether you are paying your porters by the day or by the stage, and establish beforehand the number of stages on a particular trek. The official line on porters is that they should cover between 10-13 km per day, although in practice this has little or no relevance. One option is to negotiate a fixed payment for the porters for the whole trek. Other related points to clarify before setting off include payment on rest days or in case of forced halts due to bad weather (officially full pay), payment for the return trip (officially half pay) and transport arrangements if the porters will be returning home by road. A good idea is to write out an informal 'contract' for your porters, covering all details of payment, transport, food and clothing. It is also well worth making a list of your porters so that you can get them to sign against their names (or tick them off) after paying them.

There are a number of government regulations regarding food and clothing for porters (outlined in the *Trekking Rules and Regulations* booklet). Again it is essential to establish exact arrangements beforehand. In practice porters often prefer to be paid a daily rate in lieu of their food ration and to make their own arrangements for food, particularly if trekking through their own areas where they can eat with relations and friends. Make sure though that porters take adequate food if you are heading beyond any settlements. Government rules stipulate that each porter must be equipped with rubber shoes, gloves, sunglasses and two pairs of socks, as well as a stove/fuel and tarpaulin sheet per eight porters. At higher altitudes they require in addition a jacket and, if walking on snow, proper boots. Again in practice little of this is adhered to, although the rubber boots are often expected. However, each year a number of porters die in accidents, usually related to inadequate equipment. If you are going to be trekking across ice or snow, it is your responsibility to ensure that porters have the right equipment; rubber shoes are not adequate. Indeed, rubber shoes must be the most grotesquely inappropriate kit for porters wherever they are walking; canvas shoes are not that much more expensive and are far more comfortable.

Clothing and equipment

Proper clothing and equipment is essential for trekking in northern Pakistan. It is possible in summer on lower altitude treks to get away with surprisingly little, but if the weather turns bad you could find yourself in serious trouble. At higher altitudes weather conditions can get extremely nasty very suddenly at any time of year. The following is not a comprehensive list, but covers the main essentials.

In terms of warmth, a good combination is to have a high-quality 'fleece'-type jacket and a waterproof/windproof jacket to go over it in extreme conditions. Full thermal underwear is also very warm and relatively light. It is through the extremities of the body that most heat is lost, so good gloves, socks and a woollen hat are vital. In most circumstances it can get quite hot during the daytime so light, loose-fitting, cotton clothing is the most practical. Many people swear by the traditional Pakistani shalwar kameez as the ideal loose-fitting, light-weight, quick-drying attire. A broad-brimmed sun hat is invaluable for protection against the sun.

Footwear is largely a question of personal preference. The most important thing is to have adequate ankle support, for which boots are essential. Good-quality leather boots with a metal shank in the sole are the most robust and supportive, but some people prefer to go for lighter-weight canvas or synthetic boots. Trainers can be very comfortable and perfectly adequate on many treks, but they do not give any ankle support and therefore increase the likelihood of a sprained ankle or worse. On the other hand they are very pleasant to change into after a day's walking, and invaluable for fording streams.

A good sleeping bag (minimum four-season, preferably five; a cotton sleeping bag liner will increase the warmth of a sleeping bag considerably), a sleeping mat and a tent able to withstand strong winds (domed or tunnel tents are generally the best) are essential. If you are carrying your own load, a good framed rucksack is vital and worth spending money on. Women should choose a rucksack specially designed for wider hips. If you are taking porters, a day pack is still necessary (your porters will rarely be in the same place as you en route). Other essentials include a first-aid kit, a water bottle to carry with you while walking, torch, sun cream (minimum factor 15) and sun block, lip cream (sunburnt lips are no fun), proper sunglasses and snow glasses if you are likely to spend much time above the snow-line. In an emergency, a 'survival blanket' (insulating silver sheet) and 'bivvy bag' (reinforced plastic sack large enough to crawl into) are potential life-savers; be sure to carry them with you if trekking with porters. A telescopic ski pole is useful for balance when fording rivers, traversing scree slopes and if walking on snow or ice. Other more specialized equipment, such as ice-axes, crampons, ropes etc, is only of value if you have experience in using them in the relevant conditions.

Cooking equipment is an important consideration. Kerosene or petrol stoves are most practical in that fuel is readily available, even in fairly remote areas (a fine-gauze strainer is very useful for filtering out impurities). High-tech stoves, such as the MSR, are the lightest and most efficient. Older designs or locally made kerosene stoves have the advantage of being more readily serviceable, particularly the latter, for which spares are available in any bazaar. Make sure that you have spares of all the main components before setting out; most failures are related to the pump (make sure it is properly oiled) and to blockages in the vapourising jets (take lots of needle 'pokers'). Aluminium one-litre fuel containers are best, but large groups will need a larger plastic jerry can (the latter are readily available in most bazaars in five-, 10- and 25-litre sizes). Butane/propane gas (Gaz) stoves are lighter, but finding refills is difficult (but not impossible) and you face the problem of getting them onto flights. They also generally have less heating power than kerosene/petrol. The best are those that re-seal themselves automatically when dismantled. A pressure cooker is a good idea, particularly at higher altitudes where it can save significant amounts of fuel and is the only way to force water up to 100°C. A large foldable plastic water container saves numerous trips to collect water at camp.

Hiring/buying equipment

It is best to bring your own equipment, although it is becoming increasingly possible to hire equipment in Pakistan. Many of the local trekking agencies have built up a comprehensive range of equipment from previous expeditions, including sleeping bags, tents, ice axes, crampons, ropes etc. Some agencies are in a position to fully equip a large group for even the most demanding treks. Apart from Islamabad, where the larger trekking agencies have their head offices, Skardu and Gilgit have the widest range (Chitral has relatively little).

Rawalpindi and Gilgit are the best places to buy equipment, although there is a certain amount available in Skardu and Chitral. Most readily available are army surplus items, such as sleeping bags, ground sheets, jackets etc, although all tend to be heavy. Left-over expedition equipment is sometimes available and trekking agencies are sometimes willing to sell equipment.

Whether hiring or buying second-hand equipment, be sure to check that it is in good condition. Hiring ropes is not a good idea unless you are sure of their condition. Boots are much better brought from home. Buy new boots well in advance and take time to break them in properly.

Food

The most important thing is to ensure a balanced diet (proteins, fats, vitamins, minerals, carbohydrates and fibre) and an adequate intake of calories (anywhere between 3,000 and 4,500 depending on your weight, metabolism and level of activity). Vitamin and mineral deficiencies are the most likely when trekking. Vitamin supplements are a good idea (many vitamins quickly deteriorate in even relatively fresh fruit and vegetables). Salts are rapidly lost from the body through perspiration and must be replaced. Carbohydrates (eg wheat, rice, sugar) are your main source of instant energy and need to be consumed in increased quantities; pasta is the most easily and efficiently converted carbohydrate energy source.

The main consideration in planning what food to take on a trek is whether you intend to rely on what is available in Pakistan or to bring your own supplies from home. A combination of the two gives the most flexibility and variety. The standard porters' fare of chappatis, rice, dhal, vegetables and tea (with lots of milk and sugar) is actually very nutritious and is available in any bazaar. The fastest cooking varieties of lentils are mung and masoor. It is often possible to obtain fresh dairy products from shepherds when trekking through summer pastures, but don't rely on it (remember also that milk and cheese will not have been pasteurized). Other items readily available all over Pakistan include pasta, biscuits, porridge, dried fruit, nuts and fresh seasonal fruits and vegetables, dried milk, tea, sugar, salt and spices. Items such as tinned and freeze-dried foods, stock cubes, coffee, honey and jam, yeast extract, tomato ketchup and other condiments are available in major cities, such as Islamabad/Rawalpindi, but can sometimes be found in Chitral, Gilgit and Skardu.

The most useful items to bring from home include freeze-dried/dehydrated foods (packet soups, available in Pakistan, are generally pretty foul), instant noodles, high-energy foods, such as chocolate bars, glucose tablets etc. Note that many of these items can often be found in Chitral, Gilgit and Skardu, having been left behind by previous expeditions; it is a matter of luck though as to what is actually available.

Ecology and conservation

The mountains of northern Pakistan, as well as being very beautiful, also represent an extremely fragile environment. The growth of mountaineering and trekking undoubtedly poses a serious threat to the ecology of the region. Unfortunately, climbers and trekkers often appear to be the least aware, or least concerned, about the dangers.

Firewood

The cutting and burning of firewood is perhaps the most immediate and dramatic cause of environmental degradation. Forests are all too scarce in most of northern Pakistan and are under serious threat. There is no justification for trekkers and climbers to light fires – they should have their own stoves and fuel. More importantly, they should ensure that their porters are likewise equipped. Existing forest and scrub is already under heavy pressure from local people and all of it is allocated on a collective basis to local communities. A contingent of porters arriving in another valley and collecting firewood to cook their evening meal are eating into the stock of firewood which will be collected and used during the harsh winter that follows the tourist season. It is ultimately up to you to ensure that your porters have kerosene stoves, and use them.

Pollution

Litter/waste should always be carried out with you. With just a bit of forethought it is possible to significantly reduce the amount of waste that your supplies will generate in the first place. Discard any surplus packaging beforehand and decant as much as possible into reusable containers (generally lighter and more practical anyway). Paper can be burnt, but not plastics. Remember that even biodegradable items take a long time to degrade in cold, dry, high altitude conditions. Dig a toilet pit at least 30 m from water supplies and above the high water mark of rivers. Avoid contaminating rivers, streams and water channels with detergents – they are likely to be someone's drinking water supply lower down. Burn toilet paper or better still, get used to using water instead. Anyone who has seen the toilet paper on the Annapurna trail in Nepal will appreciate the outcome.

Health

As approved by Dr Charlie Easmon, MBBS MRCP Msc Public Health DTM&H DoccMed Director of Travel Screening Services.

Travellers to Pakistan are exposed to health risks not encountered in Western Europe or North America. Business travellers in international hotels and tourists on organized tours face different risks to travellers backpacking through rural areas. There are no absolute rules to follow; you will often have to make your own judgement on the healthiness of your surroundings. With suitable precautions you should stay healthy.

There are many well-qualified English-speaking doctors in Pakistan, but quality and range of medical care diminishes rapidly as you leave major cities. If in a major city your embassy may be able to recommend a list of doctors. If you are a long way from medical help some self-treatment may be needed. You are very likely to find many drugs with familiar names on sale. Always buy from a reputable source and check date stamping. Vaccines in particular have a much-reduced shelf life if not stored properly. Locally produced drugs may be unreliable because of poor-quality control and substitution of inert ingredients for active drugs.

Before travelling

Take out good medical insurance. Check exactly the level of cover for specific eventualities, in particular whether a flight home is covered, whether the insurance company will pay any medical expenses directly or whether you pay and then claim back, and whether specific activities like trekking or climbing are covered. Have a dental check-up, and take spare glasses or a glasses prescription. If you have a medical problem, such as diabetes, heart or chest trouble or high blood pressure, get advice from your doctor. Carry enough medication to last the full duration of your trip. You may want to ask your doctor for a letter explaining your condition.

Vaccination and immunization

If you need travel vaccinations see your doctor well in advance of travel. Most courses need a minimum of four weeks. Travel clinics may provide rapid vaccination courses but are likely to be more expensive. The following vaccinations are recommended:

Typhoid Spread by poor food hygiene. A single dose injection is available (Typhim Vi) that provides protection for three years. A vaccine taken by mouth in three doses is also available, but the timing of doses can be a problem and protection only lasts one year.

Polio Protection is by live vaccine, generally given as drops by mouth. A full course is three doses with a booster every 10 years.

Tetanus If you have not been vaccinated before one dose of vaccine should be given, then a booster at four weeks and another at two months. Boosters every 10 years are strongly recommended. Children should, in addition, be properly protected against diphtheria, mumps and measles.

Infectious hepatitis If you are not already immune to hepatitis A the best protection is vaccination. A single dose of vaccine gives protection for at least a year. A booster taken six months after the first injection extends immunity to 10 years. If you are not immune to hepatitis B, a vaccine is highly effective. A course is three injections over six months. A combined hepatitis A & B vaccine is available.

Malaria For details of malaria prevention see below.

The following vaccinations may also be considered:

Tuberculosis Still common in the region. You should consult your doctor for advice on BCG inoculation.

Meningococcal meningitis and diphtheria If staying in the country for a long time, vaccination should be considered.

Japanese B encephalitis (JBE) Immunization (effective in 10 days) protects for around three years. In Pakistan there is an extremely small risk, which varies seasonally and from region to region. Consult a travel clinic or family doctor.

Rabies Vaccination before travel gives anyone bitten more time to get treatment (particularly helpful if visiting remote areas), and prepares the body to produce antibodies quickly. Three persons receiving vaccination together can share the cost of the vaccine if it is given intra-dermally.

Yellow fever Vaccinations are not required, but you may be asked to show a vaccination certificate if you have been in a country affected by yellow fever prior to travelling to Pakistan.

Common problems

Intestinal upsets

Intestinal upsets are usually due to poor food hygiene. Do not eat uncooked fish, vegetables or meat, fruit with skin on (always peel fruit yourself), or food exposed to flies (particularly salads).

Tap, stream and well **water** should be considered as unsafe. Bottled mineral water is available, but not all bottled water is mineral water (some of it is purified water from an urban supply). To avoid stomach upsets, rather than putting them in the glass, stand drinks on ice cubes.

Water can be made safe for drinking by bringing it to a rolling boil at sea level, but at higher altitudes you have to boil for longer to ensure that all microbes are killed. There are also several propriety preparations containing chlorine or iodine compounds for 'sterilizing' water. A number of water filters are on the market, available in both personal and expedition size. The general consensus is that so-called 'chemical' water filters are better than their 'mechanical' counterparts, but tend to be more expensive. Ask advice from your retailer (the brands Katadyn and Pur are highly recommended).

Unpasteurized milk products, including cheese, are sources of tuberculosis, brucellosis, listeria and food poisoning germs. Matured or processed cheeses are safer than fresh varieties.

Diarrhoea is usually the result of food poisoning, or occasionally contaminated water. It may start suddenly or rather slowly, and may be accompanied by vomiting, or by severe abdominal pain and the passage of blood or mucus (when it is called dysentery). There are various causes including: viruses, bacteria, protozoa (like amoeba and giardia).

All diarrhoea, with or without vomiting, responds to replacement of water and salts, taken as frequent small sips of some kind of rehydration solution. Proprietary preparations consisting of sachets of powder to dissolve in water (ORS, or Oral Rehydration Solution) are widely available in Pakistan, although you should bring some of your own. They can be made by adding half a teaspoonful of salt and four tablespoonfuls of sugar to a litre of safe drinking water.

If you can time the start of diarrhoea to the minute it is probably viral or bacterial, and/or the onset of dysentery. The treatment, in addition to rehydration, is Ciprofloxacin (500 mg one dose according to the UK regimes or every 12 hours for three days following US guidelines). The drug is widely available.

If the diarrhoea starts slowly or intermittently, it is more likely to be protozoal (caused by amoeba or giardia). It is best treated by a doctor, as should any diarrhoea that lasts more than three days. If medical facilities are remote a short course of Metronidazole (Flagyl) may provide relief. This drug is widely available, but it is best to bring a course with you. If there are severe stomach cramps, the following may help: Loperamide (Imodium, Arret) and Diphenoxylate with Atropine (Lomotil).

Dysentery due to salmonella infections and cholera can be devastating and it would be wise to get to a hospital as soon as possible if these were suspected.

Fasting, peculiar diets and consumption of large quantities of yoghurt are not useful in calming travellers' diarrhoea. Alcohol and milk might prolong diarrhoea and should be avoided during and immediately after an attack. Antibiotics to prevent diarrhoea are probably ineffective and some, such as Entero-vioform, can have serious side effects.

Heat and cold

Full acclimatization to high temperatures takes about two weeks. During this time it is normal to feel relatively apathetic, especially if the relative humidity is high. Drink plenty of water, use salt on food and avoid extreme exertion. When you are acclimatized you will feel more comfortable, but you will continue to need plenty of water to drink.

Tepid showers are more cooling than hot or cold ones. Remember there can be a large and sudden drop between temperatures in the sun and shade and between night and day, especially in the mountains and deserts. Dress accordingly.

The burning power of tropical sun is phenomenal, especially at altitude. Always wear a wide brimmed hat and use sun cream or lotion. Sun tan lotions up to factor seven are not much good. You will need to use types with a protection factor between eight and 25 (dependent on skin type). These are not widely available in Pakistan, so bring supplies with you. Glare from the sun can cause conjunctivitis, so wear good-quality UV protection sunglasses in snowy areas. There are several variations of 'heat stroke'. The most common cause is dehydration, so drink plenty of non-alcoholic fluid.

Insects

These can be a great nuisance and some carry serious disease. The best way to keep mosquitoes away at night is to sleep off the ground in a mosquito net and to burn mosquito coils containing pyrethrum (available in Pakistan). Aerosol sprays or a 'flit' gun may be effective, as are insecticidal tablets heated on a mat that is plugged into a wall socket. These devices, and the refills, are not widely available in Pakistan. Also remember there are regular power cuts in many parts of Pakistan. If you are taking your own make sure it is of suitable voltage with the right adapter plug.

It is better to use a personal insect repellent. The best contain a medium concentration of diethyltoluamide (DEET). These are available in Pakistan (eg Mospel, Repel), although it is recommended that you bring your own supply. Liquid is best for arms, ankles and face (take care around eyes and make sure you do not dissolve the plastic of your spectacles). Aerosol spray on clothes and ankles deters mites and ticks. Liquid DEET suspended in water can be used to impregnate cotton clothes and mosquito nets.

If you are bitten, itching may be relieved by cool baths, anti-histamine tablets (care with alcohol or driving), corticosteroid creams (great care and never use if hint of infection), or by judicious scratching. Calamine lotion and cream are no use. Anti-histamine creams often cause skin allergies and are not recommended.

Bites that become infected and infected scratches (common in Pakistan), should be treated with local antiseptic or antibiotic cream such as Cetrimide. Skin infestations with body lice, crabs and scabies are easy to pick up, particularly by those travelling cheaply or trekking to mountain grazing pastures. Use gamma benzene hexachloride for lice and benzylbenzoate for scabies. Crotamiton cream relieves itching and kills a number of skin parasites. Malathion five per cent is good for lice, but avoid the highly toxic full-strength Malathion which is used as an agricultural insecticide.

Malaria

In most of the areas covered by this handbook, malaria is not a risk. However, since it only takes one bite while travelling through one of the risk areas, you are strongly advised to protect yourself against mosquito bites and to ensure that you take prophylactic (preventive) drugs.

Malaria prevention is becoming more complex as the malaria parasite becomes immune to some of the older drugs. There has been an increase in the proportion of cases of the dangerous falciparum malaria. Some preventive drugs can cause side effects, especially if taken for a long time. Before you travel check with a reputable agency the likelihood and type of malaria in the areas you intend to visit. Take advice on prophylaxis, but be prepared to receive conflicting advice. Dr Charlie Easmon's view is that the best current options for this part of the world are either Lariam, or malarone or doxycycline.

Although less likely, you can catch malaria even when taking prophylactic drugs. If you develop symptoms (high fever, shivering, severe headache, sometimes diarrhoea) seek medical advice immediately.

Infectious hepatitis (jaundice)

The less serious but more common form of hepatitis is hepatitis A, a disease frequently caught by travellers, and common in Pakistan. The main symptoms are yellowness of eyes and skin, lack of appetite, nausea, tiredness and stomach pains. The best protection is careful food preparation, avoidance of contaminated drinking water and scrupulous attention to toilet hygiene.

A more serious illness is hepatitis B, which is acquired as a sexually transmitted disease, from blood transfusions or injections with an unclean needle, or possibly by insect bites. The symptoms are the same as hepatitis A, but the incubation period is much longer.

You may have had jaundice before or you may have had hepatitis without becoming jaundiced, in which case it is possible that you could be immune to either form. Immunity can be tested for before you travel. There are various other kinds of viral hepatitis (C, E etc) but vaccines do not exist for these.

Altitude sickness

Acute mountain sickness (AMS) can strike from about 3,000 m upwards. It is more likely to affect those who ascend rapidly (eg by plane), those not allowing sufficient acclimatization time while trekking and those who over-exert themselves. Teenagers seem to be particularly prone. It can affect you even if you have not had problems at altitude before.

Above 3,000 m, heart pounding and shortness of breath, especially on exertion, are almost universal responses to the lack of oxygen in the air. Acute mountain sickness takes a few hours or days to come on and starts with headache, tiredness, dizziness, loss of appetite, nausea and vomiting. Insomnia is common and often associated with a suffocating feeling when lying down in bed. Keen observers may note their breathing tends to wax and wane at night and their faces tend to be puffy in the morning – this is part of the syndrome. If the symptoms are mild, the treatment is rest, painkillers (preferably not aspirin based) for headache and anti-sickness pills for vomiting. Oxygen may help at very high altitudes but is unlikely to be available.

The best way of preventing acute mountain sickness is relatively slow ascent. When trekking to high altitudes some time spent in the foothills getting fit and adapting to moderate altitude is beneficial. On arrival at places over 3,000 m, a few hours' rest and avoidance of cigarettes, alcohol and heavy food will help prevent the problem. Should symptoms be severe or prolonged, it is best to descend to a lower altitude and re-ascend slowly or in stages. Symptoms disappear very quickly even with a few hundred metres of descent. If staged ascent is impossible because of shortage of time, the drug Acetazolamide is proven to prevent minor symptoms, but some people experience funny side effects and it may mask more serious symptoms. The usual dose is 500 milligrammes of the slow release preparation each night, starting the night before mg above 3,000 m. It will not prevent severe altitude sickness.

There is a further, rare hazard of rapid ascent to high altitude; a kind of complicated mountain sickness presenting as acute pulmonary oedema or acute cerebral oedema. Both are more common the higher you go. Pulmonary oedema starts quite rapidly with breathlessness, noisy breathing, cough, blueness of the lips and possibly frothing at the mouth. Cerebral oedema usually starts with confusion, going on to unconsciousness. Anyone with these symptoms should be evacuated from the mountain as a medical emergency.

Other problems at high altitude are sunburn, excessively dry air causing skin cracking, sore eyes (it may be wise to leave your contact lenses out) and stuffy noses. It is unwise to ascend to high altitude if pregnant (especially in the first three months), or if you have a history of heart, lung or blood disease, including sickle cell. Do not ascend to high altitude in the 24 hours following scuba-diving (although the opportunity is unlikely). Rapid descent from high altitude may aggravate sinus and middle ear infections and make bad teeth ache. The same problems are sometimes experienced during descent at the end of a plane flight.

Remember the mountain ranges of Northern Pakistan are very high, very cold, very remote and potentially very dangerous. Do not travel in them alone, if ill, or if poorly equipped. Telephone communication can be extremely difficult, mountain rescue all but non-existent and medical services extremely basic. Despite these various hazards (mostly preventable) of high altitude travel, many people find the environment healthier and more invigorating than at sea level.

AIDS

In Pakistan, AIDS is increasing in prevalence. It is not wholly confined to the well-known high-risk sections of the population, ie homosexual men, intravenous drug abusers, prostitutes and the children of infected mothers. Heterosexual transmission is now most common and the main risk to travellers is from casual sex (although it has to be said that for most visitors to Pakistan, the chances of casual sex are minimal). The same precautions should be taken as when encountering any sexually transmitted disease.

The AIDS virus (HIV) can be passed via unsterile needles but the risk of this is very small indeed. The chance of picking up hepatitis B or C in this way is much greater. It is sensible to check that needles have been properly sterilized or, better still, disposable needles used. If disposable needles are carried as part of a proper medical kit, customs officials in Pakistan are not generally suspicious.

The risk of receiving a blood transfusion with blood infected with the HIV virus is greater than from dirty needles because of the amount of fluid exchanged. Supplies of blood for transfusion are now usually screened for HIV in reputable hospitals, so the risk may be small. Catching the HIV virus does not necessarily produce an illness in itself; the only way to be sure is to have a blood test on your return to a place where there are reliable laboratory facilities. It takes at least six weeks for the virus to be detectable by a test.

Bites and stings

If you are unlucky enough to be bitten by a venomous snake, spider, scorpion, centipede etc, try (within limits) to catch the animal for identification. Failing this, an accurate description will aid treatment. See the information on rabies (below) for other animal bites.

The reactions to be expected are fright, swelling, pain and bruising around the bite, soreness of regional lymph glands (for example, armpits for bites to hands and arms), nausea, vomiting and fever. If any of the following symptoms appear, ensure that you get the victim to a doctor without delay: numbness, tingling of face, muscular spasm, convulsions, shortness of breath or haemorrhage. Commercial snake bile or scorpion sting kits may be available but are only useful for the specific type of snake or scorpion for which they are designed. The serum has to be given by injection into a vein, so is not much good unless you have practice in making such injections. If the bite is on a limb, immobilize the limb and apply a tight bandage (not a tourniquet) between the bite and the body. Be sure to release it for 90 seconds every 15 minutes. Do not try to slash the bite and suck out the poison – this will do more harm than good. Reassurance of the bitten person is important. Death from snakebite is extremely rare. Hospitals usually hold stocks of snakebite serum, although it is important to have a good description of the snake, or where possible, the actual creature itself. The best precaution is not to walk in snake territory with bare feet, sandals or shorts, and not to touch snakes even if you are assured that they are harmless.

Avoid spiders and scorpions by keeping your bed away from the wall, looking under lavatory seats (if you come across any), and checking inside your shoes in the morning. Dark dusty rooms are especially popular with scorpions, particularly in Chitral. If you are bitten, be sure to consult a doctor.

Other afflictions

Rabies is endemic in Pakistan. If a domestic or wild animal bites you, do not leave things to chance. Scrub the wound immediately with soap and water/disinfectant. Try to capture the animal (within limits). Treatment depends on whether you have been vaccinated against rabies. If you have, then some further doses of vaccine are all that is needed. Human diploid cell vaccine is best, but expensive; other, older types of vaccine, such as that made of duck embryos, may be the only type available. These are effective, much cheaper and generally interchangeable with the human derived types. If not already vaccinated, then anti-rabies serum (immunoglobulin) will be required in addition. It is wise to finish the course of treatment whether the animal survives or not.

Dengue fever is a viral disease transmitted by mosquito bites, and is present in Pakistan. It causes severe headache and body pains. Complicated types of dengue, known as haemorrhagic fevers, occur throughout Asia, but usually occur in persons who have caught the disease for a second time. Although it is a very serious type, it is rarely caught by visitors. There is no treatment; the only way to protect yourself is to avoid mosquito bites.

Athlete's foot and other **fungal infections** are best treated by sunshine and a proprietary preparation, such as Canesten or Ecostatin.

Influenza and **respiratory diseases** are common, perhaps made worse by polluted cities and rapid temperature and climatic changes.

Intestinal worms are common, and the more serious ones, such as hook worm, can be contracted by walking barefoot on infested earth.

Leishmaniasis can be a serious disease taking several forms. It is generally transmitted by sand flies, avoided in the same way as mosquitoes.

Prickly heat is a very common itchy rash and can be avoided by frequent washing and wearing loose clothing. It is helped by the use of talcum powder to allow the skin to dry thoroughly after washing.

Returning home

It is important to take your anti-malaria tablets for four weeks after your return. Malaria can develop up to one year after leaving a malaria area. If you do become ill, with fever, make sure your doctor knows about the areas in which you have travelled. If you have had attacks of diarrhoea, it may be worth having a stool specimen tested in case you have picked up amoebic dysentery, giardiaisis or other protozoal infections. If you have been living rough, a blood test may be worthwhile to detect worms and other parasites.

Further information

The following give information regarding well-trained English-speaking physicians throughout the world: **International Association for Medical Assistance to Travellers**, 745 Fifth Avenue, New York, 10022; **Intermedic**, 777 Third Avenue, New York, 10017.

Information regarding country by country malaria risk can be obtained from: **Malaria Reference Laboratory**, UK, T0891-600350 (recorded message, premium rate); **Liverpool School of Tropical Medicine**, UK, T0891-172111 (recorded message, premium rate); **Centre for Disease Control**, Atlanta, USA, T404-3324555. Vaccinations and returned traveller health checks can be obtained from **Travel Screening Services**, T0207-3078756, www.travelscreening.co.uk.

The London School of Hygiene and Tropical Medicine, Keppel Street, London, WC1E 7HT, UK, publishes a strongly recommended book titled *The Preservation of Personal Health in Warm Climates*. Further information on medical problems abroad can be obtained from: *Travellers' Health: How To Stay Healthy Abroad*, edited by Richard Dawood (Oxford University Press), recently updated, with good information on travel to more out-of-the-way places. A new edition of the HMSO publication *Health Information for Overseas Travel* is now available.

No 1 for travel health
No 1 for late opening
No 1 for returned travellers
No 1 for health
No 1 Harley Street

TRAVEL SCREENING SERVICES

Enjoy your trip abroad by having the best advice, the right vaccinations, and medications that suit you before you travel.

If you are unlucky enough to get ill abroad or on return we are just a click away.

call: 0207 307 8756
email: info@travelscreening.co.uk
www.travelscreening.co.uk

10% discount if you quote ad in the Footprint book Health sections by Dr Charlie Easmon of Travel Screening Services

Keeping in touch

Internet

Internet services in Pakistan improve each year, although in certain parts of the country it can still be a frustrating experience. Within the context of this handbook, the best internet facilities are in Islamabad (fastest machines, usually Rs25-30 per hour), closely followed by Rawalpindi and Peshawar (same price, somewhat slower machines). At the time of going to press, there are no public internet facilities on the KKH between Rawalpindi/Islamabad and Gilgit, and again there is no access between Gilgit and the Chinese city of Kashgar. Likewise on the road north from Peshawar to Chitral, nor indeed in Chitral itself. There are a number of cyber cafés in Gilgit (usually Rs65-75 per hour), although connections are poor, machines desperately slow and frequent power cuts mean you often have to start all over again. Kashgar has good, fast connections (¥10 per hour), although certain sites are often blocked (eg BBC, CNN).

Note that the cyber cafés in Pakistan are rarely also 'cafés' in the traditional sense. For some reason, Netscape Navigator seems to connect quicker than Internet Explorer, and mail providers such as Yahoo are easier to access than Hotmail. Information about internet connections – where they exist – is given in each town's directory section.

Post

Postal services in Pakistan are on the whole reliable, but tend to be slower in the mountainous north than in other regions. It is a good idea to take letters to a Post office where you can hand mail over for franking on the spot (to prevent your stamps being stolen!). Mail between Europe and Rawalpindi/Islamabad and Peshawar generally takes four to seven days, or seven to ten days to Gilgit and Chitral (add three to five days from North America). Outgoing mail is often slightly slower. During poor weather, when flights are cancelled and roads blocked, there are additional delays. Mail to/from China is also reliable, although the remoteness of Kashgar means it is slow to/from there.

Parcels sent from Pakistan have to be sewn up in cloth, although they must first be inspected at the post office (and have a customs declaration form completed, with one attached to the parcel itself); some GPOs have packers who will do the sewing for you (or there will be a 'little man' nearby). Sending parcels is a tedious and time-consuming process. GPOs in the larger cities also have an International Speed Post (ISP) service for parcels; parcels to Europe, USA or Australia cost Rs500 for 500 g and then Rs250 for each additional 500 g (plus Central Excise Duty of 12.5%). Parcels to Canada, France, Germany, Sweden and the Netherlands are charged 30% extra due to surcharges in these countries. NB Gilgit is a bad place from which to try and send parcels.

Poste restante facilities are available at most GPOs, and mail is held for up to three months. American Express offices also have 'clients' mail' services in Islamabad for those with Amex cards or travellers' cheques. There is a poste restante at the post office in Kashgar.

Telephone

Despite the installation of fibre-optic lines and the conversion to digital exchanges, telephone connections in Pakistan remain poor, notably in the north. Most telephone offices (sometimes called telegraph offices) have international direct dialling (IDD), but you still cannot make international calls from north of Gilgit along the KKH until you reach Kashgar (China). Hopefully, this will soon change. International telephone connections from Kashgar are pretty good.

In many telephone offices, you may find that instead of making your call from a booth, you may just have a phone pushed across a counter to you; not the most intimate setting for speaking to a loved one, or for finding out third division football results. Rates from Pak Telecom telephone offices in 2004 were as follows; UK Rs68 per minute (although to other European countries they can be much more expensive); USA Rs75 per minute; Australia Rs85 per minute. Note that there is a three-minute minimum for international calls.

Privately run public call offices (PCOs) are usually slightly more efficient. Calls are more expensive (often a flat Rs95-100 per minute), but there is no three-minute minimum. Making international calls from hotels will incur an extortionate 'surcharge'. NB It is not possible to call 'collect' (reverse-charge) from Pakistan; the nearest you can get is to phone through the number of your hotel from a telephone office or PCO and get the person to call you back there. Note also that private phone numbers in Pakistan change with irksome regularity.

The telephone number for telephone enquiries in major towns is T17. Standard emergency numbers include: Police T15; Fire T16; Ambulance T115, with local numbers for each city. Some major companies (airlines etc) now have 'universal access numbers' (UAN), allowing the same number to be dialled from any city (T111 plus by six digits).

Fax

Fax services are rapidly becoming widespread in Pakistan, with fax machines installed in many hotels. You can also send faxes from most telegraph offices and PCOs.

Media

Newspapers

There are a number of English language daily newspapers available (of which *The News* is arguably the best), but once you leave Rawalpindi/Islamabad or Peshawar they become hard to find (flights permitting, you'll find at least one title in Gilgit). They are, on the whole, disappointing, filled mainly with compilations of government and opposition press releases, poorly constructed editorials, ranting letter pages, and little 'real' journalism. *China Daily* is even worse. However, if you persevere with them, you should come across at least one article during your time in Pakistan entitled 'How I came to Islam' by Yusuf Islam (formerly Cat Stevens)!

Several of the papers can be read on-line, such as *Dawn*, www.dawn.com and *The News*, www.jang group.com/thenews/Index.html. *The Friday Times*, www.the fridaytimes.com, is a new, weekly paper containing sharp political comment. Foreign newspapers can be bought in Islamabad, or read at the British Council and American Centre (Islamabad, Peshawar). For a full list of newspapers and media links, go to www.tourism.gov.pk and follow the links, or go to http://news.bbc.co.uk /2/hi/south_asia/default.stm and follow the links in the Pakistan country profile.

Magazines

What Pakistan lacks in the quality of its newspapers, it makes up for in its magazine output. For a good summary of the contemporary political, economic, sporting and fashion scene in Pakistan, there are several informative periodicals available. *The Herald* and *Newsline* both appear monthly, covering the political and social scene in Pakistan in some depth. The reporting is of a high standard, and the contributors are not afraid to criticize the government, the opposition or the religious parties. Other interesting magazines include *Pakistan Illustrated* and *Politics and Business*. *Newsweek* and *Time* are available from some book stands.

Television and radio

Pakistan's two state-run television stations have little to offer the foreign visitor (nightly news in English at 1800 is deathly dull). Almost all upper and middle-class households, all top-end hotels and more and more restaurants, tea houses and hotels are sprouting satellite dishes, so it is now possible to sit in a chai shop in strictly Shia Muslim towns, such as Skardu, where it is rare to even see a woman on the streets, and watch uncensored episodes of 'Baywatch'. Foreign tourists, particularly women, may feel very uncomfortable watching in such situations.

Although satellite TV carries both CNN and BBC World Service Television, those who want to keep up to date with news, world affairs and sporting results, should consider carrying a **short-wave radio**. BBC World Service is strongest on the following frequencies (with lower frequencies generally better at night): 5975, 6195, 7105, **9740**, **11750**, **12095**, 15070, **15310**, 15400, 18080 (**bold** best). It is also worth tuning in to local stations, especially in the cities. Islamabad's FM101 is definitely worth a listen in the evenings for some quite lively, contemporary Pakistani (mostly Karachi) music.

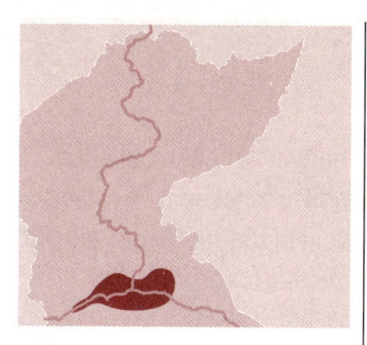

Islamabad & Rawalpindi

Ins and outs	68
Islamabad	**70**
Listings	74
Rawalpindi	**83**
Listings	85
Rawalpindi/Islamabad to	
Peshawar	**92**
Listings	94

Footprint features

Don't miss...	67
Flying into the Northern Areas	70
Arriving at night	80

Introduction

The contrast couldn't be greater between the twin cities of Islamabad and Rawalpindi (or 'Pindi). Islamabad is Pakistan's modern, neatly planned capital, built in the 1960s and laid out according to a grid pattern, with sectors for government, commerce, residential, recreational and industrial use. Rawalpindi, meanwhile, is a sprawling, congested, chaotic and typically South Asian city, with its old bazaars, Cantonment and Saddar areas. Both are growing rapidly and the master plan envisages that the two cities will one day form a single urban mass, with Islamabad encircling the central core of Rawalpindi.

Most people pass through these cities at some stage, without paying them much attention beyond organizing their onward journey. They do have some minor attractions, but for those heading for the mountains, time spent in Rawalpindi and Islamabad is time wasted.

Almost all the administrative necessities (visas, visa extensions, trekking permits etc) are to be found in Islamabad, although the greatest range of accommodation options (particularly for budget travellers) is in Rawalpindi.

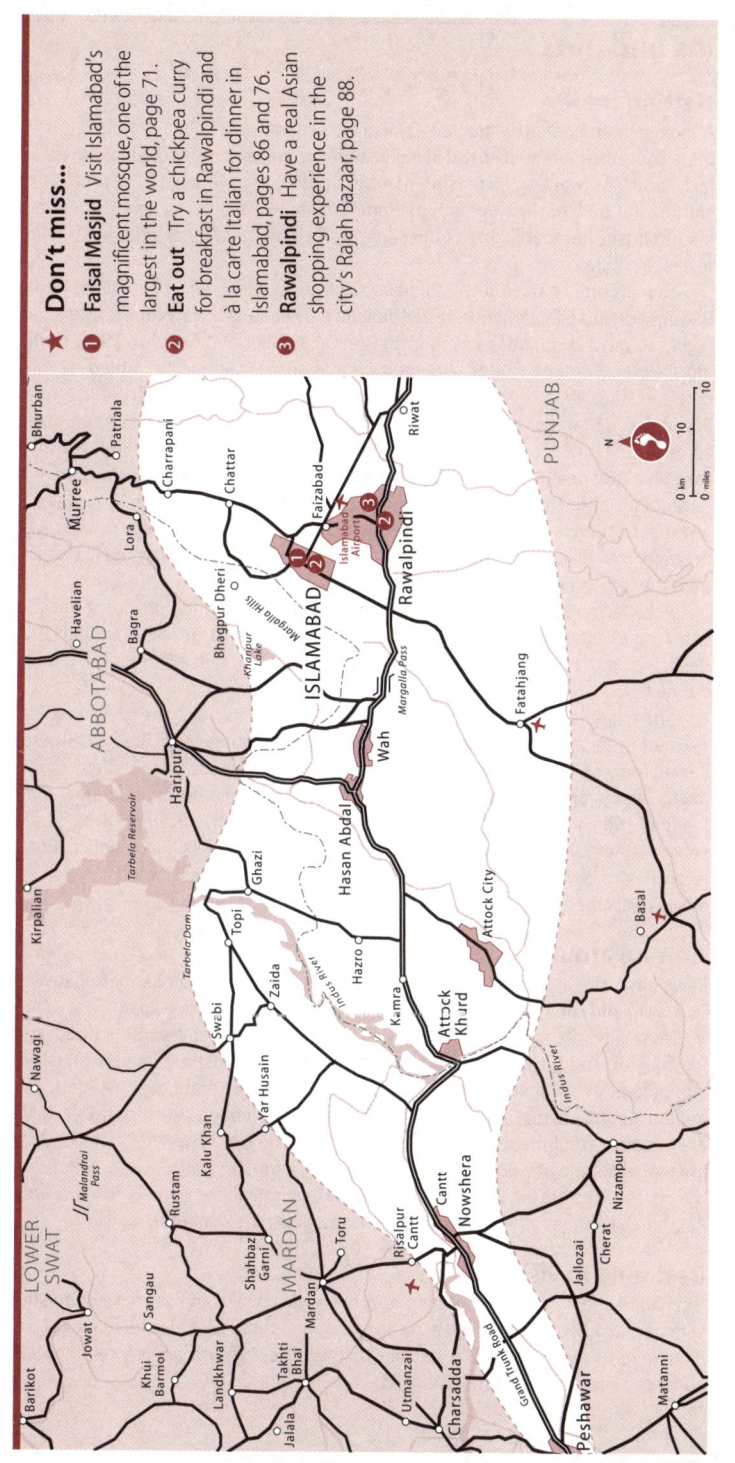

Don't miss...

★

① Faisal Masjid Visit Islamabad's magnificent mosque, one of the largest in the world, page 71.

② Eat out Try a chickpea curry for breakfast in Rawalpindi and à la carte Italian for dinner in Islamabad, pages 86 and 76.

③ Rawalpindi Have a real Asian shopping experience in the city's Rajah Bazaar, page 88.

Ins and outs

Getting there

Although international flights into Karachi are generally cheaper, Islamabad is a far more convenient point of arrival in Pakistan if you are heading to the mountains; in fact, in recent years an increasing number of airlines have begun the process of shifting the bulk of their operations from Karachi to Pakistan's capital. There are also frequent internal flights connecting Islamabad/Rawalpindi with most major towns and cities.

The **airport** is named after Islamabad, although it is in effect equidistant from Rawalpindi and Islamabad; it has improving international connections, as well as flights to most destinations in Pakistan (notably Gilgit and Skardu). Many of the more expensive hotels offer an airport shuttle service for guests. A metered taxi between the airport and Islamabad should cost around Rs150 (Rs100 for Rawalpindi). However securing a fare for less than double this at the airport takes some persistence. If you walk out to the taxi ranks in the car park you should be able to get a better deal. There are also tiny Suzukis which run between the airport and Rawalpindi (either to Adamjee Road in Saddar, or to Rajah Bazaar). These cost just a few rupees but are very cramped indeed and not really suitable if you have lots of luggage. They do not go into the airport itself, but terminate just along the main road from the airport entrance.

Pakistan's main **railway** artery passes through Rawalpindi, providing links to Lahore and ultimately Karachi (with a branch to Quetta) in one direction and Peshawar in the other, although the train is only of limited use for those exploring the north.

The long-distance **bus** network serving the twin cities has undergone a radical revision in recent years. In a move to reduce traffic congestion in the centre of Rawalpindi, all the bus, minibus and coaster services have been shifted out of town. The majority are now grouped in and around the old bus station area of Pir Wadhai (which still remains chaotic and inconveniently located), with some services (notably destinations along the GT Road between 'Pindi and Lahore) relocating to 'Swar Camp' to the southeast of 'Pindi along the GT Road.
▶▶ *See Transport, page 90, for more details.*

Getting around

Rawalpindi sits astride the old Grand Trunk Road (GT Road) on its route between Peshawar and Lahore. It is connected to Islamabad by the Murree Road.

A steady stream of intercity buses and minibuses connect Islamabad and Rawalpindi. The buses (large, brightly decorated Bedfords) are impossibly slow, stopping at every opportunity to pick up passengers, and are best avoided. The minibuses (Toyota Hiace or Ford vans) are extremely cramped but much faster. Taxis are the most comfortable option, although the 15-km trip between 'Pindi's Saddar area and Islamabad will cost Rs200 or more, as compared with less than Rs10 on the buses. Taxis are the best way of getting to and from the airport (Rs 100 to 'Pindi, Rs150 to Islamabad, but you may be asked 10 times that amount).

Best time to visit

Islamabad and Rawalpindi can both become unpleasantly hot and sticky during the summer (and even late spring/early autumn), and thus most visitors leave for the mountains as soon as possible. Daytime temperatures in winter are very comfortable, and it can even be a little chilly at night.

Tourist information

PTDC has an office in Rawalpindi ⓘ *Flashman's Hotel, T051-5581480, F051-513054*, but it is not particularly useful. **TDCP** (Tourism Development Corporation of Punjab) ⓘ *44 Mall Plaza (in shopping plaza, corner of Kashmir Rd and The Mall), T051-564824, F051-568421*, provides information and package tours to Murree and the Galis, Kaghan valley, Swat valley, Chitral, Gilgit and Hunza. Also has information and tickets for minibus to Murree and bus services to Faisalabad and Lahore.

In Islamabad, **PTDC Tourist Information** ⓘ *Supermarket, F-6/1, T051-9204027, Mon-Thu and Sat 0900-1500, Fri 0900-1200*, is useful for information on Islamabad/Rawalpindi and the immediate vicinity, and organizes tours (the main office in F-7/2 has now closed; see 'Useful addresses' for info on trekking permits). **PTDC Motels** ⓘ *F-7/2 Markaz (just west of Taj Mahal restaurant), T051-9203223, Mon-Thu and Sat 0900-1600, Fri 0900-1200*, offers advance reservations for various PTDC Motels across the country.

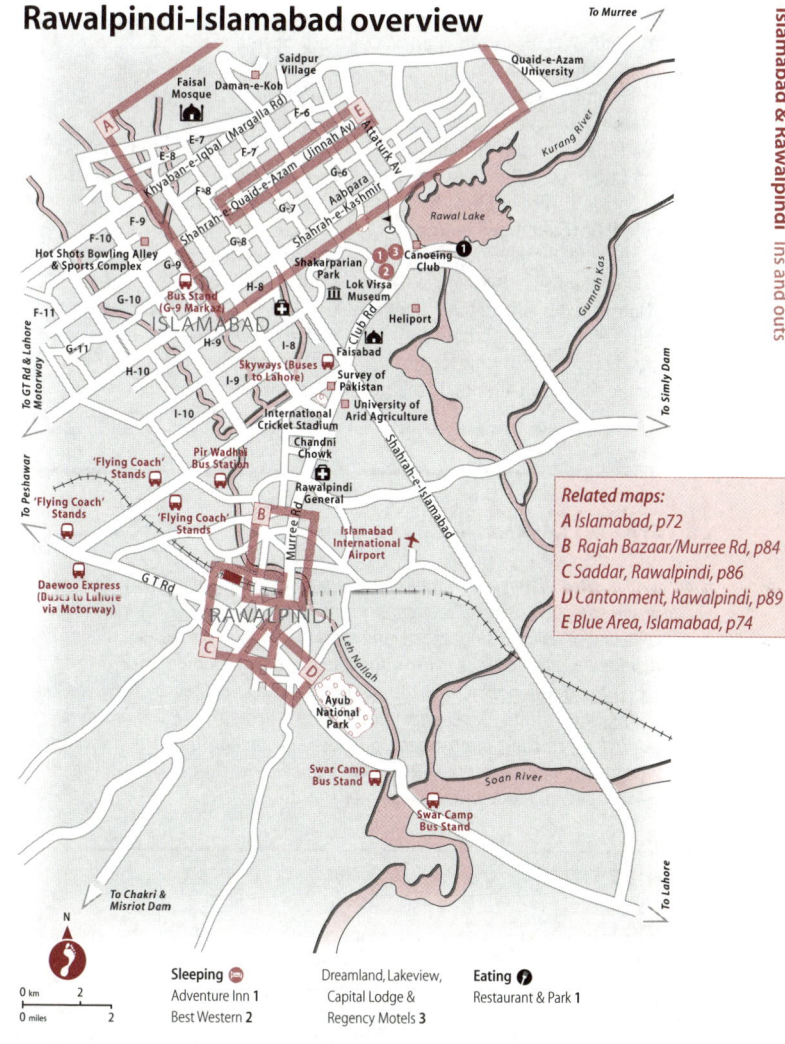

Rawalpindi-Islamabad overview

Related maps:
A Islamabad, p72
B Rajah Bazaar/Murree Rd, p84
C Saddar, Rawalpindi, p86
D Cantonment, Rawalpindi, p89
E Blue Area, Islamabad, p74

Sleeping
Adventure Inn 1
Best Western 2
Dreamland, Lakeview, Capital Lodge & Regency Motels 3

Eating
Restaurant & Park 1

⚑ Flying into the Northern Areas

One of the quickest and most dramatic ways of entering the Northern Areas of Pakistan is to fly. PIA offer one to three flights daily to both Gilgit and Skardu. If you can get a place on one of these flights, then go for it as it is a wholly unforgettable experience.

As with everything else in life there's a catch. In this case it is that not only are the flights heavily over-subscribed, but, being weather dependent, as many as 50% of them are cancelled. Sometimes these cancellations come at very short notice – when you're sitting in the plane waiting to take off, or if you're really unlucky, when the plane is already halfway to its destination! In such cases, you will have to return to the booking office in 'Pindi, where you will be reconfirmed onto the next day's flight, thus increasing the backlog of travellers wishing to fly.

Note that it is easy to buy a ticket for this flight – the difficulty is in actually confirming a seat for a specific flight. You have to do this in person at the special PIA Northern Areas booking office in Rawalpindi (round the side of the main PIA office) before 1100 on the day before you wish to fly.

The fare for foreigners is Rs2,800 to Gilgit and Rs2,750 to Skardu, and these prices increase by around 10% per year. Residents of the Northern Areas used to get a subsidized fare, but this is under review.

It's slightly easier to get a ticket (and a flight) to Skardu, since a 737 operates on this route (carrying more passengers and being less susceptible to poor weather cancellation). The flight to Gilgit on the little Fokker F-27s is more spectacular/hair-raising though, as these planes have to fly around the mountains since they can't get over them! The best views (notably as the plane skirts Nanga Parbat) are on the starboard side Ism-Gilgit, and the port side Gilgit-Ism. It's also worth asking the cabin staff if you can visit the captain and see the view from the driving seat.

Islamabad → *Colour map 1, grid C4*

Islamabad is often dismissed as a modern, bland and characterless city. Certainly, if you are wrestling with its bureaucrats or plodding round the airline offices or embassies or wherever, it's not exactly the most inspiring of places. But it does have its attractions. Its saving grace is the abundance of open woodland and greenery in amongst all the development, and the natural beauty of the nearby Margalla Hills. This is the only urban experience you'll come across in Pakistan that isn't accompanied by choking atmospheric pollution. Islamabad has a better range of mid-range to upmarket hotels than Rawalpindi, but little for the budget traveller. ▸▸ For Sleeping, Eating and all other listings, see pages 74-83.

Ins and outs

Getting there
Although there is a railway booking office in Islamabad, the train station is in Rawalpindi. Likewise, there is a small bus station (G-9 Markaz) in Islamabad, though most destinations are served by the bus stands in and around Pir Wadhai (located

between the two cities, details in the Rawalpindi section).

Arriving from Rawalpindi, brightly coloured Bedford buses link Faisabad, Zero Point, Aabpara, Supermarket, Jinnah Supermarket, Faisal Mosque and Ayub Market, and then double back along the same route. Minibuses – numbers 1 and 6, with a red stripe on the side – follow the same route, bearing east at Supermarket towards the Secretariat; number 1 goes via the GPO and number 6 via PIA's main office. **Varan** buses 1a and 2 run to Aabpara from 'Pindi. ▶ *See Transport, page 79, for more details.*

Getting around

Islamabad is too spread out to walk around; for example, it's a 45-minute walk from the Tourist Campsire at Aapara to the Chinese Embassy. The intercity buses are useful for getting between the main centres (Zero Point, Aabpara Market, Supermarket and Jinnah Supermarket). There are also local bus/minibus services to other districts of the capital, but on the whole taxis are the most convenient; if they do not have a working meter, always agree a price before getting in. Wagons and buses run along fixed routes through Islamabad, but they're crowded and not always easy to navigate.

> *An unlikely source of info on Islamabad is the website of an upmarket ice cream parlour, www.thehotspotonline.com.*

'Zero Point' was planned as the centre of the city, although the political, administrative and commercial centre of gravity has developed to the north and east. The city is divided into sectors. To the north of 'Blue Area' are sectors F-6 through to F-10 (also known as Shalimar 6-10). To the south are sectors G-6 through to G-10 (or Ramna 6-10). Sectors H and I, to the southwest of Zero Point are being developed.

Blue Area itself, running east-west through the centre of Islamabad, is the main commercial thoroughfare. Each sector has a commercial centre or **Markaz**, with its own name; F-6 is Supermarket, F-7 Jinnah Supermarket, F-8 Ayub Market, while G-6 is Civic Centre or Melody Market and G-7 Sitara Market. Aabpara, Islamabad's oldest market lies in the southern part of of G-6/1, along Khyaban-e-Suhrawardy. Government buildings – the Presidency, Parliament, Secretariat etc – and the diplomatic enclave are situated at the eastern end of the city. The intercity buses and minibuses are useful for getting between the various markets.

History

Islamabad was designated as the modern capital of Pakistan by President Ayub Khan in 1958, and was chosen to act as a counterbalance to the overwhelming economic importance of Karachi, the original capital, and the political dominance of Lahore. A number of planners and architects, including Edward Durrell Stone, Ponti and the Greek firm Doxiadis Associates were called in to plan the city from scratch. What they produced is about as un-Asian as you can imagine; a strictly geometric city of neat rectangular blocks and wide tree-lined avenues.

It's a great source of pride to many Pakistanis, but at the end of the day it's also a place far removed from the rest of Pakistan. True to its modern image, it's home to some of Pakistan's more daring modern architecture, particularly some of the foreign missions in the diplomatic enclave, as well as the government buildings which reflect the grandeur and scale of the city plan. Elsewhere there are some interesting fusions of 20th-century post-modernism and traditional Islamic architecture.

Sights

Built with funds gifted by King Faisal Bin Abdul Aziz of Saudi Arabia and designed by a Turkish architect, **Faisal Masjid** ① *at the end of Shaharah-e-Islamabad at the foot of* the Margalla Hills, you can only visit outside prayer times and not at all on Fri, free, *many of the Bedford buses from Rawalpindi terminate here,* is one of the largest mosques in the world, with 88-m-high minarets resembling rockets. It is said to hold 100,000 worshippers. The main prayer hall is an unique tent-like structure with eight faces, rising to 40 m at its summit. The raised courtyard boasts huge expanses of polished marble. There is a bookshop, library and lecture hall belonging to the Islamic Research Centre, and a restaurant to the rear. Signs state that photography is strictly forbidden, but this is applied only in the main prayer hall.

> ❗ Note that for the most part, Islamabad numbers are now seven-digit (try pre-fixing a '2' to six-digit numbers, or alternatively a '9').

Islamabad Museum ⓘ *House 41, Street 3, E-7, T051-9223826, Sat-Tue 0900-1630, Fri 0930-1230, 1430-1630, free; heading west from the east end of Gomal Road, take the first right (Street 2) and then the first left (Street 3); the museum is two-thirds of the way down on the right,* has an excellent selection of artefacts with rooms covering the prehistoric, Indus Valley, Gandharan, Arabic and Islamic periods. Although no match for the major museums at Peshawar, Lahore and Karachi, the presentation is very good. Well worth a visit, particularly if you lose interest quickly in larger museums.

The small village of **Nurpur Shahan** ⓘ *3 km to the northeast of the diplomatic enclave,* is famous for the shrine of the 17th-century saint, Hazrat Syed Shah Abdul Latif or Barri Imam (holy man of the woods), who lived for 12 years in a nearby cave. Pilgrims arrive in large numbers for the annual *Urs* (death anniversary) in May and there are music and prayers every Thursday evening. There is a path leading up to the site of his cave, on a hillside to the northeast, around two hours' walk.

Islamabad

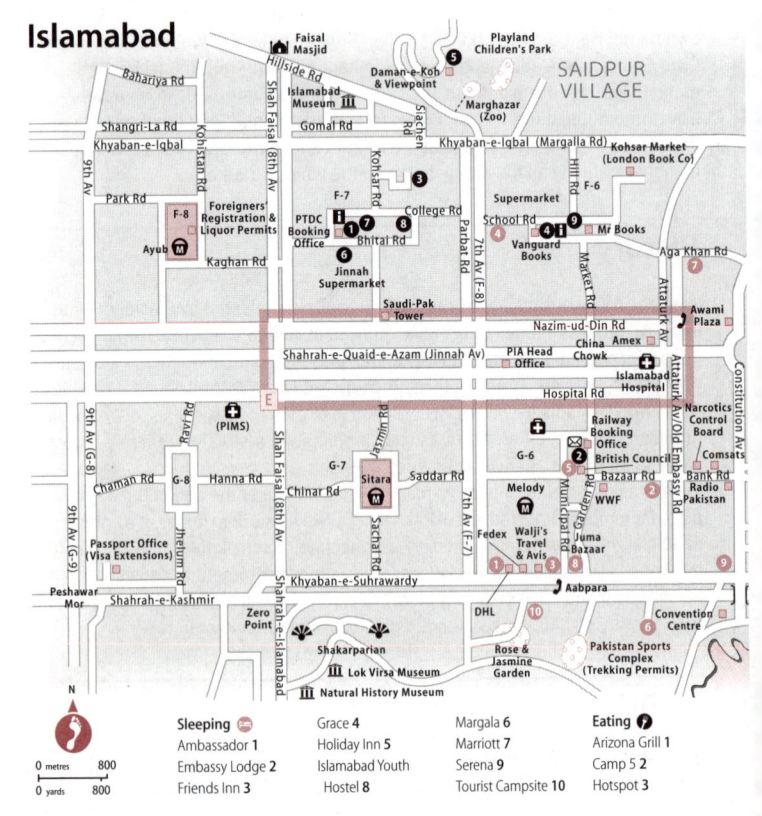

0 metres 800
0 yards 800

Sleeping 🛏
Ambassador 1
Embassy Lodge 2
Friends Inn 3
Grace 4
Holiday Inn 5
Islamabad Youth Hostel 8
Margala 6
Marriott 7
Serena 9
Tourist Campsite 10

Eating 🍴
Arizona Grill 1
Camp 5 2
Hotspot 3

Margalla Hills

ⓘ *walking distance from the northern fringes of Islamabad.*

The Margalla Hills are spread over an area of 12,000 ha, rising to a maximum height of 1,580 m. The area has been designated as a National Park in an attempt to curb the encroachment of quarrying and developers, and to protect the rich flora and fauna. The hills offer numerous opportunities for walks and longer hikes, just minutes from the city centre. It is worth visiting the offices of the **Margalla Hills Society** ⓘ *next to Vanguard Books in F-6 Supermarket, T051-9205083*. Very good detailed maps and hike descriptions can be found in the Asia Study Group's *Hiking Around Islamabad* (1992 revised edition), available from many Islamabad bookshops or from the organization's HQ ⓘ *Malik Complex, 80 West, Jinnah Av, Blue Area, T051-815891*.

The viewpoint at **Daman-e-Koh** ⓘ *follow road from the north end of 7th Av*, occupies a spur of the Margalla Hills overlooking Islamabad. A road winds its way up to the viewpoint from the north end of 7th Avenue, passing first through beautiful woods with various walking trails before climbing into the hills. There are a couple of snack bars at the turning for the viewpoint, and at the viewpoint itself there is the **Kashmirwala's** restaurant (see Eating, below), with its terrace offering great views of Islamabad. There are a number of short walks around the spur.

Saidpur Village ⓘ *to the east of Daman-e-Koh and reached by a road leading north from the top end of F-6 (the turning is signposted)*, is a small traditional village, surrounded by mango trees. It was predominantly Hindu before Partition and the springs in the area were considered holy. You come first to the school, which is housed in a former Hindu temple. If you follow the stream to the right of the school as you face it you come to a couple of potters' workshops where you can see the beautifully decorated traditional items of pottery which are still produced here.

Shakarparian Park

ⓘ *to the south of the main road between Zero Point and Aabpara*.

This low hill overlooking Islamabad has been kept as the Shakarparian Park. There are east and west viewpoints at the top, giving good views of the Margalla Hills to the north, Rawal Lake to to the east, Kahuta to the southeast (the centre of Pakistan's nuclear technology research programme) and Rawalpindi to the south. It's a very popular area for a stroll, particularly in the evening, when the lights of the city make for an attractive sight. There are various snack bars and a restaurant at the east viewpoint. The hill is forested and there are various walking trails.

Lok Virsa ⓘ *PO Box 1184, Garden Av, Shakarparian, T051-9203983, F051-920 2042, summer 0900-1900, winter 0900-1700, closed Fri and public holidays, Rs10 (students Rs5), either walk there from Zero Point, over Shakaparian hill, or take a taxi*, is Pakistan's National Institute of Folk Heritage. It is active in promoting the tremendous wealth and variety of traditional arts and crafts in Pakistan and has published a valuable range of social research material and reprints of old folk tale

Related maps:
E Blue Area, Islamabad, p74
See also Rawalpindi-
Islamabad overview, p69

Kabuli **4**
Kashmirwala's **5**
Mezzo **6**
New Afghani **7**
Pappasalli's **8**
United Bakery **9**

collections. Its sound archive is the largest existing collection of Pakistani songs, balards, interviews etc, while the video archive has films on folk performances, customs and traditions. The **museum** here houses an interesting selection of handicrafts, including some beautiful costumes, textiles, jewellery, musical instruments, pottery and carved pieces, displayed according to area, use and motif. There is also a good research **library** (incorporating the sound and video archives), an open-air **theatre** and a **bookshop**. It also has a **craft centre** in Supermarket, F-6/1 (next to **Vanguard Books**).

Pakistan Museum of Natural History ⓘ *Garden Av, Shakarparian, T051-9219983, F051-221864, Mon-Sat 0800-1800, free, either walk there from Zero Point, over Shakaparian hill, or take a taxi,* is housed in the basement of a newly built block for the natural sciences research department of Islamabad University.

Rose and Jasmine Garden ⓘ *within walking distance of Aabpara,* has shows of over 250 varieties of rose and a dozen jasmines. The best time to visit is during spring, when the gardens are in flower, out of season it is somewhat disappointing.

Rawal Lake

ⓘ *Just southeast of Aabpara, about 20 mins' walk. Suzukis running along Khayaban-e-Suhrawardy can drop you there.*

This large lake, formed by a dam across the Kurang River, is the main water supply for Islamabad. There are extensive reed-beds around the northern side of the lake, home to a wide variety of birds and wildlife. There is a restaurant and various snack bars around a terraced garden by the dam on the south side of the lake, as well as rowing boats and small motor boats for hire nearby. The Canoe Club on the track up to the dam has open membership (see Activities and tours, page 78).

Sleeping

Many of Islamabad's privately run guest houses fall into the C-D price category, although many have rooms and facilities that are easily a match for those in the A-B range. They are usually located in residential areas, and are popular with aid-workers and other expats who do not have permanent residences and wish to avoid the more impersonal large hotels. Most budget travellers stay in Rawalpindi.

NB Check to see whether hotel room charge includes taxes, since this can add 20%.
L Crown Plaza, 99-E, Jinnah Av, T051-2277890, info@hotelcrownplaza.com. Recently opened 'top end' hotel, still doesn't have the luxurious feel of the Marriott or Serena, full facilities such as central a/c, dish TV, pool, health club, conference facilities, choice of restaurants, but has a somewhat '70s look (lots of brown).

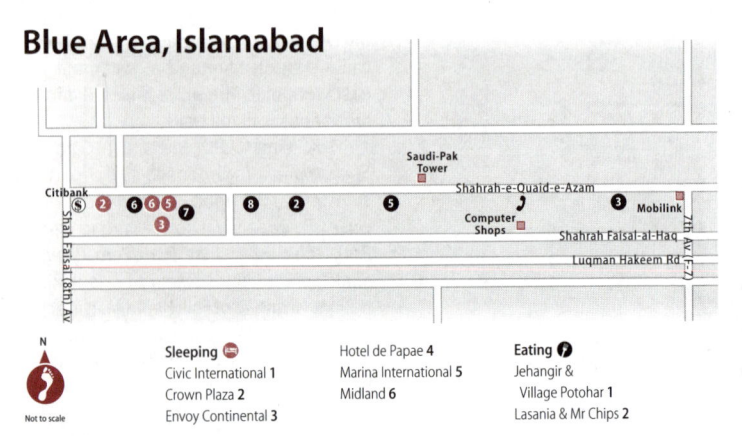

Blue Area, Islamabad

N
Not to scale

Sleeping
Civic International **1**
Crown Plaza **2**
Envoy Continental **3**
Hotel de Papae **4**
Marina International **5**
Midland **6**

Eating
Jehangir &
 Village Potohar **1**
Lasania & Mr Chips **2**

L Holiday Inn, G-6, Civic Centre, Municipal Rd, T051-2827311, holiday@isb.comsats.net.pk. Doesn't have the same sense of luxury as the Marriott or Serena, and the oft talked about ground floor renovation (indoor pool, health club etc) still hasn't happened. Central a/c, dish TV, choice of restaurants, but you can do much better than this.

L Marriott, Aga Khan Rd, Shalimar 5, T111-223344, guest@isb.marriott.infolink.net.pk. The most luxurious hotel in Islamabad before the Serena opened, with full facilities in rooms (plus suites from Rs12,000-50,000 per night), pool, health club, business centre, choice of restaurants, 24-hr coffee shop acts as an ad hoc press club, **Muddy's Café** is essentially an alcohol-free nightclub (Sat), good service. Recommended.

L Serena, Khyaban-e-Suhrawardy, T051-2874000, www.serenahotels.com/pakistan/islamabad. Now the biggest and grandest in town, 170 rooms decorated in 'Punjabi or 'Swati' style (US$200 plus tax), two types of stunning suites (US$270-350 plus tax), flat-screen dish TV and internet access in each room, IDD, varied dining options, heated outdoor pool, single-sex gyms, real sense of luxury and excellent service. Recommended, if you can afford it!

A Best Western, Club Rd, near Rawal Dam, T051-2277460, F051-2277469. Quiet location away from city centre, comfortable well-furnished rooms, a/c, dish TV, but still a little overpriced.

A Envoy Continental, 111-E, Shahrah Faisal-al-Haq, Blue Area, T051-2273971, envoycontinentalhotel@hotmail.com. Recently opened (2000), 60 rooms, central a/c, dish TV, business centre, coffee shop, beauty parlour.

A Hotel de Papae, 146-D, West Blue Area, T051-2273427, depapae@hotmail.com. Friendly and well run, but without the sense of luxury of the 'L' hotels (despite the glitzy mirrors everywhere), and a few rough edges. Large rooms with a/c, dish TV, minibar, IDD phone, small sitting area, modern bathrooms, plus a few larger 'de luxe' rooms, sitting/group briefing area on each floor, business centre, restaurant, coffee shop.

A Margala Motel, M-2, near Convention Centre, T051-2276500, isb@margalamotel.com. Professional service, quiet, leafy location, fair-sized rooms with central a/c, dish TV, business/conference facilities, 2 restaurants, not a bad deal (especially if you can get the group rate).

A-B Marina International, 109 East Jinnah Av, Blue Area, T051-2271309, F051-2876061. Central a/c, choice of suites with sitting areas (rather tatty), family and de luxe rooms, all with dish TV, fridge and modern tiled bathrooms, plus standard doubles with attached bath, public areas rather run down, but rooms with Margalla Hills views are OK, restaurant.

B Adventure Inn, Garden Av, PO Box 1807, T051-2272537, F051-2274625. Quite busy (HQ of the Adventure Foundation), and, although comfortable enough, a little overpriced for what you get. Quiet location, a/c rooms, dish TV, restaurant, nice garden.

B Ambassador, Khayaban-e-Suharwardhy, G-6/1, T051-2824011, ambassador_pk@yahoo.com. Fair-sized rooms, a/c, dish TV, small courtyard garden.

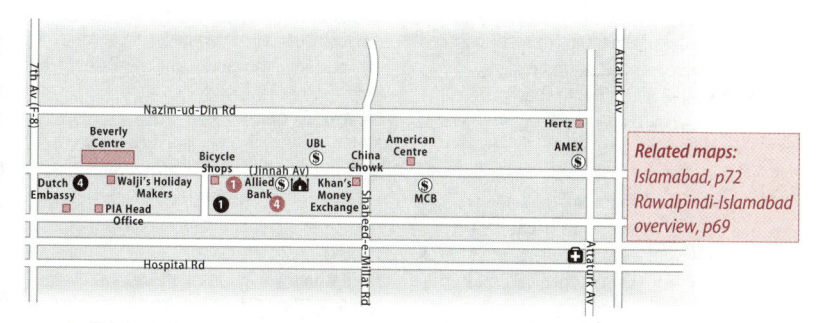

Nirala Sweets **3**
Omar Khayam **4**
Red Onion, Bolan Saltish **5**
Twenty Twenty & Dragon City **6**
Wang Fu **7**
Yummy's 36, Sogo's & Subway **8**

Related maps:
Islamabad, p72
Rawalpindi-Islamabad overview, p69

B Capital Lodge, Club Rd, T051-2823463. Like most other places in this category, quiet location but overpriced.

B Civic International, 13, West Blue Area, Jinnah Av, T051-2273740, F051-2274450. Rooms have a/c, dish TV, phone, some larger de luxe rooms, owned by neighbouring Usmania restaurant.

B Dreamland Motel, Club Rd, T051-2829072, F051-2829077. Rooms a little dark and musty for the price, a/c, dish TV, restaurant, coffee shop, conference facilities.

B Embassy Lodge, 36 Old Embassy Rd (Attaturk Av), G-6/4, T051-2272243, emblodge@comsats.net.pk. 15 a/c rooms in private guesthouse, dish TV, well furnished, modern bathrooms.

B Grace, 27 School Rd, F-6/1, T/F051-820392, grace@sparcom.net.pk. Guest house in residential location, a/c rooms, sun deck, dining room, IDD phone and internet facilities.

B Lakeview Motel, Club Rd, T051-2821386, F051-2822394. Another overpriced place in this category, could do with a good lick of paint, a/c, phone, dish TV, restaurant, conference facilities.

B Midland, 104-E, Jinnah Av, Blue Area, T051-2206740, F051-2203742. Was the Forte Crest, no real sense of luxury or quality given the price.

B Regency, Club Rd, near Rawal Dam, T051-2279275, F051-2279276. Of the 4 similar places clustered here, this is probably the only one worth considering. Rooms a/c, dish TV, IDD phone, modern bathrooms, conference facilities, restaurants, slightly newer than the others and better run.

C-D Friends Inn, Block 16, I&T Centre, Aabpara, G-6/1-4, T051-2272546. Fair-sized rooms, those with a/c also have dish TV and fridge, cheaper non a/c rooms also reasonable value, all with attached tiled bath, friendly manager, very good deal if you can negotiate a discount (or avoid paying the tax).

H Islamabad Youth Hostel, Garden Rd, G-6/4 (near Aabpara), T051-2826899. Popular with Pakistani students so often full (especially in summer), generally clean, good value, separate male/female dorms, self-catering facilities. Non-members must buy a 'welcome ticket' (Rs100), or you can buy full membership to the IYHA for 1 year (Rs450), students pay Rs45 for a bed, adults Rs75, maximum stay 3 days in the summer.

H Tourist Campsite, opposite Rose & Jasmine Garden, opposite Aabpara. This used to be dirt cheap (Rs3 to sleep under the stars, Rs8 to pitch your tent, Rs15 for a place in the huts), but prices have now leapt dramatically (possibly to get rid of the semi-permanent population since officially the maximum stay is 2 weeks). Now Rs50 for a space in one of the dormitory 'bungalows' (dirty bare floor, no beds/bedding), Rs50 to pitch a tent and Rs100 to bring in a vehicle. There are shared toilet and shower facilities. Unless you plan to camp, this isn't great value. Strictly foreigners only.

Eating

Islamabad offers some really excellent dining options.

Dragon City, East Jinnah Av, Blue Area. New, a/c restaurant, food not bad, Rs300 per head.

Dynasty at the Marriott, Aga Khan Rd, Shalimar 5, T111-223344. Probably Islamabad's best Chinese dining experience.

Hotel Crown Plaza 99-E, Jinnah Av, T051-2277890. Has a 'Lahori Night' on Thu and Fri (Rs350 per head), or try 'Greek night' (Sat and Tue) or 'Mexico & Sombrero' (Sun and Wed).

Mezzo, 15 School Rd, F-7 Markaz, T051-2650974. Thai, Lebanese etc 'nouvelle cuisine', Rs300-400 per head, nice setting.

Omar Khayamm, West Blue Area, Jinnah Av. Unprepossessing entrance disguises one of Islamabad's best restaurants. Excellent reputation amongst expat community, eat extremely well for Rs400 per head.

Arizona Grill, F-7 Markaz, T051-2824576. American-style diner offering steaks, chicken dishes, salads, plus Italian and Mexican, plus good lunchtime buffet for Rs320 (although sometimes it only comprises 5 or so dishes). Good choice for a change.

Kashmirwala's, Daman-e-Koh, T/F051-2815496. Occupies a prime position at Daman-e-Koh, with wonderful views out

● *For an explanation of sleeping and eating price codes used in this guide, see inside the front cover. Other relevant information is found in Essentials, pages 36-38.*

> ### Obtaining a Liquor Permit in Islamabad
>
> To obtain a liquor permit you must go to the Central Excise and Taxation Office, Ayub Market, F-8 Markaz. You need to get and fill out an application form, pay the Rs200 fee at the National Bank of Pakistan branch in F-8 Markaz, and submit your application along with photocopies of the relevant pages of your passport and bank receipt. Your passport will be stamped and signed and you will receive a liquor permit. Be prepared for lots of hanging around. One unit is equal to one litre of spirits or around 12 bottles of beer. The permits are valid only for Islamabad, where they can be used at the Marriott Hotel. An additional 'fee' may also be charged, although this is essentially a baksheesh.

over Islamabad, somewhat cavernous dining hall geared up to catering for special occasions and big groups, lovely terrace, buffet lunch/dinner laid on in season.

Marriott, Aga Khan Rd, Shalimar 5, T111-223344. 24-hr coffee shop serves good light meals in a pleasant a/c environment for around Rs250, or for a 'travellers' treat', try the Rs200 'high tea' buffet (1530-1830, all you can eat).

Pappasalli's, Block 13-E, Markaz F-7, T051-2650550. One of Islamabad's best and busiest restaurants (bookings recommended at weekends). A la carte menu, or excellent fixed menus to feed 2/4/6 people (Rs405/495/795). Takeaway and home delivery also available. Highly recommended.

Wang Fu, 106 West Jinnah Av, Blue Area, T051-271306. Reasonable food in plush setting (Rs275 per head).

Bolan Saltish, Jehangir (the appeal of which is the 'dwarf' doorman!), **Lasania**, **Mr. Chips**, **Red Onion**, **Sogo's**, **Village Potohar**, all at the western end of Jinnah Av in Blue Area, serve glorified fast food and most offer good value promotions (eg buy 1 pizza get 1 free).

The Hot Spot, F-7/3, www.thehotspot online.com. Tucked away in a residential area, not only offers the city's best ice cream, it's also the place where Islamabad's rich kids come to hang out in a 'Hard Rock Café' style setting.

Kabuli, F-6 Markaz, Supermarket. Setting is nothing special, although the Pakistani/Afghan food is reasonable, Rs150 per head.

New Afghan, F-7 Markaz, Jinnah Supermarket, T051-829444. Unassuming place offering excellent grilled meat, eat well for Rs150-200.

Subway, Masco Plaza, Blue Area, T051-2877248. Part of franchise, giant but pricey sandwiches.

Twelve Twenty, East Jinnah Av, Blue Area. A new-style trendy café/restaurant.

Yummy's 36, West Jinnah Av, Blue Area. Ice cream and fast food.

Camp 5 Food Court, Civic Centre G-6 (behind British Council). Range of fast food styles, dishes Rs25-90. There are also several cheap meat and chapati places in the market near the British Council.

Nirala Sweets, Blue Area. Has a good selection of pastries.

The Patisserie, at the Marriott (see Sleeping). High quality pastries.

United Bakery, Supermarket. Arguably Islambad's best, offering coffee, savoury snacks, sweets and pastries – it's a real treat when the automatic doors slide open and the smell hits you!

Entertainment

Coolabah Club, Australian High Commission, 3rd Av in the diplomatic enclave, T051-2824345. If you're really hankering for a beer and a steak, then you could try your luck here. Officially it's only open to Australian nationals (Fri night), although other nationalities are often admitted (bring your passport). It's located at the site of the old Australian High Commission (see map), but be wary of shady characters hanging around outside. Note that you are admitted as a 'guest' and not 'by right'

(best to call ahead). The clubs at the Canadian (Tue) and French (Mon, Wed and Fri) embassies are also worth trying. See box for details on obtaining a liquor permit.
Muddy's Café in the Marriott hotel, Aga Khan Rd, Shalimar 5, T111-223344. The nearest thing Islamabad has to a nightclub, strictly alcohol-free and with a policy of couples only, it can get quite lively on a Saturday night, with dancing and, gasp, women in sleeveless shalwar kameez!

O Shopping

While most foreign tourists get excited about the prospect of battling their way through the crowded chaos of Rawalpindi's **Rajah Bazaar**, most Pakistanis are far more interested in the orderly, relaxed and 'modern' shopping experience which Islamabad offers (**Supermarket**, **Jinnah Supermarket**, **Melody Market** are the commercial centres of the 'main' sectors). You can find everything here you would expect to find at home, as well as an excellent selection of Pakistani handicrafts, antiques, souvenirs etc.

Blue Area is the main commercial thoroughfare; many of the banks, travel agents, airlines etc have their offices here. The western section of Blue Area also has a number of restaurants, while around the junction of Jinnah Av with 7th Av there are several carpet and handicraft shops.

Markets
Aabpara is Islamabad's oldest market, selling household items, fabrics and spices.
Covered Market, near to Aabpara, is good for meat, fruit and veg, and the Juma (Fri) Bazaar, which can be a good place to hunt for handicrafts.
Itwar (Sun) Market is held on Sun near Peshawar Mor; primarily an agricultural market, it's worth visiting for the spectacle if nothing else.
Kohsar Market, F-6/3, has a couple of good grocery stores catering for the expat community, and an excellent bookshop (see below). There are also usually various stalls selling handicrafts.
Supermarket and **Jinnah Supermarket**, at the centre of F-6 and F-7 respectively, are both major shopping complexes, with a selection of chemists, clothing shops, convenience stores, photographic shops, handicrafts/antiques/souvenir shops, bookshops, restaurants etc.

Handicrafts
There are numerous carpet retailers in and around F-6 Supermarket.

Books
Islamabad has Pakistan's best range of bookshops (new and used).
Book City, **Book Village** and **Old Book Corner**, F-6 Supermarket. Reasonable, if eclectic, selection.
London Book Co, 3 Kohsar Market, F-6/3, T051-2823852. One of the best.
Mr. Books, F-6 Markaz, Supermarket. The best in Islamabad, also stocks *Footprint Pakistan* (Rs795).
Vanguard Books, Lok Virsa Building, Supermarket, F-6/1.

Sports goods
Pakistani (Sialkot) made sports goods are available very cheaply in Islamabad (footballs Rs450-850, wicketkeeper gloves Rs950 etc). There are also outlets in F-6 Supermarket.

▲ Activities and tours

Canoeing
Islamabad Canoe Club, Rawal Lake (contact Mike Semple, Club Secretary, Agricultural Farm No 25B, near Model Village, Chak Shahzad, Islamabad, T051-241855; or c/o Channel 7 Communications, T051-217307). Situated close to the dam, this small friendly club will allow non-members to hire out canoes for Rs50 per person per hour. Membership Rs100, plus a monthly charge of Rs300, allowing unlimited use.

Golf
Islamabad Golf Club, Club Rd, T051-829321. Next door to the highly exclusive members-only Islamabad Club, the golf club allows non-members to use the course for Rs700/500 on weekends/weekdays.

Sports clubs
Hot Shots, Fatima Jinnah Park, F-9, T111-008008, F051-251915. Daily 1000-2200. This fancy new complex features a

state-of-the-art bowling alley (Rs200 per person per game for non-members), a snooker hall (Rs75 per person per game for non-members), a small outdoor swimming pool (Rs175 per person per day, separate timings for men/women), and a health club complete with gym, aerobics, jacuzzi and steam bath (by membership only, minimum 1 month, or try negotiating a special arrangement with the management). There is also a café/snack bar and a shop.
Marriott Hotel, Aga Khan Rd, Shalimar 5, T111-223344, has a good health club and swimming pool, both of which are open to non-guests for a fee.

Tour operators
Adventure Foundation, Adventure Inn, Garden Av, T051-2272537. Organizes horse-riding around Islamabad, trekking tours in the Northern Areas, skiing near Abbottabad, ballooning near Thal and Multan, and also paragliding. With the exception of horse-riding, which can be arranged at relatively short notice, contact them well in advance if you are interested in any of these activities.
Adventure Travel, 15 Wali Centre, 86 South, Blue Area, T051-2212490, F051-2214580. Specializing in organized treks etc.
Indo Heritage, House 389, Street 21, I-9/1, T051-5534127, indoheritage@hotmail.com. Experienced and keen owner.
Hindu Kush Trails, House 37, Street 28, F-6/1, T051-2275484/2275031, www.hindukushtrails.com. Hindu Kush Trails is one of Pakistan's best and most experienced trekking and touring agencies.
Hunza Guides Pakistan, PO Box 168, G 9 Markaz, T051-2106891, www.hunzaguides pakistan.com. Very well-run French-Pakistani outfit, specializing in trekking and climbing.
North Pakistan Treks, Tours and Expeditions, PO Box 463, T051-2281655, www.north-pakistan.com. Professionally run.
Panoramic Pakistan, Flat No 1, 1st Floor, Block 19, G-8 Markaz, T051-2255838, www.panoramic.com.pk. Concentrates on the north, but also covers the rest of Pakistan.
Shangrila Resort Hotels, House 181, Street 18, F-10/2, T051-2296783, F051-2290992. Here you can book the resort's hotels in Chilas, Fairy Meadows, Skardu.
Silk Route Explorers, 32 Mezzanine Floor, Beverly Centre, Blue Area, T051-2273246, www.srexplorers.com. Very competent Aussie-Gojal-run business, excellent service.
Sitara Travel Consultants, Waheed Plaza, 3rd Floor, 52 West, Jinnah Av, Blue Area, PO Box 1662, T051-2813372, F051-2279651. Offers a wide range of services, including tours of Central Asia.
Travel Walji's, Walji's Building, 10 Khayaban-e-Suharwardy, PO Box 1088, T051-2270757-58, waljis@sat.net.pk. One of Pakistan's largest and longest running travel agents, generally reliable and efficient, also representatives for Thomas Cook. It also operates **Walji's Holiday Makers** at Office 3, Block 51, Blue Area, T051-2274340, F051-2274342.

⊙ Transport

Air
See also Rawalpindi transport section, p90.
Airline offices Aero Asia, Block 12-D, SNC Centre, Blue Area, T051-2271341, F051-2273757. **Air Canada**, 12 Shahid Plaza, Nazimuddin Rd, Blue Area, T051-2823040, F051-2824030. **Air France**, 3001 Jinnah Av, Blue Area, T051-2824096, F051-2820181. **Air Lanka**, 2 Shahid Plaza, Nazimuddin Rd, Blue Area, T051-2279795, F051-2278207. **Alitalia**, Jinnah Av, Blue Area, T051-2823442, F051-2829550. **American**, 1D Rehmat Plaza, Blue Area, T051-2273173, F051-2828844. **Bhoja Air**, 8A Potohar Plaza, Blue Area, T051-2828123, F051-2824179 (airport T051-591300, F051-590716). **British Airways**, No 10, Block 51, Blue Area, T051-2274070, F051-2274078. **Cathay Pacific**, 14 Shahid Plaza, Nazimuddin Rd, Blue Area, T051-2821936, F051-2271010. **China Xinjiang**, Shop 3, Sohrab Plaza, Block 32, Jinnah Av, Blue Area, T051-2273447, F051-2273448. Closed Wed. **Egypt Air**, No 10, Block 51, Blue Area, T051-2876019, F051-2272742. **Emirates**, 1D Rehmat Plaza, Blue Area, T051-2811677, F051-2215998. **Gulf**, Beverly Centre, Blue Area, T051-2201571. **Iberia**, 1D Rehmat Plaza, Blue Area, T051-2824718, F051-2829550. **KLM**, 1A Shahid Plaza, Nazimuddin Rd, Blue Area, T051-2829685, F051-2823795. **Kuwait**, 3 Shahid Plaza, Nazimuddin Rd, Blue Area, T051-2276450. **Malaysia**, 4 Shahid Plaza, Nazimuddin Rd, Blue Area, T051-2273382, F051-2820122. **PIA**, 49 Blue Area, T051-2816051. Open daily 0830-1800, closed

Arriving at night

No flights are scheduled to arrive at Islamabad International Airport during the 'middle of the night' (ie 2300-0500); in fact, the airport is usually closed up at this time and doesn't reopen until about 0430 (check-in time for a couple of early morning domestic and international departures). However, on the concourse outside the airport there are banks offering foreign exchange (and, in theory, a tourist information counter) that are open 24 hours, and there may be a few places open selling snacks and drinks. You won't have any problems finding a taxi or rickshaw driver to wake and take you into Rawalpindi or Islamabad.

There are no hotels within reasonable walking distance of the airport, and those a short taxi ride away are quite expensive. You should be able to wake the chowkidar and check in to almost any hotels in Islamabad or 'Pindi at any time of the night. Food-wise, few places are open after 2300.

Again, for those arriving by bus (notably at Pir Wadhai bus station) or train, you shouldn't have problems finding and waking a taxi driver to take you wherever you wish to go. Rawalpindi seems pretty safe by night (but with the obvious reservations for women); Islamabad, however, has so many wooded and parkland areas (providing cover) that walking about late at night is probably not recommended.

Fri 1230-1430. Airport counter, T051-591071, open 24 h. **Royal Jordanian**, Holiday Inn, G-6, Civic Centre, Municipal Rd, T051- 2274222, F051-2270673. **Shaheen Air International**, 104E, Unit 7-8, Jinnah Av, Blue Area, T051-2271200, F051-2271202. **Singapore Airlines**, Holiday Inn, G-6, Civic Centre, Municipal Rd T051-2821555, F051-2824413. **Swissair**, Holiday Inn, G-6, Civic Centre, Municipal Rd, T051-2822677, F051-2822798. **Thai**, Holiday Inn, G-6, Civic Centre, Municipal Rd, T051-2272140, F051-2823735. **TWA**, 12 Shahid Plaza, Nazimuddin Rd, Blue Area, T051-2823040, F051-2824030.

Bus

There is a bus station at G-9 Markaz (**Karachi Co**), with regular coasters and minivans (some a/c) to **Lahore**, **Peshawar**, **Murree** and **Abbottabad**. See also Rawalpindi, p90.

Minibus 120 runs north from Aabpara to Melody Market, then west to Sitara Market, Peshawar Mor (the junction of Shahrah-e-Kashmir with 9th Av, useful for the Passport and Immigration Office) and G-9 Markaz (known as Karachi Co).

Heading in the opposite direction from Aabpara, the same minibus runs east along Khayaban-e-Suhrawardy, and then northeast towards Nurpur Shahan village and Bari Imam, passing close to the French, German and Canadian embassies, and within walking distance of the Iranian, Indian and British embassies. Minibus 105 has the same route.

Suzukis also run due east from Aabpara along Khayaban-e-Suhrawardy (known as Embassy Road further east), passing the French, American, Chinese, Russian and Australian embassies en route to the Qaid-e-Azam University.

Car

Car hire Avis, PO Box 1088, Waljis Building, 10 Khayaban-e-Suhrawardy (next door to Travel Walji's), T051-2270751, F051-2270753. Choice of self-drive and chauffeur-driven. Cars from Rs1500 per day, plus Rs300 per day for CDW (Crash Damage Waiver) and Rs8 per km. Amex, Visa and MasterCard accepted.
Vehicle repairs Ayub, Street 23, G-8/1, T051-2280559, mobile T0333-5124284. Comes highly recommended for repairs to all types of motorbike and car.

Taxi

Taxis congregate at all the main shopping areas, as well as prowling the main streets; you may even find one with a working meter! Most journeys shouldn't cost more than Rs50, but you'll have to bargain.

Train
There is a **railway booking office** in Islamabad, on the east side of Melody Market, T051-9207474. Open daily, 0830-1630. Tickets can be booked a maximum of 15 days in advance.

ⓘ Directory

Banks American Express, 1E, Ali Plaza, Blue Area, PO Box 1291, T051-272425, F051-828783. Mon-Thu 0900-1300, 1400-1700, Fri 0900-1230, 1430-1700, Sat 0900-1300. Efficient exchange service for cash and TCs, also cash advances for Amex card holders, and Clients' Mail service. **Bank of America**, a few doors down, will give cash advances against most major credit cards for a 2% commission. There are dozens more banks spread across Blue Area, many of which also do foreign exchange. In Melody Market, behind the Holiday Inn hotel, the **National Bank of Pakistan** changes cash and TCs. **Thomas Cook** is represented through Travel Walji's (see under Tour operators). It issues TCs (through National Bank of Pakistan or United Bank Ltd) and replaces lost/stolen ones, but does not cash them or deal in foreign exchange. **Citibank**, Blue Area, has an ATM that offers cash advances on MasterCard, Visa (and those on the Cirrus network). **Chemists** There are chemists in the commercial areas at the centre of each sector, in Blue Area (concentrated around China Chowk), and at each of the hospitals listed below. **Courier** DHL, Beverly Centre, Blue Area, T051-2247790, F051-2275246. **FedEx**, 1 Ghosia Plaza, Khayaban-e-Suharwardy, G-6/1, T051-2744020, F051-274041. **TNT**, West Jinnah Av, Blue Area, T111-555111, F051-2272767. **Cultural centres** Alliançe Francaise, House 10, Street 16, F-6/3, T051-2210744. Films and other events for the French expat community. **American Center**, 60 Blue Area, Jinnah Av, T051-2824001. Periodicals, audio-visual and US Information Service materials, tight security. **Asian Study Group**, Malik Complex, 80 West, Jinnah Av, Blue Area, T051-815891. Formed in the 1970s by members of the expat community, it now has a wider membership and holds regular lectures and cultural evenings, as well as sightseeing trips and walks in the Margalla Hills. The ASG have published a number of papers and booklets. Members can make use of the small library which includes some videos. Annual membership Rs200. **British Council**, 14 Civic Centre, G-6 Markaz, T051-2829041. Geared up primarily to promote education opportunities in the UK, but tourists can browse through the British papers in the library and watch BBC World TV, Mon-Sat 1000-1700. **Lok Virsa**, PO Box 1184, Garden Av, Shakarparian Hill, T051-9203983, F051-9202042. Open 0930-1330, 1430-1700 (1900 in summer), closed Fri and public holidays. Primarily a museum and library (see under Sights, above), but also hosts occasional cultural events. **Embassies and consulates** Minivan 120 runs from Aabpara along Khyaban-e-Suhrawardy (and its continuation, Embassy Rd), looping back along Bank Rd. Varan bus 2 supposedly runs along Embassy Rd from Adamjee Rd in Rawalpindi. **Afghanistan**, House 8, Street 90, G-6/3, T051-824505, F051-824504. When run by Taliban, visas were freely issued; current situation less clear. **Australia**, corner of Constitution Av, diplomatic enclave 1, Isphani Rd, G-5/4, T051-2824345, F051-2820112. New location for embassy, Coolabah Club is still at old embassy location (see Entertainment). **Austria**, House 13, Street 1, F-6/3, T051-279238, F051-828366. **Belgium**, House 2, Street 10, F6/3, T051-827091, F051-822358. **Canada**, PO Box 1042, diplomatic enclave, T051-279100, F051-279110. **China**, diplomatic enclave, Ramna 4, T051-2817279, F051-2821116. Open Mon-Fri 0900-1200, single entry visa US$30, double entry US$60 (difficult), 6-month multi-entry US$90 (very difficult), takes 4 working days (or collect in 2 days for extra US$20 or same day for extra US$30), bring passport, 1 photo, tickets (if appropriate) and proof of funds (TCs will do), payable in rupees. **Czech Republic**, House 49, Street 27, F-6/2, T051-210195. **Denmark**, PO Box 1118, House 9, Street 90, G-6/3, T051-824724, F051-823483. **France**, diplomatic enclave, T051-278730, F051-825389. **Germany**, diplomatic enclave, T051-9212412, F051-279436. **India**, diplomatic enclave, T051-2272680, F051-2823386. Mon-Fri 0930-1100, it's chaos here with visa regulations changing regularly (plus huge crowds). Visa fee is usually on a reciprocal basis (usually 3-month single entry, though you may get 1-month), some nationalities require a 'letter of recommendation' from your own embassy; best to telephone before heading out here. **Iran**, diplomatic enclave, T051-2276271, F051-2279588. This has traditionally been a bad place to get visas (you will be told that they need to telex Tehran, with the reply never seeming to arrive; a ruse designed to put you off). Try Lahore, Peshawar or Quetta (and ask around among other travellers for the 'latest'). **Italy**, 54 Margalla Rd, F-6/3, T051-829030, F051-829026. **Japan**, diplomatic enclave, T051-279320, F051-279340. **Jordan**, PO Box 1189, House 131, Street 14, E-7, T051-823460, F051-823207. **Kazakstan**, House 2, Street 4, F-8/3, T051-262924, F051-262806. **Lebanon**, House 6, Street 27, F-6/2, T051-278338, F051-826410. **Nepal**, House 11, Street 84, G-6/4, T051-278051, F051-217875. **Netherlands**, PIA Building, 2nd Floor, Blue Area, T051-279512, F051-279513. **Norway**, House 25, Street 19, F-6/2, T051-279720. **Palestine**, House 486-B, Street 9, F-10/2, T051-291185. **Poland**, Street 24, G-5/4, diplomatic enclave II, T051-279491. **Portugal**, House 40a, Main Margalla Rd, F-7/2, T051-279530. **Russian Federation**, diplomatic enclave, T051-278671. **South Africa**, House 48, Margalla Rd, F-8/2, T051-262356, F051-250114. **Spain**, diplomatic enclave, T051-279480/827046, F051-279489. **Sri Lanka**, 315-C Margalla Rd, F-7/2, T051-828735, F051-828751. **Sweden**, 6-A Aga Khan Rd, Markaz Shalimar 6, T051-828712. **Switzerland**, PO Box 1073, diplomatic enclave, T051-279292/829001, F051-279286. **Syria**, 30 Hill Rd, F-6/3, T051-279471, F051-279472. **Thailand**, House 4, Street 8, F-8/3, T051-280909, F051-256730. **Turkey**, PO Box 2183, House 58, Attaturk Av, G-6/3, T051-278749, F051-278752. NB A new embassy is under construction opposite the Iranian delegation. **Turkmenistan**, House 22A, Nizamuddin Rd, F-7/1, T051-274913, F051-278799. **UK**, PO Box 1122, diplomatic enclave, T051-2822131, F051-2823439. **USA**, Diplomatic Enclave, T051-20802700, F051-2822632 (after hours T051-2080000), www.usembassy.state.gov/pakistan. **Uzbekistan**, House 6, Street 29, F-7/1, T051-820779, F051-278128.

Hospitals Private Hospitals Al-Shifa International, H-8, T051-446801. Islamabad Hospital, opposite American Express, Blue Area, T051-272350, F051-275846. **Public Hospitals** Capital Hospital, Street 31, G-6/2, T051-9221334. Pakistan Institute of Medical Sciences (PIMS) Hospital Complex, Faisal Av, G-8/3, T051-859511. One of the country's best. Federal Government Services Hospital (Poly Clinic), Hospital Rd, G-6/3, T051-9218300. **Internet** Islamabad probably offers the country's fastest internet connections, although some of the cafés are rather dark and seedy. **Cyber City**, Beverly Centre, Blue Area. Rs25 per hour (slow), Mon-Sat 1000-2130, closed Sun. **D&H Internet Café**, F-7 Jinnah Supermarket. Rs35 per hour, daily 1000-2400. **Super Composing Centre**, 3-D Supermarket, F-6 Markaz, T051-279349, F051-277450. Internet access Rs75 per hour. **Libraries** National Library of Pakistan, Constitution Av Building, near Parliament House, T051-812787. Mon-Fri 0900-1700. European and Oriental languages, Pakistan collection, manuscripts and rare materials, periodicals and newspapers. In addition, the **American Center**, **Asian Study Group**, **British Council**, **French Cultural Centre** and **Lok Virsa** (see under Cultural centres) each have their own libraries. Police **Emergency** T15 or T051-823333. **Aabpara police station**, Post Office Rd (next to GPO), T051-2828265. **Margalla police station**, Ayub Market, F-8 Markaz, T051-850340. **Kohsar police station**, Jinnah Supermarket, F-7 Markaz, T051-812393. **Foreigners' Registration Office**, near SSP Office, Ayub Market, F-8 Markaz (if coming by bus ask for Zafar Chowk), T051-246116 (central exchange). **Post office** GPO, Civic Centre, Municipal Rd. Mon-Thu and Sat 0900-2000, Fri 0900-1130, 1530-2000. Poste Restante and Express Post services available. There are also post offices in the major markets, including one on the southwest corner of Jinnah Supermarket. **Telephone** Central Telegraph Office, Attaturk Av, Shalimar 5. Open 7 days, 24 hours. Fax and telex services are also available at this office. There is also a telephone office at Aabpara, opposite the Tourist Camp Site (weekdays 0800-2200, Sun 1400-2000), a **Pak Telecom Customer Services Centre** in Blue Area, just west of 7th Av, and PCOs in the major markets. There are also numerous PCOs scattered around. Anyone looking to buy a mobile phone should try **Mobilink GSM** showroom in F-7 Jinnah Supermarket. **Useful addresses Visa Extensions** Passport and Immigration Office, Peshawar Mor, G-8/1, T051-260773. Mon-Thu and Sat 0800-1500, Fri 0800-1200. Tourist visas and 'landing permits' can be extended (usually 2-3 months), although the length may depend upon the whim of the person behind the desk. Bring photocopies of the relevant pages of your passport, fill out the form and you should be issued with an extension on the spot (or later that same day). To get there, catch minibus No 105 from Aabpara (or take a taxi) and ask for 'Peshawar Mor'. Holders of non-tourist visas (for example working/student visas etc) must first obtain approval from the Ministry of the Interior, Block R, Secretariat. This may also be the case if you wish to convert a single entry tourist visa to a double entry. **No Objection Certificates** Section Officer, FATA, Ministry of State and Frontier Regions, Room 232, Block S, Secretariat. The staff here deserve prizes for raising Pakistani bureaucracy to previously uncharted heights of obstructiveness. **Travel Permits** Tarbela Dam, Section Officer, 4th Floor, Block R, Secretariat, T051-920729, or contact the **Protocol Officer**, WAPDA, Tarbela Dam Project, Tarbela, T051-568941 (sometimes WAPDA will issue permits directly, at other times they require clearance from the Secretariat). **Trekking permits** The Ministry of Tourism office that issues trekking permits and delivers briefings has shifted to a new office close to the Pakistan Sports Complex ('Jinnah Stadium' on some maps), just off Shahrah-e-Kashmir (to the southeast of the Tourist Campsite, see map). The building that you want is to the east of the swimming pool and to the south of the Liaquat Gymnasium. See page 45 for full trekking info. **WWF** (Pakistan), 60 Bazaar Rd, G-6/4.

Rawalpindi → Colour map 1, grid C4/5

A sprawling, fast-growing city accounting for three-quarters of the capital area's combined population, Rawalpindi lacks any major monuments or sites of historical significance, although its lively and colourful bazaars have plenty of atmosphere. The British Cantonment area, focused on The Mall (a part of the old Grand Trunk Road), was once a separate settlement. It had barracks and a spacious residential area for the military and civilians, plus its own offices, clubs and churches. The Saddar area which developed to the northeast is the main commercial area today, with numerous hotels, restaurants, banks, shops and travel agents. To the north of Saddar, beyond the railway line and across the Leh River, is the crowded Old City, centred around Fowara Chowk and Rajah Bazaar. In addition to The Mall, the most important transport artery is Murree Road, which runs north towards Islamabad.
▸▸ *For Sleeping, Eating and all other listings, see pages 85-92.*

Ins and outs

Getting around
Within Rawalpindi you have the choice of auto-rickshaws or taxis, as well as horse-drawn tongas around Rajah Bazaar and Committee Chowk. The intercity buses are also useful for getting from Saddar to points along Murree Road. A new bus company, **Varan**, now runs a number of regular services around Rawalpindi, stopping only at designated stops. Their main departure point is from Adamjee Rd in Saddar.

Pir Wadhai bus station is difficult to reach by public transport; take a Suzuki wagon from opposite the mosque at the junction of Adamjee and Kashmir Roads as far as Fowara Chowk (Rajah Bazaar) (Rs3), and then change to another Suzuki to Pir Wadhai (Rs3). The Suzukis are so crowded this is almost impossible if carrying any luggage. A better option by public transport is to take Varan bus 3 from the stop across the road from the Varan yard on Adamjee Road. A taxi between most points in Rawalpindi and Pir Wadhai shouldn't cost more than Rs50 (but of course you'll be asked for more). Varan bus 7a runs from their yard on Adamjee Road (Saddar) to 'Swar Camp' bus station out on the GT Road towards Lahore (or Rs50 by taxi). Within specific areas of 'Pindi, walking is also an option.

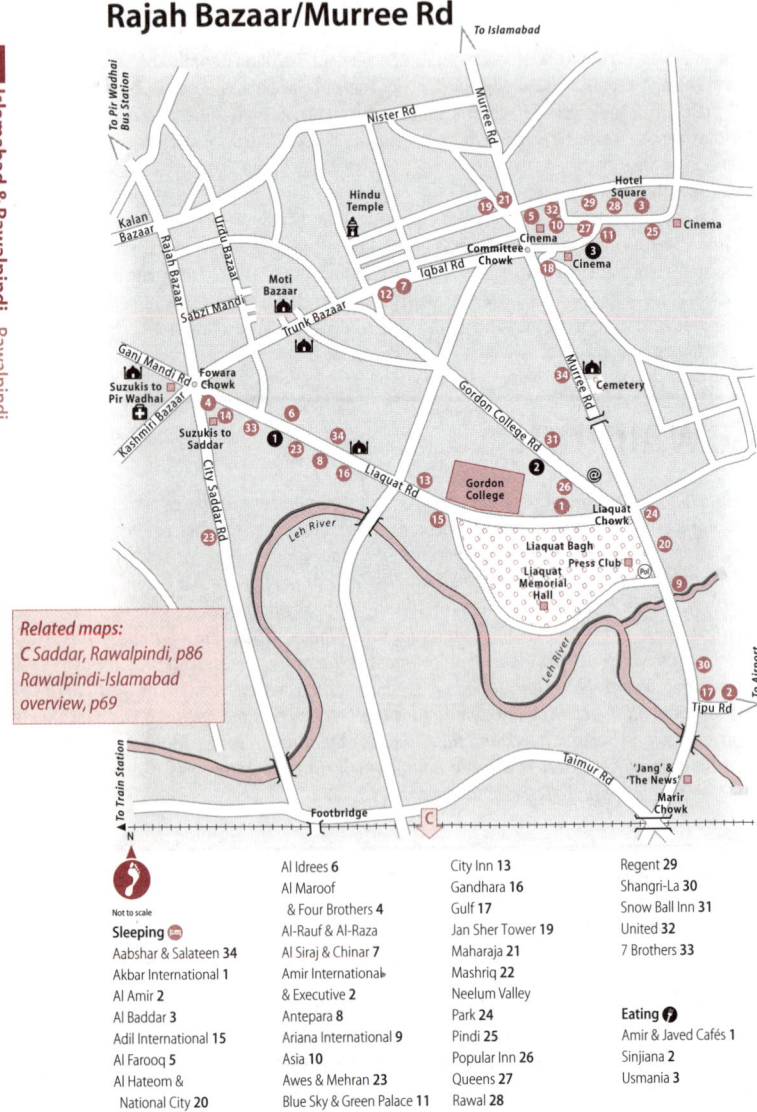

Rajah Bazaar/Murree Rd

Related maps:
C Saddar, Rawalpindi, p86
Rawalpindi-Islamabad overview, p69

Sleeping
Aabshar & Salateen 34
Akbar International 1
Al Amir 2
Al Baddar 3
Adil International 15
Al Farooq 5
Al Hateom &
  National City 20
Al Idrees 6
Al Maroof
  & Four Brothers 4
Al-Rauf & Al-Raza
Al Siraj & Chinar 7
Amir International
  & Executive 2
Antepara 8
Ariana International 9
Asia 10
Awes & Mehran 23
Blue Sky & Green Palace 11
City Inn 13
Gandhara 16
Gulf 17
Jan Sher Tower 19
Maharaja 21
Mashriq 22
Neelum Valley
Park 24
Pindi 25
Popular Inn 26
Queens 27
Rawal 28
Regent 29
Shangri-La 30
Snow Ball Inn 31
United 32
7 Brothers 33

Eating
Amir & Javed Cafés 1
Sinjiana 2
Usmania 3

History

Although there's nothing much to see in terms of historic monuments, Rawalpindi is an ancient city. There is evidence that a Buddhist settlement existed here, contemporary with Taxila. The first Muslim invader, Mahmud of Ghazni, gave the ruined city as a gift to a Ghakkar Chief, but it remained deserted until restored by Jhanda Khan in 1493.

Rawalpindi served as a strategic base for the Mughal Emperor Jahangir and later, during the 19th century, was developed as a Sikh trading centre. After the Second Sikh War the British gained control in 1849 and made Rawalpindi the Army's General headquarters for the northern region. Its importance was further increased by extending the railways to it and building a large complex of military cantonment buildings. Today it is still the headquarters of the country's Armed Forces.

Sights

The area around **Rajah Bazaar** is the commercial heart of the old market town of Rawalpindi. Five roads radiate from Fowara Chowk, and tiny alleys with crowded bazaars and craftsmen practising their skills wind their way between these roads. It's a fascinating area to explore, and to shop for anything from jewellery, handicrafts and fabrics to smuggled electrical goods. Walking east from Fowara Chowk along Trunk Bazaar/Iqbal Road, off to the left roughly halfway along you can see an old Hindu temple (one of several that once graced this area), now somewhat derelict and partially occupied as a private home.

Ayub National Park ① *on the GT Road to the southeast of the Cantonment area*, is a sprawling park, covering over 900 hectares, with a lake for boating, bridle paths, an aquarium, open-air garden restaurant and theatre, as well as a Japanese garden.

Liaquat Memorial Hall and Gardens ① *Gardens open sunrise to sunset, hall Mon-Thu 0900-1200 and 1400-1600, Fri 0900-1130, Sat 0900-1200, free, any wagon or bus passing along Murree Rd from Saddar towards Islamabad can drop you here*, was originally known as Company Bagh but renamed after Liaquat Ali Khan, the first prime minister of Pakistan, who was assassinated here in 1951. There is a library and a large auditorium where occasional art exhibitions, cultural shows and plays are staged.

Army Museum and Library ① *Iftkhar Road, Sat-Thu 0800-1400, free*. Various items of military regalia, including paintings, weapons and uniforms, and a collection of books on Pakistan's military history are on display here.

● Sleeping

Rawalpindi *p83, maps p84, 86, and 89*
There are over 250 hotels spread over Rawalpindi, a small selection of which are given below. Most of the hotels are concentrated in the **Saddar/Cantonment** area, which is Rawalpindi's real commercial centre. The more expensive ones are in the Cantonment area, along The Mall, while the mid-range and cheaper ones are in the Saddar area. There are some unappealing hotels at Pir Wadhai bus station.
L Pearl Continental (PC), The Mall, T051-5566011, smmpchr@isb.compol.com.
Easily the best hotel in town, full facilities to international standard (50% discounts can be negotiated for groups or when business is slack). Standard rooms very comfortable, or go for a Rs25,000-a-night suite. Choice of restaurants, bakery, laundry, swimming pool (Rs350 for day guests), tennis, badminton, health centre, shopping mall, travel agents, very good service. Recommended (especially for middle-budget travellers who get the big discounts).
L-A De Mall, Aziz Bhatti Rd (just off The Mall), T051-5586100, F051-5586102.

Recently opened so offering big discounts (A instead of L), although you can sometimes get rooms at the PC for the same rate. 60 doubles and 9 suites, central a/c, IDD phone, dish TV, business centre, function halls, novelty feature is the revolving rooftop restaurant.

L-A Shalimar, The Mall, T051-5562901, shalimar@khi.comsats.net.pk. Fairly comfortable hotel, although without the sense of luxury associated with the PC (which can be had for the same price if you get the discount). Central a/c, fridge, IDD phone, pool, choice of restaurants, popular with groups, bit '70s in feel.

B Rysons International, 111/10-D Murree Rd, T051-514884, F051-514914. A/c, fan, TV/dish, IDD, attached bath, restaurant, business centre, modern comfortable hotel, but a little expensive.

B-C Flashman's, 17-22 The Mall, T051-581480, F051-527846. Has seen better

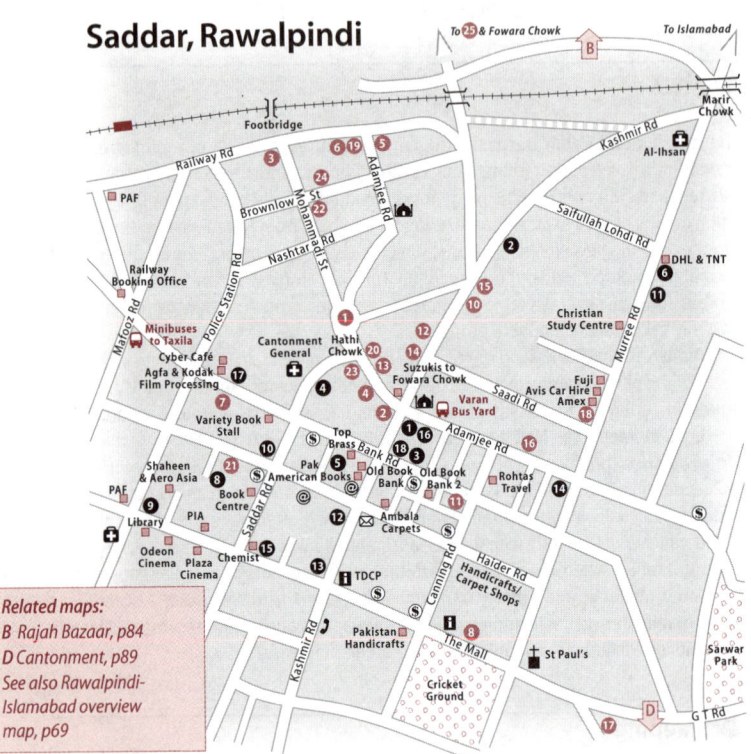

Saddar, Rawalpindi

Related maps:
B Rajah Bazaar, p84
D Cantonment, p89
See also Rawalpindi-Islamabad overview map, p69

Sleeping
Al Azam 1
Al-Falah 2
Al Shams & Al Mumtaz 5
Al-Toheed 3
Al-Umar 24
Avanti 4
Bolan 6
Flashman's &
 Pakistan Tours Ltd 8
Kamran 10
Kashmir Inn 11
Khayaban 12
Lalazar 13
Marhaba 14
Mashriq 25
New Kamran 15
Pakland International 7
Paradise Inn 16
Pearl Continental 17
Ryson's International 18
Sadia 19
Shah Taj 20
Taj Mahal &
 Sudhana Restaurant 21
Tayyaba 22
Venus 23

Eating
Anwar Café 1
Azam's Bakery 4
Café Rose &
 Data Kabawa 5
Jehangir Balti Murgh 2
Kamran Café 3
KFC 14
Kim Fah 15
Lasania 6
Mainland Chinese 7
Mei Kong 8
New Anwar 16
Pizza Kent 9
Rabat Bakers 10
Red Onion 11
Shezan 12
Taste Hunt &
 Archie's Fast Food 17
Unique Bakers &
 Burger Express 18
White House 13

days, very run down public areas, 'standard' rooms fairly large with noisy a/c, dish TV (very limited), grubby carpets, antiquated plumbing and temperamental toilet flush systems. 'New' block rooms marginally better with nicer bathrooms (tubs), plus some mini suites. Hotel has a 'permit room', restaurant, but pool is closed. All rather tatty and overpriced.

C Holiday Crown Palace, 232-B Iftikhar Khan Rd, T051-5568068, F051-5583960. Not a bad deal, central a/c, dish TV, fridge, reasonable rooms, restaurant, friendly staff.

C-D Paradise Inn, 109 Adamjee Rd, T051-5512311, F051-5567048. This is where all the taxi drivers at the airport will want to bring you, so they must pay a good commission! Some a/c rooms (C), twin or double beds, dish TV, bathrooms clean but basic, non a/c rooms (D) same but without TV, rooftop BBQ, but hotel rather overpriced.

E Avanti, Adamjee Rd, T051-5580268. Largish rooms with fan (but huge window areas so very hot), lobby looks unfinished, very expensive for what you get.

E Marhaba, 118 Kashmir Rd, T051-5566021. Essentially you're paying for the central a/c (make sure it's working) because the rooms and bathrooms are fairly grotty.

F New Kamran, Kashmir Rd, T051-582040. Singles, doubles and triples, linen clean but peeling paint and walls rather grubby, bathrooms with western WC, fan, basic restaurant, parking, friendly enough, not bad value for those wanting something a little bit above the normal grotty budget places.

F Tayyaba, Mohammadi St, T051-514591. Fairly clean rooms with attached bath, best rooms at front.

G Al-Azam, Hathi Chowk, Adamjee Rd, T051-5565901. Now run by people from Hunza so service has improved, but still very basic and grubby. Upper floors with balconies best, avoid the singles which are windowless boxes, and whatever happens do not look closely at the mattress.

G Alfalah, Adamjee Rd, T051-5580799. Fairly unappealing rooms (some windowless) with horrible toilets.

G Khayaban, Kashmir Rd, T051-568823. Basic, rather overpriced rooms, attached bath, fan.

G Popular Inn, G-261 Gordon College Rd, Liaquat Bagh, T051-5531885, saeed_nazir@hotmail.com. Most popular budget choice (only place run for 'travellers' as opposed to just being cheap), 5-bed dorms with attached bath, singles, doubles with/without attached bath, all basic but clean (including bathrooms), better rooms have balconies, restaurant serves cheap meals and other necessities (water, toilet paper etc), dish TV, library/book exchange, friendly and helpful management, taxis arranged (Rs50 from Pir Wadhai). Recommended.

G Taj Mahal, 32 Haider Rd, T051-5586802. Simple rooms, clean linen, basic but clean attached bath, fan, reasonable value (but manager asked sex of potential guests which means either there are spy holes, or he was offering the choice of twin or double beds – not sure which).

G-H Lalazar, Hathi Chowk, Adamjee Rd. Extremely run down but very cheap.

G-H Shah Taj, Hathi Chowk, Adamjee Rd. Very basic rooms with fan, basic attached bath, rock-bottom prices.

G-H Venus, Hathi Chowk, Adamjee Rd, T051-566501. Very cheap rooms with attached bath, but pretty basic and grotty.

Eating

Rawalpindi *p83, maps p84, 86, and 89*
You won't go hungry in Rawalpindi, although there are few 'outstanding' places to eat (unlike Islamabad). Cheap meat/dhal and chapati places congregate around Fowara Chowk and in the streets to the north of Hathi Chowk (Saddar). There are plenty of Chinese restaurants in the Saddar area of 'Pindi, but the food is pretty mediocre (full meal around Rs200-250 per head; if selective you can eat for much less). Almost all hotels boast some sort of restaurant. For backpackers, the Popular Inn provides for most needs (especially breakfast). There are plenty of bakeries/supermarkets scattered around the Saddar area, best of which is **Rahat Bakers**, just off Bank Rd. **Unique Bakers**, junction of Kashmir/Bank Rds, has a good selection. There are some good juice bars at the junction of Kashmir/Haider Rds (Rs20).

For an explanation of sleeping and eating price codes used in this guide, see inside the front cover. Other relevant information is found in Essentials, pages 36-38.

Pearl Continental, The Mall, T051-5566011. For the best quality cuisine (reasonably priced), try the **Marco Polo** (Pakistani, international), **Tai Pan** (Chinese), **Frontpage** coffee shop (open 24 hrs with good-value 'high tea' 1500-1900, Rs135), or the **Baker's Boutique** for pastries, cakes, ice cream, coffee. Recommended.

Blue Lagoon, Masood Akhtar Rd, opposite Pearl Continental, T051-519377. Often used for receptions and functions, or outdoor BBQ around pool.

Kim Fah, The Mall. Reasonable food, may get beer served in teapots!

Red Onion and **Lasania**, Murree Rd. Both offer fast food and Chinese, popular with families at weekends.

Shezan, Kashmir Rd, opposite GPO. Upmarket setting, reasonable quality, quite popular.

Jehangir Balti Murgh, 132 Kashmir Rd, T051-563352. Serves excellent karahis, tikkas, kebabs etc and has a pleasant garden. Gets busy in the evenings. Eat well for around Rs100-150. Recommended.

KFC, junction of Adamjee/Murree Rds, T051-5519205 (home delivery). Family meal Rs600, chicken burger and chips Rs150.

Pizza Kent, The Mall. Overpriced pizzas for the middle classes.

Sinjiang, Graham College Rd (near to Popular Inn). Serves Xinjiang kebabs, nan and noodles (the latter available without meat).

Taste Hunt & Archies, Bank Rd. Recently opened, fast food and ice cream.

Anwar Café, junction of Adamjee/Kashmir Rds. Epitome of the traditional cheap Pakistani restaurant, simple and crowded, eat well for under Rs75, breakfast channa (Rs15) is superb. Recommended.

Burger Express, Kashmir Rd. Long established, bland chicken/beef burger, chips and drink meals for Rs70-100.

Café Rose (and others), opposite Ciros Cinema. A good place for kebabs and tandoori chicken.

Kamran Café, Bank Rd, near the junction with Kashmir Rd. Clean and unassuming, good place for light meals, snacks and refreshments.

White House, Haider Rd. Basic mutton/dhal/chapati place, clean enough.

Entertainment

Rawalpindi *p83, maps p84, 86, and 89*
There's not much nightlife in Rawalpindi, and most 'cultural events' take place in Islamabad (although the Pearl Continental sometimes hosts events). There are several cinemas in Rawalpindi; those on Murree Rd tend to show Bollywood features, while those in Saddar favour Stallone/Arnie/Bruce shoot-'em-up flicks.

Shopping

Rawalpindi *p83, maps p84, 86, and 89*
Bazaars
The main shopping areas are Saddar and Rajah Bazaar. The streets and tiny alleys around **Rajah Bazaar** each contain their own smaller bazaars, with the various trades grouped together in traditional Asian style. Many of the buildings here still retain their original intricately carved wooden balconies and whenever the bazaars escape the press of modern traffic, it is easy to feel yourself slipping back a century or so.
Bara Bazaar, named after a smuggling town in NWFP near the Afghanistan border, is full of smuggled electrical goods and other items.
Bohr Bazaar contains medical shops, both western and traditional, while **Rajah Bazaar** itself centres around stalls of vegetables, spices and dried fruits and nuts, piled high.
Kalan Bazaar is the main cloth market.
Moti Bazaar is the women's market with beads, hair braids, shawls, make-up etc.
Sarafa Bazaar sells intricate hand-worked gold and silver jewellery as well as brass, copper and tin utensils.
Trunk Bazaar combines metal trunks with other items of ironmongery and practical goods; there is a good fishing tackle shop around 200 m down on the right (coming from Fowara Chowk).

Bookshops
Old Book Bank, Kashmir Rd. Best of several new and second-hand bookshops in 'Pindi. The Islamabad bookshops tend to be better.

Clothing
Top Brass Army, just east of National Bank of Pakistan on Bank Rd. Place to buy army

badges, insignia, and those 'Pakistan Army-Men At Their Best' car stickers.
Army surplus gear can be found at various shops on Mohammadi St.

Handicrafts
Pakistan Handicrafts, The Mall. Good place to get an idea of what's available and an indication of prices.
Craft House, **Kashmir Handicrafts** and **Ganemede**, towards the eastern end of Haider Rd. Between them offer a good selection of handicrafts and carpets.
Ambala Carpets, Haider Rd by the British hotel. Good selection of carpets and rugs.
  On Sun there is a **market** with handicrafts and second-hand books, which spreads out along Kashmir Rd, centred on the junctions with Haider, Bank and Adamjee Rds.

Photography
Fuji, next door to American Express, 112-D Rahim Plaza, Murree Rd, T051-581146, F051-581148. The best bet for fresh film stocks (including slide films) in Pakistan (Sensia 100 II Rs260, Velvia Rs350).

Sports goods
Pakistani (Sialkot) produced sporting goods can be found around 'Pindi, notably the 2 shops beneath the mosque at the junction of Adamjee/Kashmir Rds, plus in the places next to Old Book Bank on Kashmir Rd.

▲ Activities and tours

Rawalpindi *p83, maps p84, 86, and 89*
Sport
Rawalpindi is the venue for international one-day and test **cricket** fixtures, although the stadium itself (on Stadium Rd, off Murree Rd on the way to Islamabad) is little more than a large, glorified concrete bowl. **Golf** is available at Ayub Park, and non-guests can use the **swimming** pool at the Pearl Continental (Rs350 per day). There are more sporting opportunities in Islamabad.

Tour operators
Pakistan Adventure Travel Service, 251-B, E Block, Satellite Town, T051-414489, pak-ats@pakistanmail.com. Has been recommended by a reader.
Pakistan Guides, PO Box 1692, 3rd Floor, 62/2 Bank Road, T051-5524808, guides@isb.paknet.com.pk. Run by Kaiser Khan, 20 years' experience, offers a wide range of specialized expeditions and tours.
Pakistan Tours Ltd (PTL), Flashman's Hotel, T051-5565449, ptl@comsats.net.pk. A branch of PTDC, offers a number of package tours or tailor-made arrangements for groups and individuals, also operate several bus services (see Transport below). There are numerous other companies in Islamabad.

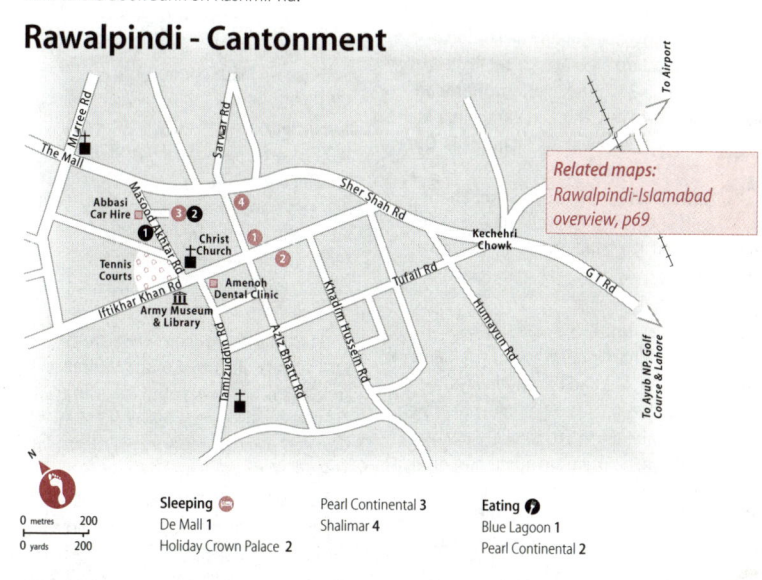

Rawalpindi - Cantonment

Related maps:
Rawalpindi-Islamabad
overview, p69

Sleeping
De Mall 1
Holiday Crown Palace 2
Pearl Continental 3
Shalimar 4

Eating
Blue Lagoon 1
Pearl Continental 2

◉ Transport

Rawalpindi *p83, maps p84, 86, and 89*

Air
Airline offices PIA, 5 The Mall, T051-5568071, F051-583793. Open daily (closed Fri 1230-1430), outside hours call airport (T051-591071). The special office for Northern Areas (Gilgit, Skardu) is round the side of the building (daily 0700-1700, closed Fri 1230-1430). All the other major airlines have offices in Islamabad. The following have General Service Agents (GSAs) in 'Pindi. **British Airways**, Pearl Continental Hotel, The Mall, T051-5566791, F051-5567710 (Mon-Fri 0900-1700). **Royal Jordanian**, World Travel Consultants, T051-563242. **Saudi Arabian**, Southern Travels, T051-814992.

Domestic Flights to Lahore, Karachi and Quetta should be booked well in advance. All flights are with **PIA** (Pakistan International Airways) unless mentioned.
Bahawalpur daily; **Bannu** (via Peshawar) Mon, Tue, Fri; **Chitral** (via Peshawar) Mon, Tue, Wed, Fri, Sat (weather permitting); **Dera Ghazi Khan** Tue, Thu, Sun; **Dera Ismail Khan** daily; **Faisalabad** daily, 2 flights Tue; **Gilgit** 2-3 flights daily (weather permitting), see box on p70; **Hyderabad** Thu, Sun; **Karachi** 5-8 flights daily; **Aero Asia** (4 flights daily, Rs4,295), **Bhoja Air** (Mon, Wed, Sat) and **Shaheen Air** (daily, Rs4,400) also run flights to Karachi; **Lahore** 7-10 flights daily; **Mianwali** Fri, Sun; **Moenjodaro** (via Karachi) 1-2 flights daily; **Multan** 2-3 flights daily; **Muzaffarabad** Mon, Tue, Wed, Thu, Sat; **Parachinar** Mon, Wed, Fri; **Peshawar** 2-4 flights daily; **Quetta** 1-2 flights daily;
Rawalakot Tue, Thu, Sat; **Saidu Sharif** daily, except Sat; **Skardu** daily; **Sukkur** Mon, Fri, Sat; **Zhob** daily, except Fri; **Air Safaris** should be booked through PIA's office in Islamabad.

International The mainstay of international flights in and out of Islamabad have been **PIA** and **British Airways**, although an increasing number of carriers are now beginning to favour Islamabad over Karachi. There are numerous travel agents selling international flights in the Mall Plaza block containing the TDCP office at the junction of Kashmir Rd and The Mall.

Bus
Local A new company, **Varan**, runs a fleet of white buses that stop at fixed bus stands on a number of routes in and around Rawalpindi. Most depart from the Varan depot on Adamjee Rd. These include: 1a Saddar- Aabpara (Islamabad); 1b Saddar-Peshawar Mor (for Passport Office, Islamabad); 2 Saddar-Aabpara-Embassy Rd (Islamabad); 3 Saddar-Raja Bazaar-Peshawar Rd (GT Rd)-Pir Wadhai; 4 Faisabad-Zero Point (Islamabad); 6 'Pindi-Taxila; 7a Peshawar Rd-Swar Camp bus station.

Long distance Almost all destinations (notably **Gilgit** and **Skardu**) are served by buses departing from Pir Wadhai bus station. With the exception of Gilgit and Skardu, you will generally find faster, more comfortable a/c buses and coasters departing from the various 'flying coach' stations now located in the vicinity of Pir Wadhai. The easiest way to reach Pir Wadhai is by taxi (about Rs50 from most points in 'Pindi, Rs75-100 from Islamabad).

Gilgit: NATCO, T051-270745, has 6 buses daily (book from the office opposite departure point at Stand 24 at Pir Wadhai). 0900 (coaster, Rs510), 1500 and 1600 (a/c, Rs560), 1700 (de luxe, Rs510), 2000 (non-stop, Rs560), 2200 (de luxe, Rs510). The 1500 and 1600 a/c buses are the best bet. **Silk Route**, T051-5479375, offers the most comfortable a/c bus from Stand 4 at Pir Wadhai (1600 and 1900, Rs560, 14-16 hrs), see Gilgit section for safety issues. **Mashabrum Tours**, T051-5463895, has 5 daily services from Stand 1 at Pir Wadhai (1200, 1400, 1800, 2100 for the normal bus, Rs500; 1630 for the de luxe a/c bus, Rs550). **Hameed Travels** has a daily coaster (Rs500, 14-16 hrs) from Pir Wadhai at 1500. You can also book seats at the Mashriq Hotel near Fowara Chowk, T051-5542970.

GT Rd (towards Lahore) Destinations, such as **Dina**, **Jhelum**, **Gujrat**, **Wazirabad** and **Sialkot**, are served from Stand 10 at Pir Wadhai, or with quicker minibuses from Swar Camp bus station out along the GT Rd (Varan bus 7a goes here).

Gujranwala Bus departs when full from Stand 2 at Pir Wadhai, or minibuses from Swar Camp bus station.

Lahore Daewoo Express, T111-007008, offers the quickest (via the motorway), most luxurious (a/c, reclining seats, hostesses) service from the bus stand on the GT/Peshawar Rd (near Kohinoor Mills and Pir Wadhai, see overview map). Regular departures 0600-1800 (Rs200, 3½ hrs). There are regular a/c coasters (Rs120, 6 hrs) from the 'Flying Coach' bus stands near to Pir Wadhai. Slower buses via the GT Rd run from Stand 6 at Pir Wadhai. **Skyways** offers 'flying coaches' (motorway or GT Rd) from its office on Murree Rd, near Faisabad Junction.

Multan Stand 33 at Pir Wadhai (Rs615, 13-14 hrs).

Peshawar Most comfortable buses are from the 'Flying Coach' bus station near to Pir Wadhai (Rs55, 3½-4 hrs), or by cheaper (Rs43) and slower (4-6 hrs) buses from Stand 13 at Pir Wadhai.

Saidu Sharif (Swat) Pakistan Tours Ltd (PTL) (see under Tour operators) runs a daily a/c service at 0800 (Rs250, 5 hrs).

Skardu NATCO, T051-270745, has a daily de luxe bus from Stand 24 at Pir Wadhai (1500, Rs500, 18 hrs). **Mashabrum Tours**, T051-5463895, has a daily bus from Stand 1 at Pir Wadhai (1400, Rs550, 18 hrs). Also **K2 Travels** has a coaster from Stand 4 at Pir Wadhai (1415, Rs550, 18 hrs).

Taxila Varan bus 6 runs from the Varan yard on Adamjee Rd. You can also flag down wagons from the junction of Bank/Mafooz Rds (near the Railway Booking Office).

Almost all other destinations (Abbottabad, DG Khan, Faisalabad, Karachi, Kohat, Mansehra, Mardan, Murree, Muzaffarabad, Sadiqabad, Sargodha) are served by buses from Pir Wadhai, or by 'flying coaches' from the bus stands close to Pir Wadhai.

Car
Car hire Abbasi, Masood Akhtar Rd, opposite Pearl Continental, T051-5516733. One of few places offering self-drive (Rs1,750 per day, unlimited mileage, insurance extra). **Avis**, 7 Rahim Plaza, Murree Rd (next door to Amex), T051-520210. Choice of self-drive and chauffeur-driven. Cars from Rs1,500 per day, plus Rs300 per day for CDW (Crash Damage Waiver) and Rs6 per km. Amex, Visa and MasterCard accepted. **Pearl Continental**, T051-566011 ext 4573. Chauffeur-driven cars only, from Rs2,500 per day.

Repairs Near the railway in Saddar, on Adamjee Rd and the road running parallel to it to the west, there are numerous vehicle breakers, car and motorcycle mechanics, tyre repair shops etc. Heading south from Fowara Chowk along City Saddar Rd there are plenty of general mechanical workshops for welding and machine tool jobs.

Taxi
Taxis are readily available throughout Rawalpindi. If they do not have a working meter always agree a price before getting in.
Auto-rickshaws are also readily available throughout Rawalpindi. They are not much cheaper than taxis, but if you can put up with their exhaust fumes they can be more convenient in some situations.
Suzuki A useful Suzuki route is between Saddar (starting/finishing by the mosque at the junction of Adamjee Rd and Kashmir Rd) and Rajah Bazaar (starting/finishing at Fowara Chowk).
Horse-drawn tongas are available at both Fowara Chowk and Committee Chowk. They have a somewhat more romantic appeal than taxis and auto-rickshaws, but are hopelessly impractical in Rawalpindi's relentless motorized congestion.

Train
Rawalpindi lies on the main Karachi-Lahore-Peshawar line, although the train is of little relevance for those only visiting the north of Pakistan (even Peshawar and Lahore are arguably more easily reached by bus). The railway station is situated on the northern edges of Rawalpindi's Saddar area. First- and second-class sleeper tickets should be bought (as far in advance as possible) at the **Pakistan Railways Booking Office** at the junction of Bank/Mafooz Rds, a block south of the station (see Saddar map). There is also a booking office at Taqi Plaza, Committee Chowk, Murree Rd, T051-5950343. Student and foreign concessions can be obtained from the Commercial Office in the building opposite the station entrance. This is just a small selection of the most convenient services:
Karachi Tezgam, 0800, 25¼ hrs; Awam Exp, 1230, 28 hrs; Chenab Exp (via Faisalabad), 0135, 34½ hrs; Khyber Mail, 0220, 28½ hrs.
Lahore All the trains for Karachi listed above stop in Lahore, except for the Chenab Exp.

They take around 5½-6 hrs from 'Pindi. In addition, there are a number of trains to Lahore only. **Multan** All the trains for Karachi listed above stop in Multan (11-12 hrs from 'Pindi). **Peshawar** There are several express service to Peshawar, eg Awam Exp, 1130, 4½ hrs; Khyber Mail, 0200, 3½ hrs; Chenab Exp, 0345, 3¾ hrs; Abbaseen Exp, 0425, 3¾ hrs, but since they all originate further down the line, they often arrive at 'Pindi late. The 211 Passenger, 0800, 5¾ hrs, takes longer but is more likely to arrive on time. **Quetta** Quetta Exp, 0540, 31½ hrs; Abbaseen Exp, 2050, 35½ hrs.

Directory

Rawalpindi *p83, maps p84, 86, and 89*
Banks National Bank of Pakistan, 55A Bank Rd, Cantt, Saddar, does not charge any fee for cashing TCs (but is painfully slow). There are numerous money changers in the Mall Plaza block containing the TDCP office at the junction of Kashmir Rd and The Mall. **Amex**, Murree Rd, offers neither foreign exchange nor clients' mail (go to Islamabad).
Chemists W. Wilson, The Mall. Pharmaceuticals plus imported toiletries (including nappies/diapers). **Embassies and consulates** See under Islamabad.
Hospitals The 2 main hospitals are the Rawalpindi General, Murree Rd, T051-5847761, and the Cantonment General, Saddar Rd, T051-5562254. Both have dispensaries, and there are various pharmacies dotted around the Saddar area. Medical facilities are better in Islamabad.
Internet Connections are far quicker than further north along the KKH, but Islamabad tends to have speedier machines. **Internet Café**, above Yasoob Travels, Haider Rd. Rs25 per hr, 7 terminals, daily 0930-2200. **Internet World**, Haider Rd. Rs25 per hr, daily 0900-2000. There is also an internet place at the GPO. **Softage Communications**, 1-135 Jlyas Plaza, Iqbal Rd, Committee Chowk, is the nearest to the Popular Inn (Rs25 per hr).
Post office Kashmir Rd, just south of junction with Haider Rd. Mon-Thur and Sat 0900-2000, Fri 0900-1130, 1530-2000. Poste Restante (at rear of building), Express Post and internet service available. **Courier** DHL, T051-823545, and **TNT**, T051-565314. Both have offices next door to each other in Gul-e-Akra Plaza, Murree Rd, south of Marir Chowk. **Telephone** Pak Telecom, Kashmir Rd. Open 24 hrs, cheapest place to make international calls (so busy), recently refurbished so a bit more privacy. There are numerous PCOs dotted around Saddar, notably in the Mall Plaza block containing the TDCP office at the junction of Kashmir Rd and The Mall. If you want to buy a mobile phone, there are lots of places along Bank Rd (especially in the block above the Taste Hunt restaurant). **Useful addresses** City Police Station, Fowara Chowk, T051-5771392; plus Police Station Rd, Saddar Bazaar, T051-564760. **Visa Extensions** See under Islamabad.

Rawalpindi/Islamabad to Peshawar → *Colour map 1, grid C4/5-C2*

Most visitors take a direct bus or train between Rawalpindi/Islamabad and Peshawar, though if you have time on your hands, there are a couple of places of minor interest imbetween. Note that the Grand Trunk (GT) Road between the cities is a fast and furious drive, lined for much of the way with industrial developments. Cyclists making this trip may prefer to take the quieter route via Swabi, Mardan and Charsadda, see Peshawar and around on page 99. ▸▸ *For Sleeping, Eating and all other listings, see page 94.*

Margalla Pass

Some 28 km from Rawalpindi, the road climbs gently up to the Margalla Pass, described by Sir Olaf Caroe as the real division between Central and South Asia. The granite obelisk here is a memorial to Brigadier-General John Nicholson CB, who played a heroic role in the two Sikh wars, the First Afghan War and the Mutiny, and died here in

1857 aged 34 while leading the column that lifted the great siege of Delhi. A walk up to the obelisk takes you onto a section of the old cobbled 16th-century Shahi road, built by Sher Shah Suri but which can trace its origins back over 2,000 years to the campaigns of Chandragupta Maurya in 324 BC (which took the Mauryan Empire onto the soils of modern Afghanistan). Look out for the troglodytes in the caves here. Just beyond the pass is the turning for Taxila, which also leads to Haripur and the KKH (see page 168).

Just after the turning for Taxila is the **Wah Cantonment** (the centre of which is off limits due to the ordnance factory). Wah is supposed to have received its name from the exclamation of the Emperor Jahangir – "wah" ('beautiful') – when he saw the beauty of the valley. The **Wah Moghul Gardens** were used as one of numerous resting places by the Mughal emperors en route to Kashmir. Today they are somewhat dilapidated and, unless you have your own transport, they are not really worth stopping for.

Hasan Abdal

The early 19th-century Sikh temple here, **Panja Sahib Gurudwara**, is the focus of the annual Baisakhi Festival (April) that attracts Sikh pilgrims from around the world. Visitors to the Gurudwara will be shown a stone with a hand imprint reputed to be that of **Guru Nanak**, founder of Sikhism. The spring which emerges from beneath the stone is said to have been created when Guru Nanak, upon asking the Muslim saint Baba Wali for a drink, placed his hand upon the rock that the saint had thrown down at his feet. Gaining entry can sometimes be difficult for non-Sikhs or Muslims. An hour's walk above the shrine, on the flat-topped hill overlooking the town, is **Baba Wali's Shrine**.

The street opposite the Gurudwara leads to the Mughal period **Maqbara** Hakiman(tomb of the hakims, or doctors). Although decayed, the brick-built lime plaster-covered structure is a good example of Mughal funerary architecture. Further on, a gate leads through into a beautiful walled garden with a simple tomb in the centre. This tomb was built for the Mughal governor Khwaja Shamsuddin Khawafi. He died and was buried in Lahore around 1599, however, and subsequently Akbar ordered that this tomb be used for the hakims Abdul and Himan Gilani.

Attock

Having crossed the Harro River and passed the town of **Lawrencepur**, the GT Road crosses the **Indus** on the Attock Bridge. To the south of the GT Road is **Attock City** (18 km), still referred to on some signs and maps as Campbellpore, and which has some interesting colonial and pre-colonial architecture. The presence here of the late

The GT Road: Rawalpindi/Islamabad to Peshawar

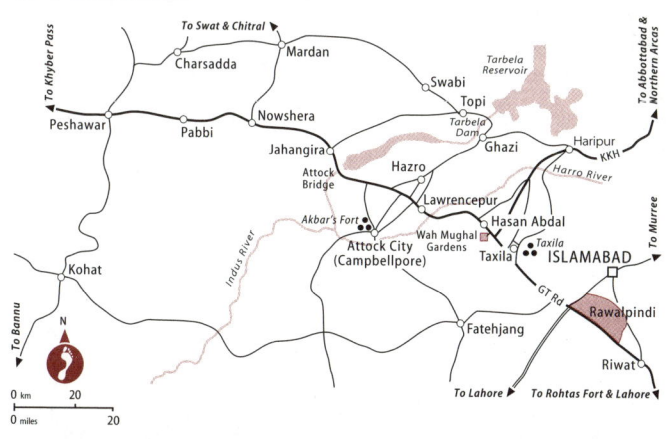

16th-century **Akbar's Fort**, with its rambling walls and large crenellations dominating the gorge, plus Sher Shah Suri's large caravanserai from the same century, indicate what a historically important crossing point this was. Today, the bridge over the Indus marks the boundary between Punjab and NWFP.

Tarbela Dam

To the north of the GT Road is the Tarbela Dam, began in 1968 as part of Pakistan's response to the Indus Waters Treaty of 1960. The world's largest earth-filled dam, it is designed to store nearly 14 million cubic metres of water and generate 2.1 million kilowatts of electricity, but is still not complete due to unforeseen technical difficulties and design defects. Some experts have criticized it as a dangerous venture in what is an unpredictable earthquake zone. The build-up of silt in the lake, reducing its storage capacity, has proved to be a far greater problem than expected.

Officially you must obtain permission from the Secretariat in Islamabad (see under Useful addresses in the Directory) in order to visit Tarbela, and make arrangements with WAPDA if you want a guided tour. In practice, however, trying to organize anything through the Secretariat or WAPDA is a waste of time unless you have someone influential behind you. Your best bet is simply to turn up at WAPDA's office in Tarbela and hope that there is someone sympathetic on duty. You can travel across the dam by public transport from Ghazi to Topi without a special permit, but this does not give you the chance to stop at the viewpoints. The viewpoints, and access to the route across the dam, are open only during daylight hours. There are regular buses from Hasan Abdal to Ghazi, and from there to Topi, from where you can return to the GT Road at Jehangira or continue west towards Mardan. There is also a direct road from Haripur to Ghazi. **NB** No photography is allowed.

Attock to Peshawar

Having crossed the Kabul River at **Jehangira**, the GT Road passes through the town of **Nowshera**, which has retained its importance as a military base from British times through to Pakistani independence (but is mostly off limits to civilians). From Nowshera it is a further 44 km to Peshawar. The road first passes through the town of **Pabbi** and then runs through an industrial landscape, before entering the suburbs of **Peshawar**.

Sleeping

Hasan Abdal *p93*
There are several places on the GT Rd by the Caltex petrol station, including:
E Frontier basic but clean, with fan and bath.
E Mesum Tourist Inn, same as above.

Attock *p93*
D Indus View on the GT Rd, east of the bridge, is the best bet.

Attock to Peshawar *p94*
On the GT Rd, there are two hotels, **E Shobra** and **F Spark**, near the bus stand at Nowshera.

Eating

Attock *p93*
There are several cheap places on the GT Rd.

Transport

Hasan Abdal *p93*
Most buses passing along the GT Rd will drop off/pick up passengers here, with the exception of the long-distance 'flying coaches' (**Islamabad/Rawalpindi -Peshawar, Rawalpindi-Gilgit**) which are generally full.

Attock *p93*
As with Hasan Abdal, picking up public transport in either direction is fairly easy.

Peshawar Valley & Chitral Valley

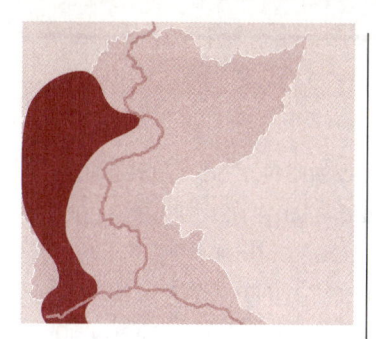

Peshawar and around	**99**
The old city and around	102
Khyber Pass	107
Darra Adam Khel	108
Listings	109
Peshawar to Chitral	**117**
Listings	121
Chitral Valley	**123**
Chitral town	126
Around Chitral town	127
Listings	138
Kalash Valleys	**132**
Exploring the valleys	137
Treks	137
Listings	138
Upper Chitral	**140**
Chitral to Mastuj	141
Yarkhun Valley	143
Turikho Valley	146
Listings	147
Chitral to Gilgit	**148**
Shandur Pass	149
Yasin Valley	153
Gupis to the Ishkoman Valley	155
Ishkoman Valley	155
Gahkuch to Gilgit	159
Listings	160

Footprint features...

Don't miss...	97
The woman's place is in the Kalash region	136
The most spectacular polo event in the world	149
A dark stain on Darkot	156

Introduction

Although the Karakoram Highway and Northern Areas draw the majority of visitors to Pakistan, a large number also spend time exploring the other great region of the north of the country – the North West Frontier Province (NWFP). Not only do the Peshawar Valley and Chitral Valley have outstanding attractions in their own right, they also provide alternative routes into the mountains to the KKH, and allow visitors to avoid retracing their steps along roads that they have already seen. The 'grand route (clockwise)' is probably the best way to explore the north of Pakistan (see suggested itineraries on page 12).

Peshawar, the provincial capital and largest city, is for many people the starting point of a visit to NWFP. An atmospheric and exciting place, the city provides a convenient base for exploring the surrounding areas (notably the Khyber Pass and Peshawar Valley). For the more adventurous still, a 12-hour journey north by road (or a spectacular one-hour flight) takes travellers to the Chitral Valley, a mountainous region of outstanding beauty, boasting endless opportunities for trekking and climbing.

The journey east from Chitral to Gilgit (the point on the KKH where things get really interesting) is not only one of the best trips in Pakistan, it also allows visitors to bypass the less welcoming lower stretches of the KKH. For details of how Peshawar and Chitral fit into a journey around northern Pakistan, see the suggested itineraries on page 12.

★ Don't miss...

1. **Peshawar's Old City** Soak up the old town's atmosphere, page 102.
2. **Khyber Pass** Take a steam train to the legendary pass, page 107.
3. **Darra Adam Khel** Visit to the gun-making town, page 108.
4. **Hindu Kush** Make use of the unique trekking opportunities, page 125.
5. **Kalash** Meet one of Pakistan's colourful religious minorities, page 132.
6. **Chitral to Gilgit** Tackle this challenging yet beautiful trip, page 148.
7. **Shandur Pass** Watch polo matches on the roof of the world, page 149.
8. **Phandur and Khalti Lake** Gawp at some of Pakistan's most jaw-dropping scenery, page 152.
9. **Yasin Valley** Relax in the tranquility of this rustic valley, page 153.

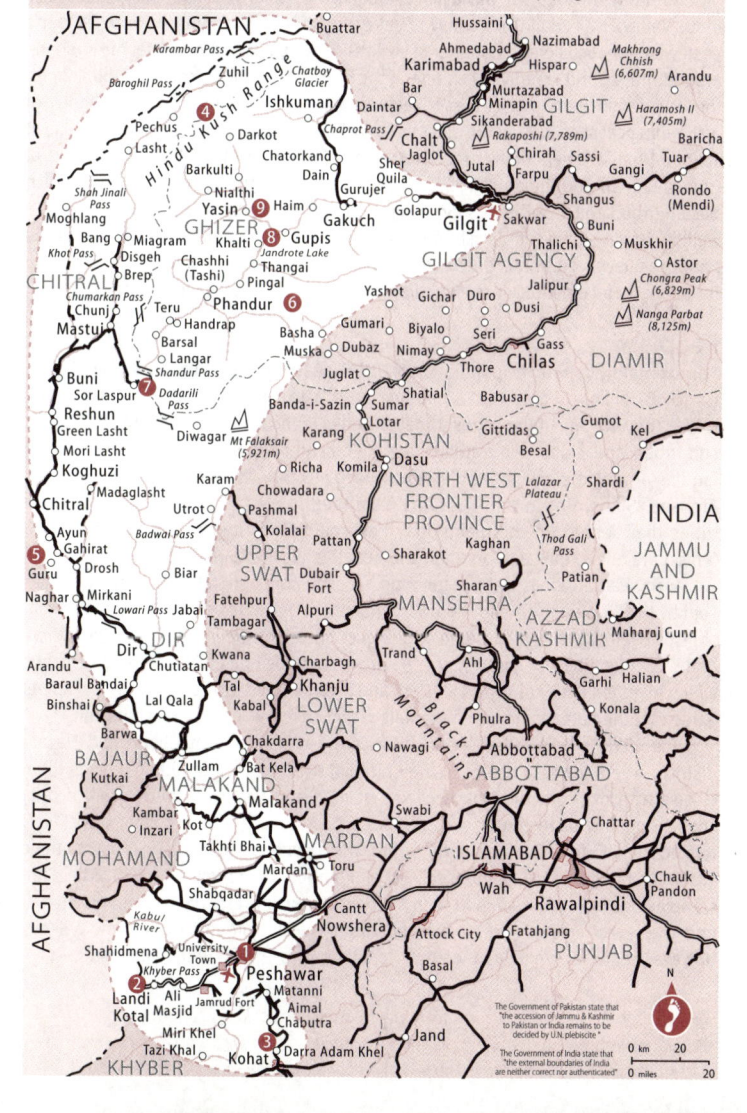

Background

The Pathan tribes that dominate NWFP have for centuries exploited its rugged terrain and thrived on banditry and guerrilla warfare, eluding the attempts of invading powers to control and pacify them. During the colonial period this frontier region grew in strategic importance and the British established their 'Forward Policy', struggling to control it as a buffer zone against Russian expansion. Despite the Durand Line of 1893 (which today forms the border with Afghanistan), they never gained full control. Even today nearly a third of the region is designated as 'Tribal Areas', with internal autonomy from Pakistani law.

Throughout history this region has existed as a turbulent zone of contact between the civilizations of Central Asia and the Middle East on one side and South Asia on the other. Yet the province also has a rich cultural history of its own, stretching back to the Indus Valley Civilization. The Peshawar Valley and hills of Swat, along with Taxila to the east, were the focus of the Gandharan civilization which flourished under the Kushans around the second century AD as one of the most important centres of Buddhism on the subcontinent. Today, these regions have the highest concentration of archaeological sites in Pakistan and some, such as the Buddhist monastery remains at Takht-e-Bhai, are beautifully preserved. Gandharan art, with its distinctive fusion of Graeco-Roman and Indian styles, is famous throughout the world. Peshawar, which became the capital of the Kushan kings, reached its zenith under Mughal rule as a wealthy trading town with lavish mosques, palaces and gardens. Tucked away in the remote valleys of Chitral, the unique Kalash tribes have existed for centuries in isolation, their colourful, vibrant culture and way of life still surviving today.

People

Approximately 90% of the population of NWFP are **Pathans** (or **Pukhtuns**). Numbering up to 18 million people and inhabiting north Baluchistan, east Afghanistan and NWFP, they are one of the largest tribal societies in the world. Divided into numerous sub-tribes and clans, the Pathans are a fiercely independent people, constantly feuding among themselves and ever hostile to any threat to their freedom. Mughals, Afghans, Sikhs, British and Russians have tried to control them, and while those tribes that settled on the plains may have paid taxes and token tribute to their temporary rulers, the semi-nomadic tribes of the hills have never been subdued.

Many Pathan tribes claim a common ancestry from a man called **Quais** who was sent by the Prophet to spread Islam in Afghanistan. One of his sons, Afghana, had four sons who left Afghanistan to settle in different parts of the province as founding fathers of the various tribes. In contrast, the **Wazirs** claim to be one of the lost tribes of Israel which migrated east, converted to Islam and finally settled in Waziristan. Most experts agree that the Pathans probably originated from an ethnic group in Afghanistan.

The NWFP's non-Pathan populations are found mostly in Chitral and Hazara districts. The **Khowar** language of the **Chitralis**, who call their land Kho, relates them closely with the nomadic groups of the Wakhan and Pamir regions. Hazara district consists mainly of **Hindko**-speaking tribes whose language and culture are closely related to that of the Punjabis to the south. The **Kalash** are a small non-Muslim ethnic group found in Chitral, in the valleys of Rumbur, Bumburet and Birir. Their fair complexions led early visitors to liken them to "handsome Europeans, with brown hair and blue eyes" believed to be descendants of Alexander's armies. It is more likely, however, that they are related to an ancient Indo-Aryan group from Afghanistan.

Although the district of Hazara, Kaghan Valley and parts of Indus Kohistan are administratively part of NWFP, these areas are dealt with in the Karakoram Highway section, since in practical terms they form part of the KKH route.

Peshawar and around → Colour map 1, grid C2

Peshawar's 'frontier' location at the gateway to the fabled Khyber Pass has endowed it with a certain sense of romance – a name to conjure up images of wild, bearded men toting guns, swaggering around the Old City bazaars (although following a government crack-down since 1999, the guns are now rarely seen in public, but beards are still in vogue). Arriving in Peshawar today, as well as confronting the usual chaos and congestion, you are engulfed by a choking, eye-stinging blue haze of fumes hanging over the city in a permanent cloud. The congestion and pollution are inescapable aspects of Peshawar but, despite this, most people quickly fall in love with the place. It's not so much that there are any great sights in the traditional sense – it's the atmosphere of the place and, in particular, the mesmerizing bazaars of the Old City, which buzz with an almost tangible feeling of vibrancy and excitement.

Peshawar is one of the ancient trading centres of Asia and today, as in the past, people are drawn from far and wide to do business. You could spend weeks exploring the narrow alleyways and covered markets, hunting out obscure treasures of antique tribal jewellery or bargaining over sumptuous Central Asian carpets, but even an afternoon spent here is enough for something of the romance of this historic frontier city to get under your skin.

There are a number of attractions in the Peshawar region, although the limited accommodation options make day trips more appealing than overnight stops. The most popular trips are to the Khyber Pass and Darra Adam Khel. Details of other sites in the Peshawar Valley (Charsadda, Mardan, Takht-e-Bhai etc) can be found in Footprint Pakistan, *alongside details of the Swat Valley.* ▶▶ *For Sleeping, Eating and all other listings, see pages 109-117.*

Ins and outs

Getting there
Although there are a limited number of direct international flights between Peshawar and the outside world (notably the Gulf), most people using Peshawar's **airport** will be travelling to/from Islamabad, Lahore, Karachi, Quetta and a number of other smaller towns and cities (the most relevant of these from a tourist point of view being the daily Fokker 27 flights to/from Chitral). The airport is very central, a Rs40-60 rickshaw/taxi ride from most hotels.

Peshawar is the terminus for Pakistan's main **railway** artery. There are two stations, Cantonment and City. The most convenient is Cantonment, both in terms of its location and because the main booking office is situated here. Trains run to Rawalpindi, Lahore and ultimately Karachi, with a branch also to Quetta. If travelling by train, bear in mind the times and distances involved in longer trips (Quetta 39 hours, 1,569 km; Karachi 36 hours, 1,676 km).

The main (general) **bus** station, on GT Road, houses a large number of private and government buses which between them offer services to most destinations north, east and southeast of Peshawar. As you reach the bus station, big buses and coasters are to the right, Hiaces to the left. Simply state your destination to a likely looking person, who will usually help you to find the right bus for you amongst the chaos. For southern NWFP (Kohat, Bannu, Darra Adam Khel, Dera Ismail Khan) and Quetta, buses and minibuses leave from the Quetta bus stand on Kohat Road, to the south of the city centre. Buses to Charsadda (and sometimes Mardan) leave from Charsadda Adha, north of Shahi Bagh. There are a couple of companies in the Old City operating direct Hiace minibus services to Chitral, otherwise the journey can be made in stages from the main bus station. A new bus station at Roadways House on GT Road offers private air-conditioned buses to the major destinations, notably Karachi, Lahore, Rawalpindi and Quetta.

Most visitors take a direct bus or train between Rawalpindi/Islamabad and Peshawar, but if you have time on your hands, there are a couple of places of minor interest in between. Note that the Grand Trunk (GT) Road between the cities is a fast and furious drive, lined for much of the way with industrial developments. Cyclists making this trip may prefer to take the quieter route via Swabi, Mardan and Charsadda. ▸▸ *See Transport, page 113, for more details.*

Getting around

Peshawar really consists of four distinct areas. In the east, to the south of the GT Road, is the **Old City**, the heart of ancient Peshawar. To the west and southwest of this are the **Cantonment** and **Saddar Bazaar** areas, which between them represent the commercial and administrative centre of modern Peshawar, with most of the hotels, restaurants, shops, banks and government offices etc. To the west of this again, beyond the airport, on the road leading toward the Khyber Pass, is the **University Town**. As well as being the site of Peshawar University, this area has developed as a focus for foreign consulates, NGOs etc. Even further west is the new residential area of **Hayatabad**. The bus system in Peshawar is almost entirely run by Afghans. Rickety Mercedes and Bedford buses run back and forth between the main bus station on the GT Road and University Town/Hayatabad, passing through the Old City, Saddar and Cantonment en route. Auto-rickshaws are also plentiful in

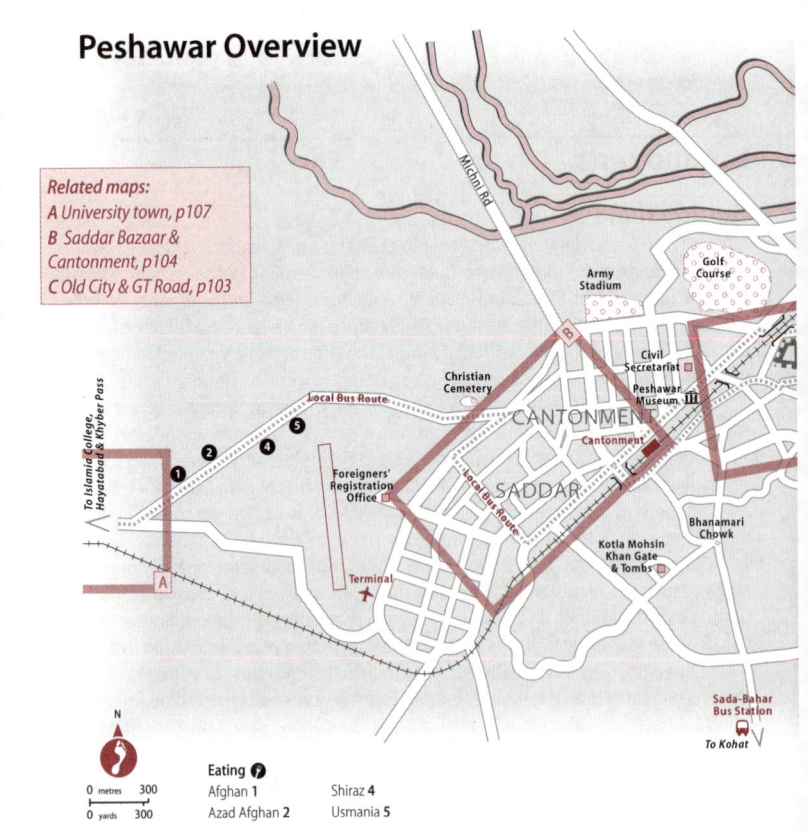

Peshawar Overview

Related maps:
A *University town, p107*
B *Saddar Bazaar & Cantonment, p104*
C *Old City & GT Road, p103*

Eating
Afghan **1**
Azad Afghan **2**
Shiraz **4**
Usmania **5**

Peshawar, and a convenient way of getting around. There are fewer taxis than in Islamabad, but in the Saddar and Cantonment areas, or outside more expensive hotels, you can usually find one without too much problem. Saddar and the Old City are both compact enough to get around on foot.

Best time to visit

The summer months are unpleasantly hot and although the traffic pollution is a year-round phenomenon, it always seems far worse at this time.

Tourist information

PTDC Tourist Information Centre ① *113 Benevolent Fund Building, Saddar Rd, T/F091-286829, Mon-Thu 0900-1300, 1400-1630, Fri 0900-1200*, has helpful, well-informed staff. Ask here for reliable information on the current situation in Khyber Agency and Darra. Also able to arrange tours of Peshawar Old City, the Khyber Pass and major sites in the Peshawar Valley (Charsadda, Takht-e-Bhai, Shabaz Ghari etc). In 2004 PTDC was charging Rs2,000 for trips by jeep to the Khyber Pass (five people, all inclusive). It also offers city tours at Rs800 for one to four people splitting the cost. To hire a Land cruiser with driver for longer excursions costs Rs3,000 per 24 hrs, all inclusive. **Sarhad Tourism Corporation (STC)** ① *Block 13-A Old Courts Building, Khyber Rd, Cantonment (near Pearl Continental), T091-9211091*, is NWFP's provincial tourism corporation but not of significant use; there is no public counter here, but you can phone up for information on the dates of the Shandur Polo Festival.

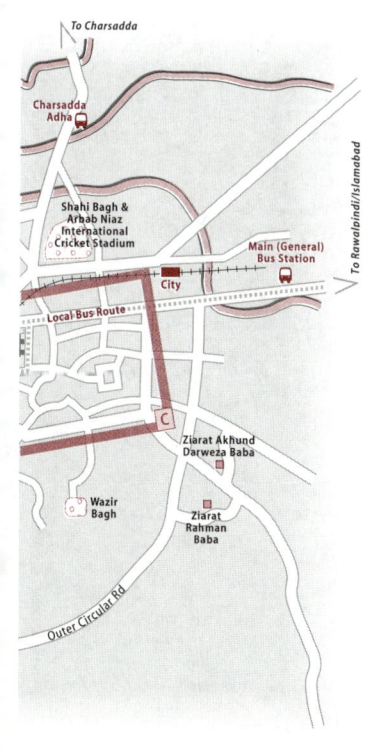

History

Although the origins of the city remain unclear, a Kharoshthi rock inscription near Attock, dated AD 119, refers to it as *Poshapura* meaning 'City of Flowers'. It's likely that the Kushan king Kanishka established his winter capital here, and indeed the famous bronze reliquary casket of Kanishka, now on display in Peshawar Museum, was discovered here in 1907 by Spooner (although nothing remains of the archaeological site, Shah-ji-ki-Dheri).

After the decline of the Kushans, Peshawar changed hands between the Sassanians and the Kidar ('little') Kushans, before being overrun by White Huns in the fifth century AD. Other conquerors included the Turki and Hindu Shahis in the sixth to seventh centuries AD, the latter shifting their capital from here to Hund, on the banks of the Indus. This was almost certainly a response to the growing infiltration of the Afghan (Pathan) tribes into the Peshawar Valley. Mahmoud of Ghazni then incorporated Peshawar into the Ghaznavid Empire at the start of the 11th century, but with the destruction of this empire, the town found itself on the margins of both the Central Asian and Indian empires.

The city next acquired importance during the Mughal period, when it flourished as a regional capital. The Mughals planted trees, laid out gardens and built forts and mosques; their monuments are among the few that survived the city's long and turbulent history. The city's name is attributed to Akbar who changed it from the Persian *Parshawar* to Peshawar, meaning 'Frontier Town'. After the decline of the Mughals, the Durranis of Afghanistan gained a firm hold on Peshawar for a time, before being driven out by the Sikh Empire of Ranjit Singh. The city was a major bone of contention between the Durranis and Sikhs, before the British, extending their empire to the north and west, finally brought it under their control.

The Old City and around

The walls and 16 gates of the Old City now survive in name only, and today the fortified stronghold of **Bala Hisar** ① *Open for visits Sat 1500-1900, Sun 0800-1900, foreigners Rs100, Pakistanis Rs20, the PTDC offer a tour for 1-4 people at Rs600 (split cost), but you won't miss much if you organize a visit yourself*, is the most imposing landmark, almost certainly standing on the site of the ancient citadel. The ramparts offer views of the Old City, while a small museum/gallery displays old uniforms, rifles, signalling equipment and photographs. Much of the present fort was built by the British, who replaced the mud walls and reinforced the Sikh construction with 'pucca' brick.

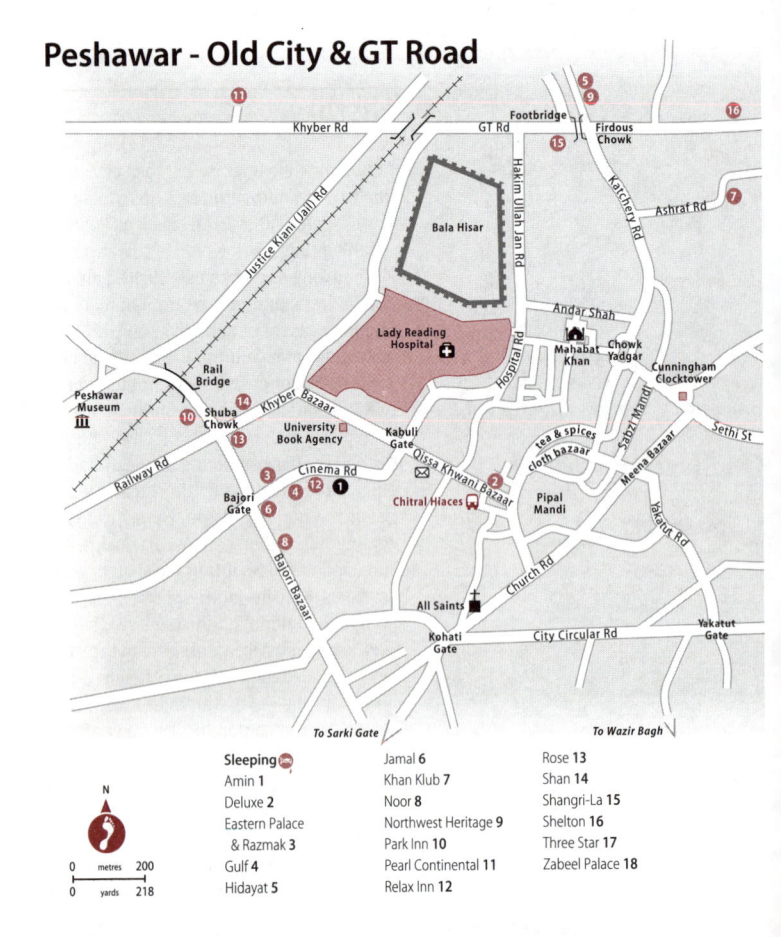

Peshawar – Old City & GT Road

Sleeping
Amin 1
Deluxe 2
Eastern Palace
 & Razmak 3
Gulf 4
Hidayat 5
Jamal 6
Khan Klub 7
Noor 8
Northwest Heritage 9
Park Inn 10
Pearl Continental 11
Relax Inn 12
Rose 13
Shan 14
Shangri-La 15
Shelton 16
Three Star 17
Zabeel Palace 18

There are traces of the many previous occupants, the fort being the key to control of Peshawar, changing hands many times. When the Mughal emperor Babur arrived in 1509, he occupied and strengthened the existing fort and laid out the Shalimar Gardens. After the decline of the Mughals, the Durranis of Afghanistan. controlled Peshawar until 1818. The fort at this time was in magnificent condition, as described by Elphinstone when he visited in 1809: "The throne was covered with a cloth adorned with pearls, on which lay a sword and a small mace set with jewels. The room was open all round. The centre was supported by four high pillars, in the midst of which was a large fountain. The floor was covered with the richest carpets, and round the edges were slips of silk embroidered with gold. The view from the hall was beautiful. Immediately below was an extensive garden, full of cypresses and other trees, and beyond was a plain of richest verdure." The Bala Hisar and the Shalimar Gardens were destroyed by Ranjit Singh who later rebuilt the fort of mud. The Sikhs named the fort *Sameer Garh* before the British took control.

> *There are few sights as such in Peshawar, but the atmosphere is a major attraction.*

The Bazaars

A wander around the bazaars of the Old City is a highlight of a visit to Peshawar. Crowds of people jostle with cars, bicycles, donkey carts and rickshaws and narrow alleys lead off from the main streets, concealing even more colourful and atmospheric bazaars selling everything from vegetables to ornate gold and silver jewellery. Trades tend to group together on the whole, but less so than in the past. A brief description of the main bazaars is given below, although there are many more; perhaps the best thing is simply to wander at will. For the serious shopper, the Old City is a wonderful hunting ground, but is not for those in a hurry. Deals are negotiated unhurriedly over cups of green tea (*khawar*) and endless small-talk interspersed with bargaining.

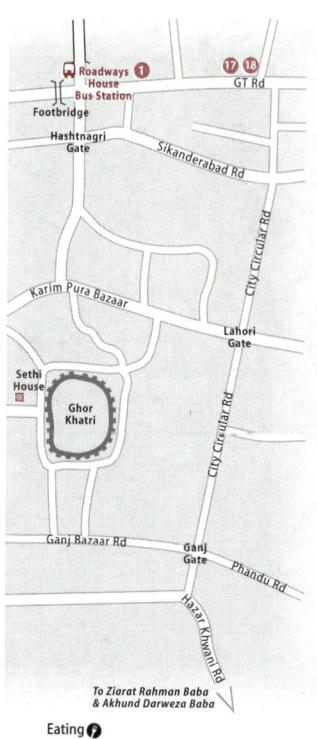

The main route into the Old City from Saddar is over **Rail Bridge**, which brings you to a busy junction known as **Shuba Chowk**. All around here are numerous carpet shops, and swarthy Pathans walking the streets with carpets on their shoulders in the hope of a quick sale. Going straight on leads to Bajori Road and **Namak Mandi**, where there are several excellent tikka restaurants. Going left into **Khyber Bazaar**, most of the street is lined with shops selling electrical goods ranging from air conditioners to hi-fi systems. Towards the end there are the dentist shops with brightly painted signs showing false teeth. The crossroads at the east end of Khyber Bazaar mark the site of the old Kabuli Gate. Turning left here leads up past Lady Reading Hospital and Bala Hisar to the GT Road. Right leads into Cinema Road and back round towards Namak Mandi; as well as its cinemas and feature bill boards, Cinema Road is a treasure trove of lurid Indian and Pakistani film-star postcards.

Eating
Salateen 1

Related maps:
Peshawar overview, p101

Straight on is **Qissa Khwani Bazaar**, or storytellers bazaar. Here were the 'Khave Khanas'; tea shops and eating houses where in the past, travellers and traders met to exchange their tales and news of faraway places. Today, the tea shops have given way to cold drink stands, as well as bookshops, clothing, luggage and general stores. Turning left at the end, the road runs up past shops selling **brass and copperware**. A fork off to the right takes you into the **Cloth Bazaar** while straight on is a bazaar selling

Peshawar – Saddar Bazaar & Cantonment

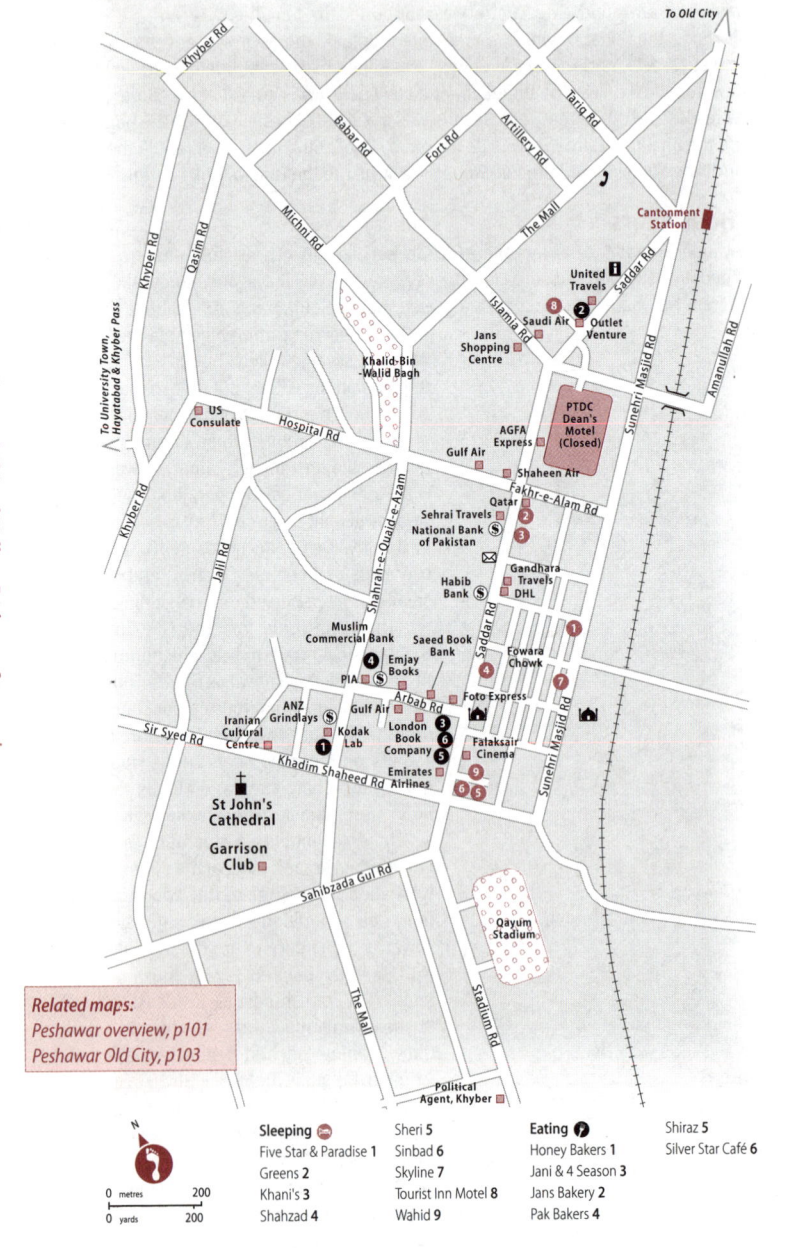

Related maps:
Peshawar overview, p101
Peshawar Old City, p103

Sleeping
Five Star & Paradise 1
Greens 2
Khani's 3
Shahzad 4
Sheri 5
Sinbad 6
Skyline 7
Tourist Inn Motel 8
Wahid 9

Eating
Honey Bakers 1
Jani & 4 Season 3
Jans Bakery 2
Pak Bakers 4
Shiraz 5
Silver Star Café 6

tea and spices. The next turning left on either leads up to Chowk Yadgar. To the south of the cloth market is **Pipal Mandi**, the main grain wholesale area where a peepul tree is believed to mark the spot where the Buddha once preached.

Chowk Yadgar lies at the heart of the Old City. Originally a memorial to Colonel EC Hastings, it was replaced by a plaza and memorial to those who died in the Indo-Pakistani war of 1965. The west side is lined with the shops and stalls of moneychangers with their displays of currencies. An underpass runs under the plaza from east to west.

Sethi Street runs east from Chowk Yadgar. This street was at the heart of the traditional business community and gained its name from the powerful Sethi family which at one time conducted highly profitable trade with Russia, China, India and Central Asia. A few of the old houses remain, some in precarious states of structural repair, with richly carved wooden doorways and ornate balconies. Inside are large airy reception rooms and deep cellars which provided relief from the summer heat. Following Sethi Street east from Chowk Yadgar, the first narrow alley on the left is the **Chappal market**, selling sandals, followed immediately by the vegetable market **Sabzi Mandi**, covered in summer with matting against the heat. Further along is **Cunningham Clock tower**, built in 1900 by Balmukund to celebrate Queen Victoria's Diamond Jubilee, and in honour of Sir George Cunningham who became Governor of NWFP. Around it tanners practise their trade, and occasionally fishmongers too.

Karim Pura, the narrow street which forks off left from Sethi Street at the Cunningham Clock tower, is also lined with ancient houses with intricately carved woodwork, which are in some ways more impressive, or at least more numerous, than those of Sethi Street. The bazaar along here is varied; everything from household goods to meat and spices. Shortly after the clock tower on the right is **Meena Bazaar** (women's bazaar), where *burqas* and veils for women are sold along with items of embroidery. Towards the end of the street, on the left, is the restored **Sethi House**, which is included in guided tours of Peshawar; if you don't want to join a tour, the beautifully restored **Khan Klub Hotel**, near Rampura Gate is, if anything, more impressive and boasts an excellent restaurant as well.

At the east end of Sethi Street is **Gor Khatri**. This large walled compound with its impressive Mughal gateway is today a police headquarters. It is usually possible to wander in and look round, although there is not much left to see. It was originally the site of the **Tower of the Buddha's Bowl** where the Buddha's sacred alms bowl was believed to have been housed. Later it became an important place of Hindu pilgrimage, perhaps as a site for funeral sacrifices or for the initiation of *Yogis*. The daughter of the Mughal emperor Shah Jahan converted it into a *caravanserai* (the existing compound) and built an accompanying mosque. During the Sikh period the mosque was destroyed and replaced with a temple of Gorakhnath (Siva) and its subsidiary Nandi shrine, the remains of which still stand.

Andarshah Bazaar (meaning 'inner city') runs west from Chowk Yadgar towards Bala Hisar. It houses the silver and goldsmiths, selling a wide range of ethnic, antique and modern jewellery. The tiny alleys that lead off to the south from the main street contain many more shops, some with quite rare antique items. About halfway along on the north side is an arched gateway into **Mahabat Khan Mosque**. Mahabat Khan was twice governor of Peshawar during the reigns of Shah Jahan and Aurangzeb, and is thought to have built it. Although much smaller, it closely resembles the Badshahi Mosque in Lahore and provides an excellent example of Mughal architecture from Shah Jahan's time. During the Sikh period, the two minarets were frequently used as gallows by the Sikh Governor, General Avitabile, a mercenary of Italian origin who joined Ranjit Singh's court following the Napoleonic wars. The Prayer Hall is decorated with intricate paint work, aging but still precise and distinct. The fire which swept through Andarshah in 1898 nearly destroyed the mosque but fortunately many of its decorative features were restored.

Other sights

South of the Old City

All Saints' Church ⓘ *Open Sun 1000-1300 when masses are held; at all other times the chowkidar in the house opposite holds the keys*, was built in 1883 and originally situated in the grounds of the nearby Edwardes High School. This church has a beautiful stained-glass chancel window and carved wooden arches.

Ziarat Rahman Baba ⓘ *situated to the southeast of Taliband City and Ganj Gate, between Outer Circular Rd and Hazar Khwani Rd, free*, is the shrine of the famous Pashto poet Rahman Baba. There is a new complex here consisting of a library, mosque and shrine, the latter with an imposing white marble dome decorated with blue tiles on the outside and an intricate mirror mosaic on the inside. The much older shrine outside has more character and is a popular meeting place in the evenings. Just before the turning right off Hazar Khwani Road to the shrine, there is a small shrine to **Akhund Darweza Baba**, a famous Sufi saint from the Mughal period.

Situated southwest of Bhanamari Chowk, just off Badshahi Road, **Kotla Mohsin Khan Gate** is a crumbling but impressive gate that once formed the entrance to a fortified residence or Kotla. The identity of Mohsin Khan is uncertain. Nearby, there are two large domed **tombs**; again it is uncertain as to whom these were for. Today, however, they are home to large numbers of bats.

Cantonment and Saddar Bazaar

British troops first set up camp in what was to become the Cantonment in 1848-49. Following the classical colonial style, ubiquitous throughout British India, a wholly independent town was built with long, wide, tree-lined boulevards designed for horse-drawn traffic and spacious bungalows set back from the road, along with all the social infrastructure of Government buildings, schools, churches, clubs etc. The railway line and station which divides the Cantonment from the Old City followed. Today, there are still many examples of the distinctive Mughal/Gothic architecture of the British period among the more modern buildings, giving glimpses of a bygone age. The oldest markets of Saddar Bazaar are to be found in the grid of narrow alleys centred on Fowara Chowk; in places these are every bit as atmospheric as those of the Old City.

Peshawar Museum

ⓘ *Sunehri Masjid Rd, en route to the GT Rd, 0900-1300, 1400-1700, closed Wed and public holidays, Rs100. Buses going northeast along Sunehri Masjid Rd pass the museum en route to the GT Rd. An auto-rickshaw from Saddar won't cost more than Rs20.* This classic piece of architecture was built in 1905 as the Victoria Memorial Hall. Some of the best artefacts from the various stages of Gandharan civilization are housed here (although many are in the Lahore Museum). This is a collection not to be missed, and the presentation is excellent. Upstairs there is an ethnographic section including wooden carvings from the Kalash Valleys.

University Town

The University Town is situated 7 km west of Peshawar on Khyber Road. The impressive **Islamia College and Collegiate School** was built in Mughal/Gothic style in 1913, and was followed by the University which was founded in 1930. Today, a sprawling residential area of red-brick buildings and well-kept lawns surrounds the University, and various Institutes and Research Councils line the main road.

Further west is the new development of **Hayatabad** and, beyond this, **Smugglers' Bazaar**, selling luxury western goods. At the end of the bazaar is a check post which marks the start of **Khyber Agency**. Foreigners are not allowed beyond this point without a permit.

Khyber Pass

Although the passes to the north and south have traditionally provided the invasion routes from Central Asia into the subcontinent, it is the Khyber Pass that has really captured the imagination. Whether or not this is due to the cinematic classic *Carry On Up The Khyber* (actually filmed in Wales!) is open to interpretation, but the British regarded it as the 'Gateway to India' and hence its fame has stuck. Nevertheless, despite being billed as the main invasion route from the west since Aryan times, the first recorded conqueror to use it was actually Babur in the 16th century. Visually it's not particularly impressive, but somehow the journey up through the barren landscape of the lawless Tribal Areas is part of the appeal, coupled with the romantic image of 'unreachable' Afghanistan that some travellers still cling to.

Ins and outs

Foreigners are required to obtain a permit to visit the Khyber Pass. They must travel by private vehicle and take an armed escort. If you wish to organize it yourself, both the permit (Rs120 per person, bring photocopies of the relevant pages of your passport) and armed escort can be obtained from the Political Agent, Khyber in Peshawar (see Directory under Useful addresses). However, the easiest way to organize a visit, and the cheapest if you can get a group of 5 together, is through **PTDC** or a reputable travel agent such as **Sehrai Travels and Tours** ⓘ *12-A Saddar Rd, T091-272085, sehrai@netzone.net.pk*. PTDC charges Rs2,000 for a half-day visit by air-conditioned land cruiser (maximum five people), including permits and escort. Sehrai Travels and Tours charges a little more per person (minimum two people). There are also plenty of taxi drivers and freelance 'guides' hanging around Saddar Bazaar who may offer to take you for less. They are less reliable and if you opt for one of these, PTDC strongly advises you to call at their office and inform them before setting off. A recently revived alternative to going by road is to travel on the famous Khyber Railway (see below). Note that at the time of writing, the Khyber Pass is open to foreigners, but whenever there is any unrest among the Afridi tribes controlling the area, the authorities are liable to close it.

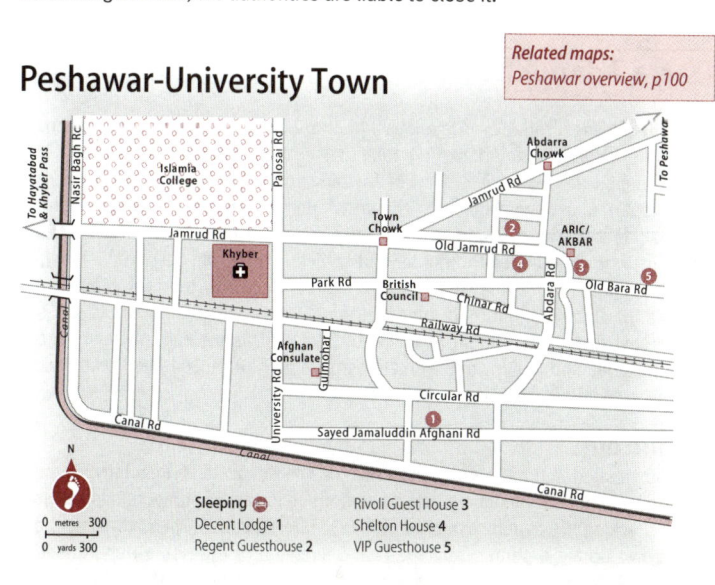

Peshawar-University Town

Related maps:
Peshawar overview, p100

Sleeping
Decent Lodge **1**
Regent Guesthouse **2**
Rivoli Guest House **3**
Shelton House **4**
VIP Guesthouse **5**

The pass

The pass stretches from Jamrud Fort to Torkham. Heading west out of Peshawar along the Jamrud Road, you pass University Town, Hayatabad and Smugglers' Bazaar, before entering Khyber Agency. **Jamrud Fort** (18 km) was built by the Sikh General Hari Singh in 1836, provoking an attack by the Afghans which cost him his life. It is of rough stonework faced with mud plaster and consists of three tiers: lower and upper forts, plus a keep. There is also a stone arched gate on the road, the **Bab-e-Khyber**, built in 1964. From the fort, the road zigzags up past viewpoints and watchtowers with good views back onto the Peshawar plain. Next is the 1920s British-built **Shagai Fort** (30 km). It is now manned by the Frontier Force and closed to the public, but in the 'Carry On' film it was manned by the Third Foot & Mouth Regiment (the 'Devils in Skirts'). In the middle of the pass is Ali Masjid (mosque) and high above it the **Ali Masjid Fort**, which defends the narrowest point of the gorge, less than 14 m wide.

From here the pass opens out into a wide valley dotted with fortified Pathan settlements. Just before Landi Kotal, 15 km from Shagai Fort, there is the **Sphola Stupa**, to the right of the road on a hillock above Zarai. It dates from the second to fifth centuries AD and is the last remains of an extensive and somewhat dilapidated Buddhist monastery. **Landi Kotal** itself is a bustling colourful market town with everything from smuggled electrical goods to drugs. Eight kilometres further on is the border town of **Torkham**, although foreigners are only allowed as far as **Michni check post**, a little beyond Landi Kotal.

Built by the British in the 1920s, the **Khyber Railway** is a remarkable feat of engineering, with 34 tunnels and 92 bridges and culverts. At one point it climbs 130 m in just over 1 km, passing through a series of switchbacks with reversing stations and requiring an additional steam engine at the back to help push the train up the steep gradient. Regular passenger services were discontinued some years ago due to insufficient usage (in practical terms it is very slow, prompting most locals to travel by bus). Recently however, **Sehrai Travels and Tours** have managed to reinstate a 'Khyber Steam Safari' for the benefit of tourists. The train normally operates at least twice a month, except in summer. This is a full-day outing costing Rs4,985 per person (including return trip by rail, refreshments en route, lunch at Landi Kotal and guided sightseeing). For more details contact **Sehrai Travels and Tours** (see Peshawar, Activities and tours). See page 111 and 112 for sleeping and eating options.

Darra Adam Khel

Darra is the biggest centre of indigenous arms manufacture in NWFP (and Pakistan for that matter). Home to the Adam Afridi tribe or *khel*, the town consists almost entirely of gun shops where working replicas of anything from pen-guns to Kalashnikovs are meticulously fashioned with only the most primitive of machine tools. These gun-making skills are thought to have arrived here in the 1890s with a Punjabi gunsmith who was wanted for murder and settled in the town, beyond the reach of the authorities. Still beyond the reach of the authorities in the 21st century, the artisans of Darra continue to produce small arms, despite attempts by the government to persuade them to make kitchen utensils instead. Meanwhile, the drugs factories and heavy arms workshops have all now moved deeper into tribal territory to avoid detection by the police and army.

Ins and outs

Darra is situated 42 km south of Peshawar on the Kohat Road. Regularly, Darra is declared off limits to foreigners, but since nothing is cast in stone in Pakistan it is worth checking the current situation at PTDC in Peshawar. If 'open', foreigners are required to obtain a permit from the Civil Secretariat of the Home Department in

Peshawar in order to visit. These are rarely, if ever, issued so most people ignore the regulations, without complications. There are regular buses and Hiace minibuses to Darra which depart from the Sada-Bahar bus stand to the south of the Old City on Kohat Road (see Peshawar transport, page 113). The journey takes around 45 minutes, and upon arrival you will be met by a 'local official' (so-called 'tribal police') who will show you around and keep an eye on you. Expect to be asked for Rs100-200 baksheesh upfront, depending on how well dressed you are. You are permitted to fire off pretty much anything you can afford (a full Kalashnikov clip costs about Rs500-600, again depending on your attire, it seems), but whatever the temptation, **do not buy anything** as a souvenir – you will almost certainly be searched on the return journey. Any northbound bus passing through Darra will get you to Peshawar. **NB** Sehrai Travels and Tours offers a day trip to a similar village in the Swat Valley when they deem Darra to be too risky.

Sleeping

Each of Peshawar's districts has its own advantages and disadvantages. The **Saddar/Cantonment** area is in many ways the most practical; here you are centrally located, with much of the city's commercial activity right on your doorstep. The **Old City** is excellent if you want to be right in the thick of it, but be warned that most of the hotels here are very noisy (unless you can get a room at the back, away from the road), and you are also in the thick of some of the worst atmospheric pollution in Pakistan. The **GT Road** is also very noisy and polluted, despite being convenient for long-distance transport, and in some instances within easy walking distance of the Old City. **University Town** and **Hayatabad** are really only of use as a base if you have business in this area, being a long way from both the Old City and Saddar/Cantonment.

Saddar/Cantonment *p103, map p104*
Most of the following have basic restaurants or can provide meals to order, but it's probably best to go outside for something approaching quality food.
B-C Greens, Saddar Rd, T091-276035, F091-276088. Most established hotel in the area but not the warmest welcome (resting on the laurels of its reputation). Standard rooms leave a lot to be desired (cockroaches seen in the wash basin). De luxe a/c rooms are much better value and more comfortable, but still a bit pricey. Lala's Grill and Greens Bakery provide decent sustenance, while the lobby houses a business centre, gift shop and a British Airways office.
D-E Khani's, Saddar Rd, T091-277513, khanishotel@hotmail.com. Decent enough carpeted rooms with dish TV, with or without a/c. Separate **Romania** restaurant.
G Five Star, Sunehri Masjid Rd, T091-276950. Cleaner than most, but very noisy with busy mosque opposite. Not unfriendly, but not recommended.
G Paradise, Sunehri Masjid Rd. 2 reception desks face each other across a dilapidated dining hall, each offering a different choice of similarly bad rooms in a hot, humid atmosphere. Bed bugs suspected. Great for a sauna and sociological study but nothing else. Avoid.
G Shahzad, Saddar Rd, T091-275741. More spacious than others in its class, but suffers from seatless western toilet syndrome, so strengthen those leg muscles in advance.
G Sheri, Khadim Shaheed Rd, T091-278449. Smiley manager oblivious to the living ant hill which is his hotel. Unaware of pretty much everything else, the manager hosts guests in basic, noisy, windowless rooms. The epitome of cheap and cheerful, although the only thing cheerful about this place is the boss.
G Sinbad, Saddar Rd, T091-275020. Grubby, noisy rooms, marginally quieter away from road but without natural light. The saving grace is the choice of five breakfasts.
G Skyline, Sunehri Masjid Rd, T091-270507.

● *For an explanation of sleeping and eating price codes used in this guide, see inside the front cover. Other relevant information is found in Essentials, pages 36-38.*

Noisy, basic, not too clean, best avoided.
G Wahid, off Saddar Rd. Basic, box-like rooms, quieter than those on the road but nothing else to recommend it.
G-H Tourist Inn Motel, 3 Saddar Rd, T091-279156. Excellent place to swap travellers' diseases in 1 of 3 filthy, dingy, bumper-to-bumper dorms (Rs100 per charpoy) offering little respite from the summer heat. Conditions are reminiscent of several POW films. Also 3 basic double rooms, common toilet and shower facilities shared by all. No food, which is possibly a blessing. Despite all this, it remains popular with budget travellers and is often full, although we have received several readers' letters recounting various horror-stories (usually involving heroin trafficking).

Old City *p102, map p103*

Do not be tempted to walk down Railway Rd to the large **Aman** and **Mengal** hotels. Neither accept foreigners.
A Khan Klub, PO Box 468, New Rampura Gate (Nevay Darwaza), T091-2567156, khan@khanclub.psh.brain.net.pk. Unique hotel, unlike anything else in Pakistan. Housed in a beautifully restored 200-year-old Sikh haveli, the 8 rooms are individually furnished and decorated using colourful, locally produced materials. A different semi-precious stone forms the central theme for each room (The Ruby Suite, Garnet Room etc), complemented by carefully chosen embroidered silks, carved wooden furniture, hand-knotted carpets etc. Downstairs there is an excellent traditional Pathan-style restaurant (see Eating). Highly recommended. Book ahead.
D-F Park Inn, near Shuba Chowk, Khyber Bazaar, T091-2560048, F091-2569172. Reasonable, comfortable rooms which could be cleaner, rates include breakfast, but watch out for the 15% tax. Rooms without a/c are better value, while those at rear are quieter, still overpriced.
D-F Rose, Shuba Chowk, Khyber Bazaar, T091-250757. Reasonable but noisy rooms, those with fan and attached bath not bad value (but double price for a/c). One of the few hotels regularly refurbished, so it is pretty clean throughout. Not a bad choice when building work not in progress.
G Eastern Palace, Cinema Rd, T091-215948. Very friendly reception when the owner's son is at the desk, but it's all downhill from there. Rooms cramped, with no natural light, clean sheets merely offset grubbiness of walls, while the western toilets are used in the eastern style.
G Gulf, Cinema Rd, T091-210103. Run-down rooms but friendly to Urdu speakers.
G Jamal, Bajori Gate, T091-213665. Small, cleanish rooms with bath in a decaying building on a noisy chowk.
G Noor, Mewa Mandi, Bajori Bazaar, T091-210916. Clean (recently repainted), cell-like, but bearable rooms with attached bath. De luxe rooms are the same with TV.
G Razmak (was Gohar Palace), Cinema Road, T091-217562, F091-2568883. Grubby rooms with bath and the claim to fame of being the narrowest bathrooms in Peshawar. Not worth a detour.
G Relax Inn, Cinema Rd, T091-215623. Musty, humid rooms with bathrooms which are better than the sleeping area (that's not to say that the bathrooms are clean.)
G Shan, Khyber Bazaar, T091-210668. Room rates rise for the dubious luxury of filthy, fitted carpets, so it's better to stay in the cheaper choice which also forgoes a shower for a bucket and jug. Rooms at rear avoid road noise, but basic facilities throughout and suspect security.
G-H De Luxe, down small alley off Qissa Khwani Bazaar, T091-216907. Ironic name for this basic of basic affairs, frequented by followers of the Taliban. Rooms are with or without bath but the cheaper choice is often all that is available. It can be very noisy as the hotel seems to be used as a thoroughfare in itself and is right in the thick of the bazaar, so may appeal to the more adventurous. Definitely **not** for single women.

GT Road *map p103*

L Pearl Continental, PO Box 197, Khyber Rd, T091-276361, hotelpsh@pes.comsats.net.pk. One of BBC journalist John Simpson's favourite places. Peshawar's only international-class hotel (although things like bathroom fittings are tattier than you'd expect), all rooms have central a/c, IDD, attached hot bath, private safe, dish TV etc. 3 good restaurants including weekend barbeque. The **Gulbar** serves alcohol to non-Muslim foreigners (show passport at bar) in a soulless atmosphere. Pool and gym available to non-residents at a price. As far removed from the old bazaars as can be, perfect if you are scared/tired of the outside world and have money to burn.

D North West Heritage, Firdous Chowk, GT Rd, T091-215881, F091-2565688, heritage@psh.infolink.net.pk. Spotless a/c rooms set around a quiet central courtyard with attached bath and dish TV, breakfast included. Restaurant menu includes 'wild sparrows, in season'. Helpful reception staff, well run, best in its class. Recommended.

D-G Amin, GT Rd, T091-218215. Not the best de luxe rooms in the class: western toilets without seats, a/c and dish TV. Some much cheaper doubles, new mid-range rooms may be worth trying out.

D-G Hidayat, Firdous Chowk, GT Rd, T091-217839, F091-2566634. Decent enough, comfortable rooms each with a minor DIY project to while away any spare time. Pseudo-plush 'de luxe' rooms with noisy a/c and dish TV, cheaper rooms may need cleaning before occupancy. Restaurant/room service with limited but adequate menu. Helpful and friendly room staff. Could be cleaner but is a reasonable, slightly cheaper alternative to North West Heritage next door.

D-G Shelton, GT Rd, T091-252337, F091-253103. Friendly reception does little to disguise overpriced and noisy rooms which, although cleanish, are dark. Cheaper rooms without TV are better value.

E-G Shangri La (not part of the chain), Firdous Chowk, T091-216409. Contains a selection of non-descript, noisy rooms ranging from cheap to overpriced with a/c.

E-G Three Star, GT Rd, T091-218160. Some decent, clean rooms with recently refurbished attached bath. Cheaper rooms are small and come with a very noisy air cooler, while 'de luxe' rooms sport a marginally quieter a/c system and dish TV.

E-G Zabeel Palace, GT Rd, T091-218236. De luxe rooms with dish TV and disgusting bathrooms, cheaper rooms with squat toilet are more sanitary and better value, but nothing special.

University Town *p106, map p107*
B Regent Guesthouse, 44 D-A, Old Jamrud Rd, University Town, T091-840670, F091-840082. A/c, fan, TV/dish, phone, attached bath. Decent rooms, but perhaps slightly below the standard of the other guest houses.

B Shiraz Inn, University Rd, T091-845544, F091-840497. Has received some good reports, especially the restaurant.

B VIP Guesthouse, Old Bara Rd, University Town, T/F091-843392. A/c, fan, TV/dish, attached bath. Comfortable, nicely furnished and well run.

C Decent Lodge, 62 D/A Syed Jamaluddin Afghani Rd, T091-840221, F091-840229. A/c, fan, TV/dish, attached bath. Comfortable and nicely furnished.

C Rivoli Guesthouse, Rehman Baba Rd, University Town, T091-841483, F091-844369. A/c, fan, TV/dish, phone, attached bath. Comfortable and well furnished.

Hayatabad *p106*
H Youth Hostel, Block B1, Plot 37, Phase 5, Hayatabad, T091-813581 (heading west past Islamia College, after crossing the Kabul River Canal, take second turning left off the GT Rd into Hayatabad, then first right; situated near water tower and National Bank of Pakistan building). Several large dorm rooms and some 3-4-bed rooms, kitchen, common room, basic but clean and good value. A long way from Saddar and the Old City (but walking distance from GT Rd and public transport), no shops nearby as yet. Small garden, parking. Camping also allowed.

Khyber Pass *p107*
PTDC Motel at Torkham, although at the time of writing, foreigners are not allowed to stay overnight.

● Eating

Peshawar is a great place to sample a Pathan favourite, the **chapli kebab**. This consists of a large, round, flat burger made with mince, chopped onions, eggs and tomato and served with naan. It certainly puts all western burgers to shame. Other meat dishes include tikka, karahi and 'roast' (usually lamb). There are lots of good cheap Pakistani-style restaurants and food stalls in the old bazaars around **Fowara Chowk**. **Namak Mandi** (Bajori Rd) has lots of excellent tikka stalls and restaurants. There are also lots of cheap places along GT Rd. **Vegetarian food** is limited to the usual daal and simple vegetable curries. Afghani pilau rice is a good variation, but take care as a 'veg pilau' often also contains meat. The Chinese restaurants listed below have a reasonable selection of vegetarian dishes. Despite the quality of Peshawar's home-grown 'fast food' offerings such as chapli kebabs, there still seems to be plenty of demand for western-style fast food.

Saddar/Cantonment *p103, map p104*

Lala Grill, Greens, Saddar Rd, T091-276035. More moderate restaurant and you can eat well for around Rs200-300 per head.

4 Season and **Jani**, on Arbab Rd in Saddar both serve the usual fare of burgers, chips, milkshakes etc.

Kennedy Fried Chicken, on Saddar Rd offers much the same.

The Shiraz, on Saddar Rd, serves good fast food in clean surroundings. Eat well here for Rs100-200.

The Silver Star, also on Saddar Rd, attempts something of a fusion between western and Pakistani fast food, serving roasted chickens, chicken spring rolls and various deep fried 'patties' of lentils, cheese.

The Honey Bakers, next door to Standard Chartered Grindlays bank on The Mall, is also good. There are several others along the central part of Saddar Rd.

Jan's Bakery, Saddar Rd, is a firm favourite with backpackers staying at the Tourist Inn Motel immediately behind.

Pak Bakers, near the PIA office, on the corner on Shahrah-e-Quaid Rd, a mini supermarket-style shop with bread, cakes and sweets among other items.

Old City *p102, map p103*

Khan Klub, T091-2567156, boasts a beautiful restaurant, traditionally furnished with low tables and cushions strewn on the floor. Serving Afghani and Pakistani cuisine, it has been listed as being among the top 10 restaurants in Pakistan by *The News*. There are live music performances (Rabbab and Tabla) at lunch and dinner. Meals cost in the region of Rs300-350 per head. Advance booking is essential. Highly recommended.

Salateen, on Cinema Rd, T091-210279. Has rightly gained a reputation for excellent Peshawari food. A good meal here will cost in the region of Rs150-200 per head.

Namak Mandi (Bajori Rd) also has lots of excellent tikka stalls and restaurants and there are lots of cheap places along GT Rd.

GT Road *map p103*

Marco Polo restaurant, Pearl Continental. At the top of the range, this restaurant serves both Pakistani and continental cuisine in elegant surroundings for around Rs500 per head. There is also an outdoor Terrace BBQ during summer weekends (Thu-Sun). The fixed-price evening buffets are great value; check with the hotel as to when these are offered.

University Town *p106, map p107*

The Shiraz, a little further along Jamrud Rd on the same side, is very similar with Pakistani food, but slightly more expensive.

Usmania, along Jamrud Rd, heading towards University Town. A comfortable a/c restaurant serving good Pakistani and continental cuisine for Rs100-200 per head.

Afghan, Serving kebabs, pilau etc.

Azad Afghan, further along on the opposite side, similar food.

Khyber Pass *p107*

Sehrai Travels and Tours, 12-A Saddar Rd, T091-272085, sehrai@netzone.net.pk, are due to open a restaurant at Landi Kotal train station to coincide with Khyber Railway trips.

Entertainment

If you are looking for a drink, the only above-board place where you can get one is at the Pearl Continental's **Gulbar**, which is open to non-Muslim foreigners daily 1000-2400. Simply show your non-Muslim passport and the bar staff will serve you with time-honoured grumpiness. The bar is usually empty and always totally lacking in atmosphere, except for when journalists or international cricket teams are in town. A bottle of Murree beer costs around Rs200.

The **music** put on each day in the **Khan Klub**'s restaurant is of a very high standard. If you fancy sampling an authentic Pakistani cinematic experience, the various **cinemas** in the Old City's Cinema Rd all have the usual selection of lurid films on offer (not recommended for women). It is worth asking at PTDC for information on any special cultural events which may be taking place.

▲ Activities and tours

The Afghan game of *bushkazi*, a more violent version of polo, using a beheaded calf, or young goat, instead of a ball and mallets, is often played during the winter months (late Nov-mid-Feb). There are several grounds around Peshawar and games, which are usually played on Sun (occasionally on Fri afternoons), are often advertised in the main tourist hotels by the PTDC.
Arbab Niaz Stadium, near Shahi Gardens, is Peshawar's international cricket venue. There is also a polo ground here.
The Garrison Club has the oldest and best swimming pool, although it is unfortunately not open to the general public.
Peshawar Golf Course, off Shami Rd. Open for guests at the Pearl Continental. Non-guests are allowed to use the Pearl Continental's swimming pool or gym for a fee.
Qayum Stadium, Cantonment, may now be a better option than that below to join in games with the locals.
Wazir Bagh, south of the Old City is a good place to watch (and join in) informal cricket, basketball, badminton, football, kabadi etc on Friday and Saturday evenings, although encroachment by buildings have reduced the space available for enjoying sports.

Tour operators
Gandhara Travels, Saddar Rd, T091-273832, F091-273124. Domestic and international flights, hotel reservations. Reliable service.
Sehrai Travels and Tours, 12-A Saddar Rd, T091-272085, F091-286077, sehrai@netzone.net.pk. Efficient and helpful, specializing in large group tours, but also offering tailor-made packages for individuals/small groups. Responsible for organizing the 'Khyber Steam Safari' (see under 'Around Peshawar', below). Also offers standard trips up to the Khyber Pass, and walking tours of the Old City. Full ticketing service for international and domestic flights.
United Travels, 6 Saddar Rd, T091-277101, F091-277105, is also worth trying for flights.

Shopping

The bazaars of the Old City are the most fascinating place to hunt for everything from carpets to spices. Note that they more or less completely close down on Fri, particularly in the afternoon. **Saddar Bazaar** has many tourist shops selling a wide range of antiques, jewellery, carpets, furniture, embroidery etc. Prices tend to be higher than in the Old City, although there is plenty of room for bargaining. A few are fixed-price. **The Outlet Venture** shop in Saddar Rd, next door to Jan's Bakery, upstairs, sponsored by the Ockenden Trust, sells high-quality carpets, rugs, embroidery, jewellery etc, all made by Afghan refugees. Prices are fixed, and on the high side, but you can browse without having to worry about any hard sell.

Bookshops
There are several bookshops on Arbab Rd, in Saddar, including:
Emjay Books, a good bet for international magazines.
London Book Co, specializes mostly in academic texts.
Saeed Book Bank, by far the best, with a good selection of books in English.
University Book Agency, on Khyber Bazaar in the Old City, is the best of several bookshops here, with a wide range of books on Pakistan's history and politics.

There are a number of **photography** shops in Saddar selling films, batteries etc, but processing rates are high.

Transport

Air
Peshawar Airport, T091-273081.
The easiest way to get to and from the airport is by taxi or auto-rickshaw. From Saddar, you should not pay more than Rs30 for an auto-rickshaw, or Rs60 for a taxi. These rates may be higher at night.

Domestic PIA operates regular domestic flights to **Islamabad** 2 or 3 times daily, **Karachi** up to 3 times a day and **Lahore** at least once a day. Heavily oversubscribed flights to **Quetta** operate each day except Tue and Sat. Flights to **Dera Ismail Khan** via Zhob are allegedly available on Wed, Sat and Sun; to **Multan** on Tue and Sat; to **Saidu Sharif** on Mon, Wed and Fri. The most popular service offered by PIA is the twice daily Fokker F27 flights to **Chitral**, (Rs2,740) although this is weather-dependent and often cancelled. If this happens, ticket holders must return to the PIA office to reconfirm for the next day's flight, or otherwise get a full refund and take alternative transport. **Aero Asia** operates flights to **Karachi** 3 times a week (Rs4,295).

International Aero Asia operates direct flights from Peshawar to **Dubai** via Abu Dhabi on Mon and Fri and to **Al-Ain/Doha** on Sat. **Emirates** flies to **Dubai** on Tue and Thu with connections to **London** and **Istanbul** as well as several of the Middle Eastern states. **Gulf Air** serves **Abu Dhabi** on Mon and Wed. PIA operates flights from Peshawar to **Abu Dhabi** (Wed), **Doha** (Fri and Sun), **Dubai** (daily), **Jeddah** (Tue), **Kuwait** (Sun) and **Riyadh** (Tue, Sat). Qatar Airways connects Peshawar with **Doha** 3 times a week.

NB Schedules change regularly, so check with airline regarding flight times and additional destinations.

Airline offices

Domestic Aero Asia, Saddar Rd, T111-515151, F091-278272. **PIA**, 33 The Mall, Cantt (entrance in Arbab Rd), T091-9212371-9, Reservations T212 or T242. Main desks open daily 0800-1800. For Chitral flights go to the 'Northern Areas Ticketing Counter' on the left side of the building 0900-1700. Both counters close for Friday prayers 1300-1400. **Shaheen Air International**, 16 Fakhr-e-Alam Rd, Cantt, T091-278409, F091-278427, airport T091-279125.

International Air France, GSA Capitol Travels, Pearl Continental Hotel, T091-273386. **British Airways**, GSA Aviona, Greens Hotel, Saddar Rd, T091-273252. **Emirates**, 95-B Saddar Rd, T091-275912, F091-276374. **Gulf**, GSA Marhaba Aviation, 8/9 Cantonment Plaza, Fakhr-e-Alam Rd, T091-287101, F091-287073. **Qatar**, next to Greens Hotel, Saddar Rd, T091-287083 or T111-310310, F091-287419, qrpew@brain.net.pk. **Saudi**, GSA Southern Travels, 6 Islamia Rd (opposite Jan's Shopping Arcade), Cantt, T091-285071, F091-285072, jangli@brain.net.pk.

Auto-rickshaws

These are the most ubiquitous form of local transport after the buses. The fare from the centre of Saddar to Khyber Bazaar in the Old City is around Rs25-30.

Bus

Local The main artery of public transport is between Hayatabad/University Town and the main bus station on the GT Rd. See the 'Peshawar Overview' map for the route. Note that heading from Saddar towards the GT Rd, buses go straight along Sunheri Masjid Rd, past the Cantonment railway station and Peshawar Museum, before turning into GT Rd near Bala Hisar fort.

Coming from the main bus station on the GT Rd, they turn left just before the Bala Hisar fort, passing right through the heart of the Old City via Khyber Bazaar and Shuba Chowk, and then continue along the south side of the railway line before crossing it by the bridge southwest of the railway station and turning left into Sunheri Masjid Rd.

The number 3 bus goes as far as the **Sada-Bahar bus station** on Kohat Rd, the number 5 goes to **Charsadda Adha**. All other local buses follow the above route.

Main (General) Bus Station This seemingly daunting bus station spreads for over half a km along the GT Rd, 3 km to the east of Bala Hisar Fort. Vehicles leave from here to the north towards **Mardan, Takht-e-Bhai, Mingora/Saidu Sharif, Timargarha** and **Dir**. This is also the place to come to for Hiaces and non a/c buses to all points along the GT Road as far as **Lahore**, including the 2-hr journey to **Rawalpindi**. As you approach from GT Rd you will find Hiaces to the left, larger coasters and regular buses on the right. Finding the right bus is simply a matter of asking someone who will point you in the right direction amid the chaos. Quite often you will be shown to an empty Hiace, which the driver and conductor will then fill, waiting time depending on the popularity of your chosen route. An auto-rickshaw from here to Firdous Chowk should be Rs20, to Saddar Rs35.

Roadways House Bus Station
Situated about 1 km east of Bala Hisar on GT Rd, this bus station is in theory exclusively used by a/c services. Several companies (with agents sat at desks) offer a/c services to **Karachi** (Rs500, 24 hrs), **Lahore** (Rs212, 8 hrs) and **Rawalpindi** (Rs85, 2 hrs), while New Qadri runs a daily service to **Quetta** (Rs450, 24 hrs). You can also find a/c services to **Faisalabad** and **Multan** here. On the forecourt in front of the bus station on GT Rd, you can sometimes pick up regular non-a/c services to **Rawalpindi** and **Mingora**.

Charsadda Adha Situated on the Charsadda Road to the north of Shahi Bagh. Local buses operate from here to **Charsadda**, occasionally continuing on to **Mardan**, although for the latter, it is much quicker to get a Hiace minibus from the main bus station.

Chitral Hiaces At the time of writing there were 3 companies based around the Qissa Khwani Bazaar (Old City) running nightly services to **Chitral**. Chitral Coach Union, T091-210503 has an office in the Spogmay Hotel, **Mayoon Coach**, T091-215545, is based in the Sultan Hotel on Qissa Khwani Bazaar and **Shaheen Coach**, T091-219516, can be found in nearby Chitrali Bazaar. All charge Rs250 for the 12-hr journey, leaving at 2000 each night. These timings (and indeed companies) change from time to time, so check with PTDC who carry up-to-date information. If the prospect of this gruelling (and hair-raising) overnight trip does not appeal, a much better option is to take a Hiace from the Main Bus Station as far as **Dir** (you may need to change in **Timargarha**), spend the night there, then continue the next day.

Sada-Bahar Bus Station Known locally as 'Ghaas Phul' or 'Wahokh Phul' (literally 'Grass Bridge' in Urdu and Pashto respectively), and situated on Kohat Rd south of the bypass, this bus terminus serves **Quetta** and the southern districts. Hiace minibuses operate from here to **Kohat** (Rs20, 1½ hours) via **Darra**.

NB You are allowed to travel direct to Kohat, even if Darra is closed to foreigners, providing you do not get off at Darra. There are also various old buses and Hiace minibuses going as far as Darra only, and on to **Hangu** and **Thal** (west of Kohat), and **Bannu** (southwest of Kohat). Coaches also operate from here to **Quetta**; they go first to **Dera Ismail Khan**, then follow the east bank of the Indus, before crossing again at **Sukkur** to go through **Jacobabad** and **Sibi**. Minimum journey time is around 30 hrs.

Car
Car hire (with driver) is available from the major hotels, or can be arranged through PTDC (Rs3,000 per day inclusive for 4WD a/c land cruisers).

Taxi
Found at the airport, outside major hotels, and around Saddar; there is a taxi rank on Fakhr-e-Alam Rd, between Sunheri Masjid and Saddar Rds.

Train
Cantonment Railway Station, T091-9211106 for reservations, or T117 for enquiries. Note that sleepers and a/c must be booked well in advance; they often sell out as soon as they go on sale (15 days before the departure date). The reservation office is open in summer 0800-1930, opening half an hour later in winter; closed for Fri prayers 1230 and 1400. Tickets for foreign tourists are discounted by 25%, whilst ISIC holders are eligible for half-price reductions (go to the Commercial Dept for your certificate).

Rawalpindi: all the services listed below to Quetta and Karachi (with the exception of the Khushal Khan Khattak Exp) stop in Rawalpindi. They take between 3½ and 4 hrs. There is also the much slower 212 Passenger, 1200, 6 hrs, which stops at all stations en route, including **Taxila**. Note that trains are liable to lengthy searches when crossing into Punjab.

Lahore: all the services listed below to Quetta and Karachi (with the exception of the Chenab Exp and Khushal Khan Khattak Exp) stop in Lahore. They take between 9½ and 10¾ hrs. The 212 Passenger takes 18 hrs for this journey.

Karachi: Awam Exp (via **'Pindi** and **Lahore**), 0845, 32 hrs; Khyber Mail (via **'Pindi** and **Lahore**), 2230, 32½ hrs; Chenab

Exp (via **'Pindi**, **Sarghodha**, **Faisalabad** and **Multan**), 2030, 39 hrs; Khushal Khan Khattak Exp (via **Attock**, **Kundian**, **DG Khan**, **Jacobabad** and **Larkana**), 1800, 38 hrs.

Quetta: Abaseen Exp (via **Lahore**), 1700, takes a mammoth 39 hrs.

Directory

Peshawar p99

Banks Habib Bank, Saddar Rd. Provides a fairly efficient foreign exchange service for both cash and TCs. **Muslim Commercial Bank**, on Arbab Rd, Saddar, has a 24-hr ATM giving cash on MasterCard and Maestro cards. **National Bank of Pakistan**, Saddar Rd boasts a 24-hr ATM which accepts Visa cards. It also changes TCs at Rs100 commission for US$, Rs500 for £ Sterling, even if the cheques are from the same company. **Standard Chartered Grindleys**, The Mall (opposite junction with Arbab Rd). Fixed fee of Rs500 to exchange TCs. No charge for cash. Able to give cash advances against Visa cards. There are numerous money changers to be found around Chowk Yadgar in the Old City. They are authorized by the State Bank to deal in foreign currency, both cash and TCs, and at the time of writing were offering dramatically better rates than the banks. You are also likely to be approached by unofficial money changers around Saddar; generally they will also try to sell you anything from carpets to hashish, and are best avoided. **Chemists** All the hospitals listed have their own dispensaries, and there are numerous chemists dotted around Saddar and the Old City. **Courier DHL**, 1080 Saddar Rd, T091-277418, F091-277417. **Dentists** Opposite the Sherpao there is a free but crowded Dental Hospital, or there are private dentists in Saddar Rd. **Embassies and consulates Afghan Consulate**, 17-C Gulmohar Lane, University Town, T091-285962. When run by the Taliban, visas were issued freely; current situation is less clear. **Iranian Consulate**, 18 Park Av, University Town, T091-845403. It may be possible to obtain transit visas here, but at the time of writing the best place to do so was in Quetta. However, it is worth checking for yourself before heading off into Baluchistan as the situation can easily change without warning. **USA Consulate**, 11 Hospital Rd, Cantt, T091-285496; Mon-Fri 0800-1630. **Hospitals** The Sherpao (also known as The Khyber Teaching Hospital or Hayat Shaheed), University Town, T091-9216340, and **Lady Reading**, Hospital Rd, Old City, T091-9211430, are the 2 largest, each with over 1,000 beds. **Mission**, Dubgari Gate, Old City, T091-9217140, is the least crowded of the main hospitals. **The Hayatabad Medical Complex**, Hayatabad, T091-818040, has a good reputation, but it is a long way from the centre of town. **The Cantonment General**, Sunheri Masjid Rd, Saddar, T091-9211825 is OK for minor problems. **The Khyber Medical Centre**, Dubgari Gate, T091-211241, is a good private hospital. There are several private practitioners around Dubgari Gate, and also in Doctor Plaza, Saddar Rd, opposite Greens Hotel. **Internet** Many cyber cafés are mushrooming around Saddar, generally charging Rs20-Rs30 per hr. University Road in University Town has a number of good facilities, but also a large number of students wanting to use them. **Libraries ARIC** (Afghan Resource and Information Centre, see Useful addresses below) has an excellent library/resource centre focusing on Afghan issues. As well as the libraries in the various cultural centres (see above), there is the **Department of Archives and Public Libraries**, next door to Peshawar Museum, T091-278944, which has an extensive collection of archival materials (of interest mostly to researchers and those with a specific area of interest). **Post** GPO, Saddar Rd. 0900-1900, Fri 0900-1200, closed Sun. Poste Restante service available. **Telephone** (Pak Telecom), 2 The Mall. Open 24 hrs 7 days. Local/international phone, fax, telegram, cable. Note that faxes can only be sent between 0900-2400, when the man responsible for the fax machine is present. Otherwise there are plenty of private PCOs around Saddar. **Useful addresses ACBAR** (Agency Coordinating Body on Afghan Refugees): PO Box 1084, 2 Rehman Baba Rd, University Town, T091-44392, F091-840471. Also the location of **ARIC** (Afghan Resource and Information Centre). **Cultural centres** Alliance

Francaise, 1 Park Av, University Town, T091-843928. **British Council**, 17-C Chinar Rd, University Town, T091-841921, F091-842633. The library (Mon-Fri 1200-1800) is geared up mainly towards providing information on study in the UK, but also has a good selection of British newspapers and international magazines. Internet access also available. **Garrison Club** (formerly the Peshawar Club), Sir Sayid Rd, near The Mall, T091-9212753. Established in 1863 for the armed forces. The Garrison Club is really for members and guests only, but you can look around the library and buildings. Facilities include tennis, squash, billiards, gym and swimming pool.

Foreigners living in Peshawar are allowed to apply for temporary membership. **Foreigners' Registration Office Special Branch**, near Shaheen Camp, T091-9210508, Mon-Sat 0800-1300. **Police** T091-9212222, Emergency T15 or T16 in Cantonment. Fire T091-279074. **Political Agent, Khyber**: (For those wanting permits for Khyber Pass), Stadium Rd, T091-9211902-3. Mon-Sat 0900-1200. Passport Office: (For visa extensions), Charsadda Rd (opposite Idgar), T091-9212516. Mon-Thu and Sat 0900-1400, Fri 0900-1200. **UNHCR** (UN High Commissioner for Refugees) Gulmohar Lane, University Town, T091-842376.

Peshawar to Chitral → *Colour map 1, grid C2-A1*

Following a Rawalpindi/Islamabad-Peshawar-Chitral-Gilgit route around Pakistan makes a lot of sense, allowing you to see some of the most appealing regions of the country before sampling the delights of the upper reaches of the Karakoram Highway (see suggested itineraries on page 12). In many regards, the Chitral Valley is the most isolated region of NWFP, physically and perhaps culturally too, and draws less visitors than Hunza, Gojal, Baltistan and other areas accessible from the KKH. However, in terms of natural beauty and trekking opportunities it is far from second best, and a visit here perfectly complements a journey along the KKH. ▶▶ *For Sleeping, Eating and all other listings, see pages 121-123.*

Ins and outs

There are two overland routes into Chitral: from Gilgit on a rough jeep track over the Shandur Pass (for further details, see page 149); and the route from Peshawar described below, over the Lowari Pass. Because of snow on the 3,118-m Lowari Pass, this route is closed from late November until May, making the daily Fokker F27 flights between Peshawar and Chitral the main link with the outside world (although even these are subject to frequent bad weather cancellations, even in summer). The only land route into Chitral that is passable in winter detours the Lowari Pass via Afghanistan, but it is usually closed to foreigners for obvious reasons. This route follows the route of the Chitral river, so it is in fact, geographically speaking, part of the Chitral Valley.

While the future of Afghanistan remains uncertain, the possibility of foreigners legitimately using this route in winter is unsure. However, during the last five or six years the Lowari Pass has been blocked for a shorter period of time, usually from December to March/April. If this local climate change continues into a pattern, then the Chitrali people may soon be able to travel home in winter without having to go abroad! Meanwhile, there is still talk of a tunnel that will bypass the Lowari Pass, but it remains just that – talk.

Most people tackle the overland route from Peshawar to Chitral in one long day, or take a night's break at Dir (although Naghar is a far more attractive option). There are, however, a number of points of minor interest along the way which are described below. ▶▶ *See Transport, page 122, for more details.*

Peshawar to Chakdara

The early stages of the journey from Peshawar to Chitral pass through some places of great historical significance, notably from the Gandharan Buddhist period (eg Charsadda and Takht-e-Bhai). Full details of these places (normally visited as an excursion from Peshawar) can be found in *Footprint Pakistan*.

Most buses from Peshawar head east along the GT Road before turning north at Nowshera for **Mardan**. However, if cycling this route it's marginally quieter to head 28 km northeast from Peshawar to **Charsadda** (with its Gandharan history) and then a further 22 km northeast to Mardan (an important military base for the last 200 years).

From Mardan, the road leads northwest for 14 km to **Takht-e-Bhai** (with its famous Gandharan Buddhist monastery), and then turns due north over the **Malakand Pass**; this was the scene of the Malakand Campaign of 1897 that is

Peshawar to Chitral

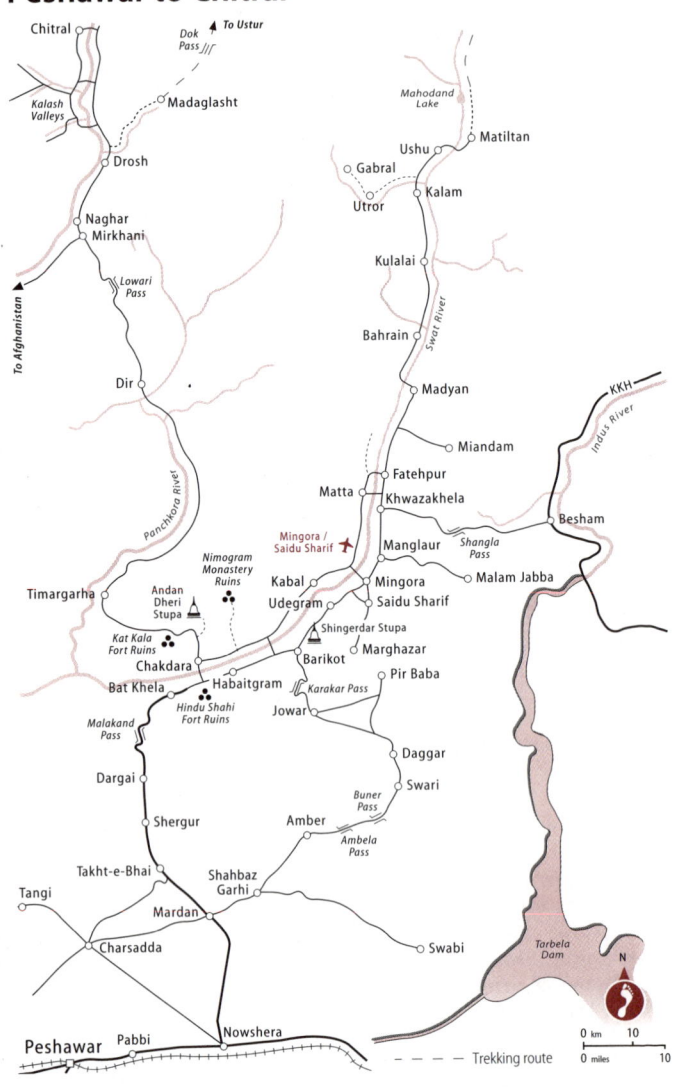

described in gushing detail by Winston Churchill (*My Early Life* and *The Malakand Field Force*). The British-built fort can still be seen at the top of the pass. This road is also the more popular route into the Swat Valley.

Once over the pass, the road descends northeast via **Bat Khela** (with the ruined Hindu Shahi fort to the east) before turning north and crossing the Swat River.

Chakdara

The bridge across the Swat River at Chakdara marks the start of Dir District, which existed as an independent kingdom for many centuries before being incorporated into Pakistan following independence. The people of Dir District are predominantly Yusufzai Pathans and away from the main road the region is today still subject only to tribal law.

Excavations on and around **Damkot Hill**, above Chakdara, have revealed evidence of settlement as early as the second millennium BC when **Aryans** occupied the site, leaving behind distinctive black and grey pottery, wood, stone and iron utensils, and copper and gold jewellery. An Aryan graveyard was also discovered at the foot of the hill, on the north side. The site then appears to have been abandoned until around the first century AD. With the flowering of **Gandharan** culture in the region, the site became an important **Buddhist** centre, and a monastery and stupa were built on the hill. This was destroyed by **White Huns** in AD 528, and in the eighth century AD the **Hindu Shahis** built an extensive fort on the ruins. This fort appears to have housed a fully fledged town, with houses, shops, stables and blacksmiths' forges. Hindu Shahi rule lasted for over 250 years until the fort was destroyed by **Mahmoud of Ghazni**, who invaded Swat in 1001. Damkot Hill itself then appears to have remained unoccupied until the arrival of the **British**, and is remembered as the site of **Churchill's Picket** (see Winston Churchill's *My Early Life* and *The Malakand Field Force*). The hill is now occupied by the military and closed to the public.

The hill on the other side of the road is the site of the **Chakdara Fort**, built by the British in 1896, on the site of an earlier Mughal fort, built in 1586 following Akbar's campaigns in the area. It is now occupied by the Dir Scouts and closed to the public.

The small **Chakdara Museum** ① *officially daily 0830-1230, 1430-1730 in summer and 0900-1300, 1400-1600 in winter; in practice you may have to track down the chowkidar, free*, has some beautiful pieces and deserves the same treatment as at Saidu Sharif. The central hall contains many small statues and small and medium-sized friezes, some very beautifully carved and well preserved. There are also some stucco pieces and one terracotta figure very similar to those found at Mehrghar in Baluchistan. However, there is no attempt to date or locate any of the pieces. The hall to the left contains impressive traditional embroidered costumes, antique guns and swords, tribal jewellery of silverwork and semi precious stones and a display of funeral burial items, all gathered from sites around lower Swat.

Chakdara to Dir

Around 8 km beyond Chakdara there is a turning right which leads to the ruins of **Andan Dehri Stupa**, less than a kilometre from the main road. Only the base remains, but it is believed to have been 24 m tall and one of the most important in Swat. This side road continues on to the village of **Shewa**, beyond which, on the range of hills marking the northern border of Dir, are the ruins of the Hindu Shahi fort of **Kamal Khan China**.

The main road bears west soon after the turning for Andan Dehri, entering the Talash Valley. To the south of the road, on the low pass separating the two river valleys, there are the ruins of the Hindu Shahi fort of **Kat Kala**, identified by Sir Olaf Caroe as the site of the ancient city of **Massaga**, captured by Alexander the Great in 327 BC. The road then bears north again, joining the Panjkora River. Across the river are the Tribal Areas of Bajour Agency. The Bajouris, along with other tribal groups from surrounding areas, particularly the Mohmands, Malazai and Kohistani Pathans, were infamous to the British for their lawlessness. The present road was built by the British close to the ridge to avoid sniping gunfire from across the river. As recently as 1977 the Pakistan Air Force was firing on 'Pathan irregulars' in a dispute over timber rights, and even today the hills of Dir and Bajour are considered a hideout for bandits.

Situated 48 km from Chakdara, **Timargarha** is the headquarters of Dir District. Across the river at **Balambat** there is an archaeological site which has revealed evidence of continuous occupation since 1500 BC by Aryans, Buddhists, Hindus and Muslims. Fire altars were also discovered, on which juniper would have been burned. Despite its administrative importance (there is also a district hospital here), the town is small and unassuming and, apart from the excavations at Balambat, there is little to stop for here. It is, however, a major transport hub.

The main road continues north following the river and passing through various small bazaars, including **Khal** (18 km), where a new bridge crosses the river, **Wara** (32 km) and **Sahibabad** (41 km), with its large new mosque and bridge across the river. Shortly after **Darora** (48 km) the road crosses a bridge and turns back on itself. Buses often stop a little further on, to take advantage of a fresh spring with sweet water; this is a good spot for cyclists to fill up their water bottles. The road continues through **Bibaware** (56 km) and **Chutiatan** (Chukyatan) (72 km), before arriving at **Dir** (78 km), by which time the valley has become narrow and thickly wooded. The journey from Timargarha to Dir takes approximately two hours. Near Chutiatan, a jeep track leads east as far as the village of **Thal**, from where it is possible to trek over into the Swat Valley. This trek passes through fairly wild tribal territory; a guide, armed escort, and permission from the Deputy Commissioner in Dir is essential.

Dir town

Although not the district headquarters, Dir seems to have more political significance than Timargarha. This was the seat of power of the Nawab of Dir, whose palace stands on the hillside above the town, still occupied by his descendants during the summer. Below it, the royal guesthouse was for many years the **Dir Hotel** (although it was forced to close in 2001 due to the death of the owner). It is a small, lively town, and an obvious place to break the journey between Peshawar and Chitral. Dir is famous for its home-grown knife industry, producing distinctive small penknives as well as larger knives and daggers. There is the potential for some pleasant walks around Dir, although a reliable local guide is essential as the area is tribal.

Lowari Pass

The main road crosses the river at Dir and continues north. After about 10 km the road becomes a rough track and begins its long climb up to the Lowari Pass, passing first through the village of Qalandar. At 3,118 m, the **Lowari Pass** is generally only open from late May/early June through to October, becoming blocked by snow during winter, although this period has shortened in recent years due to local climate change. A tunnel, visible from the road near the foot of the pass, marks the start of an unfinished project which originally aimed to make the route a year-round one; questions about the technical feasibility of the tunnel, and its cost, have put the project on hold (although in 2004 the project seemed to be on the political agenda once more). The rough track climbs up to the pass in a long series of switch-backs. Near the summit on the Dir side there are a few tea stalls which also serve simple food.

The descent down the Chitral side is even more tortuous. Near the foot of the pass there is a check post at **Ziarat** where foreigners must register. The road continues past another check post at the small village of Ashriat (often by passed), before arriving at **Mirkhani**, with its fort occupied by the Chitral Scouts. Here a road forks off to the left, following the Kunar River to the Afghan border at Arandu. During winter, under a special arrangement, Pakistanis are able to travel by this route in order to bypass the Lowari, passing through the Afghan province of Nuristan before re-entering Pakistan via the Nawa Pass and rejoining the Chitral road just south of Dir, at Chutiatan. Foreigners are officially not allowed to travel by this route. It is possible, however, to cross the pass by foot when it is still closed to vehicles. It is a long hike and you should check first with locals as to the depth and condition of the snow.

Naghar

A short distance after Mirkhani there is a bridge across to the **fort** at Naghar. The fort was built in 1919 by Shuja ul-Mulk, the then Mehtar of Chitral, for one of his sons, Jhazi ul-Mulk. Today, it is still occupied by the descendants of the royal family, who have opened a small hotel, see page 122. The fort is an almost magically idyllic place to stop for a night and it is even worth contriving to do so just to spend an evening enjoying the setting and the hospitality. Most travellers enthusiastically write of Naghar as a 'paradise' in the visitors' book. The hotel has a small, delightful garden and the rooms overlook the wide swirling waters of the Chitral River, which sweeps round the outcrop of Naghar in a huge U-bend. Behind the fort there are large, well-maintained gardens and orchards of peaches, apples, plums, pears, apricots and cherries.

Drosh to Chitral

Ten kilometres north of Naghar is the town of **Drosh**, with its large fort, which is today the headquarters of the Chitral Scouts. The fort is closed to the public and there is little else of interest in the town. Just beyond Drosh is the Shishi Valley which climbs up to the northeast. This steep, thickly wooded valley is jeepable as far as the village of **Madaglasht**, and there are opportunities for trekking beyond, although a guide is essential.

The main road continues north along the east bank of the Chitral River. Shortly before the village of **Gahiret**, an old steel girder bridge crosses the river giving access to Birir, the most southerly of the three Kalash valleys. Further on there is a turning left and a bridge across to the large village of **Ayun**, the gateway to the Kalash valleys of Bumburet and Rumbur. **NB** To visit the Kalash Valleys you must first have registered in Chitral. (For details of the Kalash Valleys, see page 132.) From the turning to Ayun, it is a further 18 km to **Chitral Town**.

Sleeping

Peshawar to Chakdara p118
Charsadda
There are several basic hotels on Bank Rd, with grubby attached bathrooms (squat toilets), including **G Al-Idrees**, T0931-63339, **G Sway Mian Sahib**, T0931-6221 and **G Zaman**.

Chakdara p119
F Jamal, 1 km beyond the main bazaar on the road to Dir, T0931-761063. Clean rooms with fan and attached bath. Also some more expensive a/c rooms with TV/dish and fridge. Restaurant, small garden.

Timargarha p120
There are 3 hotels located at the southern end of town, about half a kilometre from the bus stand.

D-F Dir Continental, T0934-821528. Variety of clean, simple rooms with attached bath, although some are a bit musty, friendly and efficient staff, restaurant and welcome water cooler in reception area, reasonable for a forced night halt.

E-G Al-Imran, T0934-821343. Clean enough rooms with fan and attached bath, those with a/c more expensive, restaurant, friendly, well run, but a bit noisy.

G New Khyber, (sign in Urdu). Located between 2 other hotels, rather more basic, also with restaurant.

Dir town p120
C PTDC Motel, T0934-880900. Situated several km north of Dir at Panakot (don't believe the distance signs in town), 200 m from the main road. 4 comfortable rooms

with attached bath (hot water in evening), very pleasant garden and terrace, quiet location, friendly manager, pricey restaurant but too far from anything else to have an alternative choice.
D Green Hills, T0934-881234, F0934-881477. Situated across the bridge to the north of the main bazaar, overlooking the river. New hotel with decent rooms, attached hot bath, some with dish TV, restaurant staffed by imbeciles, spoilt by unspirited manager more interested in recouping his large investment than in providing a welcoming ambience.
E-F Al-Manzar, T0934-880607. South of the main bazaar. Simple but well-appointed rooms with attached hot bath, roof terrace and decent food, friendly and helpful manager, local tours arranged, closed in winter, advance booking sometimes necessary. Recommended.
G Abshar, T0934-880735. Next to Green Hills. Simple but clean with some new rooms in construction with riverside balcony, attached hot bath, dining hall, friendly atmosphere.
G Al Mansor, T0934-815323. Opposite Green Hills. Just 1 grubby room with fan and attached bath.
G PIA, T0934-880872, in the main bazaar. Decent, clean rooms with large attached bath, set around central courtyard, restaurant, handy for bus stand.
G Yassar Palace, T0934-880436. Next to bus stand, entrance in main bazaar. Reasonable rooms with fan and attached bath but quite noisy due to its location, which is very handy for catching last-minute buses!

Naghar *p121*
C Old Fort Tourist Resort, T05333-450 (or book through **Hindu Kush Trails** in Islamabad, T051-277067, F051-275031). There are currently 6 rooms, with more planned. Camping is also allowed, and there is a restaurant. Recommended.

Drosh *p121*
F C & W Rest House, 4 rooms.
F Javed Palace, passable accommodation. There are a few other more basic hotels located in the bazaar.

Eating

Dir town *p120*
There are some basic chai shops around the bus stand, serving simple food.

Activities and tours

Dir town *p120*
Gypsy Travel Guide, based at Al-Manzar Hotel, T0934-880607, gipsytravelguide@pakistanmail.com. A selection of tailor-made tours on offer and may be able to arrange trips to the tribal areas if they can find a burqa in your size!

Transport

Chakdara *p119*
There is no **bus** stand in Chakdara. If you stand out on the main road you can catch local public transport bound for **Mingora** or **Timargarha** (both major transport hubs). If you are heading for **Mardan** or **Peshawar**, you may be able to find space in a **Hiace minibus** coming from Chitral or Timargarha, but it may be better to cross the bridge and pick up the more frequent transport coming from Mingora.

Timargarha *p120*
The large **bus** station at Timargarha doesn't see a lot of action although you may be able to pick up a bus or coach to **Peshawar**. A smaller yard in the bazaar, just off the main road, has regular Hiace minibuses to **Dir** (Rs30, 2 hrs), **Mardan** (Rs45, 3 hrs), **Mingora** (Rs30, 2 hrs) and **Peshawar** (Rs60, 4 hrs, although it is sometimes necessary to change at Mardan for Peshawar). There are **pick-ups** available north of the bus stand in the main bazaar, past the turning across the river. **Suzukis** operate locally through the town and across the river to **Balambat**.

Dir town *p120*
The main **bus** station is in a large yard in the centre of town. Regular **Datsun pick-ups** and **Hiace minibuses** run from here north across the Lowari Pass to **Drosh**

(Rs115, 3½-4 hrs) and **Chitral** (Rs130, approximately 5 hrs). Pick-ups on this route often carry large engine parts to be delivered to trucks which have broken down on the way up to the pass, so don't wear your best shalwar kameez! Hiace minibuses for **Timargarha** (Rs30, 2 hrs, change here for Mingora/Saidu Sharif), **Mardan** (Rs75, 5 hrs) and **Peshawar** (Rs90, 6 hrs) also depart from here.

Directory

Dir town *p120*
Post The post office is on the main road, south of the Al Manzer hotel, identifiable only by the post box outside.
Telephone There is a small Pak Telecom office opposite the Yassar Palace Hotel. More expensive, but more convenient are several PCOs in the bazaar.

Chitral Valley → *Colour map 2, grid C1*

The Chitral Valley is one of the most appealing regions in the north of Pakistan. Even the district headquarters and largest urban centre, Chitral town itself, is little more than a sleepy, overgrown village set in the heart of the Hindu Kush range. As well as the natural beauty of the mountains, which offer endless trekking and climbing opportunities, it is also home to a fascinating variety of peoples, including the non-Muslim Kalash and the semi-nomadic Wakhi. As in Hunza, the people of upper Chitral are Ismaili Muslims and quite open in their outlook. Compared with the Northern Areas, Chitral receives very few tourists, although it has just as much to offer.

Chitral is also the starting point for one of Pakistan's most rewarding journeys. Not only does the road between Chitral and Gilgit offer some of the best scenery in the country, it also provides an alternative route to the north of Pakistan that avoids the less appealing lower reaches of the KKH (see suggested itineraries on page 12). ▸▸ *For Sleeping, Eating and all other listings, see pages 138-140.*

Land and environment

The rugged and heavily glaciated **Hindu Kush** range (literally 'Hindu killer') raises a formidable barrier along the western and northern border with Afghanistan. Averaging over 4,500 m and dominated by Tirich Mir (7,787 m) and Istora Nal (7,327 m), these mountains mark the watershed between the valleys draining the Oxus and the Indus basins. To the south and east, the **Shandur** mountains (also known as the Hindu Raj or Mashabar) separate Chitral from Gilgit.

The **Chitral River**, known by four different names at various stages along its course, rises in the area of the Chiantar glacier, a 40-km sheet of ice which is also the source of the Oxus and Gilgit rivers. Here, as the **Yarkand**, it flows down from an altitude of over 5,000 m to be joined by the **Laspur River** which drains most of the northern slopes of the Shandur range. It is then known as the **Mastuj** until joined by the Lutkoh branch, draining the Tirich Mir region, where it becomes the Chitral River for much of its course until, close to Afghanistan, it becomes the **Kunar**. In total the river valley runs to over 300 km. Close to Chitral town the river plain widens to over 4 km in width and runs in a broken pattern of cultivated alluvial fans right down to Naghar, 10 km south of Drosh.

Historically, the Chitral Valley was one of the arteries of the Silk Road, across the Boroghil Pass to Yarkand and Kashgar, but was later replaced by the southern routes along the Indus and through Kashmir and Ladakh due to banditry and feuding.

History

Chitral has been a unified independent kingdom from at least the 14th century, when **Shah Nadir Rais** ruled. According to some sources, Shah Nadir Rais was descended from the Trakhan rulers of Gilgit, while others suggest that he came from Badakhshan.

Following the death of **Sangin Ali**, a powerful adviser to the Rais rulers, in 1570, two of his four sons managed to oust the Rais dynasty, establishing what became known as the **Kator Dynasty**, which ruled right up until the 1960s. The **Adamzada** clan, which form most of the upper class in Chitral, are descended from Sangin Ali's grandsons. The **Khuswaqt** family, who later emerged as rulers of Mastuj, Yarkhun and the Gilgit Valley, are similarly descended from this family. The history of the region from this time is an intricate web of intrigue and conspiracy among the various families of the ruling classes, further complicated by almost continual warring with neighbouring kingdoms.

In 1857, **Aman ul-Mulk** emerged as Mehtar (ruler) of Chitral, and by 1880 had extended his rule to include the semi-independent kingdom of Mastuj. The British, fearful of the possibility of the Russians gaining a foothold here, had already sent a mission to Chitral under **Lockhart** in 1855-6. In 1889 they provided Aman ul-Mulk with a subsidy of Rs6,000 per annum, which they doubled in 1891 on the condition that he accepted British advice on all matters connected with foreign policy and the defence of the frontier. By 1889 the **Trans-Caspian Railway** linking the European provinces of Tsarist Russia with Tashkent had been completed. Russian exploration parties visited Hunza in 1889 and Chitral in 1891, and British speculation at the threat of Russian expansion into South Asia began to appear well founded.

The death of Aman ul-Mulk in 1892, leaving anywhere between 16 and 60 sons to dispute the succession among themselves, unleashed a particularly bloody chapter in Chitral's history. Eventually, **Nizam ul-Mulk**, the eldest son, secured the Mehtarship. The British meanwhile lost no time in establishing a Political Agency in Chitral, so as to be better placed to influence events there.

In January 1895 Nizam ul-Mulk was murdered by one of his half-brothers, **Amir ul-Mulk**, triggering another round of bloody in-fighting. This time the British, in whose eyes Chitral had assumed enormous strategic significance, intervened more directly, sending a force from Gilgit under **Major George Robertson**. On his arrival he forcibly occupied Chitral Fort, a classic piece of British heavy-handedness which only served to turn all the warring parties against him. Robertson soon found himself under siege from the now reunited factions of the Chitrali royal family.

The **Siege of Chitral**, as it became known in British accounts, lasted for over a month. Major Robertson managed to hold out until at last a detachment of reinforcements sent from Gilgit under the leadership of **Colonel James Kelly** prompted the Chitrali forces to retreat. Kelly's march across the snow-bound Shandur Pass in early April, complete with two cannons, was recognized as a major achievement, and certainly took the Chitralis by surprise. Soon after, a much larger relief force arrived by way of Malakand and Dir. The British placed **Shuja ul-Mulk** (Amir ul-Mulk's brother), a boy of 14, on the throne and thereafter kept a close eye on the kingdom, supplementing the Political Agent there with a large back-up force in Drosh. Yet despite all the effort expended by the British to secure Chitral, they subsequently showed minimal interest in it, and made no real effort to develop the region.

At **Independence**, the Mehtar of Chitral acceded to Pakistan but remained in charge of all internal affairs of the former Princely State. The Pakistani government was represented by a Political Agent, an arrangement that almost exactly mirrored the system under British rule. However, in 1954 there was an internal revolt against the Mehtar, and the Political Agent took over direct control until 1969 when the state was formally merged into Pakistan (becoming a district of the newly formed Malakand Division of NWFP).

People

The Chitrali people, who call their land Kho, are not Pathan, although today there are many Pathans to be found in Chitral. Although the Chitrali language, Khowar, belongs to the Dardic group, it has strong connections with the languages of the Pamir and Wakhan regions to the north, and with Iran. There are also two minorities; the **Kalash**, who number about 3,500 and inhabit the valleys of Birir, Bumburet and Rumbur, just south of Chitral, and the **Wakhi**, a nomadic group occupying the Pamir and the neighbouring Wakhan Corridor, a thin wedge of Afghan territory between Pakistan (former British territory) and Tajikistan (former Soviet territory).

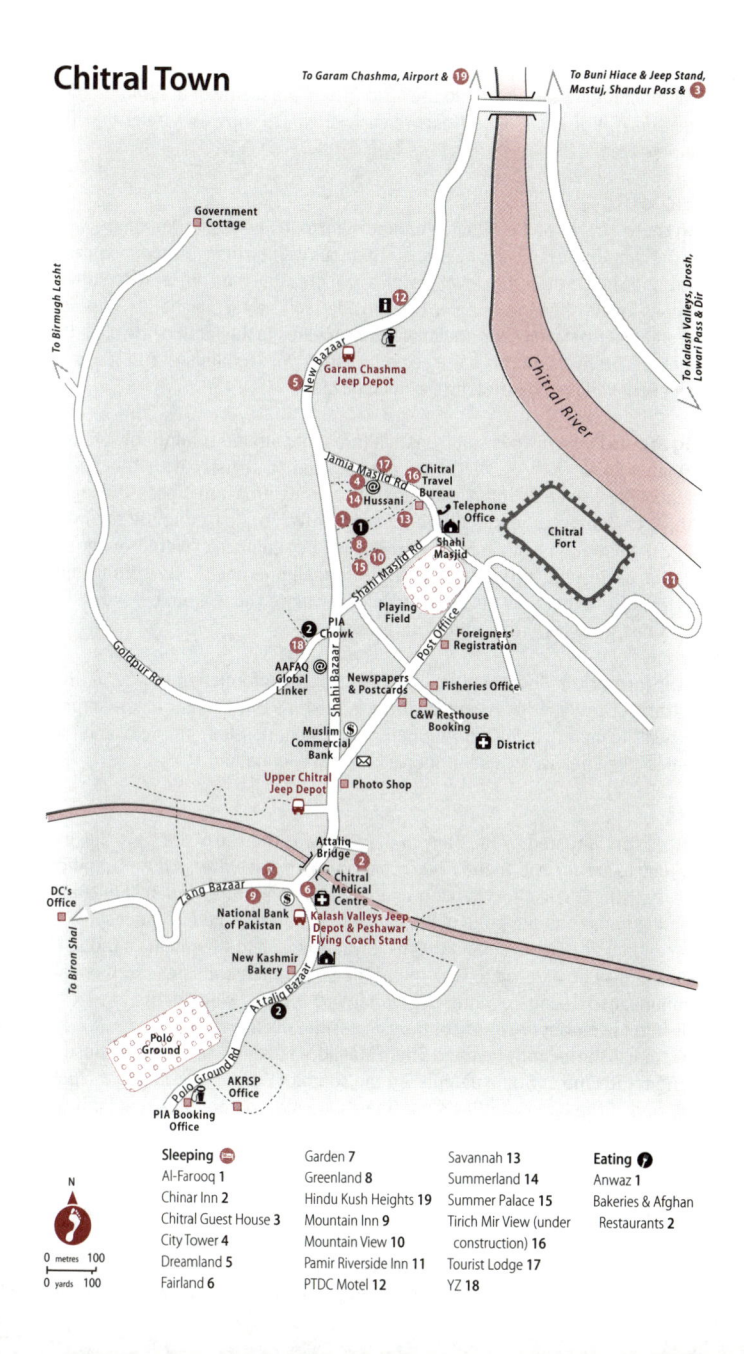

Chitral Town

Sleeping
Al-Farooq 1
Chinar Inn 2
Chitral Guest House 3
City Tower 4
Dreamland 5
Fairland 6
Garden 7
Greenland 8
Hindu Kush Heights 19
Mountain Inn 9
Mountain View 10
Pamir Riverside Inn 11
PTDC Motel 12
Savannah 13
Summerland 14
Summer Palace 15
Tirich Mir View (under construction) 16
Tourist Lodge 17
YZ 18

Eating
Anwaz 1
Bakeries & Afghan Restaurants 2

Chitral town

Chitral has experienced little of the phenomenal growth seen in Gilgit, and remains a small, friendly place where foreigners can wander around without being pounced on (or even noticed, as it often seems). What growth there has been has come mainly as a result of Afghan refugees settling here. In terms of attractions, it boasts a lively, colourful and atmospheric main bazaar, with the majestic splendour of Tirich Mir dominating the skyline to the north. There are plenty of accommodation options, and it is a good base from which to organize trips and treks into the surrounding area.

Ins and outs

Getting there The airport is situated around 3 km to the north of town, on the west bank of the river. There is always at least one minibus waiting there to meet people off the plane and shuttle them into town (Rs10), and more often than not representatives from various hotels offering a free jeep ride provided you stay at their hotel (Rs50-100 if you don't). There is a new bus station a few kilometres to the north of town, on the east bank of the river, but no one seems to use it, with minibuses and jeeps all operating from various points along the main bazaar.

Getting around The town is small enough to wander around comfortably on foot. **NB** Foreign tourists arriving in Chitral are required to register with the Superintendent of Police (see Directory, page 131). It's a straightforward process taking no more than 30 minutes and should be done on arrival, or first thing the following morning. Registration in Chitral should not be confused with Foreigners' Registration (see page 17); it is a separate formality required of all foreigners, irrespective of whether they have registered elsewhere. You will not be allowed to visit the Kalash Valleys without proof of registration.

Tourist information There is a helpful **PTDC Tourist Information Centre** ⓘ *PTDC Motel, T0933-412683, F0933-412722*. There is also a PTDC counter at the airport, open when flights arrive. Haidar Ali Shah of the **Mountain Inn**, or any of the tour companies listed below, are useful sources of local information.

Sights

The **Chitral Fort**, situated by the bank of the river, was the site of the 1895 Siege of Chitral and focus for the bloody intrigues which characterized Chitrali politics; whoever held the Fort in effect held power in the kingdom. Today, much of the fort is a crumbling ruin, although parts of it have been restored and are still occupied by the descendants of the royal family. Officially it is closed to the public, although if you ask you may be allowed to look round the abandoned parts. Inside, there are five cannons, two dating from the First World War. The best views of the fort are on the way into town from the north, or from across the river.

Next to it is the recently restored **Shahi Masjid**, a striking onion-domed mosque dating from the time of Shuja ul-Mulk. To the south of the main bazaar is the **polo ground**, one of the largest in Pakistan. Games are played here on a regular basis between March and October; check with PTDC for dates, or just listen out for the drumming which heralds the start of a match.

If you have some free time in the afternoon, there is a spot along the road north of Chitral from where **markhor** can be seen each day at around 1630. Head along the road beyond the airport, continuing past the **Hindu Kush Heights** (with the red roof, above the road) and a sign for the 'Tooshi Game Reserve' on the left. Shortly after, there is a small blue house on the opposite bank of the river. Continue for about 1 km before stopping. If you have timed it accurately and are lucky, you should see up to 30 of these sturdy beasts grazing on the steep slopes opposite and should also be able to view them drinking from the Chitral River.

Around Chitral town

Birmugh Lasht

ⓘ *It is a strenuous 3-hr walk with no shade on the way up. A steep, rough jeep track zigzags its way up to the top. Head west out of town along the road past the YZ hotel. After the first hairpin bend the jeep track forks off to the left (there is a well-hidden signpost). A privately hired jeep will cost up to Rs1500 for the return trip. The best way to arrive is by horse or pony. Ask at Hindu Kush Heights for possibilities.*

High above the town on a small plain is the former summer palace of the Mehtar of Chitral and, although now semi-derelict, it makes an ideal picnic spot with a view. The plain used to be thickly wooded with walnut trees (Birmugh Lasht translates as 'place of walnuts'), but today only a few isolated trees remain. Higher up, on top of the mountain, there is a **Wildlife Department Rest House**, bookable through the District Wildlife Officer in Chitral. A **PTDC Motel** is also planned.

Chitral Gol National Park

The small side valley (Chitral Gol) that climbs steeply up from Chitral town has been designated as a National Park, covering 7,745 ha. Rich forests of deodar (Indian cedar), blue pine, Chiligoza pine and silver fir still remain here, as well as stands of willow and birch, and some juniper scrub. In theory these are protected under the legislation governing national parks, but in practice hunting still continues, threatening the survival of many species. Encouragingly, however, there have been recent sightings of a pair of snow leopards; there are now thought to be at least three in the area. The valley also attracts many migratory birds en route between Central Asia and India, including the black throated thrush, golden oriole, grey heron, mallard and oriental turtle dove, as well as being home to an array of indigenous species.

There are several beautiful treks through the park, and some Forestry Resthouses offering simple accommodation (you need your own sleeping bag, cooking equipment and provisions). The tough but rewarding three-day trek into the Rumbur Valley is destined to become a more popular route into the Kalash Valleys. There are also a choice of attractive circuits returning to Chitral. To trek here you need a permit (from the District Forestry Officer) and a guide. See under Chitral Activities and tours, page 130, for leads on getting more information and organizing a visit to the park.

> *Snow leopards, black bears, markhor and urial are reportedly still found in the upper reaches of the valley.*

Garam Chashma

ⓘ *Regular jeeps run between Chitral and Garam Chashma (Rs25). It is a 2-day trek from Chitral to Garam Chashma and once here there are several pleasant and welcoming walks linking Ishmaili communities around the area. For guides, routes and information on safe walking, contact Chitral Travel Bureau (see Chitral Activities and tours, page 130).*

These hot sulphur springs are situated 45 km (but a two hour ride) northwest of Chitral. Approaching Garam Chashma along the narrow Lutkho River Valley, you pass an old fort still occupied by descendants of the Chitrali royal family, the civil hospital, a police post (where foreigners should register, but isn't really necessary for those on a day trip) and the fisheries department office, before arriving in the main village. There is excellent trout fishing in the area; permits can be obtained from the fisheries office on the road before the village.

Sleeping

Chitral town *p126, map p125*

A Hindu Kush Heights, Gankorini, T0933-413151 (or Islamabad T051-2275484), hotels@hindukush.isb.sdnpk.org. Set in splendid isolation high above Chitral town, this hotel is in a class of its own. Built and run by Siraj ul-Mulk, a member of the former royal family, the loving care and attention which has gone into the place is evident from the moment you walk in the door. Together with his wife, Ghazala, they are perfect hosts, while the staff provide impeccable service in a subtle manner. All rooms are tastefully furnished with Chitrali rugs and hangings, marble floors and wood-panelled ceilings, while individual balconies offer spectacular views down the Chitral Valley over the airport. Central heating in most rooms, all with attached hot bath (tubs). Hiking tours are often arranged and a stable provides horses for guests to enjoy. Open 1 Apr-31 Dec, reserve in advance. The restaurant here is excellent (see under Eating). Recommended.

B PTDC Chitral Motel, New Bazaar, T0933-412683. Decent rooms with attached hot bath and dish TV. 20% discount out of season (winter), uninspiring restaurant. Tourist information centre is based here – you will stay here if on a PTDC tour. Beware of scorpions hiding in dark corners or in clothes; treat them with respect when you find one.

B-C Pamir Riverside Inn, Noghor Gardens, T0933-412525, F0933-413365. Quiet location by the river with views of Tirich Mir from the pleasant garden, choice of rooms in rather run-down cottages or in more modern new block, although the latter is overpriced at twice the cottage rate. All rooms come with attached bath, geyser and dish TV. Restaurant serves fixed meals and can provide lunch boxes.

C Chitral Guest House, Danin, on the Shandur Rd, 1 km north of bridge, T0933-413077. Elegantly furnished rooms using traditionally hand-crafted furniture, set in 3 blocks with terraces. All rooms are spotless with attached hot bath, most with views of Tirich Mir. All have several large windows, so plenty of natural light, although the common balcony is great for relaxing and enjoying an excellent view. Plans to introduce TV with internet link. Restaurant serves fixed menus, exclusively for residents, with traditional music when sufficient guests. Used primarily for groups travelling with **Chitral Travel Bureau** (see Activities and tours below), book in advance. Recommended.

C-D Mountain Inn, T0933-412581, F0933-412668, mountain@inn.isb.sdnpk.org. Chitral's longest established hotel (1968) sees lots of return and long-stay guests thanks largely to the skill and knowledge of its host, Haidar Ali Shah. Clean and well-maintained rooms in shady, flower-filled mature garden. Recommended.

E-F Dreamland, New Bazaar, T0933-412806, dreamlandpk@yahoo.com. Reasonable rooms with fan and attached bath, but a bit dark. More expensive rooms have dish TV. Rarely used dining hall. Not a bad choice.

F City Tower, Shahi Masjid Rd, T0933-412912, djan17@hotmail.com. Reasonable, clean rooms with bath. Shared balcony with views of Tirich Mir. Restaurant.

G Al-Farooq, New Bazaar, T0933-412726. Winner of the 'popular with backpackers' award for the Chitral region. Accommodation is decent enough in itself although baths may require some self cleaning, however, the 2 terraces with views of Tirich Mir provide a laidback atmosphere for chatting with other travellers. Friendly and helpful young manager keeps his guests happy. Food available at sister concern **Anwaz Restaurant**, opposite (see Eating below). Recommended.

G Chinar Inn, off Shahi Bazaar, near Attaliq Bridge, T/F0933-412582. Clean rooms set around small garden area, but a bit soulless and overpriced. Food available.

G Fairland, Attaliq Bridge, T0933-412768. Basic rooms with attached bath. Fly-ridden restaurant.

G Greenland, off Shahi Bazaar, T0933-412084. Small rooms, basic.

G Savanna, off Jamia Masjid Rd, T0933-412294, F0933-412664. Basic rooms with attached bath set around concrete courtyard. Choice of carpet or no carpet. Restaurant. Nothing special.

G Summerland, off Shahi Bazaar, T0933-412337. Basic, grotty rooms with attached bath.

G Summer Palace, off Shahi Bazaar. Simple rooms with fan and attached bath in huge concrete building. Not the most salubrious.

G Tourist Lodge, Jamia Masjid Rd, T0933-412452. Friendly place with a small sit-out garden area, views of Tirich Mir from the roof. Rooms, set around the car park, are quite basic with seatless western toilets (promises to replace these). Restaurant.

H Garden, opposite Mountain Inn. Very basic, charpoy beds, outside toilet, wash in stream, pleasant shady garden, friendly staff, very local and often full.

H Mountain View, New Bazaar, T0933-412559. Clean, simple rooms with fan and a choice of attached or shared bath. Restaurant.

H YZ, Goldpur Rd, T0933-412690. Small, basic rooms set around small garden/courtyard. Friendly, but often full with long-term local residents.

Garam Chashma *p127*

There is 1 proper hotel here, the **F Injigaan**. Decent enough double rooms for Rs450, or dorm beds for Rs100, and meals to order. The manager claims to provide guides for local trekking/rambling. The hotel's main attraction (and the main reason for coming to Garam Chashma) is its own private, spring-fed hot water pool, a blissful way to soothe aching limbs after trekking. Non-residents are charged Rs100 to swim.

There is also a **F C & W Resthouse** and a couple of very basic Afghan-run hotels in the bazaar which serve the usual stewed mutton and naan.

Eating

Chitral town *p126, map p125*

Most of the hotels in Chitral have their own restaurant although these can all close when the roti wallahs in the bazaar go on strike. Don't expect much more than mutton or dhal dishes and it may be necessary to warn your hotel in advance if you want to eat there in the evenings.

For the spontaneous or unorganized diner, there are plenty of simple Afghan-run eating places and chai shops in the main bazaars, particularly around PIA Chowk and along the first stretch of Goldpur Rd (where there are also a couple of bakeries). There are also some at the north end of New Bazaar and around Attaliq Bridge and Attaliq Bazaar. The standard advice is to choose the place full of locals – they know best, although don't expect any haute cuisine other then the usual mutton or vegetable (with mutton) dishes. However, it's cheap and filling and does the job.

††† Hindu Kush Heights, Gankorini, T0933-412151. For a truly memorable night out for your taste buds, treat yourself to a meal here. The food here ranks amongst the best in Pakistan. If you are not staying here then it is essential to book in advance and to organize your own transport there and back to town (around Rs200 for a jeep). The fixed buffet costs around Rs300 per head and is worth every rupee.

† Anwaz, Shahi Bazaar. Comes closest to providing a travellers' menu with vegetable soups and veg spaghetti. Standard local fare (mutton curry) is also available.

▲ Activities and tours

Chitral town *p126, map p125*

Polo is played regularly at the polo ground in Chitral, see above. There is excellent **fishing** in many of Chitral's rivers. For permits and more information, contact the Fisheries Office, off Post Office Rd. Note that the closed season for trout fishing in the main Chitral River is between 1 Jun and 31 Aug. The playing field in front of the Shahi Masjid and Chitral Fort is often used for impromptu and 'organized' **football** matches.

Tour operators

All the following are recommended.
Chitral Travel Bureau, Shahi Masjid Rd, T0933-412461, chitraltravel@hotmail.com. Able to organize jeeps and treks (including porters and guides). Also has some equipment (tents, sleeping bags etc) available for hire. Syed Harir Shah, who runs this place, is very helpful and can provide local information and guides.

Hindu Kush Heights, Gankorini, T0933-413151, hotels@hindukush.isb.sdnpk.org. Specializing in trekking over the high passes connecting valleys in Chitral to valleys in Gilgit and Hunza, the owners, Prince Siraj Ul-Mulk and his charming wife Princess Ghazala, have accompanied many of the groups themselves. The company also organizes mountaineering, pony trekking and bicycle tours in the Hindu Kush region. **Hindu Kush Trails**, the main tour company in Chitral (run by members of the former royal family), has a liaison office at the **Mountain Inn**, T0933-412800, info@hindukushtrails.com. Its head office is in Islamabad, though at the time of writing they were in the process of looking for a new office, so use the above email address for new details. It is a good, reliable company, with extensive experience of organizing trekking expeditions and jeep safaris in Chitral and beyond.

Shopping

Chitral town *p126, map p125*

There are several shops piled high with a wonderful array of Afghan and Chitrali **rugs and carpets**, as well as all manner of antique tribal **jewellery**, semi-precious **stones** (particularly lapis lazuli and turquoise from Afghanistan), **embroidery** work, **carved wooden items** etc. The local Chitrali speciality is Shu, or Patti cloth, a soft hand-woven woollen material which is made into intricately embroidered long gowns (chunghas), rugs, bags, Chitrali hats etc. Most of the shops are located in **Shahi Bazaar** and **New Bazaar**, and along the first stretch of **Goldpur Rd**, before you reach the YZ hotel.

There is a limited amount of **trekking equipment** on sale in Shahi Bazaar and New Bazaar; much of it, notably sleeping bags etc, is army surplus stuff (serviceable but heavy). You can often find good second-hand boots, and occasionally bits of equipment left over from mountaineering expeditions. Alternatively, the tour operators have trekking equipment available for hire. For **provisions**, the shop next door to the Chitral Travel Bureau on Shahi Masjid Rd has a good selection of lightweight, high-energy trekking goodies. Sanitary towels are also available here and at a shop near PIA Chowk. The various **bakeries** are good for biscuits, jam, cakes etc; the **New Kashmir Bakery** in Attaliq Bazaar has a good selection.

Terich Mir Photo Studio, at the junction of Shahi Bazaar and Post Office Rd, sells slide films and camera batteries in case of emergencies, the last place to stock up before heading further north.

Transport

Chitral town *p126, map p125*

Air

PIA Booking Office, Attaliq Bazaar (by Polo Ground), T0933-412963, F0933-412563. Open daily 0800-1600. **Airport**, T0933-412547, open 1 hr before flight. Weather permitting, there are 2 Fokker F-27 flights daily to **Peshawar** at 0725 and 1000, costing Rs2740 for foreigners, Rs890 for subsidized Pakistanis. If your flight is cancelled due to bad weather and you want to try again the next day, be sure to reconfirm your seat. Foreigners are given priority on the backlog list.

Bus

Peshawar Flying Coach Stand is situated just off Attaliq Bazaar, south of Attaliq Bridge, to the right of the chai shops. Hiace minibuses run from here on a 'leave when full' basis daily 0600-1500. The full 12-hr trip to **Peshawar** costs around Rs250. You can break the journey in **Drosh** (Rs15, 1 hr), **Dir** (Rs150, 5 hrs) or **Timargarha** (Rs200, 7 hrs). Some Hiaces only go as far as these places so you may be forced to change anyway. Change in Timargarha for **Mingora/Saidu Sharif**.

Passenger and cargo jeeps

Garam Chashma Jeep Depot is situated towards the north end of New Bazaar, on the opposite side of the road between the Dreamland and PTDC hotels. Passenger jeeps operate regularly from here to **Garam Chashma** (Rs25, 2 hrs), departing when full.

Upper Chitral Jeep Depot Situated just off Shahi Bazaar, a little to the north of Attaliq Bridge. Passenger and cargo jeeps depart from here as far as **Mastuj** (Rs100, 4 hrs). Some may go as far as **Sor Laspur** (Rs100-120, 5 hrs) but services for both destinations are irregular, depending on demand; enquire a day in advance and be prepared to hang around on the day. To travel as far as **Buni** takes around 2 hrs and costs Rs35-Rs50. More regular Hiaces and jeeps exclusively to Buni also leave from across the Chitral River, just north of the bridge.

Shandur Pass/Gilgit: In the run-up to the annual polo tournament on Shandur Pass, there are regular passenger jeeps departing from here for the pass. At this time there is also plenty of onward transport from Shandur to Gilgit. At other times, it is still worth asking around at the Upper Chitral Jeep Depot in case there are any jeeps returning to Gilgit (see Private jeep hire, below). It is possible to take cargo jeeps (including empty, returning passenger jeeps on some sections) all the way to Gilgit for a total of less than Rs500, but be prepared for a lot of hanging about and less than comfortable travelling conditions. Otherwise, your best bet is to get a jeep as far as Sor Laspur, walk or hitch over the Shandur Pass, and then pick up onward transport on the other side. Or you could consider a donkey (see Mastuj Transport, page 147).

In 2003 NATCO started running a 12-seater landcruiser direct from Chitral to **Gilgit** (Rs600, weekend departure but changing schedule, 14 hrs+).

Kalash Valleys Jeep Depot Situated alongside the Peshawar Flying Coach Stand in Attaliq Bazaar, to the left of the chai shops which separate them. Regular passenger jeeps and minibuses leave from here to **Ayun** (Rs10, 45 mins). Depending on demand there are usually several direct jeeps daily to **Bumburet Valley** (generally as far as Anish or Brun, Rs30, 2 hrs). If you are lucky you may find a jeep to **Rumbur Valley** (Balanguru, Rs30, 2 hrs). The chances of finding a direct jeep to **Birir Valley** are minimal, in which case you will have to negotiate for a 'special jeep'. For the latter 2 valleys, it may be necessary to take a passenger jeep to Ayun and see what you can pick up from there. This also applies for Bumburet when it is not busy.

Private jeep hire

Jeeps can be hired privately from any of the jeep depots listed above or the manager of budget hotels can usually arrange one. See also the specialist Tour operators, above. Rates are generally fixed although it is worth shopping around and bargaining when supply outstrips demand. It's worth asking around for other travellers to split the costs. The prices quoted here are for the summer of 2004. **Garam Chashma** full-day return trip, Rs1,500; **Kalash Valleys** full-day return trip, Rs1,500; **Shandur Pass** 1-way, Rs4,000, return, Rs7,000; **Gilgit** 2 days, Rs8,000-10,000. **NB** If travelling to **Gilgit**, it's a good idea to find a jeep driver from Gilgit having to return empty. Look for the GLT number plate prefix on the jeeps. It seems that Rs1,000 per head is the going rate for the 2-day journey, while it was possible to negotiate good deals when spreading the trip over a few days. If coming from Gilgit, look for the CL (for Chitral) number plate prefix.

ⓘ Directory

Chitral town *p126, map p125*

Banks National Bank of Pakistan, junction on south side of Attaliq Bridge, licensed to deal in foreign exchange (cash and TCs). Mon-Thu 0830-1230 (1300 in winter), Fri and Sat 0830-1200. Muslim Commercial Bank, deals with cash and TCs during similar opening hours. Both charge Rs100 per TC transaction and are quite efficient and friendly. You can also find some money changers-cum-shopkeepers in Shahi Bazaar and New Bazaar; they give the going 'kerbside' rate, but will only deal with cash (US$ and £ Sterling). They also have large wads of Afghan rials for sale if you're interested! **Hospitals** The District Headquarters Hospital is off Post Office Rd. There are several **chemist** shops nearby, on Post Office Rd itself. On the south side of Attaliq Bridge is the Chitral Medical Centre, T0933-412768, with its own dispensary which is open daily 0800-1800.
Internet Aafaq Computer Centre and Global Linker, Shahi Bazaar, has 5 dedicated machines. Hussaini Internet, on Jamia Masjid Rd, has 3 terminals and will generally kick off a local student when a foreigner wants to use the internet. Both establishments charge Rs60 per hr and are open daily (Aafaq, 1000-2000; Hussaini, 0600-2400 in theory). Slightly cheaper is Radiant Computer Academy on Zang Bazaar, but it only has one terminal so expect

to wait. **Post** The GPO is on Post Office Rd, near the junction with Shahi Bazaar. It has a Poste Restante section at the rear, and you can also send faxes from here when the machine is working. Mon-Thu, Sat 0900-1500, Fri 0900-1200. **Telephone** The telephone office, for national and international calls, is in a small office off Shahi Masjid Rd, open daily, 0800-2000. The staff are helpful and rates at fixed government tariffs are much more reasonable than the private PCOs along Shahi and New Bazaars, which can cost over double. You can also receive calls on 0092-933-413367, although this number may change, so check. Fax service is also possible. **Useful addresses** Superintendent of Police Post Office Rd, T0933-412077. Daily 0800-1700 (for registering in Chitral, see under Ins and outs, above). **Deputy Commissioner** on road west of Mountain Inn, T0933-412055. If you are planning to stay for more than 15 days in the Kalash Valleys, you must obtain a permit from the DC. **Assistant Commissioner** Post Office Rd, T0933-412066. **Police** Post Office Rd, T0933-412959. **Emergency** T15. There are a number of government offices in a series of buildings off Post Office Rd, on the way to the District Hospital. The following can all be found here, although there are few signs, so you may have to ask a few people until you reach the person you need. **C&W Sub Divisional Officer**, T0933-412103. Apply here for C & W Rest House bookings. **District Wildlife Officer**, T0933-412101. Enquire here about visits to Chitral Gol National Park. **Assistant Director of Fisheries**. Ask here about trout fishing and permits in Chitral.

Kalash Valleys → *Colour map1, grid A1*

The Kalash, numbering approximately 3,500, are the smallest group among the religious minorities of Pakistan. Unlike the other minorities, they live exclusively in a particular geographical area; the three valleys of Birir, Bumburet and Rumbur in the Hindu Kush between the Afghan border and the Chitral Valley. Muslims label the Kalash 'Kafirs' ('non-believers') and their area Kafirstan. Until 1896 Kafirstan also included present-day Nuristan in Afghanistan, inhabited by the 'Red Kafirs', whereas the Kalash were called the 'Black Kafirs'. ▶▶ *For Sleeping, Eating and all other listings, see pages 138-140.*

Ins and outs

Getting there The Kalash Valleys are easily accessible from Chitral. **Bumburet** and **Rumbur** Valleys are both reached via the village of **Ayun**, situated on a large alluvial fan on the west bank of the Kunar River. Around 12 km to the south of Chitral on the main road down towards the Lowari Pass, a turning leads down to a bridge across the river and then to Ayun, around 3 km further on. The main square/jeep stop is across another small bridge over the river draining the Kalash Valleys. Regular passenger jeeps run from the jeep depot in Attaliq Bazaar (see under Chitral Transport). Most passenger jeeps run as far as Ayun, although many also continue on to Bumburet, the most popular valley. Services to Rumbur are less frequent. If there is nothing going to Rumbur, take a Bumburet jeep as far as the check post and then walk (two to three hours to Brum/Balanguru). If you arrive late in Ayun, or you wish to continue on foot in the early morning, when it is cooler, then see page 138 for accommodation options.

There are no regular passenger jeep services to **Birir** Valley, to the south of Rumbur and Bumburet, although occasional jeeps do go from Ayun, following a track along the west bank of the Kunar River. The main route is via the bridge at Gahiret, 7 km south of the bridge turning for Ayun. All of the jeep tracks up the valleys are subject to frequent blockages due to floods, landslides and earthquakes. In such cases the track to Bumburet is usually repaired within a few days, but for Rumbur and Birir Valleys repairs often seem to take much longer. The track to Rumbur has been blocked for almost three years following heavy flooding in the past.

Permits Visitors to the Kalash Valleys must pay a toll (Rs100, or Rs20 for Pakistanis, valid for all three valleys) at the check post at the junction of Bumburet and Rumbur Valleys. The proceeds from this toll are in theory channelled back into the valleys. **NB** You must first have registered in Chitral town (see Chitral Ins and outs); if you cannot produce your registration document, you will usually be turned back. However, some foreigners are occasionally allowed through on the understanding that they register in Chitral the following day. Don't rely on this, especially as the local authorities will be much more interested in who enters or leaves the valleys following recent events across the border in Afghanistan. Officially, a permit must be obtained from the Deputy Commissioner in Chitral if staying for more than a week. The latter is primarily aimed at those intending a long-term visit (anthropologists and the like). In practice though, there is generally no need for this permit for stays of up to 15 days.

History

Kalash myths tell that the Kalash originally came from **Tsiam**, thought to be near Yarkand. The Kalash oral tradition also tells that the Kalash are descended from Alexander the Great's brave general **Shalak Shah** of Tsiam, to whom Alexander gave the Chitral Valley as a reward. The Kalash language is of great interest to linguists as it belongs to the ancient Dardic branch of the Indo-European languages, suggesting a Central Asian origin. Around AD 1500 the Kalash were dominant throughout southern Chitral; the Kalash oral tradition mentions eight great Kalash kings. Local people outside the valleys often find remnants of buildings revealing evidence of former Kalash settlements.

After this Kalash period, Islam became dominant in Chitral. Islam at first seems to have been adopted by the kings who then converted their subjects more or less forcibly. The most persistent of the Kalash took refuge from conversion in the less accessible side valleys. As a result the Kalash became marginalized; a subjugated people bound to pay tributes and corvée labour to the Mehtars, economically exploited and subject to frequent raids from their neighbours in what is now Nuristan.

When the British established the Durand Line the Kalash Valleys became part of British India, and so part of present-day Pakistan. This protected the Kalash from the forcible conversions to Islam carried out by the Afghan king Abdur Rahman in 1896. Groups of Red Kafirs fled these conversions into Chitral. The refugees were given land in the upper parts of the Kalash Valleys and still have their villages there. Ironically they all later gradually converted to Islam. In 1969 the kingdom of Chitral became part of Pakistan. To the Kalash this meant a lifting of their serfdom and the enshrining of their constitutional right to practise their religion.

Religion

The Muslims label the Kalash 'Kafirs' in the misapprehension that they do not believe in God and worship only idols. In fact the Kalash do believe in God, Khodai (the Persian word for Allah) or Dezao, the creator who is worshipped everywhere. In case of a natural disaster or serious illness, the Kalash try to reconcile God by prayers and sacrifices.

Male and female Dewalok (sacred spirits) are responsible for particular parts of daily life and are addressed when necessary through prayers, offerings or sacrifices. The Kalash may ask the Dewalok to give their prayers to Dezao (in the same way as the Catholics ask the saints to do so). It is important to know and respect that the places of the Dewalok belong to the pure sphere, where only men are allowed to go. Exceptions are the temples representing Jestak, who protects the families. During menstruation and childbirth, Kalash women stay in the Bashali houses where Dejalik is represented by a carved piece of wood.

In the Kalash perception, Nature belongs to other beings than themselves. By means of offerings, sacrifices, purifications and prayers, they have to ask for permission to let the animals graze in the high pastures or cut down trees for example.

The pure/impure dualism is central to the Kalash religion. Onjesta (pure, sacred) and Pragata (impure, profane) are frequently mentioned in connection with locations as well as with acts, persons and objects. Basically the Kalash world is divided into complementary spheres of Onjesta and Pragata, with the divine, the high pastures, the men and the goats belonging to the Onjesta sphere, and the women belonging to the Pragata sphere, in particular during menstruation and childbirth. For the women, their confinement to the Bashali during menstruation provides a monthly holiday from the daily routine of hard work. Anybody entering, or touching anybody there, must be totally washed before returning to the rest of the world.

Tourists should stay away from the Bashali. If a female tourist has her period she should keep quiet about it and not leave any sanitary towels or tampons for people to find, as they are considered a strong pollutant in the religious sense (take them out of the valleys, bury them or burn them secretly, but not in a family house).

The family houses are divided into zones. The fireplace and the area behind it are Onjesta. Therefore a woman is not permitted to step over these places, but only to reach with her arms and the top of her body into the area. Inside the house, women have to pour drinking water (considered Onjesta) from the common glass into the mouth through her left hand. The valley also is divided into zones – the higher up, the more Onjesta.

As women, and also Muslims, are Pragata, they can never go to the altars and other places of the Dewalok or to the goats' stables above the villages when the goats are down, as these places are Onjesta. Acts such as washing the body and braiding the hair are also considered Pragata and have to be done at a certain distance from these places.

Purifications are an essential element in the Kalash religion. These may be done by circling burning juniper or hollyoak, by rinsing the hands in pure river water, by sprinkling goat's blood or by holding something made of iron. Of particular importance is the purification of boys during their gradual transition from the Pragata women's sphere into the Onjesta male community. Only after several purifications (after the traditional trousers dressing ceremony) at the age of about seven years, are the boys sufficiently Onjesta to go to the altars and to the high pastures. When still virgins they are very Onjesta and have special religious tasks.

Social structure

Family relations are extremely important; people rarely call each other by their name, but rather address each other in terms of their relationship to the eldest child of the family. This means that children are very important and everybody knows their names. After receiving the proper dress a child is considered a full member of the community. However, the young are expected to behave respectfully towards their elders, listening and obeying their commands.

Households generally consist of the extended family, encompassing many relations and several generations, and forming an integrated economic unit. People belong to their father's clan (even married women) which is very important in terms of identity, and involves sharing the economic responsibility in case of big expenditures such as funerals and the collection of bride price.

Important to the Kalash are the codes of honour that first of all emphasize generosity, living according to their religion, honesty in work and speech (quality of speech is better than quantity) and diligence. Greed is looked down upon – many myths tell how greed leads to disaster.

The Kalash society has no formal internal leadership. Disputes are settled and decisions made by the male clan elders in common. There are also strong personalities among the women who give their opinions and are heard. Politically the community is split into factions – traditionally around competing clan elders, but nowadays increasingly around competing politicians from outside running for the minority seat in the National Assembly. The Kalash-elected minority member of the District Council in Chitral functions as a representative and mediator with the surrounding world. The Kalash have not yet succeeded in winning the minority seat in the Provincial Assembly.

The Kalash in the 20th century

The Kalash community is at a stage of transition. The building of roads linking the valleys with the outside world has brought with it development; schools, a health system, money, commercial goods, new ideas, electricity and tourism. In particular the Kalash are a major tourist attraction and so of great economic importance for the tourist industry. Tourism is mainly outside Kalash ownership and control, which leads to concern and frustration among the Kalash, depending on the degree to which individuals feel they are harassed by or benefit from the tourists.

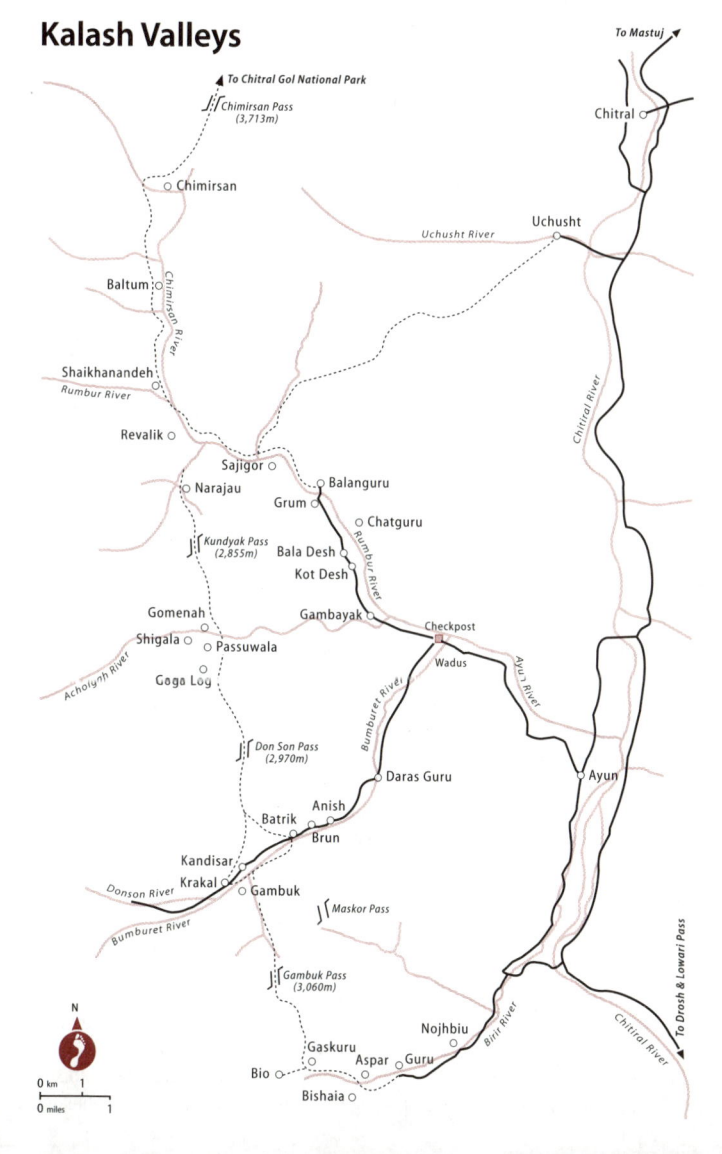

Kalash Valleys

> ### ❗ The woman's place is in the Kalash region
>
> As the women are excluded from the Onjesta sphere their living space is smaller than the men's. Women mostly stay below the highest water channels in the field and village areas. In the summer they go to the fields of the lower summer pastures. After their return to the villages in the autumn, these areas are purified and closed to the women.
>
> Although women are considered Pragata, they are not at all looked down upon; they are the common pride of the valley, and for instance have to walk first in the procession when coming to another valley for a funeral. The men talk proudly about 'our women' meaning all women from the valley or clan. They have total self-determination in all personal matters. Thus, within the strict rules governing incest and periods of abstention, a woman is able to decide whom to marry and with whom to make love. Men frequently complain of 'women's choice' saying "What can we do?" If a man dares to pull the plaits of his wife or talk rudely to her, she normally leaves the house. She can then take a lover, and nobody can force her back again. Women's elopements are one of the main reasons for community conflicts.

In general the Kalash welcome visitors if they behave with respect to the people and the culture. Less welcomed are the foreign groups who come just for a brief visit, taking pictures and behaving as if in a zoo. Least welcomed are the gangs of young men from the lowlands who confuse the women's freedom from purdah with sexual promiscuity and frequently harass the girls.

The Kalasha culture has always evolved along with the surrounding world. Some outside tourist interests want the Kalasha culture to be frozen into a museum of the living past and complain about modern innovations like electricity. Tourist interests emphasize the spectacular; the big communal rites and the material culture of dresses, houses and technology, however, leading to complaints about material changes. The Kalasha religious rites and traditions are central to the unity of the community and as these rites become redefined as tourist events, the basic functions of the rites are eroded along with the unity of the world they sustain.

So far, however, contact with other ways and norms has made the Kalash very aware of their own culture. Indeed, there is a growing cultural pride among the Kalash, partly because the interest shown by tourists has made the Kalash aware of the unique nature of their culture. Also, the religious heads tend to interpret disasters like diseases among the goats as caused by cultural slackness, which encourages the people to keep their traditions alive. An increasing dependence on tourist incomes does influence the material culture, although sometimes in positive ways. The women have learnt that their colourful costumes can earn them money, and as their incomes increase, they are able to use the extra money to further embellish them.

Perhaps the greatest threat to the Kalash is the deforestation going on in the valleys. The Kalash Valleys are among the few forested areas in Pakistan. Timber is used in increasing quantities for construction of houses for a fast-growing population, while firewood is still the main fuel source for domestic use. Far more damaging, however, is the logging carried out by external contractors. The Kalash have successfully fought to gain control over logging in the Rumber Valley, and for their legal right to royalties from the timber. However, it is still evident that there is little or no reforestation in place to keep pace with present rates of felling. Ultimately, the only way to protect the ecology of the valleys would seem to involve a complete stop to commercial logging. Without their forest cover, the steep-sided valleys with their large catchment areas are exposed to heavy erosion and flash floods, both of which are occurring with increasing intensity and frequency. The wholesale destruction of the forests in the Kalash Valleys for immediate profit seems likely to trigger an ecological disaster which will ultimately destroy the culture and community, and with it a long-term source of income from tourism for many outside the valleys.

Exploring the Valleys

Rumbur Valley

Around 45 minutes to the west of Ayun by jeep, the Rumbur and Bumburet rivers merge to form the Ayun River. Coming from Ayun, the jeep track crosses the Bumburet tributary and then forks, left up the Bumburet Valley, or right up the Rumbur Valley. Just by the fork is the check post where visitors must buy their permits. Following the Rumbur Valley, at the village of Gambayak, the Acholgah Valley branches off to the left, leading up to summer pastures. Further on, the track passes through Kot Desh and Baladesh before arriving at **Grum**, where there are some guest houses. Just across the river is **Balanguru**, a picturesque and typically Kalash village shaded by large walnut and jujube trees, with wooden houses built up the hillside, the roof of one forming the front yard of the next. Beyond Balanguru, there are beautiful walks up the valley, past the hydel plant supplying electricity to the village. Higher up the valley is the Muslim (Nuristani) village of Shaikhanandeh (literally 'village of converters'). It is also possible to trek across to Chitral town or Garam Chashma (see below).

Bumburet Valley

The valley of Bumburet is the most popular in terms of tourism and has most of the hotels. As a result, it is the most easily accessible, with the majority of passenger jeeps coming here. In some ways, this valley is also the most picturesque, being the widest of the three, with scattered villages and long, fertile stretches of cultivation strung along most of its length. From the check post at the foot of the valley, the jeep track climbs up through the villages of Wadus, Daras Guru, Gadiandeh, Anish (where the first hotels begin to appear), Brun, Sarikjao, Batrik, Kandisar, Krakal and Gambuk. At the top of the valley there is another Muslim (Nuristani) village known, as in Rumbur, as Shaikhanandeh. The village itself is to the left of the main jeep track, piled steeply up the side of a rocky outcrop. Next to the **C&W Resthouse** at the end of the jeep track, there is a trout hatchery. Permits to fish in the river can be obtained here for Rs500.

Birir Valley

Situated to the south of Rumbur and Bumburet, Birir Valley is the least visited of the Kalash Valleys. It can be reached either from Ayun, or via a bridge crossing at the village of Gahiret, further south along the road to Drosh and the Lowari Pass. From Ayun, a jeep track branches off to the left just above the main square/jeep stop and follows the west bank of the Kunar River to the foot of the valley. **Guru** is the main village and the only one with any hotels. Electricity comes on at 1900 in the evenings, or not at all, usually the latter. Bring a torch or candles.

Treks

Trekking routes connect the three Kalash Valleys. The **Kalash Environmental Protection Society** (KEPS) has introduced a small number of Kalash guides familiar with these routes. They are identified by their uniform of blue shalwar kameez, dark blue waistcoat, white Chitrali cap and a KEPS badge. Using these guides will help to keep the financial benefits of tourism within the community.

The trek between the Birir and Bumburet Valleys can be done in one day, usually in five to seven hours, depending on fitness and luggage. It is a very steep, hot climb over a 3,000-m ridge from the pass (locally known as Gumbak An or Gree An depending on whether the speaker comes from Bumburet Valley or Birir Valley respectively). Apart from the gorge on the Birir side, which follows a rocky and difficult seasonal river, there is little shade along the way. A guide is recommended as it is easy to get lost (particularly going from Birir to Bumburet). Carry plenty of water (enough for your guide also!) and start early. From Birir Valley, the path starts at the village of Gasguru and descends into Bumburet Valley at Batrik.

The trek between Bumburet and Rumbur takes two days or a very long day of at least 10 hours, crossing a 3,000-m ridge into the Acholgah Valley, and then a second ridge over into Rumbur. From Bumburet the track also starts from Batrik, ending at Balanguru village in Rumbur. A guide is strongly recommended.

From the Rumbur Valley, the trek across to Chitral town is a fairly easy two-day trek, but without a guide it is easy to get lost. The trek across the Utak Pass (4,656 m) to Garam Chashma is said to be a strenuous one taking at least three days and involving a difficult river crossing; a local guide who is familiar with the route is strongly advised.

Sleeping

Kalash Valleys *p132, map p135*
Ayun
F Paradize Motel, before the main village at the end of the first line of shops after the smaller bridge, has a few rooms around a small garden with space for camping.

Rumbur Valley *p137*
Grum
There are 3 simple hotels in Grum. Meals are prepared to order.
F Kalash Indigenous Guest House. Built in a mock traditional style, with colourful rooms (attached bath), although those at the back are quite dark. The large garden allows camping and helps to attract small group tourists.
G Kalash Home Guest House, ingenierk@yahoo.com. Decent rooms with attached bath, good views across the river, cheap camping (Rs30). Friendly Kalash owner. Not a bad choice.
H Ex-Lant (Excellent!). Small, basic, but clean rooms sharing dingy toilet/shower facilities. Garden opposite allows camping.

Balanguru
F-G Saifullah Jan's Guest House. A short distance further up the valley, across the river at Balanguru. This is the nicest place, with 5 rooms in a traditional Kalash house, right in the midst of the village. Rs250 per head including all meals and tea on request. There is also a new block nearby, containing 6 rooms with attached bath around a small garden. Saifullah Jan was the first Kalash man to receive an education outside the valleys. He speaks fluent English and acts as a spokesman for the Kalash. He has been instrumental in the struggle to protect the valleys' forests from various outside logging interests and has recently devoted his efforts to enter the local political arena.

Bumburet Valley *p137*
Most hotels listed are able to prepare food to order, even if they do not have a restaurant. Those owned and run by Kalash people are indicated, although some Muslim-run hotels are owned by Kalash, who lease them out. Camping is possible in several hotel gardens and is indicated. The going rate is Rs50 to pitch a tent.

Anish
B PTDC Motel, on the main road. Built in pseudo-Kalash style, but with an ugly iron roof, this incongruous monstrosity attracts much criticism from the indigenous population. Insensitively placed next to a Bashali and "on the flood plain", as one Kalash man happily remarked), bungalows set around a man-made garden provide a rather soulless atmosphere. Although the rooms are comfortable, with attached hot bath, they are quite cramped. The dish TV in the restaurant further alienates guests from the local culture.

E Alexanders Post, on the main road. Hideous eyesore, for some reason built in an unattractively gaudy Swiss chalet design. As if it's not ugly enough to catch the eye, the owners have draped a banner across the road to further upset the environment.

E-G Benazir, on the main road. Ridiculously overpriced rooms despite the attached hot bath and large garden area. Better value are the older rooms with shared bath, but all are quite small and nothing special.

G Jinnah Kalash, off the main road to the right, opposite Hydel station. Simple, but clean rooms with attached bathroom. Pleasant balcony and garden in quiet location, although views are somewhat let down by tin roofs of less sensitive hotels. Kalash owned, with food on order and camping possible. Recommended.

G Shalimar Tourist Inn, opposite Benazir. 4 clean rooms with attached bath, designed to be partly open to the elements. The exterior walls of this friendly place are brightly painted, making the whole resemble a box of liquorice allsorts. Food is available on order and camping is allowed. One of the better non-Kalash establishments.

G Zahid Kalash Guesthouse, on main road. Friendly Kalash-run place with simple rooms although they can appear a bit stark and bare. Food prepared to order.

Brun

E-F Foreigners Tourist Inn, on the main road. A selection of new and old rooms at negotiable rates, all clean, set around a pleasant garden. Restaurant.

G Ishpatta Inn, behind Frontier. Designed by a Japanese architect in traditional Kalash style. 3 small double rooms with attached bath. Also good-value 8-bed dorm. Camping. Food prepared to order. Kalash handicraft and doll centre. Recommended.

G Kalash Guesthouse, in the village on the hillside above main road (to the right going up the valley, turn off at Taj Mahal). Some older rooms attached to the family house and some newer ones in construction. Small garden with good views. Meals included. Friendly Kalash family. Recommended.

G Kalash View, above Kalash Guesthouse, in the same village. Simpler rooms but equally friendly, with similar views. Kalash owned. Food prepared to order.

G-H Frontier, on the main road. Clean enough, but basic rooms with attached bath (bucket). Simple food available on order.

H Taj Mahal, back on the main road. Patriotic green and white building houses some basic rooms with charpoy beds. Unorganized manager takes an age to find the right key. Food unlikely.

Batrik

E Galaxy (various spellings), on the main road. Huge ugly whitewashed concrete building with rooms beginning to show their age. Aimed primarily at domestic tourists who may appreciate the circular 'tower' restaurant, but usually empty, deservedly so.

G Green, on the main road. Cramped rooms with a small scrubby garden. Attached toilet, but shared shower/bucket facilities.

G Kalash Continental, on the main road. Spacious rooms with attached hot bath in large wooden building with garden. Joint Kalash/Lahori venture. Fixed-menu Kalash food. Pleasant location, but tin roof spoils the attractiveness of the whole.

G Peace, on the main road. Clean rooms with attached bath in wood and stone layered construction. Quite friendly. Restaurant. Jeep hire and tours arranged. Not a bad choice.

Krakal

G Alexandra, small wooden rooms on either side of the road. Camping, some tents set up on wooden shelves (!), small shop sells basic supplies. Food prepared to order.

G Jahangir, on the main road. Basic rooms with attached fungal bath. Camping.

G Lahore Motel, on the main road, opposite Jahangir. Unfriendly place with 'tents'. Food available. Camping.

G Sissojak (pronounced 'Shishoyak', Kalash for 'beautiful'), on the main road. Kalash owned. 5 simple rooms, shared bath, in traditional Kalash building with verandah. Lovely large garden (camping), complete with its own orchard. Food prepared to order. Friendly manager. Recommended.

G-H Kalash, on the main road. 3 simple rooms with western toilet. Cheaper rooms and dormitory (Rs50) in main block with shared bath. Camping. Food available. Shop. Friendly Kalash owner. Recommended.

G-H Kalash (Mountain) View, on the main road. Basic rooms with attached bath, cheaper charpoy beds downstairs. Pakistani and Afghan food.

G-H Uncle & Nephew, on the main road. Basic rooms.

Shaikhanandeh

F C & W Resthouse. Comfortable rooms with attached bath. Pleasant garden. Food prepared to order. Book through C&W Sub Divisional Officer in Chitral.

Birir Valley *p137*
Guru

The main hotels in Guru are on the south bank of the river. They will prepare food to order.

F C & W Resthouse, south bank. Log cabin style, 2 decent, clean rooms with attached hot bath (geyser). Friendly chowkidar prepares food to order. Pleasant garden. Reservations essential. Book through C & W Sub Divisional Officer in Chitral.

G Insaf (was Mehran), south bank. Run-down rooms with shared bath (bucket). Food on order, eat in the kitchen with a group of friendly, but rough looking men.

G Kalash Guesthouse, across the river on the north bank is the only Kalash-owned place, a simple but friendly place with just 2 rooms, meals included in the price.

G Paradise, south bank. Assortment of 2-, 3- and 4-bedded rooms, some with bath. Good balcony to sit out on. Food prepared.

❂ Festivals and events

Kalash Valleys *p132, map p135*

3 big festivals are of particular importance and are the milestones of the year. There are also minor religious functions during the agricultural year, like, for instance, the ploughing offering. To the Kalash these festivals are the culmination of religious life and, like the big funerals, they unite the people. Tourists should behave with extra respect if visiting the valleys during one of these big functions. As the entire community gathers for festivals, politicians often take advantage of the opportunity to use the occasion, **Joshi** in particular, as a forum for political propaganda, confusing the religious dances with an ordinary feast.

Mid-May The spring festival **Joshi** honours the fairies and so safeguards the goats and shepherds before they go to the pastures.

Mid-Aug During **Utjao**, the harvest of goats' cheese is celebrated.

Summer Tourists attracted by the vivid sound of drums may have the chance of seeing the nightly dances known as **Ratnat**, performed by the young girls and boys in order to safeguard the maize crop.

Dec At **Chaomos**, lasting most of December, the divine, the living and dead relatives, the crops and the goats are safeguarded, while the community, the village and the valley are purified before the coming year.

Upper Chitral → *Colour map 2, grid C1*

A visit to Chitral is not really complete without at least a brief foray into the heights of the north and east. Awesome, rocky mountains twisted and eroded into fantastic shapes rear up on all sides, giving occasional glimpses of majestic snowy peaks beyond. The villages along the way appear as isolated oases of rich green irrigated farmland, contrasting strikingly with the surrounding barren rock. The trekking in this region, much of which has recently been changed from a closed to a restricted zone, is particularly beautiful.

Upper Chitral is where the majority of Chitral's Ismailis live, making the area far more open and welcoming than the valleys to the south, particularly for women. The diet is simple, centred around dairy products and wheat. Chitrali bread, either in the form of Khasta Shapik or Chapouti, is baked in thick round loaves and makes a pleasant change from chappatis or naan. Machir is a thin, watery yoghurt-like drink which can be thickened into Shetu, or yoghurt, and is in turn used to make Shupinak, a delicious thick, creamy cheese. ⏵⏵ *For Sleeping, Eating and all other listings, see page 147.*

> **❝❞ Bubbling streams and irrigation channels run through golden fields of wheat and barley lined with towering poplar trees, shimmering in the sun...**

Chitral to Reshun

The task of metalling the road between Gilgit and Chitral is now almost complete. The journey from Chitral to Mastuj can, at present, be completed in around two to three hours (cargo jeeps from Upper Chitral jeep depot in Chitral). After crossing the bridge to the north of Chitral town, the road heads northeast along the east bank of the **Mastuj River**. The first village you pass through is **Koghuzi**, which boasts its own post office, health centre, a few basic shops and a local police post. About 1 km beyond Koghuzi, the **Golen Gol** drains in from the southeast. A jeep track leads up this valley as far as the village of **Ustur** (14 km). From there it is possible to trek northeast and then either bear north across the **Shakuh Pass** to Reshun, or continue in an easterly direction across the **Phargam Pass** to Harchin. Another trek leads south from Ustur, over the **Dok Pass**, and then southwest to Madaglasht at the head of the Shishi Valley.

The main road continues along the Mastuj River, through isolated patches of cultivation beneath barren slopes, passing through the villages of **Maroi (Maroai)**, **Barenis (Burnes)** and **Green Lasht**. Here, the surrounding rock suddenly becomes a strong red colour due to iron in fluvial deposits. Between Green Lasht and **Reshun**, roughly opposite the Nadir Hotel, the Barum Gol drains in from the northwest. There is a bridge across to the opposite bank and the village of Parpesh. The Barum Gol is jeepable as far as the village of Barum, or sometimes as far as Muzhen. This is the starting point of the trek across the Owir Pass and down to the Lutkho Valley.

The Owir Pass trek

ⓘ *Open zone, but permission is required from the Deputy Commissioner in Chitral. Maximum elevation 4,338 m. Aug to mid-Sep. Maps: the U502 series sheet covering this trek is restricted; Mountaineering Maps of the World, P 268 Tirich Mir and Buni Zom is reasonable. See map on p143 for orientation. See notes on trekking on p45.*

Above Barum village there is a track which is in theory jeepable as far as **Muzhen** (pronounced 'Mujen'), although the bridges along the way are often broken. Alternatively it is a 7-km walk, steep at first but gentle after the village of **Shungosh**, just over halfway. Beside the path above Muzhen there is good camping by the stream, with trees for shade. Above Muzhen the route climbs through open pastures up towards **Owir Pass** (4,338 m). There are plenty of potential camping spots on the way up. Be prepared for bitterly cold nights and high winds. The best views of Tirich Mir and Buni Zom are from a small hillock to the north of the pass itself. On the far side the descent is steep, crossing loose slate, before arriving at pastures with good camping. Further down the path passes through small settlements before arriving at **Sussoom**, the most important village in the Karimabad (previously Ozher) Valley, and the head of the jeep track up from **Shogore**, in the Lutkho Valley between Chitral and Garam Chashma. The valley below Sussoom is very narrow with sheer slate cliffs on the south side.

Reshun to Mastuj

Back on the main road, a few kilometres after Reshun, the **Turikho Valley** can be seen draining into the Mastuj River, the two valleys running almost parallel at this point. Almost opposite the junction of the two rivers is the village of **Kuragh**, with its Aga Khan school. There are a couple of small hotels here, see page 146.

At the end of the village is a police check post where foreigners must register their details. From here the landscape changes again, as the river becomes braided, with islands of silt creating multiple channels in the flow. The valley widens, and evidence of large changes in the river level can be seen in the varying heights of the alluvial deposits on the opposite bank. Just beyond the next village, **Charun**, the road crosses to the north bank of the river on a bridge. The old jeep track into the Turikho Valley branches left just after the bridge; these days it is often blocked by landslides and rarely used. The main road heads east and passes through the village of **Junali Koach**, literally just a petrol pump. A couple of kilometres further on, there is an unmarked turning to the left which is the start of the new jeep track up the Turikho Valley (see page 146).

Further on there is a bridge across to the village of **Buni**, a large, fertile settlement (the largest in upper Chitral) spread out over a wide alluvial fan (about two hours by jeep from Chitral). The main jeep track continues straight on, passing through the village of **Parwak** before crossing once again to the south bank of the river. At Parwak there is the possibility of an overnight stop, see page 146

Soon after is the junction of the Laspur River with the Mastuj, the former draining in from the south. The jeep track descends through a series of switch-backs before crossing to the east bank of the Laspur River. It then forks left past the petrol pump, which leads 3 km into Mastuj village, while the right fork is the route to the Shandur Pass (see page 149).

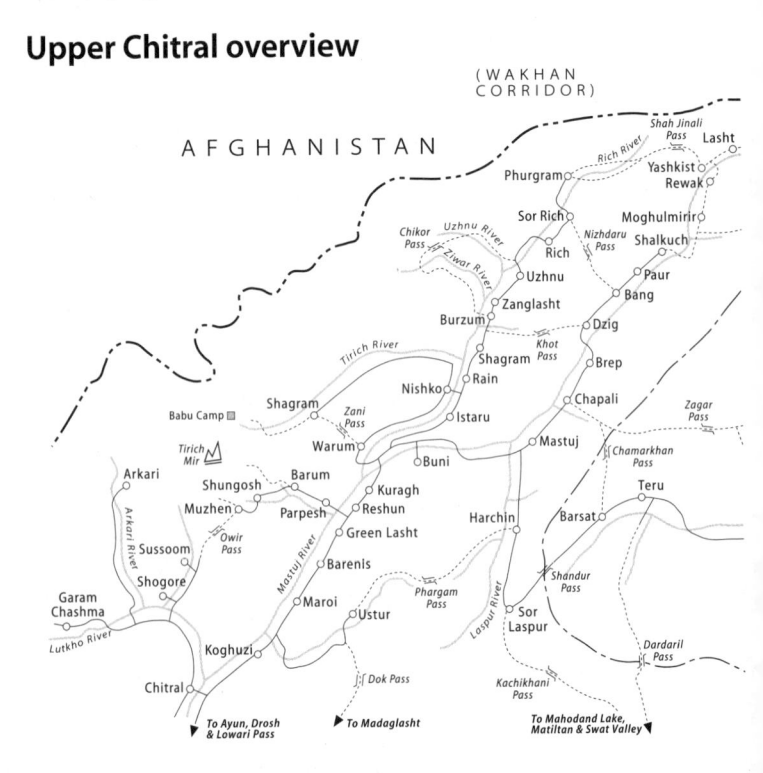

Upper Chitral overview

Mastuj

Mastuj was once the seat of power of the independent Kushwaqt principality, which in its heyday reached across into the Gilgit River Valley. **Mastuj Fort**, similar in style to the one in Chitral town, is still occupied by Colonel Khushwaqt ul-Mulk, the son of Shuja ul-Mulk, who was made Mehtar of Chitral by the British in 1895 following the siege of Chitral fort. The setting is particularly beautiful, with the village spread out across a large alluvial fan. Bubbling streams and irrigation channels run through golden fields of wheat and barley lined with towering poplar trees, shimmering in the sun and wind, while in the village apricot and jujube trees are scattered all around. There is a small bazaar, fairly well stocked with basic supplies (trekkers can stock up on flour, rice, lentils, tea, sugar etc here), a telephone exchange and a post office. The latter was established by the British and was considered to be the most far-flung post office in the Empire. For full details of the route from Mastuj to the Shandur Pass and Gilgit, see page 149.

Yarkhun Valley

North of Mastuj village, the Mastuj River becomes known as the Yarkhun. Although largely in a restricted trekking zone, some of the best treks in NWFP are here. And for those with stamina, several treks can be combined into one long trip, taking you as far as the Yasin and Ishkoman Valleys (on the Chitral-Gilgit route), or even as far as the KKH itself. See map on page 145 for orientation.

A rough jeep track follows the east bank of the river as it climbs northeast towards the Wakhan Corridor. The jeep track passes first through the village of **Chuinj**, where there is a small basic hotel.

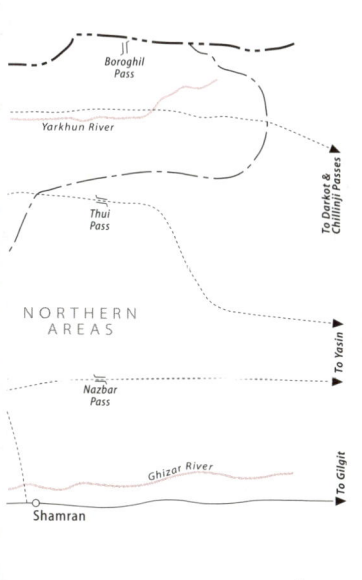

A little further on is Chapali, where a small side valley climbs up to the east, the start of the trek across the Chamarkhan Pass to Barsat, just east of the Shandur Pass (described in the opposite direction, see page 150). The jeep track continues northeast from Chapali, passing through the village of **Brep**, before crossing to the west bank of the river. Shortly after is the small village of **Dzig**, the start of the trek over the **Khot Pass** and into the Turikho Valley. Further on is **Bang**, consisting of a number of small villages spread out over several kilometres. Here, the **Bang Gol** drains in from the northwest, marking the start of the trek over the **Nizhdaru Pass** to Sor Rich in the Turikho Valley.

Beyond Bang, the jeep track winds its way through the village of **Pitrangaz**, followed closely by **Paur**, before arriving at **Shulkuch**. A few kilometres beyond Shulkuch the jeep track peters out altogether.

The Yarkhun Valley continues northeast, before swinging round to the east to run parallel with Afghanistan's Wakhan Corridor. A long, strenuous but spectacular trek (around three weeks) follows the Yarkhun Valley, passing the route north over the **Boroghil Pass** into Afghanistan, then crosses the **Karambar Pass** (4,300 m), crowned by a string of lakes, into the Karambar Valley. After crossing the snout of the Chatteboi glacier, it then climbs up over the glaciated **Chillinji Pass** (5,290 m) and crosses into the Chapursan Valley to emerge on the KKH to the north of Sust. This trek requires experienced guides and a properly organized and equipped expedition.

An alternative and more manageable trek branches northeast off the Yarkhun Valley, across **Shah Jinali Pass** and down into the Turikho Valley (see below).

Shah Jinali Pass trek
ⓘ *Restricted zone. Maximum elevation 4,259 m. Jul to Sep. Maps: U502 series NJ 43-13 Mastuj is good, although some place names are misleading; Mountaineering maps of the World, P 236 Eastern Hindu Kush is good. See map on p145 for orientation. See trekking notes, p45.*

This is a particularly beautiful (but fairly strenuous) trek and well worth the expense associated with trekking in restricted areas. Most people recommend doing it from the Turikho Valley (Rich) to Yarkhun Valley due to the steep climb towards the pass coming from the other direction. This depends, however, on whether you prefer your ascents to be short and sharp, or longer and gentler. The trek is described here going from the Yarkhun to Turikho Valley. Allow four to five days (not including rest days). Porters charge for at least six stages.

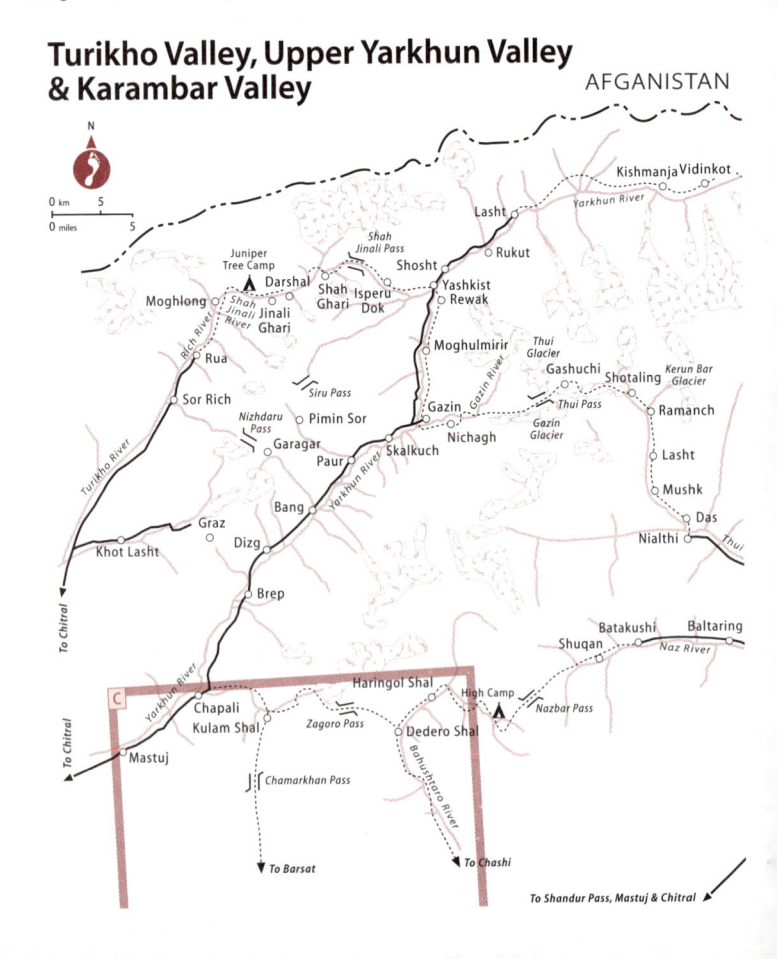

Turikho Valley, Upper Yarkhun Valley & Karambar Valley

The first section from **Shalkuch** is an easy walk, climbing gently along the east bank of the Yarkhun River, crossing the Gazin Gol flowing in from the east (the route up to the Thui Pass across to Yasin, see page 153), and passing through settlements and green, lightly wooded terrain to **Moghulmirir**, where there is good camping.

Above Moghulmirir the main path zigzags steeply up a shoulder of mountain to the village and fields of **Rewak**, situated on a beautiful small plateau with excellent views. On the other side it descends steeply through deep meadows of flowers and wild rose. An alternative route follows the river around the shoulder, but involves crossing to a shingle bank and back, and is not always passable. Further on a bridge leads across the Yarkhun River and the path doubles back before climbing up to the village of **Yashkist**. You can camp in the village, although flat ground is very limited.

Above the village the path enters the Seru Gol, crosses to the south bank of the river, recrosses further up and doubles back to enter the narrow gorge of Isperu Dok Gol. The climb up the gorge is very steep, gaining more than 800 m before arriving eventually at the summer settlement and pastures of **Isperu Dok**. There is excellent camping on a small grassy patch by the river below the main cluster of stone huts. The setting is a spectacular one and it is well worth spending a day here to explore. You can cover the section from Moghulmirir to Isperu Dok in one long day if you are fit.

Above Isperu Dok the valley divides, the left fork being the route to Shah Jinali. Cross to the opposite bank of the river and climb over a shoulder, ascending steadily

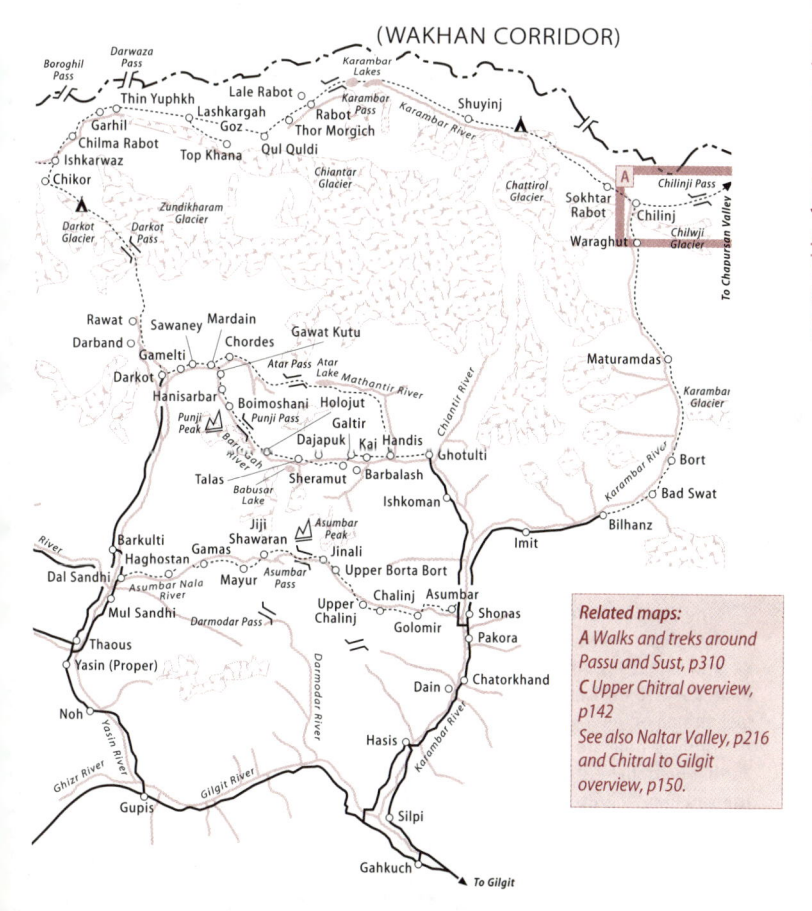

Related maps:
A Walks and treks around Passu and Sust, p310
C Upper Chitral overview, p142
See also Naltar Valley, p216 and Chitral to Gilgit overview, p150.

to the top of the pass. The **Shah Jinali (King's Polo Ground) Pass** is a beautiful area of rolling pasture, covered in flowers in early July. The greenery is broken in places by snowdrifts, small ponds and crystal clear streams. All around is an amphitheatre of icy peaks. It is a steady descent to **Shah Ghari**, another beautiful spot deep with wild geraniums, onion, hemlock and buttercups.

The next section, down to the village of **Darshal**, is subject to frequent change and can follow either bank of the river. Further on, following the right bank after Darshal, there is a precariously perched tiny camp with a rock shelter. A gully fed by a waterfall runs down from the north. The path then descends steadily, crossing to the left bank and rounding a gradual bend. On the opposite bank, where the Rahozon Gol drains in from the north, there is an area of level ground and trees known as **Moghlong**. Further round the bend, across a side-stream, there is a possible campsite. The valley steadily opens out from its narrow gorge to a wide plain. Further on the path crosses to the right bank of the river on a good bridge and eventually joins the head of the jeep track shortly before Phurgram village.

Turikho Valley

The Turikho Valley is particularly green and fertile, the irrigated patches of settlement blending into each other for most of its length. The lower section of the valley is known as the Mulkho, the middle section as the Turikho and the upper section as the Rich Valley. See map on page 145 for orientation.

From the turning just east of Khandan, the jeep track climbs steeply up to a shoulder of mountain separating the Turikho and Mastuj Rivers. On top is a small plateau with pasture known as **Kagh Lasht**, scarred by several jeep tracks which have cut through the ground cover and exposed the sandy soil underneath to erosion. The track descends to the village of **Istaru**, followed soon after by **Warkup**. Further on there is a bridge across to the village of **Nishko** on the west bank.

This bridge gives access to the **Tirich Gol** which drains in from the west, joining the Turikho River higher up, above the village of Rain. The Tirich Gol is jeepable as far as the village of **Shagram** (there are two Shagrams, the second is higher up the Turikho Valley). From Shagram a trek leads southeast over the **Zani Pass** and back into the Mulkho (Turikho) Valley near **Warum**, to join the old jeep track along the north bank of the river. Another trek leads west towards **Tirich Mir Base Camp**.

The main jeep track up the Turikho Valley continues northeast through **Rain** (pronounced 'ra-een'), **Shagram** and across a small side valley draining in from the east (the start of the trek over the Khot Pass to Dzig in the Yarkhun Valley), to **Burzum**. There is a footbridge across to the west bank of the Turikho River here, giving access to the **Ziwar Gol**, which drains in from the northwest. Further along, at **Zanglasht**, another footbridge gives more direct access. A trek follows the Ziwar Gol, branching northwest over the **Chikor Pass** and down the **Uzhnu Gol** to rejoin the Rich (Turikho) Valley at Uzhnu.

The main jeep track crosses to the west bank of the river at **Uzhnu** for a short stretch, then recrosses to the east bank to arrive at **Rich**, a scattered settlement of several villages which has a shop selling basic supplies. Further up, beyond **Sor Rich**, the jeep track crosses once again to the east bank to arrive at **Phurgram**. This last stretch of the track, crossing and recrossing the river, is frequently blocked as the bridges here are particularly rickety and easily broken during rains or floods. Further on from here is the start of the trek over the Shah Jinali Pass and down into the Yarkhun Valley.

Sleeping

Chitral to Reshun p141
Reshun
F C&W Rest House, Reshun (book through the C&W Sub Divisional Officer in Chitral). Small, overlooked by a striking array of multicoloured rock formations.

Green Lasht
G Nadir Hotel, Green Lasht, on the right-hand side of the main road. A couple of clean rooms with camp beds, in a pleasant, breezy location. Food is available. Rooms are a bit pricey, but it's a handy overnight halt for the Owir Pass trek.

Reshun to Mastuj p142
Kuragh
G Golden Inn Basic rooms around a garden with camping, food available.
G Kohistan. Basic, set around a garden (camping), also offering simple food.

Buni
F C&W Rest House. Good, with 7 rooms.

Parwak
H Glacier View Some basic rooms with charpoy beds, shared toilet and a dining hall. Worth a visit in itself is the small rickety balcony with excellent views of Buni Zom.

Mastuj p143
C PTDC Motel, situated 2 km beyond the main village, take the track to the left of the main track. Empty, lifeless place with small rooms set around a scrubby garden. The hotel itself obscures some lovely views.
F C & W Rest House. Permission to stay here is difficult to get. Try in Chitral or Buni.
F-G Mastuj Fort (book through Hindu Kush Heights in Chitral). Some simple new rooms but the main reason to stay here is the large camping area in the grounds, especially for larger groups. With your own tent, Rs200 will give you access to shower/toilet facilities.
G Foreigner Tourist Paradise, in the lane opposite Mastuj Tourist Guest House. Furnished in local style with mattresses on the floor. Food is prepared to order, camping is allowed in the small gardens. Marginally better than the Tirich Mir View.
G Mastuj Tourist Guest House. This is a well-run place with a good manager in Abu Baker. The rooms are pleasantly furnished, some with attached bath. Camping (Rs50) is possible in the small garden, while jeeps and guides can be arranged. Good communal meals at breakfast and dinner. Phone calls to Europe cost Rs250 for 3 mins. Recommended.
G Tirich Mir View, in the lane opposite Mastuj Tourist Guest House. Furnished in local style with mattresses on the floor. Food prepared to order, camping allowed in the gardens.
G Tourist Garden, in the lane to the left, facing Mastuj Tourist Guest House. 3 simple clean rooms, 1 with attached bath. Good food to order. Camping possible. Good reports in the guest book.

Yarkhun Valley p143
G Khyber, Chuinj. Small basic hotel.

Transport

Mastuj p143
Cargo jeeps are available between Mastuj and **Chitral** (2-3 hrs), although it is rare to find 1 crossing the Shandur Pass. Many people arrive in Mastuj with a **private jeep** hired from Chitral. If heading for **Gilgit**, you may be able to find an empty jeep returning from Chitral. Abu Baker at the Mastuj Tourist Guest House may be able to help you to locate one. Around Rs500 per head is the going rate for empty seats to **Gilgit**, otherwise a privately hired jeep to Gilgit will be marginally cheaper than deals offered in Chitral, but with less choice of vehicles. If you wish to break the journey at Phandur or Khalti Lake and be prepared to wait for the occasional cargo jeep heading east.

A number of 'romantic' travellers are now beginning to buy a pack **donkey** in Mastuj to carry their gear over one of the pa
sses leading into the Northern Areas. Prices for an economy-class flea-bitten model average around Rs2,000-2,500, but don't expect much more than scrap value on the re-sale in Gilgit (or along the way). Apparently, you're supposed to "look at its teeth and shake its head". To stop the beast, click your tongue several times; to get it going try "short, sharp, low guttural sounds, or a kick".

Chitral to Gilgit → *Colour map 2, grid C1-B4*

The journey from Chitral to Gilgit (or, indeed, the journey from Gilgit to Chitral in the opposite direction) is one of the most beautiful and challenging trips in Pakistan, yet relatively few foreign visitors attempt it. Admittedly, public transport along this route is not particularly reliable and accommodation options are limited, but Pakistan is supposed to be an adventure tourism destination after all. Those who do make this trip invariably agree that it is one of the highlights of their visit to Pakistan. The route crosses the famous Shandur Pass, scene of the most spectacular polo event in the world, follows the Ghizr/Gilgit River downstream past two of Pakistan's most memorable spots, Phandur and Khalti Lake, as well as providing access to the fascinating side valleys of Yasin and Ishkoman, both of which have almost inexhaustible trekking potential. Don't miss out on this one! ▸▸ *For Sleeping, Eating and all other listings, see pages 160-162.*

Ins and outs

Direction There are both advantages and disadvantages in travelling in either direction: on the Chitral-Gilgit route it seems easier to find a cargo jeep, plus it falls naturally into the best route around Pakistan (see the Grand tour clockwise on page 12); on the Gilgit-Chitral route you are more likely to find other travellers (in Gilgit) who will share the cost of a private hire jeep, you can pre-book the Inspection Bungalows, plus you can penetrate at least part of this terrain by public bus. The route here is described in the Chitral-Gilgit direction. See map on page 145 for orientation, as well as the map below.

In 2001 work began on metalling the road between Chitral and Gilgit and, at the time of going to press, the task was approaching completion. Completing the journey on **public transport** is now much easier since **NATCO** launched what in theory is a non-stop bus service (a 12-seater landcruiser) between Chitral and Gilgit, costing Rs600 and taking as little as 14 hours, but usually more. Departures are currently once a week, at weekends, although this may increase if the demand is there. The downside is that this option does not allow you to stop off and explore the wonderful places en route.

Cargo jeeps provide another public transport option, although it's rare to find one going the whole way. You could undertake the trip in a series of long and short hops (expect to spend about Rs1000 on public transport and accommodation to complete this trip in three to five days), although the disadvantage of travelling by cargo jeep is that they are horrendously overloaded. Furthermore, cargo jeeps tend to stop for the night in relatively uninteresting villages, not allowing you the option to stay at one of the beautiful lakes en route. Don't forget that there is a public (NATCO) bus service between Yasin, Gupis and Gilgit, so you have the chance to explore at least some of this route independently.

The best option, however, is to treat yourself. If you are travelling on a tight budget, then this is the one trip in Pakistan where it is worth splashing out on a **private hire jeep** – you won't regret it. It costs around Rs8,000 to hire a jeep all the way from Chitral to Gilgit (usually a three-day, two-night trip), or Rs6,000 from Mastuj to Gilgit (same rates in opposite direction). Jeeps seat four comfortably, five or six at a push, so the cost is not excessive when shared. You may get an even cheaper deal by going through a backpacker hotel manager, or if you're really lucky you may find a driver who has just made the trip and who's offering a good price in order to avoid going back empty. Or there is always the **donkey** option, see page 147. For full details of animals, buses, cargo jeeps and private hire jeeps, see Transport in the Chitral, Mastuj and Gilgit sections.

The most spectacular polo event in the world

At 3,735 m, the Shandur Pass is not particularly high, and is generally described as more of a plateau (it has two large lakes lying on it). It has, however, become the annual venue for the most spectacular polo event in the world, which has been running since 1936. Each year, the teams of Gilgit and Chitral compete as the highlight of a three-day festival when 'Shandur Top' becomes a huge tent city. In addition to the polo, there are golf and fishing tournaments, cultural shows, as well as (most importantly to some) the opportunity for the elite of Pakistan to 'be seen'. For further details on the sport, see page 44.

Unfortunately, the organization of the festival is invariably a monumental cock-up. For years the Tourism Department has been trying to fix an annual date for the event, but its attempts are frequently scuppered by the politicians who change the dates at short notice to fit in with their own plans. In 1995 the dates were rearranged with just one month's notice, and the final was played on the first day of the festival because that was the only day that the President of Pakistan could make it. In 2000, the event was cancelled altogether, in memory of those who lost their lives in the Kargil conflict, while in 2001 the festival was put forward a month at the last minute to accommodate the president's busy schedule. The PTDC has now fixed the dates of the festival as 7-9 July, with the final being played on the last day. Whether this happens in the coming years largely depends on a politician's definition of the word 'fixed', so check the dates in advance. The 500-jeep traffic jam that develops as everyone leaves at the end of the festival isn't much fun either. Accommodation, food and transport can be arranged in Chitral and Gilgit just before the festival begins. Shop around for the best deal, or bring your own equipment.

Mastuj to Shandur Pass

From **Mastuj**, the rough jeep road runs south along and above the right bank of the Laspur River through a barren landscape, only occasionally interrupted by small patches of scrub. The valley widens before entering **Harchin**, a picturesque oasis, with accommodation and a small shop selling basic supplies. On the opposite bank lies the similarly cultivated village of **Rahman**, among stands of poplar trees.

The road continues south as far as **Sor Laspur**, the last village in NWFP, 22 km from Mastuj. This is the starting point for a trek south across the **Kachikani Pass** (4,766 m) into Upper Swat (although this rarely attempted trek is best done from south to north, accompanied by a local guide and armed escort).

The track turns northeast at Sor Laspur, rising steeply at first before slowly climbing up to the Shandur Pass, a further 20 km. A 15 km section of the jeep road on either side of this pass has been left unmetalled. It's quite rough here and Sor Laspur to Shandur Top can take two and a half hours. Foreigners must register their details, including religion, at the police check post next to the polo ground.

Shandur Pass

The most famous crossing of the pass was that by Colonel James Kelly in 1895, at the head of an expeditionary force sent to relieve the British forces besieged in the fort at Chitral. Crossing in April, and faced by shoulder-deep snow, the decision to bring artillery pieces looked as if it would doom the entire expedition, but they were to prove crucial later as the force battled towards their goal. Inspired by commander, Lieutenant Cosmo Stewart, the native regiment dismantled the guns and carried them through the snow. One British officer pointed out, "Nothing can be said too highly in praise of this splendid achievement. Here were some 250 men, Hindus and Mussulmans, who, working shoulder to shoulder, had brought two mountain guns, with their carriages and supplies of ammunition, across some 20 miles of deep soft snow, across a pass 12,300 foot high, at the beginning of April, the worst time of the year." Some Chitralis still honour this achievement; the 100th anniversary of the original crossing was commemorated by a group of Chitralis who retraced the route without the guns.

Shandur Pass to Barsat

Once across the Shandur Pass, you leave NWFP and enter the Northern Areas. The districts between the Shandur Pass and Gupis are referred to as Kuh and Ghizr (sometimes Ghizer). Up until Phandur (three hours by jeep from the pass), the majority of the population of the main valley speak Khowar, and beyond Phandur it is Shina that prevails (with Burushaski and Khowar spoken in Yasin, and all three languages plus Wakhi in use in Ishkoman).

Dropping down from the Shandur Pass, the track continues to be rough and slow going, but this gives you time to appreciate one of the most impressive vistas of the journey, looking down onto a wide glacial valley, with the aquamarine Khakush River snaking its way along this charming northeast/southwest-orientated glen. With its fresh springs, trout-stocked river and lush green meadows, all set in a natural amphitheatre of snow-capped peaks, the camping here at **Langar** is superb. Langar itself is more of a point on the map than a village, since there are no buildings. A helipad and rows of electricity pylons lying at regular intervals along the valley suggest some kind of development in the near future. As the road continues along the valley floor, it becomes straighter and faster, but still rough.

Chitral to Gilgit overview

Related maps:
A *Upper Chitral overview, p143*
B *Naltar Valley, p216*
C *Walks and treks around Passu and Sust, p310*
D *Turikho Valley, Upper Yarkhun Valley and Karambar Valley, p145*

Beyond Langar is **Barsat** (3,353 m), which has a police check post just before the village. For those travelling from Gilgit towards Chitral that get stuck for transport at Barsat, there is a trekking route that is easier (and arguably more scenic) over the Chamarkhan Pass to Mastuj, via Chapali in the Yarkhun Valley, rather than across the Shandur Pass.

Chamarkhan Pass trek

ⓘ *Open zone. Maximum elevation 4,328 m. Jul to Sep. Maps: U502 NJ 43-13 map is adequate; Mountaineering Maps of the World, P 212 Central Hindu Raj is better, although a guide is highly recommended. 2 days. Read trekking notes, p45.*

From the police checkpost at Barsat, head north along the east side of the Chamarkhan River. The trail is rather confusing; when in doubt, stick to the centre of the valley. The upper meadows (after a four- to five-hour walk) make a good first night camping spot. Having crossed the 4,328-m **Chamarkhan Pass**, it is a steep descent down the east side of the river to the small settlement of Kulam Shal (3,429 m). Just beyond the settlement, the trail is joined from the east by a track towards Zagaro Pass (4,920 m). Ignore this route, and head northwest into the Zagaro River valley, staying on the true right bank of the river. After several hours walking you reach the small village of Chapali. From here it is an unrewarding 10-km walk down to Mastuj along the jeep road, although you may be able to hitch a ride on a passing jeep or tractor.

Barsat to Phandur

From the check point the jeep track rises through the village of Barsat with its cultivated land and friendly, waving villagers lining the route. The road then descends back down to the river, which by this stage cuts a steep V-shaped valley, before crossing a small stream and rising again, to **Teru** (3,065m), a long, strung-out settlement, 28 km from Shandur Pass. Here, and a couple of kilometres further on at **Teru Bahach**, there is accommodation.

As the jeep track continues east from Teru, it crosses a small pass with impressive views down onto a wide confluence as the Handrap River joins the Ghizr River. This, and the sudden starkness of the landscape, should help to take your mind off the precarious state of the road at this point. Just before it reaches Phandur this side valley leads south to **Handrap Lake**, a picturesque spot, rich in trout and a great place to camp. Officially this whole area is part of the recently created Shandur-Handrap National Park, although effectively this protected area exists on paper only. If you trek south from here, you cross the 5,030-m **Dadarili Pass** into the Upper Swat Valley, but once again this is a dangerous route requiring a local guide and armed escort.

Beyond the turning for Handrap, the road passes through the highly cultivated flood plain of the meandering Ghizr River, with the fields here tended by the people of the sprawling settlement of **Phandur**. There is a fairly steep climb up the terminal moraine of a long since receded glacier, but the view from the top of the hill is worth all the effort of getting here.

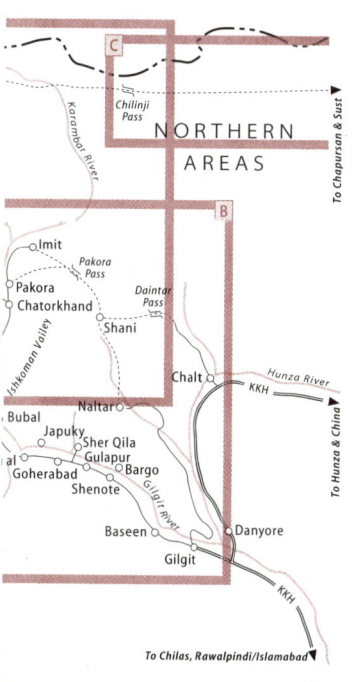

The view on the east side of the hill is equally impressive, dominated in the foreground by the deep blue **Phandur Lake**. At 2,800 m, the lake is said to be well stocked with trout, as is the river which offers some good camping spots, just before the main part of the village and immediately after the bridge. It is often possible to hire horses in Phandur, offering and almost inexhaustible series of day trips and longer excursions. Phandur is 36 km from Dahimal and about 7-9 hours from Gilgit by privately hired jeep.

Phandur to Khalti Lake

The jeep track winds its way down from the hill at Phandur, before crossing to the south side of the Ghizr River just before the sprawling settlement of **Chashi**. When Schomberg saw the small houses at Chashi, with their open skylights in the roof, "the temptation to lob stones into some of them was hard to resist".

Between Phandur and Gupis (58 km), there are numerous rock carvings, many on boulders that can be easily viewed from the road. One expert suggests that these art forms illustrate the lives of pastoral nomads who may have moved here in early Christian times, and show great continuity with similar designs found in the Pamir region. Many show mounted horsemen, solar motifs, hunting scenes and long-horned ibexes.

The valley narrows somewhat after Chashi, and the Ghizr River is augmented by tributaries from both the north and south, the latter of which provide ancient communication routes into the Tangir and Darel Valleys. From here the jeep track rises and falls more readily, reminiscent of a roller-coaster ride. Between Chashi and the next village, **Pingul**, look out for the numerous petroglyphs on the rocks.

A further 6 km brings you to **Thingai**, and then another 10 km to **Dahimal**. At this point the Ghizr River is joined from the south by the emerald green **Bathraiz River**, flowing from Swat Kohistan. The Bathraiz Valley leads south towards the Tangir Valley, although you should not attempt to follow this route. This was a route that the early Buddhist pilgrims used on their journeys from China to Gandhara, Swat and other pilgrimage sites in South Asia, as well as the means of access for invading armies from Chitral and the kingdoms to the north. Another 13 km beyond Dahimal brings you to Khalti Lake.

Khalti Lake

The lake was formed in the late 1980s following a major flood and shows no sign of disappearing just yet. Its deep blue aquamarine colour is particularly photogenic, and is a popular spot with trout fishermen. Permits should be obtained from the Fisheries Department. Ask at either of the hotels to find the local officer. At its western end, a bridge crosses the lake to the village of Khalti.

However much you travel around Pakistan, you will find few more charming spots than this.

Khalti Lake to Gupis

About 8 km east of Khalti Lake is the Chinese-constructed 96-m-long **Gupis Bridge**, which provides a diversion off the main Chitral-Gilgit route up the Yasin Valley. From this point it is 104 km to the Shandur Pass, 54 km to Phandur, 42 km to Gahkuch and 112 km to Gilgit. Beyond Gupis Bridge, the jeep track continues a further 2 km to **Gupis**. To the side of the road, about halfway between the bridge and Gupis, there is a simple stone memorial to a young Czech couple who were presumably murdered while camping at this spot in May 2001 (no trace of the man has yet been found). The police in Gupis claim to have 'tortured many suspects, but not found the culprit'. The local community was very shocked by this murder and it seems unlikely that this gruesome crime was committed by a local person, rather a passing, opportunist killer. This incident also highlights the risks of camping in isolated spots, especially next to a road.

For those carrying along the Chitral-Gilgit road and not making an excursion up the Yasin Valley, turn to page 155.

Yasin Valley

The Yasin Valley, and in particular the characters it produced, has played a leading role in the history of the region. Continually fought over by the rulers of both Chitral and Gilgit, the history of the rulers of Yasin reads like a catalogue of patricide, fratricide and avunculicide. Yasin came to the attention of Victorian Britain following the murder of British explorer George Hayward in the upper reaches of the valley. See map on page 145 for orientation.

Biddulph classifies the original inhabitants of the valley as Yeshkuns, although they refer to themselves as Boorushi. The majority of the valley are Ismaili Muslims, speaking Burushaski, although it is a more archaic dialect than the Burushaski spoken in Hunza and Nagar. The ruling class, however, speak Khowar (Chitrali), reflecting their origins in the valley to the west. Today, many residents of Yasin Valley are bilingual. The valley is sometimes referred to as Woorshigum ('Valley of the Boorushi').

The valley is well watered, and in the lower reaches in particular there is extensive cultivatable land. Yasin is probably seen at its best in late August, as the wheat and maize are approaching harvest. Locally, Yasini women have a reputation for great beauty, although it is not uncommon to find that women who originally belonged to the Khushwakht families of Chitral practise purdah.

Gupis Bridge to Yasin 'proper'

The entrance to the Yasin Valley is relatively dry and stony, until you reach the first 'green' settlements at **Damalgan** (6 km) and **Gindai** (10 km). At the time of writing, the road was metalled as far as the latter village and is expected to reach Darkot sometime in 2004. The road continues through the terminal moraine to the suspension bridge at **Noh**. Previously, NATCO bus services terminated here, although the recent construction of a more solid bridge means that the service now continues all the way to Thaous, just beyond 'Central' Yasin (or Yasin 'proper', 25 km from Gupis Bridge) where foreigners should register at the police station.

Yasin

'Central' Yasin is a long, sprawling series of settlements collectively known as Yasin. There are still remains of the fort built by Gohar Aman, one of the valley's most celebrated rulers. A member of the Khushwakht ruling family, he is remembered as much for his "cruelty of disposition" as his ability as "an able and energetic Soldier". Another commmentator, Schomberg, is more caustic in his analysis, referring to Gohar Aman as "a mighty murderer and strapping tyrant". Gohar Aman was the father of Mir Wali, the man generally held responsible for the murder of George Hayward.

Antagonistic towards Shias, Gohar Aman made many raids on Gilgit, and later had great success against the Dogra forces. However, following the eventual Dogra victory in 1863, a punitive expedition was sent to Yasin Valley to extract revenge, and it is the details of this massacre at nearby Muduri that Hayward described so graphically in *The Pioneer* newspaper (see below).

Yasin Fort ① *on the west side of the river, although you may have to enlist some local help to find it (it's close to the Tehsil Office)*, has a large tree and a new mosque within the courtyard, although the old mosque, complete with carved pillars, remains. One tower of the fort still stands and, although the door remains locked, it is possible to scramble inside where part of the wall has fallen away. Down by the river, near to the small plank bridge, is the **grave of Gohar Aman**. It is a simple Muslim shrine, surrounded by a low, jagged tooth wall.

Another place of interest close to Yasin is what is referred to as **Hayward's Rock** ⓘ *about 1 km from Yasin, on the Nazbar Rd, the chowkidar at the Inspection Bungalow can show you where it is.* Perhaps sensing that he was in some danger, Hayward carved his initials GWH, the figure 20 (the distance in miles to Darkot), and an arrow pointing in the direction he intended to travel.

Yasin to Muduri

Travelling north from Yasin, the road crosses the river on a new concrete bridge, and initially proceeds on a very high-quality jeep track. The first village north of Yasin is the sprawling settlement of **Thaous** (various spellings), which has recently seen the construction of a new hospital and a number of schools. The valley here is wide, flat and well irrigated, providing extensive wheat and maize cultivation.

Beyond Thaous, the terrain becomes barren and stony. The only greenery is provided by the settlement of **Dal Sandhi**, across the river, where camping is possible if arriving from the Ishkomen Valley via the Asumbar Pass. The small village of Muduri is just above Dal Sandhi.

Muduri

This small village has been identified with the site of the Dogra massacres that Hayward wrote about in his article in *The Pioneer* article: "They [Dogra troops] threw the little ones in the air and cut them in two as they fell. It is said that the pregnant women, after being killed, were ripped open and their unborn babies hacked to pieces. Some forty women who were not yet dead were dragged to one spot, and were there burnt by the Dogra sepoys. With the exception of a few wounded men and women who ultimately recovered, every man, woman and child within the fort, and, in all, 1,200 to 1,400 of these unhappy villagers, were massacred by the foulest treachery and cruelty."

Visiting the scene seven years after the massacre, Hayward noted "I have myself counted 147 still entire skulls, nearly all of those women and children. The ground is literally white with bleached human bones and the remains of not less than 400 human beings are now lying on the hill." The nala above Dal Sandhi runs east across the Asumbar Pass (4,560 m) to the Ishkomen Valley (and is usually attempted in the Ishkoman-Yasin direction, see page 157.

Thaous to Darkot

The river bed north of Thaous is wide and stony, with water running through only one or two main channels. The flow of the river is augmented by that of the Thui River, which joins the main river some 12 km north of Yasin at **Barkulti**. There is a new bridge that crosses the Thui Nala. The Thui Valley provides a popular and spectacular trekking route across the **Thui Pass** (4,499 m) to the Yarkhun Valley in Chitral District.

❗ *For some reason, tea-strainers have not reached this part of the world yet. If you don't want your mouth to be full of leaves every time you stop for chai, then bring your own.*

Beyond the large agricultural settlement of Barkulti, the jeep road is enclosed along a narrow lane that threads its way through a series of small settlements. About 15 km beyond Barkulti the track crosses to the east side of the river, continuing along the wide, flat flood plain. After a further 10 km a wide bowl is reached. Directly ahead is the settlement of **Darkot** (about 41 km from Yasin), while the valley joining from the east leads over the Punji Pass to the Ishkoman Valley (see page 155). The approach to the **Darkot Pass** (4,744 m) from the south side is particularly steep. Having crossed the pass into the Chapsuran Valley, you are now in a restricted area for which a permit is necessary (although there is no checkpost here). See map on page 145 for orientation, in addition to the map on page 151.

Darkot

Infamous as the scene of Hayward's murder (see box, page 156), the small village of Darkot stands at the head of the narrow gorge that leads to the Darkot Pass. It was this pass that Hayward was about to cross when he was murdered. Ostensibly on his way to the Pamirs and the source of the Oxus, possibly to 'bag' them for the British, it was no coincidence that the information that Hayward would bring back would be vital in assessing the feasibility of a Russian invasion of India through these unmapped passes.

The supposed scene of the murder can still be visited, although it is not possible to determine the exact spot with any certainty. The place is known locally as 'farang gee-bar', or the 'place of killing of the foreigner'. Local school teacher Muhammad Murad will show the spot to visitors. To find the site, turn right (east) as you cross the small wooden bridge at the entrance to Darkot, and continue up the slope as if heading for the Punji Pass. You pass a small shop in the middle of nowhere that belongs to a one-armed man, beyond which to the right is a natural amphitheatre. Follow the trail beside the nala, and the scene is just around the back. The large boulder that stood over the site has been washed away.

Gupis to the Ishkoman Valley

Returning to the main route between Chitral and Gilgit, the next settlement after Khalti Lake is **Gupis**, where foreigners must again register at the police station. Arriving from Chitral, Phandur is 58 km behind you, Teru 88 km and the Shandur Pass 108 km.

Travelling east from Gupis towards Gilgit, the jeep road improves markedly. Note also that east of Gupis, the river is referred to as the Gilgit River. A sizeable tributary from the south joins the Gilgit River just east of Gupis, while bridges cross the river to the settlements of **Moula Abad** and **Sumal** on the north bank. The cultivated fields on either side of the jeep road here belong to the sprawling settlement of **Yangal**. Beyond here the road begins to climb high above the river, and the sharp bend in the road here (just before the sign reading 'Gupis 22 km, Yangal 6 km') is the place where, in August 1995, a jeep plunged over the side killing the driver and three backpackers.

After several kilometres running high and low above the river, the jeep track drops down to a 100-m-long suspension bridge that crosses the Gilgit River, and provides access to the Ishkoman Valley. Very crowded cargo jeeps occasionally pass here on their way to Chatorkhand (Rs25, 1 hr). From this point it is 14 km to Yangal, 27 km to Gupis, 9 km to Gahkuch, 81 km to Gilgit, 20 km to Chatorkhand, 55 km to Imit and 100 km to the Pamir Border with Afghanistan. Note that there is another route (Kanchey Bridge, just beyond Gahkuch) that provides access to the Ishkoman Valley.

For those continuing along the Chitral-Gilgit route, and not making an excursion up the Ishkoman Valley, turn to page 159.

Ishkoman Valley

Although marginally less attractive perhaps than the Yasin Valley, the Ishkoman Valley is the starting/finishing point for a number of treks into the neighbouring valleys, notably Yasin and Naltar. See map on page 145 for orientation, as well as the Naltar Valley map on page 216.

Although the whole valley is generally referred to as the Ishkoman Valley, the major river that runs through the valley is the **Karamber** (which descends from the Karamber Glacier to the northeast), and some texts refer to the valley as the Karamber Valley. The actual Ishkoman River is a small tributary that joins the Karamber from the northwest, from a valley that is referred to as 'Ishkoman proper'.

A dark stain on Darkot

Of all the players in the 'Great Game', George J Whitaker Hayward must rank as one of the most extraordinary. Little is known about his early life, and even the details of his place of birth are uncertain. To add to the mystery, there only appears to be one photograph of the man, currently in the possession of the Royal Geographical Society (RGS) in London. His movements are uncertain after he resigned his commission in the Cameron Highlanders, yet in 1868 this relatively unknown man was sponsored by the RGS to undertake a journey to the Pamirs in search of the source of the Oxus.

After being given up for dead, Hayward re-emerged in 1869 to a hero's welcome, following his extensive surveys in the Pamirs and visits to the great cities of Yarkand and Kashgar, and was awarded the RGS's coveted Gold Medal.

Within a year, Hayward had returned to this dangerous and unmapped region. As Hopkirk suggests, "to a man like Hayward, the risks merely made it more attractive"; a greater insight into the man is revealed in a line that Hayward wrote to a fellow explorer: "I shall wander about the wilds of Central Asia possessed of an insane desire to try the effects of cold steel across my throat." This line was to prove prophetic. On 18 July 1870, he was murdered at Darkot.

The reasons for Hayward's murder have never really been established. One prime suspect is the Maharaja of Kashmir, embarrassed by Hayward's revelations in *The Pioneer* of the massacre at Muduri. Another prime candidate is Mir Wali, the local ruler, with whom Hayward is said to have argued in public just days before his death. Whatever the facts of the matter, it was Mir Wali who fled from Yasin, meeting a grisly end himself some years later.

Many accounts have been written of the circumstances of Hayward's death, the most fanciful of which was a cheesy poem by Sir Henry Newbolt that somehow found its way into the official report of the Gilgit Mission of 1885-6, headed by Colonel Lockhart. This tells how, upon his capture and facing certain death, he asked to be allowed to ascend a mound and gaze upon the rising sun one final time. An alleged eye-witness to the murder paints a scene that would appeal to such Victorian romanticism, describing Hayward as he walked up the mound: "as tall against the morning sky, with the rising sun lighting up his fair hair as a glory; he was beautiful to look at". Hayward is then said to have returned, said "I am ready", and was then killed. Subsequent investigations by Drew, who recovered the body, and later by Schomberg, suggest that Hayward was seized during a meal, and along with his servants, was bound and dragged to the mouth of a small nala where all were killed. Today, Hayward's body lies buried in the graveyard in Gilgit.

It is interesting to note how concerned local people are about their image to outsiders, some 130 years after the event; you may still be asked about it, and villagers are at pains to point out that those involved were not actually from Darkot.

Few foreign visitors, bar the odd trekking groups, visit the Ishkoman Valley, which is a great pity because the local people are very friendly and welcoming. The language pattern of the valley reflects the history of migration into the area and conquest by the neighbouring states of Chitral, Yasin and Gilgit, with Shina, Khowar (Chitrali), Burushaski and Wakhi all being spoken.

At the entrance to the Ishkoman Valley is a wide alluvial fan, upon which the green and well-cultivated fields of the village of **Hatoon** stand. The jeep road runs along the west side of the valley, before crossing the river on the 75-m suspension bridge at **Hasis** (8 km). Here, the jeep road joins the alternative route south via Silpi to the Kanchey Bridge. The road north up the valley continues to Chatorkhand (12 km).

Chatorkhand

This is the largest settlement in the valley, and was described by the writer Schomberg as being "famous for its pir and its bugs". The Ismaili community venerate their pirs (a hereditary position as a religious leader), and many attain considerable power and social status. The current pir, Syed Karim Ali Shah, has served as Deputy Chief Executive of the Northern Areas.

North from Chatorkhand

Several kilometres north of Chatorkhand is the village of **Pakora** (marked on some maps as Phakor or Pakor). A nala joins from the east, and you can trek east through the narrow opening to this valley across the Naltar Pass (4,710 m), sometimes marked Pakor Pass, to the Naltar Valley. Immediately beyond the Jamat Khana in Pakora, the road divides, although both forks rejoin several kilometres further north. A steep path several hundred metres along the left fork leads down to a rope suspension bridge across the Karamber River. This route leads along the west side of the valley to Ishkoman. It also leads to the valley joining from the west that provides a relatively easy five-day trek across the Asumbar Pass (4,560 m) to Yasin Valley.

Asumbar Pass trek

ⓘ *Open zone. Maximum elevation circa 4,560 m. Jul to Sep. Maps: U502 series, NJ 43-14 Baltit and NJ 43-13 Mastuj are the only ones readily available and are fairly good. See map on p145 for orientation, as well as the map on p151. Read trekking notes, p45.*

This is a relatively easy trek passing through villages and summer settlements along the way, and can be done without a guide. From Pakora village, cross to the west side of the valley. A good path heads west along the south bank of the Asumbar River, passing through stands of willow and silver birch, fields and small settlements. **Chalinj**, situated at the junction of a side valley draining in from the southwest, is a convenient overnight stop. From Chalinj you can cross the **Asumbar Pass** and reach suitable camping on the far side in one long day, or there is an area of pasture good for camping at the foot of the pass, beyond the last settlement. There are in fact two passes, separated by a rounded hill. The Asumbar is the easier of the two. The path over it climbs steadily and then branches off to the right, around the hill. There are magnificent views from the top. On the other side, the path descends to the first settlement of **Jiji Shawaran** and then crosses to the south bank of the river. A little further on is a beautiful campsite by a small lake. If you have walked all the way from Chalinj, this is the obvious place to camp. The walk down to the Yasin Valley is a pleasant one, passing through woods and settlements, with places to camp all along the route. The path crosses to the north bank of the river to arrive at the permanent village of **Chuchuanotik**, and then follows the jeep track to join the Yasin Valley at **Dal Sandhi** (see page 154).

Ishkoman 'proper'

This comprises a series of small villages along the Ishkoman River, including Jalalabad, Dalti Thupushkin, Mominabad, Faizabad, Ishkoman Bala and Ghotulti. All claim to be the original settlement of Ishkoman 'proper'. There is no accommodation in Ishkoman 'proper', and transport is very irregular.

The valley continues northwest across the 4,680-m Punji Pass (sometimes called Ishkoman Pass) to the Yasin Valley, right at the foot of the Darkot Pass (4,744 m). An alternative trek from Ishkoman Valley to Darkot in the Yasin Valley lies further to the north, across the Atar Pass (said to be easier, although a guide is essential).

Punji Pass trek

ⓘ *Open zone. Maximum elevation 4,680 m. Jul to Sep. Maps: U502 NJ 43-14 Baltit and U502 NJ 43-13 Mastuj can be used, although both have mistakes. Punji Pass is labelled as Ishkuman Aghost (and ignore what is marked as Punji Pass). See map on p145 for orientation, as well as the map on p151. A guide is essential for this trek since the trail is not always obvious. Read trekking notes, p45.*

The trek really begins at **Ghotulti** village, above Ishkoman 'proper'. Climb steeply for 50 minutes above Ghotulti to the shrine of a local saint (large circle of stones enclosed by a square stone wall). Continue west, high above the Baru Gah River for a further two hours to **Handis** (2,930 m), and then find a suitable place to camp near to the settlement. (It is from Handis that you can take the alternative northerly route via the Atar Pass to Darkot).

On the second day, head west from Handis high above the Baru Gah River on the north side as far as **Kai** (45 minutes). The trail then continues to **Galtir** (3,280 m). From here you descend to the river and cross to its south bank, pass through a juniper forest (passing a series of large cairns), then climb gently high above the river (still on its south bank). After two hours or so you reach the small settlement of Babusar, close to a small lake. Just beyond here you cross once more to the north side of the Baru Gah, and head up towards the summer settlement of Talas. Climb steeply up to the superb grassy camp site at **Holojut** (3,870 m, five to six hours from Handis). There are some great views from this spot, as well as good fresh water springs.

The third day can be a long haul, depending upon your level of fitness (five to seven hours). Head broadly northwest along the valley floor towards the small waterfall, then continue across the alluvial plain on the north side of the valley. You may need to cross and recross the stream a number of times, before climbing gently to a flower-strewn meadow. Having crossed the meadow, a series of switchbacks begin to climb to the west. The trail turns sharply east to avoid a deep ravine, before continuing northwest along a rocky ridge. Ascending the shale slope on the south bank of the stream, you climb up to the **Punji Pass** (4,680 m, marked by two cairns). There are some fine views from the top of the pass. The path from the pass descends in a northwest direction, although you will have to cross a glacier and traipse across the glacial moraine. Some trekkers camp close to the cairn here, although you are still fairly high (4,250 m). A better option is to drop down into the ravine, cross the icy stream, and continue to **Boimoshani** (3,690 m).

If coming in the opposite direction (ie Darkot to Ishkoman), this following stage should only be attempted over two days, since there is a rapid altitude gain. In the direction described here, however, this final leg can be attempted in one long day (eight to nine hours). From Boimoshani, descend gently along the north side of the river, and proceed north to the settlement of **Hanisarbar**. The route then climbs once more, up to **Gawat Kutu** (3,450 m). This is an important summer pasture area, and can seem very busy with people in a pleasing kind of way. Just to the north of here, the river (called here the Hanisar Bar) is joined from the east by another river valley, the Nyu Bar. This latter valley forms part of the alternative Atar Pass route between Ishkoman and Darkot. Having crossed the Nyu Bar, our route turns west, passing through the cultivated fields of **Mardain** village (on the north side of the valley), through **Sawaney** village, across the Alam Bar River that flows in from the north, and then via **Gamelti** (3,139 m) and **Gartens** (2,880 m), before the final dry stretch in to **Darkot** (2,760 m).

Imit

Back to the exploration of the Ishkoman Valley north of Pakora, the jeep track along the east side of the valley hugs the base of the cliffs and continues to Imit. During the summer months it is best to cross the river at this point since the high level of the water can make it difficult to cross directly between Ishkoman and Imit further up the valley.

This is the starting point for another trek across into the Naltar Valley. It is also possible to cross the Karamber Glacier, and then head west across the Chillinji Pass towards Chitral, although this is a difficult trek through a restricted area and a guide is essential (see also page 45).

Gahkuch to Gilgit

Back on the main Chitral-Gilgit route, from the suspension bridge that provides access to the Ishkoman Valley, the jeep road passes a monument to the ground-breaking of the upgraded Gakuch-Gupis-Mastuj road, which will eventually seal the road all the way from Chitral to Gilgit (except for a 15-km section over the Shandur Pass). The FWO (an army engineering regiment working jointly with NAPWD on the project) has set up camp shortly before the tiny settlement of **Damas**, which has a rickety footbridge across the Gilgit River and a mill with a 'rocket missile' coming out of its roof. From here, the road is mostly sealed already and, a little further on, reaches the district headquarters of Punial District, **Gahkuch**.

Being a relatively fertile and well-watered strip of land on either side of the Gilgit River, the former independent kingdom of Punial became a bone of contention between the rulers of Yasin and Gilgit. Both states possessed the region in turn, until it was annexed by the Maharaja of Kashmir in 1860. An important fort previously stood at Gahkuch, commanding both the entrance to the Ishkoman Valley and the Gilgit-Chitral road. It was while occupying this fort in 1893 that Durand learnt of the Indus Valley Uprising. There is a police station here where foreigners must enter their passport details; the book is usually left on the bench by the entrance. From Gahkuch it is 73 km to Gilgit.

Gahkuch to Sher Qila

About 8 km east of Gahkuch is the new, Chinese-built **Kanchey Bridge**, which provides an alternative route into the Ishkoman Valley (through the settlement of Silpi, and up the east side of the Karamber River to Chatorkhand).

The road continues to the small village of **Gulmuti**, where there is a PSO petrol pump and a basic hotel. Kuwait and Bubal, the villages on the opposite side of the river, are famed locally for their wine, reputedly so strong that they make a Western head ache for weeks.

A few kilometres further is the tiny settlement of Thing Das, followed by the larger village of **Singal**. It is often necessary to enter your passport details at the police check post at Singal (two hours by bus from Gilgit). The road then passes through Gich, 2 km beyond which is a bridge across the river to **Japuky**. Cold drinks and chai are then available at Goherabad (3 km), before the road continues to Dalnati (4 km) and the bridge across the river to Sher Qila (3 km).

Sher Qila to Gilgit

On the north side of the river, connected to the main road by a suspension bridge (with obligatory police check post), Sher Qila (38 km from Gilgit, one hours by bus) controls the western approach to Gilgit. The word 'Sher' means 'an impregnable rock', while 'Qila' means 'fort'. All that remains of the fort today is one 150-year-old watch-tower, close to the river. Sher Qila's most impressive building now is the Aga Khan High School for Girls.

The village is also home of the **Sher Qila Women's Art Group**, a women's cooperative. The inexpensive prints are available from the S.W.A.G. studio at the residence of the former Raja of Punial in Sher Qila (visitors welcome), and from a number of handicraft shops in Karimabad. For further information contact Ms Nilusha Bardai, c/o Pilot School Sher Qila, BPO Sher Qila, NA, Pakistan.

The road continues through **Gulapur**. The green and fertile village across the river is **Rashmal**, connected by a new bridge. A further 4 km leads to **Shenote**, which marks the boundary between Punial and Gilgit Districts, and another 4 km leads to a rope suspension bridge across the river to **Bargo**. This is the beginning of the home straight into **Gilgit** (27 km).

Sleeping

If you are equipped to camp, this trip from Chitral to Gilgit offers some great overnight resting places. Particularly recommended are Khalti Lake, the Phandur region, Langar and the Shandur Pass itself. If you require hotel accommodation, then some advanced planning is worthwhile.

F NAPWD Inspection Bungalows at Gulapur, Singal, Gahkuch, Chatorkhand, Imit, Gupis, Yasin, Phandur and Teru all offer comfortable accommodation, albeit with very basic food. However, they can only be booked in Gilgit (see Sleeping, Gilgit) – difficult if you are coming from Chitral. Some will accept casual callers if unoccupied. Singal, Gulmuti, Gahkuch, Gupis, Phandur, Sor Laspur and Harchin all offer some form of basic accommodation, while Mastuj offers a choice of guest houses and camping.

Mastuj to Shandur Pass *p149*
Harchin
H Yana Camping, at the start of the village on the north side.

Brock Laspur
G-H Shandur Hotel A choice of charpoys, the floor or a couple of cave-like rooms. There are tentative plans to build 6 new 'special' rooms for passing tourists, while a garden provides space for camping. Food is available.

Sor Laspur
G Hotel, Sor Laspur. Basic hotel and helipad.

Shandur Pass *p149*
Apart from during the polo festival, there are a couple of semi-permanent 'hotels' on the pass when it is open in the summer months.
H Shandoor Hotel. A few ex-army tents, Rs50 per head. Basic catering on offer.

H Shandur Inn. Also with a few ex-army tents, charging Rs50 per head. Wastes no time in showing off their impressive biscuit cabinet if you stop for chai. If you have your own equipment, there is plenty of space for camping, but remember to fill in your details at the check post.

Shandur Pass to Barsat *p150*
Barsat
For those concerned about camping in the isolation of Langar, the police are happy to let you pitch your tent next to theirs.
G Sarhad Hotel. In Barsat itself, with a couple of basic rooms.

Barsat to Phandur *p151*
Teru
G NAPWD Inspection Bungalow. 2 rooms (officially only bookable in Gilgit, although the friendly chowkidar is happy to let you stay if it's empty).

Teru Bahach
G Shandoor Inn, a couple of km further on at Teru Bahach. 1 clean, simple room with quilts on the floor. Food can be arranged, which can be enjoyed from the small sit-out area with good views, while teaching English to the owner's young son.

Phandur *p151*
C PTDC Motel, by the lake, on the crest of the hill. Superbly located, still unfinished.
F NAPWD Inspection Bungalow has a number of rooms, although a booking chit from Gilgit is pretty much essential if you want to stand a chance of being able to stay. The chowkidar, if you can find him, may be able to provide basic meals, although it is as well to bring your own.

G Over The Lake Hotel. 3 basic rooms with clean linen, a shared squat toilet (no running water, buckets supplied), occasional electricity, with basic meals available. Also a couple of expensive tents at Rs100 per head. Not the most welcoming atmosphere, thanks to the unhelpful owner.

G Phandur Tourist Inn, in the village itself, about 5 km from the lake. 3 cleanish rooms with attached bath, also a 4-bed room without bath. Food is available, the manager is friendly and there have been good reports about this place.

There are 2 **camping** areas, owned by Zafah Sanaf and Mir Bhah Shah respectively. After pitching up, the owner will approach you for the Rs50 per tent fee.

Phandur to Khalti Lake *p152*
Dahimal
G Mushraf Hotel and Restaurant, by the bridge. With 1 simple room at Rs100 per head.

Khalti Lake *p152*
C PTDC Motel. Soulless, but fairly reasonable rooms.

G Karim Lake View Hotel, a friendly, well-run and accommodating place. The rooms are clean with fresh linen and most are with attached bath. The restaurant serves decent food (speciality trout, Rs25 per fish) and there is a pleasant terrace. Note that prices go up around the time of the Shandur Pass polo (and the hotel is often full).

Yasin *p153*
F-G NAPWD Inspection Bungalow. Set in a large garden and well furnished with 2 double rooms, both joining a communal dining room, and private bathrooms. There is also a 3-room VIP block with hot bath, but these rooms must be booked in Gilgit. The chowkidar can fix meals but they are very basic. Best to bring your own food.

Thaous *p154*
E Yasin View, just after the sign for 'Bright Stars Public School'. New hotel with some clean rooms with attached bath and restaurant, but it is a bit pricey.

H Sangit Hotel (sign in Urdu). Opposite and very basic with just 1 room and no bath, but at Rs30 per head you shouldn't expect much.

Darkot *p155*
F Resthouse. Basic, but it does not get many visitors. There are also **camping** spots.

Gupis *p155*
F NAPWD Inspection Bungalow (east end of town). Decent rooms and a pleasant garden. Most of the rooms are taken up by army officers and staying without a booking chit from Gilgit is impossible.

G Dilshad, opposite the Aga Khan Medical Centre. Basic, with a couple of sorry-looking rooms with mattresses on the floor and a separate, but clean toilet with bucket and jug shower. The restaurant here has basic food and is popular with locals. Similar fare is available at the Snow Leopard Inn, nearby.

Chatorkhand *p157*
F NAPWD Inspection Bungalow. 3 VIP doubles, with eccentric plumbing, plus 2 standard rooms set in a large garden. Basic meals are available through the chowkidar, although you may well want to bring your own supplements. There are several chai shops in the village.

Imit *p159*
E NAPWD Inspection Bungalow.

Gahkuch *p159*
F-G NAPWD Inspection Bungalow. Some relatively luxurious rooms all with attached hot bath, some with TV, and a restaurant. NB They will not entertain anyone without a booking from Gilgit.

G Shandour Hotel and Restaurant, at the western end of the main bazaar. 4 basic rooms with a none-too-clean shared bath. There are also a couple of other basic restaurants in the bazaar serving the usual uninspiring cuisine.

Gahkuch to Sher Qila *p159*
Gulmuti
H New Ghizer (Nadir). New hotel which allows people to bed down for a night in a large barn-like outbuilding, but without the luxury of straw. Well what do you expect for Rs20 per head? The restaurant, on the other hand, is a decent place to stop for lunch with simple, but filling food which can be eaten next to the stream running through in a pleasant garden.

Singal
F NAPWD Inspection Bungalow.
A couple of basic restaurants in the village here too.

Japuky
F NAPWD Inspection Bungalow. Basic.

Sher Qila to Gilgit *p159*
Gulapur
F NAPWD Inspection Bungalow. Basic.
There are a couple of basic chai shops in the village where you could stay on a charpoy if you are desperate.

Eating

Eating options are fairly limited in this area unless you eat at your hotel or bring your own. See Sleeping, above.

Transport

Khalti Lake *p152*
If arriving from Chitral/Mastuj by **cargo jeep**, jump down here. Remember that if you are coming from Gilgit, you can get a **bus** as far as Gupis and then walk the remaining 10 km – it's worth the effort.

Yasin *p153*
NATCO runs a **bus** from Gilgit as far as **Thaous**, just after Yasin (Rs100, 5-6 hrs), each day at 0800 from the yard on Punial Rd (not from the main NATCO yard). The bus returns to Gilgit at 0500 and 0600, so check the night before and arrange a wake up call.

Very crowded **cargo jeeps** leave early most mornings from Punial Rd in Gilgit, and, on the return leg, from near to the Inspection Bungalow in Yasin. Note that there is very little public transport north to **Darkot**, although as the metalling of the road continues up the valley, so will the **bus** service. Expect services to Darkot by 2005. It is a full day's long walk to Darkot. Public transport is very irregular (Gilgit-Darkot Rs150 in a cargo jeep, leaving from Jamat Khana Bazaar). A **private hire cargo jeep** Gilgit-Darkot costs about Rs3,500 (9 hrs).

Gupis *p155*
A **bus** en route from Gilgit to **Yasin** (25 km) passes through Gupis at around 1400-1500 each day, plus there are 2 buses a day from Gupis to **Gilgit** (Rs85, 0600 and 0700, but confirm times locally).

Chatorkhand *p157*
There are extremely crowded **cargo jeeps** to **Chatorkhand** from **Gahkuch** (and usually 1 a day that has come all the way from Gilgit that is even more crowded). The alternative is to get off the Gilgit-Gupis-Yasin bus at the bridge and walk/hitch (20 km).

Imit *p159*
Public transport to Imit is very limited. Extremely crowded **cargo jeeps** from Gilgit pass through **Chatorkhand** between 1500 and 1600 each day, and return from Imit early the next morning.

Gahkuch *p159*
There are 2-3 daily **buses** to **Gahkuch** from Gilgit (see under Gilgit), and at least 2 daily buses from Gahkuch to **Gilgit** early in the morning (having come from Yasin and Gupis). A NATCO bus to **Yasin** generally passes at around 1130.

You may find crowded **cargo jeeps** heading up the Ishkoman Valley to **Chatorkhand** (Rs30, 1 hr).

Directory

Gupis *p155*
Hospitals As well as the civil hospital, there is also the much better **Aga Khan Medical Centre** (west end of town), T0572-45046, with 10 beds, English-speaking doctors (including 1 female) and a 24-hr emergency service. At present the centre is in a rented building; it hopes to move to a permanent building near the Gupis Bridge in the coming years.

Gahkuch to Sher Qila *p159*
Hospitals Aga Khan Medical Centre, Singal, T13 for emergencies.

The KKH: Hazara to Gilgit

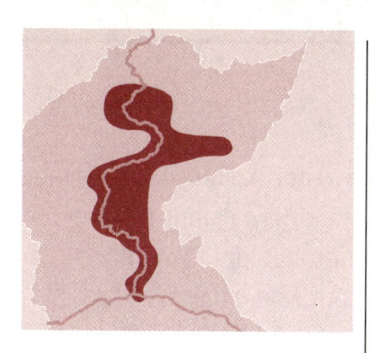

Hazara	**166**
The start of the Karakoram Highway	167
Abbottabad	168
Mansehra	170
Mansehra to Thakot Bridge	171
Listings	172
Kaghan Valley	**175**
Southern area	175
Naran	177
Naran to Babusar Pass	178
Babusar Pass to Chilas	180
Listings	181
Indus Kohistan	**184**
Thakot Bridge and Alai Valley	186
Thakot Bridge to Pattan	186
Pattan to Komila/Dasu	187
Komila/Dasu to Diamar District	189
Listings	190
Diamar District	**192**
The KKH through Diamar District	193
Chilas	195
Onwards from Chilas	197
Fairy Meadows and Nanga Parbat	198
Nanga Parbat	199
Treks and walks from Fairy Meadows	201
Raikot Bridge t to Jaglot	202
Astor Valley	202
Astor village	203
Onwards from Astor village	203
Listings	205
Gilgit District	**208**
Gilgit	208
Naltar Valley	215
Treks from the Naltar Valley	216
Danyore Valley	217
Bagrot and Haramosh Valleys	219
Treks in the Bagrot and Haramosh Valleys	220
Listings	221

⁑ Footprint features...

Don't miss...	165
Journey to the centre of the earth	188
Warning	180
Rock carvings in Northern Pakistan	197
The future of Fairy Meadows	201

Introduction

Most visitors travelling in a south to north direction along the KKH begin their journey at Islamabad/Rawalpindi, but the 'official' starting point is a small, non-descript town in the district of Hazara. After Hazara (from where there is a possible excursion off the KKH up to Kaghan Valley), the road passes through the Indus Kohistan and Diamar District on its way to the 'gateway of the north' at Gilgit.

The majority travellers along the KKH complete the trip between Islamabad/Rawalpindi and Gilgit in one long, and sometimes arduous, journey (taking upwards of 14 hours). There are several good reasons for doing this. Firstly, despite some stunning scenery en route (notably in Indus Kohistan and Diamar District, where huge peaks flanking the road compete for your attention with perilous drops into the Indus), this section is not deemed as interesting as stretches further north, where most visitors prefer to spend their valuable time. Secondly, most of the settlements along this stretch of the KKH are little more than road-stops, servicing the basic needs of travellers passing through. Furthermore, much of this part of Pakistan is tribal, and visitors are not encouraged (or advised) to stray off the main KKH.

However, full details of these regions are provided here for those who like to take their time about their travels, and for those cycling the route.

★ Don't miss...

① **Shogran** Enjoy the views from the high summer pastures about Shogran, page 176.
② **Lake Saiful Malik** See the reflections of mountain peaks in its deep blue waters, page 177.
③ **Lalazar Plateau** Bask in flower-filled meadows set in cool pine forest, page 178.
④ **Chilas** Soak up the history of the stunning petroglyphs, page 195.
⑤ **Nanga Parbat** See the world's ninth highest mountain from the charming Fairy Meadows, page 198.
⑥ **Thalichi** Get a 360-degree view of Rakaposhi, Haramosh, Dobani and Nanga Parbat, page 202.
⑦ **Polo** Watch the sport of Kings as it was always meant to be played in Gilgit, page 212.

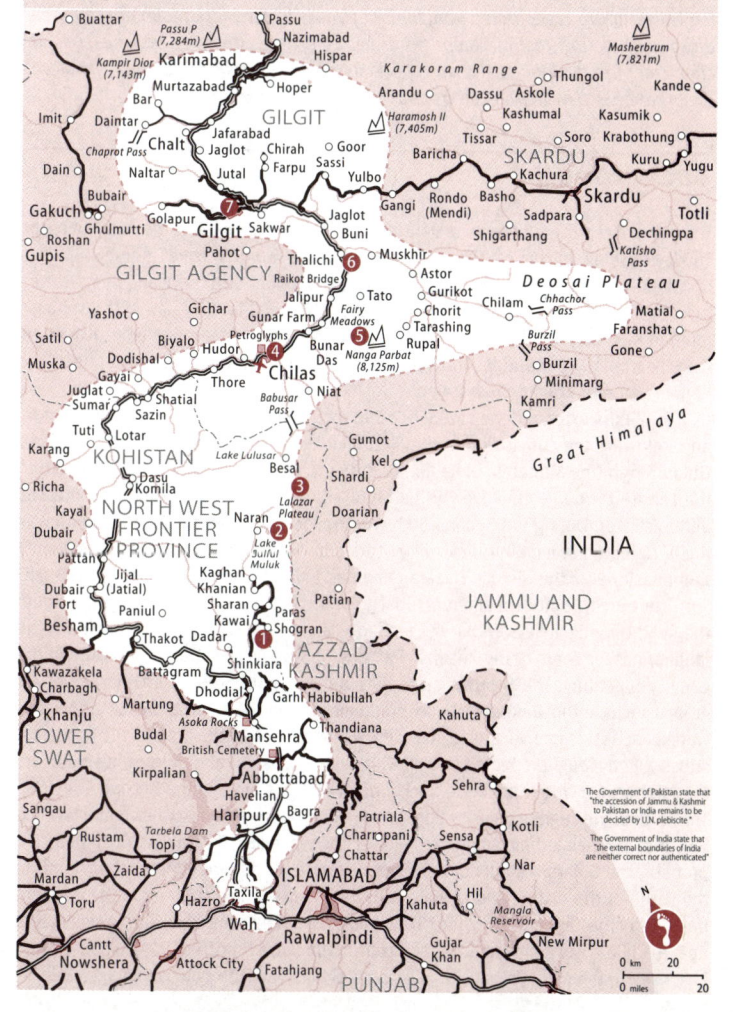

Hazara → Colour map 1, grid B4

On its journey north from Rawalpindi/Islamabad, the first stage of the Karakoram Highway (KKH) passes through the NWFP district of Hazara. Most travellers along the KKH will watch Hazara pass them by through the window of a speeding bus, usually en route direct to Gilgit. However, for KKH cyclists, or those wishing to break their journey into more digestible parts, there are a couple of places of minor interest along the way. The key settlements are the district headquarters at Abbottabad and the town of Mansehra, with its third-century rock carvings (as well as its transport links for an excursion up the Kaghan Valley).

The leading physical features of Hazara are the mountain ranges that define the boundaries on each side. To the east, the main chain is a long ridge of outlying Himalayan spurs that flank the Jhelum and Kunhar Rivers, terminating in the hills around Murree. To the northeast, in the Kaghan Valley, another small range marks the boundary between Hazara and Kashmir, and includes the 5,291-m Malika Parbat. To the west, Hazara is separated from the Swat Valley by the Black Mountains. Between these ranges, the region comprises a series of level tracts of varying size and character. The geology of Hazara reflects its position within the area of Himalayan disturbance. ▸▸ *For Sleeping, Eating and all other listings, see pages 172-174.*

Background

The name 'Hazara' is althought to date to the 15th century, following the invasion by the Turkic-speaking forces of **Timur** (Tamerlane). The word 'hazara' (thousand) is a translation of the Turkic word *ming*, meaning a regiment of a thousand men. Hazara then came under the control of the **Mughals**, to whom it formed part of the strategic route to Kashmir, but during the decline of their empire it was repeatedly invaded by Pathans from Swat (**Swathis**). In 1752, Hazara eventually came under the control of the Afghan emperor **Ahmad Shah Durani**.

The **Sikhs** extended their influence into the region at the start of the 19th century and following the conclusion of the First Sikh War in 1846, the area was ceded to **Gulab Singh** (the Maharaja of Kashmir). In 1847, however, Hazara was transferred to the Lahore Darbar – effectively British rule – and **James Abbott** was appointed as administrator. During the Second Sikh War the local ruler **Sardar Chattar Singh** was finally defeated by a mainly local army headed by Abbott, who was then made Deputy Commissioner of the district. Hazara remained in British hands until independence.

There are a number of different tribal groups in this district, many who arrived from the neighbouring valleys within the last 300 years. Most numerous are probably the **Jaduns**, descendants of the Yusufzai Pathans of Swat who migrated to Hazara in the early 17th century. The **Swathis** also share a common background. Other important groups include the **Gakhars**, found predominantly in the south. These traditionally warlike people came to the region with **Mahmud of Ghazni** around AD 1000 and subsequently fought repeated battles with the Mughals. Another interesting group are the **Mishwanis**, who formed the backbone of Abbott's army in the Second Sikh War. The north of the Kaghan Valley is populated mainly by **Sayyids**, also descendants of the Swathis, the main ethnic group in the lower Kaghan Valley. The oldest inhabitants are probably the **Gujars**, a semi-nomadic group of pasturalists who generally farm lands in the south of the district and migrate with their flocks in the summer to the northern pastures of the Kaghan Valley, into Swat, and even as far as the Darel and Tangir Valleys near to Chilas. The main language of Hazara is **Hindko**, a branch of Punjabi, but Pashtu is spoken in the main Pathan areas, and the Gujars have their own language, Gojri.

The start of the Karakoram Highway

The official starting point of the KKH is at **Havelian**, some 84 km from Rawalpindi/Islamabad. There are several options for reaching this town, although all involve travelling west from Rawalpindi/Islamabad for some distance along the Grand Trunk (GT) Road (towards Peshawar). Having crossed the Margalla Pass (see page 92), there are two options for turning north towards Havelian. Cyclists may prefer to take the marginally quieter route by turning north at **Taxila** (31 km from Rawalpindi/Islamabad), while most buses take the faster route by continuing through Wah and turning north at Hasan Abdal (a further 16 km, see Hazara map, page 167). Both roads lead to **Haripur** (a further 34 km, one to two hours by bus from Rawalpindi/Islamabad), situated in the lush Dor Valley. **Harkishangarh Fort** stands just to the east of the town. This small market town is the starting point for visits to the **Tarbela Dam** (see page 94).

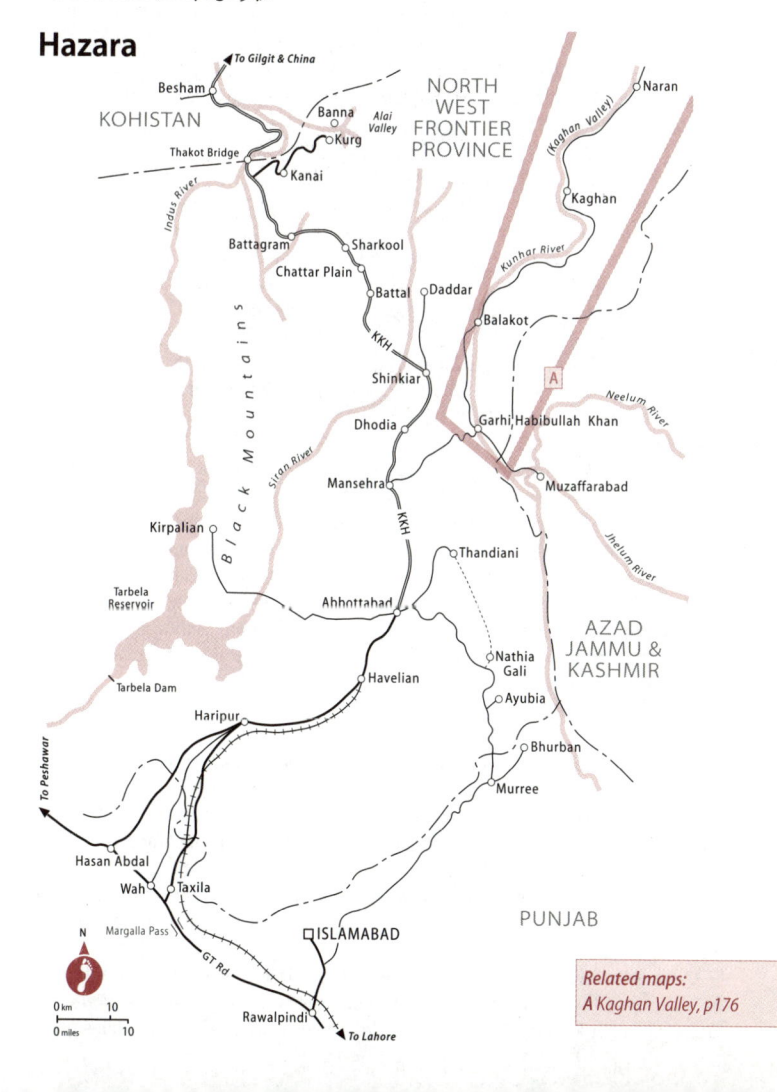

Hazara

Related maps:
A Kaghan Valley, p176

A further 20 km beyond Haripur is **Havelian**. It is the terminus for the narrow gauge railway from Taxila, and beyond the town the KKH crosses the Dor River and begins a rapid climb (unpleasant for cyclists) through the denuded hills before dropping down into Abbottabad. Islamabad/Rawalpindi is just under 100 km.

There is also a quieter, more scenic route betweeen Islamabad/Rawalpindi to Abbottabad for cyclists. This involves a steep climb up the busy road from Rawalpindi/Islamabad to Murree (64 km), before heading north via Barian, Khaira Gali, Chhangla Gali and Dunga Gali to Nathia Gali (25 km). All these attractive hill stations have some form of accommodation. From Nathia Gali to the KKH at Abbottabad is about 35 km. If doing the journey in a north-south direction, the climb up to Nathia Gali is a real killer. See Hazara map on page 167.

Abbottabad

Established as a new cantonment town in 1853, Abbottabad retains its military traditions, playing host to a number of elite Pakistani regiments as well as being the location of some of the country's most prestigious public schools. There are few places of interest in this District Headquarters town, although there is a wide choice of accommodation, see page 172.

Ins and outs
Abbottabad's various bus stations are scattered along the GT Road (known as it passes through town as The Mall), offering a variety of transport options (coasters, minibuses, wrecks) to a number of destinations. The town is compact enough to walk around, although there are Suzuki services to all the outlying spots and short excursion destinations. ▶▶ *See Transport, page 174, for more details.*

Tourist information PTDC ⓘ *Jinnah Rd, opposite Cantt Public Park, T0992-337399, Mon-Thu and Sat 0900-1500, Fri 0900-1300.* Friendly but not much help.

History
The town was established by the Deputy Commissioner of Hazara, Herbert Edwardes, who named it after his predecessor **James Abbot** (1807-96). By all accounts Abbott was a popular man in these parts, known affectionately as 'Kaka' (uncle) by local children due to his habit of distributing sweets. Indeed, when he left his post in 1853, it is said that he was followed all the way to Hasan Abdal by a weeping and lamenting crowd.

Not only was Abbott an efficient and just administrator, he was remembered by the local population as the person who liberated them from Sikh and Dogra rule, following his victory over local Sikh ruler Chattar Singh while at the head of an allied British and Mishwani Pathan army during the Second Sikh War.

Sights
Abbottabad has no real sights as such, although the **main bazaar area** is crowded and lively and contrasts markedly with the wide, tree-lined avenues of the cantonment. The latter has a number of old churches plus a morbid Christian cemetery. The **Cantt Public Park** has a separate women's section, and this whole area is a magnet for beggars on a Sunday. There is also a plaque bearing a poem by Abbott in the park.

A popular excursion from Abbottabad is to take a minivan (Rs7 from the stand on Pine View Road, or a stiff one-hour walk) up to **Shimla Peak**, the pine-covered summit of the hill that stands above the town to the west.

A pleasant little excursion from Abbottabad is to **Thandiani** ⓘ *Take a Suzuki from the stand on Eid Gah Rd, but ascertain whether it is a regular 'service' (Rs18 per passenger) or a 'special' (Rs350 to hire the whole vehicle)*, a peaceful hill-station sitting just to the northeast. Although only 26 km from Abbottabad, it takes a full hour to reach Thandiani on a long, winding road through the fragrant pine forests. There is

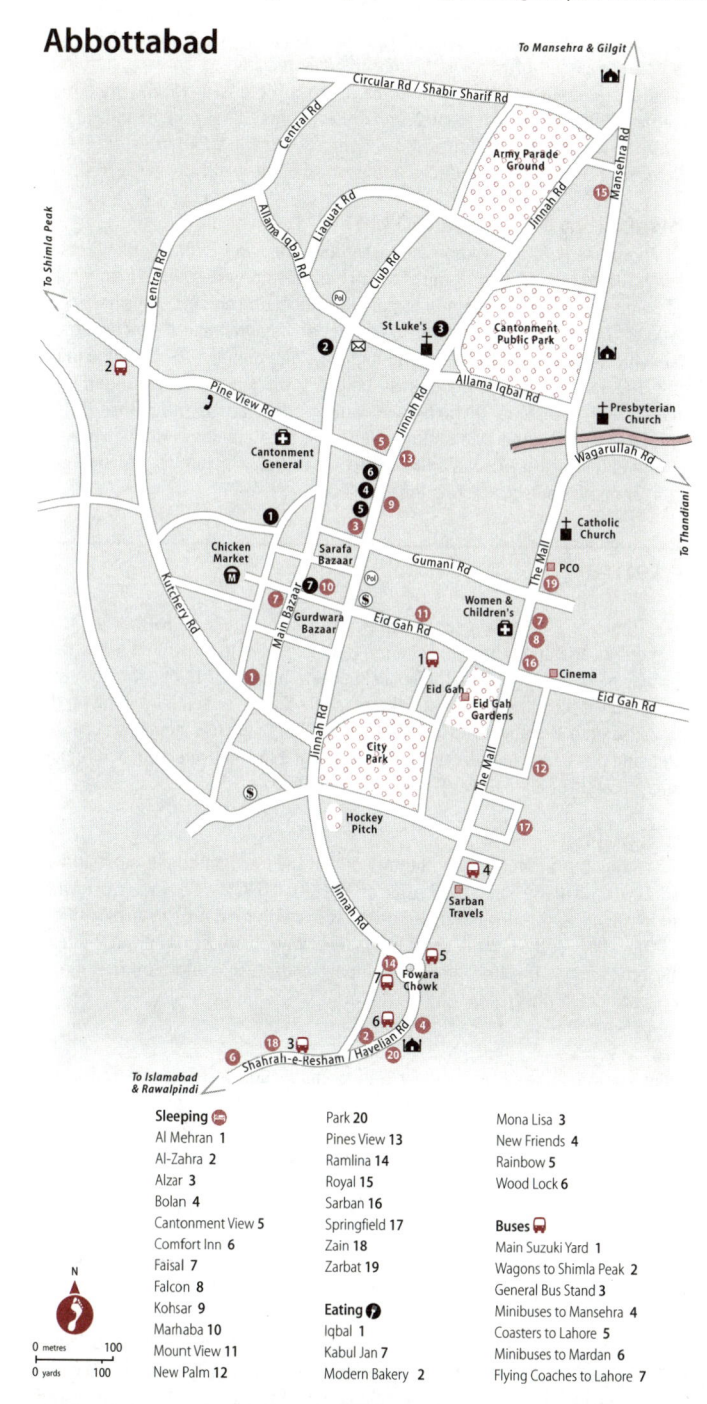

Abbottabad

Sleeping
Al Mehran 1
Al-Zahra 2
Alzar 3
Bolan 4
Cantonment View 5
Comfort Inn 6
Faisal 7
Falcon 8
Kohsar 9
Marhaba 10
Mount View 11
New Palm 12
Park 20
Pines View 13
Ramlina 14
Royal 15
Sarban 16
Springfield 17
Zain 18
Zarbat 19

Eating
Iqbal 1
Kabul Jan 7
Modern Bakery 2
Mona Lisa 3
New Friends 4
Rainbow 5
Wood Lock 6

Buses
Main Suzuki Yard 1
Wagons to Shimla Peak 2
General Bus Stand 3
Minibuses to Mansehra 4
Coasters to Lahore 5
Minibuses to Mardan 6
Flying Coaches to Lahore 7

very little to Thandiani, other than wandering through the shady forests or exploring St Saviour's Church. It is, however, extremely tranquil and very much off the beaten track and has some seasonal accommodation nearby, see page 172.

Thandiani is the most northerly of the Galis chain of hill stations, the most famous and developed of which is Murree (usually reached as an excursion from Rawalpindi/Islamabad, see Hazara map, page 167). There is a two-day hike from Thandiani to Nathia Gali, with resthouses en route at Biran Gali (1,920 m) and Palakot (2,720 m). The **Asian Study Group** ① *Malik Complex, 80 West, Jinnah Av, Blue Area Islamabad, T051-815891*, has produced a route map of the walk.

Abbottabad to Mansehra (30 km)
The KKH continues north from Abbottabad, through the two satellite settlements of Sikanderabad and Mandian, the latter of which has the impressive Ayub Hospital and Medical Complex plus several upmarket sleeping and eating options. A further 20 km brings you to Qalandarabad, which has a number of restaurants and chai houses.

Mansehra is another 6 km along the highway, although the KKH itself actually bypasses the town. The toll booth just before town marks the boundaries of Abbottabad and Mansehra Districts. Two link roads lead up from the KKH to Mansehra: the most southerly road turns off next to the **Karakuram Hotel**, while the second one is just next to **Asoka's Rock Edicts** (see below). Note that Mansehra's main bus terminal is a further 2 km along the KKH.

Mansehra

Mansehra remains a transport junction despite the best efforts to bypass it. Its development as an important trading centre (and as a garrison town) on the road to Srinagar was negated by the unnatural division of Kashmir at Partition, and now even the KKH passes it by, although it's still the place to change buses if heading up the Kaghan Valley or to Muzaffarabad in Azad Kashmir. There are few sights as such, but it's a pleasing place to wander around, with many of its recently established Afghan refugee population keen to engage you in conversation.

Ins and outs
There is a small bus stand on Abbottabad Road in the town, although most arrivals will be dropped off at the Main Bus Station on the KKH itself, 2 km beyond the town. If you ask in advance, the driver may drop you at the link road next to Asoka's Rock Edicts, from where you can walk up to Mansehra. Wagons (Rs5) run up to the town from the bus station. The town itself is compact enough to explore on foot. ▸▸ *See Transport, page 174, for more details.*

Sights
Mansehra's importance as an ancient transport junction is best reflected in the decision of King Priyadarsin (Asoka) to have a series of his edicts inscribed here in the third century BC. **Asoka's Rock Edicts** are carved onto three large boulders now adjacent to the KKH (and protected by modern roof structures), and deal with the king's opinions on subjects as diverse as 'vegetarianism', 'true glory', 'merits of piety' and the 'prompt dispatch of business', among others. Sadly, the Kharaoshthi script is so weather-beaten as to be all but invisible.

Traces of the Sikh occupation of the town can be seen in the **Gurdwara** (temple), formerly converted into a police station but now housing the municipal library. This recent restoration is most welcome, with the façade being particularly impressive; it's certainly worth going inside and taking a look around. The **Sikh Fort** has largely disappeared beneath the modern police station. See page 173 for sleeping and eating options in Mansehra. Those making the excursion off the KKH up the Kaghan Valley (or indeed those taking the alternative route north via the Babusar Pass to Chilas) should turn to page 175.

Mansehra to Shinkiari (28 km)

Beyond Mansehra the Karakoram Highway gradually begins to climb through a series of switchbacks, passing the settlement of **Dhodial** (12 km), and crossing the Siran River near to Shinkiari (8 km).

The small roadside town of **Shinkiari** (blink and you'll miss it) is home to a project that is attempting to save the national exchequer some US$200 in foreign exchange reserves annually – by growing tea! Despite the nation's taste for the stuff, tea is extremely difficult to grow in Pakistan. The ideal moist tropical climate with deep, well-drained acid soils is not encountered in Pakistan, and although NWFP has sufficient natural rainfall for tea growing, the cold, frosty winters are not suitable for the preferred Assam tea plants. Thus, Lever Brothers Pakistan Ltd, who has its

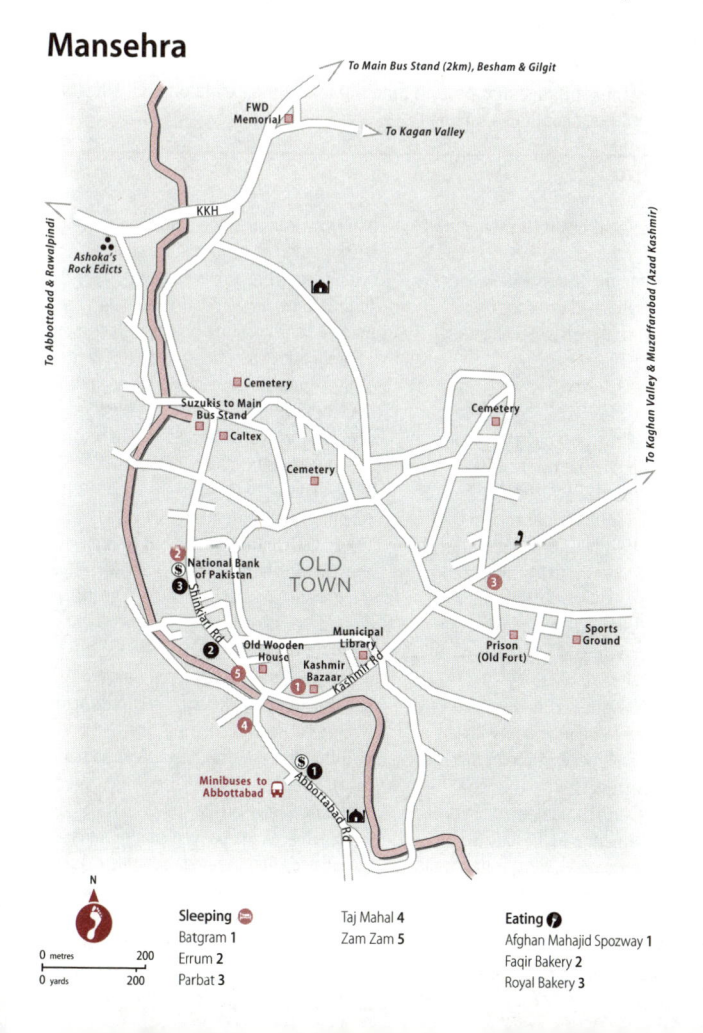

Mansehra

Sleeping
Batgram 1
Errum 2
Parbat 3
Taj Mahal 4
Zam Zam 5

Eating
Afghan Mahajid Spozway 1
Faqir Bakery 2
Royal Bakery 3

research station here in Shinkiari, has been experimenting with a China-type tea plant that is more suitable to the soil and the climate and almost 150 ha are now under cultivation. Although self sufficiency in tea is judged to be a long way off, there are hopes that some small dent can be made in the substantial tea smuggling industry that costs the government some Rs1.8 billion annually in lost revenue.

Beyond Shinkiari, a winding road leads off the KKH, following the course of the Siran River to **Daddar**. This was the epicentre of the catastrophic floods that hit Mansehra District in July 2001, causing major loss of life and damage to property. From here there are fine views of the 4,945-m Bhogarmang Peak in the neighbouring Kaghan Valley. The KKH climbs steadily from Shinkiari, after 29 km arriving at Battal. The highway then proceeds north through the fertile bowl of Chattar Plain (named after the Sikh general), and up to Sharkool, 7 km from Battal.

From here, the KKH continues to the small town of **Battagram** (14 km). Just beyond Battagram, on the west side of the road, look out for the impressive pulley cable car system over the river, that links the isolated villages to the KKH and the outside world. About 12 km beyond Battagram is a small police post, where transport heading north at night is sometimes formed up into convoys (for safety). The next 10 km of the KKH run through a notorious 'slide area' that frequently causes delays after even light rain. Some 21 km from Battagram is **Thakot Bridge**, marking the boundary between Hazara and Indus Kohistan. For those continuing north along the KKH from Mansehra to Thakot Bridge and beyond (and not taking the excursion up the Kaghan Valley), the KKH text continues on page 184.

Sleeping

Start of the Karakoram Highway p168
Haripur
G **Afaq**, near to the National Bank. Basic, doubles with attached bathroom.
G **Skabana**, near the National Bank. Basic.

Abbottabad p168
Few foreign visitors choose to overnight in Abbottabad, although it has a range of sleeping options to suit most budgets.
B-D **Sarban**, The Mall, T0992-330167. Suites and family rooms (B), de luxe a/c carpeted doubles with dish TV (C, or Rs300 less for non a/c), standard rooms with fan, dish TV and attached bathroom with tub (C), clean enough but hallways tatty, large restaurant, rooftop BBQ, parking.
C-D **Royal**, The Mall, T0992-333234, royalhotel786@yahoo.co.in. Overpriced a/c rooms (C) plus standard rooms with fan, dish TV, old-fashioned bathrooms, not great value, Chinese restaurant.
D-E **Comfort Inn**, Shahrah-e-Resham/KKH, T0992-334159. Rooms a little tatty (so negotiate a better price), some with a/c, all with attached hot bath (some tubs), dish TV, phone, can be a good deal.
E **Springfield**, The Mall, T0992-337397. Large rooms with threadbare carpets, linen none too clean, attached bath (toilet seats missing), fan, tatty corridors (looks damp), quiet location but very overpriced.
F **Cantt View**, Jinnah Rd, T0992-331346. Above a bank, small, grubby rooms, surly staff.
F **Ramlina**, KKH near bus station, T0992-334431. Unprepossessing when seen from north but OK from the south, carpeted doubles with clean enough attached bath, fan, linen could be cleaner but overall OK, terrace, parking, restaurant (check bill).
F **Zain**, Shahrah-e-Resham/KKH, T0992-335763. Friendly and keen owner who appears to add a few rooms whenever he has some spare time and money, don't go for the dingy downstairs rooms.
F **Zarbat**, The Mall, T0992-330608. Clean rooms with attached hot bath (mornings only), sometimes reluctant to take foreigners (shame since this is a good choice).
G **Abbott Inn**, Fowara Chowk. New place but still fairly basic.
G **Al-Zahra**, Havelian Rd, T0992-330155. Close to noisy bus stands, not very private, rather dilapidated but still reasonable value.
G **Bolan**, Fowara Chowk, T0992-334395. Pretty basic windowless rooms, attached bath, friendly owner (worth haggling over prices), restaurant.

G Faisal, The Mall. On noisy road, reluctant to take foreigners.
G Falcon, The Mall. Neighbour to the above, also reluctant to take foreigners.
G Mount View, Eid Gah Rd, T0992-330818. Friendly, but rather noisy and grubby, attached bath, restaurant.
G Park, Havelian Rd. Convenient for snooker hall downstairs, but basic and noisy.
G Pines View, Jinnah Rd. Verandah, not very private rooms, basic, not keen on foreigners.
G Qasr-e-Asghar, KKH near bus station. Fairly basic place above noisy music shop.

Thandiani
E-F Far Pavillions, Thandiani. Seasonal accommodation option only, generally open spring to mid-autumn. 2 cottages set in pleasant lawns, good camping.
F Shalimar, Thandiani. Seasonal accommodation option only, generally open spring to mid-autumn. Little more than a 2-room shack, clean, attached toilet is just a hole in the floor, overpriced.

Mansehra p170
F Errum, Shinkiari Rd, T0987-36245. Best deal in town, very clean singles (**G**) and doubles with attached clean bath, fan, good restaurant, friendly, recommended.
G Batgram, Kashmir Bazaar. Extremely basic and run-down.
G Parbat, Kashmir Rd, T0987-36979. Fairly grubby rooms, attached bath, dirty linen, fan, restaurant, not much English spoken.
G Taj Mahal, Abbottabad Rd, T0987-2096. Very basic, not keen on foreigners
G Zam Zam, Shinkiari Rd, T0987-2127. Rooms basic but linen clean, attached scoop/bucket shower, some even cheaper rooms (**H**) with shared bath, breezy terrace, popular restaurant, friendly, recommended.

Mansehra to Shinkiari p171
Dhodial
G Madina Hotel. New and clean.

Shinkiari
G Dubai Hotel. Basic hotel for those wishing to stay in Shinkiari.

Shinkiari to Thakot Bridge
D-E Jangal Mangal Hotel, 21 km from Shinkiari on the KKH. New hotel, clean, bare floor rooms, fan, attached bath, veranda overlooking valley, friendly staff.
F Chattar Plains Motel 5 km from Battal, KKH.
D Affaq Hotel Motel, Sharkool. Former PTDC Motel, now privately run. A little run down but reasonable value, rooms close to the road should be avoided as trucks grind up and down the hill in bottom gear.
D Green's Hotel, Sharkool, 7 km from Battal.
D Battagram View Hotel. Just to the south of Battagram, T0987-310194. Impressive but overpriced.
G Al-Faqur, main bazaar, Battagram. Modest, basic, the best of the bunch here.
G Al-Kaman, main bazaar, Battagram. Modest, basic.
G Jeddah, main bazaar, Battagram. Modest, basic.
G Khyber, main bazaar, Battagram. Filthy, not recommended.

Eating

Abbottabad p168
🍴 **Mona Lisa**, Jinnah Rd opposite the Cantt Public Park. Fast food for the middle classes ('buy 1 get 1 free' pizza deals, steak & chips, Chinese dishes, expect to spend up to Rs200 including drinks).
🍴 **Red Onion**, Jinnah Rd opposite the Cantt Public Park. Same as above.
🍴 **Café Kabul Jan**, junction of Main Bazaar and Eid Gah Rd. Meat/chicken, chapati in nicer surroundings.
🍴 **New Friends**, **New Kaghan Café**, **Rainbow** and **Wood Lock**, Jinnah Rd. Standard meat/chicken and chapati for the lower classes.
🍴 **Iqbal**, Main Bazaar. Similar food but in slightly nicer surroundings.

There are several **juice stands** at the junction of Eid Gah/Jinnah Rds, and mineral water from **Modern Bakery**, Club Rd. More upmarket fast food places can be found in the suburb of **Mandian**.

Mansehra p170
All the hotels have their own restaurants.
🍴 **Errum**, Shinkiari Rd, T0987-36245. Particularly good, inside the hotel.

There are a number of basic meat and chapati places on Shinkiari Rd plus several Afghan establishments on Abbottabad Rd. The Faqir Bakery and the place next to the Errum Hotel sell mineral water.

Transport

Abbottabad *p168*

The General **Bus** Stand to the south of town has services to all the destinations mentioned below (and more), although the buses are generally old wrecks that take forever to reach their destinations.

For buses to the **Kaghan Valley**, go to Mansehra and change. Buses from Rawalpindi to **Gilgit** (and points north of Abbottabad along the KKH) are often full as they pass through here; to get to Gilgit you usually have to change at Mansehra and then at Besham.

Lahore: Haruhito Okiyama Travel, just south of Ramlina Hotel, runs 7 coasters daily to Lahore 0900-2200 (Rs180, 8-9 hrs). Another company just south of Al-Zahra Hotel also has coasters to Lahore, as does another company on Fowara Chowk.

Mansehra: minibuses depart when full from a bus stand on The Mall opposite Sarban Travels (Rs15, 1 hr).

Mardan: minibuses depart when full from the yard next to the Al-Zahra Hotel (Rs65, 5-6 hrs).

Peshawar: minibuses depart when full from the yard next to the Al-Zahra Hotel (Rs65, 7-8 hrs).

Rawalpindi: Haruhito Okiyama Travel, just south of Ramlina Hotel, runs coasters every 30 mins from 0700 (Rs50, 3-4 hrs). Minibuses run to Rawalpindi from the yard outside the Springfield Hotel (Rs43, 3-4 hrs).

Mansehra *p170*

Suzuki wagons run from the Caltex petrol station to the Main Bus Stand down on the KKH (Rs5). The **minibus** yard on Abbottabad Road has services to **Abbottabad** only.

The **Main Bus Stand**, down on the KKH (2 km from the town), is pretty chaotic. To find the bus you want just yell out your destination and someone will kindly guide you to the right stand. Most services leave on a 'depart when full' basis, although there are several companies around the bus stand that offer scheduled 'Flying Coaches' to long-distance destinations such as **Lahore** (Rs210, 10 hrs) and even **Karachi** (Rs400, 30 hrs +).

Minibuses and bone-shaker buses run to: **Abbottabad** (Rs15, 1 hr); **Balakot** (Kaghan Valley) (Rs32, 1¼ hrs); **Besham** (Rs65, 4 hrs); **Muzaffarabad** (Rs42, 2 hrs); **Naran** (Kaghan Valley) (Rs100, 4½-5 hrs); **Rawalpindi** (Rs52, 4 hrs) and other destinations.

Buses passing through on their way to **Gilgit** can be flagged down on the KKH (arrive around 3-4 hrs after leaving Rawalpindi), but they are often already full; the best option is to go to Besham and change.

Airline offices

PIA, Abbottabad Rd (just off the map), T0987-36747.

Directory

Abbottabad *p168*

Banks There are several banks in Abbottabad, but changing money can be problematic. **Muslim Commercial Bank**, Eid Gah Rd, deals only in US$ (cash and TCs, not good rates). The main **National Bank of Pakistan** near to the courts claims to offer foreign exchange. **Chemists** Most of the chemists are located opposite the various hospitals. **Fire** T0992-336289. **Hospitals** Cantt General, Pines View Rd. Women and Children's Hospital, The Mall. Your best bet is the huge, modern **Ayub Hospital and Medical Complex** in Mandian, several kilometres north of Abbottabad along the KKH. **Police** T15 or T0992-337165. **Post office** Junction of Club Rd and Allama Iqbal Rd. **Telephones** Pine View Rd (for international and local calls). There are PCOs on The Mall and in the Main Bazaar. **Useful addresses** Conservator of Forests, Jail Rd, T0992-330728. May assist in booking the resthouses at Thandiani and in the Kaghan Valley.

Mansehra *p170*

Banks Muslim Commercial Bank, Abbottabad Rd, opposite minibus stand. Mon-Sat 0900-1230, will exchange US$ only (cash or TCs). **Post office** Kashmir Rd. **Telephones** Paktel, Kashmir Rd (look for the communications tower). Daily 0800-2200, has efficient and cheap IDD (despite the booths, you may find that the phone is just pushed across the counter to you).

Kaghan Valley → Colour map 1, grid A4

With its fragrant alpine forests, deep blue high-altitude lakes, lush green meadows, distant snowy peaks and trout-filled Kunhar River, the Kaghan Valley offers a picturesque excursion off the KKH. And for those prepared to rough it and looking for a little adventure, it provides an alternative route to the north, taking in the 4,175-m-Babusar Pass at the head of this 161-km-long valley, and then joining the KKH at Chilas. However, because of the valley's appealing alpine scenery, and its ease of access from the Pakistani plains, the need to cater to the growing numbers of domestic tourists means that development has been rapid and completely unplanned. Once you pass north of Naran, public transport all but disappears, although there's the odd cargo jeep serving the various settlements along the track. The inhabitants living just on either side of the the pass itself are not the friendliest people you'll encounter during your stay in Pakistan, so camping out along this route needs to be carefully considered. ▸▸ *For Sleeping, Eating and all other listings, see pages 181-183.*

Ins and outs

There are two entrances/exits to the Kaghan Valley. The easiest and most popular entry/exit is through Garhi Habibullah Khan at the south end of the valley, usually reached via Mansehra and the KKH. The more adventurous entry/exit to the valley is via the Babusar Pass to the north. This route is weather dependent, as well as being extremely challenging. For those planning a trip between Rawalpindi/ Islamabad and Gilgit (whether travelling north-south or south-north), travelling via the Kaghan Valley provides a more interesting (although more difficult) route than the section of the KKH between Mansehra and Chilas.

Within a few years, the Kaghan Valley will not so much be an excursion off the KKH, but an integral part of it. The road between the KKH and Naran has been recently upgraded (taking nearly two hours off the journey time from Abbottabad), with plans to provide a fully metalled road over the Babusar Pass to join the KKH at Chilas. Such a road, when completed, would cut four hours off the current Rawalpindi/Islamabad to Gilgit jouney time and relieve travellers of the trials of Indus Kohistan.

Best time to visit

During the winter months (November-March), heavy snowfall means that it is generally impossible to go any further north than Kaghan village. The Babusar Pass is usually only open to jeeps from July until early September, although it is possible to cross on foot a little before and after these dates. The summer months, May, June and July, show the Kaghan Valley at its best, allowing an escape from the heat of the Punjab plains, although the valley is more crowded with visitors. Late July sees the onset of the monsoon. Autumn can be pleasant, but cold at night.

As with other regions that are popular with Pakistani tourists (eg Murree and Swat), hotel prices in the Kaghan Valley tend to inflate in the high season, at weekends, and when the manager feels like it. It is worth bargaining at any time, particularly out of season. If you wish to stay in the better hotels at peak times, advance booking is recommended.

Lower Kaghan Valley

Although there is little to see in **Balakot** itself, it is effectively the gateway to the southern end of the valley and an important transport junction, as well as being the scene of a major battle between the Sikhs and Muslims in 1831. It is reached on a good-quality winding road from Mahsehra (39 km, 1¼ hours), which passes the bridge at **Garhi Habibullah Khan**, the junction for Muzaffarabad in Azad Kashmir. For those heading to/from Naran it may be necessary to change transport here, and, although there are plenty of accommodation options (see page 181), there are far more attractive places in the Kaghan Valley to spend your time.

Beyond Balakot, the road begins to rapidly climb high above the Kunhar River. After 24 km (1 hour), the bend in the road marks the settlement of **Kawai** (1,463 m). From here, jeeps run 10 km up the old logging track to Shogran (Rs300 one way, bargain hard), although for those who want to walk, there is a shorter, but very steep, footpath (the manager at the hotel can point you in the right direction). There is accommodation at Shogran, plus some cheaper places to stay at Kawai (see page 181).

Receiving fewer visitors in comparison with Naran, **Shogran** (2,362 m) is one of the loveliest spots in the Kaghan Valley. It has unsurpassed views in all directions, particularly if you walk up for two hours through the forest to the high summer pastures at **Seri Paya**. To the south are views of Makra Peak (3,885 m), while to the north is **Malika Parbat** (5,291 m), the highest mountain in the Kaghan Valley. Wandering through the fragrant pine forests here, or strolling through the flowers in the lush meadow, has much to recommend it (and without the commotion of Naran).

The first settlement beyond Kawai is **Paras** (6 km), often a chai-stop on the bus ride to Naran. Beyond Paras the road drops down to the valley bottom, adjacent to the river.

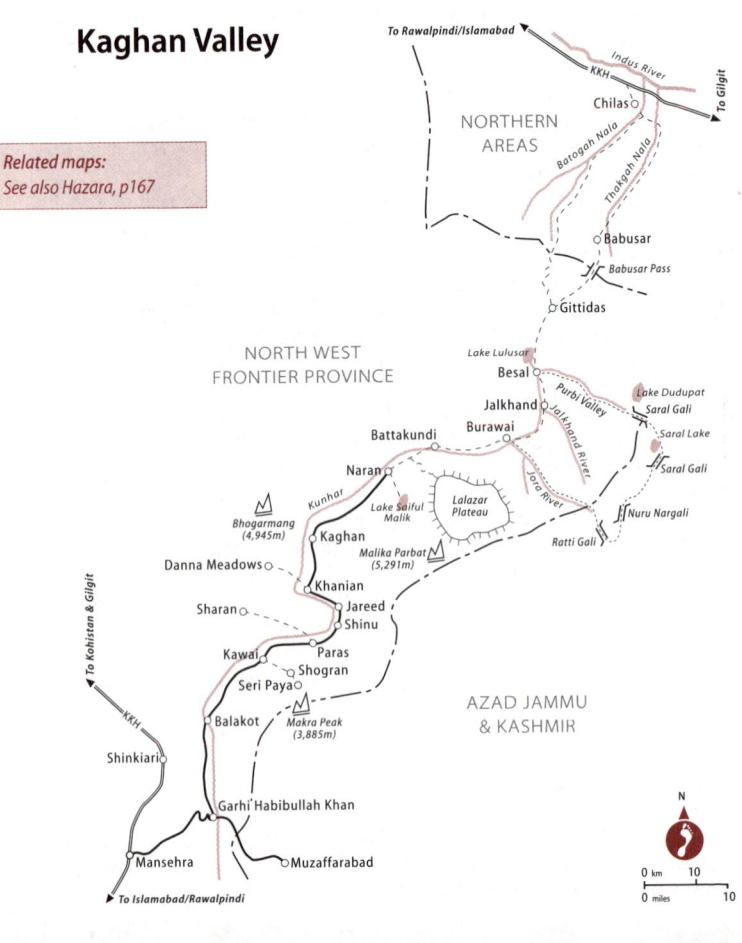

Kaghan Valley

Related maps:
See also Hazara, p167

Jeep tracks turn off right for Malakandi and Shogram, and left for **Sharan** (16 km), set in deep forest. The next small settlement is **Fareedabad** (with its new FWO cement works), and then **Shinu**, with its trout hatchery. After the extensively cultivated land of **Jareed** on either side of the road, the highway again climbs above the valley floor.

A narrow bridge crosses a tributary of the Kunhar River at the miserable settlement of **Mahandri** (15 km from Paras), and the road then continues to **Khanian**. The distinctive red pagoda-style roof here is the **Pine Parks Hotel**, used by their guests as a transit point on the way up to the beautiful **Danna Meadows**. Approachable by a jeep road one hour west of Khanian, Danna is situated in a remote side valley, surrounded by virgin forest, and set in the shadow of Bhogarmang Peak (4,945 m). It is well worth the effort of getting there. Ask at the PTDC in Balakot for more details.

A further 5 km beyond Khanian is the settlement of **Kaghan** (2,038 m), the settlement that gives its name to the whole valley. Previously, this was the most northerly point in the valley that could be reached in winter (hence the location of the valley's main civil hospital here, and not in Naran), but should the road north from Naran to Chilas be fully upgraded as planned, then much effort will be made to ensure that it is passable year round. Balakot to Naran is approximately 83 km. For details of sleeping and eating options, see page 181.

Naran

Naran is the key destination of most visitors to the Kaghan Valley – and it shows! The setting is beautiful, and there are plenty of picturesque spots a long walk or short jeep ride away. Yet the settlement itself is an unappealing collection of unattractive hotels, restaurants and numerous handicraft shops jumbled together in a haphazard, unplanned manner. Foreign visitors (and women in particular) often have to put up with persistent verbal harassment and childish jibes from the hordes of young Punjabi men who make up the majority of visitors. For sleeping options, see page 181.

Tourist information PTDC ⓘ *office at the PTDC Motel*, can arrange jeep hire throughout the Kaghan Valley (and beyond) as well as two- to five-day trips around the valley (rates on application). This is also the place to enquire about hiring guides for treks and walks in the northern part of the valley (and all negotiations should be undertaken in the presence of a PTDC staff member). For details of fishing in the Kaghan Valley, see page 183.

Lake Saiful Malik

ⓘ *The lake can be reached in a stiff 3-hr climb from Naran, or by hired jeep, generally Rs600 return, although if you only plan a stay at the lake for 20 mins or so, it is possible to hire a jeep late in the afternoon for just Rs400. The drive across the glacier en route to the lake is exhilarating/petrifying. The lake is impossibly crowded on Fri, Sat and holidays. There are a number of small snack and cold drinks stalls at the lake, and horses and ponies can be hired.*

> Note that despite the escalation in fuel prices and maintenance costs, the rates for jeep hire from Naran haven't changed since 1995 – something must give soon!

This lake could so nearly be a perfect spot. Located some 10 km to the east of Naran, at an altitude of 3,215 m and ringed by an amphitheatre of snow-capped mountains, it is not hard to see why local legends speak of princes, fairies and jealous demons who visit the lake at night to dance and bathe. Even in summer, large blocks of ice can often be seen floating in the sapphire waters, as the lake reflects the image of Malika Parbat to the south.

The fly in the ointment is not that the lake receives so many visitors, but that they seem so nonchalant about discarding their litter over as wide a space around the lake as possible – the meadows of alpine flowers really are fighting a losing battle.

Lalazar Plateau

ⓘ *The plateau is reached by a jeep track climbing up from Battakundi, a settlement 16 km north of Naran. A half-day excursion by jeep costs Rs700 return per vehicle, although you may be able to do a deal that includes Lake Saiful Malik as well.*

Located at 3,200 m, this beautiful meadow is awash with colourful alpine flowers in spring and summer, and set among the cool pine forests. A footpath leads from Lalazar Plateau down to Lake Saiful Malik, taking five to six hours.

Naran to Babusar Pass and Chilas

Naran to Buruwai (29 km)

There are plans to upgrade the current rough jeep track that crosses the Babusar Pass into Chilas with an all-weather metalled road. If and when this project comes to fruition, around four hours should be cut from the Rawalpindi/Islamabad-Gilgit journey time, as well as effecting innumerable changes in the upper reaches of the Kaghan Valley. Currently, an occasional bus runs from Naran to Jalkhand, as well as irregular cargo jeep services and trucks. In reality, however, you need your own transport to undertake this journey.

The jeep road traces the course of the Kunhar River through several excellent trout fishing reaches, passing some sublime scenery. As it begins to climb high above the course of the river, the track passes isolated summer settlements set among fields of peas and potatoes. If you look to the west, you may see nomadic Gujar communities leading their flocks across the high passes to pastures in Swat Kohistan. Just before the settlement of **Battakundi** (2,713 m) is the jeep track that leads 5 km east up to the **Lalazar Plateau**. The road then drops down into Battakundi, which has four or five small, basic hotels. Battakundi is 16 km from Naran.

Having crossed the river, the jeep road climbs steadily up the 13 km to **Burawai**, where the Jora River joins the Kunhar from the southeast, from its source in Azad Jammu and Kashmir. It is possible to hike

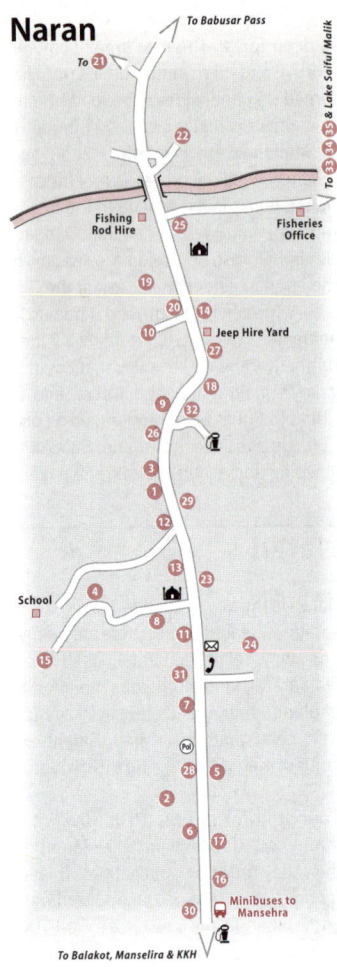

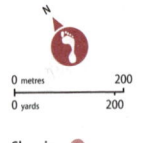

Sleeping
Babu **1**
Balakot **2**
Bilal **3**
Dreamland **4**
Errum **5**
Frontier **6**
Green Park **7**
Himalaya Inn **8**
Kashmir & Kohsar **9**
Koh-i-Toor **10**
Kunhar **11**
Lalazar & Naheem's Pizza **12**
Madina **13**
Mehran **14**
Mount View **15**
Naran **16**
New Park **17**
Pakistan **18**
Paradise **19**
Parwana **20**
PTDC **21**
PTDC (Cottages) **22**
Punjab **23**
Royal **24**
Saiful Malik **25**
Sarhad & Zero Point **26**
Shalimar **27**
Snow Land **28**
Snow View **29**
Sohrab **30**
Taj Mahal, Park & Summer Land **31**
Zam Zam **32**
Pine Park **33**
Springfield **34**
Troutland **35**

up this valley in a five-day trip which provides a more scenic route to Besal than the jeep road (see Burawai to Besal trekking route below). Burawai village is little more than a collection of low shacks, although it is possible to stay on a charpoy at one of the chai-shops overnight if you so wish. A small lodge appears to be under construction on the Battakundi side of the village. It is sometimes possible to get a public cargo jeep between Naran and Burawai (Rs60).

Burawai to Besal: jeep route (18 km)

Although the jeep road high above the river deteriorates considerably along this stretch, the scenery remains rewarding, notably the snow-capped **Dabuka ridge** (4,859 m). It's also noticeable how marked the change in scenery is beyond Burawai, with the silver fir and blue pine trees becoming scantier and the hills barer. Most surprising perhaps are the small chai stops along this isolated section of road, since there's very little passing trade.

Some 12 km or so beyond Burawai, at **Jalkhand**, the Kunhar River is joined from the east by the Jalkhand River. A new truck road heads east into Azad Kashmir from here. The valley begins to open out at **Besal**, where landscape has been likened to a "bleak Scotch moor". The jeep road drops down to the valley floor, passing tented settlements of Afghan refugees. Some 20 years ago there were at least 10 shops in Besal, but now only one shop-cum-restaurant has survived. It's possible to sleep on a charpoy here, or bivvy down in the ruins of one of the former shops; a better bet is to push on to Lulusar Lake. From Besal it is possible to make a short hiking diversion up to Lake Dudupat.

An attractive lake, **Lake Dudupat** (sometimes written 'Dudibach') lies 18 km to the east of Besal. For those attempting this excursion, hiring a guide in Besal is essential (around Rs500 per day). There are no readily identifiable permanent tracks from Besal up to Lake Dudupat; instead you will be following the temporary tracks made during the summer months by villagers bringing their flocks to graze in the Kaghan Valley. In the first 6 km (two hours) from Besal you may cross as many as five small glaciers (this is where your guide will be invaluable), before entering a 12-km-long valley. It takes four to five hours' walking through the lush green grass to reach the beautiful circular lake.

Burawai to Besal: trekking route

A very attractive alternative to the jeep road between Burawai and Besal is the four- to five-day trekking loop that takes in a couple of 4,000-m passes and two attractive alpine lakes. A trustworthy local guide should be employed.

From Burawai it is a six- to eight-hour fairly easy walk to the southeast, along the course of the Jora Valley. The meadows provide good camping. The second day involves a walk up to the **Ratti Gali** pass at 4,115 m, the boundary between NWFP and Azad Jammu and Kashmir. Follow the stream down from the pass, and where it meets another stream continue north along it to **Nuri Nar Gali** pass (also 4,115 m). This second day takes around five to six hours, and again there is good camping in the meadows (just below the pass). As you follow the stream down on the third day, ignore the Jalkhand River valley (that leads back down to the Kunhar River), and instead take the trail to the northeast over the **Saral Gali** pass (4,191 m). After four to five hours you reach **Saral Lake**, another good camping spot. Early on day four, as you follow the stream west, the trail splits. The shortest option is to take the route west across the **Saral-di-Gali** pass (4,488 m), and then along the Purbi River valley to Besal (three to four hours). Or take the trail north and camp out for a further night at Lake Dudupat. On the fifth day it's a five- to six-hour walk down the Purbi Valley to Besal.

Besal to Gittidas (12 km)

Several kilometres north of Besal (or a two-hour walk) is **Lake Lulusar**. Shaped like an irregular crescent, 2½ km long, 250 m wide and 50 m deep, Lake Lulusar is the source of the Kunhar River that flows through the Kaghan Valley. The water is deep green in

> **Warning**
>
> There have been a number of incidents where walkers and cyclists have been either robbed or threatened by armed Chilasi men while crossing the pass, or travelling between **Babusar** and **Chilas** (including a jeep load of Punjabi tourists who, in summer 2001, had all their possessions – including their jeep – stolen at gunpoint). Other travellers, while not having been actually assaulted, speak of having been made to feel very uncomfortable.
>
> Take advice, either in Naran or Chilas, before making the trip, and think seriously about hiring a local guide. This should ideally be done via the PTDC in Naran, with negotiations conducted in front of witnesses. Cyclists should note that the road is extremely rough, and is only really passable on a lightly loaded mountain bike. At a slow speed, you will be particularly vulnerable to the legendary stone-throwing kids of the Chilas region. Read trekking notes on page 45.

colour, and with the sheer mountains rising directly up from the lakeside, it is certainly as beautiful as Saiful Malik. A legend relates that a blind daughter of Emperor Akbar bathed in the waters of Lake Lulusar and her sight was restored. Remote, and at 3,350 m, there are far fewer tourists. There is excellent camping potential here, particularly on the west side (away from the road). If coming from the north, a privately hired jeep from Babusar village to the lake costs around Rs750.

Beyond the lake is **Gittidas**, the last village before the pass. The valley broadens out considerably here. This village is a summer settlement occupied by Chilasi people, who come here to graze their livestock. The village has a poor reputation and should not be approached unless you are accompanied by a reputable local guide. Camping near here is inadvisable.

A new jeep road that follows the **Batogah Nala** now links Gittidas to Chilas, avoiding the Babusar Pass. Cyclists and hikers who are travelling south from Chilas to the Kaghan Valley should make sure that they take the correct route as they leave Chilas. As you leave Chilas, you first cross the Batogah Nala. The trail leading from here is this new jeep road to Gittidas. If you want to go to the Kaghan Valley via the Babusar Pass, keep going until you meet the Thak Gah Nala.

Gittidas to Babusar Pass (7 km)

From Gittidas it is a steady climb to the summit of **Babusar Pass** ('Babusar Top') at 4,175 m (although no two sources seem to agree on this height). The actual pass is shaped like a saddle, and the best views are to be had by climbing either flank of the saddle for a further 200 m or so. There are a couple of cold drinks stands at the summit.

Babusar Pass to Chilas (50 km)

From the top of the pass it is a difficult zig-zagging descent down towards Babusar village, although the jeep track here is somewhat better than it is on the Kaghan Valley side. You will notice here how the local people have completely clear-cut the slopes – the forest of tree stumps is a staggering, but depressing sight. Government plans to reafforest the valley have so far been resisted by the villagers, who fear that in years to come they may turn round and say 'we planted the trees so the land is ours'.

The road from the Babusar Pass eventually reaches the miserable Chilasi settlement of **Babusar** (13 km). Don't be surprised if you hear 'duelling banjos' here. Foreigners will probably be asked to sign the book at the police station. You can stay here, but if you are coming in a jeep from Naran most drivers prefer to push on to Chilas.

Irregular **public cargo jeeps** run in either direction between Babusar and Chilas (Rs65, difficult to find on Fri), but it is rare to find cargo jeeps going all the way across the pass. These jeeps are uncomfortably over-crowded. **Private jeeps** can be hired in Chilas or Naran, although at Rs3,500 1 way, the trip is not cheap. A private jeep from Babusar to **Lulusar Lake** will cost around Rs750. The section of road between Babusar Top and Chilas is quite rough, and it can take up to three hours to cover the 37 km by jeep (cyclists may require 12 hours). The total journey time between Naran and Chilas in a private jeep is around nine hours.

Sleeping

Lower Kaghan Valley *p175*
Balakot
B PTDC Motel (Troutland), T0985-210208. Fairly large rooms with shared terrace, set in nice garden, restaurant, somewhat overpriced, tourist info is based here.
B-C Pine Park (New). Outer shell was completed in 1999 but it has stood empty ever since.
C-D Gateway, T0985-210591, F0985-210593. Good-sized carpeted rooms with fan, modern attached bath, large garden, restaurant.
D River View, east side of river. Recently built in location away from noise of town, reasonable rooms, restaurant, can be a good deal if you negotiate the right price (E).
D-E Pine Park (Old), T0985-210544. This was due to close when the 'new' hotel opened, but it's still clinging on with its crumbling balconies (be very careful) and damp rooms.
E Taj Mahal, T0985-210321. Rooms relatively clean compared to rest of building (but over-priced unless you bargain hard), restaurant.
F Koh-i-Toor, T0985-210263. Noisy, town-centre location (take an upstairs room), carpeted rooms with attached bath.
G Kunhar View, T0985-210229. Dark, unappealing rooms, overpriced.
G Lahore, T0985-210031. Basic rooms with attached bath, curtains too small for windows so not much privacy.
G Valley View, T0985-210505. Becomes more run down with each passing year, noisy location, rooms on upper floors are marginally better.

Shogran
L-D Pine Park Resort. Huge choice of options from VIP Suite (L) with bedroom and sitting room and Pine Villas (L), through Swiss Cottages (A), nice doubles in the Main Block (C) and reasonable value rooms in the Tourist Block (D). Restaurant, extensive gardens, vehicle hire. Good value, especially if you can negotiate the rate down by at least 1 price category.
A Lalazar Cottage, T0985-410021. Price (Rs5,000) includes rent of whole cottage (2 doubles, 2 singles, communal lounge, kitchen) plus all meals. Lovely views.
E Faisal. Rather expensive for what you get.
F Punjab Hazara. Very basic, would cost half the price anywhere else.

Kawai
F Faisal. Attractive wooden hotel on bend in the road, pretty good value, restaurant.
F Tourist Inn. Multi-storey hotel, rooms aren't bad but exterior and corridors are a little shabby, restaurant.

Paras
G Green Park Hotel. At the Naran end of Paras, this is slightly more appealing than the following option.
H Paras Hotel (Urdu sign only). At the Balakot end of Paras. Offers accommodation on charpoys in grotty cells with an unappealing shared toilet.

Kaghan
E Lalazar Hotel, T0985-420222. 24 rooms.
There are also some very basic G-H places, but it makes more sense to push on to Naran.

Naran *p177*
Prices in Naran are extremely flexible, so it is worth bargaining hard (or offering to take your business elsewhere if you can't get a good deal). Most of the young Punjabi students sleep 5 or 6 to a room, paying no more than Rs20 each. Most hotels are vastly overpriced, but during peak periods it is wise to book accommodation at the upper end of the price scale in advance. The prices below

are for the high season. Most of the hotels offer hot water, but for those without their own generator this may only be for a certain period during the day (since there is frequently no electricity during the day). You may care to pick your hotel by number and type of guests: large groups and families of Punjabi visitors = noise! Most guests eat in their hotel, although the restaurants at the Errum and Lalazar attract outside guests.

L-D PTDC. In large grounds, 'economy' rooms reasonable value (D), plus selection of self-contained cottages (L-A) and standard rooms (B). Book through Islamabad (T051-9203223).

B-C Pine Park, 1.2 km up road to lake, T0985-430045. Modern rooms with shared verandah, restaurant, own generator, unattractive red pagoda-style roof, popular so book ahead.

B-C Royal. Huge new place under construction behind post office.

B-C Springfield Bungalow, 1.5 km up road to lake, T0985-430055. Rather nice self-contained 4-room cottage with kitchen and lounge, or 4-room main block with cosy verandah. Book in advance. Recommended.

B-C Troutland, 1 km up road to lake, T0985-430088, F0985-430090. Location is good but room quality doesn't justify the price, rooms on upper floor much brighter, hot water in mornings and evenings.

C-D Errum, T0985-430028/430128. Large, well-furnished rooms, attached bath (hot water mornings only), dish TV, upstairs rooms much brighter (but more expensive), 8 de luxe rooms, generator rather noisy, prices extremely flexible (can negotiate Rs1,000 rooms down to Rs500), popular restaurant, occasional evening entertainment (sometimes featuring a dancing dwarf), look out for 'Camp Charlie', friendly. Recommended.

E Balakot, T0985-430029. Somewhat overpriced for dark rooms, hot water in mornings only.

E Dreamland, T0985-430019. Very nice building (lots of wood) but rather run down and damp inside, doubles with clean tiled bathrooms (toilet seats missing on western WCs), big room upstairs for groups, use of kitchen, Pakistani and Chinese meals, rates highly negotiable.

E Lalazar, T0985-430001. 'VIP' wood-panelled rooms on upper floors, seats missing from toilets, enclosed verandah with views of unappealing town, also basic economy rooms (F) with attached bath, grubby hallways, unattractive building, takeaway pizza restaurant (Rs100-200). Booking place for Lalazar Huts up at Lake Saiful Malik (Rs2,000 per night for 2-bed cottage, own generator, bathroom, kitchen).

E Naran, T0985-430008. Quite nice, especially upstairs rooms with breezy shared verandah, need to bargain for the best deal.

E-F Himalaya Inn, T0985-430099/430199. Recently built, 9 carpeted rooms, basic bathroom (but everything is new), western WC, 24-hr hot water, dish TV, restaurant, covered parking, keen management, reasonable value if you get off-season rate.

F Green Park, T0985-430078. Formerly the Evergreen, 10 clean carpeted rooms, double beds, modern bathroom fittings, everything new, restaurant, very good value.

F Kunhar. Unexceptional, restaurant offers fish and chips.

F Mount View, T0985-430030. 10 standard rooms, bit grubby but seen worse.

F New Park, T0985-430023. Had a recent lick of paint, rooms large with attached bath, pay the extra Rs100 for the lighter and airier rooms upstairs (downstairs ones are windowless or have internal-facing windows), terrace upstairs, restaurant, friendly, not a bad deal.

F Park, T0985-430060. Set back off main road, breezy shared verandah, rooms have bare concrete floors or very old carpets, basic bathrooms, better value than this elsewhere.

G Frontier, T0985-430015. Not a bad deal for simple rooms with attached bath, some 4-bed rooms (E), restaurant.

G Summer Land, T0985-430142. New, small basic hotel.

G Taj Mahal. Newish place, 4 rooms with attached bath, common dining area, friendly, basic but good value.

There are numerous other hotels in the G-H categories, aimed primarily at groups of Punjabi tourists sleeping 4-6 to the room. Foreign tourists (and definitely women) may feel uncomfortable in these surroundings.

Such places include: **Babu, Bilal, Kashmir, Koh-i-Toor, Kohsar, Madina, Mehran, Pakistan, Paradise, Parwana, Punjab, Saiful Malik, Sarhad, Shalimar, Snowland** (was Qareecha), **Snow View, Sohrab, Zam Zam** and **Zero Point**. If you're really skint, there are tents for hire to the south of town.

Babusar Pass to Chilas *p180*
F NAPWD Inspection Bungalow, Babusar (bookable in Gilgit if coming from the north).
Also some basic charpoy hotels.

▲ Activities and tours

Lower Kaghan Valley *p175*
Balakot
PTDC office at the PTDC Motel in Balakot, can arrange jeep hire throughout the Kaghan Valley (and beyond) as well as 2- to 5-day trips around the valley (rates on application).

Naran *p177*
Kaghan Valley has some of Pakistan's best **trout fishing** and there are 6 authorized reaches in the Naran locality. Permits are available from the NWFP **Fisheries Dept Fisheries Office and Trout Hatchery** in Naran (Rs100 per day), just to the right of the path up to Lake Saiful Malik. Several shops offer rod hire (Rs100 per day) as well as 'fishing guide' services (Rs500 per day) and lessons.

○ Shopping

Naran *p177*
If heading further north up the Kaghan Valley, this is the last place to stock up with supplies. Naran has numerous shops selling handicrafts, but none are particularly recommended.

○ Transport

Lower Kaghan Valley *p175*
Balakot
You can arrange **jeep hire** from the yard at the north end of town, or through your hotel manager. 'Official' jeep hire rates are available through the PTDC tourist office, but effectively the 'market rates' have remained the same since 1999 (listed here): **Balakot-Naran** Rs1,200 1-way; **Balakot-Shogran** Rs800 1-way; **Balakot-Chilas** Rs6,000 1-way.

Minibuses depart when full from the yard at the north end of town to **Naran** (Rs75, 3-3½ hrs) northbound and **Mansehra** (Rs30, 1¼ hrs) southbound. Occasionally there will be transport south as far as **Abbottabad** or even **Rawalpindi**, but generally you have to change first at Mansehra.

Naran *p177*
Jeep hire to **Lake Saiful Malik** (Rs600 return), **Lalazar Plateau** (Rs700 return) and **Babusar Top** (Rs2,500 return) is available from the yard to the north of town. For those continuing to **Chilas** (Rs3,500 1-way, 9-10 hrs), you can arrange a jeep through PTDC or your hotel manager. These prices have been static since 1995, so expect some increases soon.

The yard at the south end of town (next to Naran Hotel) has **minibuses** that depart when full via **Balakot** (Rs75, 3-3½ hrs) to **Mansehra** (Rs100, 4½-5 hrs); it's rare to find vehicles heading further south. Morning departures fill up quicker. A daily wreck of a bus runs north from Naran via Battakundi to **Jalkhand**.

① Directory

Lower Kaghan Valley *p175*
Balakot
Post office South of the PTDC Motel. **Telephone** Pak Telecom is located south of the Koh-i-Toor Hotel, and there are several PCOs in town. **Useful addresses** Police opposite PTDC Motel.

Naran *p177*
Banks None. Change money in Abbottabad/Mansehra if heading up Kaghan Valley. **Post Office** Opposite Kunhar Hotel. **Telephone** Pak Telecom just south of post office (wooden pagoda roof), daily 0900-1300, 1400-2200.

Indus Kohistan → Colour map 1, grid A4

Literally meaning 'Land of Mountains', Kohistan is one of the most geologically fascinating places in Pakistan. As the KKH follows the course of the deep Indus gorge, the rock formations take you on a journey from the centre of the earth to its outer crust.

As the KKH clings to the increasingly vertical sides of the narrow Indus gorge, there can be little doubt that this is travel at its most breathtaking. For long stretches, the KKH is flanked on one side by a sheer, jagged wall of rock seemingly rising endlessly above you, while the opposite flank is a neat, precipitous drop into the boiling river several hundred metres below. It's a claustrophobic environment, and despite the sense of drama, travelling through Indus Kohistan always feels like hard work, whether you're pedalling or on the bus.

The oppressive physical setting also appears to extend to the human environment. If you're looking for the answer to the nature versus nurture question, then here's your argument for environmental determinism. The Kohistani people have a warlike history, and are not known for their hospitality to outsiders – if 'children-throwing-stones-at-cyclists' were ever to become an Olympic sport, this is where Pakistan would find its gold medal winning team. It's also not recommended that you attempt to visit any of the side valleys off the KKH in Indus Kohistan. ▸▸ *For Sleeping, Eating and all other listings, see pages 190-191.*

Background

The history of the region is equally fascinating. Although referred to as Kohistan, the region has also been known as Yaghistan, or 'Land of the Ungovernable'. British influence in the region was minimal, and even today, Pakistani control beyond the Karakoram Highway is questionable. It is for this reason that tourists are advised **not** to attempt to visit the numerous side valleys away from the main KKH route.

The pattern of settlement in Kohistan has been the occupation of the numerous small valleys, where glacial streams and rivers are more controllable, as opposed to habitation in the Indus Valley itself. The mountain ranges between these valleys proved a barrier to communication, allowing the evolution of numerous independent kingdoms – effectively mini republics. The system of government was by *jirga*, or tribal assembly, but many commentators have noted that the independence of althought of the Kohistanis made the area virtually ungovernable. With the exception of Chilas, the British never really established any control over the numerous side valleys.

The situation remains pretty much the same today. Although nominally part of Pakistan, the federal government wields very little influence away from the main road. The societies are very inward looking, fiercely traditional, and reluctant to expose themselves to outside influences. One such example is in the role of women. In some of the valleys female literacy levels are as close to zero as it is possible to get.

Kohistan is an ethnically mixed area, reflecting its history of isolated valleys, with periods of hostile incursions from rival kingdoms. Thus, the reason for Kohistani insularity and apparent hostility to outsiders is perfectly understandable – with only limited resources, you have to defend what's yours. The main ethnic group is descended from the **Shins**, but also linked with **Swathis** and **Yusufzai Pathans** from the Swat Valley. Pushto, Shina and a language collectively known as 'Kohistani' (various dialects including Maiyum, Chiliss, Gauro) are mainly spoken. The area is almost exclusively Sunni Muslim.

Ins and outs

Despite the dramatic scenery, most travellers along the KKH decide to opt for the direct bus between Rawalpindi/Islamabad and Gilgit, thus viewing Indus Kohistan through a bus window (and since most buses leave Rawalpindi in the late afternoon, you will pass through this section in darkness). Further, many cyclists also skip this section, preferring to save their time and energy for more welcoming areas further north. One option is to take the day bus (although you will always end up missing some part of the journey due to nightfall), or to break the trip with a few overnight stops. The problem with this is that despite the fantastic views, none of the stops en route are particularly appealing. Another alternative to the Kohistan section of the KKH is to travel via the Kaghan Valley between Mansehra and Chilas, although this is a challenging route (see section above). Note also that if the upgrading of the Kaghan Valley road goes ahead, travellers between Rawalpindi/Islamabad and Gilgit will be able to skip the Indus Kohistan section of the KKH entirely. ▸▸ *See Transport, page 191, for more details.*

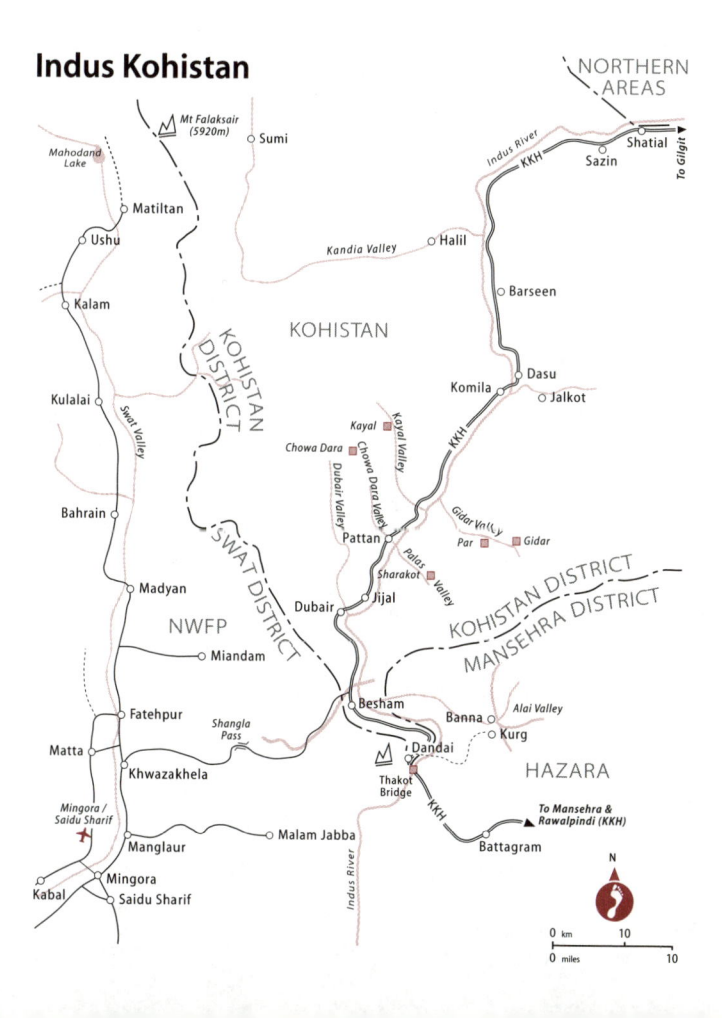

Indus Kohistan

Thakot Bridge and Alai Valley

Thakot Bridge (21 km from Battagram, see page 172) marks the boundary between Hazara and Indus Kohistan. Built by the Chinese, most of the decorative lions on the bridge's balustrade have been defaced or stolen. From the small roadside town of **Thakot** on the right bank of the Indus (and just before the Thakot Bridge), a reasonably good jeep road allows an excursion to the east, into the **Alai Valley**.

This is one of the few side valleys off this section of the KKH that it is feasible to visit, although you cannot penetrate very far and you may care to ask yourself if it is really necessary to come here. The Pathan residents of the valley certainly don't invite outsiders into their community, with a cordial greeting being about as much as any conservatively dressed visitor could expect.

Pick-up trucks from Thakot climb steeply up the mountain road, through terraced rice fields, offering fine views of long stretches of the Indus below. In summer it is particularly hot, and the pick-ups stop at every small stream to fill their radiators. The road passes through **Kanai** (19 km), where it begins to deteriorate, before dropping down to **Kurg** (29 km), where the ride terminates (Rs40, 1½ hrs). Below the bazaar is the main village, a cluster of square, flat-roofed houses near to the Alai River. A partially damaged bridge crosses the river to **Banna**, a newer settlement of mainly breeze-block and tin-roof buildings. You should not try to proceed beyond Banna without official permission.

Thakot Bridge to Pattan (63 km)

For the next 350 km or so, the KKH virtually follows the course of the Indus, with the river rarely being out of sight, and for many visitors it is here that the Karakoram Highway really begins. Having crossed the river at Thakot, the KKH passes through the village of Dandai (1 km) before continuing to **Besham** (27 km). Several kilometres south of Besham, close to the Kund Bridge and the PTDC Motel, is the spot commonly held to be the site of the Chinese pilgrim Fa-Hien's crossing of the Indus in AD 403.

The modern settlement of Besham is very much a product of the KKH, often used by academics as an example of the changing pattern of land use that is associated with road building in mountain

Besham is an important transport junction, with lots of hotels and travel options but no sights as such. See also pp 190-191.

Besham

Sleeping
Abassin 1
Abshar 2
Abu Dhabi Palace 3
Al-Hayat 4
Al-Safina 5
Continental Palace 6
Falak Sair 7
Insaf 8
International 9
Karachi 10
Mountain View Tourist Inn 18
New Hazara 11
North Inn 12
Palace Midway House 13
Paris 14
Prince 15
PTDC Motel 17
Taj Mahal 16

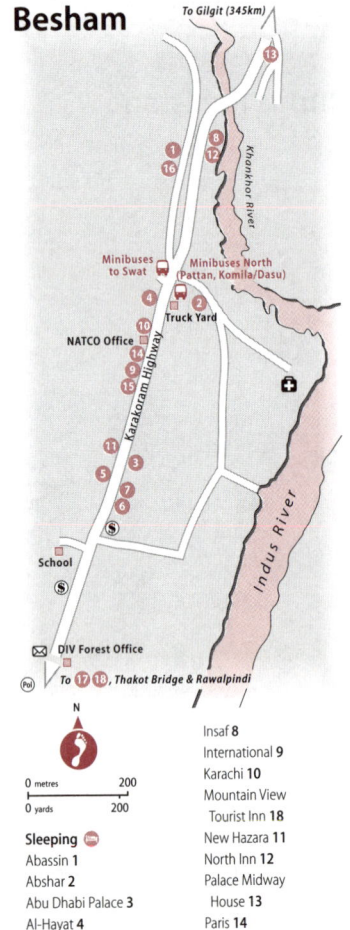

environments. Most visitors see it as a meal stop on the northbound journey between Rawalpindi/Islamabad and Gilgit, or as a place to change vehicles on a journey west across the Shangla Pass to/from Swat. It's little more than a line of hotels, shops, fly-blown restaurants and auto-repair yards, and those who choose to break their journey here (Rawalpindi/Islamabad seven hours by bus, Gilgit nine hours) may care to note that the town is noisy with traffic at all hours.

PTDC reception counter ⓘ *PTDC Motel, 2 km south of town on KKH, T0941-98*, can offer some information, or see the manager at the Palace Midway House Hotel.

The first real settlement north of Besham is **Chakai** (10 km), although this is little more than a petrol station, police post and a mosque. Some 5 km further north, the dazzlingly green Dubair River joins the Indus. The KKH crosses this tributary at **Dubair**, a busy cluster of small wooden shops and houses lining the road and sandwiched on terraces between the river and the highway. A trip up the Dubair Valley to the original settlement of Dubair (15 km) looks very enticing, but this is one of those Kohistani valleys that is definitely off limits to tourists. The Dubair Valley continues due north for some 64 km or so, with tracks leading off from the head of the valley into both Swat and Kandia Valley.

Travelling north of Dubair, the KKH continues 3 km to **Jijal**, where you should look out for the unusual coloured rocks. This stretch of the highway is geologically fascinating; the contact point between the Indian and Eurasian tectonic plates, the latter here exposing layers usually buried 30 m below the earth's surface (see box, page 188). The valley then opens out into a wide fertile bowl as the Chowa Dara River joins the Indus shortly before Pattan (17 km).

The main settlement of **Pattan** (literally 'city'), at the heart of a fertile bowl once described as "the largest and most flourishing place in Kohistan", is set below the KKH (a feeder road runs down to the village at the north end). There is a long record of human settlement here, with one artefact discovered in this area, a heavyweight girdle of gold, linking Pattan with the Scythians of the Trans-Pamir region. Weighing some 16 kg and decorated with images of men hunting various animals (and men in turn being hunted by tigers), this impressive piece can now be seen in the Peshawar Museum.

In 1974, a massive earthquake centred on Pattan buried entire villages under the rockfalls it triggered, resulting in some 5,000 dead and 15,000 injured. Today, there is little to detain visitors in Pattan (although many KKH cyclists overnight here). See pages 190-191 for sleeping and transport options in Pattan.

Palas Valley excursion

A suspension bridge 2 km south of Pattan crosses the Indus, providing access to the Palas Valley. This looks like an extremely tempting excursion off the KKH, but you should check with the Assistant Commissioner (AC) in Pattan as to whether it is safe to explore here (and he will almost certainly say no, unless you have an armed escort).

The valley stretches in a southeasterly direction, with easy access at its head to the Alai Valley. For the 40,000 or so Palasi inhabitants of the valley the forests represent the only resource, and the abundance of this resource attracted the envious gaze of the Pathans of the Alai Valley. Today, this threat comes from down-country timber merchants, although the valley now falls under the umbrella of the WWF-backed Himalayan Jungle Project.

Pattan to Komila/Dasu (38 km)

Beyond the Pattan bowl, the canyon narrows once more, forcing the KKH high on the valley side. Travelling north, the Indus canyon closes in somewhat, with the KKH perched on a narrow ledge some 300 m above the river. This is almost certainly the section of the Indus gorge that the fifth-century Chinese traveller Fa-Hien described in

Journey to the centre of the earth

Approximately 140 million years ago, a giant landmass floating on the fluid earth mantle broke away northwards from the Gondwanaland supercontinent that forms today's continents of Africa, Australia and Antarctica. About 70 million years later, this **Indian Plate** began a slow motion collision with the Laurasian landmass, or **Asian Plate**, which continues today.

At the margins of the collision the Indian Plate is subducting beneath the Asian Plate, with the resulting pressure being responsible for the mountain building process that created the Himalaya and Karakoram ranges. Trapped in the middle of the two plates is the small ocean plate that previously supported the **Sea of Tethys**, a shallow sea that used to lie between the Laurasian and Gondwanaland land masses.

In the course of the collision between the plates, a narrow chain of volcanic islands that stood in the Sea of Tethys – the **Kohistan Island Arc** – was compressed and contorted, with the result that the metamorphic rock formed at great depth below the oceanic plate has been pushed to the surface, and revealed around Jijal (just north of Besham). The younger sedimentary and volcanic materials can be seen at the northern margins of the Kohistan Island Arc, where it joins the Asian Plate near to Chalt (see page 264). Between the two, the intermediate rock stratas are revealed at the surface. As several signs along the KKH claim, 'Here Continents Collided'.

---

such detail (see quote on title page), and it's easy to draw parallels with the KKH, where men had to be lowered down from above by rope in order to place explosive charges that would blast a path out of the mountainside.

A further 9 km north of Pattan, the Kayal River joins the Indus, and the KKH temporarily detours several kilometres up the **Kayal Valley** until a bridging point on the river is reached. There is a small chai shop and police post here (NB excursions up this valley should not be attempted without a trustworthy local guide). After another 9 km, the KKH passes the police post at **Keru**, crosses the new bridge over a minor nala, then drops down nearer to the Indus (although there are still some impressive rock overhangs on the near side). On the east side of the KKH, the deep blue Jalkot Nala joins the Indus. The KKH then runs into Komila, 76 km from Besham, 38 km from Pattan.

The adjoining settlements of **Komila** and **Dasu** sprawl along either bank of the Indus, connected in the middle by the bridge over the river. Although this spot is something of a crossroads where the Jalkot and Kandia Valleys join the Indus, it's hard not to draw the conclusion that if there were no KKH, there would be no Komila or Dasu either. Dasu, on the east bank, is the administrative centre for the region with a Deputy Commissioner of Kohistan office, police post and other functionaries' offices. Komila, on the west bank, is little more than a small bazaar with a number of hotels, restaurants and transport connections north and south, see page 190. Other than cyclists who may overnight here, most travellers on the KKH will see Komila/Dasu as little more than a meal stop on the Rawalpindi/Islamabad-Gilgit bus journey (although many bus lines prefer to stop at Besham). A jeep road from Dasu leads east to Jalkot, and eventually to the Babusar Pass and Kaghan Valley, although you should not attempt to follow this ancient communications route.

● *The section of the KKH from Pattan to Komila/Dasu is said to have been the most difficult to construct, costing more lives per kilometre of road built than any other.*

Komila & Dasu

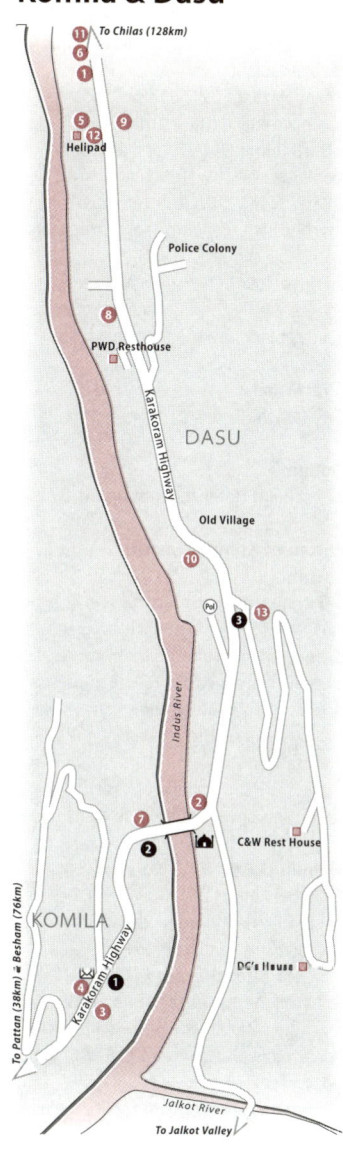

Komila/Dasu to Diamar District (47 km)

Having crossed the new bridge 1 km north of Dasu, the KKH climbs steadily to **Barseen** (10 km; the actually settlement is hidden from view). A further 1 km, the KKH crosses the new Barseen Bridge over the small nala joining the Indus from the east.

After a further 8 km, the Indus is joined from the west by the Kandia River. A joint Pak-Japanese-built suspension bridge over the Indus provides access to the extensive **Kandia Valley**, which runs due west before sharply bending to the north. A jeep track runs tantalizingly along the left bank, to Sumi at the head of the valley, from where a track then leads north around Mount Falaksair (5,920 m) into the upper Swat Valley (with another path leading into the Tangir Valley). The Kandia Valley has provided archaeologists with rich pickings from the Bronze Age, although it is best known as a well-worn Buddhist pilgrim route from the first century AD onwards, although it is strictly off limits to visitors today. The people of the Kandia Valley speak **Maiyan** (also known as Kohistani), although little is known about the 'Manzari' dialect of the language that is used here.

The Indus Valley now turns sharply to the east, with plenty of spectacular overhangs on the near side of the KKH, and is joined from the east by the **Sumar Nala**. Some enterprising individuals have set up a couple of basic meat/dhal and chapati restaurants here (a preferable location to Komila/Dasu or Shatial). Several kilometres further on, the canyon walls gradually step back (at **Sazin**) and the river widens and slows. Some 29 km from the Kandia Valley Bridge, a Chinese-built bridge provides access to the Tangir, Gayal and Darel Valleys. It is at this point that Kohistan gives way to **Diamar District**, as the North West Frontier Province meets the Northern Areas of Pakistan (for more information, see page 192).

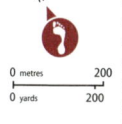

Sleeping
Afghan Afridi 1
Arafat 2
Azeem 3
Green Hills 4
Kargil 5
Khyber Lodge 6
Lalazar 7
Indus Waves 8
Manzoor 9
Moor 10
Mount View 11
PSO Motel 12
Trungpa Lodge 13

Eating
Indus Kohistan
Haz 1
Iqbal 2
Trungpa 3

Sleeping

Thakot Bridge to Pattan p186
Dandai
F Sapari Hotel. Conveniently located for the nearby gun shops.

Besham
B PTDC Motel, 2 km south of town on KKH, T0941-98. Nice quiet location, fairly comfortable rooms but very overpriced (C-D more realistic, perhaps negotiable), inconsistent restaurant, bookshop.
D Palace Midway House, T0941-597. Owned by influential local family (may be able to arrange trips to 'unvisitable' side valleys off KKH), 20 clean carpeted rooms, fan (rather hot), attached hot bath (western WC), rooms set off communal sitting area (so potentially noisy), large garden, restaurant (buffet lunch/dinner Rs230-260, breakfast Rs130), souvenir shop, popular with groups, friendly and well run.
E Mountain View Tourist Inn, KKH just south of police post, T0941-356. Quiet location, nice garden, reasonable value rooms, restaurant.
F Abshar, T0941-614. Rooms basic but clean enough, fairly modern attached hot bath, upper floors are nicer (take room at back with river view), restaurant.
F Abu Dhabi Palace, T0941-593. 10 rooms with attached tiled hot bath, fan, a little noisy, paint peeling from walls, but all in all, not bad value.
F Continental Palace, T0941-475. Huge, impressive new hotel, clean linen, modern attached small bathroom, restaurant, sitting areas, conference halls, parking, friendly staff, recommended. Most rooms are internally facing so little natural light or fresh air and rooms can be rather hot. Generally only Rs 50 more than all the other F-G hotels.
G Abasin, T0941-38. Marginally quieter location off KKH, basic rooms, fan, nice verandah, dirty water in taps, good restaurant.
G Al-Hayat, T0941-366. Fairly basic rooms, attached bath, restaurant.
G Al-Safina, T0941-64. Basic rooms around central courtyard, not very friendly.
G Falak Sair, T0941-530. Dark rooms facing onto an internal courtyard so best to choose an upstairs room.
G International, T0941-65. Not a bad cheap choice, basic but clean enough, friendly, also has a restaurant.
G New Hazara, T0941-312. Not bad when new but a little run down now.
G North Inn, T0941-679. Standard basic rooms, attached bath, restaurant.
G Paris, T0941-310. Clean, carpeted rooms, attached bath, friendly manager, restaurant, reasonable choice.
G Prince, T0941-56. Has always been popular with KKH cyclists (friendly manager), but recent massive expansion may raise prices here.
G Taj Mahal, T0941-82. Pretty basic.
G-H Karachi. Extremely basic.

Dubair
F Rest Point Hotel and Restaurant. Basic.

Pattan to Komila/Dasu p187
Pattan
E-G Kohistan Tourist Inn, T0941-542, on the KKH 1 km south of Pattan. It has 3 grades of clean rooms with attached bath, carpet, fan, a helpful manager and a restaurant, deserves to do well. There are a couple of miserable hotels on the KKH here, including the G Kohistan Inn.

There are also a couple of basic restaurants down in the village itself.

Komila/Dasu
E Khyber Lodge, Dasu, T0942-804. Despite being fairly new, paint is peeling from bedroom walls and bathrooms are bare concrete. Bargain hard to knock at least Rs200 off the quoted prices. Popular as a lunch stop for tour groups (buffet lunch Rs225, dinner Rs250, breakfast Rs100), good bookshop, breezy location.
F Trungpa Lodge, opposite police station, Dasu, T0942-889. Just above the KKH (so marginally quieter), fairly new although walls and linen are rather grubby, clean tiled bath, some squat toilets and some western (Rs100 more), should be cheaper (bargaining is recommended), restaurant.
G Afghan Afridi, Dasu, T0942-803. Cheap and basic rooms (some triples), smelly attached bath, friendly, good traditional Afghan restaurant.

G Arafat, Dasu. 4-storey block overlooking bridge, basic rooms with attached bath, linen none too clean, restaurant.
G Green Hills, Komila, T0942-632. Probably the best of the real cheapies, basic rooms with basic attached bath, fan, busy restaurant downstairs (can be a little noisy).
G Indus Waves, Dasu, T0942-968. Friendly but basic and run down, if you stay here take an upstairs room.
G PSO Motel, Dasu, T0942-626. 6 rooms at gas station, for petrol heads only.

Other extremely basic hotels (some of which won't take foreigners or are just intended as truck driver stops) include: G-H **Azeem, Kargil, Lalazar, Manzoor, Moor** and **Mount View**.

Komila/Dasu to Diamar District p189
D PTDC Motel, Barseen. Overpriced, but you should be able to negotiate a pretty big discount since few people stay here.

Eating

Many hotels and guesthouses provide food and evening meals, see Sleeping, or bring your own.

Transport

Thakot Bridge to Pattan p186
Besham
Suzukis run up and down the KKH, linking the main bazaar with the PTDC Motel (Rs5).

The **NATCO** office is little more than a desk inside the Swat Hotel (a restaurant). Very little English is spoken and tickets are not sold in advance (tell the manager where you want to go and he'll try and put you in an empty seat when the **bus** passes through).

Gilgit (Rs235, 9-11 hrs) buses pass through around 7-9 hrs after leaving Rawalpindi.

Rawalpindi (Rs185, 7-9 hrs) buses pass through some 9-11 hrs after departure from Gilgit. Other companies (**Silk Route, Mashabrum, Hameed, Sargin** etc) will pick up passengers from outside the Swat Hotel if they have seats.

It's sometimes easier to undertake your journey from Besham in a series of short 'hops' by **minibus**, rather than waiting for buses on the Rawalpindi/Islamabad-Gilgit route to pass through.

Minibuses southbound to **Mansehra** (Rs65, 4 hrs) sometimes depart from outside the Karachi Hotel. Northbound, minibuses depart when full from the north end of the bazaar (see map), although most only go as far as **Komila/Dasu** (Rs50, 2 hrs) via Pattan (Rs25, ½ hr). If there's sufficient demand, a 'special' minibus may run as far as **Chilas** (Rs150, 5 hrs) or even Gilgit (Rs250, 8½-9 hrs). Minibuses also depart when full from here across the Shangla Pass to **Khwazakhela** and Mingora in the **Swat Valley** (Rs65, 4 hrs).

Pattan
Minibuses heading south to **Besham** (Rs25, 30 mins) and north to **Komila/Dasu** (Rs25, 1½ hrs) will stop to pick up passengers outside the various chai shops on the KKH.

Komila/Dasu to Diamar District p189
Komila/Dasu
Minibuses run on a depart-when-full basis from outside the Indus Kohistan Haz Hotel (a restaurant). Northbound, few go beyond **Shatial** (Rs40, 1½ hrs), but you occasionally find a vehicle going as far as **Chilas** (Rs100, 3 hrs). Southbound, you usually have to change at **Besham** (Rs50, 2 hrs). You should also hang around the Indus Kohistan Haz Hotel (or the Green Hills Hotel opposite) in order to flag down passing buses on the Rawalpindi/Islamabad-Gilgit route (although they may be full).

Buses towards **Gilgit** pass through around 9-11 hrs after leaving Rawalpindi, while those heading south to **Rawalpindi** have left Gilgit some 6-7 hrs previously.

Directory

Besham p186
Hospitals District Hospital is off the KKH at the north end of the bazaar. **Post office** South of the main bazaar.
Telephone Until the digital exchange comes online, international calls have to be 'booked' via Islamabad; there are several PCOs in the bazaar that can do this.

Diamar District → *Colour map 2, grid C5*

Diamar District (Dyamar), one of the administrative regions of the Northern Areas, covers a vast area of sparsely populated mountainous land on either side of the Indus River. All of the side valleys off this stretch of the KKH have their own histories, although in the context of this administrative division, the history of the regional capital at Chilas is particularly important, as detailed below. The main highlight of Diamar District is the mighty peak of Nanga Parbat, with its unlimited trekking and hiking potential on all sides. ▸▸ *For Sleeping, Eating and all other listings, see pages 205-208.*

Ins and outs

Anyone taking the late afternoon overnight bus from Rawalpindi/Islamabad to Gilgit will find that, delays permitting, you should be leaving NWFP and entering the Northern Areas at around day break. This is somehow appropriate. Although the scenery along the Indus canyon in Kohistan is breathtaking, in many respects it is here, in the Northern Areas, that the fun really starts. Visitors should remember, however, that until you reach Gilgit (next chapter), the majority of the side valleys off the KKH should not be visited without first taking official advice (and even then only when accompanied by a reliable local guide). Even around Nanga Parbat, which receives many visitors, caution must be exercised (with the exception, perhaps, of the route up to Fairy Meadows which may be considered safe); a reliable local guide should be employed when visiting all the other faces of this mountain. ▸▸ *See Transport, page 207, for more details.*

Diamar District & Gilgit Sub-District

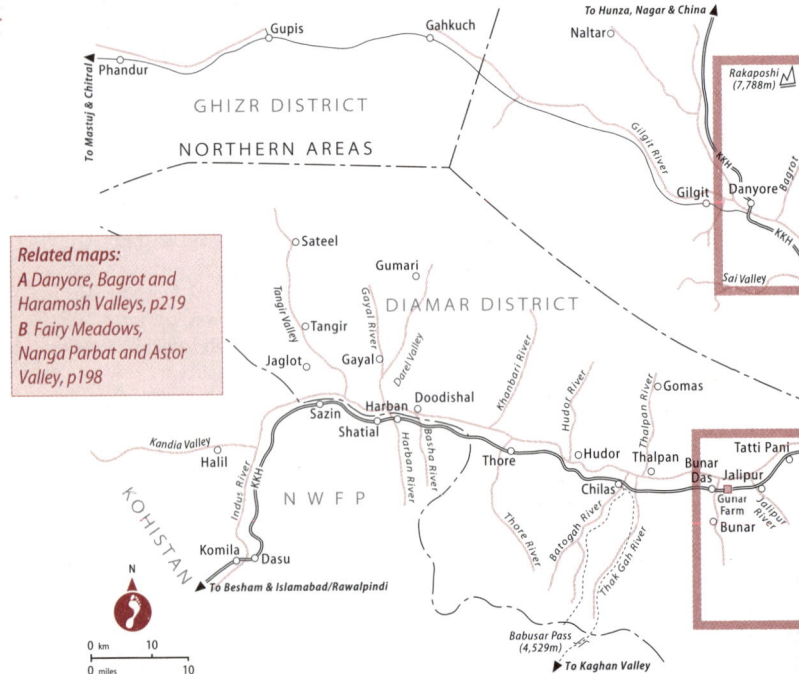

Related maps:
A Danyore, Bagrot and Haramosh Valleys, p219
B Fairy Meadows, Nanga Parbat and Astor Valley, p198

The KKH through Diamar District

Tangir and Darel Valleys

The point where the suspension bridge leads off the KKH to the **Tangir**, **Gayal** and **Darel Valleys** marks the beginning of Diamar District (47 km north of Komila/Dasu). In theory, this would be a particularly appealing excursion off the KKH: all three valleys are rich in archaeological remains from the Bronze Age, the Gandharan period, as well as the early Islamic period. Unfortunately, these once popular Buddhist pilgrim routes between China and South Asia (as used by Fa-Hien) now pass through the area christened by the British **Yagistan**; a term that can be translated as 'Unknown Track', but more often as 'Land of the Ungovernable'. Although both valleys were incorporated into the State in 1956, Pakistani central government control remains negligible.

Both valleys are extremely fertile, with their heads in particular being thicky forested, so it would seem logical for the valley inhabitants to fiercely protect their resources from predatory neighbours. Today, the forest tracts are under threat from over-logging, the evidence of which can be seen in the huge timber dumps along the KKH at the entrance to the valleys. As yet, there have been no attempts to introduce tourism to these valleys, although one guide, Mirza Baig (contact at **Madina Hotel** in Gilgit), is looking into the possibility of bringing small groups to the Darel Valley.

Shatial to Chilas (63 km)

The first settlement on the KKH in Diamar District, and thus the first settlement in the Northern Areas, is the miserable collection of shacks known as **Shatial** (about 8 km from the Tangir/Darel bridge). Shatial is famous for its extraordinary collection of **rock art**, emphasizing its former importance as a junction for a number of routes (the engravings having been made primarily by missionaries and traders). The first ones recorded here, in the Kharoshthi script, date to the first century AD, and there are also several hundred in the Sogdian language, some in Chinese, as well as many in Brahmi (dating from the fifth century AD onwards). These petroglyphs can be a little hard to find, although they are certainly worth the effort. The primary examples are to be found on a series of boulders to the left (west) of the KKH between the Tangir/Darel bridge and Shatial itself. See Chilas for a list of publications and websites that will enhance your appreciation of these rock carvings (see box, page 197). See pages 205-207 for sleeping and transport options at Shatial.

The KKH continues to follow the course of the Indus between Shatial and Chilas. Having made a huge easterly bend at Shatial, the river here is wide and gentle (in contrast to its journey through Kohistan) and frequently flanked by sandy beaches. The road crosses the Harban Nala and passes the Harban Dass police post (7 km from Shatial), and then crosses the Basha Nala (7 km). The settlement on the opposite side of the valley is Doodishal. A further 6 km along the KKH the Indus is joined from the north by the Khanbari Valley, through which flows a river renowned for its trout. The KKH begins to climb steadily through some very barren landscapes, and as you drive/ride into **Thore** (34 km from Shatial), with its petrol station and abandoned looking settlements, the impression is of arriving in a Mexican desert town (one expects tumble-weed to be blowing down the middle of the street). The only real splash of colour between Thore and Chilas is the vivid green cultivation around Hudor (17 km from Thore), across the Indus on a 650-m rope suspension bridge.

Hudor has the remains of a 10th-century fort, built in the style of the Hindu Shahis of NWFP (although it has been burnt at some stage in its history and is in an extremely poor state of repair). The name Hudor probably derives from *durga*, meaning 'fort' in a local dialect. Below the fort, towards the Indus, are numerous rock carvings that can be broadly defined into two groups. The older ones have been tentatively dated to the second/first millenium BC, and mainly feature hunting scenes of ibexes, markhors and human figures. The style of the second group suggests that Hudor was a stronghold of the Brahmin followers during the eighth century AD, with the carvings here of religious symbols, such as Saivite deities and temples, in addition to hunting and battle scenes.

For those with their own transport there are interesting petroglyphs close to the distance markers 10 km before Chilas (right side), 9 km before Chilas (left side, ie river-side), 8 km before Chilas (left side), 7 km before Chilas at the mouth of the Gichi

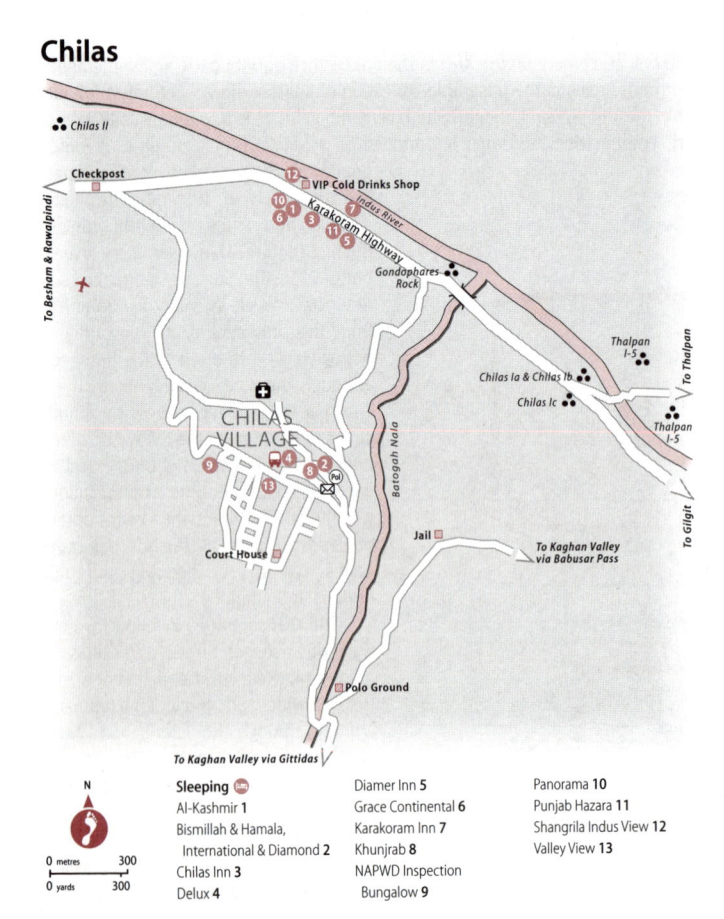

Chilas

Sleeping
Al-Kashmir **1**
Bismillah & Hamala,
 International & Diamond **2**
Chilas Inn **3**
Delux **4**
Diamer Inn **5**
Grace Continental **6**
Karakoram Inn **7**
Khunjrab **8**
NAPWD Inspection
 Bungalow **9**
Panorama **10**
Punjab Hazara **11**
Shangrila Indus View **12**
Valley View **13**

nala (left side, includes archaeological remains from the first century BC and seventh century AD, plus lots of quartz), 5 km from Chilas (left side, including a superb giant demon-god), 4 km before Chilas (both sides), and finally 1 km before the police check post (left side). The famous 'Chilas I' site is riverside (ie north) of the police check post at Chilas. Foreigners must enter their passport details at the check post.

Chilas

For KKH travellers, Chilas is usually seen as a transport junction, a possible overnight halting place, or perhaps just as a chai stop on the Rawalpindi-Gilgit bus journey. However, this district headquarters town has a long and incident-packed history, and in the collection of rock art in the vicinity perhaps the greatest archaeological testament along the entire length of the KKH.

Ins and outs

The actual town of Chilas is located some 3 km above the KKH, accessible by a link road that runs up from opposite the police check post. Many visitors never even see the town itself because most of the accommodation is down on the KKH. Chilas has something of a reputation for not welcoming outsiders (see warning on crossing the Babusar Pass on page 180), although this hostility does not apply to the hoteliers down on the KKH. It's not unusual, however, to see groups of fierce-looking Chilasi men sitting around playing Ludo!

Suzuki wagons link the KKH with the town (Rs5, a steep walk if carrying luggage). There is a minibus yard in the centre of Chilas town, with services departing when full as far as Gilgit northbound and usually Besham southbound (although some only go as far south as Komila/Dasu). Alternatively, you can flag down both north and southbound buses on the KKH. There are also cargo jeeps that run from Chilas over the Babusar Pass into the Kaghan Valley. With Gilgit airport being unsuitable for the landing of jets, there is currently speculation that the airstrip at Chilas will eventually be upgraded to become the key airport in the Northern Areas.

A recently finished jeep road provides an alternative route into the Kaghan Valley from Chilas, avoiding the Babusar Pass. This route follows the Batogah Nala to the west of the Babusar Pass, emerging into the Kaghan Valley at Gittidas. Thus, cyclists and hikers travelling south from Chilas to the Kaghan Valley should ensure that they take the correct route. As you leave Chilas, you first cross the Batogah Nala. The trail leading off from here is this new jeep road to Gittidas (not the friendliest of places). If you wish to travel via the Babusar Pass, ensure that you keep going until you meet the jeep road that runs south from the next stream, the Thak Gah Nala. Make sure that you read the warning, see box, page 180.

> ❗ It is worth stopping at Chilas just to see the petroglyphs; if you are already overnighting here, then don't miss them.

▶▶ *See Transport, page 207, for more details.*

History

As the district headquarters of Diamar (which includes the tehsils of Tangir, Darel and Astor), Chilas owes it importance to its strategic location as the gateway to the Babusar Pass (and hence the Kaghan Valley, Kishenganga Valley in Kashmir, and Hazara).

Chilas drew the attention of the British during the era of the 'Great Game', when the British were attempting to consolidate their position on the northwest frontier of the British Empire. Colonel Algernon Durand, the British Agent at Gilgit, saw the unpredictable Chilasis as a threat to the recently opened British supply line across the Babusar Pass to the Punjab. In 1892 a situation was engineered that allowed the British to march on Thalpan, opposite Chilas, and after naturally rising to the provocation, the Chilasis were subsequently defeated in battle and their town occupied.

During the Indus Valley Rising of 1893, the fort at Chilas was attacked and one-third of the garrison was killed or wounded in what was probably the British Army's most disastrous battle fought in Dardistan. For some reason, possibly the lack of food supplies, the Chilasis did not press their advantage and the garrison was relieved. Durand eventually recognized his tactical error in attempting to occupy the Indus Valley death trap; something the Dogra troops of the Maharaja of Kashmir were to experience 54 years later at Partition.

Sights

The sole attraction of Chilas is its fabulous collection of **rock art**, which also forms the main source of information on the early history of the region. These petroglyphs are in fact spread over a very wide area, on both sides of the Indus, and unfortunately there are currently no explanation boards and precious few signs indicating where the best examples are located. However, visitors who show some persistence tracking down these works of art will not be disappointed. The best sites are **Thalpan I-V**, on the opposite bank of the Indus, across the bridge to Thalpan; **Chilas I** that straddles the KKH next to the Thalpan Bridge; **Gondophares Rock**, the hillock at the mouth of the Batogah Nala; and **Chilas II-X** to the north of the check post on the KKH.

Chilas II ⓘ *This site is reached by following the path (it is signposted) north from the police checkpost towards the Indus*. The carvings here fall into two broad categories. Firstly there are those of a Buddhist nature, dating to the first century BC and with inscriptions in Kharoshthi script. They featue representations of Bodhisattva (Buddha-to-be), stupas, votive stupas, pilgrims and monks, with many of the characters actually named in the inscriptions. The second group of carvings at Chilas II feature Brahmi inscriptions, and are thus later in date. They tend to feature hunting scenes, circles, plus temples and other structures.

Gondophares Rock ⓘ *Where the Batogah Nala drains beneath the KKH, to the left (north) side of the KKH*. This large rock has two distinct parts known collectively as Gondophares Rock. The Kharoshthi inscription on the eastern section refers to 'Beloved of Vitaspa, King Gondophares', hence the name. This boulder also features several other themes (hunting, religious, names and dates) covering a variety of periods from the first century AD to at least the 15th century AD.

Chilas I ⓘ *On either side of the KKH, at the point where the link road runs down to the bridge across the Indus to Thalpan ('Chilas Ia' and 'Chilas Ib' are on the river side, 'Chilas Ic' is on the opposite side of the KKH)*. The carvings at 'Chilas Ia' date from a number of periods, notably from the seventh century AD (although many have ninth-century inscriptions). Most are devotional in nature (Buddhist), although there are some historical descriptions. One particularly important panel illustrates the Jataka story of the 'body sacrifice' of the Bodhisattva Mahasattva. The path down towards the bridge to Thalpan passes through **Chilas Ib**, which features a seated Buddha on a raised pedestal in dhyani pose (although the head is missing), as well as a seated figure of the Bodhisattva Manju Sri in the pose of fearlessness. **Chilas Ic** ⓘ *to the south of the KKH here*, features many illustrations in a seventh century AD Kashmiri style.

Thalpan I-V ⓘ *On the opposite side of the Indus, across the Thalpan Bridge*. As you cross the bridge, line up the two suspension cables on the other side. Head up the scree slope in a direct line between the cables until just before the base of the cliff – one major group is on the collection of rocks to the left (west). Some of the most impressive carvings are found here; although scattered over a wide area, there are two main concentrations. A second major group is reached by following the winding path from the bridge towards Thalpan village, on the first set of huge boulders on your

> **Rock carvings in Northern Pakistan**
>
> There are several publications which will greatly enhance your appreciation of the carvings here. The best is Karl Jettmar's *Rock Carvings and Inscriptions in the Northern Areas of Pakistan* (1982), although this can be hard to find (try via the University of Heidelberg at www.rzuser.uni-heidelberg.de, in German). Also very good is Prof. A.H. Dani's *Human Records on Karakoram Highway* (1995) or *Chilas: City of Nanga Parbat*, both of which can be found in Gilgit and Islamabad bookshops, and Volker Thewalt's *Rockcarvings and Inscriptions along the Indus: The Buddhist Tradition* (South Asian Archaeology, 1983, see the excellent www.thewalt.de/verlag.htm, also in German).

right. This latter group contains two highly significant carvings. One is a representation of the 'First Sermon of the Buddha' in the deer-park at Benares. Below the Buddha the dharmacakra is shown on a column and two deers on both sides of the wheel indicate the site where the First Sermon took place. A second shows the legend of the Buddha's temptation by the daughters of Mara but has been badly damaged by the elements. You will come across many more exciting images just by wandering around here.

Chilas to Raikot Bridge (49 km)

Beyond the police check post at Chilas, the KKH crosses the **Batogah Nala** (3 km), passes the turning for the bridge to Thalpan (1 km), and then crosses the **Thak Gah Nala** (4 km, the turning for the Babusar Pass into the Kaghan Valley). The petroglyphs that have flanked the KKH for the past 70 km or so now disappear, suggesting that the modern road does not follow the ancient route here. At **Gini** (5 km) there is a popular chai stop at a point where a cool sweet water spring runs down to the KKH (although the water is not suitable for delicate western stomachs). A jeep road runs up to the large village of Upper Gini (1½ hrs by jeep), which is situated close to a large lake. The KKH crosses the Bunar Nala, before arriving at the small settlement of **Bunar Das** (15 km).

The main settlement of **Bunar** is actually on a ridge to the south of the KKH, and often forms the finishing point of the 'Nanga Parbat circuit via Mazeno La' trek (see page 204). Those wishing to undertake this trek may like to consult Bunar's village lumdadar, Ahmed Mir (his son, Abdul Wakeel, is a registered mountain guide with **Travel Walji's**). He may also be able to arrange accommodation for those who get stuck in Bunar (his house is reached on the road signposted 'hydel station' behind the PSO).

Beyond Bunar Das there are a number of hot springs close to the road, the first being concealed among the clumps of vegetation on the right (south) side of the KKH. They are not really suitable for bathing (and certainly not for women). A further 2 km beyond Bunar Das is **Gunar Farm** (various spellings), an experimental farm development set up by the British. The settlement on the KKH now comprises a police fort, petrol station and a NAPWD Inspection Bungalow. There are also a couple of very basic charpoy places here which are used to accommodating cyclists. A further 8 km is the tiny settlement of **Jalipur**, which was used earlier this century as a British staging post. It also has a NAPWD Inspection Bungalow.

Some 6 km further along the KKH is a troublesome area around **Tatta Pani** that is plagued by landslides that often block the road, and 5 km beyond here the KKH crosses to the west bank of the Indus over the Raikot Bridge.

Raikot Bridge is the jumping-off point for **Fairy Meadows** (see below). It is also the point where the truck route heads up to the Astor Valley (it may be possible to hitch a ride from here, although most public transport runs via Jaglot/Bunji, further along the

KKH). Foreigners must enter passport details at the check post by the bridge. From the bridge, Gilgit is 78 km north, Rawalpindi 520 km south. For those not visiting Fairy Meadows, the KKH description continues on page 208.

Fairy Meadows and Nanga Parbat

There can't be many other places on earth where you can get so close to such a big mountain with such little effort. Fairy Meadows is a high-altitude alpine pasture situated among cool pine forest, with the massive north face of the world's ninth highest mountain as its backdrop – and if you take a jeep to the end of the line, you only have to walk for around two hours to reach this spot. This is quite rightfully becoming one of Pakistan's most visited attractions, and it is still easy to find some mountain tranquillity away from the crowds.

Getting there

Most visitors to Fairy Meadows actually arrive from **Gilgit** (including those travelling south-north along the KKH), since this is the best place to stock up on supplies, leave excess luggage, or to meet up with like-minded trekkers or those wanting to share transport costs. NATCO buses from Gilgit will drop passengers at Raikot Bridge (Rs55, three to three and a half hours, the best bet is the early morning Rawalpindi-bound service). Alternatively, take a Chilas-bound minibus to Raikot Bridge from Gilgit (Rs55, three to three and a half hours). Having returned to Raikot Bridge from Fairy Meadows, flag down passing transport to continue your journey (but you could have a long wait).

From Raikot Bridge (1,194 m), a jeep road leads 15 km to **Tato** (2,300 m), from where it is a further two to two and a half hours' walk up to Fairy Meadows (3,306 m). There are several options for getting there. Because the jeep road is maintained by the villagers of Tato, the unofficial 'jeep drivers' union' (or 'mafia') exercise sole

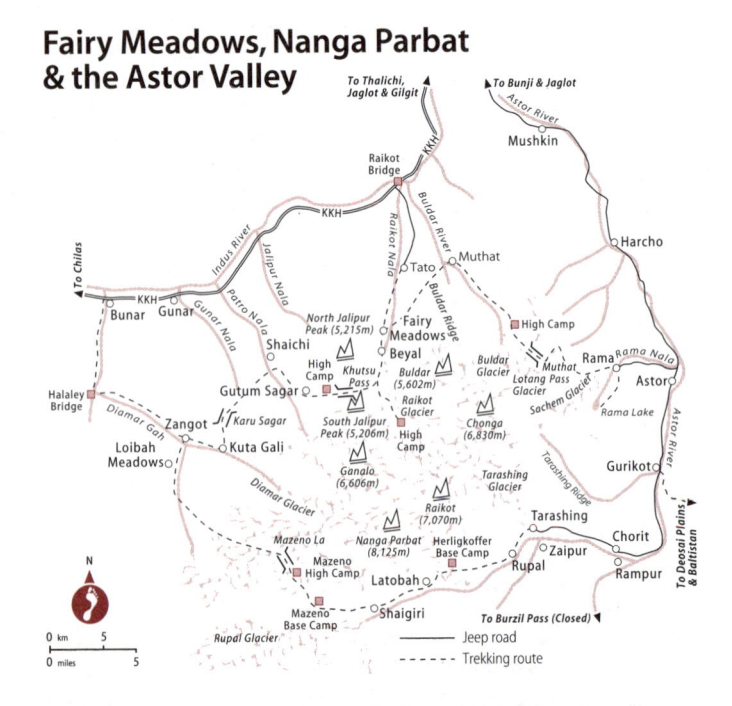

Fairy Meadows, Nanga Parbat & the Astor Valley

vehicle rights here. Thus, they have fixed the price for the jeep ride from Raikot Bridge to Tato at an extortionate Rs1,200 one way, or Rs2,000 return per vehicle (one and a half hours). They won't negotiate on this price, and seem to even resent groups of travellers banding together to share a vehicle. Individual travellers arriving at the jeep yard next to the **Shangrila Hotel** should pretend to be part of a pre-organized group if they wish to share transport costs. If taking the return trip, you need to make a note of the jeep registration and inform the driver of the date and time that you wish to be collected from Tato. If you change your plans, you'll need to send word down to that particular driver. Don't pay until you have completed your return journey. Tato jeep drivers (and people of Tato in general) have a poor reputation. Note that the government is currently building a new jeep road that will link with the existing track at a point on the way to Tato; this may eventually break the Tato mafia's stranglehold on transport. The jeep road is extremely bumpy.

An alternative to hiring a jeep to Tato is to **walk** (four to five hours). After the initial very steep climb, it's a fairly steady ascent. However, the route is very dry and very hot, and not a particularly pleasant experience (despite the views). Furthermore, if coming from Gilgit, even if you take the early morning bus, it will be warming up considerably by the time you reach Raikot Bridge. Note that Raikot Bridge to Tato is one porter stage, and a further stage from Tato to Fairy Meadows; you will be expected to pay for both stages even if your porters ride in a jeep. It is also possible to cycle all the way up to Fairy Meadows on a lightly loaded mountain bike.

The jeep track finishes at Tato (although there are vaguely talked of plans to extend it to Fairy Meadows, as it used to). There is a chai shop/restaurant at Tato (2,300 m). Having crossed the nala here, it is a steady climb (often through forest) on a good pony track to **Fairy Meadows** (3,306 m, two to three hours). You can hire a horse for this trip (Rs500), or a donkey to carry your luggage (Rs200-300, very expensive considering that this is one porter stage). NB Note the altitude gain between Raikot Bridge and Fairy Meadows (over 2,000 m).

Getting around

Those just wandering around the forests at Fairy Meadows, or continuing on to Beyal, will not require a guide. For longer trips, however, guides, porters and cooks can be arranged through the **Raikot Serai** manager (the 'middle' of the three brothers who run this place was a guide on the successful 1995 Japanese ascent of Nanga Parbat, and the expedition's cook, Shukur, also hangs around here). Sleeping and eating options are listed on page 206.

Nanga Parbat

The local name for this 8,125-m giant is Diamar (correctly Diva-Meru), meaning 'Heavenly Mount', although the mountain is almost exclusively referred to as Nanga Parbat. Kashmiri for 'naked mountain', this name is a reference to the massive 4,500-m wall of the southeast face that is too sheer for snow to stick. However, such is the reputation of the peak that it has also been nicknamed 'killer mountain'.

The mountaineering history of Nanga Parbat begins in 1895 when a British expedition attempted the peak. The leader of the expedition, the famed climber **Mummery**, along with two Gurkha porters, reached almost 7,000 m before disappearing without trace. Locals blamed the fairies, spirits and giant snow snakes that are said to inhabit the mountain, although another explanation may be one of Nanga Parbat's unpredictable avalanches.

In the 1930s no fewer than five separate expeditions attempted this *achttausender*. The **1934 Austro-German expedition** is believed to have got within several hundred metres of the summit before bad weather forced them back. Four

The future of Fairy Meadows

Christened 'Fairy Meadows' by an Austro-German expedition that attempted Nanga Parbat in the 1930s, this glorious spot has enchanted visitors for many years now. There are few high mountains that are as accessible as Nanga Parbat; the Annapurna Base Camp in Nepal is a nine- to 12-day round trip, while Everest Base Camp takes around three weeks. By contrast, you can travel by vehicle to within 2-3 hours of Nanga Parbat.

Yet despite its accessibility, and the increasing numbers of people visiting, this is still a remarkably unspoilt area. But for how long? Ever since the owner of the Shangri-La chain of hotels bought a large tract of land at Fairy Meadows in 1985, there has been talk of construction of a large, luxury hotel (indeed, they also paid to have the current jeep track constructed). Local people are now expressing opposition to this sale, attempting to return the money originally paid for the land and taking the matter before the *jirga*. The present director of the Shangri-La chain is equally adamant that the proposed venture will take place, and is confident of a verdict in his favour in the civil courts.

So, would such a development spell the end for Fairy Meadows as a quiet, picturesque mountain spot? In effect, such a process is already underway. In less than a decade, tourist infrastructure has developed from a few seasonal tents (1995) to three camps at Fairy Meadows that have both tents and wooden cabins, and another three further along the track at Beyal (2004). Indeed, some of those campaigning the hardest against the Shangri-La project are currently building cabins of their own at Fairy Meadows and Beyal. To some eyes, the main objections to the Shangri-La chain come from fear of competition, but are couched in environmental protectionist terms. Of course, the unspoken local fear is really the arrival of large numbers of domestic tourists (pejoratively referred to as 'Punjabis'), and the transformation of Fairy Meadows to something like Naran, Murree, or parts of the Swat Valley.

On a positive note, the realization at such an early stage that Fairy Meadows is under threat, and the emergence of a determined environmental lobby, may ensure that the optimum number of people can enjoy this unique place but cause the least amount of damage in doing so.

Germans and six Sherpas died in the descent. Just three years later another German party was within striking range of the summit before being wiped out by an avalanche. A later expedition found most of the men lying dead in their tents, as if asleep, their watches all stopped at 1220.

In 1950, a small British expedition attempted the mountain. A member of the party was **Tenzing Norgay**, later to find fame with Sir Edmund Hillary on the first successful ascent of Everest. However, this expedition were poorly prepared and despite a rescue attempt by Tenzing and one of the British officers, the other two members of the expedition died high up on the mountain. It was not until 1953, less than five weeks after Tenzing and Hillary had 'conquered' Everest, that Nanga Parbat was finally defeated. **Hermann Buhl,** a noted Austrian climber, eventually stood where no other person had ever been. The most recent successful ascent was by the 1995 Japanese expedition.

The current death toll on Nanga Parbat is over 50. Not only is the mountain's sheer size a huge challenge – its north face slopes down an incredible 7,000 m to the

Indus – its position as an exposed sentinel at the western end of the Himalayas has led to the formation of its own highly unpredictable microclimate. Weather conditions change rapidly, and avalanches are common and violent. Yet from both the KKH and Fairy Meadows, particularly at sunset, the ethereal beauty of the mountain is sublime.

The sole disappointment for visitors to Fairy Meadows is that the actual 8,125-m summit cannot be seen from here (and no locals, or other guidebooks, point this fact out). The highest points that you can actually see are the **N1** (7,816 m) and **N2** (7,745 m) peaks. To their left lie the twin peaks of **Silverzacken East** (7,597 m) and **Silverzacken West** (7,530 m). The huge snowfield that lies between N1/N2 and Silverzacken is the northern tip of the 3.6-km-long snowfield that leads to the summit of Nanga Parbat. The peak further left along the ridge from Silverzacken is **Raikot Peak** (7,070 m), while that furthest to the left is **Chonga** (6,830 m). The peak farthest to the right is **Ganalo** (6,606 m). The view of Nanga Parbat is still awesome, even if the summit cannot be seen (although it can from the KKH).

Treks and walks from Fairy Meadows

Beyal

The most popular walk from Fairy Meadows is the simple stroll south to **Beyal** (three to four hours). The trail follows the cliff top above the S-shaped Raikot Glacier for much of the way, before entering the cool, fragrant forest. It eventually emerges at the summer settlement of Beyal; there are several accommodation options here (see page 206) that are generally quieter and cheaper than those at Fairy Meadows. It is also possible to continue on to the **Nanga Parbat (North) Base Camp** and **Drexel Monument** (further four hours), although this is usually attempted by people staying the night there or at Beyal, rather than returning to Fairy Meadows the same day. See below for details. There is a good **viewpoint** an hour beyond Beyal that offers impressive views of the Nanga Parbat massif.

Beyal to Nanga Parbat (North) Base Camp and 'Camp 1'

ⓘ *Open zone. Maximum elevation optional (3,967-4,397 m). Jun to Sep. Maps: the 1:50,000 Deutsche Himalaya Expedition of Nanga Parbat (DAV) is excellent; U502 series, NI 43-2 Gilgit also good. Read trekking notes, p 45.*

The most popular short trek, this can be completed in two to three days. The first day is a fairly easy four-hour walk south from Beyal to a (hopefully) flower-strewn meadow. Beyond here is the **(North) Base Camp** (3,967 m) and the **Drexel Monument** to the members of the German-Austrian expedition who were killed on Nanga Parbat in 1934. There is a fresh water spring at the base camp. It is possible to push on for a further two hours to **'Camp 1'** (4,397 m, sometimes referred to as 'High Camp' and effectively the base camp for the successful 1995 Japanese ascent), although since this involves a gain in altitude of over 400 m, this trip is usually made as a day trip from Base Camp. The views of the Raikot face are particularly enthralling. It is feasible to walk down from 'Camp 1' to Beyal in one day.

Beyal to South Jalipur Peak

ⓘ *Open zone. Maximum elevation optional (4,837-5,206 m). Jun to Sep. Maps: the 1:50,000 Deutsche Himalaya Expedition of Nanga Parbat (DAV) is excellent; U502 series, NI 43-2 Gilgit also good. Read trekking notes, p 45.*

Although a short trek (two to three days), this is not for the inexperienced. From Beyal, follow the Raikot Glacier south, then follow the trail west and ascend the **Khutsu (Jalipur) Pass** (4,837 m). Most local guides select an overnight camping spot on the west side of the pass. You should not attempt the ascent of **South Jalipur Peak** (5,206 m) unless you have previous relevant experience.

Beyal to KKH at Gunar Farm

ⓘ *Open zone. Maximum elevation optional (4,062 m). Jun to Sep. Maps: U502 series, NI 43-2 Gilgit is reasonable. Read trekking notes, p 45.*

This trek provides an alternative route back to the KKH from Fairy Meadows/Beyal. There are several options for completing this trek – the route you take will depend largely upon your guide. Note that there is no regular public transport available for you at **Gunar Farm**.

NB For details of the **Rupal Valley** trek and the **Nanga Parbat Circuit via Mazeno La** trek, both of which are on the south side of Nanga Parbat, see below under the **Astor Valley** section, page 202.

Raikot Bridge to Jaglot (30 km)

Back on the KKH, just to the north of Raikot Bridge, the Indus is joined by a minor tributary from the east, the **Liachar Nala**. In 1841, a massive land-slide (probably triggered by an earthquake) completely dammed the river, creating a giant lake that stretched almost 50 km back to Gilgit. The dam, several hundred metres thick, is said to have raised the water up to 300 m above its normal level. When breached in early June 1841, having held for several months, the resulting flood is said to have washed away an entire Sikh regiment camped downstream at Chach.

If the weather is clear, this stretch of road has some of the best views on the entire length of the KKH. Directly to the north is the magnificent **Rakaposhi** massif (7,788 m), flanked by **Dobani** (6,134 m), with the serrated ridges of **Haramosh** (7,409 m) to the northeast. Directly behind you, to the south, is the massive north (Raikot) face of **Nanga Parbat** (8,125 m). A small sign at the settlement of **Thalichi** (10 km from Raikot Bridge) reminds you to look. For sleeping options here, see page 207.

Across the Indus from Thalichi is the entrance to the **Astor Valley**, gateway to a trekking route round to the naked southeast (Rupal) face of Nanga Parbat. **Thalichi** is in fact the boundary between Diamar District and **Gilgit District**, although the Astor Valley (see page 202) is part of Diamar. For details of the journey north towards Gilgit turn to page 208. A new suspension bridge linking Thalichi to Bunji recently opened, obviating the need to continue further to cross via Jaglot/Bunji.

Just before **Jaglot** (50 km from Gilgit), a suspension bridge crosses the Indus (look for the sign marked 'NLI Centre'), and a road runs back south through **Bunji** to the Astor Valley.

Astor Valley

The Astor Valley was once part of the primary trade and supply route between Gilgit and Srinagar (Kashmir), but Partition effectively closed this passage. However, the valley remains the starting/finishing point for trips across the Deosai Plains to Baltistan, as well as offering some excellent trekking around the eastern and southern sides of Nanga Parbat. For orientation, see map on page 198. Sleeping, eating and transport options are on pages 205-208.

Ins and outs

There are three transport access points to the Astor Valley. One is from the Deosai Plains of Baltistan (see page 244). The second (and least used) is the truck road from Raikot Bridge (see page 198, although there is no public transport on this route and hitchhiking is difficult). Finally, there is the recently upgraded road that connects Astor (via Bunji) with the KKH at Jaglot (and hence Gilgit). Minibuses and landcruisers now link Astor with Gilgit in just four hours – a considerable improvement upon the previously gruelling six- to seven-hour cargo jeep ride. Note also that there is a new bridge linking the KKH at Thalichi with the Astor road, avoiding the need to continue to Jaglot/Bunji if arriving from the south. The first settlement along the jeep road is **Bunji** (6 km). From there it is a further three hours or so to the village of **Astor**, via **Mushkin** and **Harcho**.

Tourist information Those considering visiting the Astor Valley (or trekking here) may care to consult **Keiko** ⓘ *newtouristcottage@hotmail.com* or **Pakistan Adventure Heights** ⓘ *akhtarhussain60@hotmail.com*, which are based at **New Tourist Cottage** in Gilgit; they have lots of experience in this region. NB It is essential to hire a reputable guide for trekking in the Astor Valley; in 2001, a Japanese girl who ignored pleas not to trek alone was found murdered here.

Bunji

Strategically placed at a crossing point of the Indus, and guarding the entrance to the Astor Valley, the small, nondescript settlement of **Bunji** has played a remarkably significant role in the recent history of the Northern Areas. This was the furthest outpost of the Kashmiri state, beyond which lay 'Yaghistan'.

The British built a fort at Bunji in order to protect the route across the Burzil Pass into Kashmir, the main supply line between British India and the outpost of the Empire at Gilgit. During the Gilgit uprising at Partition, Bunji's strategic importance at the head of the the pass into Kashmir was re-emphasized and was said to be the deciding factor in the whole game of Gilgit's freedom struggle.

Although the route across the Burzil Pass into Indian-occupied Kashmir is closed, Bunji still maintains its strategic significance controlling a vital supply line to Pakistani troops stationed on the Siachen Glacier. It is also the headquarters of the Northern Light Infantry, the successors to the Gilgit Scouts.

Astor village

The village (2,345 m) is perched high above the river on the shoulder of a mountain, its small and crowded main bazaar consisting of a series of impossibly steep and narrow streets. The restaurants and snack places are fairly basic, and the range of goods on sale in the shops makes stocking up in Gilgit a good idea for trekkers (and those heading across the Deosai).

From Astor it is possible to walk up to the beautiful **Rama Lake** (3,482 m), about four to six hours away through dense pine forest (note the altitude change). There are some superb camping options here. For sleeping options in the village and by the lake, see page 205.

Ins and outs The easiest way to reach Astor is by taking a minibus (or occasional long-wheelbase landcruiser cargo jeep) from the Diamar Hotel in Gilgit (Rs110, four hours, usually at 0800, 0900, 1000, reserve the night before). Minibuses return to Gilgit from Astor in the afternoon. There are also wagons and minibuses that link Jaglot (on the KKH) with Astor (Rs85, three hours). A privately hired jeep between Gilgit and Astor costs around Rs2,000. ▸▸ *See Transport, page 208, for more details.*

Onwards from Astor village

Continuing south from Astor village, the jeep track descends back down to the river level, passing through the village of **Gurikot** (9 km). The track then crosses and recrosses the river, before dividing sharply after the second bridge. The main jeep track bears gradually east, climbing steadily upwards towards the **Deosai Plateau** and crossing eventually into Baltistan. The last village before the Deosai is **Chilam**, a tiny, rather forlorn place, swelled in size only by the military presence here. For full details of this extraordinary trip across the Deosai (described in the opposite direction) see page 247.

The road to Tarashing also follows the same route to **Gurikot** (9 km), taking the right fork just after the second bridge. **Tarashing** (2,911 m) is the starting point for the excellent Rupal Valley and Mazeno Base Camp trek around Nanga Parbat (see below). For details on how to get here, see Astor above. Astor to Tarashing is 40km. **NB** A guide is essential for any explorations in this area. See page 207 for sleeping options.

Rupal Valley trek

ⓘ *Open zone. Maximum elevation optional (4,000 m). Jun to Sep. Maps: the Deutsche Himalaya Expedition of Nanga Parbat is excellent; U502 series, NI 43-2 Gilgit also good. Read trekking notes, p 45.*

This trek is a popular with trekking agencies, as well as with self-organized trekkers. This trek begins at **Tarashing** (2,911 m). There are always plenty of guides and porters available here, as well as horses and donkeys for hire. It takes around four to five days to reach Mazeno Base Camp and return by the same route.

The trail climbs the lateral moraine of **Tarashing Glacier** before crossing the glacier on a good path to reach the settlement of **Rupal** (3,155 m), divided into upper and lower villages. There is good camping beyond the upper village, or further on at **Herligkoffer Base Camp** (3,656 m), an ideal spot with woods, flowers and clear spring water. The path then crosses the Bazhin Glacier (again, this is a relatively easy glacier crossing). On the far side, below the lateral moraine, is another good camping place known as **Tupp Meadow**, surrounded by summer settlements where sheep, goats, dzo and horses are brought to graze. An alternative route from Rupal village crosses to the south bank of the river on a good bridge and skirts the snout of the Bazhin Glacier to arrive at Tupp Meadow. From here the trail continues up the Rupal Valley, passing several possible campsites, to **Shaigiri** (3,655 m) which offers the best camping and excellent views of Nanga Parbat's south face. The trail then follows lateral moraine as it climbs up to **Mazeno Base Camp**.

Beyond, the trail bears sharply north and begins its steep ascent to Mazeno Pass (5,385 m). About a third of the way up is **Mazeno High Camp** (4,700 m). It is possible, instead of returning to Tarashing, to trek over Mazeno Pass and descend into Daimer Valley, which gives access to the KKH via the Bunar Valley (see trek below).

Nanga Parbat circuit via Mazeno La

ⓘ *Open zone. Maximum elevation optional (5,385 m). Jun to Sep. Maps: the Deutsche Himalaya Expedition of Nanga Parbat is excellent only as far as Mazeno La; U502 series, NI 43-2 Gilgit also good. Read trekking notes, p 45.*

This demanding trek offers numerous possibilities and alternatives, although it should be noted that it doesn't make a complete 'circuit' of Nanga Parbat (despite often being referred to as the 'around Nanga Parbat' trek). The first four to five days follow the Rupal Valley trek as far as **Mazeno Base Camp** (see above). You should be fully acclimatized before attempting the six-hour climb up to **Mazeno High Camp** (4,700 m). The following day is long and difficult, and again you should be fully acclimatized. Ascending along the northeast edge of the Mazeno Glacier, you cross it and then head for **Mazeno La (Pass)** at 5,385 m. The descent from Mazeno La is particularly difficult, largely because the north side is heavily crevassed. Trekkers should have experience of such conditions, and should always be roped (300 m of rope is recommended). Just to make this trek more complicated, it is often necessary to change porters here (from Tarashing villagers to Bunar residents), although these rules generally only apply to particularly large trekking parties. Having made the descent, the trail meets the Loibah Glacier, which you then follow to the **Upper Loibah Meadows**. The following day features a more relaxing downhill walk to the Loibah Meadows, from where the trail turns north to **Zangot** (2,400 m).

From Zangot there are two options. You can trek for two days down to the KKH at **Bunar**, camping at **Halaley Bridge** on the way (Abdul Wakeel, son of Bunar's lumbador, who is a registered mountain guide with **Travel Walji's**, is very experienced along this route, Gilgit T05811-2665, Islamabad T051-820908). The second option is to extend the trek by six days, and continue on to **Fairy Meadows**. This option involves overnight camps at **Kuta Gali** (four hours); **Shaichi** via the **Karu Sagar Pass** (4,800 m), large parties may have to change porters at Saichi (Bunar to Gunar); **Gutum Sagar** (3,500 m), six hours; **Jalipur High Camp** (4,400 m), six hours; before the long descent down to **Beyal** (with a possible side trip to **Nanga Parbat Base Camp** and **'Camp 1'**, see above).

Continuing on the KKH from Jaglot to Gilgit

Some 4 km north of Jaglot is the confluence of the **Indus** and **Gilgit Rivers**; a sign marks this place as a 'unique spot', at the confluence of two rivers and three mountain systems. A further 4 km along the road (and 38 km from Gilgit), the KKH leaves the Indus and branches along the west bank of the Gilgit River. The **Skardu** road crosses the Gilgit River here on the **Alam Bridge**, and follows the course of the Indus Valley east to **Baltistan** (see page 232).

The long splash of vegetation on either side of the road a further 7 km along the KKH is **Pari**, which has a NAPWD Inspection Bungalow (officially book in Gilgit) and a few restaurants on either side of the new mosque. The KKH passes a Frontier Constabulary fort a further 5 km along the KKH; the valley opening seen to the east across the Gilgit River here is the Haramosh Valley (see page 219).

A further 11 km along the KKH (and 17 km south of Gilgit) is another 'unique spot'; it is known locally as the '**Ambush Point**' and is marked by a memorial raised by the NLI in 1997 to indicate the place where in 1852 the 'Dards' ambushed and annihilated the Sikh garrison of Bunji Fort. Opposite, across the Gilgit River, is the entrance to the Bagrot Valley (see page 219).

The KKH continues through another police check post (foreigners are sometimes required to register), before turning north shortly before the confluence of the Gilgit and Hunza Rivers. The KKH crosses the river on a long suspension bridge, and proceeds north for **Hunza** and **China**, while the left fork enters **Gilgit** through its eastern suburb of Jutial.

Sleeping

Shatial *p193*
There are 2 basic, unfriendly H 'hotels' in Shatial, **Ittefaq** and **Swat**, although you should avoid both if possible.

Chilas *p195*
Chilas has an excellent range of upper-middle and middle-priced hotels (B-E) down on the KKH, and a miserable collection of basic F-H places up in the bazaar of the main town. You may find the hotels down on the KKH are desperate for business and hence some excellent discounts are available to those prepared to haggle. All the hotels have their own restaurants. It may be possible to book the **NAPWD Inspection Bungalow** in Babusar village from Chilas.
A-C Shangri-La Indus View, KKH, T058120-235. Good-value beautiful new VIP rooms (A) in 'traditional' style with mud walls, hessian flooring, rugs and furniture, modern bathroom, de luxe rooms (B) off a communal veranda are wood panelled with traditional fireplaces, tiled bath, air cooler, plus some poor-value uncarpeted budget rooms (C) with air cooler, but no real views, restaurant, garden overlooking river. Mixed reviews for its service, but the VIP rooms are very nice.

C-D Chilas Inn, KKH, T058120-211. Large rooms in main block (D) with air cooler, clean linen, hot bath, dressing table, de luxe rooms in new block out back have nice beds, air coolers, furniture, modern tiled bathrooms, but are a little overpriced. Large garden, own generator, sitting area in the lobby, air-cooled restaurant. A better deal with group discount.
C-D Panorama, KKH, T058120-340. The price you pay and level of service very much depends upon how many groups are staying. 12 rooms in new block (C, overpriced without the discount) are larger, carpeted, with new tiled bathroom and dressing room, 24 other rooms are the same price but with less modern bathrooms (negotiate down to D-E price at least), all rooms have (noisy) air coolers, not exciting Rs300 buffet dinner, you need to bargain hard to get the best deal here (Rs500-600 for a room when business is slack).
E Grace Continental, KKH. 2-storey hotel with tin roof (hot upstairs), 11 plain, carpeted rooms, air cooler, new tiled bathroom, restaurant, lawn.
E Karakoram Inn, KKH, T058120-212. 15 rooms, modern attached bath, air cooler, most with river view (those upstairs can get hot), some suites (C), good restaurant (Pakistani/Chinese), discounts available (15%), good value, friendly manager.
F-G Al-Kashmir, KKH, T058120-315. Basic old rooms (G) have peeling walls and grubby linen, attached bath, fan (power only in evenings), newer rooms (F) have air coolers and are marginally cleaner, garden, restaurant, not much English spoken.
G Punjab Hazara, KKH. Rather run down.
H Diamer Inn, KKH. Often used as a chai stop by buses, a few extremely basic rooms plus a not very private camping area.

There are several basic hotels in the bazaar up in Chilas proper. Of these, the **G Valley View** is probably the best, followed by **G Delux** or **G Diamond**, with **H Bismillah**, **H Hamala International** and **H Khunjrab** being only for those who are desperate or on a miniscule budget.

Raikot Bridge *p198*
Accommodation is available at the
B-C Shangrila Hotel, although several guests have written to say that the hotel and restaurant here are overpriced and bad value.

Fairy Meadows *p198*
A Shangrila Fairy Meadows, on hill above Raikot Serai. At the time of going to press construction was still underway. Plans for 40 double-storey wooden chalets, double bedroom with bathroom on each floor, verandah, own generator for 24-hr electricity (and hot water), price is for whole unit (sleeps 4, 25% discount for groups), large panoramic restaurant with trademark pagoda roof, some tents (or pitch your own), horses for rent, subsidized transport here.
C-E Raikot Serai, c/o Fairy Meadow Tours, Link Rd, Gilgit, T05811-4126, fmtours@glt.comsats.net.pk. Longest established camp here, 7 wooden cabins (C) attached bathrooms soon to be 'online', plus 10 large upright tents (D), 2 beds in each, warm blankets, coir-matting floor, plus 30 low-slung tents (E), not much room for 2, separate toilet huts and shower huts. You can also pitch your own tents in the meadow (H). Large dining hall, communal dinner a little expensive (Rs255), breakfast likewise (Rs160), budget visitors may be able to negotiate. Very friendly management, very well run (by brothers, Rehmat Nabi and Aziz Rehman Raees), good location (can watch sunrise/sunset on Nanga Parbat from your bed). Recommended.
E Fairy Meadow Cottages, T05811-2418 or T051-255990. In a clearing in the forest 5 mins beyond Greenland (views of Nanga Parbat above treetops), 11 sparse 2-bed cabins (E), verandah, shared toilet, can pitch own tent (H), dining hut, pleasing location.
E-F Greenland, T058120-382, T05811-2367. Currently 3 wooden cabins (E), 2 beds in each (blankets provided), bare wooden floor, separate toilet and shower, 2-person bell tents with sleeping bags and mats (F), or pitch your own tent (H), dining hall.

Beyal *p201*
E-F Jilper Inn, T05811-4126. 5 cabins (E) with 2 beds, blankets, rug, separate toilet and hot shower huts, 5 small 2-person tents (F) with sleeping bags and mattresses, or pitch own tent (H), dining hall being built, nice location.
E-F Parbat Serai, T05811-2418, F05811-2367. 6 2-bed huts (E), although there are plans for some 'VIP' huts with attached bath (D), some tents for hire (F) or pitch your own (H).

The owner of Greenland at Fairy Meadows is building some huts at Beyal.

Raikot Bridge to Jaglot *p202*
Thalichi
There is a very pleasant
G NAPWD Resthouse here, popular with cyclists, beautifully furnished, although you may have to be in your room by 2100 (no camping allowed). Food can be arranged, but it's best to bring your own supplies. No power, but a lantern (and water) are provided. Bookings should ideally be made through the Executive Engineer in Chilas or the Chief Engineer's Office in Gilgit, but it normally accepts casual callers.

Astor Valley *p202*
Harcho
G Saiful Malik Inn. Basic.

Astor village *p203*
F Kamran. The best hotel, situated above the bazaar and offering clean, pleasant rooms with fan, attached bath.
F-G Dreamland Hotel is overpriced, but still recommended, quiet, good food, reliable manager, basic rooms with attached bath, nice garden area and views.
G NAPWD Inspection Bungalow. Up on another hillside, away from the bazaar. 2 rooms. (should really be booked in Gilgit, but you can try just turning up).
G-H New Ropal Inn. Very basic with pokey rooms.

Rama Lake
B-C PTDC Motel in the forest below Rama Lake. Big luxury motel.
The camping here is superb, although it is possible to stay at the
F NAPWD Inspection Bungalow about halfway between Astor and the lake (bookings in Gilgit).

Onwards from Astor Village *p203*
Gurikot
G-H Lalazar Inn. Very simple, comprising a restaurant and a couple of rooms upstairs.

Tarashing
G Nanga Parbat Tourist Cottage. Basic.
A new hotel and campsite are also under construction in Tarashing.

Jaglot to Gilgit *p202*
Pari
G NAPWD Inspection Bungalow. Officially, book this in Gilgit.
There are a few restaurants on either side of the new mosque.

Transport

Shatial *p193*
If your public transport terminates in Shatial, there is usually transport available north to **Chilas** (Rs70, 2 hrs) and south to **Dasu/Komila** (Rs40, 1½ hrs).

Chilas *p195*
Gilgit The best option is to walk up to the bus yard in Chilas itself and take one of the depart-when-full minibuses (Rs75, 3½ hrs). If they don't fill up quickly, these services will drive down to the KKH to pick up passengers (but the best seats will have gone). Or you can stand down on the KKH and flag down passing buses (NATCO, Silk Route etc), which pass through some 10-12 hrs after leaving Rawalpindi.

Besham Minibuses depart when full from the bus yard in Chilas (Rs150, 5 hrs), but many only run as far as Komila/Dasu (Rs100, 3½ hrs).

Rawalpindi/Islamabad Either take a series of short trips via Komila/Dasu and Besham (see above), or wait for the NATCO, Silk Route etc buses originating in Gilgit to pass through on the the KKH (Rs360, 10-12 hrs, buses arrive 3½-4 hrs after leaving Gilgit, but there is no guarantee of there being available seats).

Babusar Pass (Kaghan Valley) A very crowded public cargo jeep leaves Chilas bazaar very early most mornings (except sometimes Fri) going as far as Babusar village (Rs65, 4-5 hrs).

From Babusar, there is rarely any public transport going over the pass into the Kaghan Valley (a private hire jeep as far as **Lake Lulusar** will cost around Rs750, and about Rs3,500 as far as **Naran**). A privately hired jeep from Chilas to Naran costs Rs3,500 (9-10 hrs). See below and warning box, page 180. Note that there are plans to upgrade this route into an all-weather metalled highway, making it the main route between Rawalpindi/Islamabad and Gilgit.

Astor village *p203*

There are up to 3 cargo jeeps per day from Astor to **Tarashing** (Rs60, 2 hrs), or you could hire your own jeep (up to Rs1,000). A privately hired jeep all the way from Gilgit to Tarashing costs around Rs3,000. It is very difficult to find any public transport in Astor that is crossing the Deosai Plains to **Skardu**; you normally have to book such transport in Gilgit. It is possible to hire a jeep from Astor up to **Rama Lake** for around Rs800.

Directory

Chilas *p195*
Hospitals Civil Hospital On the road up to the main town, but in emergencies you will be better off in Gilgit (or Islamabad, if getting there is a possibility). **Post office** In the main bazaar, Chilas town.
Telephone The PCO, located just east of the Chilas Inn, offers international phone calls.

Gilgit District → *Colour map 2, grid B4*

Gilgit District is arguably the most important of the five administrative divisions that comprise the Northern Areas (Gilgit, Diamar, Ghizr, Skardu, Ghanche), with the seat of the regional capital at Gilgit town. Gilgit District stretches all the way up to the international border with China, and is divided into a number of sub-districts (Gilgit, Hunza, Nagar 1, Nagar 2, Gojal), all of which have their own sections within this guide. This section deals with Gilgit sub-district, and in the context of this administrative division, the history of the regional capital at Gilgit town is particularly important.

Gilgit sub-district is an ethnically and religiously mixed area, reflecting its geographical and political importance as the regional focal point. The indigenous language is Shina, although the influx of outsiders means that such diverse tongues as Pashto, Burushaski, Wakhi, Khowar, Chilasi, Kohistani, Urdu and English are all spoken here. Likewise, the various religious groups (Sunni, Shia, Ismaili), who all have their own well-defined turf across the rest of the Northern Areas, live in close proximity here, which sometimes leads to sectarian strain.

For those travelling along the KKH from south to north, you will suddenly find that the side valleys off the KKH are now accessible, while the towns and villages on the highway itself are more geared up for tourism than those further south in Hazara, Indus Kohistan and Diamar District. ▸▸ *For Sleeping, Eating and all other listings, see pages 221-228.*

Ins and outs

For those travelling along the KKH from the south, there is a seamless join in the journey between Diamar District and Gilgit sub-district (there isn't even a sign to announce your arrival in a separate district). It's also possible to arrive in Gilgit sub-district by air (directly into Gilgit town from Islamabad), from the west (along the Chitral-Gilgit road), from the east (from Baltistan), and from the north (from China, via Gojal, Hunza and Nagar). ▸▸ *See Transport, page 226, for more details*.

Gilgit

From the numerous territorial disputes between the rival petty kingdoms in the surrounding valleys, through the imperial rivalry of the era of the 'Great Game', up until the Partition war between Pakistan and India and the continuing antagonism between the two states, Gilgit has held its place at the centre of local history. John Keay described it as "the hub, the crow's-nest, the fulcrum of Asia" (*The Gilgit Game*, 1979), and, although it is now the regional capital of the Northern Areas, it derives its importance today as the key northern junction for travel to all points of the compass.

Almost all visitors to the north of Pakistan pass through Gilgit at some stage of their journey, however, despite having arguably the best choice of budget and medium-priced accommodation in the country, the region's best shopping (handicrafts and trekking supplies), a wide choice of trekking and travel agents, and transport connections all across the region, Gilgit has few real 'sights' as such. In fact, in terms of tourism, Gilgit's greatest utility is as a base to visit nearby attractions, arrange transport to other places in the Northern Areas, or prepare for a trekking expedition.

Ins and outs

Getting there

Gilgit is linked by **air** to Islamabad (two to three flights per day, see page 226 for more details), although these flights are weather dependent and hence regularly cancelled (up to 50%). Land has been bought to extend the runway, enabling jets to land here, although this is highly unlikely ever to happen. Two jets have successfully used the airport here but pilots claim that the take-off is just too dangerous. Because of the hills that enclose Gilgit, if you have an engine failure you have nowhere to go except into the hillside. It's more likely that the airstrip at Chilas will be upgraded but not in the immediate future. See also box, page 70, on flying into the Northern areas.

Gilgit is the **bus** transport hub of the Northern Areas. In order to reduce traffic congestion in town, a new multi-company/destination bus station has been built in the eastern suburbs at Jutial (just off the Gilgit map). Almost all bus services leave/depart from here, the most notable exceptions being **NATCO** services west towards Chitral (Gahkuch, Gupis, Yasin) that run from a yard on Punial Road (see map). Most of the bus companies still have booking offices in the town centre. A Suzuki from downtown to Jutial costs Rs6 per person (or Rs60 in a taxi). ▸▸ *See Transport, page 226, for more details.*

Getting around

The centre of Gilgit is compact enough to negotiate on foot, although some care is necessary, especially when walking on the road to avoid pavement vendors. **Suzuki minivans** run up and down the main road, linking the post office in the west with Jutial in the east (Rs6 for full journey), and can be flagged down anywhere along this route. Occasionally, if a lone western woman gets in, all the men get out and the driver will insist that you hire the whole vehicle ('special'). A 'special' suzuki will cost around Rs30 for most journeys within Gilgit (eg the airport to your hotel), although it's Rs60 out to Jutial bus station. Suzuki minivans also run from Garhi Bagh, via Babar Road, across the Jinnah Bridges to Danyore.

Best time to visit

Because Gilgit sits in a bowl surrounded by bare brown hills that reflect the sun's heat and because, at around 1,500 m above sea-level, it's not particularly high, it can become unpleasantly hot in summer (temperatures of 40°C are not unknown). It's very cool in the winter, and due to the drop in the river level, water and power shortages are common. It has also had more than its fair share of sectarian violence, and as tensions between the Sunni and Shia communities are at their highest around key religious dates (notably Ashoura and the end of Ramadan), Gilgit is best avoided at these times.

Tourist information

PTDC ⓘ *PTDC Chinnar Inn, Babar Rd, T05811-4262/2562, F05811-2650.* Typical government appointee, you'll find out much more from a backpacker hotel manager or through other travellers.

History

The record for the early and medieval history of Gilgit is rather incomplete, largely because the oral tradition, as opposed to the written form, has been the primary source of transmitting information on the period. The oral tradition has left us with some amusing titbits, however, such as the story of the last Buddhist ruler of Gilgit, Sri Badad (although some sources claim he was Hindu). It is suggested that such was his taste for the flesh of young children, that he ate nothing else!

> *The phone code for Gilgit is 05811. Old 4-digit numbers are now prefaced with a 5. At time of going to press, the 0572 code still worked.*

The **Trakhans** were the dominant dynasty during Gilgit's medieval period, ruling for eight distinct phases from some time in the eighth century until 1840. It is from the Trakhan line that the rival ruling families of Hunza and Nagar have evolved.

The end of the Trakhan dynasty saw some very unpleasant rulers in Gilgit, notably **Gohar Aman**, during whose unopposed rule between 1852 and 1860 over half the local population were sold into slavery. Following Gohar Aman's death, the Dogras assumed control of Gilgit, since the Dogra Raja of Jammu, **Gulab Singh**, had 'bought' Kashmir from the British as part of the Sikh war reparations from the First Anglo-Sikh War of 1846. Thus, for the first time since the rule of Sri Badad some 11 centuries earlier, Gilgit found itself under the yoke of a non-Muslim ruler.

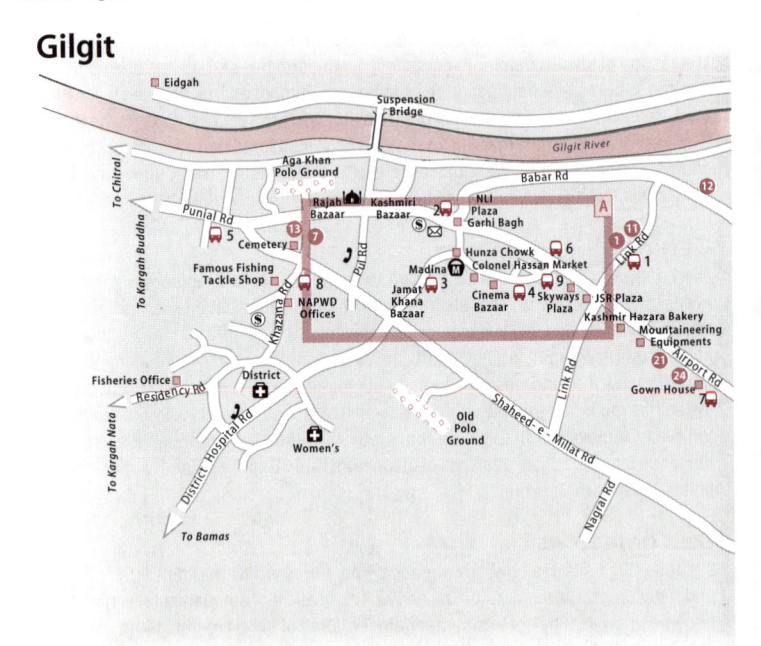

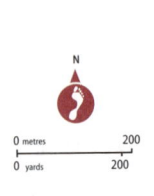

Gilgit

Sleeping
Alflah 1
Chinese Lodge 3
Dreamland 5
Gilgit Gateway 6
Golden Peak 7
Horizon 8
Hunza Inn 9
Hunza Tourist House 10
Mir's Lodge 11
Mountain Refuge 12
NAPWD Inspection Bungalow 13
North Inn 14
Park 15
PTDC Chinnar Inn 16
Riveria 17
Rupal 18
Shaheen International 19
Serena Lodge 20
Top Moon 21
Tourist Cottage 22
Tourist Hamlet 23
Vershigoom 24

Growing British concern over the perceived threat of a Russian invasion of the subcontinent through the unmapped passes to the north resulted in the creation of the **Gilgit Agency**, an administrative division established in 1877 in an attempt to increase British influence in the region. A series of 'Political Agents' were appointed to Gilgit, notably **Colonel Algernon Durand** (see box, page 275). Although in theory just representatives of the British government on the frontier, these political agents became the de facto military commanders of the region, and as such were the key policy makers. This system of 'dual control' between the British and the Dogra rulers of Kashmir was soon deemed unworkable, and in 1935 the then Maharaja of Kashmir, Raja Hari Singh, was 'encouraged' to sign a document leasing the Gilgit Wazarat to Britain for 60 years. This is how the position of Gilgit stood at the Partition of the subcontinent in 1947, and the creation of the state of Pakistan.

The key event in the recent history of Gilgit has been the development of transport infrastructure in the region, in particular the Karakoram Highway. Gilgit is now a major staging post in the border trade with China, and potentially with Central Asia in the future. It is also a key market for goods from both China and down-country Pakistan, as well as a local centre for labour.

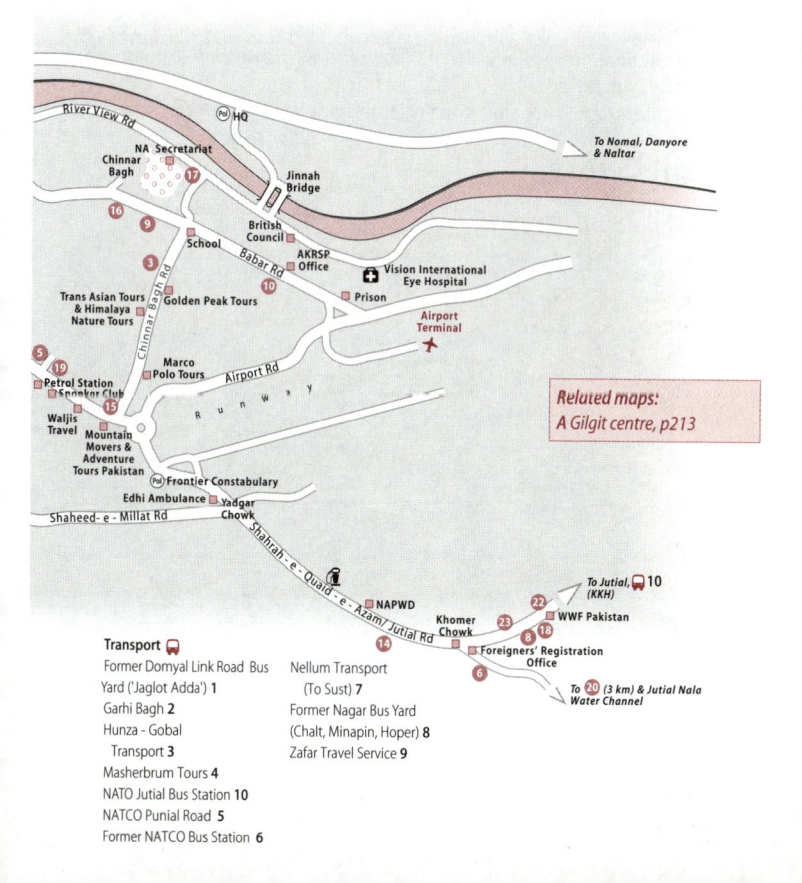

Related maps:
A Gilgit centre, p213

Transport

Former Domyal Link Road Bus Yard ('Jaglot Adda') 1
Garhi Bagh 2
Hunza - Gobal Transport 3
Masherbrum Tours 4
NATCO Jutial Bus Station 10
NATCO Punial Road 5
Former NATCO Bus Station 6
Nellum Transport (To Sust) 7
Former Nagar Bus Yard (Chalt, Minapin, Hoper) 8
Zafar Travel Service 9

Gilgit is one of the places that you are most likely to see the swashbuckling version of **polo** that is played in the north of Pakistan (see page 44). There are several polo federations based here and a number of different clubs. The most famous teams are those run by the police, armed forces and NAPWD, although transfers between sides are common. There are also a number of privately run sides, including, until recently, the plaything of a wealthy European woman who had a taste for the sport.

The two most important polo events of the year are the Gilgit versus Chitral matches ('A' team, 'B' team, youth games etc) held at the Shandur Pass each year (usually second week in July, see page 149), and the week-long festival beginning 1 November that celebrates the Gilgit Uprising. There are also generally matches around Pakistan Independence Day (14 August). In the days leading up to the big tournaments, there are plenty of late afternoon practice matches (usually around 1600-1700). These tend to be held at the Old Polo Ground (see map), little more than a section of street that is closed off during matches. Important matches are held at the Aga Khan Polo Ground (see map). Enquire about fixtures at the Tourist Office, ask your hotel manager, or try contacting the **Karakoram Polo Development and Youth Welfare Organization** ⓘ *House 571, Street 53, G-9/1 Islamabad, T051-2252360, kpdywo@yahoo.com*.

The most famous grave in the Christian, or so-called **'British' Cemetery** ⓘ *Khazana Rd to the west of town (ask for ghora cabrestan)*, is that of British explorer George Hayward (see page 156), although the original headstone that was installed by the Maharajah of Kashmir (a suspect for Hayward's murder) disappeared in the 1970s and was replaced by the present Royal Geographical Society-sponsored stone in the 1980s. The graveyard is also the final resting place of a number of servants of the British colonial machine (included a Major Ian Galbraith, of whom all that could be recovered from the river in which he drowned was his wooden leg), as well as several young men killed in climbing accidents in the region.

If the gate is locked ask around at the local shops for Ghulam Ali, who has taken

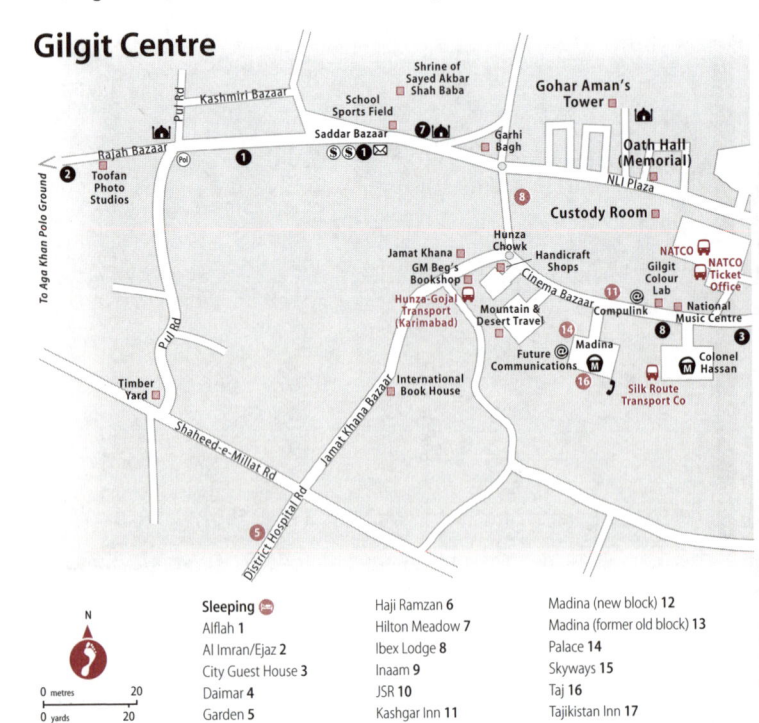

Gilgit Centre

Sleeping
Alflah **1**
Al Imran/Ejaz **2**
City Guest House **3**
Daimar **4**
Garden **5**
Haji Ramzan **6**
Hilton Meadow **7**
Ibex Lodge **8**
Inaam **9**
JSR **10**
Kashgar Inn **11**
Madina (new block) **12**
Madina (former old block) **13**
Palace **14**
Skyways **15**
Taj **16**
Tajikistan Inn **17**

over from his father the task of maintaining the cemetery. It seems he receives no salary for this, so donations are accepted (and solicited). He also sells (Rs50) a brochure produced by **BACSA** ⓘ *76 Chartfield Av, London, SW15 6HQ*, which provides some interesting background detail on those buried here.

There are a number of monuments dedicated to the **Gilgit Uprising**, including a memorial in **Chinar Bagh**, the municipal gardens down by the river, where the graves of two of the key players are located. The recent redevelopment of the Northern Light Infantry's former barracks into a shopping plaza means that you can now visit the **Custody Hall** where Brigadier Ghansara Singh was imprisoned, although the **Oath Hall** where the officers of the Gilgit Scouts pledged their allegiance to Pakistan has recently been replaced by a memorial stone. Neither are particularly inspiring. The shopping plaza redevelopment also means that you can now see the sole remaining tower of the **fort** that Gohar Aman built in the 1850s (but look out for wasp nests!).

A popular **walk**, giving good views of the 'bowl' in which Gilgit sits, involves a stroll along the **Jutial Nala** above Gilgit to the south. You can extend the walk by continuing along the Jutial water channel, even continuing to the Kargah Buddha (see below). Depending upon which option you follow, this can be a half or a full day's walk. Take plenty of water. **NB** Do not attempt these walks if it has rained recently – there may be the danger of land-slides and rockfalls. Women should not attempt this walk alone.

Take a Suzuki from central Gilgit up to the junction for the Serena Lodge (look out for the ibex statue), and then walk up the hill past the hotel. About 500 m past the Serena Lodge turn right (west), and follow the irrigation channel (for directions just ask for the 'nala'). For **Jutial Nala**, head for the cleft in the rock near the beginning of the irrigation channel. Follow the goat path into the steep-sided gorge, sticking to the right of the stream. The gorge climbs for some 6 km up to pine forests and green pastures, with great views back north to Rakaposhi.

Less ambitious walkers can ignore the temptation of climbing up the Jutial Nala, instead continuing west along the **water channel**. There are good views from here down to the Gilgit 'bowl', particularly early on misty mornings. After several kilometres you reach the village of Barmas, a suburb of Gilgit. From here you can drop down into Gilgit (emerging onto Hospital Road, see map), or continue along the channel to the **Kargah Buddha**.

Kargah

ⓘ *Kargah is about 8 km from Gilgit, and can be reached on foot, or by Suzuki. Passenger Suzukis heading for Baseen village can be taken from Punial Rd in Gilgit, but they are few and far between. You may be encouraged to hire one (Rs200 1 way). There are two options for walking there. Either head west along Punial Rd from Gilgit towards Kargah village, before turning left (south) along Kargah nala, or incorporate the Buddha as part of the Jutial Nala/Water Channel walk (see above).*

Thought to date to the seventh or eighth centuries, and showing marked similarities to Tibetan carvings found in Baltistan, this large image of a standing Buddha (in *abhaya*, or fearlessness, pose) is found on a cliff face at

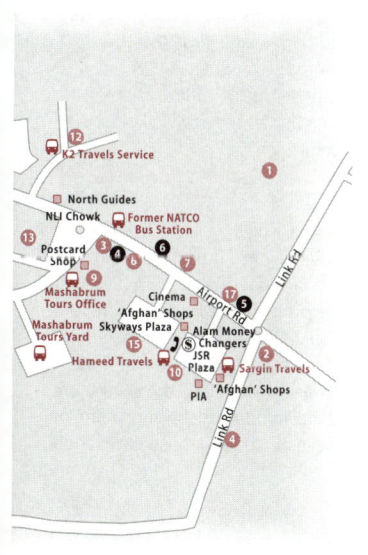

Eating 🍴
Chai Shops **1**
Haidry Tea Shop **2**
Indus **3**
Juice Shop **5**
Madina Supermarket **4**
Pathan **6**
Safdar Ali Bakers **7**
Unamed Thai Shop **8**

Partition and the Gilgit Uprising

A radical reinterpretation of the 1935 lease agreement meant that when British paramountcy over India lapsed on 3 June 1947, the whole of the Gilgit Agency was handed over to the Maharaja of Kashmir. His representative, Brigadier Ghansara Singh, took over as governor of the area on 1 August 1947, two weeks before the date set for the independence of India and Pakistan. This was despite the fact that all the civil and military officers had expressed a preference to the British to join Pakistan. The local population had not been consulted at all.

On the night of 26 October 1947, Maharaja Hari Singh announced his accession to India. How much this decision was influenced by Pathan Afridi tribesmen from NWFP proclaiming a jihad on his doorstep is open to historical debate, but in Gilgit plans for this eventuality had obviously already been made. A small group of army officers serving in the Gilgit Scouts had already secretly pledged their allegiance to Pakistan and made plans for the liberation of Gilgit. In the early hours of the morning of 1 November 1947, Ghansara Singh was arrested at his home and placed in custody. He was made to sign a surrender document and the Pakistani flag was raised over Gilgit.

Within four days the Chilas Scouts had captured the fort at Bunji, thus gaining control of the vital line of communication, and potential counter-attack, with Srinagar. Meanwhile in Gilgit, a Provisional Government had been set up and assistance requested from Pakistan, although this fledgling state's meagre resources meant that the support given was generally moral as opposed to tangible. Major Mohammad Aslam Khan (later proprietor of the Shangri-La chain of hotels) was flown in to coordinate the military defence of the country so far acquired, and to 'liberate' as much territory as possible. Not only did his forces succeed in holding the territory gained, they also managed to liberate Baltistan and occupy parts of Kashmir. In January 1948 a UN-sponsored cease-fire ended the war, leaving the Line of Control as the de facto border between Pakistan and India.

Kargah, several kilometres west of Gilgit. There is an excellent local legend that provides a far more amusing explanation for the carved figure. The image is actually that of a giant who used to terrorize the local population. A passing saint was enlisted by the terrified villagers to deal with the menace, and he succeeded in pinning the giant to the rock face. The saint explained that the giant would remain pinned there for as long as he was alive, and they would continue to be safe if they buried the saint at the foot of the cliff upon his death. The resourceful villagers killed the saint there and then, and buried him at the foot of the cliff! Several hundred metres upstream of the Buddha are the remains of a monastery and several stupas, whose excavation revealed a number of Sanskrit Buddhist texts.

Kargah nala trek
① *Open zone. Maximum elevation about 4,000 m. Jul to Sep. The only person who seems to be regularly offering this trek is Altaf Hussain (contact through the Madina Hotel). Read trekking notes, p 45.*
This straightforward six- to seven-day trek (can also be completed in four to five days) is aimed at beginners who want to get off the beaten track. It takes in some pleasant alpine meadows, several waterfalls, plus good fishing streams and lakes.

From the **Kargah Buddha**, it is a two-and-a-half-hour jeep ride (Rs1,200) past the Giglit hydel stations and several waterfalls to **Jute**. The campsite here is used in summer by Gujar shepherds (there is a good water source here). You can either camp here, or climb gently for three to four hours to the meadow on the edge of the forest at **Chowk**. There is a Forest Police check post here that keeps an eye on incursions from Kohistan. There is good fishing at Chowk. Those who camped at Jute can usually reach **Chilalee** in one long day (further three and a half hours of gentle, then brief steep climbs from Chowk). Again, there is good camping at Chilalee, hopefully in flower-strewn meadows that are used for summer grazing by Gilgit livestock. An alternative camping spot is at **Chilalee Lake**, two and a half hours above Chilalee, with the option of a further climb for good Rakaposhi views. The return from Chilalee to Jute can be completed in two days.

Naltar Valley

Lying to the north and northwest of Gilgit is the beautiful Naltar Valley. An area of glacial lakes, pine forests and alpine meadows penned in by snow-covered peaks with seasonal skiing, this is ideal camping country (and other accommodation is also available). There are a number of short hikes that can be made from here, in addition to two short treks.

Ins and outs
The road to **Naltar Valley** leaves Gilgit by the Jinnah Bridge, but turns north (left) at the Frontier Constabulary post, rather than crossing the suspension bridge to Danyore and the KKH. This route used to form part of the Old Hunza Road prior to the construction of the KKH. The route is dry and dusty until you reach the extensive cultivated area of **Nomal**. There is a NAPWD Inspection Bungalow here, as well as a dubious looking footbridge across the Hunza River to the KKH.

At Nomal a rough jeep track turns west, up the Naltar Valley. After 10 km you reach '**Lower' Naltar**, or Naltar Paen. '**Upper' Naltar** is a further 10 km up the valley. The main settlement at 'Upper' Naltar is often referred to as **Dumian** (2,820 m). ▶▶ *See Transport, page 226, for more details.*

Upper Naltar and Naltar Lake
The lower reaches of the Naltar Valley are confined within a hot, rocky, narrow canyon, but at Upper Naltar the valley opens out to reveal lush green alpine pastures and pine forests surrounded by spectacular snowy peaks. In winter, the scene is entirely different, and it is here that the Pakistan Air Force maintains a winter survival school. Note that Lower Naltar is Shia, while Upper Naltar is Sunni.

The beautiful **Naltar Lake** is a gentle 12-km walk beyond Upper Naltar, and can be reached in three to four hours. The path passes through pleasant meadows and scattered pine forests, although there is some scrambling over loose scree and boulders at the start of the trek. The gradient is quite modest. It is worth noting if you are returning the same day that the numerous streams that you have to hop across are considerably higher by late afternoon. There are actually several lakes in the upper part of the Naltar Valley, although the first one that you come to is probably the most attractive. Set in a hollow of terminal moraine deposited by a long since retreated glacier, Naltar Lake is a stunning vision of colour, with exquisite aquamarines, electric blues and vivid greens. In places it is unbelievably clear. Potential swimmers should note that it is very deep and very cold. Diving in may cause unhealthy rapid changes in body temperature. It can also take longer to climb out than you think, so don't leave it until you are turning blue before attempting to scramble out. It is quite possible to camp at this idyllic spot, see Sleeping, page 221. The two other lakes beyond Naltar Lake are said to offer the best fishing.

Beyond the series of lakes, there are two more strenuous trekking opportunities. One route travels over the 4,710 m Naltar (or Pakor) Pass into the Ishkoman Valley, and the other crosses the Daintar Pass (4,500 m) to Chalt. Sleeping options for Naltar and Naltar Lake are on page 223.

Treks from the Naltar Valley

The Naltar valley gives access to two possible treks, one leading over the **Daintar Pass** and via the Daintar Valley to Chalt in the Chaprot Valley, the second leading over the **Naltar (Pakor) Pass** into the Ishkoman Valley. Although in an open zone, a guide is recommended for both treks since the routes across the Daintar and Naltar Passes are not obvious and it is easy to get lost. Both treks are quite strenuous, although they offer excellent views and welcome relief from the heat of Gilgit. The Naltar Valley, as well as being significantly cooler higher up, receives considerably more rainfall than Gilgit and is thickly wooded. There are plenty of Gujar nomads in the upper reaches of the valley. Large trekking parties may have to hire an even split of Shia porters from Lower Naltar and Sunni porters from Upper Naltar and there may be some tension between the two groups during the trek. You need to allow at least six days for the Daintar Pass trek, and five days for the Naltar Pass trek (not including rest days).

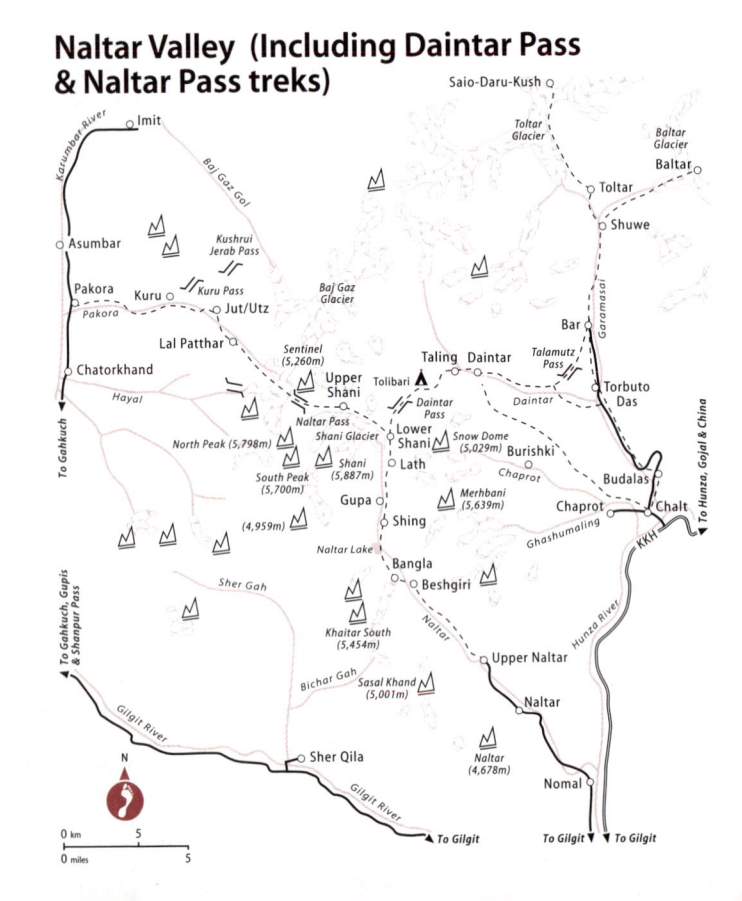

Naltar Valley (Including Daintar Pass & Naltar Pass treks)

Daintar Pass trek

ⓘ *Open zone. Maximum elevation 4,500 m. Jul to Sep. Maps: Swiss Foundation are good; the U502 series, NJ 43-14 Baltit is not adequate for this trek. Read trekking notes, p45.*

From Naltar it is a three-and-a-half to four-hour walk up to **Naltar Lake**. The jeep track is rarely passable as far as the main lake, which offers the best camping. North of Naltar Lake the path crosses the east bank of the river and climbs through pastures and moraine to **Lower Shani** (3,690 m). There is good camping along the way, and at Lower Shani. This is where the paths for Naltar and Daintar Passes fork.

Climb up onto the ridge to the east of Lower Shani and head north to a flattish shoulder of mountain known as **Daintar Base Camp**. From here the path climbs steadily, following the shoulder, up to **Daintar Pass** (4,500 m). A thick snow cornice forces you to bear off to the right following the crest to its highest point. A little further on it becomes possible to descend a very steep shale gulley to a large snowfield. Lower down there is a large summer pasture offering camping in good weather. The recognized campsite is further down at the shepherds' settlement of **Tolibari**. From here the path along the south bank of the river runs through woods and pastures, fording two side streams and then enters a narrow gorge before arriving at the village of **Taling**, where the Daintar River flows down from the north. There is a polo ground above the village. Taling is at the head of the jeep track, although it is often blocked lower down and jeeps rarely come up this far (if you are planning to arrange for a jeep to pick you up from here, check first as to the condition of the track). It takes around three hours to walk down to Torbuto Das, from where there are fairly regular passenger jeeps. At Daintar just past Taling, a path on the opposite (south) bank of the river climbs up to the ridge behind and leads down to Chaprot village, 3 km above Chalt (see page 264).

Naltar (Pakor) Pass

ⓘ *Open zone. Maximum elevation 4,710 m. Jul to Sep. Maps: as for Daintar Pass. Read trekking notes, p 45.*

From Lower Shani (3,690 m, see above) the path heads west on a good path alongside the Shani Glacier to **Upper Shani** (4,230 m), a large area of summer pasture at the foot of the pass. Higher up there is another area of summer pasture on a plateau, also good for camping. **Naltar (or Pakor) Pass** (4,710 m) is wide and flat topped, with no definite path across it. Shortly after the summit the route bears off to the right (north) across crevassed snowfields, crosses a small side glacier and then follows the crest of lateral moraine before arriving at a meadow surrounded by trees, plus large red boulders known as **Krui Bokht** (in Khowar language, or **Lal Patthar** in Urdu). From here the path follows the Pakora River, passing through pastures, woods and summer settlements, crossing the river three times. The lower section of the valley enters a narrow gorge, with the trail gently climbing up to the Gujar huts at **Jut/Utz** (3,390 m). The descent towards Pakora is fairly steep, and also hot and dry, before the valley opens out as it approaches Pakora village, at the junction with the Ishkoman Valley (see page 155).

Danyore Valley

Most visitors only see **Danyore** (Dainyor) as a small roadside village on the KKH on the way to Hunza. However, this small village actually stands at the head of a little-explored valley – **Danyore Valley** – that provides one of the best views of the South Face of **Rakaposhi**. What is more, there is a relatively easy trek in the Danyore Valley that provides a close up view of the Rakaposhi South Face. Suzuki minivans run via the Jinnah Bridges and another dramatic suspension bridge to Danyore from Gilgit's Garhi Bagh (near Saddar Bazaar). For orientation see map on page 219.

Danyore Valley Trek (Rakaposhi South Face)

ⓘ *Open zone. Maximum elevation circa 4,000 m. Jul to Sep. Maps: Swiss Foundation good; U502 series, NI 43-2 Gilgit and NJ 43-14 Baltit are adequate. Read trekking notes, p 45.*

This trek is an excellent way of getting in shape for more strenuous treks: it does not involve crossing any passes and, although the lower sections of the valley are hot and dry, higher up there are beautiful alpine woods and pastures in the ablation valley alongside the glacier flowing down from Rakaposhi. Allow two days (three if you are going slowly) to reach the head of the valley, and two (or one very long day) for the return trip.

The path into the valley climbs up through **Danyore village**, heading towards the Danyore Hydel Project on the right bank of the river. It takes four to five hours in a baking hot, bare rock canyon to reach the first spring water. The path then crosses the river three times before climbing steeply over a shoulder and descending once again to the river. Further on, across a wide stony plain, a rock cairn marks the point where a small spring emerges at the base of the low cliffs by the river. The path then climbs steeply up to **Barit village**, situated on a small plateau. Rich green terraced fields extend up the side valley flowing in from the west. The path crosses the side valley on a wooden bridge and then climbs steeply to rejoin the main valley, running along an irrigation channel. It then continues past three bridges giving access to cultivated summer settlements on the east bank before climbing up through pine forests to a small summer settlement high above the river. There is spring water available here. After

Danyore, Bagrot & Haramosh Valleys

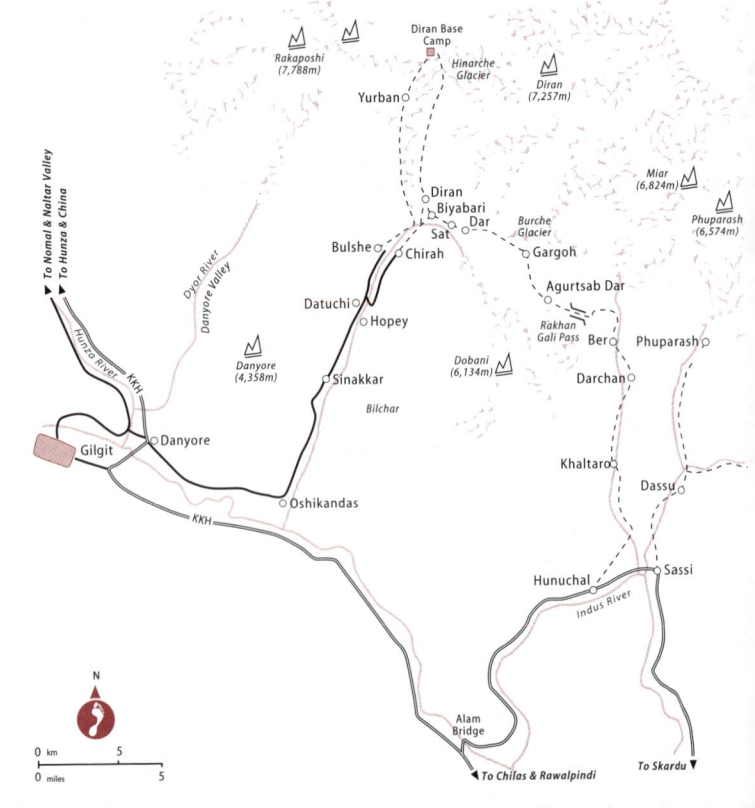

descending back to the river level, cross to the east bank of the river. The path, marked by stone cairns, runs through lightly wooded, rocky terrain. It crosses a small side stream and then climbs onto the ridge of the glacier's lateral moraine. Follow the ridge until the ablation valley to the right widens out into a large area of alpine pastures, woods and streams, offering numerous idyllic camping spots. It is well worth spending a day or two here to explore and take in the awesome scenery.

Bagrot and Haramosh Valleys

Located to the east of Gilgit, the Bagrot Valley runs roughly southwest-northeast for 20 km or so, before turning east and providing a route into the Haramosh Valley. In addition to offering fine views of the south face of the Rakaposhi Massif (including Diran), this little-visited valley offers some excellent walking and trekking.

The 6,134-m Dobani (Bilchar) Peak at the centre of the valley is said to be inhabited by fairies, and the belief here in the power of shamans is strong. The population of the valley are Shia Muslims and traditionally provided the backbone of the army raised in times of war by the rulers of Gilgit. When Durand visited the valley in 1889 he found evidence of an earlier raid by Gohar Aman, a prince of Yasin, in which it is estimated that two-thirds of the population had been killed or carried off into slavery. Few people visit this valley, although in recent years a large number of anthropologists have been studying the rapidly changing social structures within the valley.

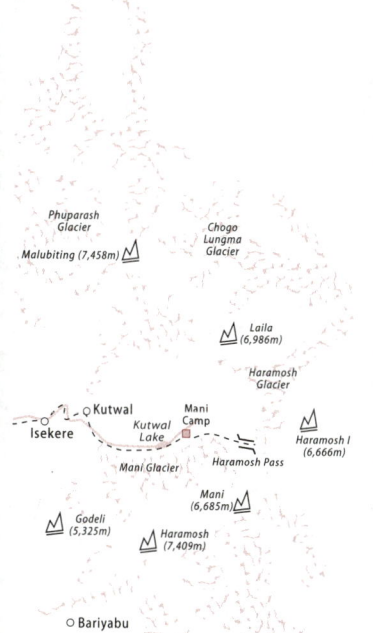

The highly cultivated entrance to the valley is usually reached from Danyore, on the KKH, although public cargo jeeps are irregular. It may be possible to take a very crowded cargo jeep (Rs50, 1400) from Garhi Bazaar in Gilgit – otherwise you will have to hire a vehicle (Rs1,400 one way, two hours, Rs1,600 round trip). **Bagrote Serai** sometimes has a jeep that transfers tourists from Gilgit (contact via the **Madina Hotel**). All food supplies should be purchased in Gilgit before setting out for the valley. This whole area around the sprawling settlement of **Oshikandas** was bare mountain in the early 1960s, the current highly cultivated environment being a testament to the skill of the many Ismailis from Hunza who came to settle here.

The first few kilometres of the valley are rocky and barren, as the jeep track winds its way through the lateral moraine, but after **Sinakkar** this soon gives way to intensively cultivated agricultural land. The jeep track runs as far as **Chirah**.

Beyond Chirah there are walks up to the summer pastures, and a demanding trek across the Burche Glacier into the Haramosh Valley (see below). Those looking for a simple afternoon's stroll should head up the valley from **Bagrot Serai**. After 30 minutes the path passes some weighing scales. Just beyond is the river where, in winter, the

Bagrotis cut the ice into blocks for sale in Gilgit and around (hence the scales). It's sold at Rs1 per kg locally, but costs Rs4 per kg by the time it reaches Gilgit. The path climbs up the hillside, heading up the valley, revealing a face of Diran (7,257 m) that looks very different to the perfect pyramid shape that it reveals to those viewing it from the KKH. As the path rounds the bend that leads into the Haramosh Valley, Diran is now obscured by foothills, although Rakaposhi (7,788 m) appears to the left (west) and Phuparash (6,574 m) to the right (east).

The path continues through a livestock gate, and then presents walkers with several options. Those trekking into the Haramosh Valley via the Rakhan Gali (Pass) bear east towards the distant settlements of Sat and Dar (see details below). Those undertaking the Diran Base Camp trek should cross the river and continue north along the east side of the Hinarche Glacier (see below). Those just undertaking a short walk can go part of the way along either route.

Treks in the Bagrot and Haramosh Valleys

Diran Base Camp
ⓘ *Open zone. Maximum elevation circa 4,000 m. Jun to Sep. Maps: Swiss Foundation good; U502 series, NI 43-2 Gilgit and NJ 43-14 Baltit are adequate. Read trekking notes, p 45.*

This is a fairly straightforward short trek, although a local guide should be employed to take you across the Bagrot Glacier. It provides some wonderful views of the less commonly seen faces of Rakaposhi and Diran. Note that Diran Base Camp is referred to locally as **Hinarche Harai**. Perhaps the only drawback to this trek is that the best campsite (**Biyabari**, just below Diran settlement) after leaving the trailhead at **Chirah** is only a two- to three-hour walk, making the first day very short and the second very long. The second day involves an unrewarding walk (seven to eight hours) along the east side of the **Hinarche Glacier**. Once across the glacier it is a further one and a half hours to **Diran Base Camp** (Hinarche Harai). Return by the same route. **NB** The route via the west side of the Hinarche Glacier (via Yurban) is heavily crevassed at the north end.

Bagrot Valley to Haramosh Valley
ⓘ *Open zone. Maximum elevation 4,548 m. Jun to Sep. Maps: Swiss Foundation good; U502 series, NI 43-2 Gilgit and NJ 43-14 Baltit are adequate. Read trekking notes, p 45.*

This little attempted trek provides a route from the Bagrot Valley to the Haramosh Valley via the **Rakhan Gali (Pass)**, and is usually attempted from west-east. A guide is essential (Mirza Baig at Gilgit's **Madina Hotel** comes highly recommended here). Note that upon crossing the pass, large parties will have to change porters.

The first day involves climbing gradually along the lower east side of the Hinarche Glacier from **Chirah**, before bearing east along the north side of the Burche Valley. Beyond **Dar** (three hours) the trail continues along the **Burche Glacier**. After 2 km the trail divides. Following the branch to the right (heading southeast), it takes two tricky hours to reach the shepherd's hut at **Gargoh**. There is good camping here. The second day involves a short but steep climb up to the camp site at **Agurtsab Dar**. The third day is the most arduous of the trek. It's a three-hour slog over the scree up to the **Rakhan Gali (Pass)** (4,548 m), and then a very steep three-hour drop down to **Ber**. The best camping is a further hour or so down the valley at **Darchan**. The final day is a fairly unrewarding seven-hour hike via **Khaltaro** down to **Hanuchal** on the Gilgit-Skardu road. Buses running between Gilgit and Skardu provide onward transport, although there's no guarantee that seats will be available.

Kutwal Lake and Mani Camp

ⓘ *Open zone. Maximum elevation optional (3,260-4,800 m). Jun to Sep. Maps: Swiss Foundation good; U502 series, NI 43-2 Gilgit and NJ 43-14 Baltit are adequate. Read trekking notes, p 45.*

It is essential that potential visitors seek reliable local advice before visiting this area, and employing a reliable local guide seems particularly wise (Mirza Baig at Gilgit's **Madina Hotel** comes highly recommended here).

The trailhead is just beyond **Sassi** on the Gilgit-Skardu road, and can be reached by taking one of the buses running between these towns. This trek can also be tagged on to the end of the Bagrot Valley to Haramosh Valley trek above. From the bridge on the main Gilgit-Skardu road, head north along the east side of the Phuparash River as far as **Dassu**. On the second day continue north from Dassu (the climb is quite steep), then bear east towards **Isekere**, where there is some good camping. On the third day, cross the river above Isekere and follow the winding trail to the summer pastures at **Kutwal**. There are several options beyond Kutwal. Those with time to spare can camp at both **Kutwal Lake** (3,260 m) and **Mani Camp**, both along the north side of the Mani Glacier. The very experienced (and well prepared) can continue across the difficult 4,800-m **Haramosh La (Pass)** onto **Laila Camp** and the **Chogo Lungma Glacier** (although this route is usually attempted from Baltistan). Otherwise, follow the same route back to the trailhead at Sassi.

> ❗ *Before considering this trek, you should bear in mind that 2 Americans were shot while camping at Mani Camp in the upper reaches of the Haramosh Valley in mid-1998; 1 of them subsequently died.*

Sleeping

Gilgit *p208, maps p211 and 213*

Although lacking a truly international-class 5-star hotel, Gilgit has arguably Pakistan's best range of accommodation options. It is particularly strong in the B-D categories, while for those travelling in a south to north direction along the KKH it is probably the first place where the budget hotels are actually run with backpackers in mind. Some excellent discounts can be negotiated, especially in the middle price brackets. Most budget places haven't raised prices for years, so are in no real position to discount room prices. Those seeking long-term accommodation may like to contact Abdul Qayam at **Xama Stores** (near Park Hotel), who rents out a beautiful house (with swimming pool) up in Jutial.

NB Gilgit is the only place where you can officially make bookings for the **NAPWD Inspection Bungalows** in the surrounding area. In some of the more remote areas, particularly to the west between Gilgit and Chitral, this is the only accommodation available. Tourists take the lowest priority behind visiting dignitaries and NAPWD employees, and your booking can be cancelled without notice if someone higher in the pecking order turns up unannounced.

If you do not have a booking (very likely if coming from Chitral side), you will generally be able to use the resthouse if it is unoccupied. Villages that have Inspection Bungalows, but limited alternative accommodation include Babusar, Imit, Gahkuch, Gupis, Yasin, Darkot, Phandur, Singal and Gulapur. Those in particularly choice locations, eg Naltar, seem permanently full. Bookings should be made through Administrative Officer (Mr Aktar Hussain), Office of Chief Engineer, NAPWD, Khazana Rd, T05811 3375. Fees are generally Rs200 for a double room, Rs300 for a VIP room, and the receipt must be given to the chowkidar at the bungalow. Bedding is provided and the chowkidars are usually able to arrange basic meals, but it is certainly worth taking your own supplements.

A-B Rupal Inn, Khomer Chowk, T05811-55161, sales@rupalinn.com. Huge, multi-storey place but without any great feel of luxury, de luxe (A) rooms large, well furnished, dish TV, attached tiled bath and scrappy shared balconies (not suitable for children), standard rooms (B) over furnished, all have good modern showers but none have a/c and the fans are puny, large restaurant, bookshop.

A-B Serena Lodge, Jutial, T05811-55894/9. Comfortable rooms but small and hot in summer, private terrace, heating, dish TV, phone, room service, Dumani restaurant is highly recommended for good-value buffets, Jutial coffee lounge, tennis, foreign exchange.

B-C PTDC Chinnar Inn, Babar Rd, T05811-54262, F05811-52650. 44 rooms, de luxe rooms (B) bigger with newer furniture, all with dish TV, fans, attached hot bath (own generator), quiet location, nice garden, useless tourist info office, reasonable value.

B-C Riveria, River View Rd, T/F05811-4184. 13 good-quality rooms with 8 more planned, 24-hr hot water (own generator), dish TV, overland companies often camp in the extensive gardens, very good restaurant, BBQ in garden, well run. Recommended.

C-E Mir's Lodge, Link Rd, T05811-2875, mirlodge@glt.comsats.net.pk. Little difference (except more furniture) between de luxe(C), standard(D) and budget (E) rooms, dish TV, 24-hr hot water, restaurant recommended but better deals around.

C-E Palace, Madina Market, Cinema Bazzar, T05811-2266. Not that old but a little tatty, standard rooms (E) overfilled with furniture, de luxe rooms (C) large with air cooler, dish TV, phone, large bath, 24-hr hot water (own generator), some family rooms (D), panoramic rooftop 24-hr restaurant, reasonable value if it gets spruced up a bit.

D Canopy Club, River View Rd. Series of wooden cottages under construction right on the river bank, see the Palace Midway House in Besham for details (same owner).

D City Gate, Airport Chowk. At the time of going to press hotel had been built, but was yet to open. It may also be named 'Royal' or 'Jamial'.

D Gilgit Continental, River View Rd, T05811-3569, continentalgilgit@yahoo.com. Recently opened, experienced owner (very friendly), pretty good-value large rooms, some with river views, carpeted, dish TV, modern tiled bath, rooftop BBQ (Rs270 buffet), panoramic restaurant, not a deal.

D-E Panorama, Jutial, T05811-55715. Simple rooms with air cooler, attached bath, panoramic restaurant (a/c), rooftop BBQ, but rather overpriced.

D-E Park, Airport Rd, T05811-2379, F05811-3796. Increased competition has forced rate cuts here. 26 standard rooms (E), 20 de luxe rooms (D), all with air cooler, dish TV, tiled bath, plus 4 suites (C), à la carte restaurant downstairs with group buffet (dinner Rs265) upstairs, reasonable value despite rather noisy generator.

D-F Gilgit Gateway, Khomer Chowk, off Jutial Rd, T05811-55014. Built for a tourist boom that never came, very tatty, poor value. Doubles downstairs, with damp walls; dusty rooms on upper floors.

E Hunza Tourist House, Babar Rd, T05811-52338. 16 rooms set around a nice garden, fan, heated in winter, 24-hr hot water, good restaurant. Recommended, if the price is right. Used to be popular with NGO staff, now rather frayed and they stay elsewhere.

E Yunas, Shahrah-e-Resham, Cantt, Jutial. 7 km from town centre, close to bus station, large carpeted rooms, dish TV, restaurant.

E-F Hunza Inn, Babar Rd, T05811-3814. Nice 'luxury' rooms (E) with attached hot bath, reasonable-value simple rooms, quiet location, restaurant.

E-G Tourist Hamlet, Jutial Rd, T05811-55538. Several dusty 'VIP' doubles (E) with sitting room, some standard rooms (F) with attached 24 hr hot bath, plus some basic rooms (G) with attached bath, large garden (pitch your own tent, H) with nala-water swimming pool (cold), restaurant, bit run down but reasonable value.

F Haji Ramzan, NLI Chowk. New 'skyscraper', double rooms with attached bath, fan, popular restaurant on ground floor. Mainly used by Pakistanis.

F North Inn, Khomer Chowk, Jutial Rd, T05811-55118. Old rooms downstairs are rather dark and run down, those upstairs much better, good restaurant, garden.

F Taj, Madina Market, Cinema Bazaar, T05811-53716. Fairly basic (but cheap) doubles with choice of attached western or squat WC, some triples and quads, plus a restaurant.

G Garden, District Hospital Rd, T05811-52898. Formerly the New Lahore, 12 dusty, basic rooms with attached run-down bathrooms, saving grace is the tatty but tranquil garden with its running water, shady fruit trees and colony of ducks.

G Golden Peak Inn, Khazana Rd, T05811-3519. Former summer residence of Mir of Nagar, 2 doubles with attached bath in old building, 4 doubles with en suite in

new block, plus 2 cool 5-bed dorms (H) in the old building, nice garden, restaurant.
G Ibex Lodge, NLI Plaza, T05811-52334. Formerly the NLI barracks, rather run-down doubles and triples, some en suite some shared bath, rooms are either windowless and dark or have too many windows and no privacy, popular restaurant, internet café.
G JSR, JSR Plaza, Airport Rd, T05811-2308. Cheap doubles with attached bath, rooms with dirty shared bath Rs50 cheaper, some triples and quads (F). Rather worn out.
G Skyways, Skyways Plaza, Airport Rd, T05811-3026. Above a very noisy bazaar, popular with Pakistanis, double rooms with attached bath, fan.
G-H Horizon Guest House, Khomer, Jutial Rd, T05811-55516, bari@glt.comsats.net.pk.Used to be Tourist Cottages,10 good-value rooms that remain cool in summer, some attached some shared bath, cheap dorm (H), a little run down but has character, nice garden, recommended Lost Horizon Treks & Tours based here.
G-H Madina, NLI Chowk, T05811-52457/3536. Pakistan's most popular backpacker hangout, and for good reason. Very good-value carpeted triples, doubles and singles with attached bath, cheaper rooms with shared bath, 4-bed dorm (H), or pitch your own tent (H). Some cheaper rooms at the 'old block'. Rooms, bathrooms and bed linen all very clean, hot water available mornings and evenings (electricity permitting). Communal sitting area where a very good meal is served at 2000 each evening (Rs90, very cheap à la carte menu throughout the day), several shaded sitting areas scattered throughout the garden. Highly recommended.
G-H Mountain Refuge, Babar Rd. A really nice place, set in the tranquil 'Sufi Garden', run by the experienced and entertaining Ibrahim Baig, has a real family atmosphere, 7 simple doubles with attached bath, some even cheaper rooms with shared bath, 4-bed dorm (H) or sleep on the verandah or pitch your own tent (H), restaurant (set meal Rs80), kitchen, popular with cyclists, trekkers and those after some peace and quiet. Recommended.
G-H New Tourist Cottage, Chinnar Bagh Rd, T05811-54255, newtouristcottage@ hotmail.com. Japanese owner Keiko has been running a 'home-from-home' for her compatriots for many years now (other nationalities made very welcome), very cheap doubles and singles, some shared some attached bath, dorm (H), Japanese set dinner (Rs150, book by 1600, not Sun), tempura/teriyaki/nan-ban set meals Rs200, jeeps/guides/trekking can be arranged (Astor Valley a speciality). Highly recommended.

There are also many G-H hotels that are rarely used by foreigners, including: **Alflah, Al Imran/Ejaz, Diamar, Gilgit-Chitral Tourist Inn, Hunza, Inaam, Kashgar Inn, Rama, Tajikistan Inn, Top Moon, Varshi Goom.**

Naltar Valley *p215*
Naltar
F Pasban Inn. Large rooms with attached bath, restaurant with a good menu, dish TV.
F Prince. A couple of triples, with separate open-air toilet, restaurant and garden.
G Hilltop. Has a 4-bed dorm and a 3-bed dorm, both with attached bath, restaurant and walnut garden.

Naltar Lake
It is quite possible to camp at this idyllic spot, or to use the tents provided by the
H Lake View Hotel, or **Red Stone Huts**. Both also serve food.

Bagrot and Haramosh Valleys *p219*
Chirah
E Bagrote Serai, which has 2 wooden cottages (you see the sunrise/sunset on Rakaposhi from 1 cottage, but it obscures the mountain view from the other!). There is a separate hot shower/toilet block. It is also possible to camp here (H) or hire a tent (G, mattress and blankets included). The owner is friendly, but bargain hard. He also has a good restaurant.

Eating

Gilgit *p208, maps p211 and 213*
All the hotels have their own restaurants, and there are a few where the food is a cut above the rest. Other noteworthy hotel restaurants include the ♥♥ **Riveria**, ♥♥ **Park Hotel**, ♥♥ **Mir's Lodge**, ♥ **North Inn**, and ♥♥ **PTDC Chinnar Inn**. The buffet at the ♥♥♥♥ **Serena Lodge** (especially the 'specials' on Sunday) is good for a treat (Rs350). Hygiene

is a concern in some of Gilgit's restaurants, so make sure what you order is properly cooked and served straight off the hot plate. Vegetarians will find little succour outside the backpacker hotel communal dinners.

New Tourist Cottage, Chinnar Bagh Rd, T05811-54255, has a Japanese set menu for Rs150 (book by 1600), and a cheap à la carte menu during the day.

Haidry Tea Shop off Rajah Bazaar. You may read elsewhere that this place serves the best cup of chai in town; Footprint, and many Gilgit residents, disagree. An unnamed place on Cinema Bazaar, diagonally opposite the National Music Centre, holds this honour. The unsmiling owner is said to never forget a face, and will reproduce your favourite blend without asking. At one time he used to have an old wind-up gramaphone and stack of 78s, and was also able to recall each customer's favourite tune; as you walked in the door, he'd fix your brew and pop your preferred disc on the turntable!

Haji Ramzan, Airport Rd. Recently supplanted the Pathan Hotel (see below) as the place to feast on grilled and braised meat thanks to excellent chicken karahi (Rs200 for 2), chapli kebabs etc, but in a slightly cleaner environment.

Madina, NLI Chowk, T05811-52457, offers an excellent-value and very sociable communal meal served at 2000 (Rs90, rice, chapatis, 3-4 veg and meat dishes, custard, tea), non-guests should book by 1600 if possible. Cheap à la carte menu during the day (eat well for under Rs50).

Pathan Hotel, Airport Rd. For many years Gilgit's meat/chicken and chapati eating male population gathered in numbers here, although some connoisseurs suggested that the standard was never quite the same following the death of the head chef in the sectarian gun battles of 1993.

Festivals and events

Gilgit *p208, maps p211 and 213*
Jul-Sep The recently established **Silk Route Festival** has a rolling programme of events across the region Jul-Sep. It generally involves polo matches, cultural shows, artisans at work, a trade fair, plus food fairs. Advance notice of the programme can be obtained from its organizer, Uxi Mufti (nmufti@apollo.net.pk).

For details of **polo** matches that accompany **Independence Day** (14 Aug) and the **Gilgit Uprising** (1 Nov), see under sights above. During the annual **Ashoura** procession during the month of **Muharram**, foreigners are usually confined to their hotels (go to Ganesh if you want to witness it). Likewise, the end of **Ramadan** also experiences sectarian tensions, so avoid Gilgit then.

Shopping

Gilgit *p208, maps p211 and 213*
Bookshops
GM Beg's, Jamat Khana Bazaar, T05811-2409, F05811-3695. Formerly the best bookshop in the Northern Areas, but now eclipsed by those in Karimabad.
International Book House, Jamat Khana Bazaar, has a small selection.

Clothing
If arriving from China, Gilgit is usually the first place where you can buy a shalwar kameez (a very sensible investment). They are available made-to-measure or off-the-peg from numerous places in Saddar and Rajah Bazaar.

Handicrafts, gemstones, carpets and jewellery
There are now numerous shops in Gilgit selling 'handicrafts', much of which is mass produced outside the region. As ever, it's a matter of deciding if you really want something, and what price you're prepared to pay. Most of the places are around Hunza Chowk, JSR Plaza and Madina Market.
Xama Stores, Airport Rd, near Park Hotel. One of Gilgit's longest established handicraft emporiums, trustworthy owner has gems, carpets, old flintlocks muskets, and many other items.

Maps
Best to bring them from home. **GM Beg's** has a small selection.

Music
National Music Centre, Cinema Bazaar. More than just a shop selling tapes of local music, this is also a repository for the region's musical heritage. Those interested in local music should talk with Karim Mutrib at the

Madina Hotel, or alternatively look at www.monoreality.org.

Photography

If possible, bring supplies from home (and get films processed there as well). The most reliable, or least unreliable, place is the new shop with the 'Kodak' sign at NLI Chowk. Most film sold in Gilgit is poorly stored. The only slide film you can generally find is a very reddish Konica effort (Rs300; you may get Fuji Sensia in Karimabad, but the Fuji HQ in Rawalpindi has the best stocks).

Toofan Photo Studios in Rajah Bazzar has an interesting window display dedicated to the region's unfortunates.

Supermarkets

There are several places around town, including **Kashmir Hazara Bakery** and **Madina Supermarket**, both on Airport Rd, that sell a few imported items alongside the locally produced biscuits, jam, chocolate, and other trekking necessities.

Trekking gear

Gown House and **Long Life Mountaineering Equipments**, both on Airport Rd, have an eclectic collection of equipment left behind by expeditions and trekkers, which can be bought or rented (Gown House is better). Sleeping bags (Rs50-100 per day), tents (Rs100-200 per day), sleeping mats (Rs20-30 per day), plus waterproofs, boots, packs, cooking gas. It usually works out cheaper to buy the stuff then sell it back later than it does to rent (rental deposit is the selling price). Check the gear before you take it away (eg make sure tents have the right poles). Mirza Baig at the Madina Hotel also has some gear (including some specially designed tents manufactured in Lahore).

▲ Activities and tours

Gilgit *p208, maps p211 and 213*
Fishing

Licences should be obtained from the Fisheries Office, Napur Rd, T05811-2374 (Rs100 per day). They have some gear for rent here, or you could try the **Famous Fishing Tackle Shop** on Khazana Rd.

Horseriding

Probably the best tour agency through which to organize this is **Walk & Ride**, see under Tour operators.

Whitewater rafting

The only company in Gilgit really set up to offer this is **Walji's** (Adventure Pakistan), who have limited opportunities between 1 Mar-end May and 15 Sep-end Oct. Most trips require min 4 and max 8 persons. Half-day (Rs1,200 per person), 1-day (Rs1,600 pp) and 2-7 day (Rs1,500 pp per day) trips can be arranged on the Hunza River (Sust-Khaibar) and Gilgit/Ghizr River (around Phandur and Singal-Gilgit).

Tour operators

Adventure Center Pakistan, Jamat Khana Bazaar (at GM Beg's Bookshop), T05811-2409, ikram@ acp-glt.sdnpk.undp.org. Run by the experienced and efficient Ikram M Beg. Recommended.
Fairy Meadow Tours, Link Rd, T05811-4126, fmtours@glt.comsats.net.pk. Owners of Raikot Serai at Fairy Meadows (can book here), also offer full range of other services.
Gilgit Travel Consultants, Airport Rd, T05811-58050, www.geocities.com/ gtcs2001. Owner Hidayat Hussain is extremely experienced in the travel industry, offers trekking and mountaineering possibilities.
Himalayan Nature Tours, Chinnar Bagh Link Rd, T05811-2946/55359, F05811-55900. Treks, tours, guided expeditions.
Mountain Movers, Airport Rd, T05811-2967. Long established, have a long list of suggested tours (6 days Rupal Base Camp US$530 for 1 person, 4 days Fairy Meadows US$200 for 1 person, 4 days Rakaposhi Base Camp US$200 for 1 person; prices come down for larger groups).
Pakistan Adventure Heights, c/o New Tourist Cottage, akhtarhussain60@ hotmail.com. Good for visiting Astor Valley.
Paradise Tours, opposite Park Hotel, Airport Rd, T05811-2292, paradise@glt.comsats. net.pk. Recently established, friendly and professionally run.
Travel Adventure Pakistan, Airport Rd, T/F05811-4290, top1glt@hotmail.com. Full range of treks and tours.

Walji's (Adventure Pakistan), Airport Rd, T05811-2665, waljis@comsats.net.pk. Probably the best and most reliable, prices a little high but service good and reliable.
Walk & Ride, Airport Rd, T05811-52205/53171, www.walkandridepakistan.com. One of the best-run small agencies in Gilgit (joint Hunza-Italian run), specializes in horse/yak trekking (especially in the Chapursan Valley, or between Gilgit and Chitral), can also arrange all other tourist requirements, very friendly. Recommended. Budget travellers (and others) may care to employ one of the highly recommended guides, Altaf Hussain, Karim Mutrib, Nasir Ahmad and Mirza 'Chillim' Baig, who operate out of the Madina Hotel (each has an area of speciality).

Transport

Gilgit *p208, maps p211 and 213*
Air
There are 3 daily flights to **Islamabad** (2 on Sun and Thu) at 0700, 0745 and 1000 (earlier ones are the most reliable), with the tourist fare being Rs2,800 1 way (this increases by about Rs150 per year). **PIA**, JSR Plaza, Airport Rd, T05811-3390. Open daily 0800-1500.

Bus
There are numerous bus companies serving a variety of destinations. Other than the depart-when-full services, it is best to book your ticket at least a day in advance. Unless otherwise stated, buses depart from the bus station in Jutial.

Astor: 3 minibuses daily (Rs110, 4 hrs, 0800, 0900, 1000) plus some long wheelbase landcruisers from the Diamar Hotel on Link Road and Rama Hotel on Airport Road (book the night before).

Besham: For **NATCO** services see under Rawalpindi (Rs235, 9-11 hrs). There are sometimes 'depart when full' minibuses from the Jutial bus station.

Chalt: There is a daily minibus at around 0900 (Rs40, 1½ hrs). The Sust-bound **NATCO** bus (0700) passes the turning for the Chalt bridge (Rs40, 1½ hrs).

Chilas: For **NATCO** services see under Rawalpindi (Rs100, 3½-4 hrs). There are also 'depart when full' minibuses (Rs75, 3½-4 hrs).

Chitral: New weekly non-stop 12-seater landcruiser service from the **NATCO** yard off Punial Rd (Rs600, 12+ hrs , Sat 0800, they sometimes run twice a week if the demand is there).

Ganesh (for Karimabad): The Sust-bound **NATCO** bus (0700) also stops at Ganesh (Rs60, 3 hrs).

Gahkuch: 2 daily buses run to Gahkuch from the **NATCO** yard off Punial Rd (Rs50, 2-3 hrs , 0800, 0930).

Gupis: 2 daily buses go to Gupis from the **NATCO** yard off Punial Rd (Rs75, 5-6 hrs, 0800, 0930).

Hoper: Daily minibus goes to Hoper at around 1000 (Rs80, 3½ hrs).

Karimabad: Hunza-Gojal Transport have minibuses that depart when full (Rs60, 3 hrs). See also under Ganesh, above.

Minapin: Daily minibus at 1400 (Rs60, 1½-2 hrs). See also under Pisin below.

Nagar ('proper'): Daily minibus at around 0900 (Rs70, 2½ hrs), and sometimes an afternoon service too.

Naltar: See under 'jeep hire' above.

Passu: The Sust-bound **NATCO** bus (0700) stops at Passu (Rs85, 4½ hrs). **Taus Transport** minibuses en route to Sust (see below) also stop here.

Pisin (for **Minapin**): The Sust-bound **NATCO** bus (0700) stops at Pisin (Rs55, 2½ hrs), from where you walk to Minapin.

Raikot Bridge (Fairy Meadows): Take a Chilas-bound minibus (Rs55, 3½ hrs). For **NATCO** services see under Rawalpindi (Rs55, 3½ hrs).

Rawalpindi (Pir Wadhai): An a/c de luxe or de luxe is the most comfortable option on this route. **NATCO** has recently had to upgrade its fleet (to meet the competition), but it still has the steadiest drivers. It has 8 daily vehicles to Rawalpindi (0900, coaster, Rs510; 1100 and 1300, 'deluxe', Rs510; 1500 and 1600, 'a/c deluxe', Rs560; 1700, 1900, 2100, 'deluxe', Rs510; all take 15-17 hrs). **Silk Route**, Colonel Hassan Market, T05811-55234, undoubtedly has the most comfortable buses, but a series of crashes soon after setting up business and stories of hair-raisingly terrifying rides makes it hard to recommend this company. It runs 2 buses daily (Rs560, 14-16 hrs, 1530, 1730). **Hameed Travels**, JSR Plaza, runs 3 coasters daily (Rs450, 14-16 hrs, 0800, 1500, 1700).

Sargin Travels, JSR Plaza, runs 3 coasters daily (Rs500, 14-16 hrs, 0600, 1600, 1800). **Mashabrum Tours**, Cinema Bazaar, has 5 services daily ('big buses' at 1200, 1400, 1800, 2000, Rs500; a/c bus at 1600, Rs560). All leave from the Jutial bus station.

Skardu: A 'big bus' or coaster is the most comfortable on this route. **NATCO** has 3 services daily ('big bus' at 0600, special ½ price at Rs75; coasters at 0800 and 1300, Rs150; all 7 hrs). **Mashabrum Tours** runs 3 daily minibuses (Rs150, 6 hrs, 0800, 1000, 1300). **K2 Travels Service** has 4 daily minibuses (Rs150, 6 hrs, 0700, 0900, 1100, 1300). All leave from the Jutial bus station.

Sust: NATCO has 1 service daily ('big bus', Rs105, 6 hrs, 0730), via Pisin, Ganesh, Gulmit and Passu. **Taus Transport** has minibuses that depart when full (mornings are best) for Sust (Rs100, 5 hrs); these buses stop en route at destinations in Gojal. All leave from the Jutial bus station.

Yasin: 1 daily bus from the **NATCO** yard off Punial Rd (Rs95, 7-8 hrs, 0800).

Jeeps/Car hire

There are a number of destinations around Gilgit (usually trekking trailheads) where hiring a jeep is the simplest option for getting there. A privately hired jeep is an extremely pleasant way to travel, offering great flexibility. Hire charges for certain routes are more or less fixed, although you may get a slightly cheaper deal by going through a hotel manager at a backpacker hotel. You'll probably get a more reliable vehicle (and steady driver) by going through one of the reputable travel agencies. Official jeep hire rates are around Rs350 per day (plus Rs350 for overnight), and Rs8-10 per km. Effectively, certain 'fixed rates' to specific destinations have evolved over time. Diesel and vehicle maintenance costs have rocketed in recent years, but because there are so many jeeps chasing so little work, hire charges have remained static for some time.

Bagrot/Haramosh Valleys: For cargo jeeps ask the shopkeepers near Garhi Bagh (usually 1 per day at 1400, Rs50). A day return trip to Chirah (Bagrot Valley) costs around Rs1,600 (Rs1,400 1 way, 2 hrs).

Chitral and Mastuj: Although jeep hire prices have recently increased, it's still possible to hire a jeep for this trip for Rs9,000 1 way (3 days/2 nights), or Rs7,500 to Mastuj. You can find a jeep through a travel agent or, more likely, through your hotel manager. If you got to Chitral with a company like **Walji's**, you're looking at Rs11,000 (2 days/1 night) to Rs12,000 (3 days/2 nights), or Rs9,200 to Mastuj (2 days/1 night). For more details, see page 148.

Ishkoman: Cargo jeeps and long wheelbase landcruisers depart according to demand (book the night before) from the yard beneath the Gilgit-Chitral Tourist Inn just off the Punial Link Rd (Rs3,000 per vehicle, or Rs120 per person).

Karimabad: A private jeep will cost around Rs2,000 1 way, or Rs2,800 same day return.

Khunjerab Pass: A 1 way drop costs Rs5,800, or Rs6,300 for a 2 day/1 night return trip.

Naltar: Cargo jeeps to Lower Naltar run from the 'Jaglot Bus Stand' ('Jaglot adda') on Domyal Link Road (Rs75), although some continue to Upper Naltar (another Rs75). There is a least 1 daily (around 1400). A privately hired jeep to Upper Naltar will cost arond Rs1,300 (or Rs1,700 same day return). You may get a same day return jeep to Naltar Lake for Rs3,000.

Raikot Bridge (Fairy Meadows): Rs1,000 1 way to the bridge (but then you must change transport).

Rawalpindi: About Rs11,000 1 way (this will probably be a car, rather than a jeep).

Naltar *p215*

Naltar's cargo jeep drivers have a well-deserved poor reputation, and are keen to fleece visiting tourists. You may be asked to pay for a 'special booking' only to find another 16 passengers sharing your jeep. If travelling from Gilgit, it is essential to establish whether the fare is to Lower or Upper Naltar. The fare from Gilgit to Lower Naltar is Rs75, and you may be asked for the same again to continue to Upper Naltar.

Cargo jeeps leave from the Jaglot Bus Stand on Gilgit's Link Rd. A private jeep from Gilgit to Upper Naltar costs Rs1,300 1 way, Rs1,700 same day return. Return jeeps leave Upper Naltar early in the morning.

ⓘ Directory

Gilgit *p208, maps p211 and 213*

Banks Foreign exchange rates in Gilgit are marginally inferior to those available in Rawalpindi/Islamabad, but better than those offered further north along the KKH. The nearest places for official credit card advances are Rawalpindi/Islamabad and Kashgar. Some local handicraft shops will offer an 'unofficial' advance on credit cards, but there are lots of stories about fraudulent debits being made. **Alam Money Changer**, JSR Plaza, T05811-4148, and a branch next to the post office, offers the best rates on cash and TCs, and the quickest service. Most hotel managers will also change cash (and maybe TCs). **Allied Bank** and **Soneri Bank** near the post office offer foreign exchange facilities. **Chemists** Opposite the hospitals and at various places in Cinema Bazaar. **Hospitals District Hospital**, District Hospital Rd, extreme cases are often flown out to Islamabad. Women should go to the **Women's Hospital** opposite, where they should ask to see a female doctor. Certain cases will, however, be referred to a (male) specialist at the District Hospital. **Internet** Internet access remains frustrating (and Gilgit is currently the only place online between Rawalpindi/Islamabad and Kashgar). Slow machines (it can take 20 mins to reach your inbox) and the risk of power cuts makes it unreliable. The most reliable place is at the office of the ISP, **Comsats**, (Rs90 per hr, 5 terminals, claims to stay open 24/7, battery back-up) up in Jutial (take a wagon, it's 50 m past the Indian helicopter). **Compulink**, Cinema Bazaar. 4 slow terminals, Rs75 per hr. **Cyber Net Internet Café**, Yadgar Chowk, 6 slow terminals and unreliable power (Rs65 per hr, daily 0800-2300). **Future Communications**, Madina Market (under Palace Hotel). **Ibex Lodge**, NLI Chowk, has 5 terminals (Rs60 per hr). **Libraries Gilgit Municipal Library**, Upper Khazana (Bank) Rd (Mon-Thu and Sun 0900-1500, Fri 0800-1200). Has an excellent range (borrowers welcome for a small deposit), particularly strong on local history. Sherbaz Ali Khan who runs the library is extremely helpful. **Police**, T05811-4007/3266, the headquarters are on the other side of Gilgit River, across Jinnah Bridges. **Post office** Saddar Bazaar (Mon-Thu and Sat 0800-1500, Fri 0800-1200). Go to the 'poste restante' office round the back to get all stamps franked. Gilgit to London takes 7-10 days, slightly quicker in the opposite direction. For poste restante take the little alley up the side of the building, and enter through the last door round the corner on the left. Mail is kept in a small basket and you are free to browse. Notes addressed to 'Poste Restante-Gilgit' saying "please forward all my mail to ..." end up filed in the basket with all your mail! Avoid at all costs sending parcels from Gilgit (read the warning poster on the wall at the Madina Hotel). **Telephone** Even as the digital exchange comes online, making calls from Gilgit remains problematic (cheap rates on Sun and after 1800 weekdays make these bad times to attempt international calls). The most efficient PCO is the one on JSR Plaza (international calls Rs95/min, booths available, clear line). The army-run main **Telegraph Office** is on District Hospital Rd (open 24 hrs); calls are cheapest from here, but queues are longer. **Useful addresses** Aga Khan Rural Support Programme (AKRSP), PO Box 506, Babar Rd, T05811-2480, F05811-2779. Has an excellent 'development' library, and you may find someone who will explain the organization's role in the Northern Areas. International Union for the Conservation of Nature – Pakistan (IUCN), in the former Alpine Hotel out in Jutial (opposite Panorama Hotel). **Visa extensions** It should be possible to extend visas (including the 30-day 'landing permit') at the DC's office near Yadgar Chowk (see map), although this can only be done by the DC in person. It's a straightforward process, although you should note that although the DC is authorized to extend visas and 'landing permits' for up to 3 months (and to issue re-entry visas), it takes some gentle persuasion to obtain anything more than a 30-day extension. Open Mon-Fri 0900-1200.

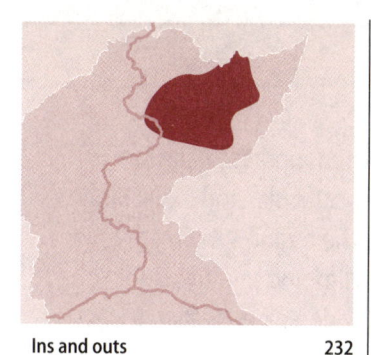

Baltistan

Ins and outs	232
Background	233
Gilgit to Skardu	234
Skardu	**235**
Around Skardu	238
Listings	239
The Deosai plateau	**244**
Deosai National Park	246
Skardu to Astor	247
Deosai plateau treks	247
Shigar River Valley	**248**
Shigar village	249
Excursions from Shigar	251
Treks in the area	252
Listings	254
Khapulu	**255**
Skardu to Khapulu	255
Khapulu	257
Listings	258
Hushe Valley	**259**
Khapulu to Hushe village	259
Treks from Hushe village	261

Footprint features...

Don't miss...	231
Organising your trek from Hushe Village	262

Introduction

At the very heart of the Karakoram mountains, Baltistan possesses a landscape that is as spectacular and exhilarating as it is forbidding and inhospitable. The region's main attractions are the opportunities it offers for climbing and trekking. You don't need to be a mountaineer or dedicated walker to appreciate the beauty of these mountains since many of the most attractive areas are easily accessible by bus or jeep, including Shigar, Khapulu, Hushe and the Deosai plateau.

Most of the treks here are fairly challenging, requiring guides and often porters and permits, but the rewards of trekking through the very heart of the extraordinary Karakoram range are immense. Indeed, some of these treks, notably those along the Baltoro Glacier to Concordia and K2 Base Camp and to Gondogoro La, rival anything else on earth. There are also a number of shorter, less challenging, treks through "open zones".

Another great Baltistan adventure is the jeep safari across the Deosai Plateau, where the stunning open landscape is complemented by floral and faunal delights. Those of a less adventurous nature will certainly still enjoy the region, with many opportunities to explore the unique culture of Balti village life, and an inspiring backdrop of great mountains.

Baltistan is not just about awesome mountain scenery; it is also home to the Balti people, whose hardy resilience is matched only by their warmth and friendliness. The history and culture of this region, stretching back to Buddhist times and earlier, is also still very much in evidence in the local architecture, language and traditions of its people.

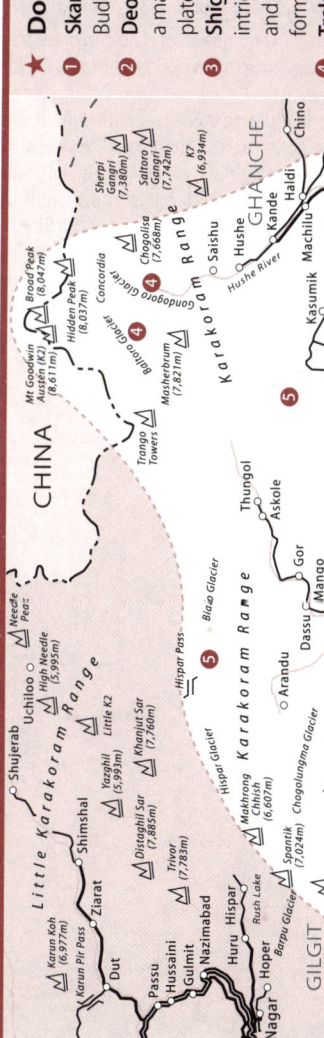

★ Don't miss...

1. **Skardu** Take a short excursions to the Sadpara Buddha carving and Sadpara Lake, page 235.
2. **Deosai Plateau** Get a sense of landscape on a massive scale on this uniquely beautiful plateau, page 244.
3. **Shigar and Khapulu** See centuries-old, intricately-carved wooden palaces, mosques and Khanquahs, lovingly restored to their former glory, pages 249 and 257.
4. **Trekking** Hike some of the best routes in the world, notably the Baltoro Glacier trek to Concordia and K2, page 252, and the Gondogoro La trek, page 260.
5. **Open zone trekking** Enjoy some other great treks, such as the Biafo-Hispar traverse, page 253, and the Thalle La trek, page 256.

Ins and outs

Best time to visit

The best time to visit is from mid-May to mid-October. The trekking season lasts from early June to late September. During summer (July-August) it gets quite hot during the day, with temperatures reaching well over 30°C, and even touching 40°C on occasion. Temperatures, however, drop considerably if there is cloud or rain. Nights are generally pleasantly cool. During winter it is bitterly cold, with temperatures drop as low as -30°C.

Land and environment

To the north, the **Karakoram** mountains dominate the region, a huge tangle of rock and ice with 12 of the 30 highest recorded peaks in the world. At its core is the **Baltoro Glacier**, covering some 1,200 sq km, and four peaks exceeding 8,000 m; **K2**, the second highest mountain in the world at 8,611 m, **Gasherbrum I** (8,068 m, also known as Hidden Peak), **Broad Peak** (8,060 m) and **Gasherbrum II** (8,035 m). There are also dozens of 7,000-m peaks and literally hundreds of 6,000-m ones, the majority unnamed. To the south is the **Deosai**, an expanse of high plateaux, all above 4,000 m.

Flowing through the middle of Baltistan and dividing these two main features is the **Indus River**. Entering the region from the south across the ceasefire line with India, it then wends northwest, at one point spreading out over a wide glacial plain around Skardu, before raging through a narrow gorge till it loops sharply south to emerge near its confluence with the **Gilgit River**. Joining it from the east is the **Shyok River**, while near Skardu the **Shigar River** flows in from the north. Although lesser in size, the latter two are of crucial importance for the opportunities for settlement which they afford.

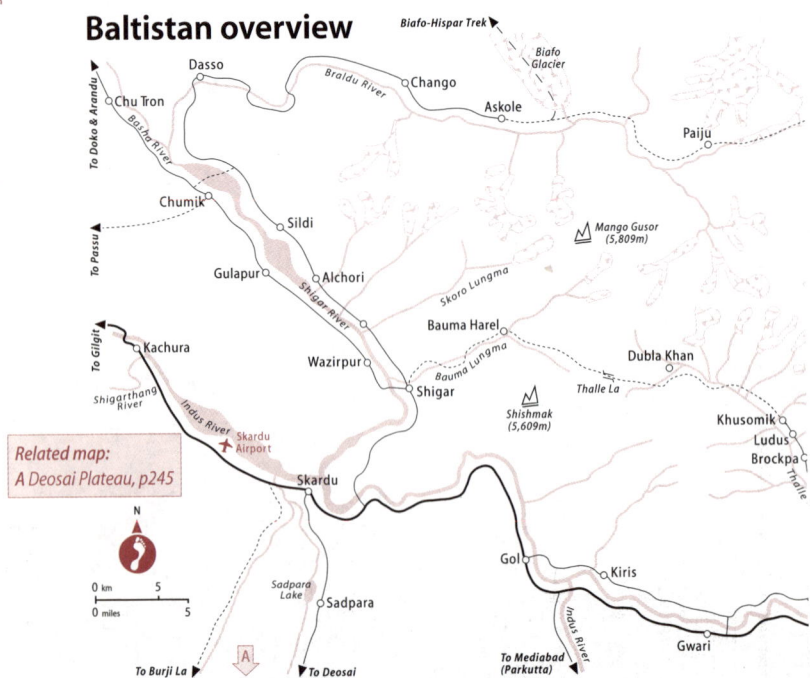

Baltistan overview

Related map: A Deosai Plateau, p245

Background

Early history

The first references to Baltistan as a distinct region date from around the 5th century. At this time it was known as **Great Bolor** in Arabic literature or **Po-lu-lo** in Chinese accounts. Buddhism had reached Baltistan some two centuries earlier, although was not firmly established until the Tibetan invasion during the 8th century AD. It wasn't until the decline of Tibetan power around the beginning of the 10th century that the region established some real degree of independence, notably with the emergence of the **Makpon** dynasty, although their origins are unclear and are variously attributed to either the White Huns, Egypt, Kashmir and the Tibetan frontier regions.

The rule of the Makpon dynasty reached its peak under **Ali Sher Khan Anchen** (1595-1633), when control was exercised over all the minor kingdoms of Baltistan. Ali Sher Khan ('Anchen' was a title that was added later, translating as 'great') also waged war with Ladakh attacked Gilgit, Chilas and Astor, and even campaigned as far as Chitral.

Close relations were established between the Mughals and the Makpon rulers in the period following Akbar's conquest of Kashmir in 1586. According to a local legend, a Mughal princess by the name of Gul Khatoon was given in marriage to Ali Sher Khan (although historical sources suggest that he married a Ladakhi princess). Whoever his wife was, she was responsible for building the aqueduct which still survives in Skardu, and for laying out a Mughal-style gardens (unfortunately these gardens are no longer remaining) fed by its waters. Ali Sher Khan's death was followed by a period of feuding which resulted ultimately in the Mughals estab- lishing suzerainty over Baltistan, but they barely interfered in the internal affairs of the region and the semi-independent kingdoms were left to fight among themselves.

The rule of **Shah Morad Khan** in Skardu (1660-80) was considered to be another golden age; fortresses and palaces were built, craftsmen brought from Kashmir and trade extended as far as Tibet and Kashgar.

Sikhs and Dogras

The Sikhs, who took power in Kashmir in the second half of the 18th century, extended their control into Ladakh by the start of the 19th century and made several attempts to capture the capital Skardu and subjugate Baltistan. This was finally achieved in 1840 by the Raja of Jammu **Gulab Singh**, a Rajput Hindu and member of the Dogra tribe. Gulab Singh forged close links with the **British**, and at the conclusion of the First Anglo-Sikh War in 1846, the British 'sold' Kashmir to him when he stumped up for the Sikh war reparations (using money he'd looted from the Sikh treasury!). Although he taxed Baltistan heavily, the indigenous rulers were allowed to remain in place, watched over only by a small force commanded by a Kardar (a kind of political agent).

Independence and Partition

At Partition, the people of Baltistan followed the lead taken in Gilgit and revolted against their Dogra rulers. While the battle was a swift one in Gilgit, in Baltistan the Dogra army resisted until 1948 before being finally driven out. It was not until January 1949 that a cease-fire was declared between India and Pakistan, with the line of control becoming the de facto border between the two countries. The line of control divided a geographically and culturally integrated area and severed an important trade route from Kashmir through Baltistan to the Punjab.

Religion, culture and society

The majority of people in Baltistan are **Shia Muslims**. According to local legend, the Shia faith was brought to Baltistan by a man named Amir Kabir Syed Ali Hamadani, who is said to have arrived in Shigar (from Iran, via Kashmir) around 1379 AD. Nearly 150 years later, a second Muslim missionary, Mir Shamsuddin Iraqi, spread the faith in Baltistan, and Buddhism finally died out.

The **Nurbakshi** faith of the people of Khapulu and Hushe is traditionally attributed to Hazrat Syed Mohammad Nur Baksh, who preached between 1438-1448. this faith is closely linked to the Shia faith, and according to some historical sources, Nur Baksh was a pious Shia whose teachings were later spread in somewhat adapted form by Mir Shamsuddin Iraqi and subsequent missionaries, giving rise to the Nurbakshi sect.

The early spread of Islam, which at the time had a strong **Sufi** element to it, originally involved a synthesis of the Muslim faith with the cultural heritage of the region. Traces of Sufism can still be seen in the old mosques of Shigar and Khapulu for example, which are known as Khanqahs or monasteries, and include special cells for meditation and prayer as well as a distinctive square chimney-like 'tower' on the roof.

However, the Shia faith as it is practised in Baltistan today is very strict and, apart from in Nurbakshi areas, one is very unlikely to see any women at all. This is a relati- vely recent phenomenon, and many observers have linked the decline in traditions of music, dance and folk literature to the revolution in Iran, the politicization of religion and the emergence of more militant sectarian groups in Pakistan as a whole.

Gilgit to Skardu

It is possible to fly into Skardu directly from Islamabad, and since the daily flights are on a 737, the flight is marginally less weather dependent than the Fokker flight to Gilgit. However, most visitors still arrive by road from Gilgit. This route is a spectacular one, following the narrow gorge of the Indus as it cuts its way through sheer rock mountains. The right side of the bus gives the best views, but is not for sufferers of vertigo.

The Skardu road leaves the KKH 38 km to the south of Gilgit, joining the Indus River at **Alam Bridge** and giving anxious travellers a worrying view of the broken and warped old bridge. There are several rock carvings and inscriptions by the turning. The route first bears northeast, giving excellent views of the Nanga Parbat massif, followed by a glimpse of Rakaposhi. After passing through the first village of **Hanuchal** (end point of the Bagrot-Haramosh trek, see page 220), the road then bends sharply southeast at **Sasli** (27 km, also known as Sassi). There are tea shops and a petrol pump (with squat toilet) here. At the bend in the river, a steep side valley enters from the north, leading up towards the north face Base Camp of **Haramosh**. From here the road enters a narrow gorge and the Indus roars past as a raging torrent.

After the small settlement of **Shangus**, a daring cable and pulley system crosses the river giving access to some improbably sited dry-stone huts on the opposite bank. These are occasionally used by small-scale gemstone miners as a base for their explorations. A little further on is another cable and pulley to the cultivated village of **Subsar** which also has the luxury of a rope suspension bridge, as does **Yulbo**, the next settlement on the left bank.

Shortly after **Gangi** (with excellent views for the mountain-lover), most buses stop for lunch at **Astakk Nala**; a convenient halfway point in the journey where the **Indus** and **Midway** hotels provide basic meals and drinks on either side of a fast-flowing tributary. There is also a **Culture and Tourism Centre** here in a new stone cabin, although what use, if any, it will be to passing visitors is unclear at the time of writing.

As the road continues, the gorge widens a little to reveal a wall of snow-capped peaks ahead. At **Tuar** (or Thowar), the largest village en route which has shops, engine workshops and some basic food and chai places, the valley widens a little further revealing large patches of cultivation. A little further on is **Rondu**, capital of the former kingdom of the same name, perched high up the steep valley side on a flat shelf across the river. Further east, at **Kachura**, the road crosses to the south bank of the Indus by means of a large suspension bridge. Foreigners must register here at the 'Tourists Facilitation Point'; the police will bring the registration book to your vehicle. From here the mountains fall back and the river spreads lazily across a wide open plain with rolling sand dunes, as it quietly delays its entrance to the raging gorge.

Just east of the bridge the road passes Kachura village where there is a sign-posted turning to **Kachura Lake** and the luxury **Shangrila Tourist Resort** (see Around Skardu, page 238). From Kachura it is a further 32 km on to Skardu, across the parched and sandy plain. The road first takes you past **Skardu Airport,** 13 km west of the main town.

Skardu → *Colour map 2,/3 grid C6*

Skardu is the administrative centre and largest town of Baltistan. Although of no great interest in itself, its setting is a dramatic one and the town provides a starting point for some of the most spectacular trekking and mountaineering that Pakistan has to offer. The town is a small, dusty place, growing rapidly along its one main street, but still utterly dwarfed by the towering amphitheatre of imposing rock mountains all around and by the broad sweep of the Indus. Dominating the town on the north side is the huge rocky outcrop of Karpochu. To the west and east are rolling sand dunes stretching out into the distance. To the south the wide stony course of the Sadpara Nullah, an irrigated oasis scattered with trees and fields, fans down from Sadpara Lake. Hidden from view by the surrounding mountains is the vast tangle of high Karakoram to the north, and the equally vast high plateaux of the Deosai to the south.

The modern town of Skardu is seen by most as a place from which to set off from and return to, rather than a destination to visit in itself. It does, however, have a certain amount of atmosphere and there are parts of it that can be well worth exploring. There are also several short half-day or one-day excursions that can be made from here, to Sadpara Lake, Sadpara Buddha and Kachura Lake. ▶▶ *For Sleeping, Eating and all other listings, see pages 239-244.*

Ins and outs

Getting there
The easiest way to get to Skardu is via the daily weather-dependent flights from Islamabad. The main land route into Baltistan is the road along the Indus River linking Skardu with the KKH. There are regular bus services between Gilgit and Skardu (a six- to seven-hour journey depending on the bus), and less regular services between Islamabad/Rawalpindi and Skardu (a gruelling 18-24-hour journey). The only other route into Baltistan is by way of a rough jeep track which follows the Astor Valley southeast from the KKH at Jaglot and climbs up over the Deosai Plateau before descending eventually to Skardu. This is a demanding two-day journey for which you should be properly acclimatized. There is no regular public transport along this route.

Getting around
There are sometimes Suzuki minivans waiting outside the airport terminal to ferry people into town for Rs10 as well as representatives from the various hotels who will take you for free provided you stay at their hotel. A shared taxi should cost Rs30-Rs50 per person depending on bargaining skills. Otherwise you will have to negotiate a fair rate for a taxi where the driver may demand an inflated rate for a whole taxi even although you have to cram yourself in with half a dozen locals. From town out to the airport it's easy to get a taxi for Rs100. During the day Suzukis ply

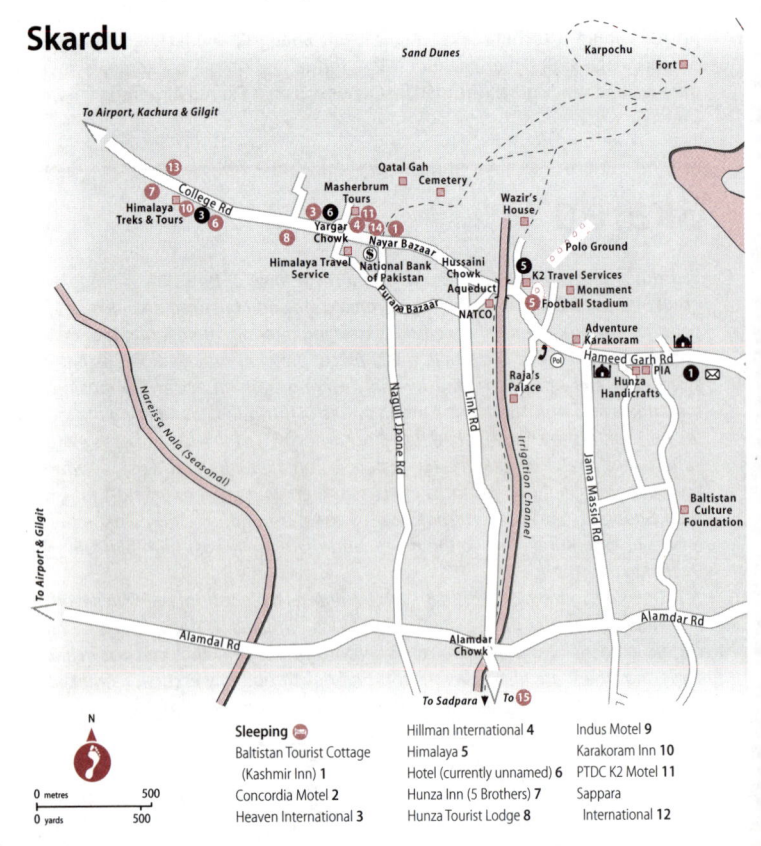

Skardu

Sleeping
Baltistan Tourist Cottage (Kashmir Inn) **1**
Concordia Motel **2**
Heaven International **3**
Hillman International **4**
Himalaya **5**
Hotel (currently unnamed) **6**
Hunza Inn (5 Brothers) **7**
Hunza Tourist Lodge **8**
Indus Motel **9**
Karakoram Inn **10**
PTDC K2 Motel **11**
Sappara International **12**

back and forth along Skardu's main street, running between Yadgar Chowk and the district hospital at the east end of town (Rs5), or there are plenty of taxis around Naya Bazaar. ▶▶ *See Transport, page 242, for more details.*

Tourist information

PTDC Tourist Information Centre ⓘ *K2 Motel, T0575-50291, F0575-50293, Mon-Thu 0800-1500, Fri 0800-1230*. Helpful staff who will point you in the right direction for organizing treks etc. They can also arrange private jeep hire (see Transport for rates).

Sights

Running in a short arc to the south of Naya Bazaar, **Purana (old) Bazaar** gives something of the flavour of the town before the arrival of jeeps and concrete, with its wooden houses and shops selling basic supplies, clothes, shoes and household goods. Local women are not permitted in either bazaar. Foreign women are tolerated, but reminded by hand-painted signs to dress respectfully.

The large **polo ground**, just east of the old aqueduct, is a lively social focal point during the summer when polo matches are held. There is usually a major tournament around Independence Day (14 August); check with PTDC for details. At other times the polo ground is host to informal cricket and football matches, while 'serious' competitive football matches are now played at the adjacent stadium below the road.

Just north of Naya Bazaar next to a sandy cemetery, **Qatal Gah** is a colourful copy of Hussain's shrine in Karbala, Iraq. It is a popular pilgrimage and meeting place (especially for women, who are banned from Skardu's *purdah* bazaar). Foreigners may enter the courtyard if dressed respectfully. It is the focus of the self-flagellating Ashoura procession in the month of Muharram, when you should take caution.

You can climb as far as the partially restored remains of the old **Dogra Fort** ⓘ *a short way up the eastern side of Karpochu, on a good footpath; the most direct path is just east of the aqueduct, beside K2 Travel Services, passing the old 2-storey Wazir's House, Rs50 for foreigners*. The Dogra fort replaced one built by Ali Sher Khan Anchan in the 17th century, although some date the first fortress here to the time of Makpon Bokha in the early 16th century. The views from here down onto Skardu are excellent.

At the fort itself, the chowkidar will enthusiastically show you the local royal family tree. Take care when walking on the ramparts as the supporting roof already has many holes and one false step could easily create another human-sized one. The fort is on the **AKCSP** (Aga Khan Cultural Services Pakistan) 'things to do' list, but while it remains in the hands of the army the likelihood of much needed renovation is slim. Some visitors like to walk around Karpochu

Wazir **13**
Yurt & Yak Sarai **14**

Eating 🍴
Askari Bakers **1**
Concordia **2**
Indus **3**
PTDC **4**
Tibet Fast Foods **5**
United Bakers **6**

Rock itself, through the edge of the sand dunes and along the south bank of the Indus. This walk takes around three to four hours and is a good way to get fitness levels up while acclimatizing. To reach the top of Karpochu, you need to start from the western end, near the Sadpara International hotel. It is a long, dry, exposed climb, and very difficult in places (some tricky rock climbing is required in places, so not recommended for novices) although the views from the top are spectacular. There are further ruined fortifications here of uncertain origin.

Around Skardu

Sadpara Lake and Buddha

① *It is a 3-hour walk to the lake, or you can hire a Suzuki or jeep (for around Rs350 direct as a half -day excursion, Rs450, including a detour to the Sadpara Buddha), or try hitching. By foot the most scenic option is to follow the aqueduct from the centre of town, continuing to follow the irrigation channel from Alamdar Chowk.*

Shortly after joining the main stream, a bridge crosses to the left bank with access to the **Sadpara Buddha** ① *the chowkidar will be hanging around somewhere in the vicinity, with the key and a Rs20 entry coupon*, a meditating Maitreya Buddha surrounded by Bodhisattvas carved into a large boulder, thought to date from around 900 AD. The rock has been allotted, on a 90-year lease, to the Baltistan Culture Foundation, who hope to buy some land and build a permanent enclosure around the Buddha to protect it from tree felling and rock blasting in the vicinity.

From here you can rejoin the irrigation channel towards the main jeep track, or stay on the left bank and take the high track to the right of the village used by tractors collecting building rocks. Better still, when the river is not in full flow (June-July), skirt around the village through the area of boulders and pick up the narrow irrigation channel high above the river. Take care with your footing and cross to the jeep track on the other side at the weir, after the hydel plant opposite. From the weir the jeep track to the lake is a further 3 km, while the path on the left bank quickly becomes impassable.

Situated 8 km south of Skardu, **Sadpara (Satpara) Lake** is a beautiful, tranquil spot and well worth a visit. The lake is fed by the mountain torrent which flows down from the Deosai plateau to the south, and dammed on its northern edge.

The lake is well stocked with trout. **Fishing** permits can be obtained from the local Fisheries Official, who will be found for you or will find you, or from the office in Skardu (US$10 or Rs500 per rod). Equipment (including rowboats) can be hired from either of the two hotels on the western side. Note, however, that fishing is not permitted from November to March, as this is the breeding season. It is a further 7 km to the picturesque Sadpara village above the lake. The people of Sadpara are Shina speakers, known in Balti as Brokpas (literally 'settlers of high places'). There is a check post on the road by the turning to the village marking the start of the Deosai National Park (see page 246).

Returning from Sadpara, the jeep track offers impressive views over Skardu, Karpochu Rock and surrounding mountains. As you reach the outskirts of town, you may also pass some of the local football 'academies'.

Kachura Lake

The village of Kachura is situated 32 km west of Skardu, just before the main road to Gilgit crosses to the north side of the Indus River. A turning leads south off the main road up through the village, with its rich fruit orchards, to the luxury **Shangrila** resort, which features its own private lake (see under Sleeping, below).

A much more attractive option is to continue on to the far more beautiful and unspoilt **Upper Kachura Lake** (known locally as Foroq Lake). Continue past the turnings for the **Shangrila** resort and **Tibet Motel** and cross the bridge to reach the village of Karpia. Bear right in the village to follow a very narrow, rough track for around a kilometre and then take a path off to the left which leads steeply down to the lake (ask directions from the village as the route is not particularly obvious, although by following the white painted 'arrows' the lake will appear in view). There are a couple of simple snack places here which open during the summer season only, but otherwise the lake is completely undeveloped.

By taking the left fork at Karpia you can walk up the **Shigarthang nullah**, which drains into the Indus just to the east of Kachura and is the starting point for treks up onto the Deosai plateau. There are also plenty of beautiful short walks in the area.

Sleeping

Skardu *p235, map p237*

A Hotel (currently unnamed), College Rd. New hotel due to open soon, destined to be the first luxury hotel in town. Locally hand-crafted carved wooden furniture and decor. Rooms at the rear with balconies will provide good views of Sadpara Nullah and towards Kachura. Front rooms overlook a petrol station, so not so appealing. Room rates likely to reflect high investment.

B PTDC K2 Motel, off Hameed Garh Rd, T0575-50291, F0575-50293. Excellent location with relaxing garden overlooking the Indus, remains the traditional focal point for mountaineering and trekking groups and serves as a good place to get up-to-date information. Rooms comfortable with fan and hot water geyser, although equally comfortable rooms can be found cheaper in town. Slightly cheaper rooms in old block. Decent restaurant (see Eating below). Camping possible (Rs100 per tent including use of toilet/shower facilities). PTDC Information Office and some Kashmiri souvenir shops are also located here.

C Concordia Motel, off Hospital Rd, near Heliport, T0575-52582, F0575-52547. Clean, comfortable rooms with fan and attached hot bath, peaceful location with a choice of garden or terrace views of the Indus and surrounding mountains, restaurant, friendly staff; overall rooms are rather overpriced.

C Yurt and Yak Sarai, Link Rd, T0575-52856. Collection of luxury metal-framed Mongolian-style yurts, a bit of a glorified campsite for those with dreams of being a modern-day Genghis Khan, restaurant, quite a hike to town centre.

D Pioneer, near Airport, T0575-55188. Clean, comfortable rooms with bath, garden, restaurant, some way from town so a bit isolated (advantage of proximity to airport is negated if flight is cancelled, as you must go into town to reconfirm next day's flight).

E Hilton International, Hussaini Chowk, overlooking Football Stadium, T0575-55581. Newish hotel, better rooms overlooking football and polo pitches, although small, with attached hot bath, 2 restaurants (upper 1 for guests only), roof terrace.

E Indus Motel, College Rd, T0575-52608. Friendly hotel with discounts when quiet, rooms clean, fan, attached bath (hot in mornings), those at the rear have good views over Sadpara Nullah, good restaurant with huge portions and flavoursome dishes. Recommended.

E Sadpara International, College Rd, T/F0575-52951. Simple but well-furnished clean rooms, fan, attached bath, set around central courtyard and small garden area. Also some cheap and basic rooms, restaurant tries its best without winning any awards. Overall, it is well run and not a bad choice.

E Wazir, opposite National Bank of Pakistan, T0575 55445. Entrance in side street to this randomly built newish hotel, rooms clean with attached bath, although better with Pakistani toilet, large restaurant serves reasonable food.

F Heaven International, near Yadgar Chowk, College Rd, T0575-50450. Fairly new, claiming to be the first in Skardu with many features, destined to become another crumbling concrete mess. Rooms with attached bath already grubby, restaurant with Balti music at weekends (allegedly).

G Baltistan Tourist Cottage (Kashmir Inn), Yadgar Chowk, T0575-52707. Rooms from the basic end of the basic range on the

For an explanation of sleeping and eating price codes used in this guide, see inside the front cover. Other relevant information is found in Essentials, pages 36-38.

luxury scale are grubby to say the least. Cramped dorm (H) still popular with backpackers, good place to link up with other trekkers and source of information, the 'purdahi' office of Ali Haider Sadpara is here (see Tour operators below) as well as Mohammed Iqbal, the friendliest hotel boss in town. Restaurant with a terrace overlooking the bazaar serves the usual fayre including a half-decent tomato soup, if you like garlic.

G Hillman International, Yadgar Chowk, T0575-52175. Rooms are simple but clean with attached bath, restaurant.

G Himalaya, College Rd, T0575-52576. Simple, not too clean rooms with attached bath, those at the back with balconies and views over Sadpara Nullah marginally better, basic restaurant.

G Hunza Inn (5 Brothers), College Rd, T0575-52570. Basic, small rooms arranged around a garden/courtyard behind restaurant, nothing special but cheap and negotiable.

G Karakoram Inn, Yadgar Chowk, T0575-55438. Modelled on the set of 'Prisoner Cell Block-H', although the rooms on the top floor are clean and decent enough. Take breakfast on the terrace since the restaurant is dusty; food is mediocre.

Sadpara Lake and Buddha *p238*

B PTDC Sadpara Motel, the eyesore on the northwest side of the lake, linked to the main jeep track by a bridge upon arrival. Opening significantly delayed due to the government failing to pay large contractors' debts, comfortable rooms and variable restaurant, although somewhat overpriced.

E Sadpara Lake Inn (NB Sign above entrance reads 'PTDC Hut Satpara' at time of writing, 2 rooms were rented out to PTDC), situated by the lake, just off the main jeep track. Comfortable rooms with pleasant lakeside garden and restaurant, camping possible and trekking equipment (including tents) available for up to 25 people, boats for hire, friendly manager.

F-G Lake View Motel, by the lake, on the main jeep track, before Sadpara Lake Inn. 2 simple rooms, 1 with attached bath, the other with views across the lake, pleasant garden, food prepared to order, cheaper camping allowed, trekking equipment, rowing boat and fishing gear for hire.

Kachura Lake *p238*

L Shangrila, T0575-55191, resorts@isb.comsats.net.pk (or book with Travel Walji's in Islamabad). This fancy resort now charges Rs100 for day-trippers to keep the riff-raff out. Chalet-style rooms and VIP suites arranged in a complex stretching around 80% of the lake, prices range from Rs4,000 for a single to Rs12,000 for the apartment-like 'Presidential Suite'. 3 restaurants including a pagoda on the lake and a café in the fuselage of a DC-3 aircraft. Also conference facilities, boating and a small, sorry-looking zoo. Some readers have suggested that it's not as luxurious as the price tag suggests, with unreliable power supply and dangerous electric fittings.

C Tibet Motel, occupying a small corner on the southern edge of the lake, T0575-52585. 30-room extension recently completed, original 2 rooms rather overpriced, restaurant, boating, camping (H, with access to toilet and shower facilities).

● Eating

Skardu *p235, map p237*

Almost all the hotels in Skardu have their own restaurant and non-guests are free to eat at any of them, although the choice and quality of most is mediocre at best. At the cheaper end, there are several local-style restaurants in Naya Bazaar, Hameed Garh Rd and around Yadgar Chowk. Many incorporate Punjab in their names although this doesn't necessarily reflect the style of cuisine. Hygiene standards are not what they could be, so it's best to choose one which is full of locals. There are several bakeries from Yadgar Chowk down towards the GPO. The best of these is **Askari**, near GPO, Hameed Garh Rd, with excellent freshly baked cakes and biscuits as well as trekking supplies. Recommended. **United Bakers** is a bakery-cum-supermarket offering similar goods in a more convenient location.

ΨΨΨ Concordia Motel, off Hospital Rd, near Heliport, T0575-52582, F0575-52547. Evening buffet (if enough guests are staying), book in advance if non-resident.

ΨΨΨ PTDC K2 Motel, off Hameed Garh Rd, T0575-50291, F0575-50293. Evening buffet (Rs250 per head) and occasional barbeques (Rs300) when around 30 people are staying. Non-residents must book in advance.

🍴 **Indus Motel**, College Rd, T0575-52608 One of the better quality restaurants in town with huge portions (1 plate of rice is ample for 2 people) and dishes cooked with care and attention.

🍴 **Tibet Fast Food**, near aqueduct. Does reasonable soups and snacks.

O Shopping

Skardu *p235, map p237*
Souvenirs, jewellery, antiques
There are several tourist-oriented shops along Naya Bazaar selling antiques, souvenirs, jewellery, precious and semi-precious stones etc. Most are concentrated around Yadgar Chowk; eg **Baltistan Gems**, near Baltistan Tourist Cottage, **Pakiza**, next to National Bank of Pakistan or **Topaz Gems**, below Karakoram Inn. Another place worth trying is **Shahbaz Jewellers and Antiques**, on Hameed Garh Rd. Precious and semi-precious stones available include, among others, Ruby, Amethyst, Emerald, Topaz, Garnet, Turquoise, Aquamarine (mined locally around Baltistan), Tourmaline and Lapis Lazuli. Some of the antique jewellery and other artefacts are quite striking. **Hunza Handicrafts**, next to PIA, Hameed Garh Rd, has a good selection of carpets and other souvenirs, while a row of small shops in the **PTDC K2 Motel complex** is another option. For traditional embroidered handicrafts, try the **Baltistan Culture Foundation** (see Directory) who are empowering local women by teaching them traditional Balti techniques and motifs and paying them for their produce. Over 200 local women are employed by the Foundation's 'Baltistan Handicrafts Development Programme', which also encourages the revival of local music and dance.

Trekking supplies and equipment
Purana and Naya Bazaars are the best place to shop for basic trekking supplies. All staple foods, biscuits etc are readily available (try **Askari** or **United Bakers**), as well as cooking implements (including pressure cookers) and kerosene stoves. High-energy and freeze-dried foods are more difficult to come by, although left-overs from previous expeditions sometimes find their way into stores; College Rd and Naya Bazaar are the best place to look for these. If you are looking for trekking equipment (tents, sleeping bags etc), **Ali Haider Sadpara** has a small office at Baltistan Tourist Cottage and can rent out equipment. **Mountaineering Equipment Shop**, next to Shahbaz Jewelers on Hameed Garh Rd is a new concern worth checking out, with trekking and mountaineering gear for sale and hire. Otherwise, try renting it from 1 of the tour operators (see below).

Rockmans, Hameed Garh Rd (next door to Travel Waljis), has a good selection of postcards, T-shirts and various handicrafts/souvenirs, as well as a selection of apricot products (dried apricots, apricot candy bars, apricot kernel oil etc). Also sleeping bags and some trekking equipment for sale. Further east from Rockmans on Hameed Garh Rd, by a crossroads, there are a couple of large metal tanks where kerosene is sold. If there is no one on hand, ask around in the surrounding shops or try a little further on where another pair of tanks are on the right after the mosque.

▲ Activities and tours

Skardu *p235, map p237*
Fishing
There is good trout fishing on many of the rivers and lakes of Baltistan during the season, which stretches from 10 Mar-9 Oct each year. Most notable in the Skardu area are the lakes at Sadpara and Upper Kachura while Kachura Nullah provides a faster flowing challenge. Permits cost US$10 or Rs500 per rod per day, whichever is cheaper. A maximum of 6 fish per day are allowed to be landed but they must be over 9 inches (23 cm) long. Permits are available from the Office of the Assistant Director of Fisheries on Link Rd, T0575-50300 or more conveniently from local Fisheries Inspectors at the sites themselves.

Trekking
The main reason for people coming to Skardu is for the trekking and mountaineering territory in Baltistan. For any of the treks in the area, Skardu is an essential starting point and is the place to get up-to-date information on routes and to link up with others if travelling alone. There are also a number of shorter

walks around Skardu which can be useful to tackle while acclimatizing for more strenuous higher altitude treks.

There is no shortage of people in Skardu claiming to be guides; only go with someone who has references proving they have done the trek. Ali Haider at Baltistan Tourist Cottage can advise.

Spectator sports
During the summer months and during festivals, there are occasional **polo** matches at the polo ground (see Sights) while the adjoining **football** 'stadium' hosts regular games between local teams. These are generally quite popularly attended with most spectators watching from the side of the road close to the aqueduct.

Tour operators
Adventure Karakoram, PO Box 626, T0575-55144. Run by Mr Abbas Kazmi, one-time manager of the Baltistan Tourist Cottage, now head of the Baltistan Culture Foundation, a local scholar specializing in Baltistan's pre-Islamic history and culture. Offers a wide range of organized/tailor-made treks and jeep safaris.

Ali Haider Sadpara, Hameed Garh Rd. Ali Haider Sadpara, a mountain guide of over 25 years' experience can be found at Baltistan Tourist Cottage. He is very helpful for information and can organize good guides, especially for new routes in the Deosai plateau. Good recommendations. Also trekking equipment for hire.

Full Moon Night Trekking Service, PO Box 603, Satellite Town, T0575-55256, www.fmn trekking.co.pk. Very well run, specialises in eco-tours and treks. Recommended.

Himalaya Treks and Tours, College Rd, T0575-52528 (Liaison Office, 112 Rahim Plaza, Murree Rd, Rawalpindi T/F051- 5563014). Mountaineering/trekking expeditions, jeep safaris, equipment hire available for up to 50 people. Good reputation.

Travel Walji's, Hameed Garh Rd, T0575-53468 (Head Office 10 Khayaban-e-Suhrawardy, PO Box No 1088, Islamabad, T051-2270757-8, F051-2270753). This is Pakistan's largest tour operator. It is not the cheapest, but generally gives a good service.

Other tour operators include **Baltistan Tours**, T0575-52626, local handlers for **KE Adventure Travel**; **Hushe Treks and Tours**, Muheb Rd; **K2 Treks and Tours**, Al Abbas Market; **Mountain Travels**, College Rd and **Nazir Sabir Expeditions**, Hameed Garh Rd, T0575-52778. Shop around for the best deal. PTDC K2 Motel should be able to give a good benchmark figure for the trek or tour you are interested in. There are several others not mentioned here, but some are difficult to find since the police insisted that signboards are not allowed on the street.

Transport

Skardu p235, map p237
Air
PIA Booking Office, Hameed Garh Rd, T0575-50284. Daily 0800-1600. Airport T0575-50285. Weather permitting, there is 1 Boeing 737 flight daily to **Islamabad**, departing at 1040 (50 mins). The decision on whether the flight goes or not (based on cloud density around Nanga Parbat) is usually known shortly after 0900, the scheduled departure time of the outward bound flight from Islamabad. Cost is Rs2,770, or Rs3,745 for 'Club Class'. Pakistani fares are subsidized. A taxi to the airport from town is around Rs100.
NB All tickets must be reconfirmed the day before the scheduled flight. If your flight is cancelled you must return to town to reconfirm at the PIA Office – there is usually a rush between 0930-1000 on these days, but it's just a matter of ticking your name off the list and changing the date on your ticket. Passengers from cancelled flights are given priority on the next available flight, while foreigners are put at the front of this list, so when a flight does leave, a non-Pakistani passport should ensure a seat if you have reconfirmed. After a few days of bad weather a back-log quickly builds up, so leave time to take the bus if you have a tight schedule.

Bus
There are 4 companies operating from Skardu to 4 regular destinations. **Himalaya Travel Service**, T0575-55414, and **Masherbrum Tours**, T0575-55195, both close to Yadgar Chowk in Naya Bazaar. **K2 Travel Services**, T0575-55584, and **NATCO**, T0575-50289, lie immediately to the east and west of the aqueduct respectively. All buses leave from outside their respective office. It is

wise to book at least 1 day in advance and to check departure time when booking.

Rawalpindi All 4 companies operate services to Rawalpindi with **Himalaya** (at 1300), **K2** (1400, 1500) and **Masherbrum** (1200, 1300) running coasters on the 18-hr journey at Rs550 per seat. Masherbrum also offers the gruelling 24-hr option on a full-size bus at 1400 each day for Rs490, while **NATCO** provides a so-called de luxe (ie big) bus departing at 1300 each day for Rs500.

Gilgit K2 and Masherbrum both run Hiace minibuses on the 6-7-hr journey at Rs150 per head. K2 services depart at 0700, 1900, 1100 and 1300 each day. Masherbrum Hiaces leave at 0800, 1000 and 1200. A cheaper option is to take the daily NATCO Hiaces at 0800 and 1200 for Rs105 or if you're really strapped for cash it also runs a de luxe bus at 0530 for Rs75.

Khapulu K2 offers jeeps for the 3-hr journey at 0700 and 1100 at Rs75 per head. Masherbrum runs a coaster at 0600 for Rs60 while NATCO provides bus services at 0600 and 1000 at Rs53 per seat.

Shigar Only NATCO runs an afternoon bus at 1430 at Rs15 for the 1½-hr trip. However, the road is often blocked by land-slides, when it is necessary to hire a jeep that can usually still negotiate the precarious old road.

Cargo Jeep

This is the cheapest way of getting to places not served by public bus. Finding a cargo jeep going to your destination can be difficult, particularly as everyone will try to persuade you to hire a private jeep (a 'special' or 'booking'). They run on an irregular basis up the Shigar Valley at least as far as **Dassu** or **Chutron**, across the Deosai to **Astor** and east towards **Khapulu** and up to **Hushe**. The most regular services are to **Kachura**, **Shigar village**, **Doghani** (at the foot of the Thalle Valley) and **Khapulu**. They leave from various places along Naya Bazaar, particularly around Hussaini Chowk; ask around.

Private Jeep Hire

The tour operators listed below in the Directory, PTDC Tourist Information and most hotels can all arrange private jeep hire, although it may be worth asking jeep drivers in the bazaar for cheaper deals if on a tight budget. The following rates are from PTDC and represent the maximum you should pay at that time: **Askole** (drop) Rs3,500; **Gilgit** Rs3,500; **Hunza** (2 days) Rs6,000; **Hushe** Rs3,200; **Khapulu** Rs2,200; **Khunjarab Pass** (2-3 days) Rs10,000; **Kachura Lake** (half-day excursion) Rs800; **Sadpara Lake** (half-day excursion) Rs350-450, the latter price including a diversion to the Sadpara Buddha rock; **Shigar village** (half-day excursion) Rs800. PTDC also has fare stages to various points across the **Deosai plateau**. The following rates are for 1-way drop only: **Deosai Top** (seasonal hotel and campsite near Ali Malik Mar) Rs1,800; **Shatung La** (campsite) Rs2,200; **Bara Pani** (seasonal hotel, campsite and Himalayan Wildlife Project Research Station) Rs2,500; **Sheosar Lake** (campsite) Rs3,500; **Chilam** Rs4,500; **Astor** Rs7,000. The 2-day trip to Gilgit across the Deosai costs Rs10,000. All of these rates are negotiable with other jeep operators as is the number of days spent on the road; if you've come all this way there's not much point in zooming across the plateau in a day and a half.

❶ Directory

Skardu *p235, map p237*

Banks Alam Money Changer, College Rd, is the best bet for changing currency notes and TCs at slightly below the 'kerbside' rate in Islamabad. Daily 0800-1800. **National Bank of Pakistan**, Naya Bazaar, T0575-52958 will only change US$ cash and TCs at a lower rate with a longer wait. Mon-Thu 0900-1330, Fri and Sat 0900-1230. Most hotels can change or arrange to change small amounts of US$. Try in the PCOs and shops in Naya Bazaar where unofficial money changers may also change cash. **Chemists** There are several chemists opposite the hospital, and some in Naya Bazaar. **Hospitals** The District Headquarters Hospital, east of the main town, beyond the PTDC K2 Motel, on Hospital Rd. Al-Abbas Hospital, Alamdar Rd. **Internet** There is currently no public internet access in Skardu. **Police** Hameed Garh Rd, T0575-50114. **Post** office Hameed Garh Rd, east of the PIA office. Mon-Thu and Sat 0800-1600, Fri 0800-1200. **Telephone** The army-run SCO

telephone office is next to the red and white transmitter tower on Hameed Garh Rd, east of the aqueduct, daily 0600-2400. You can make national and international calls, although faxes can only be sent within Pakistan. International calls must go via Islamabad so when the line is 'engaged', it usually means that there is no connection to Islamabad. Rates vary between Rs50 and Rs60 per min for most European countries and the USA (clearly listed on a wall chart), timed on a stopwatch. There are also a few PCOs in Naya Bazaar and around Yadgar Chowk but these charge nearly double the SCO rate on international calls, although they do have the advantage of direct dialling and allow call-back facilities. **Useful addresses** Baltistan Culture Foundation, a 10-min walk from PIA office, PO Box 636, T/F0575-55141. Active in reinvigorating and supporting traditional Balti culture including music, dance and women's handicrafts. Also attempting to restore valuable heritage buildings. Run by Abbas Kazmi, an enthusiastic and knowledgeable expert who knows as much about the area's history as anyone. Technical expertise and generous donations would help the many worthwhile projects initiated by this seriously under-funded NGO. **Foreigners' registration** Superintendent of Police, Hospital Rd, T0575-52424.
NAPWD Link Rd, T0575-50225, for booking NAPWD Resthouses. **Deputy Commissioner** Hospital Rd, T0575-50100, Res: T0575-50102. In the past, the DC was authorized to issue visa extensions, although this has been (temporarily?) suspended.

The Deosai Plateau → *Colour map 2, grid C6*

This is a uniquely beautiful region, covering an area of 400 sq km, and all of it over 4,000 m. In Chinese the word 'Deosai' translates literally as 'giant's abode', and in a landscape on such a massive scale it isn't hard to see why. Likewise, the Balti name for the region, 'Bhear Sar', meaning 'place of flowers', is entirely appropriate, in summer at least. You experience an unmistakeable sense of elevation here, in the huge expanse of the horizon, the wide open space and the clarity of light and colour. Gently rolling hills, clothed in a soft cladding of vegetation and carpeted with brightly-coloured flowers in summer, extend into a ring of jagged, rocky mountains in the far distance, while the plateau's rivers flow past, crystal clear and icy cold.

Ins and outs

There is a jeep route across the Deosai which links Skardu with Astor and goes down to the KKH at Jaglot. From Skardu to Astor is 115 km, which is feasible in one very long day, but much more enjoyable if spread over two days with an overnight stop on the plateau. There are comfortable hotels at Sadpara and Astor, and during the summer there are several temporary places on the plateau with food and basic accommodation in tents. Even so, you are strongly advised to bring your own supplies. It is essential that you are properly equipped for high altitudes. If you have flown directly up from the plains and are planning a visit to the Deosai, acclimatization is an important consideration.

During the summer, cargo jeeps make the journey from Skardu as far as Chilam or Astor on an irregular basis. Astor is linked by regular public transport with the KKH and Gilgit. Renting a private jeep is fairly expensive (Skardu to Astor is around Rs7,000), but worthwhile, particularly if you can split the cost between several people. Alternatively, the Deosai plateau can be visited as a round-trip excursion from Skardu. This is possible in one long day, but again is better spread over two days or more. Part of the Deosai has been designated as a National Park and an attractive option is to arrange a visit through the staff who run it.

Best time to visit

The Deosai is at its best from mid-July to late August. While the weather can be glorious in daytime during this period, temperatures drop dramatically at night and it can also turn nasty very quickly, with intense windstorms often sweeping across the plateau. Note that rivers can be impassable in a vehicle when in spate (usually during June and early July). Take local advice and find out about the current state of the jeep track before setting out. Mosquitoes are a major problem during the early part of the season (June/July) and strong repellent or mosquito nets are essential. On the other hand, this is also when the plateau is in full flower. From November through to May the Deosai is completely snow-bound.

Land and environment

The Deosai closely resembles the Tibetan plateau in its topography and environment, although local claims that it is the world's highest plateau are not accurate since the Qinghai-Tibetan Plateau averages over 4,500 m. It is of enormous significance in hydrological terms, acting as a huge water store. As it gradually melts, the snow that has built up here over the winter accounts for over 5% of the total discharge of the Indus. The data from weather stations monitoring snowfall on the Deosai is used to predict the peak flow of the Indus later in the year.

Frozen beneath a deep blanket of snow for much of the year, the Deosai is surprisingly rich in plants and animals, bursting into life during the brief spring and summer months. The plateau is home to the Himalayan brown bear (*Ursus arctos Isabellinus*), a species of bear unique to this part of the world but under serious threat due to illegal hunting. Rough estimates place the total number still surviving in Pakistan at around 30-40, with all or most of them inhabiting the Deosai. There have been no sightings in the Biafo Glacier area for some years now, although some may remain in Khunjerab National Park. Other mammals include the golden marmot (in large numbers), Tibetan wolf, Tibetan red fox, Himalayan ibex, Ladakh urial and various small rodents, including voles and shrews.

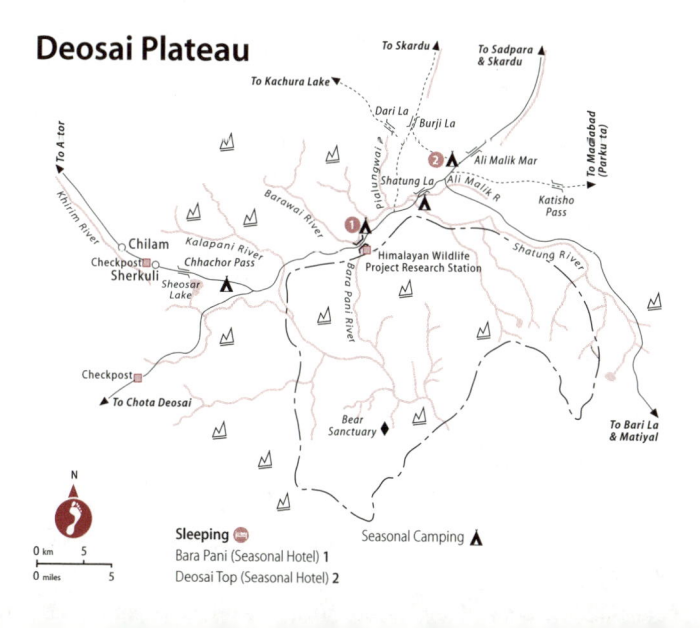

Deosai Plateau

Sleeping
Bara Pani (Seasonal Hotel) 1
Deosai Top (Seasonal Hotel) 2

Seasonal Camping

Reptiles include lizards such as the Himalayan agama, ground skink and glacial skink. The unique snow carp is found in the Deosai's rivers. Below 3,000 m, in the nullahs leading down off the plateau, the Himalayan otter feeds on the snow carp. This altitude zone and habitat is also home to some snow leopards and musk deer, particularly in birch and juniper forests. The recently discovered alpine toad has now qualified as a separate species.

The plateau provides spring and summer breeding grounds for many of Pakistan's birds, including the Himalayan golden eagle, lammergeier (bearded vulture), northern hobby (a falcon), kestrel and long-legged buzzard, as well as larks, wagtails, warblers and sand plovers. It also lies on the flight path of a number of migratory birds which can be seen from late September to mid-October on their return from Central Asia to the plains of the subcontinent. Species include the osprey, damoselle crane, little turn, great black-headed gull and ducks such as the common teal, pintail, shoveller and marganzer.

More than 100 species of plants and grasses are found on the Deosai, including colourful flowers such as aconitum, rheum, iris, astragalus and spiraea. There is also a wealth of herbs and medicinal plants, including ginger, primula, geranium, mint, artmesia, rubus and barberry. At lower altitude on the peripheries wild rose is found, as well as trees such as juniper, blue pine, spruce, pencil cedar, white birch, Himalayan poplar and chinese salix.

Deosai National Park

In an attempt to provide some sanctuary to the remaining brown bears, and to monitor them and learn more about their behaviour and habitat, the Deosai National Park was established in 1993 by the Himalayan Wildlife Project, in collaboration with the Northern Areas Forestry, Parks and Wildlife Department and local communities. The park has a semi-official status and an important part of the management plan involves gaining official recognition and ensuring proper implementation of recommendations for the protection of the brown bear and its habitat.

Visiting the park

There is a check post at Sadpara village, and another one near Sherkuli village, between the Chhachor Pass and Chilam. The hunting of bears or other wildlife and carrying of firearms is forbidden in the park area (line-fishing is allowed with permit). Vehicles are not allowed off the main jeep tracks. People are asked to camp at the recognized campsites, or within 60 m of the track. There are four seasonal campsites (usually May-October); at Deosai Top near Ali Malik Mar, Shatung La, Bara Pani and Sheosar Lake. Those at Deosai Top and Bara Pani have a couple of fixed tents for those without their own. Entry into the 'Bear Sanctuary' area (see map) is restricted and permits ('local community ticket', US$4) must be obtained from officials at the Research Station at Bara Pani. Otherwise, permission may be obtained from the Conservator of Wildlife in Gilgit.

If you want to gain some insight into the wildlife and ecology of the Deosai, or would just like to catch a glimpse of a brown bear, the staff of the Himalayan Wildlife Project, who are fully trained, familiar with the terrain and experienced in tracking the animals (safely), will take people on tours of the protected area. They have a research station at the Bara Pani bridge crossing, which is manned throughout the season. To organize a visit, contact ⓘ *Himalayan Wildlife Project, Centre One, House 1, Street 15, Khayaban-e-Iqbal, F-7/2, Islamabad, T051-276113, F051-824484.* Alternatively, it may be possible to arrange a visit by contacting the staff at the check posts at Sadpara or Sherkuli or at Bara Pani, depending on who is available at short notice and at the time.

Skardu to Astor

From Skardu the jeep track goes up past Sadpara Lake (see page 238) and, further on, Sadpara village. Above the village, on the jeep track, is **Sadpara check post**, marking the start of the National Park area. As well as the accommodation down by Sadpara Lake, there is a spare tent at the check post which is able to sleep up to four people (bring your own bedding), or you can pitch your own tent. The check post is recommended as an overnight acclimatization stop. Above the check post, where a small nullah joins the main stream, there is an area of cultivated land strewn with several great boulders covered in pre-historic, Buddhist and Islamic rock inscriptions.

Beyond the check post the jeep track climbs steeply up the Sadpara Nullah. After the track crosses to the west bank of the stream, the course of the old jeep track which continued along the east bank can still be seen in places. If the new track feels scary, you can comfort yourself with the fact that it is infinitely less hair-raising than the old one. At the top (around two to three hours' drive from Skardu) is **Ali Malik Mar** (4,080 m), the pass marking the start of the Deosai proper, also known locally as **Deosai Top** for the tourists' benefit. From here, the track descends for a short way to a designated camping site with a seasonal hotel consisting of a couple of tents. Tea and basic meals can be obtained here when it is open.

After half an hour, the jeep track forks; the right fork is the main route to Chilam and Astor, while the left fork heads southeast towards Matiyal. The latter route is closed to foreigners beyond **Bari La**, a one-and-a-half-hour diversion by jeep from the main track, with views of glaciers and six lakes. Taking the right fork, further on the track fords the Ali Malik Mar and Shatung streams shortly before they converge. This fording is the hardest on the route. There is a camping site here at **Shatung La**. The track then goes along the main river to the bridge-crossing at **Bara Pani** (about an hour's drive from Ali Malik Mar). By the bridge there is another camping site and a seasonal hotel with a couple of tents for sleeping and a kitchen tent for tea and basic meals. Around 500 m to the south of the bridge (to the left as you face the bridge coming from Skardu) is the summer camp/research station of the Himalayan Wildlife Project.

After crossing the bridge, the track climbs gently but steadily over a watershed and down to the **Kalapani River**. The track crosses the river and then forks further on. The right fork is the Chilam/Astor route, while the left fork leads to the area known as **Chota (small) Deosai**, currently closed to foreigners and guarded by an army check post. Taking the right fork, the main track continues on to the beautiful **Sheosar Lake** (around an hour's drive from Bara Pani), where there is good camping. Immediately after is the **Chhachor pass** (4,230 m), after which the track begins to descend. Around an hour beyond the pass is the **Sherkuli check post**, marking the entrance to the Deosai National Park from the Astor side. Soon after is the small village of **Chilam**, situated near the top of the Das Khirim Valley. It takes a further two to three hours to reach the village of Astor. For details of Astor and the Astor Valley, see page 202.

Deosai Plateau treks

ⓘ *Open zone. Maximum elevation optional (4,080-4,820 m). Aug. Maps: the U502 series, NI 43-3 Mundik and NI 43-2 Gilgit are not accurate enough to be relied on for treks on Deosai. See trekking notes, p45.*

Skardu-Astor

The jeep route between Skardu and Astor can also be done as a trek; allow around five to seven days between Skardu and Chilam. This route has also begun to attract adventurous mountain bikers in search of something really challenging.

Burji La

The most popular trek is a short loop from Skardu, climbing up past Sadpara Lake, across Ali Malik Mar, then doubling back across Burji La and down to Skardu. This takes around four days. It is advisable to do the trek in this direction as the ascent from Skardu to the 4,820-m Burji La is extremely steep and involves an altitude gain of nearly 2,500 m in just two days. In either direction, it is essential to acclimatize properly first; do not be tempted to do this trek if you have just flown into Skardu. The approach to Burji La from the south does not follow any clear path and the route across the pass itself can be difficult to determine. A guide is strongly recommended.

If walking from Skardu, the best place to camp for the first night is by the check post on the jeep track above Sadpara village. The second day takes you over Ali Malik Mar (4,080 m) to the camping site and seasonal 'hotel' just beyond the pass. From here follow the jeep track on for a short distance and then branch off sharply to the right to head due north towards Burji La (if you reach the main fork in the jeep track you have gone too far). The approach to the pass leads past two small lakes with options for camping wherever there is water. The pass itself gives spectacular views of the Karakoram mountains to the north (including K2 and Masherbrum on a clear day) and south back onto the Deosai. It is feasible to reach Skardu from the top of the pass in one long day; an overnight stop halfway down is preferable, but make sure you have sufficient water with you as there is none along the way.

Shigarthang Valley

From near Kachura Lake trekking routes lead up the Shigarthang Valley onto the Deosai. Higher up, the valley divides. The left fork climbs southeast over the **Dari La** and on to the Deosai. From here you can angle sharply northeast over the **Burji La** and drop down towards Skardu, or else join the rough Skardu-Astor jeep track to the south. The right fork continues southwest up the main stream, crosses the **Alam Pir La**, and then follows first the **Bubind** and then the **Das Khirim** valley down towards Astor. An alternative route branches west above the first fork in the valley, across the **Banak La** and descends the **Parishing River** directly to Astor. We have not covered these routes, but a survey of the literature reveals some confusion as to names and exact routes; a guide familiar with the area is strongly recommended.

> ❗ Foreigners are not permitted to go south or east of the jeep track between Ali Malik Mar and Chachhor Pass without a permit, except as far as Bari La on the road to Matiyal.

Shigar River Valley → Colour map 2, grid B/C6

The Shigar River flows into the Indus just north of Skardu. The valley is wide and fertile, carpeted by gently terraced fields of wheat, barley and maize, and rich orchards of apricot, mulberry, peach, plum, apple and pear. Once a powerful independent kingdom, this valley is the gateway to some of the most spectacular treks in northern Pakistan, including the famous Baltoro Glacier trek up to Concordia and K2 base camp and the increasingly popular Biafo-Hispar trek across Snow Lake. The village of Shigar, near the foot of the valley, is worth a visit in itself and is easily accessible from Skardu. ▶▶ *For Sleeping, Eating and all other listings, see page 254.*

Background

Shigar was one of the most powerful semi-independent kingdoms after that of the Makpon rulers of Skardu. A local legend traces the ancestry of the ruling family to a man named **Cha Tham** (or Shah Tham), who was deposed as the ruler of Nagar during the second period of the Trakhan dynasty in Gilgit. He crossed over to Shigar by way of the Hispar and Biafo glaciers and subsequently established the Amacha dynasty which continued to rule right up until the Dogra period. It was to Shigar that the Muslim missionaries Amir Kabir Sayed Ali Hamadani and Mir Shamsuddin Iraqi are first said to have come, in the 14th and 16th centuries respectively. Following Sultan Abu Said Khan's invasion of Baltistan in 1532, which brought him by way of the Braldo Pass to Shigar, strong links were forged with Yarkand to the north. Later these were replaced by ties with the Mughals of Kashmir. **Imam Quli Khan** (1634-1705) is considered the greatest of Shigar's rulers. He forged close links with the ruler of Skardu, Shah Morad Khan, helping him with his campaigns against Khapulu, Ladakh and Gilgit. During the rule of his son **Azam Khan** Skardu fell under the control of Shigar for a short period.

Skardu to Shigar

From Skardu, the road east towards Khapulu passes through the villages of Hassainabad and Thorgu. There is a left turn for Shigar just after Thorgu, about 12 km from Skardu. The old wooden suspension bridge across the Indus has now been supplemented by a much more solid-looking Chinese-built bridge right next to it. From this point it is 20 km to Shigar, 70 km to Dassu and 112 km to Askole. After crossing the river, the road is slowly being metalled but quickly turns to a decent jeep track which runs north across a level plain before climbing over a shoulder of mountain, giving excellent views back down onto the Indus and up the Shigar Valley. The road then descends to Shigar village, 32 km from Skardu. Quite often there are land-slides on this section, blocking the road for long periods. Jeeps can usually cope with the occasionally unlikely looking old road at these times, passing through the village of Kothang; buses are suspended for the duration. Scrabble aficionados can confidently place 'dzo' on a triple word score after a visit to this valley, since there are many examples of the cow/yak hybrid around Shigar village itself and all the way further up towards Askole and beyond. ▸▸ *See Transport, page 258, for more details.*

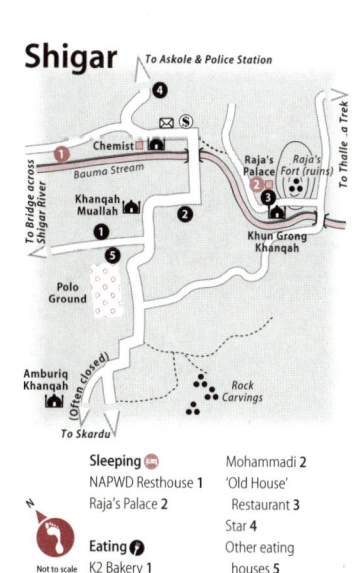

Shigar village

This picturesque village, shady, cool and green with irrigation channels and the Bauma Lungma (lungma meaning 'stream') briskly flowing through, was once the capital of the ancient kingdom of Shigar. Today it retains much of its charm. Many of the houses are still built of wood, with intricately carved doorways and windows, while the locals, including the women, are friendly, curious and welcoming. The kids seem to say 'one pen' more as a greeting than as a demand.

Ins and outs Visiting Shigar village as a day-trip from Skardu by public transport is a little tricky, especially when the road is blocked, but with a privately hired jeep (maximum Rs800) it is an easy half-day excursion. The bus goes right into the main

Sleeping
NAPWD Resthouse 1
Raja's Palace 2
Mohammadi 2
'Old House' Restaurant 3
Star 4
Other eating houses 5

Eating
K2 Bakery 1

bazaar. A good place to wait for cargo jeeps is near the polo ground, by the turning leading to the bridge across the Shigar River, or ask around the restaurants.

Sights

The largely destroyed ruins of the **Raja's Fort** stand on a sharp outcrop of rock overlooking the village. It is possible to climb, and to enjoy some excellent views, by following the jeep track to the east of the rock to pick up a path up to the ruins.

Below it, a short way up the Bauma stream is the former **Raja's Palace (Fongkhar)**, in the same style as those at Baltit and Altit in Hunza. It is believed to have been built around 1640 by Hassan Khan, the 20th ruler of the Amacha dynasty. The palace is a three-storeyed cribbage construction, consisting of three separate buildings built adjacent to each other in different periods. The whole appears as one, with a beautifully carved entrance doorway and carved wood decoration in the outside wall. It is presently undergoing extensive renovation by **AKCSP** (Aga Khan Cultural Services Pakistan). The plan is to transform it into an exclusive 13-room guesthouse with the grand audience hall and the ante rooms serving as a museum of Balti woodcarving and local living traditions. The audience hall and the court of the Fort-Palace may also be used for concerts of traditional music. Museum visitors can also see unoccupied historic rooms.

The raja's **'Old House'**, which has less historic value, is being converted into a reception and restaurant compound, with the restaurant, the kitchen and service rooms occupying the former stable on the ground floor, while the lounge, a conference room and a manager's office occupy the upper floor.

Nearby, overlooking the Bauma stream, is the **Khlin Grong Khanqah**, a small, beautifully carved wooden mosque.

By the roadside in the centre of the village there is the much larger, wooden **Khanqah Muallah**, now used as the Juma Masjid, where Friday prayers are still held. This is the largest mosque in Shigar, with a three-tiered roof built by Kashmiri craftsmen. Its construction is generally attributed to the Muslim missionary Mir Shamsuddin Iraqi. It is hoped that **AKCSP** (Aga Khan Cultural Services Pakistan) will soon undertake restoration work on the building and a nearby *astana*.

Upper Shigar Valley & around

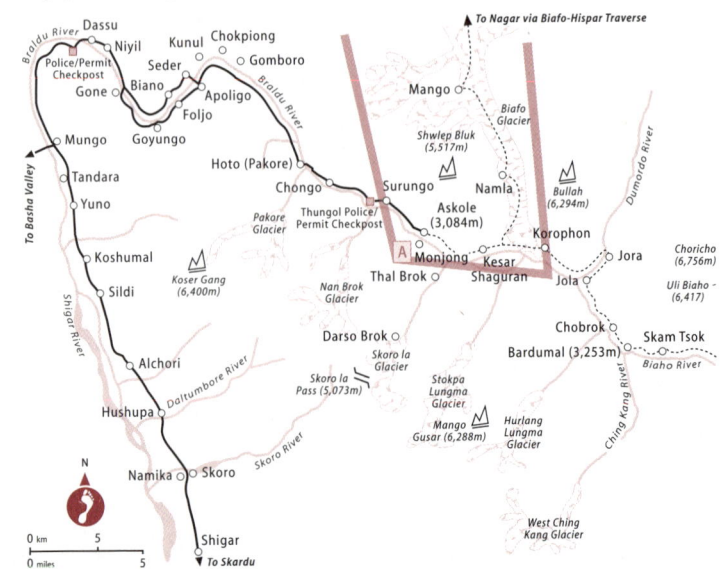

At the southern end of the village, **Amburiq Khanqah** is a smaller structure, but well restored showing the cribbage structure using wooden beams supporting wattle and daub. Unfortunately, entry to any of these mosques is forbidden to non-Muslims. On the opposite side of the main road, scattered around a low ridge to the south of the main village, are numerous **rock carvings** depicting ibex, Buddhist stupas and other symbols, although these are difficult to find. The ruins of a **Buddhist monastery** have also recently been excavated in the area.

Excursions from Shigar

Chhurka Khanqah ⓘ *8 km north of Shigar, further up the valley off the main track – take the left fork under concrete water channel and park vehicle shortly after the underground apricot processing plant on the left; from here, walk a short distance across fields past the new mosque*, is another interesting example of an old *khanqah*, unique in that it has a large plane tree growing from the inner courtyard, dominating the traditional place of worship, while there remains evidence of delicate carvings on the doors and the triple balcony at the front. Despite a new mosque in the village, the *khanqah* still remains a social focus, but non-Muslims are sadly not allowed inside. The AKCSP hopes to complete restoration soon.

The side valley climbing up to the east from Shigar village is known as **Bauma Valley**. A jeep track leads up as far as the hydro-electric plant at Chaupi Ol that provides Shigar with electricity. This is the start (or finish) of the Thalle La trek (see page 256 for a description of the trek going from the Thalle Valley to Shigar). If you do not want to undertake the full trek, it makes for a very pleasant walk to follow the valley up as far as feels comfortable and then return to Shigar. From the hydro-electric plant to the picturesque settlement of Ol is around two hours' walk away. A little further on there is a bridge across the stream. If you double back along the opposite bank here you can reach the equally picturesque settlement of Anisgal. Both settlements offer good camping.

Related maps:
A Biafo-Hispar Traverse, p253
B Hushe Valley, p260

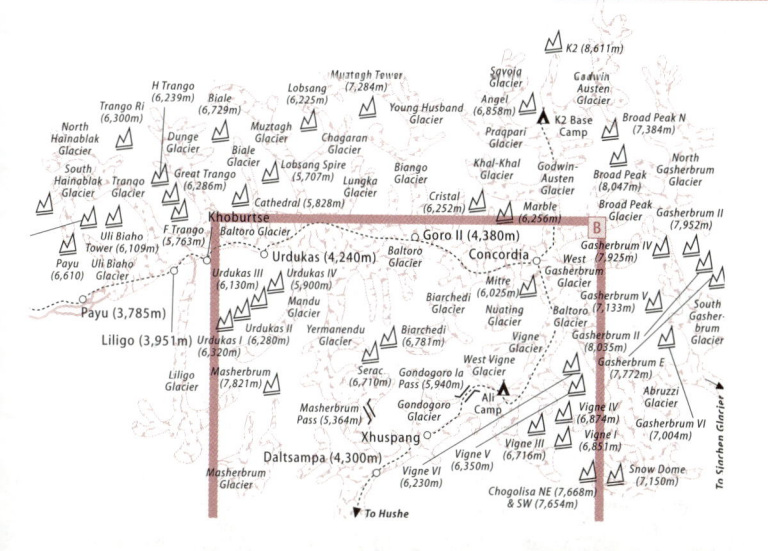

There is a bridge crossing just to the west of Shigar village and a jeep track leading up the west bank of the river, giving access to the **Basha Valley** which branches off to the northwest. At **Chu Tron**, 8 km into the Basha Valley, there are hot **sulphur springs** with separate bathing huts for men and women. There is also a **NAPWD Resthouse** adjacent, bookable in Skardu (also worth trying without a booking). The jeep track continues up the valley as far as the beautiful village of **Doko** (20 km). It is a long day's walk (or two fairly easy days) to **Arondu**, a tiny village at the snout of the awesome 40-km **Chogo Lungma Glacier**. North of the village, the glaciated Kero Lungma Valley leads up to the extremely difficult and deeply crevassed Nushik La, and over to the Hispar Glacier. The pass was once used as a route connecting Nagar with Baltistan, but is today considered to be impassable.

The main route up the Shigar Valley continues up the east bank, passing through several green and fertile villages along the way. At the confluence of the Basha and Braldu Valleys, a series of bridges provides an alternative point of access to the Basha Valley, although after heavy rains the crossing is often impassable. **Dassu**, 11 km into the Braldu Valley where the jeep track crosses to the north bank, is the first village. This was originally the starting point for the trek to K2, but the jeep track has now been extended as far as **Askole** (up to Rs3,500 jeep drop from Skardu). This last section of jeep track is still unstable in places and subject to frequent closures due to land-slides. A little way beyond the village of **Chango**, above the jeep track, there are hot sulphur springs suitable for bathing.

Treks in the area

Baltoro Glacier trek: Concordia and K2

ⓘ *Restricted zone. Maximum elevation optional (5,000 m plus). Jun to mid-Sep. Maps: Swiss Foundation are the best; Leomann's sheets 2 and 3 are also good; U502 series, NI 43-3 Mundik and NI 43-4 Chulung are adequate; the excellent 1977 Japanese-Pakistan K2 1:100,000 map covers the Baltoro Glacier only. For orientation, see map p251. See trekking notes, p45. See above for details of the route from Shigar to Askole.*

Since this trek is in a restricted zone and therefore requires a permit and registered guide, no detailed route description is given here. In practice it is only possible to obtain a permit through a recognized trekking agency. This is far and away the most popular trek in Pakistan, attracting large numbers of trekking groups (all the major trekking agencies bring groups here) as well as numerous mountaineering expeditions en route to peaks around Concordia. As a result it can get seriously crowded and some of the main campsites have become heavily polluted, especially after Gokus. The Falchen Kangri Association has installed an incinerator at Payu (Paiju) which should be used to dispose of all local burnable rubbish.

The trek along the Braldu and Biaho Rivers, and then the **Baltoro Glacier** is a long and very demanding one. The reward is, however, spectacular, taking you right into the heart of the Karakoram mountains at **Concordia**, where the Godwin-Austin Glacier descends from **K2** to join the Baltoro. Surrounding these huge expanses of ice are some of the highest peaks in the world, with seven of them (K2, Broad Peak, Gasherbrum IV, Mustagh Tower, Golden Throne, Chogolisa and Masherbrum) clearly visible.

Notwithstanding land-slides and blockages, the jeep track now extends as far as **Askole**. The trek from Askole to Concordia takes around eight days, not including rest days. Porters on this trek can be difficult, often striking for increased pay, or refusing to go beyond the lower stages of the trek. There are nine recognized stages between Askole and Concordia: Askole-Korophon-Jola-Barduman-Payu-Liligo*-Urdukas-Biango*-Goro-Concordia. Those marked with an asterisk are usually bypassed for camping. It takes a full day to trek up to the K2 base camp from Concordia. Count four to six days for the return trip.

Another option which is becoming increasingly popular is to trek out of Concordia into the Hushe Valley over the **Gondogoro Pass**. At 5,500 m the route across this pass is extremely strenuous. There is now a fixed rope up to the pass, installed by the local mountain rescue team who demand Rs2,500-5,000 to cross, depending on whether there are five group members or more. An alternative route across the Masherbrum pass is slightly lower (5,364 m), but extremely difficult, involving technical sections on the descent through an icefall on the far side and requiring ropes, crampons and ice axes, and specialist high-altitude porters.

Biafo-Hispar Traverse

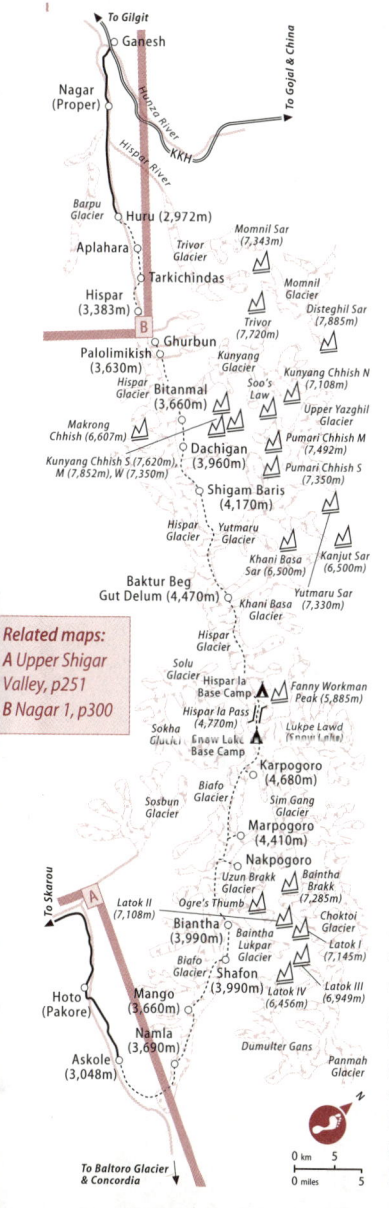

Biafo-Hispar trek: Askole to Nagar

Open zone. Maximum elevation 5,150 m. Jul to mid-Sep. Maps: Swiss Foundation are best; U502 series, NI 43-3 Mundik, NJ 43-15 Shimshal, NJ 43-14 Baltit reliability poor but adequate. For orientation, see map, page 253. Read trekking notes, p45.

Although this trek is in an open zone, it is an extremely strenuous one, involving long stretches of glacier-walking along this 115-km ice corridor; a guide is essential, and so are crampons and ropes. The trek takes you far from any permanent settlements and is also rich in wildlife. However, Himalayan brown bears have sadly not been spotted on this route for over five years now. Starting at **Askole**, the route follows the K2 trek for a short way before branching up the **Biafo Glacier**.

The first part of this trek, up the lower sections of the Biafo Glacier, is particularly difficult. Above the junction of the Sim Gang and Biafo Glaciers, off to the north as you approach Hispar Pass, is **Snow Lake**, an expanse of ice covering around 80 sq km. Known locally as Lukpe Lawo (the name of the pass on the lake), it was named Snow Lake in 1892 by the British explorer Martin Conway. The 5,150-m **Hispar Pass** has stunning views in good weather; west down the Hispar Glacier towards Hunza and east back to the peaks around Snow Lake and Sim Gang Glacier. The trek to Hispar village along the north edge of the Hispar Glacier is difficult in places, crossing four- side glaciers en route. Between these there are several beautiful ablation valleys (small valleys running parallel to the glacier), rich in alpine flora and with plentiful water.

Hispar village, the first permanent settlement after leaving Askole, is at the head of the jeep track which runs up past **Nagar village** from the KKH opposite Karimabad. There is no regular public transport up to Hispar, so unless you have organized a jeep to meet you at Hispar, it is still another two days' walk down to Nagar, where you can count on finding public transport, although it may be possible to pick something up in Huru on the way. The trek between Askole and Hispar villages takes around 12 days (not including rest days) and involves around 22 porter stages: Askole-Korophon-Namla-Mango-Dongbar-Shafon-Biantha-Nagporo-Marporo-Karporo-Snow Lake (base camp)-Hispar Pass-Hispar Pass Base Camp-Khaniblansa-Khani Glacier-Jutanma-Big Glacier-'Another' Glacier-Buttonmul-Ta Shing-4th Glacier-Hispar. Few people now attempt this route in the opposite direction due to difficulties with Nagari porters.

Sleeping

Shigar village *p249*

L-C Raja's Palace (Fongkhar). Good-quality accommodation. Cosy rooms and suites retain much authentic character of the Fort/Palace, but with modern bathrooms. Minimal modern furniture and facilities in rooms, many rooms feature spectacular original or restored woodwork and are complemented by traditional craft objects and artefacts from the region.

F NAPWD Resthouse, pleasantly situated by the Bauma Lungma. 2 rooms, clean and comfortable with a nice garden (camping allowed), book through NAPWD in Skardu or else just turn up, the chowkidar is not fussy and will give you a room if available. Food prepared to order.

Eating

Shigar village *p249*

'Old House' Restaurant, in front of the Fongkhar, offers traditional Balti food. The management here is overseen by the Baltistan Culture Foundation, which ensures that it is run by the local community for their own benefit.

There are also a few basic restaurants in town offering chewy mutton and not much else, such as the **Mohammadi** and **Star**, plus a couple of unnamed ones.

Transport

Shigar village *p249*

When the road is clear, there is a daily **NATCO** bus service from **Skardu** to Shigar village, departing at 1430. This journey takes around 1½ hrs and costs Rs15. The bus remains in Shigar overnight and returns to Skardu at around 0600. Cargo jeeps operate fairly regularly on this route, mostly leaving Skardu in the late morning or early afternoon (try asking around the aqueduct or Yadgar Chowk), the frequency depends on demand. They cost around Rs30, taking about 1 hr overall for the journey.

Cargo jeeps also pass through Shigar on an irregular basis (they usually pass through in the afternoon) en route for **Askole** in the Braldu Valley, and to **Chu Tron** in the Basha Valley. The fare from Shigar to Askole is around Rs200-225. To Chu Tron expect to pay Rs80-100. Unless you are prepared to hang around forlong periods, it is a better idea to hire a jeep privately to get to these places, although this is normally part of the deal for trekking expeditions booked through a decent agent. Half-day jeep excursions to **Shigar village** from Skardu will set you back around Rs800.

Khapulu → *Colour map 3, grid C2*

Khapulu formed one of the major kingdoms of Baltistan and is now one of the region's administrative divisions. Most of the population of Khapulu belong to the Nurbakshi sect of Islam, similar to the Ismailis of Hunza and Chitral in their more progressive outlook on life. They are warm and friendly and the women go about their business freely, without observing purdah. The regional capital is the sleepy little settlement of Khapulu, where the Raja's Palace can still be seen, an ideal place to visit for those not up to the rigours of trekking. ▶ *For Sleeping, Eating and all other listings, see pages 258-259.*

Ins and outs

There are regular bus, Hiace minibus and cargo jeep services between Skardu and Khapulu, which make the journey in two and a half to three hours. Private jeeps will cost at least Rs2,000. Unless you are really pushed for time, an overnight stop here is recommended. Arriving from Skardu, you pass first the AC's and DC's houses, a petrol station and the police station. A little further on, the road forks up from the main road to the main bazaar in the lower part of the village, where the cheaper hotels, bank, post office, PCO and bus station are located. ▶ *See Transport, page 258, for more details.*

History

Khapulu formed the third major kingdom of Baltistan. During the rule of **Bahram** (1494-1550), the Muslim missionary Mir Shamsuddin Iraqi is known to have visited Khapulu. According to some sources it is he who was responsible for establishing the Nurbakshi sect. Many folk tales talk of the great theological debates which took place at this time. Khapulu was subject to repeated attacks from Skardu, although at a later stage, under the rule of **Hatim Khan** (1650-1715), who was considered the greatest of the Yabgu kings, Khapulu in its turn attacked Skardu. Later, in the early 19th century, Ahmed Shah of Skardu once again attacked Khapulu, installing his own governor, or Kharpon. The divisions this caused among the people ultimately paved the way for the Dogra invasion of Baltistan.

Skardu to Khapulu

The road east from Skardu to Khapulu is now metalled for most of the way. After passing the bridge-turning to Shigar, the road bends southeast across a stony plain to **Gole** (30 km). Just before the village, beside the road, several large boulders feature weather-beaten **inscriptions** in Tibetan and carvings of **Buddhist stupas**, tridents and other symbols. A bridge at Gole crosses the Indus giving access to a rough jeep track running along the north bank of the Shyok River.

A few kilometres beyond Gole, the Shyok River drains into the Indus from the east. A suspension bridge crosses the Indus just south of its confluence with the Shyok. There is a check post at the bridge; foreigners must register their details. The road southeast along the Indus (closed to foreigners) passes through the villages of **Mediabad** (formerly Parkutta), **Totli** and **Kharmang**, once centres of tiny independent kingdoms, and leads towards the Line of Control (effectively the border) with India. The main route east to Khapulu crosses the Indus on the suspension bridge and follows the south bank of the Shyok River. This first stretch of the Shyok was once the home of the tiny kingdom of **Kiris** (the village is on the opposite bank). Beyond was the powerful kingdom of Khapulu, second only to Skardu, guarding the old route to Ladakh.

Just to the east of **Ghowari** village there is a bridge across to the north bank of the Shyok. Between the villages of **Yugo** and **Karphok** there is a second bridge. Hidden in the mountains above Karphok there is a large lake fed by glacier water. A few kilometres beyond Karphok, there is a third bridge across the Shyok which gives direct access to the village of **Doghani**, at the foot of the Thalle Valley. Higher up this valley is the start of the **Thalle La** trek. The main road continues along the south bank of the Shyok, passing through **Bara**, a cluster of villages stretching over several kilometres, before arriving at Khapulu, 103 km from Skardu.

Thalle La trek

ⓘ *Open zone. Maximum elevation 4,572 m. Jul to Sep. Maps: Swiss Foundation are the best; U502 series, NI 43-3 Mundik is reasonably accurate topographically, although place names are mostly redundant. Read trekking notes, p45.*

This trek is easily accessible from Skardu and is ideal if you are looking for something not too demanding, or wish to acclimatize and improve your fitness. It can be done in either direction; the ascent to the pass is gentler from Shigar side, although if you cannot afford to organize jeeps to pick you up at the end of the trek, it is probably best to finish in Shigar, where public transport back to Skardu is readily available (on the Thalle side you are likely to have to walk all the way down to **Doghani** before finding any public transport). The trek is here described from Doghani to Shigar. If you are fit and determined, the trek can be done in three days; four days is more manageable, or five if you wish to go slowly and have time to relax at the end of each day's walking.

From **Doghani**, the jeep track continues up the Thalle Valley as far as **Khusomik**, the last permanent village. Up until about 50 years ago, the side valley that drains in from the east at Khusomik was used as a route across to Kande in the Hushe Valley. Glacial advance and deep crevasses have made this route no longer passable.

From Khusomik the trail crosses the side valley on a foot bridge and climbs gently past two small areas of fields and pasture and then crosses to the west bank of the valley. The side valley that leads off to the southwest from here is a trekking route across to Kiris, on the north bank of the Shyok near where it joins the Indus. The trail continues up through beautiful summer pastures with rich green meadows, flowers (July and early August), fields and scattered seasonal settlements of tiny stone houses and animal enclosures. There are numerous places to camp along this stretch. Higher up, near **Metsik Pa**, which consists of two animal enclosures with huts, the valley forks. The left fork is the route up to Thalle La, while the right fork leads up to the much higher and more difficult **Tusserpo La** (5,048 m) which provides an alternative route over to Shigar. Metsik Pa means 'place of fire' in Balti, and according to locals this area was thickly wooded until around a hundred years ago, when a huge fire which raged for more than a month completely destroyed the forests.

The trail continues along the left bank of the stream to **Dumsum** (literally 'junction'), where there are shepherds' huts, before crossing to the right bank. There is one more potential camping place higher up at **La**, again a small seasonal settlement of shepherds' huts, before the final ascent up to **Thalle La** (4,572 m). From the top of the pass it is a long steady descent along the right bank of the stream. The pastures on either side of the pass abound in marmots. Lower down, the vegetation gradually gives way to stunted woods of pine, juniper and wild rose. There are three small settlements in close succession, offering good camping places, before reaching **Bauma Harel**, at the junction of the Thalle La and Tusserpo La Valleys, again a good camping spot. From Bauma Harel it is a steep descent down the **Bauma Lungma**, which is a narrow, rocky and dry gorge for much of the way. The path follows the right bank, crosses to the left and then back to the right bank. Beyond the second bridge, on the left bank, is the picturesque settlement of **Anisgal**. Further on, the trail passes **Ol**, before finally reaching the hydro-electric power station at **Chaupi Ol**, from where it is a short walk along a jeep track down to Shigar village.

Khapulu village

Khapulu (Khaplu) is beautifully situated, spread across a wide alluvial fan which slopes steeply down from an amphitheatre of mountains towards the south. It is surprisingly green, with numerous irrigation channels feeding terraced fields and orchards which abound in apricots, apples and even oranges (these are harvested from late August to early September). At an altitude of 2,600 m, it is also pleasantly cooler than Skardu in summer. There are numerous walks along tree-lined paths and irrigation channels and good fishing in the calmer bits of the Shyok River. Like the village of Shigar, it is a picturesque place where you can experience something of the flavour of traditional Balti culture.

Sights

High up on the alluvial fan overlooking the village (a pleasant 45-minute walk from the main bazaar) is the **Raja Mahal**, or Raja's Palace ① *visitors are asked to buy an entry coupon for Rs50 from the chowkidar, whose family live in the palace's compound, and is usually on hand to open it up.* The palace is althought to have been constructed by Kashmiri craftsmen for Yagbu Silim Lde in around 1460, although not in its present location. When the Dogras conquered Baltistan in the 1840s they either burnt down the former rulers' strongholds or allowed them to be brought down into the main villages to avoid revolt. Consequently, Khapulu Palace was shifted down the valley to its present location about 150 years ago. It was occupied until recently by three brothers of the old ruling family, but is now owned by **Baltistan Culture Foundation** who hope to raise funds for its much-needed restoration.

From the outside, the most striking feature of the palace is a four-storey carved wooden balcony, although, true to form, the local PWD has whacked an electric cable right across the façade. Inside, you can see the beautiful, intricately carved Kashmiri woodwork decorating the doors, windows and some of the ceilings of the various rooms. Overall, however, the palace is very dilapidated and heading steadily towards dereliction (take great care if you go up onto the roof). It stands out as a fascinating and potentially very attractive monument urgently in need of the required restoration.

On the way up through the village en route to the Raja Mahal you pass two old wooden mosques by the track. Further on, below the track, is another large wooden mosque, the **Khankha Masjid** (Khankha being the name of the village), with some particularly fine carved decoration. Next to this mosque is a recently restored four metre square wooden **astana**, a type of shrine. Around 15 minutes' walk beyond the Raja Mahal, in Chakchan village, the similar **Chakchan Masjid** is also worth a visit. Unfortunately, non-Muslims are not allowed to enter any of these mosques.

To the southeast of the main village, up on the shoulder of mountain reaching

Khapulu

N
Not to scale

Sleeping
Citizen 1
K7 Motel 2
Karakoram Lodge 3
Khaplu Inn 4
Kunais 5
PTDC Motel 6

down to the river, is an area of summer pasture with shepherds' huts, known as **Hanjore**. From here you can cross the fields at Kaldaq to the village of Surmo from where there are excellent views of **Masherbrum** (7,821 m) above the Hushe Valley to the north. Further up, towards the glacier above the pasture, there is a lake. Golden marmots are easily spotted on this route. To reach Hanjore, follow the old jeep track which branches off by the polo ground near the Raja Mahal. It is a long and fairly strenuous (but rewarding) climb. This is a full day's hike, although you can return more quickly by following the main track back down to Khapulu.

Another full-day, but worthwhile, hike starts from the Chakchan Masjid and crosses the villages of Hippi and Gharbunchhung, before ascending the **Thor-ste-khar rock tower**. From here the original foundations of the Raja Mahal can be seen, along with a preserved mosque. Good views over Khapulu to the Karakorams can also be enjoyed from this vantage point. For both of the above day walks it is advisable to take a local guide who knows the way. Ask at your hotel to recommend someone.

Sleeping

Khapulu *p257, map p257*

C PTDC Motel, T0575-77110, F0575-77162. On main road below village, 10-min walk past the turning to the main bazaar. Newish, tastefully built stone-clad complex, comfortable chalet-style rooms with attached hot bath and individual terraces, pleasant sit-out garden, restaurant.

C-E Karakoram Lodge, T0575-77111, btadvent@karakoram.sdnpk.undp.org. 15-min walk above the main village, towards Chakchan. Clean and comfortable carpeted rooms with attached bath, restaurant and garden with good views down to the confluence with the Shyok River. Camping possible at Rs100 with own tent. The lodge is primarily aimed at organized trekking groups.

E K7 Motel, above the main village, near the Raja Mahal. 4 rooms with small sofa-beds, attached hot bath and individual balconies, excellent views, restaurant and garden which permits camping.

G Khaplu Inn, in the main bazaar. Not much to look at, but contains some reasonably clean rooms with attached bath (room 209 has an excellent view over a small patch of shitting ground, if you like that sort of thing!). Decent restaurant serving simple spicy food, friendly, helpful manager.

H Citizen, T0575-77119, main bazaar, entrance on path leading to post office. Passable rooms, some with attached bath, most without, arranged around a small courtyard, owner has made an effort to attract backpackers with trekking info and an ambitious menu.

H Kunais, main bazaar. Most basic rooms in town, but cheapest, with shared toilet/shower facilities, restaurant.

Eating

Khapulu *p257, map p257*

†††-†† PTDC Motel, on main road below village, 10 min walk past the turning to the main bazaar, T0575-77110, F0575-77162. The most comfortable, when there are guests they serve a fixed evening menu (Rs250 per head) although you must book in advance if you are not staying here.

†† Karakoram Lodge, 15 min walk above the main village, towards Chakchan., T0575-77111, btadvent@karakoram.sdnpk.undp.org. Does little for the vegetarian but has good views. Again, book in advance if not staying.

† Khaplu Inn, in the main bazaar. Popular with bus and jeep drivers and serves the usual simple but tasty meat and rice dishes. Vegetable 'du jour' is well spiced and not overcooked mush.

Otherwise, there are a couple of places in the main bazaar selling simple snacks (bhajis, samosas etc). There are also a couple of bakeries where you can buy biscuits etc, and shops selling rice, lentils, onions and whatever fruits/vegetables are in season.

Transport

Khapulu *p257, map p257*

NATCO runs 2 buses per day to and from **Skardu**, while **Masherbrum** have a daily coaster for the 3-hr journey. **K2** provides 2 cramped jeeps each day. The buses depart from near the NATCO booking office in the main bazaar of Khapulu. Times are variable, so ask in this area or get up early for morning departures to Skardu. Jeeps may leave from lower down, before the cheap hotels, so ask around. Cargo jeeps run mainly on demand, generally leaving late in the day from Skardu, and a little earlier for the return journey. A private jeep will set you back Rs2,200 for the 1 way trip from PTDC in Skardu, although it will cost less from jeep-drivers in the bazaar.

Hushe Valley → *Colour map 3, grid B1*

North of Khapulu, the Hushe Valley (pronounced 'Hooshay' and now often spelt Hushey) climbs gently for 30 km up to Hushe village. A rough jeep track, very difficult in places, reaches as far as the village, leading past spectacular views of snow-capped peaks on all sides, with Masherbrum to the north dominating. As in Khapulu, the people are predominantly Nurbakshi. Being the only approach route to Masherbrum, as well as numerous other major peaks in the area, the Hushe Valley has for a long time attracted mountaineers. With the discovery of the Gondogoro La route across to Concordia and the Baltoro Glacier, the valley has become of major importance, at least in terms of mountain tourism. Trekkers can now make the 10-12-day trek from Askole to Concordia, and then instead of doubling all the way back, climb up over the Gondogoro La (a very strenuous and in places technical 5,500-m pass) and down into Hushe Valley. ▸▸ *For Sleeping, Eating and all other listings, see pages 264-264.*

Ins and outs

Finding public transport heading up the Hushe Valley is something of a hit-and-miss affair. Cargo jeeps run on an irregular basis from Skardu or Khapulu to various villages in the valley. Those coming from Skardu are likely to be already full when they pass Khapulu (wait for them on the main road below Khapulu if you want to try). You will probably have better luck asking around in the main bazaar in Khapulu. Fares are open to negotiation; from Khapulu as far as Kande should cost around Rs100, and as far as Hushe village up to Rs200, although the road is often blocked at Kande. Jeeps are readily available for private hire in Khapulu's main bazaar; as far as Hushe village will cost at least Rs1,500, although this depends on your bargaining skills.

The other option is to walk. From Khapulu to Hushe is feasible in one very long day if you are fit, but two days is more realistic. There is accommodation at **Machilu** and **Kande**, and plenty of places to camp all the way up the valley. The first section between Khapulu and Machilu (around four hours) is the least interesting; if possible, it is worth getting transport for this stretch, or at least across to Saling. From Machilu to Kande is around three to four hours, and from Kande to Hushe the same again. ▸▸ *See Transport, page 264, for more details.*

Khapulu to Hushe village

Just east of the PTDC Motel there is a military check post where foreigners must register. The guard here will enlighten you with the advice "not allowed Siachen"! Originally locals would cross the Shyok River from Khapulu on rafts known as *dzaks*, made of inflated goatskins, walking several kilometres upstream before paddling their way furiously across the fast-flowing river. Until very recently this was continued, with inner-tubes replacing the goatskins, but the regular fatalities, particularly when the river was swollen, finally convinced the authorities to build a bridge. Completed in 1992, this bridge crosses the Shyok 4 km east of Khapulu, giving direct access along a pebble-dash road to the village of **Saling** on the west bank of the Hushe River.

From Saling, the track, now mud and stone, climbs up into the valley, becoming progressively rougher and precarious. At the village of **Machilu** (Machulo) there is a resthouse. In the village itself, the focus point is an impressively renovated *khanqah*-style mosque, superbly situated overlooking the wide confluence of the Saltoro and Hushe Rivers. Opposite is the village of Haldi, on the banks of the Saltoro River where it drains into the Hushe River from the east. The Saltoro River Valley is currently closed to tourists due to the border dispute with India over the Siachen Glacier. The valley is particularly stunning in places with sheer granite

Hushe Valley

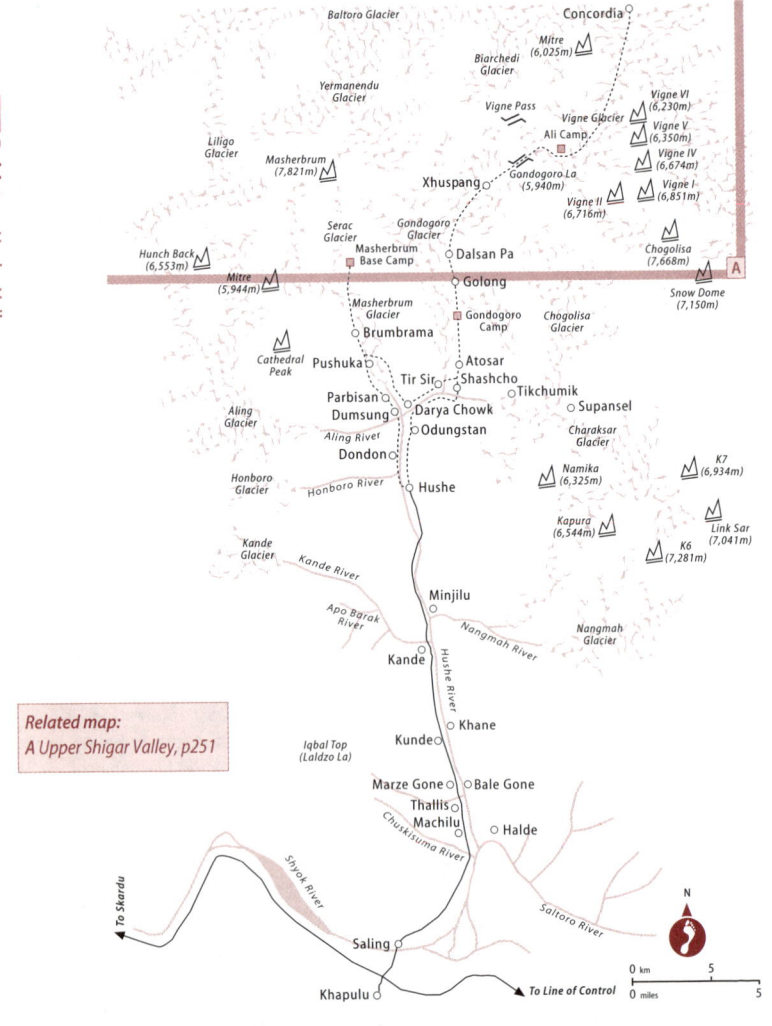

Related map:
A Upper Shigar Valley, p251

pinnacles rising to nearly 1,000 m above the valley floor. Higher up, the valley divides, the north fork being the **Kondus Valley**, while that to the south keeps the name of **Saltoro** (giver of life). Both valleys have the potential for some beautiful trekking and climbing.

The main track up the Hushe Valley passes through **Thallis** (with its colourful *khanqah*) to **Marze Gone**, where a bridge crosses to the east bank village of **Bale Gone**. From Bale Gone a jeep track leads south back to Haldi. The track north along the east bank is impassable except on foot.

The main track continues north, passing the village of **Khane** on the east bank, reached only by a footbridge, before arriving at **Kande** (pronounced and now often spelt 'Kandey'), a reasonable sized village with a small hotel. If you are walking up to Hushe, this is a good place to break the journey, but check the bill carefully since everything has a price tag.

The village itself is frequently the victim of flash floods and land-slides. In 1997, 20 houses were destroyed with most of the others suffering some kind of damage. With 130 houses destroyed by the flood of 2000, the village was pretty much wiped out. The rebuilding has now split the village into two with 'New Kande' (or Kabbirabad) located just to the north of the original village with a better chance of avoiding the next great flood.

Since most treks from the Hushe Valley are restricted, local guides have been active in finding new routes in the open zones of the side valleys. From Kande a number of such treks have been identified. You may well be offered a trek to **Iqbal Top**, named after a local guide (by himself), although other villagers claim that this point has actually been known as **Laldzo La** for generations. This three- to four-day trek heads west from Kande. From the pasture at the top, views of K2, Broad Peak, Gasherbrum I & II, Chogolisa, K6, K7, K12 and K13 can all be seen when the weather is favourable. It is possible to continue on this route to join up with the Thalle La trek (see page 256) although this is a difficult proposition. To the east of Kande, a week-long trek up the **Nama Valley** leads to a cauldron of 7,000-m-plus mountains, including **Amin Barkk**, a demanding challenge for rock climbers.

Above Kande, the jeep track (which is often blocked by rock falls) continues on for a while before crossing to the east bank on a wooden bridge and climbing the final stretch up to Hushe village. When the track is blocked it is necessary to walk or negotiate a 'special' jeep, which will cost up to Rs1,000 and be full of locals anyway.

Hushe village (pronounced 'Hushey') is beautifully located on a small hillock, surrounded by rocky peaks and pinnacles, with Masherbrum visible from here in all its splendour. This is the starting point for numerous beautiful treks and walks. The village is steadily gearing itself up to the increased flow of trekkers and climbers, with every other man in the village claiming to be a guide. Each year, over a thousand people are estimated to pass through, going to or coming from Concordia over Gondogoro La. Some years this figure has topped 1,100, with around 80% arriving from Askole across the Baltoro and Gondogoro Glaciers.

Treks from Hushe village

Gondogoro La Trek

ⓘ *Restricted zone. Maximum elevation 5,500 m. Jun to Sep. Maps: Swiss Foundation are the best; U502 series, NI 43-3 Mundik is adequate as far as Dalsan Pa. For orientation, see Hushe Valley map, p260. See trekking notes, p45.*

This is a very beautiful trek. From the top of Gondogoro La there are excellent close-up views of K2 and a host of other high peaks (provided of course the weather is clear). The panorama is truly breathtaking. It is also an extremely strenuous climb (particularly without the benefit of a couple of weeks walking and acclimatizing that

Organizing your trek from Hushe

The village of Hushe marks the start of treks north towards the glaciers of Aling, Masherbrum, Gondogoro and Chogolisa, and numerous peaks in the area. **NB** All these treks, with the exception of the trek to Aling Glacier, have now been officially classified as restricted, requiring trips to Islamabad for briefing and debriefing before and after the trek. However, this is a development which is being strongly contested by the freelance guides in Hushe, who argue that they should be allowed to take trekkers on round-trip treks from Hushe without having to obtain permits. In practice, many trekkers do go up the Gondogoro Valley and towards Masherbrum Base Camp without a permit. However, you are advised to obtain a permit if you intend to go to the top of Gondogoro La. On no account should you consider crossing into Concordia without a permit; you are very likely to get caught and are liable to be helicoptered back to Skardu at your own expense (in the region of US$6,500).

Each of the campsites in Hushe is owned by a government-registered guide, and there are several others from Hushe, including Anwar Ali, a freelancer with plenty of experience and good humour. In fact almost every other man in the village will claim to be a guide recognized by the government, so check that they are registered and have the relevant paper from the Culture, Sports and Tourism Division. It's also worth asking for recommendation letters from previous trekkers. Official rates are Rs240 per porter per stage. Guides ask for Rs600-700 per day. There is a considerable amount of equipment available for hire, including tents, sleeping bags, crampons, ice axes, ropes etc. Hamza Ali has a good selection of equipment, as does Ashraf Hussain, and the K2 Shop claims to have enough to equip a party of 12. The latter, and also a couple of other stores, usually have a reasonable selection of high-energy, freeze-dried and tinned foods leftover from previous expeditions. Unless a large group has hired everyone and everything (fairly unlikely), it is usually possible to simply turn up in Hushe and organize guides, porters, equipment and food. However, this is not much use if you want to attempt one of the restricted treks as you have to all go down to Islamabad for your briefing.

---

you get if you come from the Baltoro side). The top of the pass is at an altitude of 5,500 m (another 500 m and it would qualify as a mountain), and involves a climb along the glacier and a snow traverse. A guide and proper equipment (high-altitude clothing/bedding, crampons, rope) is essential if going this far. The trek to Dalsan Pa (the last stop before heading onto the glacier) is far less demanding but still very beautiful and well worth considering.

From **Hushe** it is three stages up to Dalsan Pa (three to four days), and a further three stages to the top of the pass (two days). From Hushe the path heads north along the east bank of the river through fields and stands of willow and wild rose. It then bears east along the south bank of the Charaksar River, passing through a summer camp used by shepherds. Just beyond where the Gondogoro River joins from the north, a bridge crosses to the north bank to reach **Saishu**, where there is good camping. A rubbish pit and latrines have been dug here, and in season there are even a couple of simple 'restaurants'. The path then climbs up the east side of

Gondogoro River and glacier, following lateral moraine and stretches of ablation valley. There are several possible camping places, the main one being at **Gondogoro summer settlement**. Above here there is a difficult stretch down beside the edge of the glacier before climbing back onto the lateral moraine and then passing through a beautiful meadow area and up to **Dalsan Pa**. Dalsan Pa is particularly beautiful, with two small lakes and a meadow that is carpeted with flowers in spring. The last three stages from Dalsan Pa (onto the glacier, up to **Gondogoro base camp** and then to the top of the pass) is where the going gets really tough. A fixed rope is now in place across the pass, see Baltoro Glacier Trek, page 252. An alternative route around here crosses the extremely difficult and technical **Masherbrum La.**

Chogolisa and Charaksar Glaciers

From Saishu a route continues east along the north bank of the Charaksar River and then along the north side of the Charaksar Glacier to its junction with the Chogolisa Glacier. The valley is more barren than the Gondogoro or Masherbrum, and the main attractions are the opportunities for climbing **K6** and **K7**.

Masherbrum Base Camp

ⓘ *Restricted zone. Maximum elevation optional (up to 4,200 m). Jun to Sep. Maps: as for Gondogoro La. For orientation, see map, p260. See trekking notes, p45.*

This trek bears off to the northwest above Hushe and follows the left side of the Masherbrum Glacier up to the base camp. Cross the footbridge just north of Hushe village to the west bank of the river. The path crosses the Honboro River, passes through a seasonal settlement and then crosses the Aling River. Higher up is **Dumsung**, and a little further on is **Parbisan**, both good camping spots. As far as Parbisan (one stage) is easy and pleasant, passing through fields and stands of wild rose, willow, juniper and tamarisk. Above Parbisan, there is a difficult section up onto the lateral moraine. Once on top, it is a beautiful walk along the lateral moraine to **Brumbrama**, situated on a wide sandy area between the lateral moraine and the mountains. It is possible to reach this in one day (two stages). A little higher up is **Chogospang**, with a few stone huts where in summer women tend large flocks of sheep and goats, as well as yaks, cows and dzo. Above Chogospang the path follows the lateral moraine before dropping down onto the glacier itself to reach Masherbrum Base Camp I (4,200 m). This is one stage; the walk to Base Camp II is a further stage.

Aling Glacier

A trekking route follows the north bank of the Aling River as far as the summer settlement of Ghazala, on the north side of the Aling Glacier. Allow two days to trek as far as here. This is the only trek to the north of Hushe officially classified as being in an open zone.

Honboro Glacier

To the west of Hushe, this trek is also in an open zone, reaching Kande via the Honboro Glacier. Local guides are constantly trying to find new routes in the area which don't involve the trip to Islamabad that restricted treks require, so ask around for alternatives, checking that the guide has done the route in advance.

Sleeping

Khapulu to Hushe village *p259*
Machilu
F NAPWD Resthouse. Officially this should be booked in Skardu, but in practice you can just turn up and providing there is room (which there usually is) you will be allowed to stay in 1 of the 2 rooms. Food is also available.

Kande
G K6 Hotel. 1 double room and 1 'dorm' room (sleep on the floor). There is a restaurant and small shop with basic supplies. Tents can be pitched on the roof.

Hushe village
NB It is necessary to register with the local police who will generally find you at your campsite. There are 4 **campsites** allowing camping with your own tent, or tents can be provided. They all consist of a small walled yard with toilet/shower facilities and can provide simple meals. All are in the main village.
H Gondogoro, owned by Ashraf Hussein.
H Gondogoro La, owned by Farhat Ali.
H K6-K7, owned by Mahmood Hassan. If you don't want to camp, you can doss down on the floor of the restaurant here.
H Leyla Peak, owned by Hamza Ali.

Biscuits, snacks etc (often including foreign chocolate and other goodies) can be found in the small stores in the village.

There is also an **open campsite** (no charge) just beyond the village, down near the spring, but don't expect any privacy or respite from boisterous, inquisitive and demanding children.

Transport

Hushe village *p261*
Cargo jeeps run on an irregular basis down to **Khapulu**, or it is often possible to negotiate something with private jeeps heading back down to Khapulu or **Skardu**, having dropped their trekking groups at the road head. However, jeep drivers in Hushe tend to charge somewhat inflated prices for private bookings (up to Rs1,500 to Khapulu after bargaining).

If you cannot find a cargo jeep or negotiate a reasonable deal on a private booking, it is worth walking down to Kande or further, since cargo jeeps from Khapulu often do not go all the way up to Hushe village. When the road is blocked at Kande it is usually possible to travel as far as the blockage on either side, at a price. A private jeep from Skardu will cost around Rs3,000 for the 1-way trip to **Hushe village**.

The KKH: Lower Hunza to Gojal

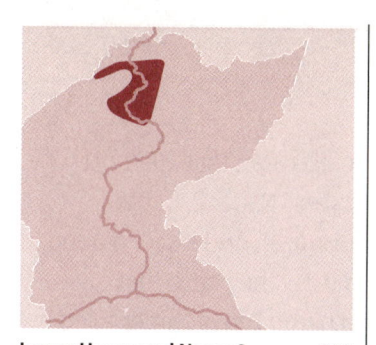

Lower Hunza and Nagar 2	**268**
Gilgit to Chalt	269
Chaprot Valley and Bar Valley	270
KKH: Chalt to Ghulmet	272
Minapin and Rakaposhi Base Camp	273
Rakaposhi/Diran Base Camp trek	274
Other walks around Minapin	276
Pisin to Hasanabad	277
Listings	277
Central Hunza	**279**
Hasanabad Nala	279
Hasanabad Nala to Aliabad	280
Listings	281
Karimabad	**282**
Listings	285
Around Karimabad	**290**
Altit	290
Duikar	292
Ganesh	295
Ganesh to Nazimabad/Shishkut	297
Listings	298
Nagar 1	**300**
Ganesh to Hoper	302
Treks from Hoper	303
Nagar 1 via Shayar, Askordas and Sumayar	304
Listings	304
Gojal (Upper Hunza)	**305**
Gulmit	305
Short walks around Gulmit	306
Gulmit to Passu	307
Short walks around Passu	309
Treks in the Passu area	311
Listings	313
Shimshal Valley	**315**
Passu to Shimshal village	316
Treks from Shimshal	317
Passu to Sust	318
Listings	319
Chapursan Valley	**319**
Sust to Zood Khun	320
Around Zood Khun	321
Zood Khun to Baba Ghundi	322
Treks from Baba Ghundi	323
Listings	324

Footprint features...

Don't miss...	267
Hunza and Nagar regions explained	296
'The fighting of giants, not men'	275
Some tips for shoppers in Karimabad	288
Keeping the language alive	293
Baba Ghundi and the legend of Ravai Lake	322

Introduction

This section deals with the parts of Pakistan that are most popular with visitors: Lower Hunza and Nagar 2, Central Hunza, Nagar 1, and Gojal (Upper Hunza). And it's for a good reason that these places appeal most – they have that winning combination of stunning natural environment and a friendly welcome from its inhabitants.

In addition to the main valley that the Karakoram Highway follows, there are numerous side valleys to explore that, unlike others further south along the KKH, are safe to visit. Although trekkers rave about the possiblities here, there are still opportunities for less experienced hikers. Indeed, some of the best walks in this region can be completed in a single day , and there are also options of jeep, horse and yak safaris.

Here is a region of Pakistan (and the world) that should not be missed, and if possible, should not be rushed either.

★ Don't miss...

1. **Chalt and the Chaprot Valley** Visit this village and valley for which the word rustic could have been invented, pages 270 and 271.
2. **Minapin** Sit pool-side in a flower-filled garden, gazing up at the mighty Rakaposhi, page 273.
3. **Rakaposhi Base Camp** Make one of Pakistan's easiest treks to see Rakaposhi up close, page 274.
4. **Baltit Fort** Take a guided tour around this superbly renovated fort, with stunning views across the valley, page 283.
5. **Altit** Visit this charming village, a scaled-down version of its neighbour, Karimabad, page 290.
6. **Duikar** Watch sunrise or sunset from Hunza's finest viewpoint, perched high above Altit and Karimabad, page 292.
7. **Ganesh** See a little bit of living history and culture at the restored heart of the village, page 295.
8. **Hoper** Get up close to an active glacier, page 302.
9. **Rush Phari** See the 360° panorama that includes K2, Broad Peak and Gasherbrum IV, page 303.
10. **Hussaini bridge** Have heart-stopping moments crossing the 'Indiana Jones'-like bridge, page 306.
11. **Shimshal Valley** Experience transhumance in all its glory in this remote and little-visited valley, page 315.
12. **Chapursan Valley** Become a travel pioneer by exploring the valley that runs across the top of Pakistan, page 319.

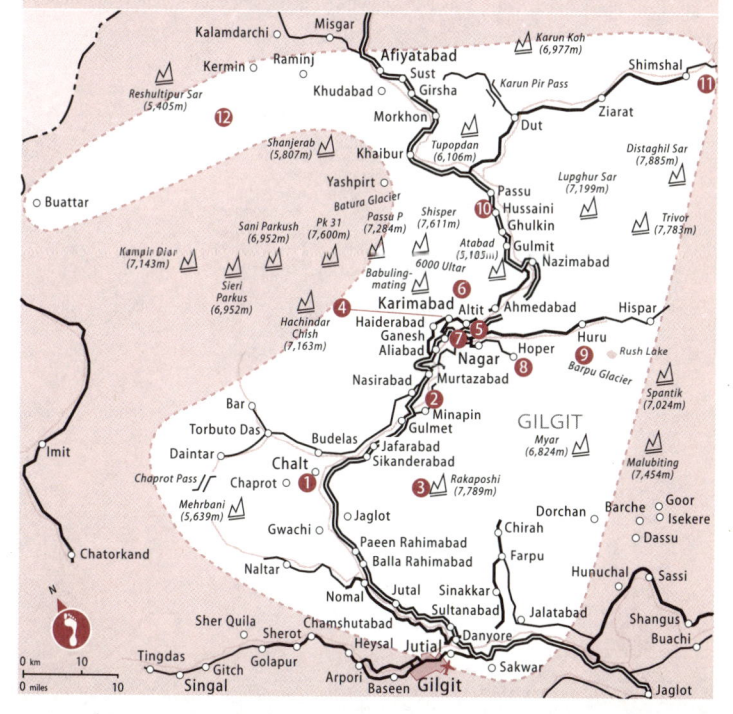

Lower Hunza and Nagar 2

→ Colour map 2, grid B3/4

For the majority of foreign visitors to Pakistan, reaching Hunza is one of their main aims. With a reputation for outstanding natural beauty, welcoming people, endless trekking and hiking potential, and a tourism infrastructure that is sufficiently developed that you don't have to rough it – but not so developed that it attract hordes of package tourists – Hunza is often considered to be the centrepiece of the North's tourism industry.

Hunza is all these things, although the general term 'Hunza' can be a little misleading (see box, page 296). The areas that most visitors are interested in are Central Hunza and Gojal (Upper Hunza); for the more adventurous (and trekkers in particular), there are plenty more delights to seek out, notably in Nagar 2. Most visitors to Northern Pakistan usually take a bus or jeep directly between Gilgit and Karimabad (in Central Hunza), although there are a number of attractions in between, all of which can be reached by public transport. Of these, Minapin, with the chance to trek up to Rakaposhi Base Camp, should not be missed ▸▸ *For Sleeping, Eating and all other listings, see pages 277-279.*

Lower Hunza, Nagar 2, Central Hunza & Nagar

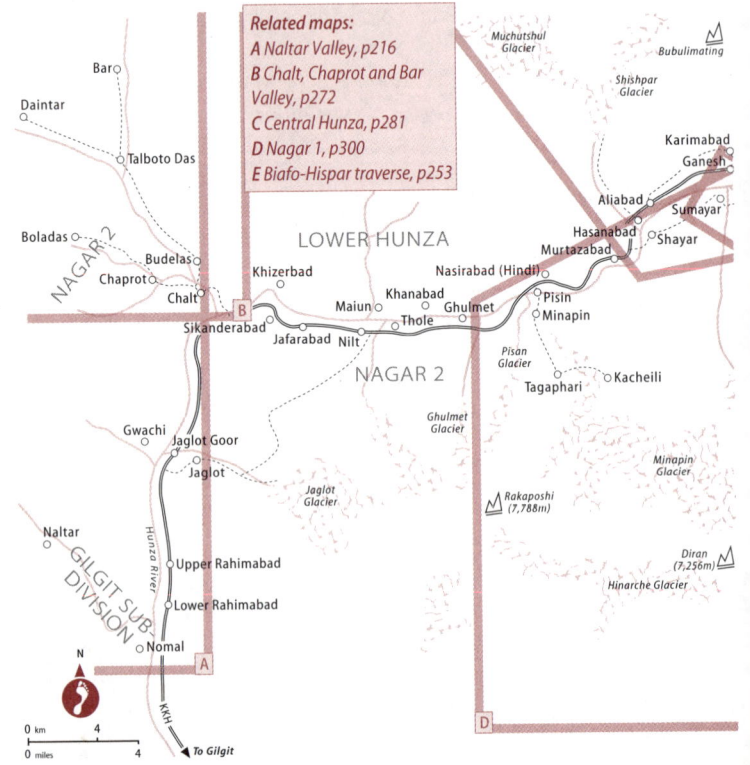

Related maps:
A Naltar Valley, p216
B Chalt, Chaprot and Bar Valley, p272
C Central Hunza, p281
D Nagar 1, p300
E Biafo-Hispar traverse, p253

History

Hunza and Nagar were formerly princely states, each ruled by an unbroken line of thums (kings) who first occupied their positions some time during the fourth period of Trakhan rule in Gilgit (1241-1449). Both houses of the two ruling families (Ayash in Hunza, Maglot in Nagar) are descended from a pair of brothers. Like many of the other semi-independent kingdoms in the Northern Areas, internecine fighting was the usual mechanism of succession. Despite periodic inter-marriages between the two houses, a great rivalry, frequently resulting in open hostility, has continued between the two kingdoms. Yet as the British found out when they annexed the region in 1891-92, the two were prepared to unite against a common enemy.

Hunza in particular emerged as a powerful kingdom in the region, establishing relations on equal terms with both China and Kashmir. It was partly persistent caravan-raiding, and partly perceived closening links between Hunza and Russia during the era of the 'Great Game' that precipitated the 1891-92 'Hunza Campaign' that resulted in the British annexation of the two states.

Hunza and Nagar both retained a semi-autonomous status in British India until Partition, and then became independent princely states within Pakistan. Reforms of 1973-74 eventually abolished the feudal authority of the Mirs (rulers) and incorporated the princely states within the Northern Areas of Pakistan, so ending the longstanding hereditary rule of the two families.

The recent construction of the Karakoram Highway has brought great change to the region, although this is only a part of the process of 'development' here. It is also interesting to note how Hunza and Nagar have developed at disparate rates, and in different ways (but it's over-simplistic to claim that this is due solely to the differing outlooks of the Shia-Ismaili communities).

Gilgit to Chalt (63 km)

Travelling north to Hunza there are two roads out of Gilgit. Jeeps and Suzukis leave Gilgit by the Jinnah Bridge across the Gilgit River, and then run parallel to the river, before encountering a spectacular suspension bridge across the Hunza River that disappears into a tunnel through the hillside. Vehicles to **Nomal** and **Naltar Valley** continue along the west side of the Hunza River, while those travelling to Hunza cross a suspension bridge that disappears into a tunnel in the cliff face. The tunnel emerges into the village of **Danyore**.

Larger vehicles (including buses and minibuses) travelling north leave Gilgit via Jutial, on the road leading to the KKH. Several kilometres beyond Jutial, the KKH forks right (south) for Islamabad/Rawalpindi and left (north) for Hunza/Nagar and China. Travelling north, the KKH crosses the confluence of the Gilgit and Hunza Rivers and continues along the east bank of the Hunza River. The village of **Danyore**, 6 km north of Gilgit, is the gateway to some simple trekking in the Danyore Valley (see page 217). Beyond Danyore, the landscape is quite barren on either side of the KKH, with sandy dunes flanking the road in places. Across the river, running like a long scar along the mountainside, you can make out the Old Hunza Road.

Just north of Sultanabad, with its LPG storage depot, the KKH passes through the first real splash of greenery at **Jutal** (15 km). On the opposite side of the river are the sprawling agricultural lands of the village of **Nomal**, gateway to the **Naltar Valley** (see page 215). An incongruously positioned 'bus shelter' several kilometres north of Jutal marks the spot where a steep footpath leads down to a rickety bridge across the river to Nomal. Several kilometres further along the KKH is a memorial to the 103 Corps of Engineers "who preferred to make the Karakorams their permanent abode", now just an army-run 'rest stop' and cold drinks stand.

The next village on the KKH is **Rahimabad** (40 km from Gilgit), situated on either side of a small bridge (the **Garden restaurant** in 'Lower' Rahimabad is sometimes used as a meal/drinks stop). A little further along the KKH is **Jaglot**, where foreigners are sometimes asked to register passport details at the check post at the far end of town. Just beyond Jaglot (and about 45 km from Gilgit) is **Jaglot Goor** (Jaglotah), site of an FWO base, a new fish farm, plus several small shops and chai stalls. The **New Krakoram Hotel** (sic) and **New Hunza Hotel** often serve as chai stops on the Gilgit-Karimabad bus ride, and both serve a tasty meat and gristle pie, although if you see how the meat is stored here, you're sure to decline. Both have charpoys upon which it would be possible to overnight (if desperate).

Beyond Jaglot Goor the canyon wall closes in on the right side, and a 'slide area' begins. Here Gilgit sub-district ends and the KKH enters **Hunza and Nagar** (a sign welcomes visitors to Nagar). As well as being an administrative boundary, this is also a geological boundary – the northern limit of the '**Kohistan Island Arc**' (see page 188).

As the KKH leaves Gilgit District and enters **Nagar 2**, the KKH takes a sharp bend to the right, following the course of the Hunza River. To the left, a jeep road drops down to the river and crosses on a new bridge to the village of **Chalt**, 58 km from Gilgit. There is a second bridge 5 km further on (marked by a huge boulder at the side of the KKH; from here it's a 40-minute, 3-km walk to Chalt). This is the gateway to the **Chaprot Valley** and **Bar Valley**. Those continuing along the KKH, turn to page 264.

Chaprot Valley and Bar Valley

This whole area has a wonderfully rustic feel to it, reflecting the availability of fertile, well-irrigated agricultural land. Remarkably few visitors come here, and thus it may be considered to be the Northern Areas best-kept secret. The main valleys here (Chaprot, Ghashumaling and Bar) offer simple day walks along narrow country lanes, plus some more adventurous treks.

Ins and outs
There are direct minibuses to Chalt from the Jutial bus station in Gilgit. Alternatively, vehicles along the KKH can drop passengers at the link road that leads down to the Chalt bridge (look out for the huge boulder shortly before the petrol station).

Background
The availability of so much agricultural land was one reason that the Chaprot Valley was a source of contention for so long between the rival kingdoms of Gilgit, Hunza

● *A large metal sign at the entrance to Nagar used to declare "Here continents collided", but*
● *it has now been destroyed by the very actions that it sought to describe.*

and Nagar. Furthermore, the fort at Chalt used to strategically control the main southern approach to both Hunza and Nagar. In 1886 the then Mir of Hunza, Ghazan Khan, was so desperate for the restoration of Chaprot to his control that he begged of Colonel Lockhart "Give me Chaprot and my people shall carry you through the Killik snows as if you were women", adding that the forts at Chalt and Chaprot were "as dear to him as the strings which secured his wives' pyjamas".

Today, the valley belongs to Nagar and the population is predominantly Shia. Although remarkably friendly, the local people have less experience of dealing with foreign tourists than the people of, say, Hunza, and it is vital that visitors show a sensitivity to local customs, particularly in terms of modest dress.

Chalt

The main settlement and junction point for the Chaprot, Ghashumaling and Bar Valleys is Chalt, although once you see how small this village is you'll soon realize just how 'rural' the rest of this area is. Immense pleasure can be derived from looking upon the bare, craggy peaks that surround the village; they may not be the snow-capped glories seen from elsewhere in Hunza and Nagar, but they still have their appeal. There is also a distinct satisfaction in the knowledge that in a few days time you could be sitting in Minapin or Karimabad, gazing upon a different set of peaks entirely. There are no real 'sights' in Chalt as such, but it does provide a base for some short walks in the Chaprot and Bar Valleys.

Short walks in the Chaprot Valley

The small village of **Chaprot** in the Chaprot Valley is about an hour's walk beyond Chalt. From Chaprot it is possible to continue southwest along the **Ghashumaling River**, where you will find excellent walks through orchards, pine forest and fields of wild strawberries.

From Chaprot it is also possible to take the path northwest to **Daintar**, and make the trek over the Daintar Pass to **Naltar** (see page 215), or to head east (then north) from Daintar to link up with the Bar Valley trek.

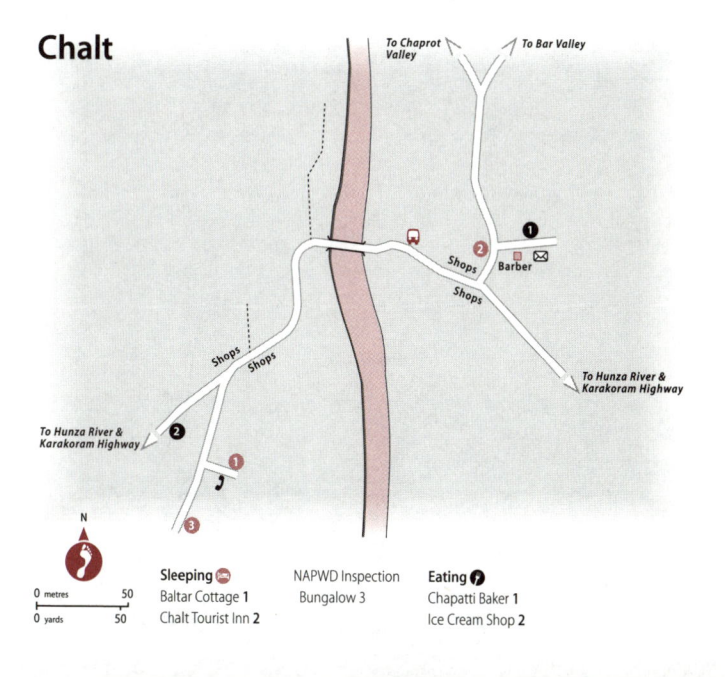

Chalt

Sleeping
Baltar Cottage 1
Chalt Tourist Inn 2
NAPWD Inspection Bungalow 3

Eating
Chapatti Baker 1
Ice Cream Shop 2

Another option is to head up the **Budalas** or **Bar Valley** from Chalt (follow the Bar signpost). Several kilometres beyond Budalas there is a hot, sulphurous spring, said to have healing qualities. At **Torboto Das** the path divides, with the right fork continuing to **Bar** (18 km from Chalt, see Bar Valley trek below), and the left fork leading to Daintar – starting point for the trek across the 4,500-m Daintar Pass (see page 217).

Bar Valley trek

ⓘ *Open zone. Maximum elevation 4,000 m. Jul to Sep. Maps: Swiss Foundation are good; the U502 series, NJ 43-14 Baltit is just about adequate for this trek. Read trekking notes, p45.*

There are two options for trekking in the Bar Valley, although day hikers can easily reach Bar in one day. The first involves an eight-day return trip from **Torbuto Das**, via **Bar**, heading along the Garamasai River to **Toltar**, before bearing northwest along the Toltar Glacier to **Saio-daru-kush**, from where you retrace your steps. The camping around the **Bar-daru-kush Lake** (3,200 m) and pastures (beyond Toltar) is sublime. Note, however, that crossing the Toltar Glacier to reach Saio-daru-kush can be treacherous.

The alternative is to head up the Garamasai River from Bar to the summer pastures at **Shuwe**, and then continue northeast to the Baltar Glacier and **Baltar**. This return trip can be completed in three days. See the maps on page 272 and 216.

KKH: Chalt to Ghulmet (13 km)

Returning to the route along the KKH, as the Hunza River and the KKH make a 90° bend, there are views of Rakaposhi straight ahead. Although the KKH continues on the Nagar 2 side of the valley, across the river the first **Hunza** village (Khizerabad) can be seen.

Chalt, Chaprot Valley & Bar Valley

The first major settlement on the KKH in Nagar 2 is **Jafarabad** (previously known as Tondas). This is the headquarters of an impressive indigenous NGO, the **Naunehal Development Organization**, which has already initiated a number of self-help projects throughout Nagar in the fields of education, health care, conservation and tourism promotion. Those seeking to learn more about the organization's work can call here, or chat with the manager of the **Diran Guest House** in Minapin (Israr Hussein).

Beyond Jafarabad is the small settlement of **Nilt** (1,425 m), scene of the pivotal battle in the 1891 Hunza and Nagar Campaign, although next to nothing remains of the famous fort (see box, below).

The green, fertile lands on the Hunza side of the river belong to the small villages of **Maiun** and **Khanabad**. To the left of the KKH at **Thole** is the small, green-domed roof tomb of **Sayyid Shah Wali**, a 16th-century preacher from Badakhshan who settled in the area. On the first bend on the KKH out of Thole there is a fine view up to Rakaposhi. The cold drinks and snacks stand here is said by many to offer the best *chhapshuro* ('Hunza pizza') in the region. The next miniscule settlement on the KKH is **Qasimabad**, after which a short 'slide-area' begins (Nagaris often stop to make a donation at the roadside shrine here). A further 1 km brings you to **Ghulmet** (not to be confused with Gulmit in Gojal).

If you pass this spot at night, the impression is somewhat akin to driving through the Nevada Desert and suddenly coming across the bright lights of Las Vegas. By day, however, it is easy to see why several entrepreneurs have constructed a number of hotels and restaurants seemingly in the middle of nowhere. Immediately to the south of the KKH are impressive views up the Ghulmet Glacier to the peak of **Rakaposhi** (7,788 m). It is possible to trek up to the Japanese Base Camp (1979 expedition) from Ghulmet in a hot, dry four hours (two hours return). In fact, many of the entrepreneurs running the cafés and hotels here were employed as porters and guides on the 1979 Japanese expedition. This is a popular overnight spot for cyclists, and a regular cold drink/lunch/photo stop for tour groups, although those on public transport tend to speed straight through.

Just beyond Ghulmet on the KKH is the small settlement of **Pisin**. This is the jumping off point for those wishing to visit **Minapin** (and the Rakaposhi Base Camp trip). For those not visiting Minapin, the journey along the KKH continues on page 277. A short distance along the road to Minapin, on the left, is the site of **Nagar Crafts**, a handicrafts centre set up by the Naunehal Development Organization that provides income generating opportunities for local women. The centre itself employs five salaried women, but also provides materials for homeworking (with training provided by Hunza's successful **ThreadNet** programme). The handicrafts that the women make are then graded and sold in the fixed-price shop here (also available at Ghulmet and at the **Diran Guest House** in Minapin). Designs are traditional, but with some modernization.

Minapin and Rakaposhi Base Camp

In recent years, Minapin has become one of the most talked about spots in the north of Pakistan; and for good reason. It is the starting point for a trek (some would say a hike) that provides stunning views of two grand peaks (Rakaposhi and Diran, plus the ice wall that joins them), but entails relatively little walking; in fact, many people visit Rakaposhi Base Camp as a day trip from Minapin. Since there are some facilities available at the Base Camp (tents, hot food etc), this is a trip that can be made even by those who haven't brought their own gear.

For those who don't have the energy for the Base Camp trip, there are plenty of short walks in the vicinity of Minapin (ask the owner of the **Diran Guest House** for advice). Alternatively, there is much to be said for just sitting pool-side in the hotel's charming garden and gazing up at the high peaks around you; it's a splendid place to sit, relax and admire the views. Although Minapin currently has only one place to stay, it caters for all budgets, is extremely well run, and perhaps justifies a visit to Minapin in its own right, see Sleeping for full details.

Ins and outs
Minapin is reached by a link road from the KKH at Pisin. The sign says that it is 4 km from the KKH, but it is more like 6 km. There are now direct minibuses linking Minapin and Gilgit (see transport, page 279), or you can get off passing services at Pisin and walk.

Rakaposhi/Diran Base Camp trek

① *Open zone. Maximum elevation optional (2,400-4,400 m). Apr to Oct. Maps: Deutsche Himalaya Expedition map of Minapin is excellent; Swiss Foundation good; U502 series, NJ 43-14 Baltit is reasonable. For orientation, see map, p300. There is also a very good sketch map of the route in the visitors' book at the Diran Guest House. Read the trekking notes, p45.*

This is the ideal introduction to trekking. The most popular option is the relatively straightforward walk up to Tagaphari (known as 'Rakaposhi Base Camp') in four to five hours, spending one night there, then descending back to Minapin the following day (another four to five hours). This trip can be done in 'sports sandals' but this is not recommended (especially the descent). Further options from Tagaphari include crossing the Minapin Glacier to Kacheili ('Diran Base Camp', three to four hours), with perhaps a visit to Kacheili Lake thrown in, with the second night spent at either Kacheili or back at Tagaphari, before returning on the third or fourth day to Minapin. Those with little time to spare (but boundless energy) have been known to visit Rakaposhi Base Camp from Minapin, and then return again in the same day. This is perfectly feasible, although rather rushed.

Another option (often used by groups) is to camp at Hapakun, a spot about halfway between Minapin and Rakaposhi Base Camp, although this does make the first day very short. Since the route as far as Tagaphari is fairly straightforward, and there are no glacier crossings, it is possible to do this trip without a guide (and without porters if you carry your own gear). For those continuing to Diran Base Camp near Kacheili, a guide is essential to lead you across the Minapin Glacier.

Another reason why this trek is so popular is because there are tents, sleeping bags and hot food available at both Tagaphari and Hapakun, meaning that you do not need to carry a heavy pack of equipment. Note, however, that the set-up at Tagaphari is due to change soon (for the latest arrangement consult the manager at the **Diran Guest House** in Minapin). The present practice is for the community (who own the land at Tagaphari) to lease the meadow to an individual for the season. Thus, the success (or otherwise) of this operation is dependent upon the competence of the person leasing the campsite. Plans are afoot to stake out a proper campsite at Tagaphari, and employ a salaried manager to run it. There is even talk of investing in a selection of tents, rather than the leftovers currently available, and running the place more professionally. This may sound like 'over-development' to some, but it could be a positive step in limiting environmental damage at this beautiful spot. Sleeping options are detailed below.

The route
Most walkers begin from the **Diran Guest House** in Minapin. Turn right out of the gates and follow the road for 50 m or so. As the road bends to the right, a 3-m-wide path heads off to the right. Follow the water channel to where it turns left, cross the channel and ascend the path ahead (passing an old mud/stone house to your right). Cross the mound and follow the path down the other side, turning right along the path that

> ### ❗ 'The fighting of giants, not men'
>
> Although relatively insignificant amongst the many great battles that the British Army fought during their period of conquest of South Asia, the battle for the fort of Nilt on 1 December 1891 is recorded in British military history as an action in which two Victoria Crosses were won. In fact, such was the bravery on display that one local ruler is reported to have commented "This is the fighting of giants, not of men".
>
> Having crossed the Hunza River, the British expeditionary force was stopped in its tracks by the seemingly impregnable stone fortress at Nilt. With the seven-pound guns making no impression on the fort walls, the defenders were able to pick off the British troops at will through the narrow peepholes. In fact, the British commander Colonel Durand, who refused to take cover by crouching behind a rock, received a bullet in a delicate part of his anatomy that meant he had to do quite a lot of crouching in the future!
>
> With casualties mounting, the order was given to blow the main gate. The special correspondent for the Times, E F Knight, witnessed the battle and described what happened next as "one of the most gallant things recorded in Indian warfare".
>
> Rushing through a hail of bullets to the gate, Captain Fenton Aylmer, two subalterns and a Pathan orderly laid an explosive charge, lit the fuse and retreated along the wall to await the explosion. Aylmer was hit by a bullet at such short range that the powder charge singed his uniform, and then to make matters worse, the fuse went out. Risking what Knight thought was certain death, the wounded Aylmer returned to the gate, trimmed the fuse and relit it.
>
> While doing this, a heavy rock dropped from above by the fort's defenders crushed one of his hands. This time the fuse was good, and with the gates blown, the three British officers and six Gurkhas dashed into the fort. Unfortunately, the rest of the British force did not realize that the walls had been breached, and for many minutes the storming party were isolated. It wasn't until Lieutenant Boisragon, one of the subalterns, dashed back to the breech, thus exposing himself to the fire from both sides, that the British realized their colleagues were inside. Within minutes the reinforcements had stormed the fort and the battle was over. For their gallantry, both Aylmer and Boisragon received the Victoria Cross.

leads along the base of the cliffs that stand behind Minapin. Follow the path for 20-25 minutes until you come to a **wooden bridge** across the Minapin Nala (if you look downstream to your right, you'll see the new bridge that you crossed when arriving in Minapin from Pisin).

Having crossed the bridge, the first long climb begins. The path ascends through a series of steep switchback turns. It can get very hot here, although the compensation is the view of Ultar Peak (7,388 m) behind you. This section is particularly tough on the knees during the descent. After an hour of continual climbing, the trail then flattens out for an hour's gentle climb through scrubby juniper forest. The pyramid-peak of Diran (7,257 m) first comes into view along this stretch (ahead, to the southeast). Some two to two and a half hours from Minapin, you reach the shepherds' huts at **Bungidas** (where cold drinks are usually available). **NB** Plans are under consideration to construct a jeep road from Minapin as far as Bungidas. A further 30 minutes' gentle climb brings you to **Hapakun** (it is one full porter stage from Minapin to Hapakun). Many tour groups choose to overnight here. **Green Garden** has several two-man tents (Rs100 per tent), or you can pitch your own for Rs50 in the meadow. There is a latrine tent here; the advertised 'local shower' is effectively a bath in the stream. Food is available (dhal and chapati Rs60; rice, dhal, veg, soup, chapati, dessert Rs100; mineral water Rs50; coke Rs30; milk tea Rs15). Just above the **Green Garden** is **Savannah**, although this is really just a meadow where you can pitch your tent for Rs50 or order meals (similar prices). The only downside to this charming spot at Hapakun (2,850 m) is that there are no Rakaposhi/Diran views.

Beyond Hapakun the trail begins to climb steeply once more, although this time through some pleasant pine forest and pasture. If you look behind you, across to the Hunza side of the river, there are superb views of **Sangemarmar Sar** (7,050 m). As you begin to emerge from the forest, you'll see the peak of **Rakaposhi** (7,788 m) ahead of you. There are two route choices here. You can continue to follow the steep switchback path up to the right, or if you're impatient, you can scramble straight ahead up to the ridge in front of you (at about 3,300 m). Either way, the view when you crest this ridge of lateral moraine is breathtaking. Below you, in all its glory, is the huge **Minapin Glacier**. To your left is Diran, to your right is Rakaposhi, and directly ahead is the 35-km **ice and rock wall** that joins the two. Continue right along the ridge, but take care as you traverse the scree slope; in places the donkey track becomes a goat track, narrowing to just 30 cm with a rock wall to your right and a long, steep drop down to the glacier on your left. There are plans to upgrade this short stretch of track. Having safely traversed this section, it is a short walk through the meadow to **Tagaphari** (or **Rakaposhi Base Camp** as it is better known). Hapakun to Tagaphari takes about two hours (one full porter stage). If this is as far as you intend to go, it is well worth spending a day or two here exploring the area and taking in the scenery (the possibilities are limitless). Note that it gets very cold here at night. It is worth making this trip even if it's cloudy when you leave Minapin; you may get lucky and wake up to find the sun's early morning rays striking the top of Rakaposhi.

From Tagaphari, it is possible to cross the Minapin Glacier to **Kacheili**, a grassy summer pasture with superb views of Rakaposhi that is usually referred to as **Diran Base Camp** (four to five hours). It is perfectly feasible to walk from Tagaphari to Kacheili and back to Tagaphari in a day (two full stages), although a guide is essential to help you negotiate the glacier (Rs500 for a group). It is also quite feasible to walk down from Kacheili to Minapin in one very long day. There is also the option of continuing from Kacheili up to the beautiful **Kacheili Lake** at around 4,400 m (one hour). Those who have a guide can make an alternative descent from Kacheili Lake to Minapin, but this can only be attempted at certain times of the year when the streams are lower.

The route down to Minapin from Tagaphari is the same as the ascent, although it takes four to six hours and can be rather hard on the knees.

Other walks around Minapin

Modestly dressed visitors are welcome to wander around the village, discovering different aspects of Nagari life (but you should not attempt to photograph women). One pleasing short walk is to turn right out of the **Diran Guest House**, follow the jeep road as far as the water channel, then follow the path as it climbs through the terraced fields above Minapin. You can continue for as long and as high as you wish. From this viewpoint above Minapin, the KKH across the river looks particularly insignificant.

Another short walk from Minapin (three to four hours) is the hike up to **Shuli**. This begins from the bridge at the entrance to Minapin (on the road in from Pisin). Follow the path from the bridge up past the huge rock. Shortly it comes to a jeep road; turn left and begin to climb. Cross the supposedly gold-rich Pisin Nala by the wooden bridge and follow the steep jeep road up to the second bridge (next to a small mud and stone water-driven flour mill). Having recrossed the nala, there are two choices.

The jeep road heads left, eventually meeting a water channel. You can follow this water channel to a viewpoint over the Pisin Glacier (1½-2 hours); this is in fact an alternative three-day route up to Rakaposhi Base Camp.

The other choice from the second bridge is to follow the track to the right (Diran peak comes into view shortly). The trail divides once more. The right fork leads down via the hamlet of Chaetti to the Pisin-Minapin jeep road. The left fork, however, climbs steeply for a further 30-45 minutes to the settlement of Shuli. Rakaposhi comes into view during this climb, while the Pisin Glacier can be seen from Shuli (this is a particularly good spot for sunsets). Those wishing to continue on from Shuli can either climb up to the meadow at **Bekitchang Woton**, or cross the bridge and climb steeply to a viewpoint over the Minapin Glacier. There are superb front-on views of Rakaposhi.

Pisin to Hasanabad (14 km)

Returning to the KKH, a little beyond Pisin the road leaves Nagar 2 and crosses the Hunza River by way of a Chinese-built bridge onto the Hunza side of the river. From here, it is 80 km south to Gilgit and 21 km north to Aliabad.

The first village in Hunza on the KKH is Hindi, now known as **Nasirabad** (1,500 m). Nasirabad 'buys' much of its irrigation water from Minapin, in Nagar, although after 10 difficult years in the making, a new AKRSP-funded irrigation channel is about to be launched. Some of the very best Rakaposhi and Diran views are here, particularly from the flower-filled garden of the **Eden Gardens** cold drinks stand. A native of Nasirabad, Karim Mutrib (contactable at the **Madina Hotel** in Gilgit), is developing some treks from here that lead up to some high pastures and disused polo grounds on the way to Hasanabad Nala; they feature panoramic views of Rakaposhi, Diran, plus the whole Batura Wall.

Just beyond Nasirabad is one of the worst 'slide areas' on this section of the KKH; indeed, across on the Nagar side of the river you can still see evidence of the massive 1935 landslide that destroyed so much cultivated land and partially dammed the river. The next settlement on the KKH is **Murtazabad**, whose population is split roughly 50-50 between Ismaili and Shia Islam. There are hot springs here, although they are used predominantly for laundry purposes.

Just beyond the village there are splendid views of the daunting Ultar Peak (7,388 m) straight ahead, before the KKH begins to turn into the Hasanabad Nala. A jeep track leads down to the right, crossing the river on a rope suspension bridge to Shayar, on the Nagar side (the bridge is not immediately visible from the KKH). For details of a long, but enjoyable, walk from Shayar on to Askordas and Sumayar, see page 304. As the road enters the mouth of the Hasanabad Valley, you pass from Lower Hunza into **Central Hunza**.

Sleeping

Gilgit to Chalt p269
Danyore
F-G Travel Lodge. Has rooms with attached bath, shady garden and a quiet location, but is often closed up.

Chaprot Valley and Bar Valley p270
Chalt map p271
G Chalt Tourist Inn. Converted school building, a triple and 2 doubles, basic but clean enough, attached bathrooms with bare floors, little privacy and odd smelling water. Simple food in the restaurant, large pleasant garden (with sheep and fruit trees).
G NAPWD Inspection Bungalow. Book in Gilgit (although casual callers often accepted), 2 rooms set in private garden, arrange meals through the chowkidar.
H Baltar Cottage. 3 extremely run-down rooms, very basic shared bath, have to be very desperate to stay here (although the owner is very friendly).

Chalt to Ghulmet *p272*
Ghulmet
Until very recently, Ghulmet was little more than a few tented camps and some cold drink stands. Now, most of the tents have been replaced by concrete hotels with names along the Rakaposhi theme (Rakaposhi Paradise, Rakaposhi Zero Point, Rakaposhi Main Point, Rakaposhi Echo, Rakaposhi Vieweria; Rakaposhi View Point etc, the latter being the longest established). The best bet is to look at them all and see which is offering the best deal (usually in the F-G price bracket, or H to pitch your own tent); not many people overnight here so good prices can be negotiated.

Minapin *p273*
D-H Diran Guest House, T0572-2949, diran_gh@hotmail.com. Currently the only place to stay in Minapin, and with prices to suit all budgets, this is also one of the best places to stay in the whole of Pakistan. Set in a huge garden filled with flowers and fruit trees, with magnificent views of Rakaposhi, the 'old block' has 4 budget doubles and triples with attached hot bath (G), a cheap dorm (H), plus an appealing 5 mattress-dorm in an old Nagar style traditional house (H). The 'new block' features 16 comfy doubles with clean linen, dressing room and modern tiled bath with excellent hot showers (sinks have plugs!). Rooms are priced in the D-E price range, but backpackers may be able to get them for an E-F price. The guest house even has a clear (but cold) water phallic-shaped swimming pool. The restaurant is recommended, and the manager (a relative of the ruling family of Nagar) is both informative and entertaining (check out his little shrine to Diana, Princess of Wales!). Highly recommended.

Rakaposhi/Diran Base Camp Treks *p274*
Tagaphari/Rakaposhi Base Camp
The present campsite at Tagaphari is called **H Green Garden Hotel**. Comprises 4 ancient, cramped, and not necessarily waterproof 2-man tents (Rs100). You can pitch your own tent here for Rs50, or for free if you pitch it outside the demarcated camping site. The tents have very thin sleeping mats, or you can hire warm but smelly sleeping bags for Rs60 per night. If all the tents are occupied it is possible to sleep in the kitchen tent for Rs50. Food is reasonably priced given the transport costs involved (dhal and chapati Rs80; full dinner of rice, dhal, veg, chapati, tea Rs120; mineral water Rs50; coke Rs35; milk tea Rs15).

Eating

Chaprot Valley and Bar Valley *p270*
Chalt *map p271*
There are a surprising number of basic meat and chapati restaurants in the village (most with dish TV). Several shops sell biscuits and mineral water, although trekkers should really bring their own supplies.

Activities and tours

Bar Valley *p270*
The villagers in the Bar Valley, who are keen to promote tourism here, have gone as far as forming the 'Bar Valley Conservation NGO' and producing leaflets extolling the virtues of the valley. They are also encouraging local people to accommodate tourists in their homes, or allow them to camp on their land (nominal charges). In fact, it is sometimes possible to arrange all-inclusive **trekking packages** in the Bar Valley (guides, accommodation, food etc) from as little as Rs500-600 per day; ask around in Chalt.

Horseriding can be arranged (Rs650 per day), as well as cultural events such as **polo matches** (Rs11,000), **mock marriage ceremonies** (Rs6,000) and **dancing** (Rs5,500). They can be contacted in Barkot village (Bar, 2,200 m), or through the WWF office in Gilgit (543-A, Shahrah-e-Quaid-e-Azam, Khomer, T/F0572-4127). The WWF are involved locally in setting up a 'Sustainable Wildlife Project' based on management and use of the Siberian ibex, including **trophy hunting** (Dec only, US$3,000 licence fee, 75% goes to the local people).

Transport

Chaprot Valley and Bar Valley *p264*
Chalt *map p271*
There is at least 1 daily minibus to Chalt from the Jutial bus station in Gilgit (Rs40, 1½ hrs). Minibuses back to **Gilgit** from Chalt run

intermittently 0600-0900 (from outside the Chalt Tourist Inn). There are also early morning minibuses from here to **Hoper** (Rs100, 3 hrs) via **Pisin** (for **Minapin**) (Rs20, 30 mins) and **Ganesh** (for **Karimabad**) (Rs60, 1½ hrs). Or walk up to the KKH and hitch.

Minapin *p273*
There is a daily minibus to Minapin at 1400 from Jutial bus station in **Gilgit** (Rs60, 1½-2 hrs), that returns from outside the Diran Guest House at 0700 each day. Alternatively, the 0700 **NATCO** bus from Gilgit to **Sust** will drop passengers at **Pisin**, from where you can walk. The Gilgit-Karimabad minibuses will also drop you at **Pisin**, but you may have to pay the full Karimabad fare. It is also possible to flag down north and southbound buses along the KKH at Pisin.

Central Hunza → *Colour map 2, grid B4*

Comprising the land above the Hunza River between Hasanabad Nala and Nasimabad/Shishkut (where Gojal begins), this is the region most visitors think of when they talk of 'Hunza' (it is sometimes called Hunza 'proper'). The setting is superb: a natural amphitheatre formed by a series of snowy peaks, with seemingly dry and barren canyons opening up to reveal grassy pastures, orchards and ingeniously terraced fields. The people living here, predominantly Burushashki-speaking followers of the Ismaili sect of Islam, have a reputation for openness, and visitors are well catered for in a variety of hotels and guest houses. The Karakoram Highway snakes through the centre of this region, following the course of the Hunza River, on its journey up to Gojal (Upper Hunza) and on to China. ▶▶ *For Sleeping, Eating and all other listings, see pages 281-282.*

Hasanabad Nala

The invisible line dividing Lower and Central Hunza passes along the **Hasanabad Nala**. The mouth of the Hasanabad Nala is one of the most treacherous 'slide areas' on the KKH, and if you look down towards the river there are numerous house-size boulders scattered throughout the settlement. **Hasanabad** (Ismaili, with one Shia family) is the site of the Norwegian-built power station that provides a regular supply of electricity to the Karimabad/Central Hunza region. The new **VIP River View** cold drinks spot has been set up by the power station. At the apex of the bend, behind the road maintenance depot, several trails lead north along the Hasanabad Nala; these are the starting points for treks to the Shishpar Glacier and the Muchutshil Glacier.

Shishpar Glacier trek
ⓘ *Open zone. Maximum elevation 3,600 m. May to Oct. Maps: Deutsche Himalaya Expedition map of Hunza is good; Swiss Foundation good; U502 series, NJ 43-14 Baltit is unreliable; all the maps have some mistakes, or incorrectly labelled names. For orientation, see map on p281. Read trekking notes on p45.*

This is not a particularly demanding trek (although at some times of the year it is hot and dry), yet it offers alternative views of mountains that become familiar to those staying in Karimabad. Most trekkers complete this trip in four days (two out, two back). From the road maintenance depot on the KKH it is a fairly unrewarding four hours' walk along the east side of the Hasanabad Nala to **Bras 1**. The camping site is just above the terminal moraine on the east side of the Shishpar Glacier, although you have to go down to the glacier itself for water. The following day involves a five-hour trek along the east side of the glacier moraine to the summer pastures at **Khaltar Harai**, from where there is a different view of Ultar Peak that is denied to those in Karimabad. To return, follow the same route.

Muchutshil Glacier trek

ⓘ *Open zone. Maximum elevation 3,600 m. May to Oct. Maps: Deutsche Himalaya Expedition map of Hunza is good; Swiss Foundation good; U502 series, NJ 43-14 Baltit is unreliable; all the maps have some mistakes, or incorrectly labelled names. For orientation, see map on p281. Read trekking notes on p45.*

This six-day trek also offers rarely seen views of commonly seen peaks, and is again fairly undemanding, although a guide is necessary to cross the glacier. From the road maintenance depot on the KKH, head along the west side of the Hasanabad Nala, camping on the first night below the mouth of the glacier. The second day is fairly long (six to seven hours), beginning with a crossing of the **Muchutshil Glacier** (shown on some maps as the Muchuhar Glacier). The pastures at **Gaymaling** provide the second night's camping. The reward at the end of the third day (six hours) is the camping at **Shandar**, just below **Sangemarmar Sar** (7,050 m); it is worth spending a couple of days here before the three-day walk by the same route back down to the KKH.

Hasanabad Nala to Aliabad (7km)

As the KKH emerges from the Hasanabad Nala bend, the Nagar face of **Distaghil Sar** (7,885 m) can be seen ahead in the distance. The road passes a Frontier Constabulary check post where foreigners sometimes have to enter passport details. Just beyond the check post, a link road to the left runs the 10 km up to Karimabad (this is called the 'Aliabad link road', although it is no longer the main route used up to Karimabad). The main KKH continues through Aliabad (incorrectly signposted as being at 2,500 m).

Aliabad

The town of Aliabad has found a new role for itself. The settlement pre-dates the construction of the KKH, but attracts few foreign visitors as nearby Karimabad offers better views and more peace and quiet. But with land prices rising alarmingly in

Central Hunza (Including Hasanabad Nala & Ultar Nala treks)

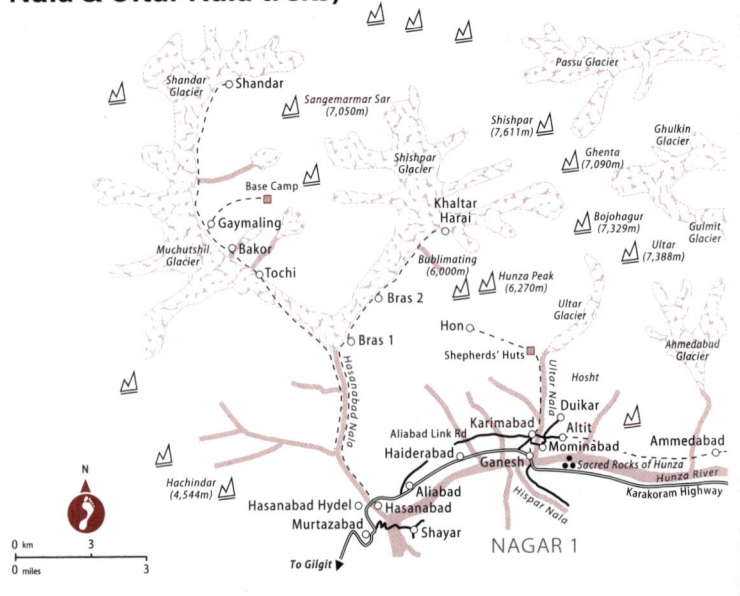

Karimabad, most non-tourist related businesses have set up here; Aliabad has become the regional market place where Hunzakuts come to shop. It also has Hunza's best hospital, the Aga Khan Health Services clinic to the west of town. Those trekking in the Hasanabad Nala area can ask the hotels here for guides and porters.

Aliabad is also an important transport junction, and most visitors see Aliabad as a place to change vehicles, or more likely, as a meal stop on the bus journey between Gilgit and Sust. There is a PCO in the centre of the village (south side of the road) that supposedly offers international calls. ▸▸ *See Transport, page 282, for more details.*

Aliabad to Ganesh (5km)

The first settlement after Aliabad is **Dorkhan**, a predominantly Ismaili village (with 10 or so Shia families) nestling below the KKH. The next settlement, just above the highway, is **Haiderabad**, while strung along the riverside of the KKH are **Aksur Das** and **Garelht**.

Just beyond the **PTDC Motel** are more excellent views of Rakaposhi and Diran. The road that leads off to the left (north) is the new link road up to **Karimabad** (which most of the traffic now uses). Halfway up this link road, the right fork leads via Mominabad (see page 293) to Altit (see page 290).

The **KKH**, meanwhile, enters into a large S-bend around the village of **Ganesh** (see page 295). North and southbound buses will drop off and pick up passengers at the KKH Memorial/**Karakoram Highway Inn** here. There is a steep road ('Old Ganesh Road') that leads up to Karimabad from here. For those continuing their journey north along the KKH to Gojal and China, turn to page 305.

● Sleeping

Hasanabad Nala to Aliabad *p280*
Aliabad
There are a few places to stay in Aliabad, but Karimabad and Altit have better options.

F Silk Route. Recently opened, doubles and triples with attached bath, nice garden.
F Village Guest House. Traditional Hunza-style house that sleeps 6, also 2 doubles, food by arrangement.

There are several very basic places (a few grubby rooms attached to a restaurant), including G-H **Dumani**, **Prince/Swat**, **Shishper** and **SR**.

Garelht
B-C PTDC Motel Hunza, T0572-69. 29 carpeted rooms with hot bath, panoramic views from the restaurant, plus laundry and vehicle hire services. Overall, it's reasonable value for money, but gets busy, so book in Islamabad if possible.
F-G Golden Peak View Hotel. Opposite the above, sadly offers no views of Golden Peak at all!

● Eating

Hasanabad Nala to Aliabad *p280*
Aliabad
The restaurants here are basic meat, chapati and dhal places; the unnamed place where most bus services stop for meals has a 60-channel dish TV system.

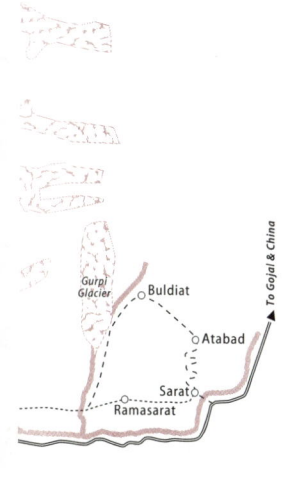

Transport

Hasanabad Nala to Aliabad p280
Aliabad
Passing services on the Gilgit-Sust-Gilgit route will pick up passengers in Aliabad, with many (including **NATCO**) stopping for lunch here. The northbound **NATCO** bus passes at about 1000, southbound at 0730-0830, with private minibuses regularly passing through in either direction from about 0600-1600.

There are also minibuses via Gulmit and Passu to **Sust**, and via Pisin to **Gilgit**, that originate in Aliabad; if you can't find a minibus in Karimabad, hop on a wagon (Rs10) to Aliabad and change.

Karimabad → Colour map 2, grid B4

Karimabad has always been considered the centrepiece of the tourism industry in the Northern Areas, and perhaps the whole of Pakistan. Its charms are immediately apparent: panoramic views across the Hunza and Nagar Valleys incorporate three snow-capped peaks over 7,000 m and provide a contrast to a colourful natural environment that includes orchards of fruit trees, forests of poplars and 10,000 other trees. Karimabad is the base for a number of short walks and excursions, as well as being a popular place with visitors to relax and unwind.

Old hands will tell you that the village has become spoilt or over commercialized, and true, while there are over 30 hotels and a similar number of 'handicraft' shops competing for your business, tourist levels are nothing like those that are experienced in similar places in, say, India, so it's still possible to enjoy the scenery in peace here.
▶▶ For Sleeping, Eating and all other listings, see pages 285- 290.

Ins and outs

Most visitors arrive by minibus directly from Gilgit (three hours) and are dropped off in the centre of the village. Those coming from the north (Sust, Passu etc) are more likely to be dropped off down on the KKH at Ganesh. Likewise, those coming from Gilgit on the NATCO bus will also be dropped off at Ganesh. It's a very steep walk (or an extortionately priced ride) up from Ganesh to Karimabad. There are also wagons which link Karimabad with the transport hub at Aliabad.

The number of jeeps roaring in and out of Karimabad can become rather unpleasant; there's no excuse not to get around on foot here. ▶▶ *See Transport, page 289, for more details.*

Background

More than 95% of the population of Karimabad belong to the Ismaili religion, with **His Highness Shah Karim al-Husayni Aga Khan IV** as their spiritual head. Traditionally there were only two classes in Hunza: the Mir's family and courtiers, and the agriculturalists. There is no hereditary occupational class structure (except for the Dom, see box, page 293), with the village hierarchy cutting across a system of clans of different origin, and no obligation to marry within the clan. Unlike the Nagar subdivision to the south, there is no purdah system in Karimabad and women work alongside the men in the fields. Some may argue that the women do all the work.

The predominant language in Karimabad is Burushashki, but increasing opportunities in education and government service mean Urdu and English are widely spoken. The people of Karimabad are proud of their educational achievements, and as 95% of all children attend school, the implications for future literacy rates are encouraging.

History

The village now known as Karimabad has absorbed the *khun* (cluster of households) around the fort at Baltit, as well as the Khurukushal and Dhirimshal khuns, and has expanded greatly from being just the settlement around the new palace of the *Mir* (King) that was built in 1923.

The state of Hunza was ruled by the same family for 960 years, with their seat of power being the **Baltit Fort**. Famous for their incessant caravan-raiding and constant wars against the rival state of Nagar, the modern history of the Hunzakuts of Karimabad begins in 1891-92 when the British occupied the fort at Baltit. Hunza became a princely state within British India, and then retained a similar status within Pakistan following Partition. The 1973-74 administrative reforms of Zulfikar Ali Bhutto abolished the feudal authority of the Mir and incorporated Hunza within the Northern Areas of Pakistan.

The nature of the terrain has played a large part in determining the social economy of Karimabad. With annual precipitation below 150 mm, rain-fed agriculture is not possible and so an intricate network of glacier-fed irrigation channels serve the limited agricultural land. Previously a subsistence economy based upon agriculture and pastoral activity, but producing no surplus, evolved. The most pressing social necessity for a household in Karimabad was to be self-sufficient in every way.

The improvement of access to the area, in association with other processes of socio-economic change, has had a major impact upon the economy of Karimabad. Previously self-sufficient, Karimabad is now dependent upon food imports, particularly cheap subsidized food grains imported from down country. A new middle class has emerged, and now about 70% of all families have some family member engaged in trade, commerce, tourism related activity, artisanal work, or in government service. Earnings in administrative sectors, service sectors (including tourism) and in trade and commerce are seen as far more lucrative and requiring less physical work than farming, and interest in agriculture has declined. With the population growing so rapidly, and the emergence of an educated class, more and more young men are seeking employment down country.

There have been attempts to control the development of the built environment here, notably through the work of the Karimabad Planning Support Services (KPSS), but it is not just the desire to build new hotels, shops and restaurants that is threatening Karimabad's beauty. More and more families are looking for bigger, more modern homes and are choosing to build on what was previously cultivated land.

Sights

Located on a large rocky outcrop at the base of the Ultar Nala, **Baltit Fort** ⓘ *T0572-77110, summer daily 0900-1300, 1400-1730, winter daily 0930-1600, foreign tourists Rs300; groups can book evening dinners on the roof of the fort (catering by the Baltit Inn, music and dancing also provided)*, dominates Karimabad and the view of the Hunza and Nagar Valleys from the roof is superb. The exact origins of the fort are unclear, although the foundations are thought to be around 750 years old. The main section was seemingly built some time in the 17th century as part of a dowry accompanying a Baltistan princess who came to marry the Mir, with the architecture reflecting Baltistan's ancient links with Tibet. It is primarily built of mud plaster, stone and timber beams. Many changes were made during the course of the 20th century that reflect the influence of British rule (and hence architecture) in the region, notably in the addition of the balconies, bow windows and the exterior white paint job. The fort remained the official residence of the Mir of Hunza until the 1960s,

● *Local myths and folklore that pre-date Islam – particularly belief in wizards (bitten), fairies (paris) and the power of the shaman – are an important cultural aspect of Hunza life.*

although in reality the ruler had been living in a new palace in Karimabad since 1945.

Formerly in the possession of the Mir, the fort has been donated to the **Baltit Heritage Trust**, a semi-governmental organization entrusted with the running and maintenance of the building. In 2000, the restoration project won the British Airways 'Tourism For Tomorrow' global award. Local young men now provide an informed guided tour of the fort, as well as some of the surrounding traditional houses. As well as the fine views, an eclectic slide show is the highlight.

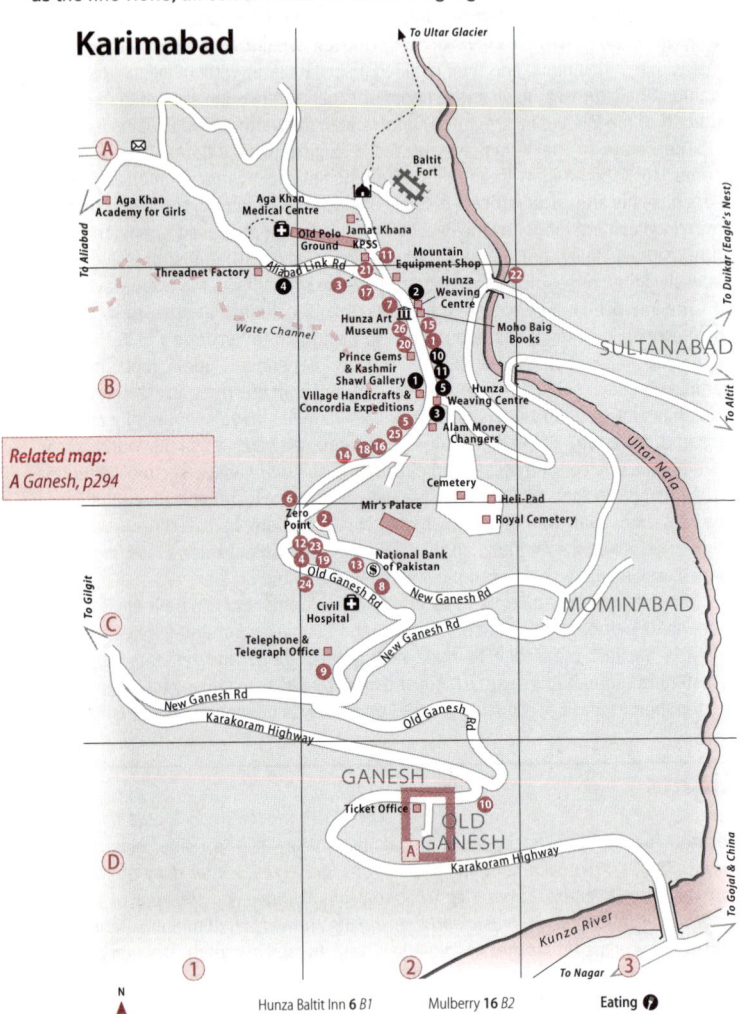

Karimabad

Related map:
A Ganesh, p294

Sleeping
Blue Moon **1** *B2*
Darbar Hunza **2** *C2*
Garden Lodge **3** *B2*
Haider Inn **4** *C2*
Hill Top **5** *B2*
Hunza Baltit Inn **6** *B1*
Hunza Lodge **7** *B2*
Hunza View (new) **8** *C2*
Hunza View (old) **9** *C2*
Karakoram Highway
  Inn (Ganesh) **10** *D2*
Karim **11** *A2*
Karimabad **12** *C2*
Khusho Sun Guest
  House **13** *C2*
Lady Finger **14** *B2*
Lucky Star **15** *B2*
Mulberry **16** *B2*
Mount Everest **17** *B2*
New Hunza Tourist **18** *B2*
Old Hunza Inn **19** *C2*
Punjab Sindh **20** *B2*
Rainbow **21** *B2*
Relax Inn **22** *B2*
Rest House
  (NAPWD) **23** *C2*
Tourist Cottage **24** *C2*
Tourist Park **25** *B2*
World Roof **26** *B2*

Eating
Amjad Soup Corner **1** *B2*
Baltit Bakery & Al Rahim
  General Store **2** *B2*
Café de Hunza & Ali
  Book Store **3** *B2*
Café de Mountain **4** *B1*
Friends **5** *B2*
Sunshine & Eagle's Nest
  Office **10** *B2*
Ultar **11** *B2*

In addition to sitting around admiring the view, you can undertake a number of **short walks** around Karimabad. More sedate strolls can be taken along the numerous water channels, or down to the neighbouring village of **Altit** (see below). More energetic visitors may wish to visit the summer pastures below the Ultar Glacier.

Ultar Glacier hike/trek

The view from the pastures sited below the imposing Ultar Peak is one of the highlights of a visit to Karimabad. The main **Ultar Peak** (at 7,388 m, the 73rd highest mountain in the world) was for a long time one of the lowest unclimbed peaks that had been attempted. Having claimed a number of Japanese lives, it has now been conquered, although it is said that the local people do not broadcast this fact so that the mountain can retain some of its mystique. **Bubulimating** (also known as Lady's Finger), the 6,000-m-high granite spire to the left, is so sheer that it cannot hold snow. Viewed from Nagar, however, this granite finger looks entirely different. To the right (northeast) of Bubulimating is the 6,270-m **Hunza Peak**. For those camping at the meadow, prepare to have your sleep interupted by the creaking Ultar Glacier and the sound of distant avalanches. You can get similar views with marginally less effort from the viewpoint of Hosht, above Duikar (see page 292).

There is some dispute as to whether the trip up to Ultar Glacier is a 'hike' or a 'trek'. It can be visited as a (long) day trip (ie a 'hike') from Karimabad, although you will almost certainly enjoy the trip more if you camp up at the meadow for at least one night (ie a 'trek'). It is not essential to take a guide up to Ultar, although if you feel more comfortable taking one they are not difficult to find in Karimabad (expect to pay about Rs500). It should be noted that the number of rockfalls that have occured in recent years means that the route is no longer as clear as it once was. Do not, however, go alone. Ask around at the various hotels and see if you can team up with others who are making the trip. An early start is advised, and you should carry plenty of water. Stick to the west (left) side of the stream on the way up – the route is not always obvious. Do not make the trip after heavy rain, or during high winds, since there is a great risk of rockfalls. while up at the meadows, do not attempt to go down onto the glacier.

Although the nala, or canyon, that leads to the Ultar Glacier from just behind Baltit Fort looks quite narrow at the entrance, a strenuous climb of three to four hours along the lateral moraine reveals a wide grassy bowl, surrounded by a spectacular mountain amphitheatre. Shepherds occupy the stone huts during the summer, and are keen to sell chai and fresh dairy products to visitors. It's possible to camp here (at about 3,000 m), although if you are too close to the huts and the corals holding the 600 or so sheep and goats, you may wake up the next day scratching. You should ask permission from the shepherds before camping near to their huts.

A small place among the shepherds' huts called **Lady Finger Restaurant** offers mattresses in a crowded tent for Rs70 each (blankets provided), lunch for Rs70, tea for Rs15, coke for Rs35, all served on tables and chairs made from the rocks. There is sometimes a temporary 'tea shop' on the way up to the meadows from Karimabad.

A further four hours up to the left of the shepherds' huts brings you to **Hon** (4,600 m), which offers even better views. There is no water on this route, and it should only really be tackled if you are overnighting at the meadow. There is a rock shelter near the top, plus some obvious camping spots just below. You can walk down from Hon to Karimabad in one long day (six to eight hours). For orientation, see map, page 281.

● Sleeping

Karimabad *p282, map p284*
Karimabad has so many hotels (notably at the budget end) that you can find a good deal by shopping around. Note that many of the hotels are rented by a manager for a single season; if they can't make a success of it, they often move on (hence frequent name changes).

The **Haider Inn**, **Old Hunza Inn** and **Tourist Cottage** are particular favourites of the Japanese (especially smokers), cyclists and those on a rock-bottom budget.

A Darbar Hunza, T0572-77105, hunza@isb.apollo.net.pk. Sadly dominates the skyline, grand entrance hall and pleasant lobby area, 40 rooms (5 de luxe and 5 suites) nicely furnished, picture windows, dish TV, fridge, but no fan or a/c, surprisingly small bathrooms, cracks in plaster and repaired bed sheets, bar, large restaurant (buffet breakfast Rs210, Chinese/Pak/continental dishes from Rs200). Despite significant discounts for groups this place has a reputation for poor service.

B-C Hunza Baltit Inn, T0572-77012, serena@glt.comsats.net.pk. Serena-run so high standards of service. 20 very small rooms, bathrooms recently upgraded, restaurant is one of the best in Karimabad. Discounts for groups. Ask here about group dinners at Baltit Fort.

C Hunza View ('new'), T0572-77146, F0572-77141. Formerly the **Mountain View**, this is one of the older hotels in Karimabad. Some rooms have view blocked by the restaurant, and all have vista impeded by new mobile phone mast. 4 VIP rooms (same price) are best bet, 24-hr hot water in bath. You can find much better value than this.

C Hunza View ('old'), T0572-47098, F0572-3695. Actually the newer of the 2, large over-bearing building, fair-sized rooms, well furnished, reasonable restaurant, large discounts for groups.

D-E Hill Top, T0572-77129. 36 rooms, not all have a view, rooms reasonable size (those on upper floors are a little dark), bathrooms modern but small, fan, restaurant (buffet dinner Rs250, breakfast Rs110), occasional cultural shows for groups.

D-E Tourist Park, T0572-77087. 15 doubles with attached bath, restaurant, garden.

D-E World Roof, T0572-77153. 8 fair-sized doubles with nice balconies, don't bother with the 3 cheaper rooms at the back, bath, 24-hr hot water, restaurant, rooftop BBQ, would be a better deal if slightly cheaper but is often full.

E Blue Moon, T0572-77115. Hopelessly overpriced, 7 rooms with fan, paint peeling from walls, grubby linen and blankets, half-tiled bathrooms, all rather jerry-built.

F Hunza Lodge. 4 fairly basic carpeted rooms with small shared balcony, attached hot bath, experienced owners.

F Karim, T0572-77091. 5 doubles and 2 triples with attached bath, basic but clean, 6-bed dorm (H) in traditional Hunza room, rooftop restaurant has one of Karimabad's best views.

F Khusho Sun Guest House. 5 triples with attached hot bath (F) plus a dorm (H), plans for a new block, small terrace garden, offices of *Indus Guides*, slightly sleazy atmosphere.

F Mulberry. 4 plain doubles, reasonable size, carpet, hot bath, restaurant and tented rooftop BBQ, could bargain price down a bit.

G Garden Lodge, T0572-77019. 3 small doubles and 1 crowded 5-bed dorm (H), rather basic with grubby walls but remains very cool in summer, camping, quiet and pleasant terraced garden, restaurant.

G Hill View, Aliabad Link Rd. Was the Asia Star, peeling paint and cracked walls, no real views, no restaurant, poor choice.

G Lady Finger. 4 basic rooms with attached bath, restaurant upstairs.

G Lucky Star. Building used to be the post office. 4 slightly grubby rooms, 3 with basic attached bath and 1 with shared bath, fan, friendly owner but a little overpriced.

G Mount Everest. Was the Mountain Refuge, 3 grubby rooms so cramped you can barely move around, fan, attached bath, view obscured by trees, cheap but not good.

G New Hunza Tourist. Long-established hotel, some new carpeted rooms with attached hot bath, some cheaper standard rooms with attached bath, 3-bed dorm (H), restaurant, garden, not a bad deal.

G Punjab Sindh. 5 grubby and smelly rooms with attached bathrooms featuring dangerous-looking hot water boilers.

G Rainbow. Foreigners rarely stay here, basic rooms, used more as a restaurant/meeting place with blaring dish TV.

G-H Haider Inn. Run by Ali Haider, 5 doubles with attached bath downstairs (G) and 3 4-bed rooms with attached bath upstairs (H, pay per bed). A changing communal meal (Rs70) served each evening.

G-H Karimabad. 3 basic doubles (or pay per bed), looking rather forlorn.

G-H Old Hunza Inn. 5 simple doubles with basic attached bath in new block below the road (G), plus 5 3-bed dorms (H) with

attached bath in old block above road, camp site, communal dinner in evenings (Rs70).
G-H Tourist Cottage. 4 basic triples (G) with bath or pay per bed (H), rather run down.

Eating

Karimabad *p282, map p284*
Common practice seems to be for visitors to take lunch in one of the restaurants along the main street before retiring to their own hotel for communal dinner in the evening. See also under Supermarkets in Shopping.

A lot of foreign visitors get ill in Karimabad; it could be the mica-filled water supply that the locals drink with relish, and to which they attribute good health. Bottled water is readily available for those in doubt. Likewise, fresh apricots and mulberries that will be showered upon you are virtually guaranteed to give you diarrhoea.

TTT Darbar Hunza, T0572-77105, hunza@isb.apollo.net.pk. The grandest of the hotel restaurants (serves alcohol), although it frequently receives poor reviews.

TTT Hunza Baltit Inn, T0572-77012, serena@glt.comsats.net.pk. The best food (Rs200+ per dish) of the hotel restaurants.

TT Ultar. Long-established place serving Hunza dishes, although the prices are now on the expensive side.

T Café de Hunza. Just about the nicest place to sit with your coffee (Rs25, or Rs50 for cappuccino or espresso) and enjoy some homemade brownies (or walnut cake, Rs40). It's also Karimabad's best bookshop.

T Friends. Local dishes in a pleasant setting

Pubs, bars and clubs

Karimabad *p282, map p284*
Not really the place for nightlife, although the **Darbar Hunza** has an overpriced bar (Hunza water Rs600, can of Chinese beer Rs350); officially it's for residents only, although diners can usually order. Some of the supermarkets on the main street now sell cans of Chinese alcoholic beer. Your hotel manager may be able to procure some 'Hunza water' for you (about Rs600 for a litre bottle), but it's not to everyone's taste and there are inherent risks in drinking home-brew.

Festivals and events

Karimabad *p282, map p284*
Feb Bo Pho/Taghun (late Feb/early Mar) celebrates the first ploughing/sowing of the year (wheat).
Mar Nauroz (21 Mar) marks the pre-Islamic vernal equinox (arrival of spring).
Jun Ginani/Chinir (late Jun/early Jul) marks the first wheat harvest of the year.
Jul Taqt Nashina (11 Jul) is fervently celebrated to mark the ascension of the present Aga Khan to the position of leader of the Ismaili community.
Oct Hunza Didar Sal Gira (23 Oct) commemorates the Aga Khan's first visit to Hunza, in 1960.
Dec Birthday Sal Gira (13 Dec) celebrates the Aga Khan's birthday, in Ismaili areas. **Tumishiling** (21 Dec) is a festival held to celebrate the death of Shri Badat of Gilgit. For full details, see Festivals and events, page 39. At least once a year there is a grand festival of music and dancing (timings vary), but it is designed with local people in mind; it's held on the old polo ground, and only villagers are admitted.

Shopping

Karimabad *p282, map p284*
Bookshops
Ali Book Stall inside the Café de Hunza, is the best place to browse and probably has the best selection of books too.
Baltit Book Centre has pretty much the same selection as the others: a few novels, travel literature generally related to South Asia, plus a number of books on Pakistan (notably this region) that are out of print elsewhere.
Mohd Book Stall is a branch of G.M. Baig & Sons, but is better run than the Gilgit branch.

Handicrafts
Hunza Fabric has benefitted from AKRSP support, also has a showroom here (*pattu* weaving specialists).
Hunza Weaving Centre (several branches) is run by the son of one of Karimabad's master weavers; he is one of the few owners here who will tell you the exact origin (and quality) of the stuff he is selling.

Some tips for shoppers in Karimabad

Karimabad has always catered for visitors seeking souvenirs from their visit, but it could be argued that things have gone too far: now the main street is an almost unbroken line of shops selling various handicrafts, with ever more new places under construction. What's more, many of the storekeepers have adopted the custom practised elsewhere (notably India) of calling out to passers by to entice them in.

In general, the usual rules on bargaining apply (see page 43), although there are a couple of fixed-price places. Bear in mind that not all the goods that you see are produced locally (shopkeepers used to tell you exactly where their stuff came from, but many are now being rather creative with the truth); much is from NWFP, a little from Afghanistan, some from Kashmir and some from India. It is also worth noting that should your tour guide take you to (or recommend) a particular shop, then the chances are that he's receiving a commission from them (which ultimately you pay for).

Gems, jewellery, carpets, clothing and general handicrafts are all available; take your time and decide for yourself how much the item is worth. The shops mentioned below have been personally recommended to Footprint by satisfied customers, readers' letters and storekeepers in the business.

Prince Gems/Prince Handicrafts has been recommended by a number of readers; the owner also has a branch at the **Eagle's Nest Hotel** in Duikar.

Threadnet Hunza Carpet is part of the *Karakoram Handicraft Development Programme* (KHDP), and run under the auspices of the AKRSP. It is a community-based programme aimed at reviving the traditional mountain culture and crafts of Hunza. The vegetable-dyed carpets, made by local women from Haiderabad, are superb but not cheap (a 3-m-sq wool carpet can cost US$1,200, or US$2,000 for a similar size in silk). Bargaining is expected and credit cards can be used. Other 'fixed-price' merchandise is also sold here. The main showroom is on the main street, but it's possible to visit the project HQ on the Aliabad Link Rd.

Photography
Film choice is generally better than Gilgit and Kashgar but inferior to Rawalpindi/Islamabad. Many places store their stocks poorly (eg in the windows). Colour print film is widely available, with a few places selling slide film (Fuji Sensia II, Rs400). **Sharma Movie Maker**, up the road to the fort, is your best bet.

Supermarkets
There are half a dozen or so general stores (eg **Baltit Bakery**) selling cold drinks (including, sometimes, Chinese beer, Rs300 a can), biscuits, processed cheese and other items of interest to trekkers. Note that local people travel to Aliabad to buy most of their 'groceries' (cheaper).

Trekking gear
Export Quality Jacket House has a few items (jackets, sleeping bags, tents) that may be of some interest to trekkers.
Mountain Equipment Shop has the best (of a bad bunch) selection of trekking gear (jackets, rucksacks, sleeping bags) for those who have arrived unprepared. There is also a reliable trekking agency based here (see below).

▲ Activities and tours

Karimabad *p282, map p284*
A recommended local guide (usually contactable at **Concordia Expeditions**) is the English, German and Japanese speaking Illias Khan, who started in the business as a tourist-pesterer as a small child but now has great experience with trekkers and groups. Rehmat Karim, based at **Mountain**

Equipment Shop on the road up to the fort, has also been personally recommended.
Concordia Expeditions, Hill Top Hotel, T0572-47010.
Eagle's Nest Hotel, T0572-77074. Based in Duikar, it also has a booking office on the main street here. As well as jeep hire services (see below), it also does bookings and transport for the hotel in Duikar.
Hunza Guides Pakistan has an office in Altit (see below).
Sitara Travels, near Karimabad Hotel, T0572-47010.
Travel Walji's, Tourist Park Hotel.

Transport

Karimabad *p282, map p284*
Jeep hire
Just about every hotel can organize jeep hire. Note that recent sharp increases in diesel prices and vehicle maintenance costs have yet to be fully passed on to travellers; this is largely due to the oversupply of jeeps in the region. A standard fixed price to most destinations has been established by jeep owners. The sample list here has been provided by the Eagle's Nest Hotel office on Karimabad's main street; they have been found to be very reliable providers of jeeps:
Ganesh-Karimabad Rs150; Karimabad-**Altit** Rs400; Karimabad-**Duikar** Rs750 return, Rs500 1-way (see notes on Duikar below); Karimabad-**Hoper** Rs1,100 same-day return; Karimabad-**Minapin** Rs1,000; Karimabad-**Gulmit** Rs1,000; Karimabad-**Borit Lake** Rs1,200; Karimabad-**Passu** Rs1,200 (Rs1,500 same-day return); Karimabad-**Sust** Rs1,500; Karimabad-**Khunjerab Pass** Rs3,500 same-day return; Karimabad-**Gilgit** Rs1,500. Overnight charge is Rs300. Other rates available on request.

Bus
Gilgit: Minibuses of Hunza-Gojal Transport from Gilgit drop passengers along the main street in Karimabad. However, to ease traffic congestion they do not return to Gilgit from here. There is a daily minibus from outside the Rainbow Hotel at 0600 (Rs60, 3 hrs). Alternatively, take a Suzuki wagon down to Aliabad on the KKH (Rs10) from where minibuses run to Gilgit (originating from Aliabad, or passing through en route from Sust). You can also walk down to Ganesh and flag down passing traffic (minibuses from Sust pass through from around 0600-1430, the **NATCO** bus at around 0800).
Gojal (**Gulmit**, **Passu**, **Sust**): To reach destinations in Gojal (Gulmit 1 hr, Passu 1½ hrs, Sust 3 hrs) it is necessary to go down to the KKH. Passing vehicles en route from Gilgit to Sust (stopping at points inbetween) can be flagged down at either Aliabad or Ganesh, although they are often full (early to mid-morning is the best time). Alternatively, there are some minibuses that originate in Aliabad (morning departures are more common). The **NATCO** bus on this route usually reaches Aliabad at around 0930-1000 (it often stops here for chai), reaches Ganesh some moments later. There's not much traffic northbound in the afternoon.
Pisin (for **Minapin**): Eventually someone will set up a direct service on this popular tourist route; in the meantime it's necessary to flag down Gilgit-bound services down on the KKH at Aliabad or Ganesh, go as far as Pisin, and then walk the last 4-6 km to Minapin. Minibuses may be reluctant to take passengers such a short distance (perhaps insisting on the full Gilgit fare); there are no such problems with the **NATCO** bus (at about 0800).
Chalt: Gilgit-bound services down on the KKH at Aliabad or Ganesh will drop passengers at the turning for the Chalt bridge (then a 40-min walk), although minibuses may be reluctant to take passengers such a short distance; there are no such problems with the **NATCO** bus (at about 0800).
Nagar/Hoper: There is usually at least 1 early morning minibus (and several cargo jeeps) daily from Ganesh to Hoper (via Nagar). See also under Jeep hire.

Directory

Karimabad *p282, map p284*
Banks Rates are inferior to those found in Gilgit. Northbound, this is the last place to reliably change money before Sust.
Alam Money Changers, T0572-47109, opposite the Tourist Park Hotel, offers the quickest service for cash and TCs.
National Bank of Pakistan, New Ganesh Rd,

T0572-47050, changes cash and TCs at a snail's pace. **Chemists** Several on the Aliabad Link Rd (or go to Aliabad). **Hospitals** Civil Hospital, Old Ganesh Rd, below village, is of limited use. **AKHS clinic** in Aliabad is a far better bet in an emergency if you can't get to Gilgit. **Internet** Not here yet! Gilgit is the closest place southbound (a real nightmare) and Kashgar northbound (good service). **Libraries** The Baltit Library has recently opened on the road up to the fort (eclectic collection of books and magazines, aimed at local market). **Post office** New location out on Aliabad Link Rd. Mon-Thu and Sat 0900-1600, Fri 0900-1300 (1-2 days for mail to reach Gilgit). **Telephones** The PCO on Aliabad Link Rd has to book international calls via Gilgit (usually unsuccessfully). Gilgit is the nearest place southbound (and Kashgar northbound) to reliably make international calls. The ugly, new mobile phone mast just below Karimabad may soon change this.

Around Karimabad → *Colour map 2, grid B4*

There are a number of wonderful places in the immediate vicinity of Karimabad, all of which can be reached on foot (although jeeps could be hired for the less mobile). These include Altit, a mini Karimabad; the marvellous viewpoint (and hotel) at Duikar; the restored old village of Ganesh; plus the ancient and not so ancient petroglyphs known as the Sacred Rocks of Hunza. This section concludes with the resumption of the KKH journey from Central Hunza to Gojal (Upper Hunza) at Nazimabad/Shishkut.
▶▶ For Sleeping, Eating and all other listings, see pages 298-299.

Altit

The charming village of Altit is a smaller, quieter, scaled-down version of Karimabad, but without the same level of tourism development. There are a number of pleasant walks around the neighbourhood, and a fort dramatically positioned on the cliff 300 m above the Hunza River. Altit is located 1½ km to the east of Karimabad. Altit hotel owners may tell you it's nearer to encourage you to go there, while Karimabad hotel owners may tell you it's further in order to dissuade you from visiting!

The heart of Altit is the rather run-down cluster (*khun*) of settlements around the fort, although lack of space and poor sanitation has forced many villagers to build new houses on their outlying agricultural land. An ambitious programme operated by the **Aga Khan Trust for Culture** is now seeking to redress these problems. By rehabilitating the cluster, it is hoped that villagers will be encouraged to resettle here, rather than using valuable agricultural land for house building. There is also talk of relocating the unappealing 'high-rise' government school and hospital buildings, thus restoring the traditional polo ground; not necessarily for polo, however, but as a community meeting place where village events can be held. The final piece in this four-year jigsaw puzzle will be the restoration of the fort, to increase the tourism appeal.

The people of Altit are aware of the impact that tourism is having on neighbouring Karimabad, and although some members of the village are seeking to embrace the business, others are concerned about its impact on traditional ways of life. For this reason, there are some signs on display requesting visitors not to wander around the narrow alleys at the heart of the old village.

Ins and outs
Most visitors approach on the road that leads from halfway up the hill that is Karimabad's main street (just below **Ultar restaurant**). It's a simple walk, although a

jeep will take you for a pricey Rs120. Altit can also be approached via Mominabad, on the link road that leads down to the KKH (see map, page 284). ▶▶ *See Transport, page 299, for more details.*

Sights

Altit Fort ⓘ *usually entered through the gate next to the Original North Gems shop. The AKTC offices are in a room in the charming orchard here, and will gladly explain the project's progress. Conservation work commenced in 2004 and completion is likely in 2008. Visitors are not permitted to look around the fort until all work is completed, when entry fees will be around Rs200-300,* is thought to be about a hundred years older than the one at Baltit, and prior to the annexation of Gojal (Upper Hunza), it marked the northernmost extremity of the state. The fort is currently engaged in a lengthy restoration programme, aiming to conserve it in its raw state, to give visitors an authentic impression of the original structure and materials. An existing traditional building in the garden beneath the fort may be converted into a restaurant/café, and separate guest rooms may be constructed on a lower terrace behind the restaurant.

It is now known that the original base of the fort, dating from some 850-900 years ago, is actually standing upon two separate rocks; thus the need to securely pin them before further work could progress. The tower was begun some 50 or so years later, probably by Balti craftsmen. Its wooden frame has acted as an effective anti-seismic device, for without this it would no longer be standing. Current plans envisage a realignment of the door and window frames, plus a cosmetic paint job. The fort evolved through three further stages of construction, with the addition of a small mosque, modifications to the tower (around the 16th century), the provision of more storage space, until its present form was reached just 50 years ago when the guest quarters were added.

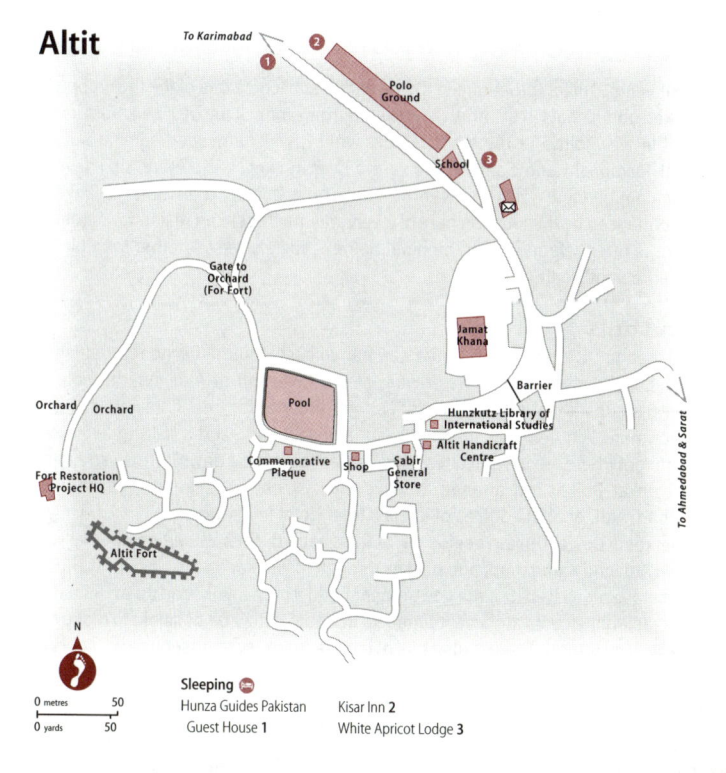

Altit

Sleeping
Hunza Guides Pakistan Guest House **1**
Kisar Inn **2**
White Apricot Lodge **3**

The fort is an intricate maze of rooms connected by small doorways, ladders and trapdoors, built on three levels. The dungeon, said to be the scene of one of the many cases of fratricide that litter the history of the ruling families of Hunza and Nagar, remains sealed off. The watchtower provides stunning views down the Hunza Valley, although a glance down the 300-m vertical cliff face to the river below is not recommended for sufferers of vertigo. From the balcony of the modern royal apartments there is a tremendous view down to the cluster of houses of old Altit village. Because the densely packed rooftops are regularly used by women for drying fruit and washing, photography of this very appealing scene is forbidden.

Walks around Altit

Small groups of modestly dressed visitors can look around the **tank** (pool) area at the heart of the cluster, although diversions up the narrow alleys leading off from here are frowned upon. It is polite to ask before photographing anything, and you should not point your lens at women or young girls; Hunza remains a conservative place, despite what you read elsewhere about the veil-less womenfolk. A pleasant way to spend some time is to wander out the other (east) side of Altit, along the quiet track to **Ahmedabad** (about 7 km). This village is also the starting or finishing point of the Buldiat Valley trek (see page 298).

Informal cricket matches are held most evenings on the old **polo ground**, and talentless foreigners are encouraged to participate. The grandly titled **Hunzkutz Library of International Studies** comprises a small collection of books on local history and some bestsellers (tourists can rent books for Rs5 per day). Staff here are extremely keen to promote the use of English among the younger population and this is a good place to leave books that you have finished with.

Duikar

In recent years, Duikar (pronounced 'Dwee-kar') has become one of the most popular and talked about spots in the north of Pakistan. This is one of the best and most easily accessible viewpoints in the whole Hunza Valley, with unrivalled sunrise/sunset views of Rakaposhi and Spantik across the river in Nagar. There are also several highly recommended walks that can be made from Duikar. The whole package is further enhanced by the location here of a very well-run hotel and restaurant; indeed, this spot is often referred to by the hotel name – Eagle's Nest – rather than by the small settlement's name.

Ins and outs

A hired jeep to Duikar (2,825 m) from Karimabad costs around Rs750 return (Rs500 one way), although backpackers staying at the **Kisar Inn** at Altit may be able to negotiate a substantial discount or indeed get the ride for free if staying for three nights or more. Alternatively, it is a stiff but enjoyable one-and-a-half- to two- hour climb on foot (there are several alternative routes for coming down). Those spending a night up at Duikar can arrange to leave their excess baggage at their hotel in Karimabad/Altit, or at the offices of **Eagle's Nest Hotel** in Karimabad.

The road up to Duikar begins at Sultanabad, the small settlement halfway between Altit and Karimabad, and passes through Melishkar on the way up. The local villagers have requested that the government build a proper link road up to Duikar (to reduce tractor hire costs at harvest time), so in future it may be possible to make the trip cheaply by Suzuki. There is also talk of Japanese money sponsoring two flights of steps up to Duikar from Altit (one from near the Kisar Inn, the other from the Jamat Khana). Another rumour speaks of a link road from the wooden bridge on the Karimabad-Altit road (next to the Relax Inn) up to Duikar.

> ## Keeping the language alive
>
> The interesting little village of Mominabad, with some 65 or so households, is located between Altit and the link road down to the KKH at Ganesh (see map, page 284). Its inhabitants are the Dom, the hereditary lower caste members of Hunza society who occupy the lower professions (such as those of blacksmiths, cobblers and musicians). They have their own language – Domiki – although the higher caste Burushaski speakers refer to this language in a derogatory way as Beriski (and to the people as Berichos).
>
> Less than a decade ago, many commentators were viewing the Doms as a community in crisis. Believing that the villagers would continue to be regarded as lower class citizens if they persisted in using their own language, the elders made a conscious effort to encourage the next generation to improve their Burushaski, Urdu and English language skills. Linguists noted that the Domiki language could well be dead within a single generation, and there was some comment upon this being an interesting reversal of the normal pattern of a language going out of general usage as the younger generations usually make the decision to dispense with the traditional language.
>
> There are now encouraging signs that this heritage will not be lost. Thanks in part to the work of the AKCSP, and other associated bodies, there is a recognition that each distinct culture is something to be proud of, and use to your advantage. The villagers of Mominabad are now proudly highlighting their cultural identity, most notably their role as musicians. Musical workshops have been initiated, and there are more and more opportunities for the musicians to perform, both for tourist groups and for local festivities. Anyone interested in further information should consult with Karim Mutjib (usually found at the Madina Hotel in Gilgit); although not part of the Dom, he is very much involved in Hunza musical affairs.

Sights

The main **viewpoint** (2,900 m) is a 10-minute climb through the eroded rock formations above the **Eagle's Nest Hotel** (although the views are almost as good from the hotel's restaurant, or indeed from your bed). Although many tour groups now arrive for sunrise, lunchtime and sunset viewing sessions, it only takes a five-minute walk to get away from the 'crowds'. The key event at sunrise is when the 7,788-m peak of Rakaposhi is first illuminated by the sun's rays, with the golden glow striking Ultar Peak, Hunza Peak and Bubulimating shortly afterwards. At sunset it is the turn of Spantik (7,027 m) to shine (literally). This mountain, far away to the east (left), is known locally as 'Golden Peak' for reasons that soon become obvious. Bring plenty of film (turn off your flash if it's one that fires automatically and bracket your exposures if you have manual exposure control on your camera: under expose by -1 and -2 stops to avoid the snow highlights from being burnt out).

Beyond Duikar, a two-hour walk heading east from the Eagle's Nest Hotel will take you to the **Hazrat Abbas shrine** near Shabbat village. From here there are impressive vertical views down to the KKH, as well as across to Golden Peak.

Walk to Hosht

This strenuous walk is highly recommended. It gives similar views to the Ultar Glacier hike (see page 285), but from above rather than at the heart of the Ultar bowl. If you are beginning this hike from Karimabad or Altit, it is a fairly exhausting day trip; if you spend the night up at Duikar it is far more manageable. It's pretty hot and dry here so take plenty of water.

There are several routes up and down, with the trail not always being obvious; you tend to come across the white painted arrows by chance, rather than actually following them. You can get general directions from the owner of the Eagle's Nest, or hire someone to show you the way for Rs200-300. It takes about two to two and a half hours of almost continual climbing to reach the viewpoint at **Hosht** (about 3,600 m) from Duikar, although you can continue higher and further if you wish. The short-cut route down is not recommended.

Begin the hike by heading northwest from the Eagle's Nest Hotel (if the hotel is the centre of a clock, aim for ten o'clock). Climb steadily up the hill to the ridge, before doubling back in a northeastly direction (ie two o'clock). Follow the zig-zagging path up and through a series of dry stone walls before traversing the ridge to the west (left). This section is well marked by cairns. It's a steady uphill climb for the next two hours or so until you suddenly crest a ridge (Hosht) and the whole Ultar canyon and sweeping glacier comes into view. Those with energy remaining can continue along the ridge to a small memorial stone, from where there is a view down to the shepherds' huts at Ultar meadow.

Ganesh

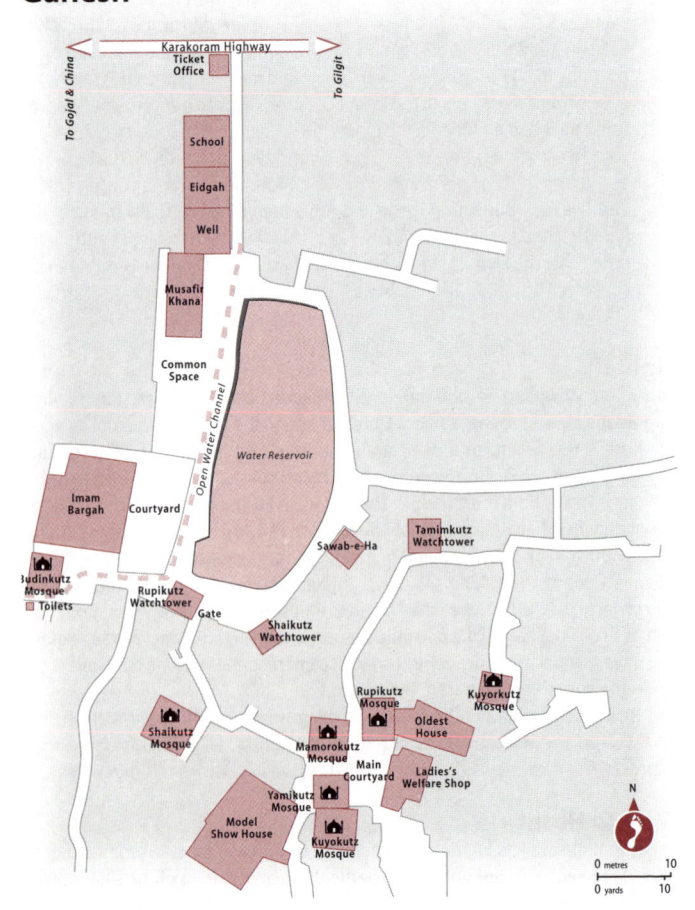

Ganesh

Ganesh is one of Central Hunza's best-kept secrets. Thanks to the expertise and assistance of the **Aga Khan Cultural Service Pakistan** (AKCSP), the ancient heart of this old settlement has been restored and refurbished, and is slowly beginning to entice a steady stream of inquisitive visitors keen to experience something other than Hunza's physical attractions. Until very recently, the village of Ganesh was considered by most outsiders as little more than a place you passed through as you continued your journey along the KKH; if you did stop here, then it was to change vehicles. However, Ganesh is finally being recognized for what it is: the oldest permanent settlement in Hunza (established some 1,000 years ago), with some of its most interesting historical architecture. The restoration programme in Ganesh won an 'Award of Distinction' in the 2002 UNESCO Asia Pacific Heritage Awards for Cultural Heritage Conservation.

Ins and outs

The large settlement of Ganesh sprawls for some distance along and below the KKH, although the part of the village of most interest to visitors sits within the large S-bend cut by the KKH road builders. At the western end of the 'S' is the new link road up to Karimabad (New Ganesh Road), while at the centre of the bend stand a few shops, a hotel, and the KKH Memorial. This is where passing buses normally drop and pick up passengers. Close to the KKH Memorial is a steep, dusty path up to Karimabad (Old Ganesh Road). ▶▶ *See Transport, page 299, for more details.*

Information on Ganesh (including protocol for observing the Ashoura procession) can be obtained from Iftikhar Hussain, secretary of the **Heritage and Social Welfare Society** ⓘ *iftihussain14@yahoo.com* or *www.hunza.8k.com*, or through Rowena Newberry, a British woman who has lived in Ganesh for some years from where she runs an NGO ⓘ *jeep8060@yahoo.co.uk*.

Background

Part of the reason that Ganesh has been ignored for so long is down to its status as home of Hunza's largest Shia population. Following the arrival of Islam in the region, almost the whole of Hunza was under the influence of the Shia sect. The majority of Hunzakuts and Gojalis converted to Ismailism some time in the 18th century, but Ganesh bucked this trend, along with about half of Murtazabad and Garelth, three-quarters of Giram Ganesh, plus a number of families who have settled in Hasanabad, Dorkhun and Aliabad. There are also about a dozen Ismaili families in Ganesh itself, and it has a Jamat Khana.

Of course, Ganesh has not been ignored because the majority of villagers are Shia *per se*; it's due to outsiders' pejorative views of this branch of Islam. True, Ganeshkuts have looked on the effects that tourism has had on places such as Karimabad with some degree of suspicion, but now there is a growing realization that outside influence can bring positive as well as negative benefits. Modestly dressed visitors are now encouraged to visit the architectural highlights at the heart of the 'old village' and, as if to finally dispel the notion of 'unfriendly Shia Ganesh', this is one of the few places in Pakistan where respectful foreigners are encouraged to observe the annual Ashoura procession during Muharram.

Sights

The heart of **Old Ganesh** ⓘ *summer daily 0900-1300, 1400-1730, winter daily 0930-1600; foreign tourists Rs200; photography is permitted (but not of women); modest dress please*, is approached halfway through the huge S-bend that the KKH

> ### Hunza and Nagar regions explained
>
> **Lower Hunza** Comprises the villages on the north side of the Hunza River between Khizerabad and Hasanabad. The majority of villagers here are Shina-speakers (and the area is often referred to locally as Shinaki). Details of this region are in this Lower Hunza and Nagar 2 section.
>
> **Central Hunza** Sometimes referred to as Hunza 'proper', this is the area above the Hunza River between Hasanabad and Nasimabad/Shishkut. Its capital was Baltit, which has now been largely integrated within Karimabad. Most of the inhabitants are Burushaski speakers. See page 279.
>
> **Gojal** Also known as Upper Hunza, this is the area further north along the Hunza River (and KKH), between Nasimabad/Shishkut and the Khunjerab Pass (into China). Most of the inhabitants are Wakhi speakers. See page 305.
>
> **Nagar 2** Comprises Chalt and the Chaprot Valley, plus the Bar Valley, as well as the villages along the south side of the Hunza River as far as Minapin. Most of the villagers are Shina speakers. This region is sometimes referred to as Lower Nagar. Details of this region are found in the Lower Hunza and Nagar 2 section.
>
> **Nagar 1** Comprises the villages on the south side of the Hunza River, from Minapin to the Hispar Glacier. Its capital was the village of Nagar, sometimes referred to as Nagar 'proper'. The main language spoken here is Burushaski. See page 300.

has cut through the village. A new wooden hut acts as the ticket office. The path leads along the open water course, passing the **Eidgah**, the Spanish-funded USWA school and the **well**, before arriving at the **Musafir Khana**, or old travellers' rest house. An interesting feature of the **'common space'** here are the panels in the floor. These are in fact 'Ganesh fridges', where villagers store butter wrapped in birch bark. Some of this butter is over 20 years old, and is only taken out of the 'fridge' for ceremonial use on special occasions (eg birth of a son). Those blessed with a son during the previous year also have to pay a tax (in butter) to the labourers who clean the communally owned water channels each spring.

The **courtyard** beyond the 'common space' provides access to the comparatively modern (80 years old) **Imam Bargah**, which houses a special 'community coffin'; there is even a special version for any unfortunate tourists who happen to croak during their visit! The chenar tree in front of the building is said to be the oldest in Ganesh, with one main branch for each of the five leading families of the village. Just behind is the 400-year-old **Budinkutz Mosque**, which like all the mosques here takes its name from the family that endowed it. It's currently awaiting further restoration work. The modern visitors' toilet block, however, is fully functioning. The **water reservoir** at the heart of the settlement has an interesting history: it is claimed that it was previously used to teach boys and young men how to swim, in preparation for raids on the rival kingdom of Nagar. Despite the Nagaris also following the Shia sect, Ganesh has always been on the side of Hunza in this cross-river rivalry. The original reservoir was dug some 500 years ago, with the removed earth being used for construction purposes. On the southeast side of the water reservoir it's possible to see the **Sawab-e-Ha,** or old caravanserai, the upper storey of which is presently used as a school.

The gate ('himaltar') at the southern end of the reservoir provides access to the main *khun*, or cluster of old settlements. It is flanked by the 700-year-old **Rupikutz watchtower**. Originally the village had some 14 watchtowers, but over the years most have been lost;

the great Shimshal River flood of 1963 claimed a number (plus much village land), as did the construction of the KKH, with others simply succumbing to old age. The narrow alleyways and ladders within the *khun* lead first to the **Shaikutz Mosque**, tentatively dated as being 400-500 years old. The wood carving here, recently restored, is first rate.

The main **open courtyard** ('chataq') features four old mosques, superbly restored in 2001 under the technical direction of the AKCSP (and using Noraid money). All are believed to be about 500 years old. Clockwise, from the southwest corner of the courtyard, they are **Kuyokutz Mosque**, **Yamikutz Mosque**, **Mamorokutz Mosque** and **Rupikutz Mosque**. The east side of the courtyard is occupied by the **Ladies' Welfare Shop**, where Ganesh handicrafts can be purchased, while the northeast corner of the courtyard leads on to the village's **oldest house**, which is currently awaiting refurbishment. Three storeys high, visitors are shown the various spring/autumn, summer and winter quarters, and the various sitting areas for men, women and guests. A number of chogras and weapons are on display here. It may even be possible for small groups to stay overnight. There are some 40 or so houses in the cluster, of which 25 are currently still occupied. Just off the square to the southwest is the home of Ibrahim Khan (financial secretary of the Heritage & Social Welfare Society), whose residence is used as a modern model show house.

For the best view over the *khun* it is recommended that you climb to the roof of the 600- 700-year-old **Shaikutz watchtower**; there are even plans for group dinners to be served here. Away to the east is the 500-year-old **Kuyorkutz Mosque**, currently awaiting restoration work, while located just to the northeast is the 700-year-old **Tamimkutz watchtower**.

Sacred Rocks of Hunza

Although the best, and arguably the most significant, petroglyphs along the KKH are at Chilas and Shatial, the examples of rock art found here are probably the most accessible. The images of ibexes predominate so thoroughly that this place is known locally as *Haldeikish*, or 'the place of the male ibexes/rams', recalling the local tradition of the ceremony of ibex hunting (*thuma saling*).

In addition to the ibex and mounted hunters, there are numerous lists of kings, princes, ambassadors, governors and simple pilgrims who passed this way, with scripts ranging from Kharoshthi, Gupta Brahmi, Sogdian, through Chinese and Tibetan, with dates ranging from the second century AD right through to the graffiti written by Chinese KKH construction workers at the end of the 20th century.

The Sacred Rocks can be reached in a 45-minute walk from Karimabad (although it's an hour's climb back up again). For further detailed information consult Karl Jettmar's *Rock Carvings and Inscriptions in the Northern Areas of Pakistan* (1982) – this can be hard to find, try via the University of Heidelberg at www.rzuser.uni-heidelberg.de. Also very good is Prof. A.H. Dani's *Human Records on Karakoram Highway* (1995) and Volker Thewalt's *Rockcarvings and Inscriptions along the Indus: The Buddhist Tradition* (South Asian Archaeology, 1983, see the excellent www.thewalt.de/verlag.htm website).

Ganesh to Nazimabad/Shishkut (31 km)

Returning to the KKH, just beyond Ganesh, the highway crosses to the south side of the Hunza River. The jeep road to the right directly after this bridge leads southeast to **Nagar** and **Hoper** (see page 302). Above the KKH to the north are great views of **Altit Fort** (see page 291) and Ultar peak. The KKH then passes the **Sacred Rocks of Hunza**, and the Chinese-built brick factory (soon to be closed since it is unprofitable). A further 4 km from the Sacred Rocks a jeep road drops down to the left and crosses the Hunza River, linking **Ahmedabad** to the KKH (this village is usually visited by walking from Altit, see page 290).

Also visible across the Hunza River from the KKH is the **Gurpi Glacier** and the peak of **Ultar II**, and then the village of **Salmanabad** (10 km from the Sacred Rocks). A further 5 km along the KKH is the jeep road to the left that crosses the Hunza River, then climbs spectacularly through a series of hairpin bends up to **Sarat**, 21 km from Ganesh. This is the starting point for an excellent, although little attempted, trek through the Buldiat Valley, see below.

The KKH continues past the Sarat turning, passing through some rugged scenery on its way to the splash of greenery that is **Ayeenabad** (7 km, various spellings, eg Aienabad). A further 4 km beyond here is the small settlement of **Nazimabad**, formerly known as **Shishkut**. Some cyclists choose to break their journey at the simple G Paradise Hotel here. Sarat to Nazimabad/Shishkut is 11 km. The bridge across the Hunza River 2 km beyond Nazimabad marks the boundary between Central Hunza and Gojal ('Upper Hunza'). The KKH journey through Gojal resumes on page 301.

Buldiat Valley trek

Details of this trek have been provided by a reader of *Footprint Pakistan*. It is described as being "ideal for those looking for something a little different in Hunza, away from the crowds but without having to march far to find some solitude". The owner of the **Eagle's Nest Hotel** in Duikar may also be able to provide further details (and arrange camping in relatives' gardens or home-stays).

There are two options for getting to Sarat, the start of the trek. You can either walk 7 km east from Altit to Ahmedabad (see page 292), before continuing for a further 7-8 km via Ramasarat to Sarat. Alternatively, there are wagons available in Ganesh (from outside Sanghir Khan's General Store) that run 20 km north along the KKH, before crossing the bridge over the Hunza River to Sarat. The **NATCO** bus between Gilgit and Sust will also drop you at this bridge. From **Sarat** it is a very steep one-and-a-half-hour switchback climb up to **Atabad**. This is possible in a jeep (Altit to Atabad is Rs800), although it's not for the faint-hearted (it's claimed that only local drivers can safely negotiate this climb). You may be able to arrange accommodation in Atabad by first speaking with local jeep driver Saif Khan (contact him through his relative at the **Prince Gems** shop in Karimabad).

It's a five- to six-hour walk from Atabad up to the flower strewn meadows and ancient forest at **Buldiat** (approximately 4,200 m), where the camping is superb (with plenty of spring water). This is in fact a very popular picnic spot for local people (although they don't usually take so long to get here!). A further climb of a couple of hours gives superb views of the Ultar massif.

From Buldiat the trail descends towards the **Gurpi Glacier**, crossing the nala lower down and continuing to Ahmedabad (and then Altit). It is not impossible to walk down from Buldiat to Altit in a single long day.

● Sleeping

Altit *p290, map p291*
E White Apricot Lodge. Large, carpeted rooms with attached hot bath, place is rarely used after construction of new school and clinic obscured its views.
F Hunza Guides Pakistan Guest House, T0572-77076, www.hunzaguides pakistan.com. Formerly the Amir Jan Village Guest House No 1, now the base for this well-run French-Pakistani tour company. 3 nice doubles with bath (hot water morning and evening), 1 triple and 1 single, rooms open onto communal dining area, guest house set in pleasant, flower and fruit tree-filled garden. Recommended.

F-H Kisar Inn, T0572-77074. Currently run by the brother of the owner of Eagle's Nest at Duikar (enquire here about backpacker discounts, see below), this is one of the best and longest established backpacker hangouts in Pakistan. It is worth paying that extra Rs50 more than in Karimabad for the added cleanliness, service and location. 7 rooms with bath (1 with hot water); 2 front-facing doubles; 2 cheaper doubles; 1 single; a 6-bed Hunza-style dorm plus a 3-bed dorm. Restaurant serves one of Hunza's best evening communal dinners (Rs110), cheap à la carte menu during the day. Recommended.
G Relax Inn. This is the place next to the bridge, on the road from Karimabad to Altit; it started life as a 'cool spot' selling drinks, but there are now 2 basic rooms with shared bath. Views are nice at sunset, but it's a little remote and the waterfall is noisy!

Duikar *p292*
D-G Eagle's Nest Hotel, T0572-77074. This hotel receives rave reviews from tour groups as well as being a good place for backpackers to treat themselves. The 8 rooms are often full, so advance booking is recommended (there's an office in Karimabad's main street where you can also organize transport, or enquire at the Kisar Inn). When business is slack, backpackers may be able to negotiate a decent discount. The rooms are large with picture windows providing superb views (Rakaposhi sunrise from your bed), clean linen, large bathrooms with hot water, and a shared verandah. There are also some modern tents with blankets and thick mattresses for those on a tighter budget. The restaurant offers good buffet meals (breakfast Rs180, lunch Rs220, dinner Rs280) and cheaper à la carte, and is a great place to sit with a pot of tea or a cold drink. Highly recommended.
G Edelweiss Hotel. Good budget option on road up to Duikar, views of Golden Peak (but 15-mins' walk for best panoramic views), 2 basic double rooms with attached cold bath, food sometimes available.
G-H Sun Rise campsite. Often used as an overspill from Eagle's Nest (or by those on a smaller budget). Here you can choose to either pitch your own tent or take a mattress in one of theirs. They have shared cold showers but no restaurant.

Ganesh *p295, map p294*
F-G Karakoram Highway Inn, near KKH Memorial, T0572-47072. Several fairly basic rooms with bath, restaurant. There's better choice (and value) in Karimabad and Altit.

◉ Transport

Altit *p290, map p291*
A **minibus** leaves for Gilgit (Rs60, 3 hrs) from outside the Kisar Inn at 0500 each morning. Otherwise see under Karimabad.

A **jeep** ride up to **Duikar** costs Rs750, although you may get it for Rs300-350 if you're staying at the Kisar Inn (or even free if you book for 3 days or more).

Ganesh *p295, map p294*
NATCO **buses** on the **Gilgit-Sust** route will set down and pick up passengers near the KKH Memorial in the S-bend at Ganesh (the southbound service arrives around 0730-0800, northbound around 0930-1000); there are usually spare seats.

Minibuses on this route will also pick up passengers, although they often pass through full; it may be easier to take a wagon to **Aliabad** (Rs5), from where some services originate. At least 1 minibus per day that leaves Gilgit at around 1400 passes through Ganesh some 3 hrs later on its way to **Hoper** via Nagar; there may be others earlier in the day, some of which have originated in Chalt.

There are also some **cargo jeeps** each day to **Hoper**, although there is not a fixed schedule. You can also find wagons running as far as **Sarat**, for the Buldiat Valley trek (see page 298).

Nagar 1 → *Colour map 2, grid B4*

In many regards this is the 'forgotten' part of the Northern Areas. A combination of factors has meant that Nagar rather missed out on the tourist boom that Hunza experienced, although there are now attempts to promote the former kingdom (both Nagar 1 and Nagar 2) as a less spoilt and more authentic alternative to its rival across the river. It still has some way to go to achieve this, but with its trekking options and hamlets and villages barely touched by tourism, there is more than enough rural appeal to draw the visitors.

Sometimes referred to as Upper Nagar, Nagar 1 includes all the land from Minapin to the Hispar River on the south side of the Hunza River, including Nagar proper, Hoper village and Hispar village. Nagar has a greater land area than Hunza, and since it receives more rainfall (and snow melt), the area of land under cultivation is also greater. The region is famous for its apricots, which are dried and exported to the Punjab in considerable quantity, while the streams are supposedly rich in gold. ▸▸ *For Sleeping, Eating and all other listings, see page 304.*

Ins and outs

There are several entry points into Nagar 1. Most visitors (especially day-trippers) arrive via the jeep road that leads off the KKH just east of Ganesh (directly after the KKH crosses the Hunza River). This route leads via Nagar (proper) and the junction for the track to Hispar before continuing to the end of the line at Hoper. Most public transport uses this route. An alternative entry point from the KKH is via the bridge just to the west of Hasanabad, which crosses the Hunza River to Shayar (for Askordas and Sumayar), although few people use this route (see page 304).

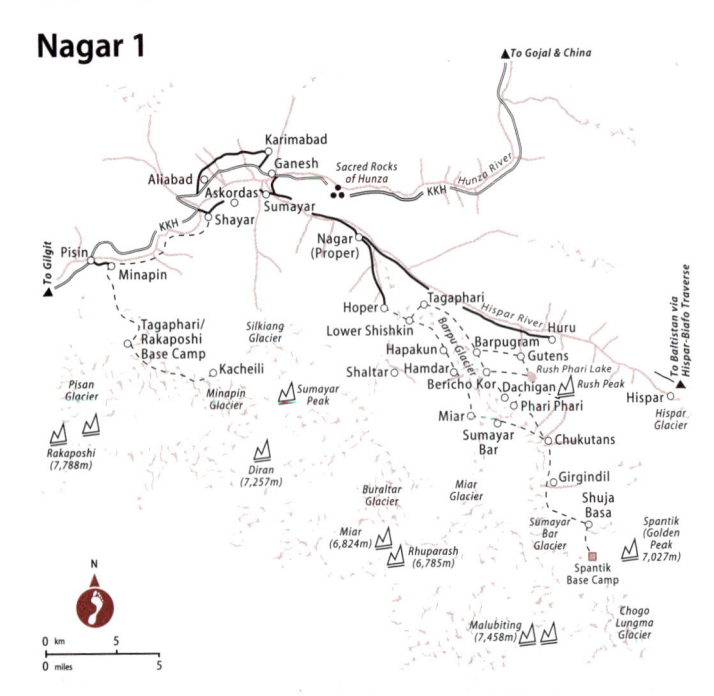

For those arriving from Minapin in Nagar 2, there are a series of jeep roads and tracks that lead along the south bank of the Hunza River to Nagar (proper) and Hoper, although most of these roads are poorly maintained and some have been swept away altogether; for example, public transport from Minapin to Hoper goes via the KKH. See map, page 300, for orientation. A small number of trekkers arrive at Hispar each year, having walked in from Baltistan along the Biafo and Hispar Glaciers (see page 253 for map and trek details).

There are direct services to Nagar and Hoper (via Ganesh and the KKH) from the Jutial bus station in Gilgit, as well as from Chalt and Minapin (both in Nagar 2). There are also some services originating in Ganesh. ›› *See Transport, page 304, for more details.*

Background

Nagar's history has been inextricably linked with that of its neighbour (and rival) across the river, Hunza, and it is very difficult to separate the two (see box, page 296). Unfortunately, there is a real danger that Nagar gets subsumed under all things Hunza. There are a variety of reasons for this. As mentioned elsewhere, Hunza has generally been considered the dominant partner in this rivalry, even if history does not always bear this out. The key battle (at Nilt) of the British Hunza Campaign of 1891-92 to subjugate the region, for example, was in fact fought in Nagar. Hunza is, however, the more evocative name of the two, and Hunzakuts have done little to dispel this notion. You'll often find official government tourism brochures with pictures of 'Rakaposhi, Hunza' when it is indisputably located in Nagar, because Hunza has more tourist appeal.

This is due, in part, to the fact that tourism established itself in Hunza long before Nagar recognized its potential. The route taken by the KKH (itself often said to have been determined partially by religion), the fact that Nagar has more cultivatable land available (plus greater rainfall) and thus less need for other income-generating activities, as well as this whole idea of the 'myth' of Hunza, have all been influences.

Nevertheless, Nagar is now making great strides to get on the development bandwagon, with tourism being seen as one such medium through which this process can take place. Through the work of a number of NGOs in the area, the residents of Nagar are beginning to assert their own cultural identity. Locally produced postcards sporting spectacular views of Rakaposhi, Diran and Golden Peak now proudly, and prominently, bear the word 'Nagar'. Perhaps the 'Welcome To Nagar' sign on the KKH as you leave Gilgit sub-district is the most obvious manifestation of this process. It's just a cosmetic issue, but does underline a genuine effort by Nagaris to express a distinct cultural identity.

Nagar has a number of problems, and perceived problems, to overcome if it is to compete with Hunza on an equal footing. Over the years, porters and guides have developed a reputation for being keen to overcharge. In fact, the people keenest to spread negative stories about Nagari porters, children and 'unfriendly' people in general have often been those with a stake in tourism in Hunza. There has now been a realization that Nagari porters are on the verge of 'killing the goose that lays the golden egg', and hence great efforts are being made to clean up their act. Likewise, children are being educated in the ways of foreign tourists, and are being actively encouraged not to beg and generally hassle visitors. Of course, respect for alien culture is a two-way business, and visitors to Nagar have a responsibility too. This is a conservative area, and thus visitors must be respectably dressed (no bare flesh, on either sex), not indulge in public displays of affection, and be careful about who and what they photograph (make sure that you ask permission, particularly when women are around).

Ganesh to Hoper (25 km)

Shortly after leaving Ganesh on its way to Gojal, the KKH crosses a bridge to the south side of the Hunza River. A jeep track leads off to the right here, running in a southeasterly direction along the Hispar River. This is the main route into Nagar 1, and the one used by almost all the public transport.

Several kilometres up this canyon, on the opposite side of the river, there is a tall, prominent cliff face, known locally as **Burrum Char** ('white rock'). Local legend claims that it was from the top of the cliff here, during times of war with neighbouring Hunza, that captured Hunzakuts were tossed into the river below to the accompaniment of drums and music. Perhaps showing a superior business sense, Hunzakuts preferred to sell their captured Nagaris into slavery.

The road is sealed as far as the bridge across the Hispar River (6 km). It then climbs steeply up the other bank to **Nagar Khas** (the disused road that continues along the bank of the Hispar River is the old route to Hispar). To the left of the road here, close to the new mosque, is one of the first **Imam Baras** built in Nagar (date unknown, although probably around 1700); the carved wooden door is particularly impressive. Just beyond the new mosque (but before the clinic) a path winds upwards (just beyond a blue and white sign saying 'USWA Public School'). Nagar's old fort used to stand on the plateau here, although the only antiquity to be seen today is the **Shah Kamal Mosque**. Made of mud and plaster (but with a modern, temporary roof), the date 1117 A.H. is carved on the lintel (making it contemporary with the Imam Bara down below). There are good views of Spantik (Golden Peak) from here.

Nagar Khas ends just beyond the Civil Hospital and Distighil Hotel with the village of Nagar proper beginning at the police station (foreigners sometimes have to register here). Ganesh (on the KKH) to Nagar proper is about 10 km.

It is hard to believe that **Nagar proper** was once the capital of an independent kingdom, although the former Mir does still retain a 'palace' here. The jeep track that leads off in a southeasterly direction (left) here is the new road via **Huru** to **Hispar** village. It is a couple of kilometres down this road that you take the left fork to the **Mir of Nagar's palace**. The last Mir, His Excellency Mir (Brig rtd.) Shaukat Ali Khan, still passes the summer months at the modest palace here. It is occasionally possible to visit and view the eclectic collection of photos, hunting trophies, weaponry and citations that line the walls, although the golden bed given as a present when the last Mir's son married the daughter of the last Mir of Hunza is not on display. Most of the palace dates to the 20th century, although outside in the gardens lies the carved wooden 200-year-old **audience chamber** that remained in active use until some 30 years ago. It has a pleasing panoramic view over Golden Peak.

A further 15 km beyond Nagar proper, through colourful cultivated fields, the jeep road enters an impressive wide fertile bowl ringed by high peaks. The five small hamlets clustered together here (Shakoshal, Hakalshal, Borushal, Holshal and Ratal) are collectively referred to as **Hoper** (or 'Hopar'). Listen out for 'duelling banjos' here. Hoper is the starting/finishing point for a number of impressive treks (see below; for details of the Biafo-Hispar Traverse, see page 253). Those with limited time can still admire the dirty **Bualtar Glacier** down below, and the **Barpu Glacier** on the other side. **NB** Do not go down onto the glacier without a reliable guide.

Unfortunately, Hoper does not always show the people of Nagar in the best light, but there are some mitigating circumstances. The majority of visitors to Hoper are day-trippers from Karimabad (and since the jeeps are hired there, Nagaris rarely derive any income from this). The majority of these visitors spend just long enough to drink a coke and peer down to the Bualtar Glacier for a couple of photos. Thus, the traders and businessmen in Hoper have little more than 20 minutes to make any money. As a result, there is a tendency for the restaurants to grossly overcharge, while the abiding memory of most visitors is of persistant hustlers trying to flog them 'gemstones' and souvenirs. Until Hoper can attract visitors for longer periods, this sorry situation is set to continue, although improved transport links here does mean that a day trip in a jeep is no longer the only way of getting here.

Treks from Hoper

Barpu Glacier/Spantik Base Camp trek

ⓘ *Open zone. Maximum elevation 4,000 m. Mid-Jun to Oct. Maps: Swiss Foundation reasonable; U502 series, NJ 43-14 Baltit is unreliable. For orientation, see map on p300. Read trekking notes on p45.*

This trek is usually undertaken in six days, although it does involve nine stages. The walking is fairly easy, but the fact that there are five glacier crossings makes a guide essential. Leaving Hoper (2,790 m), you cross the **Bualtar Glacier**. The trail across changes daily, and it can take anywhere between 20 minutes and two hours to cross. Make sure that you are carrying water since there is none until the first night's camp. Having crossed the Bualtar Glacier to **Lower Shishkin**, you must then cross the **Barpu Glacier** to **Tagaphari**. Proceed in a southeast direction along the ablation valley via the shepherds' huts at **Barpugram** (45 minutes), and camp the first night at **Bericho Kor** (3,300 m), a further one hour, and four to five hours from Hoper altogether. From here there is the option of a strenuous two-day climb up to Rush Phari (see below).

The second day is a simple, straightforward two-hour hike via **Dachigan** to **Phari Phari** (3,450 m). The third day is particularly pleasant, passing through the grassy meadows of **Chukutans** to the pastures at **Girgindil** (four hours). From here it is possible to make a two-day detour up to **Spantik Base Camp**, known locally as Shuja Basa (a further six stages). To return to Hoper you need to retrace your route back down to Chukutans, then cross the **Sumayar Bar Glacier** to the shepherds' huts at **Sumayar Bar** (five hours). On the fifth day, cross the **Miar Glacier** to **Miar**, then follow the Barpu Glacier via **Hamdar** (two hours) to **Hapakun** (one hour). On the final day, walk down to **Lower Shishkin**, recross the Bualtar Glacier, and return to Hoper (four hours).

Rush Phari trek

ⓘ *Open zone. Maximum elevation 4,694 m. Mid-Jun to Oct. Maps: Swiss Foundation is usable, although it has some mistakes; U502 series, NJ 43-14 Baltit is unreliable. For orientation, see map p300. Read trekking notes on p45.*

This is a fabulous extension to the Barpu Glacier Trek, although several serious considerations must be borne in mind. **Rush Phari**, a breathtaking turquoise lake from where a 360° panoramic view takes in all the most spectacular peaks of the region (including K2, Broad Peak and Gasherbrum IV), is located at an altitude of 4,694 m. Consequently, it is only for trekkers who are already acclimatized. There are also long stretches on this trek where water is not available.

Follow the first day description of the Barpu Glacier Trek from **Hoper** to **Bericho Kor** (3,300 m). The second day involves an altitude gain of over 1,100 m, and should only be attempted by those who are fully acclimatized. What's more, this five- to six- hour climb is very hot, and has no water en route so you should stock up in Bericho Kor. The first four hours of the climb up from Bericho Kor heads east, up to a 4,020-m ridge (marked by a cairn). If you experience altitude sickness, you will have to descend since there are no alternative camping options. Having reached the ridge (where a trail joins from Gutens, to the northeast), head southeast along the ridge to the camping spot near shepherds' huts at **Chidin Harai** (two hours, 4,400 m). There is water here.

The following day it should not take more than two hours to reach **Rush Phari** (4,694 m), although the trail is not always obvious. It is worth spending some time here, perhaps an extra day, in order to ascend some of the surrounding hilltops (eg Rush Peak) in order to get even better views. Note that it can get very cold and very windy at Rush Phari.

There are two options for the return trip: you can descend the way that you came, or you can make the steep descent down to Phari Phari (three hours). See the Barpu Glacier Trek details above for the return to Hoper.

Nagar 1 via Shayar, Askordas and Sumayar

Another access point to Nagar 1 is via Shayar, Askordas and Sumayar, the latter being the small village perched on the wide alluvial fan that you seen when looking south accross the Hunza River from Karimabad. The most interesting way to approach the village is from the west, via Shayar and Askordas. This involves hiking (or hitching) south along the KKH, to the point where the road emerges from the entrance to the Hasanabad Nala, see page 279. A snaking jeep road drops down to the Hunza River, crosses via a suspension bridge, and then up to the settlement of **Shayar**. From here, it is an enjoyable one-and-a-half-hour walk along the track to **Askordas**. This small village is notable for its ostentatious new mosque, built with proceeds from the rich mineral strike above Sumayar. There's a small chai shop in Askordas. A further hour brings you to **Sumayar**. The camping site up above the village is a fine place to stop. The more energetic may like to continue up the hillside along the Sumayar Nala to Mamubar, the former hunting grounds of the Mir of Nagar. Some four hours above Sumayar are the summer pastures of Madur Kushi, where it is also possible to camp (although the Mir of Nagar is still entitled to collect rent from campers here). It is high up here, above the Sumayar Nala Valley and Silkiang Glacier, that Nagar derives much of its wealth: the aquamarine crystal mines at Chuman Bakhur (a further two hours up the mountain). In theory, there is a three-day trekking route from here to Hoper, although it is rarely used and a guide is essential. From Sumayar it is a two-hour walk down to Nagar proper. From here, you can return to the KKH, or head up to Hoper.

Sleeping

Nagar 1 p300, map p300
Nagar Proper
G **Khunery Inn** at the junction with the road to Hispar. Presently just 1 basic room, but owner plans expansion.
G **NAPWD Inspection Bungalow** in Nagar (book in Gilgit).
G-H **Distighil Hotel** at Nagar Khas, very basic rooms, restaurant.

Hoper p302
The owners of the 2 hotels here are not necessarily the best advertisment for Hoper; you may find them literally fighting each other for your custom. They may also tempt you to their place by the offer of 3 (as opposed to 2) eggs in your omelette! Note that when ordering food and drinks, nothing on the menu is priced. This system is designed to allow the owners to charge you what they think you will be prepared to pay;

fix all prices in advance and double-check your bill. Prices at both are negotiable.
F **Hoper Hilton**. 4 new rooms with attached hot bath, plus 2 older triples, restaurant.
F-G **Hoper Inn**. 3 bare doubles with attached bath, some tents, restaurant, plans for further expansion.

Transport

Hoper p302
A day trip by jeep from Karimabad costs Rs1,100, although you only get about ½ hr here. There is an early morning minibus to Gilgit each day (Rs120, 4-5 hrs), returning from the Jutial bus station each afternoon. Cargo jeeps operate on a depart-when-full basis between Hoper and Najad Ali's jeep workshop in Ganesh (Rs30), and there are also some minibuses to/from Chalt.

Gojal (Upper Hunza) → Colour map 2, grid B4

The upper part of Hunza is referred to as Gojal (Guhjal), and comprises the area along the upper section of the Hunza River from the village of Shishkut/Nazimabad up to the Khunjerab Pass. It also includes the Shimshal Valley that lies to the east of the KKH, and the Chapursan Valley that lies to the west of the KKH along the border with China (towards Afghanistan's Wakhan Corridor).

Gojal is populated by Wakhi-speaking communities who settled here several generations ago. Originally nomads from the grazing pastures of the Upper Oxus, they are thought to have arrived through the Irshad Pass which connects the Wakhan, Yarkun, Ishkoman and Chapsuran Valleys, and settled down to sedentary agriculture. They were previously ruled by their own Raja but later came under the suzerainty of the Mir Of Hunza. The people are almost exclusively Ismaili.

Gojal offers some of the most exciting attractions in the north of Pakistan. There are plenty of good treks, but what makes Gojal particularly appealing is the spectacular one-day hikes on offer for those who do not wish to do a full-scale trek.

The southern limit of Gojal is the village of Nazimabad, where the KKH crosses to the west bank of the Hunza River. A further 3 km along the KKH is a police station, defining the southern limits of Gulmit. Most of the hotels are found a further 2 km along the KKH, with the main village itself positioned just above the KKH. ▶▶ *For Sleeping, Eating and all other listings, see pages 313-315.*

> **Related maps:**
> *A Walks and hikes around Passu and Sust, p310*
> *B Shimshal Valley and Shimshal Pamir, p317*
> *C Sust to Kashgar, p332*

Gulmit

Former summer residence of the Mir of Hunza, Gulmit (2,370 m) is a sleepy village set amid productive agricultural land, and offers some easy short walks. The main village is centred around the old polo field several minutes' walk above the KKH. As recently as the 1950s, the polo ground was a lawn of lush grass hosting regular matches, although the arrival of the internal combustion engine made the keeping of horses an expensive luxury as opposed to an everyday necessity.

Ins and outs

NATCO buses running northbound and southbound between Gilgit and Sust will drop and pick up passengers at Gulmit. There are also Sust-bound minibuses from Gilgit that will drop passengers here; services running in the opposite direction may ask passengers to pay the full fare as far as Karimabad at least. It is a short walk up from the KKH to the polo ground at the heart of the village. ▶▶ *See Transport, page 314, for more details.*

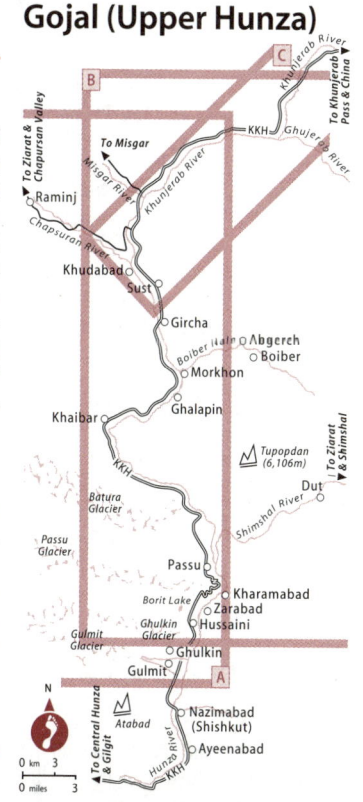

Tourist information

The current phone system requires you to dial the exchange number (T77238) and then ask for the extension number. A new digital exchange is under development.

Sights

The charming one-room **Cultural Museum** ⓘ *Rs25 for tourists; ask for key at Hunza Marco Polo Inn if museum is shut*, has recently been 'refurbished', but has lost none of its eccentric appeal. It contains an unusual assemblage of artefacts ranging from local cooking utensils, household objects and clothing, through a stuffed snow leopard (the only one, living or stuffed, that you're likely to see in Pakistan) to the gun that is said to have caused Colonel Durand's unusual limp (see box, page 275). The 'refurbishment' has consisted of putting a few dusty items into dusty showcases and adding labels. You may be given a commentary in English by someone who probably doesn't understand a word of the speech that he is making.

At the northern end of the polo ground are the scant remains of the original village, sometimes referred to as **Old Gulmit** (between 100 and 200 years old). The **Aga Khan Cultural Service Pakistan** (AKCSP) has recently turned its attention to Old Gulmit, with plans in hand for a restoration project along the lines of those accomplished in Baltit, Ganesh and underway in Altit. The former **Mir's Palace** is currently being restored and may one day be turned into a guest house. There are also plans to restore the polo ground. Likewise, the traditional-style **Oldest House** has now been occupied by **ThreadNet**, and it is possible to come and watch the 25 or so women employed here creating locally designed products on the looms. The labyrinth of alleyways running between the old stone, mud and wooden houses of Old Gulmit covers a very compact area only, but it is interesting nonetheless. There is also an old Shia mosque that predates most of the other buildings here.

Short walks around Gulmit

Kamaris, Gulmit Glacier and Andare Fort

It is possible to walk up to the **Gulmit Glacier** above the village as a long day trip, or as an overnighter. The track behind Gulmit climbs steeply to the small village of **Kamaris**, from where a footpath continues for some four hours or so to shepherds' huts on the south side of the Gulmit Glacier. On your return, it is possible to take the path leading down to the east of Kamaris, past the insubstantial remains of the 200-year-old **Andare Fort**, and back to Gulmit. **AKCSP** (Aga Khan Cultural Services Pakistan) are discussing a restoration programme for the fort.

Ghulkin, Ghulkin Glacier and Borit Lake

The small village of **Ghulkin** can be reached by either crossing the snout of the Gulmit Glacier, or from a link road off the KKH, 500 m north of Gulmit.

From Ghulkin a footpath crosses the snout of the **Ghulkin Glacier**, before climbing up the lateral moraine. If you are unsure about crossing the glacier, ask for local advice or hire a guide. A further two and a half hours' walk brings you to **Borit Lake**, a large brackish glacial lake that attracts a number of migratory birds in February to June and September to November. From the lake you can either return to Gulmit (four hours), or continue on to Passu (five hours – route described in Passu section). To walk from Gulmit, via Borit Lake, to Passu all in one day is quite a slog, although you can stay at Borit Lake, see page 313.

Hussaini Bridge

This is a popular day excursion from Passu (see page 307), although the southernmost of the two suspension bridges on this walk (Hussaini) can be reached from Gulmit by walking 5 km north along the KKH. You could also continue on to Passu from Hussaini, although it's a fairly unrewarding 9-km uphill walk.

Gulmit to Passu (14 km)

Returning to the KKH, 1 km north of Gulmit is a jeep road turn-off for **Ghulkin**. After a further 2 km you cross the snout of the Ghulkin Glacier via a pair of iron girder bridges. At the bend in the road 2 km from here you come across the large village of Hussaini, just below the KKH on the river side. At the southern end of the village, a track leads down from the KKH to the much-photographed suspension bridge across the Hunza River. This bridge is usually visited as part of a long day walk from Passu.

The KKH continues to climb from Hussaini, passing the turn-off for the jeep road to **Borit Lake** (1 km) a further ½ km down the highway (see page 310). The KKH climbs for much of the remaining 7½ km through a series of sweeping bends to the southern outskirts of Passu.

Passu

Passu offers some of the best walking in the whole of the north of Pakistan, from half and full day trips, to short multi-day walks, right through to long strenuous treks. And

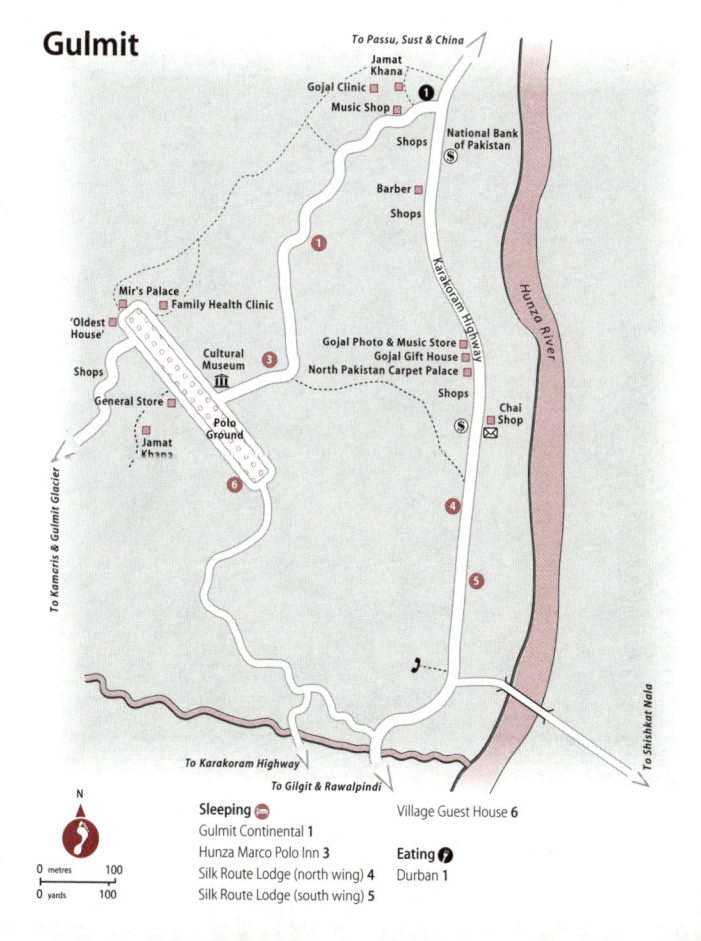

Gulmit

Sleeping
Gulmit Continental **1**
Hunza Marco Polo Inn **3**
Silk Route Lodge (north wing) **4**
Silk Route Lodge (south wing) **5**
Village Guest House **6**

Eating
Durban **1**

to the delight of backpackers, few tour groups stop here and it has attracted none of the tourism-related development that has blighted Karimabad; it remains little more than a sleepy village with a few good-value guest houses.

The village (2,543 m) is located to the east of the KKH, with houses scattered among the irrigated fields and orchards on the wide alluvial fan. Flooding that follows periodic damming of both the Shimshal and Hunza Rivers has done irreparable damage to the agricultural system in Passu, and greatly reduced the amount of land available for cultivation; the village has received a 30 lakh Rupees government grant to build a new bund in order to counteract the flood threat. There are also plans to bring the wide stony plain to the north of the village under cultivation with assistance of the **AKRSP**, but this has proved to be a slow process fraught with technical difficulties.

To the south of the village, the KKH bridges the stream of the **Passu Glacier**, strikingly white in contrast to the dirty grey morainal glaciers common to this region.

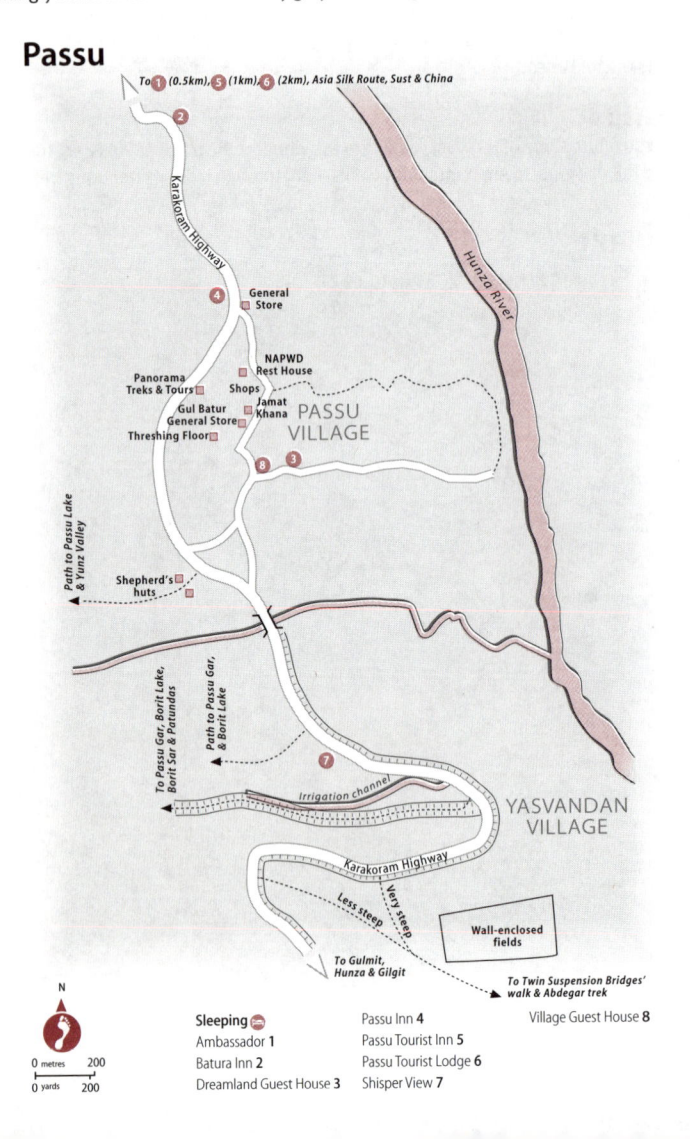

Sleeping
Ambassador 1
Batura Inn 2
Dreamland Guest House 3
Passu Inn 4
Passu Tourist Inn 5
Passu Tourist Lodge 6
Shisper View 7
Village Guest House 8

To the north of Passu is the immense **Batura Glacier**, stretching some 58 km from the Batura Muztagh group of peaks to the west, right down to (and sometimes through) the KKH. Across the river is a huge and ruggedly beautiful multi-pinnacled ridge of crumbling granite spires, that is sometimes referred to as 'The Cathedral' but is known locally as **Tupopdan**.

Short walks around Passu

Warning Glaciers are active and highly unstable, especially in summer. Note that if a foreigner is killed or injured on the glaciers, the local people tend to get the blame from the authorities. It is for this reason that they are so insistent on you taking a guide. Those planning to hike or trek should note that the trails change somewhat from year to year. For example, the catastrophic rains of September 1992 changed some routes significantly, and you should be sceptical of any route descriptions written before then. Check the latest 'rumour books' in the various hotels.

Twin suspension bridges

Probably the most popular day hike from Passu, this trip crosses and then recrosses the Hunza River on two dramatic suspension bridges, passing through some delightful Upper Hunza villages and affording fine views of the Passu Glacier. The one drawback to this marvellous day out is that in order to complete the loop back to Passu, the last leg of the trip is a fairly unrewarding 8-km hike back along the KKH from Hussaini Bridge (the further south of the two). Presuming you get a lift back to Passu from Hussaini, this walk takes around 5-6 hours. One alternative is to hire a jeep (Rs150) from Passu as far as Hussaini Bridge, then walk back from there via the villages on the east bank of the river and the northernmost of the two bridges. Even if you don't have the energy to make this hike, it is still worth spending some time watching the comings and goings at Hussaini Bridge. **NB** This trip is quite hot and dry so take plenty of water. See map on page 310 for orientation.

> *On hot days, come and stand by the stream of the Passu Glacier to appreciate the icy drafts.*

South of the **Shisper View Hotel**, just past the first hairpin out of Passu (and just before the second hairpin), follow the path down from the KKH (it may be marked by some white cairns). Follow the path, and don't be tempted to drop down to the river too early. A series of rockfalls has largely obliterated the path along the river bank, so care should be taken while scrambling over the boulders. The route is clearly marked by a series of cairns. About 45 minutes downstream, you come to the **first bridge**, sometimes referred to as Shisper Bridge. Irregular planks and branches, in places up to a metre apart, supply the footholds, while two rusty metal cables provide a handrail. The bridge sways as you walk across it, even more so on a windy day or if more than one person attempts to cross at a time. Of the two bridges, this is the most difficult one to cross, but the bridge at Hussaini is probably more photogenic (and busier).

Having crossed the river, continue straight ahead across the rocky, alluvial fan, heading for the large pile of boulders at the top. To the left is the route to Abdegar (see below), via the Passu-owned lands of Kharamabad. Aim to cross the ravine to your right as high as possible, but before the large pile of boulders. Avoid at all costs the extensive thorn forest across the ravine; the way through it is neither clear nor painless.

Once across the ravine, you pass through highly cultivated land belonging to the village of Hussaini, on the opposite side of the river. The settlement here is known as **Zarabad** and is particularly photogenic in autumn when the crops are ripening against the distant white background of the Passu Glacier. Follow the path through the village and then descend by way of the steps cut in the cliff face to the **Hussaini Bridge**. There are two bridges here, although the one furthest downstream is too dangerous to use. Across the river is **Hussaini**, another small village situated below the KKH. Near to the bridge are some hot springs with segregated bathing times for men and women. From Hussaini it is about 8 km to Passu along the KKH, although you should be able to hitchhike quite easily. You could also continue on to Gulmit (5 km), or to Borit Lake (1½ km, see pages 306 and 310).

Passu Gar (and Borit Lake/Borit Sar)

By expending a little energy you can get great views of the Passu Massif and the Passu and Batura Glaciers in an eight- to nine-hour round trip. There is also the option of continuing on to Botit Lake (and eventualy Gulmit, if you so wish), as well as Borit Sar. The beginning of this hike is also the start of the Patundas trek (see below). **NB** This trip is quite hot and dry, so take plenty of water. See map on page 310 for orientation.

To save energy and time it is important to find the right trail straightaway. Head south along the KKH beyond the **Shisper View Hotel**. Above the road is a line of vegetation running along the cliff (it's actually following a water channel). The water channel eventually reaches the KKH and runs alongside it for 30 m, before going under the KKH. Continue along the KKH for a further 30 m and you'll see a distinct path climbing up the cliff. Follow this in the direction of the electricity pylons until you reach a low saddle. The trail that heads off left (southeast) continues to **Borit Lake** (a further two hours). The trail that ascends straight ahead (west) continues for a further one hour to a large slate platform (2,730 m) from where there are good views down to Passu Glacier and Passu Lake. There are two options here. A stiff three hours straight up the

Walks & treks around Passu & Sust

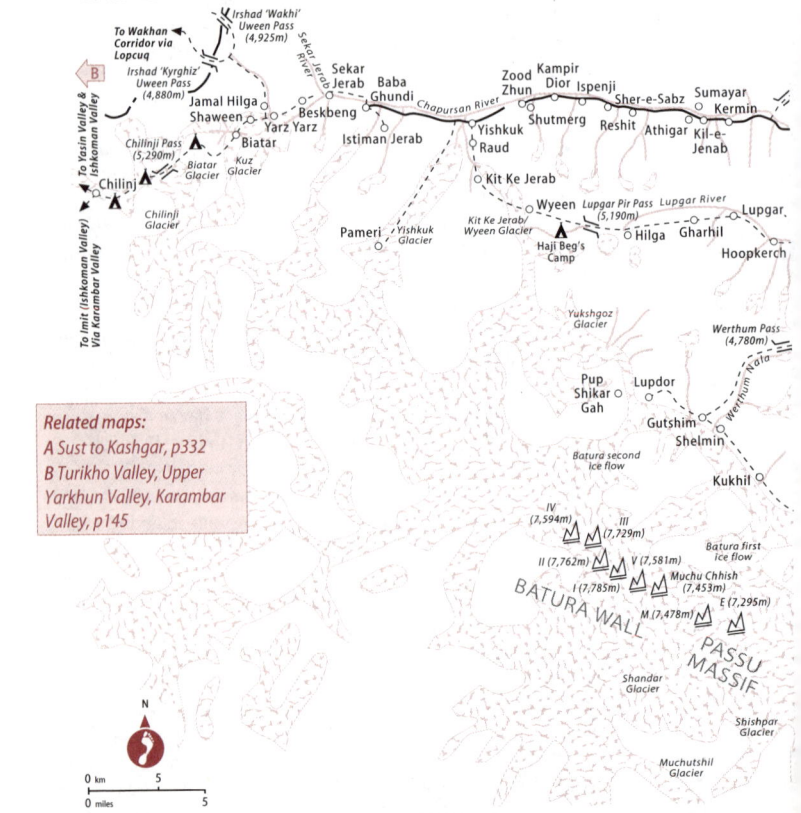

Related maps:
A *Sust to Kashgar, p332*
B *Turikho Valley, Upper Yarkhun Valley, Karambar Valley, p145*

slate-covered mountainside leads you to **Borit Sar**, the viewpoint overlooking Borit Lake and the Passu and Ghulkin Glaciers. Alternatively, head from the slate platform along the old water channel above the Passu Glacier for half an hour, then climb sharply at the end of the ablation valley to a distinct rest point. A second abandoned water channel heads west along the ablation valley, after 40 minutes or so arriving at the shepherds' huts at **Passu Gar** (3,100 m). You can camp here, or return to Passu in four to five hours. This is the usual first night camp on the Patundas trek (see below).

Yunz Valley

The one-day, but hot, dry and strenuous walk through the **Yunz Valley** offers good views of the Passu and Batura Glaciers. The route passes behind Skazart, the massive yellow rock that looms over Passu, and takes between eight and ten hours depending upon how many of the 'viewpoints' you make it to. There is a beautifully painted map of the route, complete with cut-aways and highlights, in the 1995 'rumour book' at the **Batura Inn**, although all the text is in Japanese. **NB** This is one of the routes that was affected by the September 1992 rains. See map on page 310 for orientation.

Walk south through Passu until you reach some stone huts near to the KKH bridge across the Passu Glacier stream. Head up towards the Passu Glacier until you reach the small Passu Lake. Walk around the west side of the lake, ignoring the old route along the water channel high to your right (this now ends in a precipitous drop), until you reach its north side. This lake was formed 10-15 years ago by the retreat of the Passu Glacier. The water is not suitable for drinking and it is very cold. Follow the cairns (small, route-marking piles of rock), and climb up the steep path into the Yunz Valley (2,775 m, the route is not always obvious). A couple of hours along the valley is a detour to the right, which leads to a viewpoint above the Hunza Valley. This will add one and a half hours to your journey. At the north end of the valley, descend the moraine to the left of the stone huts, and follow the path of the Batura Glacier back down to the KKH.

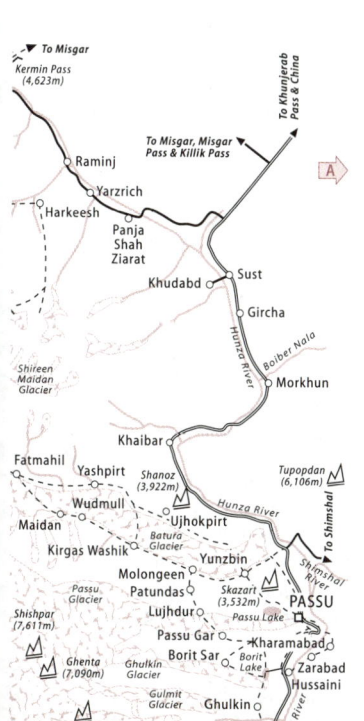

Treks in the Passu area

Batura Glacier trek

ⓘ *Open zone. Maximum elevation optional (up to 4,000 m). Early Jun to late Sep. Maps: the Chinese Institute of Glaciology map of Batura is excellent; Swiss foundation is good; U502 series, NJ 43-14 Baltit is just about adequate. See map on p310, for orientation. Read trekking notes on p45.*

The Batura Glacier trek is a popular one and relatively easy, apart from the crossing of the glacier at the beginning of the trek. It can be completed in six to eight days, although you may want longer to explore higher up the glacier. An increasing number of walkers are extending the trek by continuing north from Lupdor and heading up into the Lupgar River valley. Once there, it's possible to continue into the Chapursan Valley via the east (Raminj) or west (Yishkuk); see page 319 for further details.

There are two ways to start the trek, either via the **Yunz Valley** (see Short Walks around Passu), or by following the south side of the Batura Glacier from the KKH to the north of Passu. If taking the latter route it is well worth trying to find transport to drop you off by the Batura Glacier itself. Both ways lead to the shepherds' hut at **Yunzbin**, where you can camp. From here the main route crosses to the north side of the Batura Glacier, although it is possible to continue along the south side as far as **Kirgas Washik** and then cross near there. The exact route across the glacier from Yunzbin changes each year and is marked by small stone cairns set up by the locals at the beginning of the season. A guide is recommended for the crossing unless you have experience of glaciers; the most difficult part is getting off the glacier again from its northern edge. Once off the glacier, the path climbs through a series of lightly wooded ablation valleys to **Yashpirt**, the main summer settlement for the people of Passu. There are spectacular views from here of the glacier and surrounding mountains; it is also a beautiful place to spend a day or two exploring. The path continues up through the summer pastures and settlements of **Fatmahil**, **Kukhil** and **Shelmin** to **Gutshim**, the last summer settlement. All of these are good for camping. Higher up at the pasture of **Lupdor**, the ablation valley ends and the only way to continue further is on the glacier. The return journey is back along the same route (unless you're heading north into the Lupgar and Chapursan Valleys). Another alternative extension to this trek is to head northeast from Gutshim along the **Werthum Nala**, cross the **Werthum Pass** (4,780 m), before emerging via **Harkeesh** into the Chapursan Valley at **Raminj**.

Abdegar trek

The walk up to **Abdegar** is one of the most strenuous short trips from Passu, and, although the views are rewarding, it is only for the very fit. From the 4,000-m ridge across the river from Passu, there are incredible panoramic views back towards the entire Batura Muztagh cluster, including Passu Peak (7,284 m), **Batura Muztagh** itself (7,785 m), numerous other 7,000-m and 7,500-m peaks, plus the Passu and Batura Glaciers. It is also worth checking the 'rumour books' at Passu hotels for comments on the best route. See map below for orientation.

This is really an overnight trip for which you should be fully prepared. Whatever the daytime temperature, it will be freezing cold at night so a good sleeping bag and a tent are essential. It is also worth bearing in mind that you will be sleeping almost 1,500 m higher than you were in Passu, and the dangers of altitude sickness are very real. There is water at the campsite, and at the foot of the hill, but none in between. The route up the scree to the campsite is not always obvious, and in order to avoid needless backtracking it may be wise to hire a local guide. Having said all this, the views on a clear day truly are magnificent.

> ❗ For those wanting an idea of the view, there is a panoramic photo of the scene on the reception counter at the Batura Inn.

Having crossed the rope bridge to Zarabad, bear left towards **Kharamabad** village, and head up to the bottom of the main hill. There is a freshwater spring emerging out of the cliff next to the waterfall pool. Cross the stream, and the path upwards begins 100 m downstream of the waterfall. It is a pretty vertical three and a half hours to the campsite at 3,600 m (six hours in total from Passu). The following morning you can climb for a further three hours up to the viewpoint (4,000 m), but if you don't really feel up to it, take some consolation in the fact that the view from the campsite is 90% as good. It takes one and a half hours to descend from the ridge to the campsite, and then four hours back to Passu.

Patundas trek

ⓘ *Although this trek is fairly short (3 days, 4 stages), it is not for novices. You will need an experienced guide to cross the extremely dangerous Passu Glacier (you will need to be roped, and crampons are recommended), and since there is a rapid altitude gain* you will need to be already acclimatized (many people attempt this trek on the back of the Batura Glacier trek, see below). Note that you will have to use Ghulkin guides and porters for this trek. See 'Walks and treks around Passu and Sust' map for orientation. For the description of the first day, see under 'Passu Gar' above. The second day begins with the difficult crossing of the dangerous Passu Glacier (a feat that takes anywhere between one and three hours). From here, your guide will lead you the three hours or so via Lujhdur (3,400 m) to the pastures at Patundas (4,100 m). Note that water supplies are problematic along this entire trek. The return to Passu is via the same route, but it can be done in one day.

Sleeping

Gulmit *p305, map p307*

C Silk Route Lodge (south wing), KKH, T77238 ext 18, himalaya@glt.comsats.net.pk. 20 double rooms with small balcony (upper floor more private), fairly basic for the price, check bed linen before committing, modern hot bath, airy restaurant (dinner buffet Rs280), large garden, mainly used by groups.

C-D Hunza Marco Polo Inn, T77238 ext 7, marcopoloinn@a1.com.pk. 20 rooms with shared verandah (D), attached bath, good value when compared with rivals, also a VIP guesthouse block with traditional Hunza-style room (sleeps 5), plus 5 doubles (C) with bath, sitting and dining rooms, kitchen. Good restaurant, handicraft shop, all very well run, in large, flower-filled garden.

D Gulmit Continental, T0572-3569 (Gilgit), continentalgilgit@yahoo.com. Currently the 12 rooms are carpeted, with clean linen, tiled hot bath, western WC, soap and towels provided, although still a little overpriced (bargain a possibility since hotel is rarely busy). Restaurant offers Pakistani and Chinese dishes (Rs110 per plate), veg dishes (Rs5-60), American breakfast (Rs120) etc.

D-H Silk Route Lodge (north wing), KKH, T77238 ext 19, himalaya@glt.comsats.net.pk. Rooms to suit most budgets. 12 rooms (D) in main block (choose the largest, or one with best view), all with hot bath, 3 overpriced doubles (D) with bath in front block (backpackers should negotiate a 50% discount), plus traditional Hunza house that sleeps 4-5 (H, pay per bed), and 1 spartan double with bath (G). Restaurant (buffet dinner Rs280), 2 gift shops, friendly management, can be a good deal.

E-H Village Guest House, T77238, ext 12. Set in large pleasant gardens (can pitch your own tent or take a place in one of theirs). New block has 4 large but musty-smelling doubles. The old block has a traditional-style room upstairs (wooden columns, sofa, great views), but a little over priced as the bathroom is shared, plus 3 doubles with shared bath. If it's a busy tour group year this place can be overpriced, but if business is slack some good deals can be found.

Gulmit to Passu *p307*
Ghulkin

E Village Guest House at Ghulkin.
F-G Al-Rahim Hotel, both at the link road turn-off on the KKH.

Borit Lake
G Borit Lake Hotel. Basic hotel. There is also some good camping here.

KKH
F-G Al-Rahim Hotel, at the junction of the KKH and the jeep turn from Ghulkin. Recently refurbished.

Passu *p307, map p308*

NB An ongoing matter of debate in the Passu village committee meetings is the location of several guest houses in the heart of the village itself. Local women in particular are nervous about coming across (male) tourists while going about their daily business. At time of going to press, the village-based hotels had been closed down, but the matter is subject to appeal.

D Asia Silk Route/Ambassador, KKH 1½ km north of Passu. Recently completed, although little thought seems to have gone into the design. For some reason the verandahs all face inwards towards the central restaurant block, thus denying guests any views. Name is subject to change.

D Passu Tourist Lodge, KKH 2 km north of village. 20 rooms that look like an army barracks from the outside but are clean and carpeted inside, bath, western WC, 24-hr hot water, excellent restaurant, not a bad deal.

E-G Passu Inn, KKH, T1. 6 carpeted rooms (E) upstairs with hot tiled bath, western WC, plus 4 rooms with flaky paint and cold baths downstairs (G). Restaurant, garden, good place to recruit guides and porters.

E-G Village Guest House, Passu village. 3 doubles with bath (overpriced), 1 triple with shared bath (F; or pay per bed, G), plus 7 mattresses in traditional Hunza room (G, pay per bed), although this room is used for communal dining so early nights and privacy are out. With its nice location at the heart of the village, cosy dorm, good food and friendly owner, this place has become very popular and receives good recommendations, but often full and prices are creeping upwards.

F-H Dreamland Guesthouse, Passu village. 1 double with bath (F), 2 with shared bath (G) plus cosy dorm in traditional Hunza room (H), a little more basic than other guest houses in the village, but much cheaper.

F-H Passu Peak Inn, KKH, 1 km north of village. In the middle of nowhere so very quiet, 4 doubles (G) with concrete floors, clean linen, bath, new carpeted double with tiled bathroom under construction (F) plus 6-bed dorm with bath planned (H). Very friendly owner serves up huge portions of veg food for dinner (Rs70). Recommended.

G Batura Inn, KKH, just north of village. The friendliness of the welcome and the excellence of the communal dinner (Rs75) cannot make up for the fact that the 8 'cells' formerly used for housing Chinese KKH construction workers are exceedingly run down. Rooms are dark, bare, with sagging beds and attached bathrooms that don't do justice to the word 'basic'.

G Shishper View, KKH south of village. 8 reasonably clean carpeted doubles with basic bathrooms (some with hot water), evening communal meal, large garden.

Eating

Gulmit to Passu *p307*
Passu
Most guests dine at their hotel, with communal evening dinners (veg and non-veg) being particularly popular. For a treat, try the **Passu Tourist Lodge** (spaghetti carbonara Rs160, crumbed fried chicken Rs160, club sandwich Rs140, plus Pak and Chinese dishes). A general store opposite the Passu Inn sells cold drinks, mineral water, biscuits and most trekking supplies.

Shopping

Gulmit *p305, map p307*
North Pakistan Carpet Palace, on the KKH, offers handicrafts (gems, carpets etc), plus cold drinks, mineral water, biscuits and limited trekking supplies.
ThreadNet sell their products at the Oldest House, see page 306.

Transport

Gulmit *p305, map p305*
Northbound travel involves flagging down passing traffic from Gilgit to **Sust** (or Aliabad to Sust) on the KKH. The best place to stand is opposite the National Bank.

A few **minibuses** starting from Aliabad may appear early morning, but most don't start passing through until midday. The NATCO bus comes through around 1230-1300 (**Passu**: Rs15, 30 mins; **Sust**: Rs35, 1½ hrs). **Passu** is a fairly unrewarding 14-km walk along the KKH (but you do pass the famous Hussaini Bridge, see p309), or you could walk there via Borit Lake. It's also fairly easy to hitch northbound (sometimes you'll be asked for the equivalent bus fare).

Southbound you are waiting for transport heading from Sust to **Gilgit** (stand outside the National Bank). **Minibuses** start coming through from 0600, with the NATCO bus arriving about 0700 (Ganesh, for **Karimabad**: Rs30, 1 hr; **Gilgit**: Rs90, 4 hrs).

Passu *p307, map p308*
Northbound travel involves flagging down passing traffic from Gilgit to **Sust** (or Aliabad to Sust) on the KKH.

A few minibuses starting from Aliabad may appear early morning, although most don't start passing through until midday. The **NATCO** bus comes through at around 1300 (**Sust**: Rs30, 1 hr). It's also fairly easy to hitch northbound (although sometimes you will be asked for the equivalent bus fare).

Southbound you are waiting for transport heading from Sust to **Gilgit**. Minibuses (often already full) start arriving very early, with the **NATCO** bus steaming through at about 0630 (Ganesh, for **Karimabad**: Rs35, 1½ hrs; **Gilgit**: Rs100, 4½ hrs).

ⓘ Directory

Gulmit *p305, map p307*
Banks National Bank of Pakistan has a branch in what used to be the Evershine Hotel. Mon-Thu and Sat 0900-1330, Fri 0900-1230. Offers foreign exchange (poor rates, sluggish but friendly service). **Post office** KKH, Mon-Thu and Sat 0830-1630, Fri 0930-1200. **Telephones** There's a temporary PCO just off the KKH, behind the abandoned Horse Shoe Motel building; a new digital exchange (offering international calls) is being built near the police station at the southern extremity of the village.

Shimshal Valley → *Colour map 2, grid B5*

Shimshal receives relatively few visitors, which is a shame since the trekking is superb and the Shimshali guides and porters are among the finest specimens of mountain men. The valley offers several strenuous but rewarding treks, with alternative routes out for the really adventurous. The summer pastures up at Shewert (Shimshal Pamir) are particularly memorable, and have already been the subject of several fascinating natural history documentaries. Some advanced planning is required before visiting the Shimshal Valley, but nobody leaves disappointed.

Potential visitors to Shimshal need to prepare in advance; a guide is mandatory for all trekking here (including the walk in), and the guide must be a local person (although Passu porters can work up to Shewgarden). Guides and porters can be recruited in Passu. There is also a general store in Passu that stocks most supplies, but there's more choice in Gilgit. ▸▸ *For Sleeping, Eating and all other listings, see page 319.*

Ins and outs

Just after the point where the KKH crosses the snout of the Batura Glacier three kilometres to the north of Passu, a bridge crosses the Hunza River and a jeep track heads up the narrow Shimshal Valley defile. This is the main route into Shimshal, but there is a difficult alternative route in via the Boiber Valley and Kurunpir Pass (see page 318). For those continuing north along the KKH, go to page 318.

Background

This remote valley was once used by the Mirs of Hunza as a penal colony and was for a long time unknown to people from outside the region. The secrecy of this valley was put to good use by the Hunzakuts: it became the route by which they could raid the Kashmiri and Ladahki caravans before disappearing back into the mountains. Thus, late in the 19th century, the British sought to learn the whereabouts of the secret pass.

The man chosen to undertake the task of exploring and mapping this region was **Younghusband**, one of the greatest British explorers of the Victorian age. After many adventures (and a spiritual awakening) in the knot of mountains and glaciers to the east of the Shimshal Pass, he approached this fabled defile in the late summer of 1889, suggesting that "a fitter place for a robbers' den could not be imagined."

Tourism is still in its infancy here today so outsiders should strive hard to leave a good impression and all foreigners must be accompanied by a local guide.

The walk in: Passu to Shimshal village

Part of the reason so few outsiders come here is because Shimshal is so difficult to reach. In fact, you have to trek just to get there. For a decade or so the local villages have been constructing a jeep road along the 60 km to link them with the KKH, and the outside world. The road is a miracle of engineering, and, although it now reaches **Uween-a-Ben**, the nature of the terrain means that it is often blocked by land-slides beyond **Dut** (a distance of some 15 km, or one and a half hours, from the KKH). Very crowded cargo jeeps run intermittently from Passu to Uween-a-Ben, but if you are carrying all your food and equipment for a trek, you'll probably have to hire a vehicle (Rs1,500, or Rs750 to Dut).

If you are walking in, it's two hours of fairly easy walking from the KKH to **Jurjur** (2,450 m). There is water available at Jurjur but then nothing until Dut, another two hours along the track. Note that there is considerable rock-fall risk along this stretch of the valley. It is two porter stages from Passu to Dut. There are a number of huts at Dut (2,580 m) where travelling Shimshalis overnight. You can use the communal cooking facilities, although obviously you must clear up after yourself.

Locals are often known to walk from Dut to Shimshal in a single long day (it's three porter stages), although foreigners generally only make it as far as **Ziarat** (2,600 m) in five to six long hours. Obviously, if you manage to get a jeep as far as Uween-a-Ben (halfway between Dut and Ziarat), then you're laughing, although it is a tough ride. If travelling on foot, a local guide is essential for this section not only to assist with the multiple river crossings, but also to alert you to the very real danger of rock-falls. There are some well-equipped huts at Ziarat and it is customary to leave a donation.

It's a very long nine-hour day from Ziarat to Shimshal, with the route sometimes

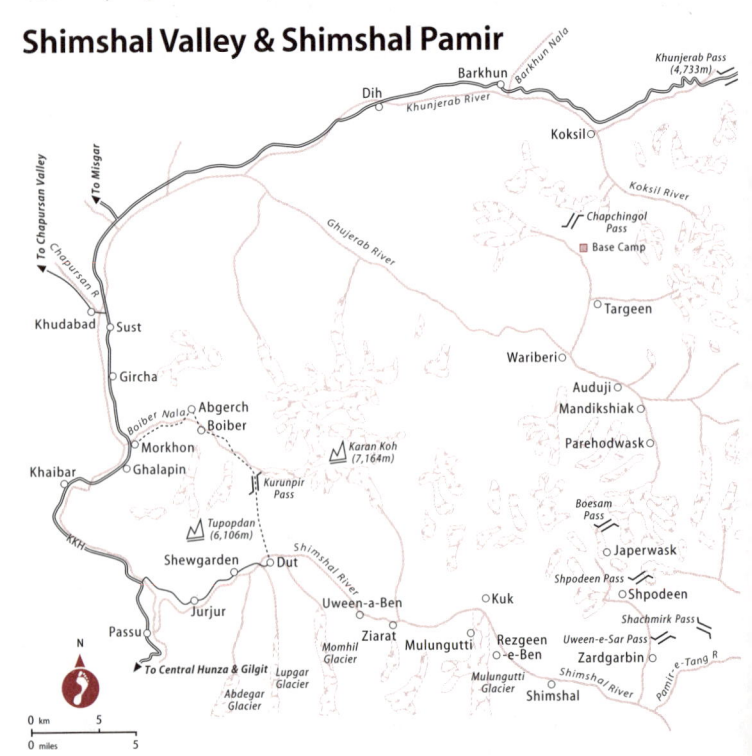

Shimshal Valley & Shimshal Pamir

changing daily. An early departure is necessary in order to make the river crossings easier. **Kuk** is three to four hours away, with a number of streams and high scree slopes that need to be negotiated en route. There are some hot springs and clear water streams here, and this is a good camping spot for those who do not plan to march from Ziarat to Shimshal in a single day. Depending upon the trail in use when you travel here, it may be necessary to cross the snout of the **Mulungutti Glacier**, before climbing the terrace up to **Rezgeen-e-Ben** (2,820 m). From here it is a relatively straightforward three-hour walk to **Shimshal** (2,880 m).

There isn't much to Shimshal village itself, although visitors are warmly welcomed. Once you're here although, it seems a shame not to press on to Shewert (see below), although since this is a long and strenuous trek you should have made your preparations (guides, food, equipment etc) before having left Passu.

Treks from Shimshal

Shimshal Pamir trek

ⓘ *'Restricted' zone. Maximum elevation optional (4,420 m if going all the way to Shewert). Jul to Aug. Maps: Swiss Foundation is adequate, but there are several glaring inaccuracies; U502 series, NJ 43-14 Baltit and NJ 43-15 Shimshal likewise.* **NB** *Although not officially listed as being in a restricted zone, you must take a local guide for all treks from Shimshal village. For orientation, see map, p316. Read trekking notes on p45.*

The trek from Shimshal to Shujerab is a demanding one, crossing three passes and taking eight days for the return trip. It is also very beautiful. Porters charge for 12 stages for the return trip. The path leads east from the village (entering the Khunjerab National Park) and then crosses to the north bank of the river on a good bridge. Further on it climbs steeply north up the west bank of the **Zardgarbin** Valley before crossing to the east bank and climbing east to an area of pasture with good camping by a large boulder below **Vween-e-Sar Pass** (4,420 m, also referred to as Zardgarbin Pass or Wyeen Pass). Another route continues up the Zardgarbin River, across the Boesam Pass (4,725 m) and follows the Ghujerab River to rejoin the KKH to the north of Sust (see trek below).

The climb over Vween-e-Sar Pass is strenuous and, immediately after the steep and difficult descent from the pass, it climbs once again, zigzagging steeply up the mountainside to cross the **Shachmirk Pass** (4,160 m), marked near the summit by a wooden gateway. On the far side there is camping at the foot of the pass at **Targeen** (3,597 m), near a side river which flows into the Shimshal River from the north. Alternatively, continue for an hour on to **Purien-e-Ben** (3,322 m). The path then runs along a barren plateau, through an area which was once well wooded, following the Shimshal River to arrive at the shepherds' settlement of **Shujerab** (4,084 m) with its complex of small stone huts.

From here, the path climbs up to the pastures of **Abdullah Khan Maidan** (4,389 m). You can now relax and enjoy a pleasant stroll through the pastures to the **Shimshal Pass** (4,402 m), a beautiful open plateau with two lakes. A little further on is the main summer settlement of **Shewert**. Here, huge numbers of sheep, goats and yaks are tended by the women of Shimshal, who collect the milk to produce butter and cheese. The sight of the animals returning to their night enclosures in the dying light of the sun is a spectacular one. Lovingly referred to by Shimshalis as their 'Pamir' (upland grazing area), this area is incredibly beautiful, although extremely harsh as well. The minute the sun drops below the mountains, temperatures fall dramatically.

It is possible to continue southeast from Shewert and then follow the Braldu River south to the Braldu Glacier and over the Lupke Pass to Snow Lake, joining the Biafo-Hispar Glacier trek. This is an extremely difficult and technical route which should only be attempted by properly equipped, experienced mountaineers and with an experienced guide familiar with the route. To return to Shimshal village take the same route.

Boesam Pass, Ghujerab Valley and Chapchingol Pass trek
ⓘ *'Restricted' zone. Maximum elevation 4,725 m. Jun-Sep. Maps: Swiss Foundation has many inaccuracies; U502 series, NJ 43-14 Baltit and NJ 43-15 Shimshal likewise. NB You are required to take a local guide for all treks from Shimshal village. For orientation, see map, p317. Read trekking notes on p45.*

This difficult seven-day, 12-stage trek should only be attempted by the most experienced and fully equipped trekkers, who are accompanied by a local guide who is well acquainted with the route. There are two high passes to cross, a river to ford, as well as some roped ascents/descents and glacier crossings. The trek is done from south to north and emerges at Koksil, on the KKH above Sust. You will have to arrange transport in advance to collect you.

Passu to Sust (40 km)

Returning to the KKH, north of Passu the road continues its steady climb towards Sust. The first settlement on the road is **Khaibar** (sometimes 'Khyber') after 18 km, where it is possible to overnight. Beyond Khaibar, the local people are predominantly Wakhi Tajiks and sometimes refer to this area as Upper Gojal. The next hamlet is **Ghalapin**, before you arrive at **Morkhon** (13 km) and the adjacent settlement of Jamalabad (9 km south of Sust).

Visitors to Pakistan are always looking for new valleys to explore and new treks to make, and recently the **Boiber Valley** has attracted the attention of intrepid travellers. Following the footsteps of traders, slavers and caravan raiders of old, several local guides now offer visitors the chance to follow the route that Shimshalis used to reach the Hunza River from their mountain stronghold. For orientation, see map, page 317.

It is possible to hike up the valley from Morkhon (2,743 m) to the original settlement of **Abgerch** (3,200 m) in two to three hours, then climb for a further hour and a half as far as the summer settlement of **Boiber** (3,505 m). Day-trippers can make it back to Morkhon and the KKH the same day, although trekkers may like to camp here before proceeding the following day. It is a steady climb through the ancient juniper forests to the pastures at **Maidun** (3,989 m), and those with time on their hands may prefer to camp here. Alternatively, it is a further hour-and-a-half climb to the meadow at **Zardgarbin**, before a long, steady climb (three to four hours) up the scree slope to the **Karun Pir Pass** (4,873 m). The views from here are terrific. The trail, if it can be called that, eventually leads to **Dut** on the current access route into Shimshal. From there, it is 15 km on the jeep road back to the KKH. A guide is essential on this trek (even if you're just making the daytrip up to Boiber). You should be able to find one in Morkhon, where you can also find accommodation.

Beyond Morkhon, the KKH continues through the other 'Abgerchi' village of **Gircha** to **Sust** (9 km). As well as being the transport and administrative junction for those continuing their journey into China, Sust is also the jumping off point for the Chapursan Valley. For details on the border town of Sust, and the route to Kashgar, see page 328.

Sleeping

Shimshal village *p317*
Accommodation and food is usually arranged by your guide (often with his family), but a few guesthouses are springing up.
G Disteghil Cottage, The longest established guesthouse, although arrangements here are little different than staying with your guide's family. If meals are offered, note that high transport costs should be incorporated into the price you pay.

Passu to Sust *p318*
Khaibar
G Khyber Inn. Located opposite the school. Basic.

Morkhon
G Greenland Hotel. Basic.

Gircha
G Dreamland Hotel. Basic.

Chapursan Valley → *Colour map 2, grid B4*

Running along the top of the country, parallel to the Chinese and Afghan borders, the 70-km-long Chapursan Valley is the "next big thing" waiting to be discovered by adventurous visitors to Pakistan. The meaning of the valley's name, 'chi purson', is said to translate as 'what else do you need?', and the friendly communities here seem to live by this motto. The valley comprises 11 small villages, with 300 or so households and a population of less than 2,000 principally Wakhi people who migrated here from Gojal, plus a few arrivals from Hunza and Wakhan respectively.

In terms of transport and accommodation, tourism is still in its infancy here, while the trekking is superb with seemingly limitless options. The actual Chapursan Valley itself is just 70 km or so long, and it connects via a number of passes to so many other valleys that it is actually possible to spend three or four weeks walking all the way across the top of Pakistan; a number of large trekking companies already offer this trip. Those not wanting to trek, or who want just to make shorter day walks, can take public transport from Sust as far as Zood Zhun and base themselves there.

There still remains some doubt as to the official status of the region. Previously a 'closed zone' due to its proximity to Afghanistan, locals will tell you that is was declared 'open' in 1999. However, some officials at the Ministry of Sports and Tourism may tell you otherwise; certainly there's nobody checking for permits in the Chapursan Valley itself, but once you trek further west into the Upper Yarkhun Valley there are a number of routes that are 'restricted' and 'closed'. ▸▸ *For Sleeping, Eating and all other listings, see page 324.*

Ins and outs

There are cargo jeeps from outside the **Sky Bridge Inn** at Sust as far as Zood Khun ⓘ *most days at around 1300, Rs60, 2½-3 hrs*, although they are rather crowded and thus quite uncomfortable. A privately hired jeep as far as Zood Khun will cost around Rs1500-1800 (two hours). **NB** Visitors are advised to bring their own supplies of food since there are no shops in the valley (although cigarettes, sugar and biscuits can be found in Reshit). A sleeping bag is recommended (and essential after September).

Modest dress is essential (shalwar kameez recommended), and permission should be sought before taking photos (particularly of women and religious places).

Entering the valley from the east (via Sust, on the KKH), the most westerly point is Baba Ghundi (70 km). However, if you trek beyond here it is possible to cross the Chilinji Pass to Chilinji, where you can turn south along the Karambar River Valley into the Ishkoman Valley, or continue west to the Karambar Lakes below the Karambar Pass. West of here lies the Broghil Pass, one of the easiest access routes into northern Afghanistan. South of here is an exit route into the Yasin Valley via Darkot (see page 155), or you could continue westwards via the Upper Yarkhun Valley, linking up with the Turikho Valley and the plethora of treks in this region (Thui Pass, Shah Janali Pass etc). Of course, all these treks are also available in the opposite direction and large parties may have to change porters when entering different valleys.

All these routes and valleys and passes may sound a little confusing at first, but it becomes clearer when you examine the maps in this guide and see how they join up. From east to west, start with the Walks and treks around Passu and Sust map on page 310, and follow it west to see where it links up with the Turikho Valley, Upper Yarkhun Valley and Karambar Valley map, page 145.

Best time to visit
The best time to visit the valley is during one of the festivals, notably the pilgrimage to Baba Ghundi Ziarat or the autumn harvest festival. The principal festivals are listed below; plus polo in September and October and weddings which take place from October to December.

Tourist information
A good source of information on the Chapursan Valley (and a contact for arranging transport) is the manager at the **Sky Bridge Inn**. Alternatively, a Gilgit-based company called **Walk & Ride** ⓘ *T0572-52205, www.walkandridepakistan.com*, specialize in this valley, offering budget trekking (including horse/yak safaris).

Sust to Zood Khun

Five minutes north of Sust along the KKH, a signposted jeep track crosses the Hunza River and heads west towards the Chapursan Valley. After 45 minutes' travelling the jeep track passes the **Panja Shah Ziarat**, easily spotted due to the number of colour flags here; the scratches on the rock inside the shrine are said to be the handprint of the saint himself. Above the ziarat is an old defence post that provides a wonderful view of the whole valley.

Several minutes further along the track is **Yarzrich**, the first settlement in the valley. The first major settlement beyond here is **Raminj** (15 minutes), although the actual village itself is hidden from the road (it can be seen from Yarzrich). The population of this village are all Hunzakuts, including Nazir Sabir, the second Pakistani to summit K2. Raminj is the starting/finishing point for a number of treks. Some trekkers are now extending the Batura Glacier trek (see page 311) by continuing northeast from Gutshim along the Werthum Nala, crossing the Werthem Pass, and then linking up with the Lupgar River valley that runs parallel to the south of the Chapursan Valley (see map on page 310). This trek then finishes at Raminj. Another option is to trek the entire length of the Lupgar Valley between Raminj and Yishkuk, although this route is usually attempted in the opposite direction (see page 323).

A further 30 minutes by jeep from Raminj is **Spandrinj** (a few forlorn huts). A rarely attempted trek heads northeast from here over the Kermin Pass (4,023 m) to Misgar (although the Kilik and Mintaka Passes into China beyond here are in a 'closed' zone). Just beyond Spandrinj is a cluster of three villages known collectively as **Kermin**. A further 30 minutes by jeep (two hours from Sust) is the central village in the valley, **Reshit**. This is the site of an old fort as well as the **Jamal Khan Istan shrine**, which features the rock imprint of a hand holding a riding crop (although unless you were told what it was you'd never guess). Just beyond here, at **Sher-e-Sabz**, is the new Jamat Khana shrine.

The next cluster of villages along the jeep road (around two and a half hours from Sust) includes **Ispenji**, **Shutmerg** and **Kampir Dior**. There is an interesting legend relating to one of the houses in Kampir Dior, in some instances featuring Baba Ghundi (see above and page 322), and in others a nameless saint. It tells how the saint arrived in the rich, fertile valley, going from house to house begging alms. Only one old woman was obliging, offering her precious sheep's milk – her only source of food. As a punishment to the rest of the valley dwellers, who apparently were not the most pious of people, the saint called down a great flood that swept through the valley, destroying everything but the old woman and her house. The effects of catastrophic flooding from this heavily glaciated region are immediately apparent still.

The final village in the valley is **Zood Khun**, a little further down the jeep road (two to three hours from Sust, depending upon the type of vehicle you take). There isn't a great deal to it, but it forms a good base from which to explore the surrounding area. There are lots of short day walks, plus any number of overnight or two- to three-day trips. Lying at about 3,550 m it is the highest permanently inhabited village in the valley. A number of villagers are now taking in paying guests.

Around Zood Khun

About two hours' walk from Zood Khun (or 30 minutes by jeep) is the glacial-formed **Ravai Lake** (Ravai Jhui), now little more than a dry depression in the ground, see box on page 322. Because of the boulder-strewn terrain the camping here is not great; if you continue walking for another half hour you will find some suitable flat ground near the river. There is an even better spot to be found if you follow the river or climb above the glacial moraine for a further hour to an ancient birch forest. There are some shepherds' huts here and lots of birds.

The meadows at **Yishkuk** (3,450 m) are less than two hours' stroll along the Baba Ghundi track, with excellent views of the glacier (the subject of many local legends) and across the whole Chapursan Valley. There is a fresh water spring hidden among the rubble to the right of the jeep road.

The idyllic area of **Jhui Sam**, opposite the Yishkuk glacier, is an hour's easy stroll from Zood Khun, and is the location for a great camping spot among hidden, crystal-blue lakes.

There are also several short treks available from Zood Khun. A local guide is required. For orientation, see the map on page 310. Read trekking notes on page 45. This is also ideal horse trekking terrain.

Pamiri

This three- to four-day trek takes you into ibex and snow leopard habitat, following the ablation valley of the Yishkuk Glacier to Zood Khun's favourite summer pasture. It's also possible to extend the trek to Zood Khun Sar base camp.

Dilisangsar base camp

This moderate (but unexplored) three- to four-day trek takes you to the base camp of the 6,200-m Dilisangarsar, a beautiful peak known locally as Little K2. Here you can camp among the ancient juniper forests. This trek can be extended for a difficult two to three days by travelling to Baba Ghundi via Sek Sar base camp.

Baba Ghundi and the legend of Ravai Lake

The famous saint of the Chapursan Valley, Baba Ghundi, features in a legend surrounding Ravai Lake. It is said that in order to placate the ashdar, or dragon, that lived in the lake, villagers had to take daily turns to feed the monster with a meal of bread, meat and a live person. Eventually came the turn of a man and his wife who, not wishing to sacrifice their only child (a particularly beautiful girl), decided to present themselves to the dragon. However, their daughter would not hear of this so instead offered herself. As she was waiting at the lake for the dragon to devour her, a saint, Baba Ghundi, appeared.

On hearing the girl's sad story he immediately slew the dragon with his sword and ordered the girl back to her parents home. However, fearing that nobody in the village would believe her story of the dragon's demise, she refused to go. Baba Ghundi eventually sent her packing, presenting her with his shoes and sword's scabbard as confirmation of the events that had occured at the lake. The news caused much rejoicing in the village, and in true Cinderella style, the girl's parents offered her hand in marriage to the person whose feet fitted the shoes and sword fitted the scabbard.

The legend gets a bit vague here, but it seems that Baba Ghundi himself appeared in the guise of a beggar but was denied any refreshments by the now extremely drunk villagers, and his claims to the girl were dismissed even although his feet and his weapon were both a snug fit. In disgust, Baba Ghundi summoned up one of his specials – a great flood courtesy of the Yishkuk Glacier, so hence the boulders and rubble strewn around the valley that you see today. There is also a scattering of 'dragon bones' in the dry bed of the Ravai Lake (actually coral).

Zood Khun to Baba Ghundi

The jeep road through the Chapursan Valley terminates at Baba Ghundi, 10 km beyond Zood Khun. A hired vehicle will cost you about Rs1,200 one way for this trip (45 minutes by jeep, over an hour by tractor), although you can walk it in four to five hours (or two to three hours on horse). An alternative route for those not keen on walking along roads is to follow the shepherds' trail via Band-e-Ben along the opposite side of the Chapursan River (the trail is steep and faded in parts, but not too difficult to find – ask someone to set you on it at Zood Khun). It's a stiff six-hours' walk in total, although a nice option is to camp a night at Jhui Sam (see page 321). There is a third, longer route (via Shigard), but you'll need a guide.

At Baba Ghundi is the **Baba Ghundi Ziarat**, a small shrine said to contain the sword and holy books of the preacher from the Tajik village of Ghund who entered Chapursan from Afghanistan some time in the 16th century. Baba Ghundi is credited with supernatural powers and the subject of a number of legends relating to the valley, and the shrine is a popular place of pilgrimage at the end of the autumn harvest (late September to early October), particularly with couples praying for children. It is said that devoted Ismaili and Shia Muslims will try to make this pilgrimage at least once during their lifetime, with many coming from as far away as Baltistan. The current shrine was built by the Mir of Hunza in 1924 (and renovated in 1999), but is not a tomb and does not contain the body of the saint. A small path (lined with ibex horns) leads from here to a 'holy spring', said to originate directly from the shrine.

Treks from Baba Ghundi

There are some excellent (although challenging) treks from Baba Ghundi. **NB** A local guide is essential. For orientation, see the maps on page 310 and page 145. Read trekking notes, page 45. This is also ideal horse trekking terrain.

Irshad Pass(es) trek

This is a popular trek through amazing scenery, including multi-coloured mountains. Some trekkers have been known to enter Afghanistan via the Irshad Pass, before returning to Pakistan via the Broghil Pass to the west, but this is illegal.

Some locals claim there are two distinct passes here: the more southerly **Irshad 'Kyrghiz' Uween Pass** (4,880 m), used primarily by the Kyrghiz, and the **Irshad 'Wakhi' Uween Pass** (4,925 m) which is in the domain of the Wakhi people. In recent years, however, what little traffic passes this way has tended to use the latter. Those thinking of visiting here should consult the **Walk & Ride** tour company in Gilgit or Alam Jan/Sarfraz Khan in Zood Khun.

Ghulam Ali Pass

This three- to four-day trek has several highlights, notably superb views of the Batura Group and Chapursan's highest mountains, the red canyon at Sekr Jerab, plus access across a narrow pass (Ghulam Ali) into Afghanistan. The trek is quite demanding and involves glacier crossing (rope, crampons and ice axe may be needed).

Kuz sar base camp

This moderate three- to four-day trip is recommended for those without the time or stamina for Chilinji (see below), but leads trekkers to Chapursan's summer yak pasture (features easy glacier crossing).

Chilinji Pass trek (and beyond)

ⓘ *Open zone. Maximum elevation 5,160 m. Early Jun to late Sep. Maps: Swiss Foundation is best, despite inaccurate place names; the Leomann has faults but is OK and U502 Baltit (NJ 43-14) is useless. For orientation, see the maps on page 310 and page 145. Read trekking notes on p 45.*

This is a trek to undertake if you love to walk and walk, being part of the great route all the way across the 'top' of Pakistan (see Ins and outs on page 319 for further details). It is three days from Baba Ghundi as far as the 5,160-m **Chilinji An** (Chilinji Pass), and then a further day and a half's walk to the summer Gujar settlement of **Chilinji** (3,450 m, six porter stages). Once here it seems a shame to turn back, so you have the options of turning south along the Karambar River valley into the Ishkoman Valley, or continue west to the Karambar Lakes below the Karambar Pass (and on to the Upper Yarkhun Valley, or down into Yasin Valley via Darkot). Note that west of Chilnji, you may have to change porters.

Lupgar Valley trek

ⓘ *Open zone. Maximum elevation 5,190 m. Early Jun to late Sep. Maps: Swiss Foundation is best, despite inaccurate place names; the Leomann and U502 Baltit (NJ 43-14) are useless. See the map on p310 for orientation. Read trekking notes, p45.*

A west to east route is recommended for those who prefer descents to ascents, although acclimatization is necessary before setting off. The trek begins at **Yishkuk**, crosses the **Wyeen Glacier** to **Haji Beg's Camp** (4,680 m), crosses the 5,190-m **Lupgar Pir Pass** before descending through the Lupgar Valley via **Hoopkerch** and **Harkeesh** to **Raminj**. The trek usually takes six days (about eight stages), but some days are fairly short in order to allow for acclimatization. Obviously, an experienced guide who knows this route is essential and this is not a trek for novices. Note that Harkeesh is also the point where this trek links up with the Werthum Pass route to the Batura Glacier (see page 311).

Sleeping

Zood Khun *p308*
H Pamir Serai. Run by genial Alam Jan, guests sleep in a common Wakhi-style room for as little as Rs50 per person. He provides food (breakfast Rs20, lunch Rs40, dinner Rs50, you can cook your own if you wish), information, guide services and indispensable trekking advice.

Ghulam Ali also takes in paying guests. He has a modern house with a traditional interior (but you can't cook for yourself).

Baba Ghundi *p322*
H M&M Block. Run by Alam Jan of Zood Khun, providing simple accommodation in a concrete room with kitchen and bathroom ("no electricity, no nothing, except the spirit of Baba Ghundi and sublime mountain scenery").

Trekking

Fees in Chapursan are as follows: **Guides**, Rs800 per day (1-3 clients), Rs1,000 per day (4-6 clients), Rs1,100 per day (7+ clients); **Porters**, Rs280 per stage; **Horse safari**, Rs600 per day (plus Rs250 per day for horse man); **Yak safari**, Rs750 per day (plus Rs250 per day for yak leader); **Yak/horse/ donkey hire** (for luggage), Rs280 per stage (per 25 kg). Always agree on fees and stages before your departure.

Zood Khun *p308*
Alam Jan's brother, Safraz Khan, lives close to the polo ground and is one of the valley's most experienced guides. This is the man to talk to about horses and yaks.

Festivals and events

Dates vary according to the Islamic calender, weather, astrology etc. The following are celebrated in the Chapursan Valley.
Mar 15-20, **Kut-e-Dthit** (Spring Cleaning), once-yearly removal of soot and dust caused by smoke of stoves; 21, **Chey-Sol** (New Year).
Apr 5-8, **Tagum** (Sowing Festival), communal gathering to bless grains prior to ploughing and sowing, special sweet dish called *semen* is served.
Jun 18-21, **Kuch** (Transhumance), livestock is brought up from lower pastures and then moved to high summer pasture.
Jul 11, **Salgira**, celebrates inauguration as iman of the present Aga Khan, features polo, speeches, school plays etc.
Aug 8-10, **Chinir** (Harvest Festival), strands of ripe wheat are cut and brought to the houses for decoration, special foods prepared and shared.
Sep/Oct Mid-end, **Kuch** (Transhumance), livestock brought down from high summer pastures (although yaks spend the winter in the lower pastures of the Wakhan Corridor); last Thu in Sep/first Thu in Oct, **Jumarat** (pilgrimage to Baba Ghundi Ziarat), biggest celebration in the valley.

The KKH: Sust to Kashgar

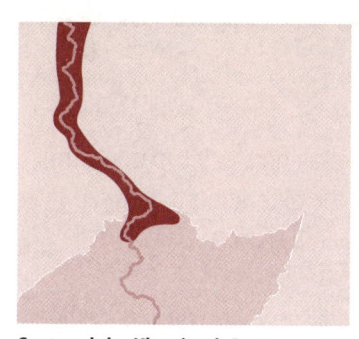

Sust and the Khunjerab Pass	**328**
Sust and around	329
Sust to Khunjerab National Park/Dih	331
Khunjerab National Park	331
Listings	334
Into China	**336**
Khunjerab Pass to Tashkurgan	336
Tashkurgan	339
Kara Kuli and around	341
Kara Kuli to Kashgar	342
Listings	343
Kashgar and beyond	**345**
Travelling on from Kashgar	351
Listings	351

Footprint features...

Don't miss...	327
Note for cyclists travelling from Pakistan to China	330
Travel tips for visitors to China	337

Introduction

This section is for those travellers making a day trip up to the Khunjerab Pass, or for those who are extending their KKH adventure into China's Central Asian region.

In addition to the romance of traversing what is reputedly the highest paved border-crossing route in the world, this is one of the most spectacular and exceptional sections of the entire Karakoram Highway journey. Not only is the scenery exhilarating and unlike anything else along the rest of the KKH, there is also a marked cultural change from Pakistan, giving most visitors their first taste of the magic of Central Asia.

Although it is usually two days of pretty hard travelling by public transport from Sust to Kashgar (breaking the journey and changing buses in Tashkurgan), or a week or so for cyclists, it is certainly worth the effort. Kashgar is still one of Central Asia's more exotic destinations, while the scenery around Kara Kuli lake makes breaking your journey there all the more appealing.

★ Don't miss...

1. **The Khunjerab** Traverse what is believed to be the highest paved-road international border crossing, page 328.
2. **Kara Kuli Lake** View the magnificent peak of Muztagh Ata reflected in the waters of one of the KKH's most beautiful spots, page 341.
3. **Chinese beer** Your rendez-vous with a 650ml bottle of beer, page 345.
4. **Kashgar** Get a perfect introduction to Central Asia at Kashgar's famous Sunday market, page 350.

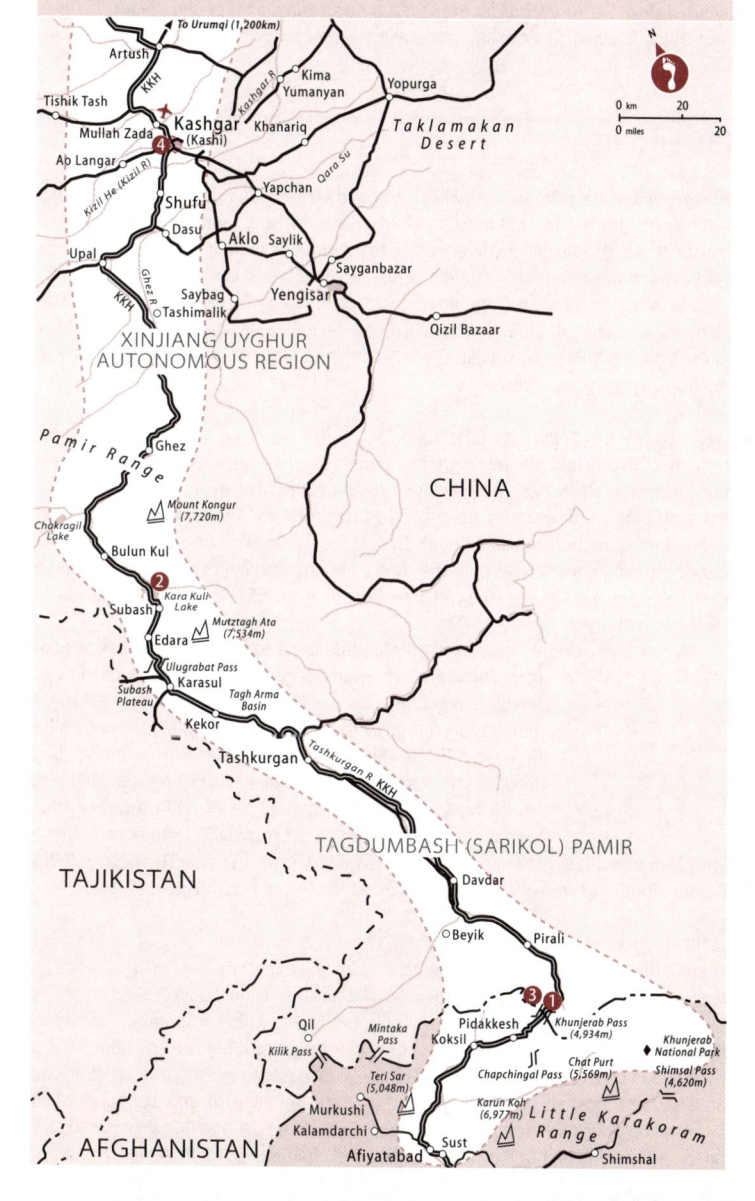

Sust and the Khunjerab Pass

→ *Colour map 2, grid A/B4*

Sust is the border town in Pakistan where formalities are completed for those either continuing on to China, or for those who have just arrived from Pakistan's neighbour country. It is also the transit point for day-trippers to the actual Pak-China border on the Khunjerab Pass and the jumping-off point for visits to the Chapursan Valley. However, unless you plan on undertaking one of these four options, Sust is best avoided since like many border towns it is a noisy, dirty, unappealing place. If this is your point of arrival in Pakistan, don't worry – things get much, much better! ▶▶ *For Sleeping, Eating and all other listings, see pages 334-336.*

Ins and outs

Those arriving by bus from China will be dropped off in the Customs Yard in 'New Sust' (where entry formalities will be completed). Buses arriving from the south will drop passengers in the old village (if requested to) before terminating outside the customs yard. Few people spend more than one night in Sust if they can help it.

For details on transport connections from Sust to Tashkurgan, see page 334. See also pages 17 and 338 for further details on border formalities. See below for day trips to the Khunjerab Pass from Sust. Cyclists contemplating the journey should refer to the box on page 330.

Leaving Pakistan for China

Note that the official opening time for foreigners to cross the international border via the Khunjerab Pass has recently been extended (1 May to 31 December); only Pakistanis and Chinese can cross outside these dates. This crossing is weather dependent though; it's usually open by 1 May, but snow often shuts it before 31 December. You should also note the time zone change when you cross into China (see box, page 337). Make sure you have kept Rs250 (US$4) to pay the entry 'tax' to the Khunjerab National Park at Dih.

It can take several hours for the entire bus to clear Pakistani customs at Sust when leaving the country, although Westerners' luggage is rarely checked in any detail. Make sure you get an exit stamp from Pakistani immigration, otherwise you will not be able to enter China (Chinese officials will check for an exit stamp at the various check posts en route to Tashkurgan). It is not possible to bring private vehicles into China unless arranged in advance (this can take months and is very expensive). Details of Chinese entry/exit formalities at the border post at Tashkurgan are discussed on page 338. **NB** Do not attempt to smuggle illegal drugs into China – the penalties are severe.

❗ *Those intending to travel on to China should note that visas are not issued on the border (the nearest embassy is in Islamabad).*

Arriving in Pakistan from China

Those arriving from China should note that because the bus is often hours late in leaving Tashkurgan, you may find the immigration and customs post at Sust closed by the time you arrive (officially it's open 1300-1700 Pakistani time in summer, 1300-1600 in winter). It may remain open an hour later in emergencies, but the bus often arrives two to three hours late. In such circumstances, your passport will be collected from you at the check post at the entrance to Sust, and returned to you stamped when immigration opens the next day (0900-1200 daily). In theory, your luggage has to stay on the bus overnight, but if you make a fuss it is often waived for foreigners.

The immigration post at Sust used to enjoy a fair degree of autonomy, but this has now changed and 30-day 'landing permits' are issued at Sust whenever this policy is in operation in the rest of the country. Of course, it's always useful to have visas in advance, although the only Pakistani embassy in China is in Beijing. For further details on crossing the border between Pakistan and China, see page 26 in Essentials.

Tourist information

PTDC have a tourist information office ⓘ *PTDC motel, flexible hours*, with information about daytrips to the Khunjerab Pass and for buses to China. The current phone system requires you to dial the exchange number (T77239) and then ask for the extension number. A new digital exchange is under development.

Sust and around

Since the construction of a new customs and immigration house 2 km to the north of the original village (Old Sust), a whole new town has sprung up around it (sometimes referred to as Afiyatabad or New Sust). Built entirely to cater for the cross-border trade, it is a jumble of hotels, restaurants and shops selling imported/smuggled

Old Sust & New Sust (Afiyatabad)

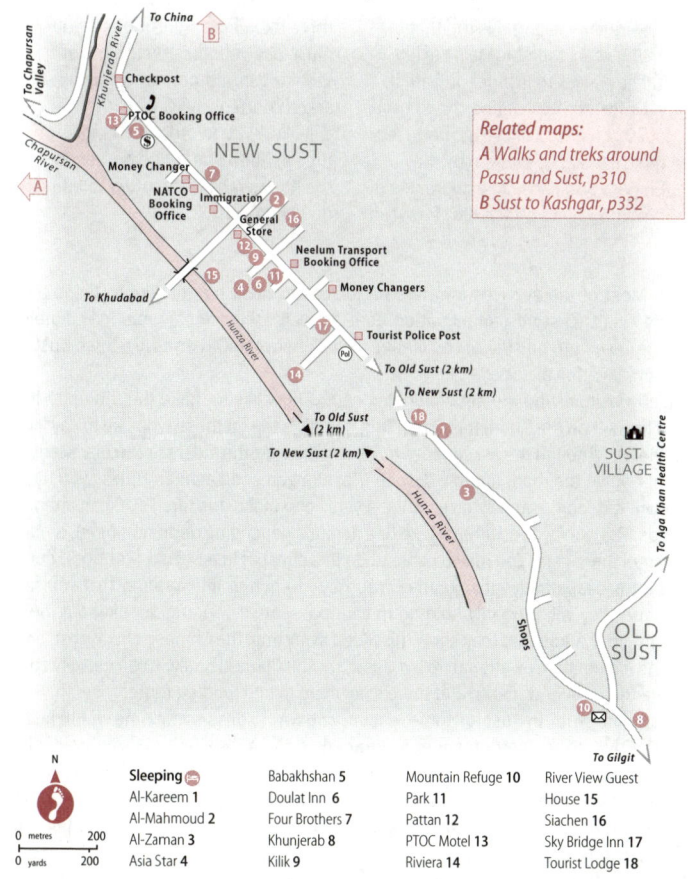

Related maps:
A Walks and treks around Passu and Sust, p310
B Sust to Kashgar, p332

Sleeping
Al-Kareem 1
Al-Mahmoud 2
Al-Zaman 3
Asia Star 4
Babakhshan 5
Doulat Inn 6
Four Brothers 7
Khunjerab 8
Kilik 9
Mountain Refuge 10
Park 11
Pattan 12
PTOC Motel 13
Riviera 14
River View Guest House 15
Siachen 16
Sky Bridge Inn 17
Tourist Lodge 18

> ### Note for cyclists travelling from Pakistan to China
>
> For many cyclists, pedalling over the Khunjerab Pass and crossing from Pakistan into China (or vice-versa) is one of the highlights of cycling the KKH route. However, there has always been some uncertainty in the eyes of the Chinese authorities about the status of cyclists attempting this journey. For example, on most Chinese visa application forms it specifically states that it is not permitted to bring a bicycle into China without special, rarely granted, dispensation. Furthermore, there is also some ambiguity about whether the route between Kashgar and Pakistan is 'open', 'restricted' or 'closed' to cyclists. Nevertheless, such has been the volume of foreigners making this trip that for many years the Chinese have left these crazies to just get on with it.
>
> Unfortunately, during the summer of 2001 a group of cyclists betrayed the trust placed in them by the Chinese and chose to explore one of the side valleys off the KKH between the Khunjerab Pass and Tashkurgan. As a result of this incident, the Chinese have reaffirmed the ban on cycling between the border with Pakistan on the Khunjerab Pass and the town of Tashkurgan (and also place a soldier on each bus making this trip). If you're travelling northbound, you will have to load your bike on the bus at Sust (you aren't generally charged for this) and won't be able to get on it again until the immigration post at Tashkurgan. The Pakistanis will permit you to cycle up to the Khunjerab Pass as a day or overnight trip, but you must leave your passport in Sust – you cannot get on the bus on the Khunjerab Pass and continue from there into China. Southbound, you must load your bike on the bus at Tashkurgan, although most drivers (if asked courteously well in advance) will allow you to offload your bike on the Pakistani side of the border on the Khunjerab Pass in order to ride down into Sust.

goods. Most of the services are here (eg places to book bus tickets to China and towards Gilgit, customs, immigration etc), as well as the more upmarket hotels. Unless you want to pay Rs50, you'll have to walk between Old and New Sust. Sust is sometimes written as 'Sost'.

Many visitors who are not continuing on to China like to make the trip up to the official frontier on the **Khunjerab Pass**. This is really a trip for those who like to say 'I've been there'. Although the ascent does have its moments, the most spectacular scenery is further down the road, notably between Tashkurgan and Kashgar. Unless you have your own transport, you will have to hire a vehicle to make this trip. PTDC can arrange day-trips (Rs1,500-2,000, either a jeep or a minibus depending upon numbers), as can most hotel managers. You may be able to do this cheaper in a Suzuki (Rs1,000), but it would be a desperately slow journey. You have to inform immigration that you are going, and they will probably hold on to your passport. If you are camping out there overnight, make sure that they know this. Keep away from the Chinese check post, and under no circumstances attempt to bypass it or enter China illegally. It can get very cold up there (especially at night), and there's nowhere to find food en route.

If you are stuck in Sust for some reason, one way to pass some time would be to cross the river to the settlement of **Khudabad** on the opposite bank. Alternatively, you could consider walking up to the village of **Sust** itself (largely hidden from the KKH). The huge rock that stands above Sust actually sports a cricket pitch on its flattish summit! A far better way to spend your time is to head up the **Chapursan Valley** (see page 319).

Sust to Khunjerab National Park/Dih (35 km)

Having completed customs and immigration formalities at the yard in Sust, the bus heads north for all of 20 m before coming to a halt; exit stamps are then inspected at the check post at the north end of town before the bus can proceed. If you are heading to the Khunjerab Pass just for the day, you may have to produce a receipt to confirm that you have left your passport at immigration. If coming from China and your bus has been delayed en route (meaning that immigration is now closed), your passport may be collected from you here and returned to you at immigration the next day.

The KKH to China travels north, entering a narrow canyon about 1 km above Sust. Here, the Hunza River is joined from the west by the Chapursan River, with a jeep road disappearing to the west up the **Chapursan Valley** (see page 319). A further kilometre along the road to China is a petrol station where most vehicles stop to fill up. A little further along the canyon, a jeep road leads off to the west along a side valley for 17 km to **Misgar** (3,708 m). An ancient strand of the Silk Road trading route used to run north from Misgar, crossing into Chinese territory by way of either the **Mintaka Pass** (4,709 m) or the **Killik Pass**. These two passes were of great strategic concern to the British who feared a Russian invasion of India in the 19th century, particularly when they received a report in 1874 claiming the Killik Pass to be "remarkably easy of access". When the KKH was being constructed, the route through the Mintaka Pass was considered but rejected as lying too close to the Afghan and Soviet borders.

The KKH now begins a steady climb, entering the Khunjerab Buffer Zone that adjoins the National Park established here. Above the junction of the Chapsuran and Killik Valleys, the Hunza River is referred to as the **Khunjerab River**, and the KKH now runs through this narrow gorge (one of several 'slide-areas' on this route) in a northeasterly direction before turning north at the Khunjerab River's confluence with the **Ghujerab River**. The bridge here marks the entrance to the **Khunjerab National Park**. The road here is still a very gentle incline as it runs into **Dih** (35 km from Sust).

Khunjerab National Park

The collection of huts at Dih (or 'Dhee') is the base for the KKH road maintenance crew and the Khunjerab Security Force (KSF), the latter of whom's task is less protecting the border and more attempting to stop illegal activity in the **Khunjerab National Park**.

The establishment of a national park here has always been a controversial matter, but it is now tourists on their journey between Pakistan and China (and vice-versa) who are joining with local people in opposing some of the measures imposed by the park management. The park comprises some 2,270 sq km of land on either side of the KKH between Dih and the Chinese border on the Khunjerab Pass, and until the administrative reforms of the Zulfikar Ali Bhutto in 1973 this was the domain of the Mir of Hunza. Following the abolition of the Mir's feudal authority, the noted biologist George Schaller, with the best of motives, suggested that this whole area should become a protected area, offering a refuge for threatened species such as Marco Polo sheep. Unfortunately, in those less enlightened times, notions such as 'community-based conservation programmes' were all but unknown and although a National Park was declared, it effectively comprised a ban on local communities exercising their traditional grazing rights on park land. Furthermore, the promised compensation for these lost rights never materialized. Of course this alienation of the local population did little to discourage illegal hunting in the region.

Over the years the concept of consultation with local communities has gained more ground, with the realization that cooperation with those who traditionally use the land is essential if a conservation scheme is to succeed. A key issue has been

Sust to Kashgar (China)

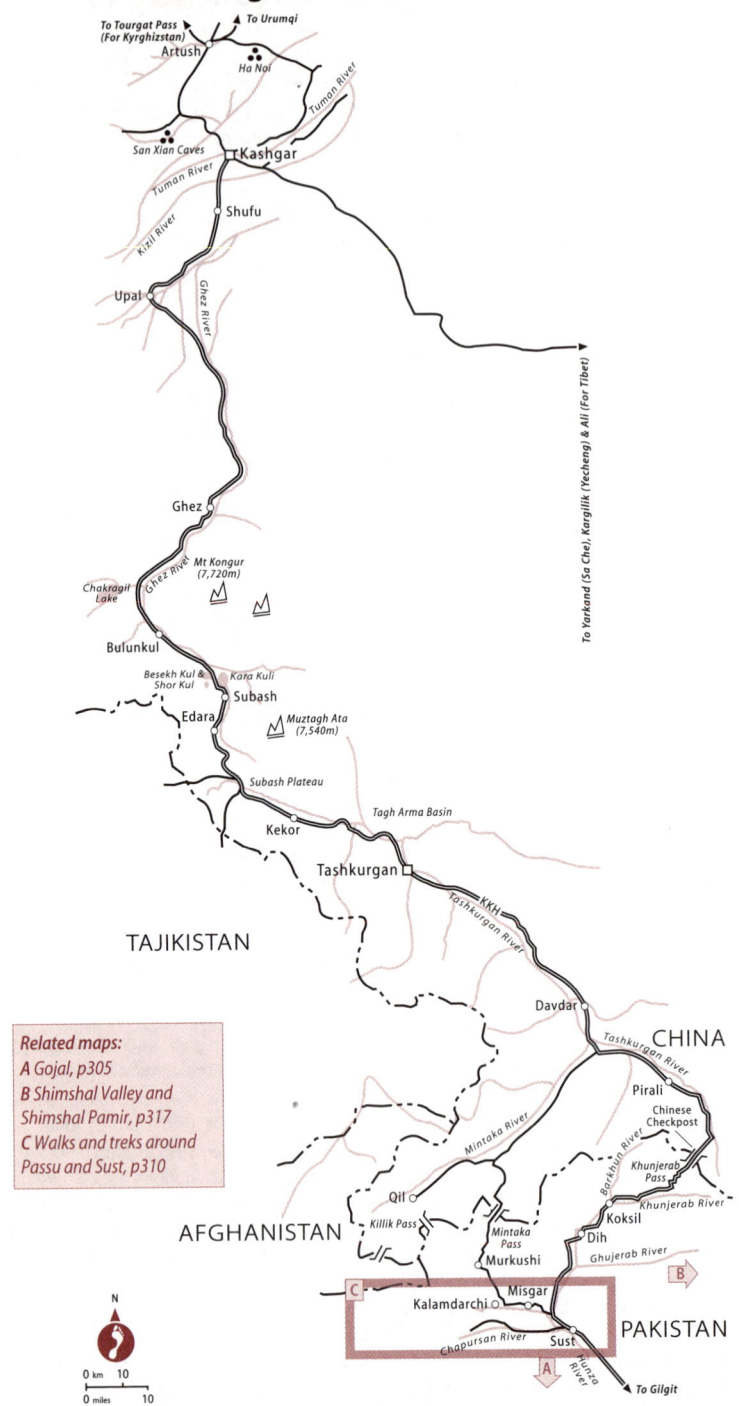

alternative income and employment opportunities for those denied their traditional grazing rights here, and thus many local villagers have been trained for jobs in park management and wildlife conservation. There is some opposition to the whole national park idea here, particularly among Shimshalis, with much ill-feeling caused by remarks attributed to a WWF official who seemed to imply that the Shimshalis' livestock were responsible for the spread of a disease that was killing the region's famous blue sheep.

Since September 1999, foreign tourists have been drawn into the argument about park policy by the sudden imposition of a US$4 'tax' for entering the park (additionally galling since Chinese and Pakistanis pay just Rs20, and when you consider that a hefty tax is already included in the ticket price for the bus journey between Sust and Tashkurgan). Part of the opposition to this fee is the feeling that you're actually getting nothing for your money. If you travel between Sust and Tashkurgan (or vice-versa) you have no option but to pass through the National Park (and thus pay the 'tax'), yet there is practically zero chance of seeing any wildlife from the bus window and it is impractical to head off wildlife spotting here as you will almost certainly be denied permission to explore the park. Of course, the idea is that the revenue created here will be shared with the villagers who have lost their grazing rights in the park and used for wildlife conservation, but many foreigners feel that the money will simply be embezzled somewhere along the way.

The officers at the Dih check post who record your passport details, collect the fee (in Rupees or US Dollars) and issue the receipt are used to foreigners complaining long and hard about this policy, but everyone has to cough up eventually otherwise the bus doesn't move. Note that the fee is valid for one day only, so if you're just cycling up to the pass and coming back down the next day, in theory you will have to pay twice (you may be able to negotiate here). There is a **Rest House** at Dih, although it is invariably occupied (and rarely accommodates cyclists).

Dih to Khunjerab Pass (51 km)

Beyond Dih the KKH continues its gentle climb, shortly re-crossing to the west bank of the river. This section of road is particularly susceptible to land-slides and flooding, and local people still rub their hands with glee at the memory of the money they made carrying bus passengers' baggage around the major blockage that occurred in 1998! The Khunjerab River is then joined from the north by the Barkhun Nala at **Barkhun**, where there is a rarely manned anti-hunting check post. The KKH begins to climb steadily here, although there are sections where it drops back down to the river.

Some 34 km from Dih, the road begins to climb up to the abandoned work camp and check post at **Koksil**. From here there are beautiful views of a snow-capped Matterhorn-style peak that lies along the Koksil Valley, to the south-southeast. Koksil is in fact the finishing point of the little- attempted Boesam Pass, Ghujerab Valley and Chapchingol Pass trek that provides an alternative route out of the Shimshal Valley (see page 318). Permission is rarely granted to begin the trek from Koksil. For those cycling up to the Khunjerab Pass from Sust, Koksil is the usual overnight halting place (and it is usually possible to camp in the check post's garden).

The real work for cyclists (and bus drivers) begins immediately after Koksil, as the KKH rapidly gains altitude through a dozen or so long, steep switchback turns. Cyclists may care to note that if there's a strong headwind, freewheeling back down is not necessarily an effort-free endeavour. As the bus struggles up the incline, look out for the golden marmots on either side of the road. It has been suggested that they must taste disgusting, otherwise the Chinese would have eaten them to the point of extinction.

Khunjerab Pass

Having negotiated the steep climb, the KKH eases gently up to the top of the **Khunjerab Pass** (86 km and three hours by bus from Sust, 125 km and two and a half to three hours by bus from Tashkurgan).

The Khunjerab Pass (sometimes referred to in Pakistan as 'Khunjerab Top') is reputedly the highest paved-road international border in the world. No two sources quite seem to agree on the exact altitude of the pass, although 4,733 m is generally accepted as being about right. Those expecting a narrow ravine through which to pass from one country to another will be disappointed, since Khunjerab Top is a broad, grassy saddle flanked on all sides by snowy peaks.

The pass is significant in terms of physical geography in that it marks the continental watershed (with rivers to the south flowing down towards the Indian Ocean, and rivers to the north flowing into the Tarim basin), as well as a convenient junction between two major mountain chains, the Pamirs and the Karakorams. The physical terrain varies considerably on either side of the pass, with the tight, narrow canyon valleys that have been the main feature of the KKH on the last 650 km of its journey through Pakistan giving way to wide, grassy high-altitude plateaux on the Chinese side.

Until falling within the remit of the Khunjerab National Park (on the Pakistani side of the border at least), this whole area was considered to be the private grazing lands of the Mir of Hunza, with *Khun jerab* supposedly being Wakhi for 'Valley of the Khan' (king). An alternative translation of the Wakhi name as 'Valley of Blood' is a sinister reminder of the Hunza slave caravans that passed through here.

> If you are just on a day trip up here, on no account attempt to bypass the check post and enter China.

A number of stone markers indicate the international border between the two countries, and a recent wire fence has appeared, should anyone be in any doubt as to who owns what. Bus drivers (travelling in either direction) may pause for a very quick 'photo stop' here. If you stay on the bus, you're unlikely to feel the effects of the altitude here, but once you get off and start to move around a bit it suddenly hits you.

● Sleeping

Sust *p328, map p329*
New Sust (Afiyatabad)
Most of the hotels have been built around the customs yard in New Sust. Unfortunately, this area is noisy and rather polluted. It is convenient for transport services, and because of all the competition, prices have dropped and good bargains can be struck.

B-D Riveria, T77239, ext 44, riveriasost@yahoo.com. Best in town. Value for money if you get the 'group rate' (D instead of B). 14 fair-sized rooms, dish TV, VCR, fan, bath with 24-hr hot water (own generator), intercom, restaurant (buffet breakfast Rs120, lunch Rs230, dinner Rs250), 24-hr room service, keen, friendly manager.

C PTDC Motel. 24 not particularly large rooms, small balconies, modern bathrooms that leak, dish TV in reception occupies staff, restaurant, not a great deal.

F River View Guest House. Recently opened but carpets already worn and linen grubby, 7 basic doubles with attached squat WC, 3 with western WC, hot water, restaurant with dish TV, keen owner.

F-G Sky Bridge Inn. Best deal in New Sust, good-sized doubles (F) with clean linen, bath (hot water mornings and evenings), 3-bed dorm (G) and plans for a big dorm (H), cheap restaurant, friendly manager is a good source of information on the Chapursan Valley. Recommended.

F-H Asia Star. 11 rooms (more planned), carpeted doubles with attached bath (F), slightly more basic rooms at the back (G), triples where you pay per bed (H), friendly owner. Quieter location off main road.

G Al-Mahmoud. If you must stay here (mainly triples), go for one of the marginally lighter and airier rooms upstairs.

G Badakhshan. 15 simple rooms around courtyard, linen clean enough, basic attached bath, cheap restaurant with dish TV, best of the rock-bottom hotels.

There are several other very basic unappealing hotels in New Sust, including **Doulat Inn, Four Brothers, Kilik Inn, Pattan, Park** and **Siachen**.

Old Sust
Many of the original hotels in Old Sust have now closed down, or been turned into

truckers' rest stops. This area is quieter than New Sust and you may find a good deal.

E-F Khunjerab. Located just outside Sust, ambitiously priced but usually empty so good scope for bargaining.

F-H Mountain Refuge, T77239, ext 18. Most popular choice with backpackers, good range of budget options. 6 doubles and 2 triples with carpet and attached hot bath (F) in separate block, 4 simple doubles with cold bath (G), 3-bed dorm (H) plus similar 4-bed dorm (H). If unoccupied, it is usually possible to take a hot shower in one of the upmarket rooms. Hotel offers free drop-off service to/from New Sust, and sells commission-free tickets to China. Foreign exchange is also available. Restaurant. Recommended.

G Tourist Lodge. Sensibly slashed prices in recent years, but the rooms are little more than tin shacks so are desperately hot and hard to recommend.

Other even more basic places here include **Al-Kareem** and **Al-Zaman**.

Eating

Sust *p328, map p329*

F-H Mountain Refuge, Old Sust, T77239, ext 18. Most popular choice with backpackers. Restaurant serves good-value communal dinner (Rs150 with meat, Rs95 veg), snacks (Rs30-50, plus a lunch-box for those heading to China (Rs110, 6-7 items).

Transport

Sust *p328, map p329*

Those heading up to **Tashkurgan** in China (from where you get onward transport to Kara Kuli and Kashgar) should book their ticket as soon as they arrive in Sust in order to try and reserve a good seat. This route is at its busiest Thu-Fri, when everyone is aiming to catch the Sunday Market in Kashgar; transport may not run due to lack of demand on Sat and Sun. Note that there is nowhere to buy any food or drink between Sust and Tashkurgan. Don't forget to keep Rs250 (or US$4) for the 'tax' payable at Dih; this is in addition to the departure tax that is incorporated into your ticket price.

There is rarely connecting transport in Tashkurgan to take you on to **Kashgar**; you will almost certainly have to spend the night there. For further details on departing for China/arriving in Pakistan, see page 328.

To Tashkurgan (China) with **PTDC**: The best option for the 5-6-hr (but sometimes 7-8-hr) trip to Tashkurgan is the PTDC coaster (book as early as possible at the PTDC transport office outside the PTDC Motel). It seats 20 passengers, although they only require 6 to justify the trip. The only disadvantage is that if it can't get 6 passengers together, everyone is shunted onto the **NATCO** service, and in all likelihood all the best seats will have gone. The advantage with the PTDC service is that the absence of Pakistani traders means that it tends to clear Customs and Immigration quicker on departure, and it will also make photo-stops on the way to Tashkurgan. It costs the same fare as NATCO (currently Rs1,210, although this fare increases by about Rs60 per year) and departs at 0900 (subject to border formalities).

To Tashkurgan (China) with **NATCO**: it sends a combination of buses, coasters and landcruisers on a daily basis (subject to demand); book at the NATCO office at the customs yard. All services cost the same (currently Rs1,210, but this fare increases by about Rs60 per year) and depart at 0900 (subject to border formalities). Before you request a seat in the landcruiser (up to an hr quicker than the bus), note that a vehicle that in the west would hold 4-5 passengers plus luggage, here holds 10 plus baggage. Avoid at all costs the inward-facing seats in the luggage area, the two middle seats in the second row, and only sit up front if you know (or want to get to know) your neighbour very well. You need to assemble at 0800 for a departure 30 mins later (but you usually wait for up to 3 hrs for all border formalities to be completed). Note that for this journey in reverse (ie Tashkurgan to Sust) you pay the equivalent of Rs1,800 in yuan.

To Gilgit: Neelum Transport runs minibuses south to Gilgit (Rs120, 5-6 hrs) via Gojal (Passu, Gulmit, see below), and Ganesh (for Karimabad) on a 'depart when full' basis from 0500 until mid-afternoon. There are then further minibuses (depending upon demand) once the bus from China has arrived. They usually take a meal break in Aliabad. The yard is diagonally opposite the customs yard, outside the Siachen Hotel.

To Gojal: Gilgit-bound **Neelum Transport** minibuses (see above) go via Passu (Rs30, 30 mins), Gulmit (Rs35, 45 mins).

To Karimabad: Gilgit-bound **Neelum Transport** minibuses (see above) go via Ganesh (Rs60, 2½ hrs), from where you can walk up to Karimabad.

To Minapin: Gilgit-bound **Neelum Transport** minibuses (see above) go via Pisin (Rs80, 3-3½ hrs). From here you can walk to Minapin.

Directory

Sust *p328, map p329*
Banks National Bank of Pakistan, near PTDC Motel, always seems to be closed when you need to use it (Mon-Thu 0900-1330, Fri 0900-1300, Sat 0900-1230), and it generally only deals in TCs. Note that rates get better the further south you travel. Many of the shops around the customs yard (and most hotel managers) will change money, offering better rates and keeping longer hours. Chinese currency is also available, and you can dispose of unwanted yuan. Check rates first with other travellers. **Hospitals** There is an Aga Khan Health Centre in Old Sust village; otherwise go to Aliabad (or better still, Gilgit). **Internet** Gilgit offers the nearest on-line facilities. **Post Office** Next to the Mountain Refuge in Old Sust.
Telephones The PCO (in the white building in the truck yard, opposite PTDC Motel) claims to offer international calls, but it's a very hit and miss affair; there are plans to build a new digital exchange.

Into China → *Colour map 4, grid B6*

For those equipped with a visa for China, a whole new world of possibilities opens up to travellers on the Karakoram Highway. The KKH doesn't just stop at the Pakistan-China border, but terminates (or begins, if you're heading north to south) at Kashgar, and from here one can travel on to the various 'stans' of Central Asia (Kyrghizstan, Uzbekistan and so on), east into Tibet, or carry on further into China. A good many travellers who haven't quite had enough of Pakistan, and who have had the presence of mind to obtain a double-entry visa in advance, turn round after visiting Kashgar and head back to Pakistan.

Travel in China is very different to travel in Pakistan. Language difficulties aside, there are great cultural differences, and perhaps the most obvious of these is the way in which foreigners are regarded by the Chinese. Unlike Pakistan, where almost everyone takes an interest in you and wants to be your friend, travel in China can be quite hard work; basic things such as buying bus and train tickets, checking into hotels, eating out and asking directions can often become frustrating experiences. Perseverance, and an optimistic outlook can help you deal with such trials on the road.

This section deals with a very small part of China. The journey described here from the Pakistani border town of Sust up to, and including, the city of Kashgar, is really a part Pakistani, part Central Asian and part Chinese experience, showing the best of all these worlds. ▶▶ *For Sleeping, Eating and all other listings, see pages 343-345.*

Khunjerab Pass to Tashkurgan (125 km)

As the bus crosses the pass, it makes a dramatic swerve across the road from left-hand-drive Pakistan to right-hand-drive China. Just below the border on the Chinese side is a small Chinese check post where exit stamps from each respective country are checked. Occasionally bags will be searched and Pakistani traders encouraged to give 'gifts' to the Chinese border guards. There are also stories of some foreigners accepting hospitality here, then being presented with an extortionate bill for that friendly cup of tea. Following the actions of a number of cyclists on this route (see box on page 330), a grumpy, nervous soldier accompanies each bus from the

Travel tips for visitors to China

Time zones On entering China you move into a different time zone. In theory, the whole of China operates on official Beijing time which is three hours ahead of Pakistan time. There is also an unofficial Xinjiang time, two hours behind Beijing time.

In general, when dealing with officialdom (eg plane, train and bus times, office opening hours etc) you will be quoted Beijing time. Check this although, especially when discussing transport departure times; you may be quoted a departure time in Beijing time only to find Xinjiang time written on your ticket!

Unless otherwise stated, information given in this guide uses Beijing time.

Money The Chinese unit of currency is the Yuan (¥), sometimes referred to in the slang term as *kwai*, although officially titled *Renminbi* (RMB, or 'people's money'). The policy of charging foreigners double, treble, quadruple and beyond for goods and services is in operation in Xinjiang at least. Banks in the major cities (including Kashgar) change travellers' cheques, with small commission charges. The current approximate exchange rates for cash are as follows: £1 = ¥15; US$1 = ¥8.30; €1 = ¥10. You get slightly better rates for travellers' cheques.

Sleeping Most hotels listed offer a range of accommodation options to suit all budgets. You do not usually get given your own room key – you have to rely on the floor attendant to lock and unlock your room. In theory, this should make your room more secure, but in practice it is not to be trusted: never leave valuables in your room. Take care of valuables when using communal showers. Toilet facilities can be interesting.

Eating In the areas of China covered by this guide, few restaurants will have menus in English (or even understand English), so it is generally a matter of going into the kitchen and pointing at what you want. Make sure the price is clearly established.

Kashgar and Tashkurgan provide the opportunity to try some regional cuisine, notably Uiygur cooking. All Uiygur dishes are accompanied by *nan*, a thick bread similar to its counterpart served in Pakistan. The other staple is *shashlik*, skewers of barbecued mutton or minced meat served with nan. Hygiene is always a consideration when you order this dish (or anything containing meat).

The other Uiygur speciality is *laghman*, the thick noodles that you see being spun out by the food stall holders. They are often served as part of a spicy soup. Other ubiquitous dishes around Kashgar include *chuchureh* (the boiled dumplings with a minced meat filling) and *samsa* (a Central Asian style of samosa). The region is famous for its variety of melons, and fresh slices are extremely cheap.

---

border to Tashkurgan; he will ensure that nobody wanders far from the bus when it stops. It usually takes two and a half to three hours by bus from Khunjerab Pass to Tashkurgan, and often longer in the opposite direction.

The KKH begins to descend through a long series of bends on the Chinese side of the border, after 30 km passing the former immigration and customs post at **Pirali** (4,100 m); all that's left now are a few abandoned, glass-strewn buildings. It is also noticeable how the road deteriorates markedly on the Chinese side, with little of the pride in the KKH that is shown in Pakistan being evident here; in fact, it is rarely referred to as the 'Karakoram Highway' on this side of the border. The KKH runs in a broadly northwesterly direction along the floor of the Tashkurgan River valley, and although giving the impression of being flat and straight, the road is remarkably bumpy. The mountains on either side of the road step back somewhat, with the scenery now comprising a mixture of green pastureland grazed by yaks, dzou (a yak/cow cross- breed), cattle, sheep and goats, followed by long stretches of high-altitude sandy desert. A number of jeep roads head off into distant Pamir side valleys, like one that follows the Mintaka River towards the Killik and Mintaka Passes into Pakistan, and the Wakhjir Pass into Afghanistan. As tempting as these trips look, they are strictly off limits to foreigners.

> ! Twin-humped Bactrian camels are a common sight, as are the spectacularly dressed nomadic Tajik horsemen. If you are lucky, you may now begin to see a few grazing yaks.

Some 47 km below the Khunjerab Pass, the KKH passes through the large Tajik 'town' of **Davdar**, before bumping its way a further 78 km past several other settlements and into the Chinese customs and immigration yard 1 km south of Tashkurgan.

Ins and outs

Arriving in China from Pakistan
Chinese entry and exit formalities are completed at the immigration and customs house a kilometre south of Tashkurgan. **NB** Please note that no visas are granted upon arrival, and that it is not permitted to bring private motor vehicles into China without prior arrangement.

For those arriving in China, you will first have to fill out a **health declaration form**, and then a **landing card**. You then pass through immigration, before having to fill out a **customs declaration form** detailing your foreign currency and expensive consumer items. You should keep the stamped copy until you depart China. Westerners rarely have their bags checked by hand, but luggage will have to pass through a suspicious-looking X-ray machine (discreetly put all your film in your pockets). Some readers have written to say that if you're delayed en route from Sust, the immigration post may be shut when you arrive. Your bus (and luggage) plus passports may be impounded until next day. By the time the immigration post opens next day, the Kashgar bus may have gone. You then have the option of staying in Tashkurgan, or hiring a vehicle to Kashgar. It is worth buying your bus ticket for onward travel the next day as you may be able to reserve a better seat.
» For further information, see Transport, page 344.

Leaving China for Pakistan
Exiting China can be a long, slow, frustrating exercise, with formalities dependent upon where passengers boarded the bus. If you boarded the Kashgar-Sust bus in Kashgar itself, your name and passport number will already appear on the passenger manifest; anyone else who boarded en route, eg Kara Kuli or Tashkurgan, will then have to be added (a long and seemingly complex process). Note that when you board this bus in Kashgar, you do not have access to your luggage when the bus makes its overnight stop in Tashkurgan. However, when the bus rolls up to customs the following morning, everyone must remove their luggage for inspection, including X-ray checks. All the luggage then needs to be reloaded upon clearing customs, and when you see the amount of baggage that Pakistani traders are carrying, you can see why the bus often leaves here up to four hours late. The situation is not helped by the time it takes for the traders to negotiate a fee with the baggage handlers to reload their goods. There may also be an additional delay while cyclists who intended to peddle this route have their mounts loaded onto the bus. At the time of writing, there was no additional price to pay for carrying bikes, but it will probably come.

Tickets for those boarding the bus in Tashkurgan are sold at the counter at the customs hall. You are not generally allowed through Immigration unless you have southbound transport arranged. The **NATCO** landcruisers and buses generally return to Pakistan empty, and they are not allowed to take passengers unless the uncooperative Chinese immigration officials give their permission.

Tashkurgan

Tashkurgan is the capital of the 'Tajik Autonomous County within the Xinjiang Uiygur Autonomous Region of the People's Republic of China', yet despite this grand title it is a miserable little town that travellers on the Pakistan-Kashgar journey are invariably forced to stop in overnight. If it wasn't for the construction of a new hotel a short distance to the south of the main drag, Tashkurgan would very much fall into the category of a 'one-street town'. Despite being of historical interest, there is little to occupy visitors while they await their transport connections the following day, the accommodation is not particularly appealing unless you're prepared to spend a lot, and the restaurants have a reputation for overcharging tourists. So, after such a negative introduction, things can only get better, no?

The town has a long history and is said to have been mentioned in the second century AD writings of Ptolemy. The intrepid Chinese Buddhist pilgrim **Xuanzang** (Hiuen Tsiang) spent a month here during his great 16-year journey in the seventh century AD (although he probably wouldn't stay so long today!). At the time of the pilgrim's visit, Tashkurgan was something of a minor seat of Buddhist learning, boasting the monk Kumarajiva (one of the great translators of Mahayana Buddhism) among its residents.

Tashkurgan is today home to some 6,000 people of predominantly Tajik stock, although there are representatives of other minorities such as Uiygurs, Kyrghiz, Uzbeks and of course, Han Chinese. It is located at an altitude of some 3,200 m.

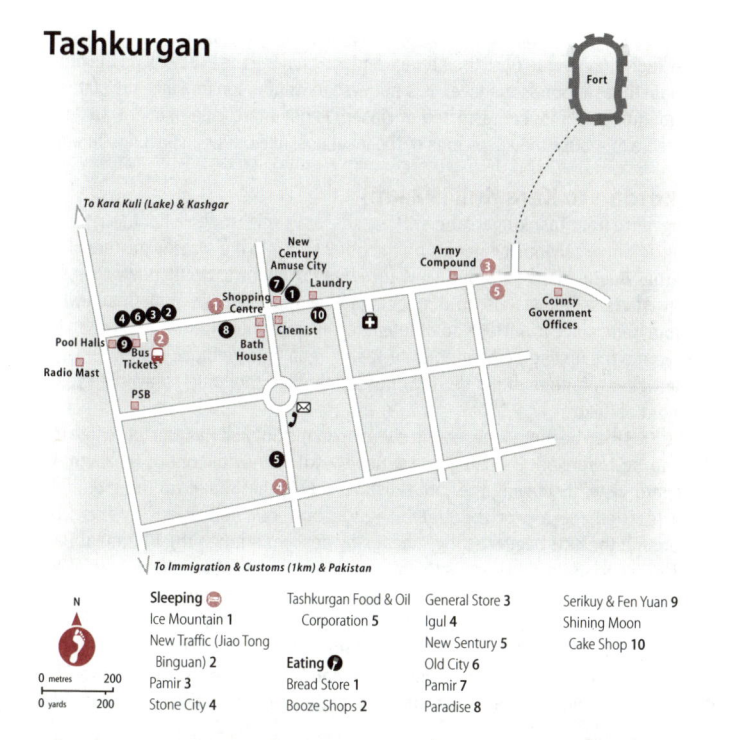

Tashkurgan

Sleeping
Ice Mountain 1
New Traffic (Jiao Tong Binguan) 2
Pamir 3
Stone City 4
Tashkurgan Food & Oil Corporation 5

Eating
Bread Store 1
Booze Shops 2
General Store 3
Igul 4
New Sentury 5
Old City 6
Pamir 7
Paradise 8
Serikuy & Fen Yuan 9
Shining Moon Cake Shop 10

Ins and outs

If you arrive from Pakistan you will be dropped at the customs and immigration hall, a short 1-km walk to the south of town. If coming from the north (ie Kashgar or Kara Kuli), you will almost certainly be dropped at the New Traffic (Jiao Tong) Hotel on the main street. Everything in Tashkurgan is within short walking distance, with the post office and phone office on the parallel street one block south of the main road. The bus waiting outside the customs house will give you a lift into Tashkurgan, although it's usually quicker to walk.

Sights

The name Tashkurgan is usually translated as 'stone fortress' or 'stone city', with the main attraction here being a **stone and mud-brick fortress** ① ¥5 *entry fee*, of indeterminable age. A fortress has stood in Tashkurgan for at least 1,300 years, possibly a further 1,000 years too, but the present structure is thought to date to the 14th or 15th century. Much of its outer walls and battlements are intact, although the interior is little more than a pile of rubble and hardly justifies the entrance fee. There is a good view of the surrounding flood plain from the hill upon which the fortress stands.

The most famous 'Stone Fortress' to have stood in Tashkurgan is the so-called Maiden's Castle, the ruins of which Xuanzang visited and described. Legend tells how a Chinese princess of the Han dynasty was on her way to marry the king of Persia when she was unexpectedly detained in Tashkurgan because of the presence of robbers on the road ahead. For her own protection she was placed by her escort on an isolated peak here, guarded by rock precipices. According to a 1904 account, when peace was restored, and the journey to be continued, the king's envoy in charge of the bride discovered that she was pregnant. Upon further enquiry he found that the sun-deva had visited the lady every day at noon, and that it was by him that she was with child. This event so impressed the local people that they begged her to stay and become their queen, with all the subsequent rulers of the region being offspring of the sun-god's son.

Although there is precious little else to see in Tashkurgan, those detained unexpectedly may care to pass their time wandering among the livestock on the broad flood-plain that surrounds the town. It is not wise to wander too far since the status of the surrounding area (open, restricted or closed) is not entirely clear, and it would be unadvisable to arouse the suspicions of the local possible or Public Security Bureau.

Tashkurgan to Kara Kuli (92 km)

Heading north from Tashkurgan, the KKH passes for 17 km through a flat basin before entering a narrow canyon. It emerges on the other side into the marshy pasture of the **Tagh Arma Basin**, allowing a first view up ahead of the rounded, snowy peaks of Mustagh Ata (see below). It is worth noticing the shape of this great mountain when seen from here, since it will look so different further into your journey. Another 10 km brings you to the first settlement north of Tashkurgan (a large block of new houses), and then after a further 10 km the KKH passes through the long, sprawling Kyrghiz settlement of **Kekor**.

The KKH then begins a long, gentle climb up to the **Subash Plateau** (although this is said to be hard work if cycling into a headwind). A new picture of Muztagh Ata comes into view, displaying the three distinct ridges that make up the mountain. Having reached the top of the plateau (about an hour and a half by bus from Tashkurgan), the KKH begins a long, zigzagging descent through the **Ulugrabat Pass** to the basin floor. Directly ahead is the huge 7,720-m bulk of **Mount Kongur**, while on either side of the road is the endearing sight of numerous Kyrghiz summer settlements, scattered among the herds of grazing yaks. The first of these settlements (2 km to the east of the KKH) is **Edara**, the jumping-off point for trips up to Muztagh Ata's base camp. The major settlement on the road here is **Subash**, shortly before the KKH arrives at the southern end of Kara Kuli (about two hours by bus from

> **❝ Kara Kuli is one of the most stunning places on the Karakoram Highway, as the dark, deep waters of the lake reflect the giant peaks that flank two sides...**

Tashkurgan). The small settlement around the police post here is **Upalu**, and there are three restaurant yurts (**Sabut's Café**) on the bend in the road here. Buses drop passengers at the hotel area on the southwest corner of the lake.

Kara Kuli and around

Without doubt, this is one of the most stunning places on the entire length of the Karakoram Highway, as the dark, deep waters of the lake reflect the giant peaks that flank two sides. It is a photographer's dream, with the local Kyrghiz population being as photogenic as the remarkable scenery. It is certainly worth planning your journey so that you get to spend a few days here.

Although long used as a grazing spot by the Kyrghiz, it first came to the attention of Europeans in 1886 when the British explorer Ney Elias was mapping the adjacent **Muztagh Ata** mountain. This massive, 7,540-m bulk of snow, rock and ice is probably the most attractive peak in the entire Pamir range, its geological age accounting for the rounding of its peaks (the Pamirs being considerably older than their Himalayan and Karakoram neighbours). The mountain is popular with **ultimate skiing** enthusiasts, and a great source of revenue for the Chinese government, although this commercial exploitation does not sit well with the local Kyrghiz who revere the holy spirits that are said to live on the summit.

Ins and outs

Kara Kuli is on the route of the Tashkurgan-Kashgar (and vice-versa) bus, but if heading from Pakistan up to Kashgar and then back again, it is usually easier (and cheaper) to arrange onward transport by stopping at the lake on your way back. This is largely because bus drivers (or vehicle drivers who offer a lift in return for payment) make up their own prices, so it is usually cheaper to be ripped off on the shorter Kara Kuli-Tashkurgan trip than the longer Kara Kuli-Kashgar ride. See Transport, page 344, for full details. The only drawback to this plan is the unpredictable nature of the weather here, but bad weather can change to good remarkably quickly here (and vice-versa).

An 'Alien Travel Permit' is no longer officially needed for Kara Kuli, although the Public Security Bureau (PSB) in Kashgar or Tashkugan will sell you one if you ask. Treks that lead you any real distance away from the lake, however, are another matter, and enquiries should be made with the PSB in advance.

Exploring the lake

The lake is called a variety of names along the Kara Kuli theme (Kara Kul is Uighur for 'black lake'), although we refer to it here as Kara Kuli (or 'little' Karakul Lake) in order to distinguish it from the more famous Kara Kul in Tajikistan. Despite the beauty of the place, the Chinese (and to some extent the local Kyrghiz) have done their best to spoil it. The small, built-up area of the lake where the hotel and restaurant complex is located has become rather polluted. And to cap it all, the Chinese authorities have put a fence up around the lake so that they can charge foreigners ¥20 for the privilege of visiting this scenic area. Perhaps if this fee was being put to good use in maintaining the area visitors would be less reluctant to part with their cash, but this obviously isn't happening. Note that the fence around the lake is fairly porous, and if you stay away from the hotel complex area, you should be able to avoid the ticket seller. During the daytime, when the tour groups are expected, dozens of stalls selling junk are set up by the entrepreneurial Kyrghiz youth, who also bring their horses and camels and offer rides to visitors (see page 344). It can all get a bit touristy, but a five-minute walk in any direction will get you away from the crowd.

There are lots of options for those wishing to explore the area, but you should note the effects of altitude before planning anything too ambitious. The altitude here approaches 3,700 m. Also note how quickly the weather changes here; even if it's hot and sunny when you set off, make sure that you have sufficient warm and waterproof clothes with you for that sudden change in conditions.

A nice introduction to **Kyrghiz life** can be had by walking to the settlement about 30 minutes north of the hotel complex, although don't expect an experience untouched by tourism. You will be invited in to the yurts here (circular nomads' tents), and you should expect to pay for any tea/food that you are offered (and your host will probably also try to sell you some trinkets too). A little further north from here are two more smaller lakes (Besekh Kul and Shor Kul), which are also rather photogenic. Another good walking option is a trip right around the lake, although you should note that this takes five to six hours at least, with the soggy marsh terrain to the south of the lake adding considerably to your walking time. From the village on the other side of the lake (or even from Subash), you can also hire a horse to visit the high pastures (¥100).

Those who are equipped with tents, stoves and cold weather gear may like to visit **Muztagh Ata base camp** (officially you need a PSB permit for this, but only rarely is there anyone around to demand to see it). The base camp is reached by heading roughly southeast for 15 km from Edara (a settlement some 14 km south of Kara Kuli along the KKH); it is a long, steady climb up to about 4,500 m.

Kara Kuli to Kashgar (193 km)

North of Kara Kuli, the KKH passes through a mixture of pastureland and stony river plain, after half an hour or so (by bus) passing the small settlement of **Uzantal**; there is a small yurt restaurant here (but the bus doesn't stop here). Having made a number of short but steady climbs and descents into a wide, marshy basin (with sand dunes to the west), the KKH enters the southern reaches of the rocky canyon of the **Ghez River** (sometimes referred to as Tiger's Mouth Gorge, about an hour by bus from Kara Kuli). The road here is rough in parts, and subject to rock falls and land-slides.

After a long descent, the KKH arrives at the small Kyrghiz settlement of **Bulunkul**, about an hour and three-quarters north of Kara Kuli by bus. Passports are examined at the police check post, and photogenic young children sell cold drinks and snacks, like delicious parathas stuffed with spicy fried vegetables. Toilets here are not pleasant.

The road through the canyon is very rough, although the views are endearing. The enclosing mountains are highly folded, with stratas of multicoloured sandstone providing a dramatic impression. Some of the deep burgundy reds are particularly striking. After 70 km or so (and three hours), the KKH begins to emerge from the north end of the Ghez Canyon. There is a military check post at **Ghez**, at the north end of the canyon, although passports are not checked.

The KKH finally leaves the canyon, continuing for the last 80 km to Kashgar along a wide, flat plain. Trees line the road that links the smaller oases to the major city of the region. Away from the oases it's fairly bare and dry, an unmemorable stretch of road for cyclists, even if it is fairly flat. Frustratingly, the bus always seems to stop for a meal break at **Upal**, just an hour short of Kashgar (even if you're heading southbound). The road then enters **Kashgar** on a grand, eight-lane freeway that is almost traffic free.

◎ Sleeping

Tashkurgan *p339, map p339*
For notes on sleeping, see box, p337.
Ice Mountain, T0998-3422668. Best deal in town for budget accommodation. Luxury rooms a little overpriced (¥100), doubles have TV and bath and you can usually pay per bed (¥30). The 3- and 4-bed dorms (¥20, ¥15 and ¥10 per bed) are similar to those at the Traffic Hotel, although you can usually use one of the private showers. Also has a reasonable restaurant.
New Traffic (Jiao Tong Binguan), T0998-3421192, F0998-3421576. Used to be one of the worst hotels in China, now the best deal in town for a private room (¥100 for a double) since the rooms were renovated with new beds, clean linen, colour TV, hot shower and toilet. Everything is listed on a card, and the room will be checked for any breakages or missing items (everything from the colour TV at ¥2,000 to the toothbrush mug at ¥6 is priced; and don't think about stealing the card as a souvenir since that is listed too!). The dorm rooms here are not such good value at ¥10 per bed in a 4-bed dorm (linen not always clean). There are no showers and the shared toilets are repulsive. Pakistani and western guests are usually separated, and women may be able to request a 'women only' dorm. Don't leave valuables in your room. If you don't have any Yuan, you can usually pay in Rupees. Even if there are only 4 people in the whole hotel, the staff usually put them all in the same room.
Pamir, T0998-3422348, F0998-3421085. This used to be where all the tour groups stayed, although the Stone City and even the New Traffic are now much better bets. Basic doubles (¥150) with dirty carpets, very old bath tubs and antiquated plumbing are grossly overpriced.
Stone City, T0998-3422600. Recently opened, this is the place to stay if you want some luxury. Very plush suites (¥368), well furnished, plus very nice doubles (¥180).

Kara Kuli *p341*
There are some 10 or so pseudo-yurts at the complex on the southwest shore of the lake. They sleep 4-8 people, although they come priced at an extortionate ¥40 per person. The yurts contain a pile of thick quilts and blankets (warm, but of variable cleanliness), but no other facilities (bar an electric light). Note that if you stay at the yurts here, it is difficult to avoid paying the ¥20 'scenic area' entrance fee. If you want to bathe, the only option is in the lake (rather chilly), and the public toilets are very unappealing. **NB** Do not leave any valuables in the yurt, even if you have secured it with your own padlock.

A further sleeping option is to stay in the yurt of a **Kyrghiz family**; there are 3 such places some 250 m north of the hotel complex. Their starting price is now ¥30 for a full-on travel experience, living cheek by jowl with a Kyrghiz family, huddling round the stove for food, and wrapping up in smoky quilts for the night. Once the family are settled in for the night, it can get quite crowded, and this is an experience that may not appeal to the introverted. Meals are available (set prices in advance).

The final sleeping option is to camp.

◎ Eating

Tashkurgan *p339, map p339*
For notes on eating, see box, p337.
Many of the restaurants in Tashkurgan have reputations for fleecing foreigners, but it is difficult to warn about specific places to avoid since few have signboards in English. The best advice is to choose what you want by going into the kitchen, then making very clear what the price is to be. The way the meat is stored (wrapped in a cloth and hung from a tree in the street) may persuade you to become vegetarian while in Tashkurgan.
Ψ Ice Mountain Hotel. The restaurant here isn't bad, and usually has a priced menu from which to choose.
Ψ Igul (?) opposite the New Traffic (signboard has a picture of 2 goats butting in front of a sun). Run by a smiling gold-toothed Tajik lady who serves up a plate of spicy vegetables and noodles for ¥5, and beer for ¥4.

Note that food stops en route to Kashgar are extremely limited (and non-existent on the road to Pakistan). There are several shops along the main street where you can stock up on rudimentary supplies, or there are a couple of stalls that set up outside the New Traffic early each morning. Fresh bread (¥1) is available early every morning from the bakery just after the main junction to the east of the **Ice Mountain** hotel.

Kara Kuli *p341*
♦♦♦ The **restaurant at the lake** charges an extortionate ¥25 for a meal of meat/veg/noodles, ¥10 for spicy noodle soup, ¥15 for veg and noodles, plus ¥5 for coffee and ¥5 for fried bread at breakfast time. It is a good idea to bring your own supplies from Tashkurgan/Kashgar.
♦ **Sabut's Café** at the 3 yurts just south of the lake offers noodle soup for ¥5, veg/noodles for ¥10, and ¥5 for a coke.

Most of the **family yurts** will offer meals, although you should clearly establish what you are getting and how much you should pay. Salty tea and bread is usually ¥5.

▲ Activities and tours

Kara Kuli *p341*
A horse or camel ride around the hotel complex will cost around ¥10 for 10 mins, although this is more a photo opportunity than a serious exploration; it will cost around ¥100 to hire a horse for a 5-hr trip part of the way round the lake (perhaps to Subash and some of the large yurt settlements).

⊖ Transport

Tashkurgan *p339, map p339*
Bus
It is advisable to buy your onward ticket to **Kashgar** at the counter in the customs hall as soon as you arrive. It costs ¥62, journey time is 7-8 hrs (often more in the opposite direction as the bus is so loaded down) and the bus departs at 0900 Beijing time. You can buy a ticket on the morning of departure from the small office by the gate of the NewTraffic; this is also where the bus departs from.

Although there is a 10 kg baggage allowance, you may be asked for money if someone loads your bag onto the roof for you. Seat numbers on tickets are not always respected and drivers on this route are fantastically bad tempered. This route is particularly busy Thu-Sat, when more than 1 bus may make the journey. This is also the bus for **Kara Kuli** (lake), see below.

Occasionally, when you arrive at the customs hall there is a bus waiting to leave for Kashgar immediately, although this is demand driven and the fare depends upon how many passengers there are.

Kara Kuli (lake): If you are heading from Pakistan to Kashgar and then returning back to Pakistan, it is more convenient (and often cheaper) to stop at Kara Kuli on the way back. Officially, the fare from Tashkurgan to Kara Kuli (on the Kashgar-bound bus) is ¥25, and then a further ¥43 from the lake to Kashgar. However, when you hail the bus at the lake, the drivers make up their own fares, typically asking ¥40 southbound and ¥100 northbound! You may get a better deal (be prepared to haggle), but don't bank on it.

Sust (Pakistan): The bus to Sust is the one that has originated at the international long-distance bus station in Kashgar (¥270 from there, or ¥225 from Tashkurgan). Tickets from Tashkurgan can be bought on the morning of departure at the counter inside the customs hall (your name will be added to the existing passenger manifest, see Leaving China, p338). Those who have travelled on this bus from Kashgar usually re-board at the New Traffic hotel, while those joining here have to walk out to the customs hall. This bus is generally pretty full already and, although luggage is often rearranged in order to squeeze a few more bodies in, you will have to pay the full fare even if you don't get a proper seat. Note that seat numbers occupied from Kashgar are not always respected when new arrivals join the bus at Tashkurgan. This journey southbound often takes longer than in the opposite direction (it's usually grossly overloaded), and what with departure delays, it often arrives in Pakistan after the immigration and customs offices there have closed (see p338). Occasionally, if there's sufficient demand, there is a second Sust-bound bus that originates in Tashkurgan. The journey takes about 8 hrs and departure time is scheduled for 1000 Beijing time

---

● *Prices categories for restaurants in China are* ♦♦♦ *¥20 and over;* ♦♦ *¥10-20;*
● ♦ *¥10 and under.*

(although with all the delays at the customs yard it rarely departs before 1300 Beijing time). The bus journey from Tashkurgan to Sust is a quarter more expensive (in Rupee terms) than the journey in the opposite direction.

Jeep
The price quoted for a privately hired landcruiser to **Kashgar** is ¥1,000, but many Pakistani traders group together to hire a private car when they arrive in Tashkurgan, and claim to only pay ¥100 per person.

Kara Kuli *p341*
Northbound
The 0900 (Beijing time) **bus** from Tashkurgan to Kashgar will drop passengers off at **Kara Kuli** (¥25, 2 hrs).

Continuing north to **Kashgar**, you will have to stand by the road and flag this bus down (presuming it has seats, which it usually does, although it is at its busiest on Fri and Sat). It passes through at about 1100 (Beijing time) and although the official fare is ¥43, the drivers often demand more than double this. You can usually bargain, but it's rare that you pay the correct fare.

You could also **hitch-hike**, although you should establish in advance how much you are expected to pay (the bus fare, at the very least). Although China is safer than most other countries in this regard, it is better for women not to hitch alone.

Southbound
The 'international' bus to **Pakistan** (via Tashkurgan) is scheduled to pass through Kara Kuli at around 1700-1800 (Beijing time), although it often leaves Kashgar well after its scheduled 1200 (Beijing time) departure time. If arriving at Kara Kuli from Kashgar, make sure that you tell the driver (on departure and again as you draw near) that you want to get off at the lake (¥43 from Kashgar), and take your luggage inside the bus with you. The official fare from Kara Kuli to Tashkurgan is ¥25 (2 hrs+), but your driver may initially ask for double that. You could hitch-hike, but you should agree in advance how much you are expected to pay (the bus fare, at the least).

Directory

Tashkurgan *p339, map p339*
Banks The Bank of China counter beyond customs and immigration has disappeared, and the Uiygur-run bank rarely seems to open. Staff at the counter selling bus tickets will change money for you, seemingly at the going bank rate (certainly for US$ cash, possibly for US$ and £ TCs too).

Kashgar and beyond → *Colour map 4, grid A5*

Kashgar is one of those evocative sounding destinations, like Timbuktoo or Kathmandu, that seems to appeal to travellers. Indeed, this oasis town has lain on a branch of the ancient trans-Asia trading route, later dubbed the Silk Road, with its strategic location inviting a long and varied list of visitors and conquerors. Nowadays, Kashgar still welcomes weary travellers, many of whom have come to witness its famed Sunday Market. For many it provides not just their first contact with Central Asia, but with Han Chinese society too. Few leave disappointed.

Recent arrivals from Pakistan revel in the availability of cheap Chinese beer while being shocked at the lack of clothes worn by tourists and Chinese women alike. Despite being a predominantly Muslim town, there is little reaction to tourists (including women) wearing shorts – hardly surprising when most young Han Chinese women are wearing shorter and shorter miniskirts.

Kashgar is predominantly populated by Uiygurs (pronounced 'Weegur'), a Turkic-Muslim race thought to have arrived in the area around 700 years ago, and there is a significant number of minority groups in Kashgar. Although Mandarin Chinese is the official language, Uiygur (written using the Arabic script) is the most widely used in the bazaar. ▶▶ *For Sleeping, Eating and all other listings, see pages 352-356.*

Ins and outs

Getting there

It takes some pretty hard travelling to get to Kashgar, although each year the transport links improve somewhat. There are daily flights to Kashgar's airport, 12 km northeast of the town (taxis from ¥30, although **CAAC** often have a shuttle bus running to their offices in town). Kashgar also now has a rail link with Urumqi, offering a quicker (24 hours) and more comfortable journey between the two cities, although at a higher price than the bus. The railway station is around 3 km east of the town, and can be reached by taxi (¥10) or bus 28 (¥1.50).

There are a number of places where the bus may drop you if arriving from Tashkurgan (and Kara Kuli). In theory, the bus should drop you at the new international bus station, but it occasionally drops passengers at the old long-distance bus station and regularly drops them at a yard on the western outskirts of

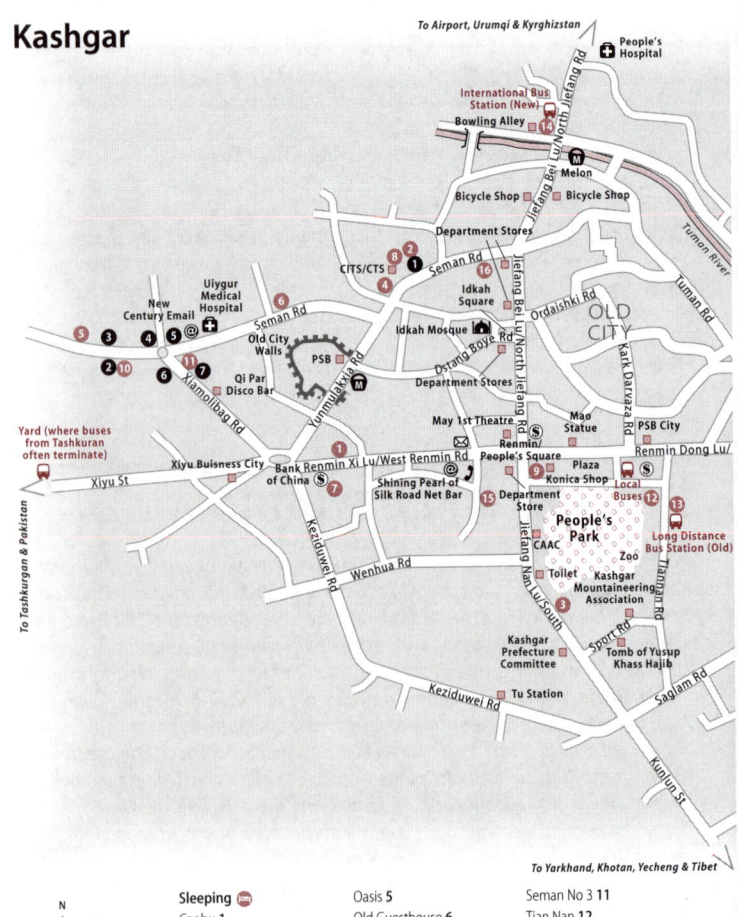

Kashgar

Sleeping
Caohu 1
International 2
Labour Union 3
New Yield Fast Foreign Executive Centre 4
Oasis 5
Old Guesthouse 6
Qian Hai 7
Qiniwake/Chini Bagh 8
Renmin/People's 9
Seman 10
Seman No 3 11
Tian Nan 12
Traffic 13
Tuman River 14
Wuzi 15
Xin Yi 16

Kashgar (¥5 taxi ride to hotels). Passengers on the sleeper-bus from Urumqi should be dropped at the international bus station, but other services (including those from Yarkhand, Khotan and Artush) may well terminate at the old long-distance bus station on Tiannan Road. Kashgar is located at an altitude of 1,289 m.

Getting around
Buses around town are now far easier to negotiate. They are clearly numbered, with bus stops displaying bus numbers, route maps and the name of the next stop in clear English. There are plenty of taxis available, although Kashgar remains a pleasant city in which to cycle. It's also a fairly compact place, so with the exception perhaps of the Sunday Market and Abakh Hoja's Tomb, everywhere can be reached on foot.

Best time to visit
When the border crossing with Pakistan is closed (officially 1 January- 30 April, although weather often closes the pass beyond these times) there are less foreign tourists in evidence at the Sunday Market (though even at peak visiting periods it's hardly swamped by them). Summer can be hot and dusty in Kashgar (as opposed to cold and dusty during winter).

Tourist information
There is no tourist information office as such, although there are a couple of tour operators (see below) who offer free advice (as well as 'fixing' nearly anything that you need doing).

History

By the first century AD the **Han Chinese** had grabbed control of Kashgar, following the extension of the Great Wall westwards and the construction of a chain of beacons that warned of attack by marauding raiders. However, following the collapse of the Han Dynasty in the third century, Kashgar was sacked by the Huns and a great period of instability ensued. It wasn't until the end of the seventh century that the **Tang Dynasty** re-imposed Chinese rule in the region, although they were to be defeated by an alliance of Western Turks and Arabs in 752 AD. The **Arabs** had the upper hand in this one-sided alliance, and subsequently Islam became the dominant religion in the region.

In 1219 the city fell to the great Mongol ruler **Genghis Khan**, as he established an empire that stretched from Asia to eastern Europe. Ironically, the fear generated by the Mongol Horde brought great stability to the whole region and trade along the Silk Road flourished. In 1265 **Marco Polo** visited Kashgar, registering his comments on the

Eating
Beer Shops 6
Caravan Café & Asian Explorations Travel Co 1
John's Café 7
Kashgar Café/Bar of Wein 2
Oasis Café & Daniel's 3
Various Uiygur Restaurants 5
Zilala 4

city. As the power of the Mongol empire waned towards the end of the 14th century, the city was sacked by **Tamerlane**. However, his death in 1405 marked the beginning of another era of instability that was to last almost 350 years.

In the middle of the 18th century, the Manchu Dynasty of the **Ching** returned to the Tarim Basin, ending the isolation from China imposed by the insular Ming Dynasty. The Ching rule over the region was tenuous, however, and in 1865 the Turkic leader **Yakub Beg** crossed the Pamirs, seized control of 'Kashgaria' and declared it independent. In 1868 the first British visitor, a tea planter-cum-adventurer named Robert Shaw, arrived in Kashgar, followed closely behind by George Hayward (see page 156).

The Great Game

In the era that followed, Kashgar became the furthest extension of the rival British and Russian empires, acting as a listening post in the 'Great Game' of imperial rivalry. A British mission headed by Sir Douglas Forsyth had been received at Kashgar in 1873 by Yakub Beg. However, in 1877 the Ching army put down Yakub Beg's rebellion and Kashgar was incorporated within the Xinjiang ('New Frontier') Province of China. As a snub to the British for their dealings with Yakub Beg, in 1882 the Chings let the Russians open a consulate there, not sanctioning a British one until eight years later.

The first British representative was the 24-year-old **George Macartney**, who was to remain in Kashgar for the next 28 years. A shrewd tactician and 'Great Game' player, Macartney is remembered as one of the most extraordinary characters from the latter era of Kashgar's history. In 1898 he returned from brief home leave with a young wife, **Catherine Theodora Borland**, and so began the dramatic transformation of the consulate building, the Chini Bagh (Chinese Garden), into a little island of Britain in the heart of Central Asia. Catherine was later to write a book, *An English Lady in Chinese Turkestan*, detailing such exploits as culinary disasters with soggy Christmas puddings.

In 1908 the Chinese finally recognized the British representative in Kashgar as a Consul, although within three years the Manchu government had fallen and China was declared a republic. In the resulting upheaval the Manchu appointed ruler, the Taotai, was subsequently murdered and Kashgar threatened to descend into another period of savagery. Order was only restored at the intervention of Russian troops.

As the 1917 Russian Revolution spread slowly eastwards towards Kashgar, the Russian Consulate there was briefly a refuge for White Russians. By 1924, however, the Bolsheviks had taken over. Kashgar, meanwhile, continued to be ruled from Urumqi by Governor Yang until his assassination at a banquet in 1928. In the resulting bloody conflict between the Han Chinese and the **Tungans** (Chinese Muslims), Kashgar was briefly captured in 1934 by the Tungans, but they were soon driven out by a local warlord backed by the Soviets. The warlord, **General Sheng Shih-tsai**, appointed himself Governor of Xinjiang and ruled until he was pensioned off by the Chinese in 1944.

Recent history

Following Indian independence and the creation of Pakistan, the last British Consul-General, Eric Shipton, left Kashgar. Within a year **Mao Zedong** had declared the foundation of the People's Republic of China and a major modernization of Kashgar began. Much of the old city, including the 500-year-old city walls, were bulldozed to make way for uninspiring concrete blocks. In recent years there have been reports of Uiygur uprisings in Kashgar, although news of such incidents is suppressed. A building opposite the **Seman Hotel** was supposedly blown up, although it has since been rebuilt, but foreigners who hang around there asking questions and taking photos seem to end up down at the PSB answering questions themselves. Although there is resigned acceptance of Chinese rule, the Uiygur population still resent the influx of Han Chinese into the region, now believed to be 38% of the population of Xinkiang province.

Sights

Central Kashgar

When the original **Idkah Mosque** ⓘ *entry ¥10*, was built in 1442 it was located on the edge of town, but Kashgar's gradual expansion means that the mosque is now pretty much at the centre of town. The mosque currently standing is considerably larger than the original, and has been rebuilt or repaired many times. The main features are the now restored yellow-tiled tower gate, a victim of the excesses of the Cultural Revolution, and the large 16,800-sq-m courtyard, said to be capable of holding 20,000 worshippers. Visitors are welcomed if respectfully dressed (arms, legs and women's heads covered), and the quiet atmosphere in the shady courtyard is well worth the fee.

The main **Idkah Square** outside the mosque, and the surrounding street markets, are really interesting (not least the fabulous shots taken by the portrait photographers around the clocktower). Check out the card schools, pigeon swaps or the old bearded men hanging about. The barbers' chairs near the mosque draw photographers.

With the exception of the livestock market, a mini version of the Sunday Market seems to occur every day within the old city area. To the east of Idkah Square lies the **old city**, a narrow labyrinth of mud-brick houses, shops and mosques built on an Islamic city design of enclosed courtyards, tight passages and numerous cul-de-sacs. On the edge of this old town lie the bazaars, selling all manner of products. The hats, knives and handicrafts are probably a better bargain here than at the Sunday Market.

One of the best ways to pass time in Kashgar is to visit the various parks and watch the Uiygurs and Chinese at leisure. The central **People's Park** ⓘ *¥2, maybe the best value ¥2 that you spend during your stay in Kashgar*, is a large shady area full of picnicking families, youths shooting pool (don't play them – they cheat like mad!), modest courting couples sharing a blanket in secluded spots, old men drinking beer and gambling away the house-keeping at cards, plus a number of amusement park-style rides and stalls. The plaza at the entrance to the park, opposite the giant **Mao statue**, is a popular place in the evenings, especially when the colourfully lit fountains are playing. Less appealing is the cruel and depressing **zoo** ⓘ *in the southeast corner of the park, ¥2*, the place to come and see the locals taunting, spitting and throwing things at miserable creatures in tiny, filthy cages. The latest addition is a lion, housed in a cage no bigger than 2 m by 1 m, while the Himalayan brown bear has been pacing the same cage since 1990 at least.

Built during the Song Dynasty circa 1130, the **Tomb of Yusup Khass Hajib** ⓘ *Daily 0930-2000, ¥10, camera fee ¥2*, was superbly rebuilt and restored in 1993. An 11th-century Uiygur poet and philosopher, Yusup Khass Hajib was the author of what is considered to be the most important Uiygur text ever produced, *The Wisdom of Royal Glory*. He was born near to the Central Asian city of Tokhmakh in 1019, but later moved to study at the Royal Islamic College in Kashgar. He wrote his 13,290-line didactic lyric epic in 18 months in 1069-70 and presented his work to the Great Khan of the East Karakhanid Dynasty. He was rewarded with the title of 'Khass Hajib', or Privy Chamberlain (King's adviser). A political, economic and cultural history of the Karakhanid Dynasty, the original manuscript of *The Wisdom of Royal Glory* has never been found, although three ancient copies survive in Vienna, Cairo and Namangan, in the Fergana Valley. Yusup Khass Hajib died in 1085 and was buried in Kashgar, but when the tomb was destroyed by a natural disaster he was reburied at the present site.

The shrine is entered through the large tiled north gate. The main façade of the tomb features superb blue and white tile work, and is topped by a tall, blue-tiled dome. The restoration work really is first rate. Inside the chamber, the sarcophagus stands on a large plinth. The walls are engraved with fine calligraphy and excerpts from the Qu'ran in Arabic, Chinese and romanicized Uiygur. In the surrounding cloistered courtyard is a small exhibition on the life and work of Yusup Khass Hajib.

East of the centre

Without any doubt Kashgar's prime attraction is the weekly **Sunday Market**, and the city seems to fill with tourists in the days leading up to the event, and empty shortly afterwards. No doubt some will claim that the market is too touristy, but the sheer scale of it, particularly the livestock market, is still able to accommodate the large number of visitors. **NB** The volume of tourists is far lower outside the May-December period when the Khunjerab Pass route to Pakistan is open. Alternatively, you could visit one of the weekly markets in the less visited southern Silk Route towns (Khotan, Yarkhand etc).

The main market grounds are within a walled area to the east of the old town, but on a Sunday the entire surrounding area is one enormous donkey-cart and pedestrian traffic jam. Along a side road, just to the west of the main market, is the most fascinating part of the whole spectacle – the livestock enclosure. Throughout the morning, from 0600 onwards, it slowly fills with sheep, goats, donkeys, horses, bullocks, cows, buyers, sellers, hangers-on, sightseers and tourists, until there's no more open space bar the run where men test-drive the animals. It truly is a photographer's dream, with some fascinating faces and a superb collection of old bearded men. The livestock deals are so important, and the negotiators so intent upon their bargaining, that they hardly seem to register the presence of hugely expensive Japanese photographic technology on display.

> ❗ Beware of pickpockets. Food served at the Sunday Market always looks a bit dodgy, and there is little on offer for vegetarians.

The main enclosed market grounds contain an astonishing array of goods, from avenues of brightly and elaborately coloured cloth, through fruit and veg, to electrical goods. There are also traditional Uiygur handicrafts, such as elaborately carved knifes and daggers, as well as numerous types of hats. The area behind the main market, outside the walls, is where the poorer dealers trade, some of whose stock merely comprises several odd shoes; it's quite depressing.

It's best to arrive at the market as early as possible (before most of the tour groups), so you can watch it gradually filling up. Shared rickshaw taxis can be hired from outside the main hotels (about ¥5 per person from the **Seman**), and bicycles are not recommended. **John's Café** sometimes arranges a free shuttle bus.

Probably dating to the 18th century, although some sources place it earlier, the beautiful **Tomb of Abakh Hoja** ⓘ *to the east of the town, several km beyond the Sunday Market grounds, best reached on a pleasant bicycle journey around 45 mins from the Seman Hotel, ¥15,* shows a distinct Persian influence in its use of green and blue tile work on its façade and dome. Although there are some 70 graves in the main domed chamber, the tomb is named after a local Uiygur aristocrat, Abakh Hoja, sometimes referred to as the patron saint of Kashgar.

The tomb is also claimed to be the burial place of Abakh Hoja's granddaughter, popularly known as Xiangfei, or Fragrant Consort. Legend suggests that she was the leader of a failed Uiygur uprising in 1759 and was subsequently carried off to the imperial court of the Qing Emperor, Qian Long, to be a concubine. The Emperor is said to have become so besotted by his new acquisition that his mother, fearing the growing influence of Xiangfei, ordered her to commit suicide. The large Muslim graveyard located behind the tomb is particularly attractive during the late afternoon, although the main tomb may be closed by then.

The park around the **East Lake** to the east of the city centre is popular at weekends.

Ha Noi and Mor Pagoda

The insubstantial remains of this Tang dynasty town (seventh-11th century) lie some 35 km northeast of Kashgar, and are usually reached as part of an organized tour (usually around ¥150 for a vehicle seating four). The remains are barely worth the effort of getting here, and if you're going to Urumqi by train the line actually passes within 200 m of the site (east – right – side of the train).

San Xian (Three Immortals) Caves

The three caves here, 20 km north of Kashgar, feature the rapidly deteriorating remains of a number of Buddhist frescoes. They are usually reached as part of an organized tour (around ¥60 for a vehicle seating four).

Travelling on from Kashgar

Towards Urumqi

In many regards, all roads (and rail lines) lead to Urumqi (see Transport, page 354). An alternative to the usual route from Kashgar to Urumqi is to travel via an old branch of the Silk Road that passes along the south side of the Takla Makan Desert. First stop is **Yecheng** (270 km, also jumping-off point for Tibet), although it is possible to get a bus from Kashgar all the way to **Khotan** (Hetian, 12 hours). The latter also has an engaging Sunday market and is a local centre for the carpet-making industry. Both towns have pretty basic hotels and restaurants. From Khotan you can take the bus to **Mingfen** (Niya), from where a new road runs across the heart of the **Takla Makan Desert** to **Korla**. From here you can continue to **Urumqi** or **Turufan** (Turpan).

Kyrghizstan

What appears on paper (and on maps) to be a simple crossing from China into Kyrghizstan (or vice-versa) is complicated by the fact that the crossing point, the **Tourgat Pass** (3,572 m) lies within a closed military area on either side of the border. There is a bus service between Kashgar (China) and Naryn (US$25) and Bishkek (US$50) on the Kyrghiz side, but only locals can use it.

Note that you will require a visa whichever direction you are coming from; Chinese visas are definitely not issued on the border, although a Kyrghiz one may be if you offer a big enough bribe (but the Chinese may not let you proceed without a Kyrghiz visa, and will not let you back in if the Kyrghiz turn you away). The Chinese will not let you in if you don't have the relevant travel documents to pass through the restricted zone. See page 356 for details on obtaining permits.

The road to the pass from Kashgar (160 km, six hours) is pretty poor, although it is being improved. Chinese formalities are completed at Topa, 60 km south of the pass, and the pass is only open until 1300. You cannot walk across the pass, so if you haven't hired your own transport, you will be quoted outrageous prices for the ride across to the Kyrghiz side (there may be a shuttle bus). From the Kyrghiz side, where extravagant attempts will be made to garner bribes from you by the customs and immigration officials, you can hire a taxi to Naryan for about US$15, and then take a public bus to Bishkek for US$5. ▶▶ *See also Transport page 351.*

Tibet

The journey from Kashgar into Tibet is one of the most difficult, but spectacular, trips for any traveller.. The problem with this route is that it travels via China's Western Military Road across the Aksai Chin, the ownership of which is disputed between China and India. This whole region is often declared 'closed' to foreigners, although at other times those usually hard-to-obtain travel permits are issued freely. In fact, just before this guide went to press, an increase in the severity and frequency of fines levied on truck drivers carrying foreigners eastwards from Ali meant that either few were prepared to risk taking passengers, or the price had now become prohibitive: this is not an easy route to attempt. Yet the starting of a sleeper bus service between Ali and Lhasa (with tickets being sold to foreigners) would suggest that this trip is becoming more accessible. Further information on cycling this trip can be found at www.pedalglobal.net. ▶▶ *For detailed information on Tibet, consult Footprint Tibet.*

● Sleeping

Kashgar *p345, map p347*
For notes on sleeping, see box, p337.

International, 144 Seman Rd, T0998-2833235. Large carpeted doubles with attached bath, TV, some with fridge and a/c are ¥240 (but inspect room first).

New Yield Fast Foreign Executive Centre, Seman Rd, T0998-2837388, F0998-2831859. Large, well-furnished rooms, with TV, phone, small but modern bathrooms, ¥350 and ¥280, some de luxe rooms for ¥680 and huge suites for ¥1,280, plush, attentive restaurant, massage room, keen staff, although not much English spoken.

Qian Hai Hotel, 199 Renmin Xi Zu, T0998-2822584, F0998-2820644. Large hotel with central a/c aimed at the party cadres, standard doubles from ¥240 and suites for ¥460, set back from road, restaurant, not much English spoken.

Qiniwake/Chini Bagh, 144 Seman Rd, T0998-2842299, F0998-2823842. On the site of the former British consulate, this hotel is currently undergoing a major renovation. Currently, there are 3- and 4-bed dorms on the upper storeys (¥40 and ¥35 per bed sometimes half those prices) with bare floors and fairly basic bathrooms. Lower floors in the new block have some large suites (¥580), doubles (¥300) and singles (¥260). The 'old' block has slightly more basic rooms, but at a cheaper price (suites ¥480, doubles ¥260, singles ¥140). There are several restaurants in the grounds, plus an office offering phone calls, fax, internet (¥10 per hr).

Renmin/People's, Renmin Dong Lu, T0998-2823373. Now seems to accept foreigners, small doubles for ¥168, larger doubles for ¥268-288, plus suites for ¥680, but all overpriced.

Seman, Seman Rd, T0998-2822147, F0998-2822861. This huge hotel is where most visitors to Kashgar stay. Divided into various blocks according to price. In the main block you pay ¥15 for a sagging bed in the dorms; some have 3 beds and others 10. Linen is not necessarily changed between visitors. Slimy shared toilets and showers on each floor with hot water in the mornings and evenings. Be careful with valuables. You pay a ¥50 deposit upon arrival plus another ¥20 for the dorm padlock key deposit, and settle your bill on departure. The main block also has doubles sharing the same bathrooms for ¥60, and doubles with bath and TV for ¥150. Block 'A' is for tour groups, with carpeted doubles (¥280) and de luxe rooms (¥388). Block '1' is part of the old Russian Consulate, and has luxury suites with antique furniture, TV, phone, fridge and bath for ¥466 and ¥588. The rather expensive Seman Restaurant is aimed primarily at tour groups. The hotel offers foreign exchange, a travel service, shops, overpriced fax, telephone and email services, and a recently opened nightclub.

Seman Hotel No3, Seman Rd, above John's Café, T0998-2825969. This is probably the best bet for those after a budget private room. Reasonable doubles with attached bath and ancient TV cost ¥80, but this hotel is often full. NB It's run separately from the Seman Hotel across the road.

Tuman River, Jeifang Bei Lu, T0998-2822912, F0998-2822952. Convenient for the international bus station (though little else), doubles with smelly attached bathrooms for ¥280 and ¥160 (overpriced), some clean 3-bed dorms (¥30 per person) with shared bathroom, plus more basic 4-bed dorms with not very private shared toilets (no doors).

● Eating

Kashgar *p345, map p347*
For notes on eating, see box, p337.
There are plenty of places serving authentic **Chinese food** scattered across the city, although few will have menus in English (or even understand English), so it is generally a matter of going into the kitchen and pointing at what you want. Make sure the price is clearly established. There are any number of upmarket Chinese restaurants along the fashionable Renmin Xi Lu,

---

● *Prices categories for restaurants in China are* ¶¶¶ *¥20 and over;* ¶¶ *¥10-20;*
● ¶ *¥10 and under.*

although most have prices to match. Cheaper dining halls can be found at many of the hotels, eg **Tian Nan** and **Chini Bagh**. The night market on Yunmulakxia Rd is another place to experience Chinese food.

Kashgar is not unlike a much scaled-down version of Kathmandu or Bangkok, with restaurants offering sanitized versions of local dishes, plus those good old traveller favourites such as banana pancakes, fruit salad and yogurt, muesli etc. Most of these places are clustered around the **Seman Hotel**. Note that some of these places have several different menus (they're colour coded), with tour group ordering from à la carte with the marginally higher prices.

The night markets around Idkah Square or along Yunmulakxia Rd are the best places to try Uiygur dishes, and are as interesting for their atmosphere as their food. Make sure any dishes that you order are freshly cooked and served hot. The dining halls at the **Seman** and **Chini Bagh** hotels provide a good introduction to Uiygur food. Fresh fruit and vegetables are sold each evening at the informal market on Yunmulakxia Rd.

Caravan Café, outside Qiniwake/Chini Bagh hotel. Excellent new place (open 0900-2400, closed Wed) offering range of coffees (espresso/latte ¥15-18), pizzas ¥20, sandwiches ¥12, plus cakes and pies ¥2-18, a little expensive but very good quality.

John's Café, Seman Rd, T0998-2551186. Similar menu to other places nearby, main meat dishes ¥22 (steak etc), main Chinese dishes ¥12-20, Kashgar pizza ¥12, fruit yogurt ¥5, coffee ¥6, beer ¥4, rather slow service.

Kashgar Café/Bar of Wein, in the grounds of the Seman Hotel. Welcomes foreigners and is arguably the best of all these places. Main meat and chicken dishes ¥12-15, fruit salad and yogurt ¥5, noodle dishes ¥5-8, beer ¥4, etc. The lady who runs this place, Fen, is the beauty referred to in anecdotes that fill the hotel rumour books the length of the KKH.

Oasis Café, opposite the Seman Hotel. Offers an almost identical menu at fairly similar prices.

Old City, next to the Overseas Chinese Hotel. Good place to try reasonably priced Uiygur food (¥7-15 per plate), although little English is spoken so you'll have to go into the kitchen and point.

● Entertainment

Kashgar *p345, map p347*
Cultural shows
If there is a big tour group staying, there is often a Uiygur cultural show at the Seman Hotel; ask at reception for details.

Nightclubs
There are plenty of nightclubs in Kashgar, although you should be wary of hidden cover charges or expensive drinks. Note that many of the places in and around Seman Rd that masquerade as nightclubs/bars are actually brothels. For example, the place at 313 Xiamolibag Rd (red sign with image of waitress carrying drinks).

Qi Par Discobar, 314 Xiamolibag Rd. If you're lucky, you may have a fantastic night out here. ¥10 entrance fee includes first drink (beer subsequently ¥8), features a sunken pit with sprung dance floor (!), and if you're lucky the DJ will do his solo Michael Jackson routine. Best nights are at the weekend, when there may even be a Uiygur dancing floor show. Crowd is a Chinese-Uiygur mix, and the music Chinese rave. Magic.

Sports
Bowling alley behind the Tuman River Hotel.

● Shopping

Kashgar *p345, map p347*
Clothing
Renmin Xi Lu Upwardly mobile young Chinese women shop for latest fashions in this 'trendy' place.

Chinese army surplus is available from a store close to the PSB on Yunmulakxia Rd (although large sizes are hard to find). The spectacularly colourful cloth bazaars are located on the arcade running north from the post office.

Department stores
Although it's unlikely that you'll actually find anything worth buying (apart from perhaps a few toiletries), strolling around Kashgar's department stores is a great way to while away the hours. Unattractive products displayed in unappealing ways, sold by poorly motivated sales staff.

Handicrafts

The stalls around Idkah Square (notably Dstang Boye Rd, which leads off the square to the south of the mosque) are the places to hunt down souvenirs of your visit to Kashgar, but be prepared for some hard bargaining. Hats, knives and brassware are the most popular choices, with a few places selling miniature and full-size musical instruments. Ordaishki Rd, leading off from the square to the northeast, is also a good place for hats and knives. Note that many countries ban the import of fur products, from which many of the hats are made. Prices are probably better here than at the Sunday Market. Carpets are probably best seen at the business park next to the Sunday Market grounds. Gold and jewellery are best displayed in the arcade running north from Idkah Square.

Photography

The best place to buy film, batteries and camera gear is the Konica shop just east of Renmin/People's Hotel on Renmin Square. It has Fuji Sensia slide film for ¥65, colour print film for ¥19-25, most batteries, plus some fairly current photographic equipment.

▲ Activities and tours

Kashgar *p345, map p347*

Caravan Café, outside Qiniwake/Chini Bagh Hotel, T0998-2841864, F0998-2842196, caravan_cafe@yahoo.com. Efficiently run, the company (Asian Explorations) arranges permits and transport for the Tourgat Pass (see p351), transport as far as Sust (¥2,900 for up to 5 passengers in a landcruiser, there in 1 day), overnight trips to Kara Kuli (¥1,200 for vehicle hire), plus trips to Takla Makan Desert (itineraries on request) and transport to Ali (¥18,500 by landcruiser).

China International Travel Service (CITS), Qiniwake Hotel, 144 Seman Rd, T/F0998-2828473. Government-run agency can arrange most things (air/train tickets, tours, various permits), but at a price. Full-day city tour (including all meals, guide and vehicle, but not entrance fees) from ¥370 per person (minimum 2, discounts for larger groups); 1-day return trip to Kara Kuli ¥1,000 (landcruiser seats 4); Takla Makan Desert tours from ¥400 per person per day; Tourgat Pass permits (see p351). Open daily 1000-1330, 1600-2000, good English spoken.

China Xinjiang Kashgar Mountaineering Association, 45 Tiyu Lu (Sport's Rd), off Jiefang Nan Lu, T0998-2523660, F0998-2522957, www.ksalpine.com. Advice on climbing and trekking in the region (notably Muztagh Ata), plus help with permits etc.

John's Café and Information Service, Seman Rd, T0998-2551186. John Hu has a string of cafés/travel agencies (Kashgar, Turpan, Urumqi), dispensing free advice as well as arranging air/bus/train tickets for a small commission. He can also arrange tours, transport and permits. The success of the operation, however, depends upon whether you actually get to speak to John himself (or his wife), or one of his less efficient managers.

● Transport

Kashgar *p345, map p347*

Air

Xinjiang Airlines/CAAC have 1-3 daily flights to Urumqi, depending upon demand (usually mornings and evenings). Fare is ¥980 plus ¥50 tax. Book as far in advance as you can.

Airline offices **China Xinjiang Airlines**, T0998-2826188, has a non English-speaking counter just inside the Renmin Hotel. **CAAC**, Jiefang Nan Lu, T0998-2822113. Open Mon- Sat 1000-1300, 1630-1930, Sun 1100-1300, very inefficient office (try John's Café).

Bicycles

Can be hired from outside the Qiniwake/Chini Bagh Hotel (¥20 per day, ¥100 deposit, check condition of bike and lock). **John's Café and Information Service**, Seman Rd, also rents out bikes. Don't cycle to the Sunday Market (it's just too crowded). Those looking to buy a bicycle (and perhaps ride it back to Pakistan) should try the shops on Jeifang Bei Lu, between Idkah Square and the intersection with Seman Rd (eg no. 228); the best 18-speed Chinese-made mountain bike costs around ¥500.

Buses

Local Bus 28 is probably of most use to visitors, running from Idkah Square to the train station (¥1.50). Bus 7 runs to the Sunday Market grounds (but gets very crowded). Bus 9 runs along Seman Rd and up past the international bus station.

Long distance There are 3 main bus stations in Kashgar. Of most interest to foreigners (for Pakistan, Tashkurgan, Kara Kuli and Urumqi) is the **new international bus station** on Jeifang Bei Lu. Many other services still run from the **old long-distance bus station** on Tianan Rd, although foreigners may experience some frustration buying tickets there. The small **bus stand** near to the People's Park is for buses in and around Kashgar. Check whether the departure time you are given is Beijing or Xinjiang time; those given below are all Beijing time.

Sust (Pakistan): The through bus to Pakistan (overnighting in Tashkurgan) departs daily from the international bus station at 1200 (¥270, plus ¥2-3 for luggage). Buy your tickets in advance whenever possible (this route is busy immediately after the Sunday Market). Take your passport when you buy the ticket because your details have to be put onto the passenger list. Actually boarding the bus can be chaotic (seat numbers are rarely respected), and it frequently departs hours late since it takes forever to load the Pakistani traders' luggage (including the paying of bribes to customs officials, transport managers and luggage handlers). Safety and comfort are not respected on this route, with the passengers playing second fiddle to freight transportation. The journey should take 5-6 hrs to Tashkurgan (but often takes 7-8), then a similar journey time to Sust the following day. Note that when overnighting in Tashkurgan, you do not have access to luggage loaded onto the bus roof.

Kara Kuli: This is the same bus that is heading for Pakistan. Make sure that you take your luggage inside the bus with you, and check that the driver knows that you want to get off at the lake. Journey time is usually about 5-6 hrs and the fare ¥43 (but few get to pay the correct ¥25 fare when trying to continue their journey from Kara Kuli to Tashkurgan).

Tashkurgan: This is also the Pakistan-bound bus, although if heading across the border it is better to buy a through ticket to Sust, and if you wish to break your journey Kara Kuli is a nicer option. Fare to Tashkurgan is ¥65. In theory, there is also a daily bus to Tashkurgan (via Kara Kuli) from the old long-distance bus station, but foreigners may have difficulty buying a ticket for this service.

Urumqi: There are at least 5 different bus options to Urumqi. Most comfortable is the 36-hr 'sleeper bus', which has semi-reclining beds as opposed to seats. It appears that the special 'foreigner fare' (¥380/440) is no longer being charged on this service, with foreigners only having to pay the standard ¥179 for a 'lower' berth and ¥159 for an 'upper' place. Note that some of the other buses between Kashgar and Urumqi take 3 days, stopping overnight at disgusting hotels in boring towns where you have no access to your luggage. These cheaper services generally leave from the old long-distance bus station. Buy your tickets in advance whenever possible (this route is busy immediately after the Sunday Market).

Other destinations: **Yarkhand** (Shache), **Yecheng** (Kargilik) and **Khotan** (Hotan/Hetian), as well as other spots on both the northern and southern Silk Road are served by daily buses (try the international bus station first; if no luck, go to the old bus station).

Kyrghistan: Although there are buses to Bishkek (US$50) and Naryn (US$25) from the international bus station, tickets are not sold to tourists. See p351 for further details.

Taxis

Less than a decade ago, donkey-cart taxis were seen all over the city but are now just in the old city. These were replaced by George and Mildred-style motorcycle-sidecar combination taxis, although these too are now an endangered breed. Small red taxis are now everywhere (many of which are driven by women). Agree the fare in advance. ¥10 should take you most places.

Train

The line linking Kashgar to **Urumqi** (and the outside world) is now open. The grand train station (worth a visit in itself, probably bigger than Islamabad's airport!) is located some distance to the east of town (¥10-15 by taxi, or take bus 28 from Idkah Square). Buying tickets can be a hassle, so it's an idea to pay a small commission and go through an agency (eg **John's Café**, see under Activities and tours above). There is a morning (about 0900) and a late afternoon (around 1600) train daily for the 24-hr trip to Urumqi (although tickets can be hard to come by for the days immediately following the Sunday Market). Soft sleeper ¥529, hard sleeper ¥345, hard seat ¥180. The train is more comfortable and quicker than the bus, but more expensive.

Kyrghizstan *p351*

Permits and **transport** for crossing the **Tourgat Pass** (in either direction) can be arranged at a number of places in Kashgar (see under tour operators above for contact details).

For example, **Asian Explorations** at the Caravan Café charge the following fees for the 160-km journey from Kashgar to the pass (including all documentation): 1 passenger US$186, 2 passengers US$190, 3 passengers US$225, 4 passengers US$260, 5 passengers US$325, 8 passengers US$60 per head.

Once across the Tourgat Pass, onward transportation is organized through **Edelweiss**, who charge US$235 for 1 passenger (or US$295 for up to 4 passengers) for the 2-day trip to **Bishkek** (or US$100 per vehicle as far as **Naryn**). Since it's cheaper to travel as a group, potential travellers can hook up by leaving messages at places such as John's Café in Kashgar. It may take up to 14 days' notice to organize the permit.

ⓘ Directory

Kashgar *p345, map p347*

Banks Bank of China, Renmin Xi Lu, Mon-Fri 0930-1330, 1600-2000, Sat 1100-1500. Offers efficient foreign exchange for cash and TCs, plus ¥ cash advances on Visa/Diners/Amex/MasterCard at 3% commission (counter 1). Hotel reception at the **Seman** and **Chini Bagh** change cash and TCs at the set bank rate. Uiygur money changers hassle anyone walking past the **Chini Bagh** hotel, but you take an unacceptable risk by changing money in this way.
Hospitals Renmin Yiyuan/People's Hospital, T0998-2822337, to the north of Kashgar (see map). The Uiygur Medical Hospital, 272 Seman Rd, is unappealing. There's a **clinic** at the Seman Hotel.
Internet Internet connections in China are far better than those in Pakistan (especially the Northern Areas), although you may find certain sites (BBC, CNN) blocked, and if there's any negative news about China around, messaging systems such as Hotmail may also be down. **Shining Pearl of Silk Road Net Bar** (!), Renmin Xi Lu (next to China Mobile). 10 fast terminals, daily 1100-2300, ¥8 per hr, probably the best bet. New Century, Seman Rd. ¥6 per hour. John's Café and Information Service, Seman Rd, T0998-2551186. Slow connections, ¥10 per hr. Many of the hotels now have internet facilities, and there are various other places scattered across town. **Post office** 40 Renmin Xi Lu, Mon-Sat 0930-2000, Sun 1000-1930. Upstairs for international mail and poste restante (small fee charged for collecting each item of mail). **Telephones** China Telecom, off Renmin Xi Lu. This is just off the main street (next side street along from 'China Mobile' shop), has 5 not very private booths, daily 1100-2300, ¥8-21 per min for international calls, depending upon destination. John's Café also has international call service with a small mark-up. **Useful addresses** Public Security Bureau ('regional') (PSB) for **visa extensions** is located on Yunmulakxia Rd (efficient, prices according to nationality). This is where 'Alien Travel Permits' are issued (Mon-Fri 0930-1330, 1600-1930). Note that if, for example, the Chinese embassy in Uzbekistan only issued you with a 10-day visa, you may find the PSB here only offering a further 10-day extension. The **PSB** ('city'), where you report crimes, lost passports etc, is on Renmin Dong Lu, opposite Tiannan Rd.

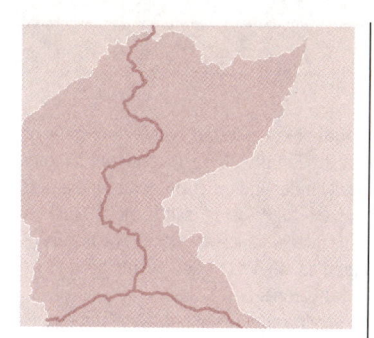

History	358
Culture	368
Land and environment	374
Books	378

Background

History

The majority of places described in this handbook are found within the state of Pakistan, a nation born out of the partition of the South Asian subcontinent in 1947 when the British transferred power to the newly independent countries of India and Pakistan. And although the modern Islamic Republic of Pakistan is little more than half a century old, the land and people certainly have far more ancient origins. The history of this region is complicated and has been shaped as often as not by events beyond its borders, in Central Asia, China, Persia, India and Europe.

Numerous empires have operated within varying spheres of influence across this region, with contemporary empires frequently being unaware of each other's presence; hardly surprising when much of the terrain covered by this handbook comprises a dense complex knot of mountains, glaciers and valleys unlike any other found elsewhere on the planet. Yet well developed communications routes link many of these geographically remote regions, and interactions (whether it be war, commerce, shared religion) have drawn often culturally disparate groups into a common history.

This section aims to provide a brief overview of the region's past: more specific regional histories can be found in the travelling text of the major regions covered. The books section (page 378) can also point you in the direction of some suitable background material, both 'academic' and 'readable'. *Footprint Pakistan* also has an extensive historical overview.

Prehistory

Settlement

The prehistory period in Northern Pakistan is poorly documented (largely through lack of research), although there is evidence of the cave dwelling 'Rock Art People' (Dani, 1991) subsequently being replaced by the so-called 'megalith builders'. Although the latter practised a productive system of terraced-field agriculture irrigated by glacier melt, the nature of the terrain meant that no great expansive civilizations were established, as the adoption of settled agriculture had led to elsewhere on the subcontinent. Thus, great societies, such as the **Indus Valley Civilization** (peak 2500 BC, in terminal decline by 1750 BC), based upon the spread of settled agriculture and so important in the history of South Asia, had little impact on the lands covered here.

Aryan arrival

The arrival of invaders from the northwest of what is now Pakistan around 1700 BC had a major impact on the future history of the subcontinent. The origins of the **Aryan** invaders are not precisely known, although it is clear that they did not belong to one single ethnic group. However, by 1500 BC the Indo-Aryan language had begun to develop and although the centre of population shifted east from the banks of the Indus to the land between the Ganges and Yamuna (in what is now modern day India), the Aryans left their mark upon the landscape and culture of the more southerly parts covered in this guide (eg in the Peshawar Valley), laying the foundations of what would ultimately become Hinduism. The situation in the mountainous northern areas through which the Karakoram Highway now snakes is less clear, although suffice to say that any empires and dynasties established were extremely local in nature, generally confined to the particular valley in which they were established.

Early history

Ancient empires

In the period that followed the Aryan colonization of large parts of South Asia, a number of empires and dynasties with varying spheres of influence became established in the region of modern Pakistan. The Persian Empire of the **Archaemenians**, for example, established itself in the Indus basin, with **Taxila** evolving as a great cultural centre; the empire's tentacles may even have reached as far north as Gilgit.

However, when **Alexander the Great** marched his army through Bactria and into modern-day North West Frontier Province in 326 BC, he rapidly subjugated the territories that were within the Archaemenian Empire. The furthest north he marched along what is now the Karakoram Highway was Aornos (variously identified with Thakot and Buner), although this doesn't stop the people of Hunza and Nagar claiming descent from five soldiers of one of Alexander's generals. In reality, with the exception of the Hellenistic influence in the distinctive style of Graeco-Indian art (later termed Gandharan), Alexander's brief stay in the region made little impact, with the vassals that he placed on their thrones in the lands he conquered being swiftly defeated and replaced by other dynasties shortly after his departure. Indeed, this Hellenistic influence is often traced to the Bactrian Greeks who arrived over a century later. Still, Alexander the Great is an evocative name, and the Hunza-Nagar geneology an amusing tale.

Following Alexander's departure, **Chandragupta Maurya** established the first indigenous empire to control most of the South Asian subcontinent (c. 310 BC) with the **Mauryan** Empire reaching its zenith in the third century BC under one of South Asia's greatest kings, **Asoka**. Yet the horrors of war witnessed by Asoka in creating this vast empire left a lasting impression upon him and, although it is still unclear whether he embraced Buddhism fully, he certainly adopted many of its pacifist doctrines. He left a series of edicts in the form of inscriptions on rocks and pillars right across the subcontinent (some of which can be seen at Mansehra, see page 170). Yet within 50 years of Asoka's death in 232 BC, the entire Mauryan Empire had disintegrated.

Around this time in China, the **Han Dynasty** (206 BC- AD 220) was establishing a series a trade routes radiating from its capital at Chang'an (X'ian). The most famous of these led west, skirting the Takla Makan Desert to Kashgar, from where routes run further west into Central Asia and Iran (eventually reaching the eastern Mediterranean), or south through the remote mountain passes into Kashmir and Ladakh. In the years to come, and in tourist brochures ever since, these various strands became known collectively as the **Silk Road** (or 'Silk Route'); at the time, they provided a means of exchanging ideas as well as goods, with the added advantage of providing a living for the various regions' bandit population.

> There are several excellent books on this period listed on page 378.

In the northwest margins of the subcontinent, a series of invaders from the northwest attempted to exert their hegemony over the region. After the **Bactrian Greeks**, the **Sakkas** (or **Scythians**) arrived in the region in the first century BC, according to the *Wei-lio* (written history of the Chinese Wei Dynasty) via the Boroghil Pass and Yasin Valley. Indeed, Kharoshthi inscriptions and rock carvings at Chilas depict the surrender of the local king to 'Moga', ie Maues the Scythian ruler. This empire was itself replaced some time in the first century AD by that of the **Parthians** (they of the 'parting shot'), with details of their rule in the region also being gleaned from rock carvings (notably Gondophares Rock at Chilas). Dani (1991) also notes a distinct change in the rock art style of the Parthians, with the lean towards Iranian features suggesting that this empire "was responsible in interlinking Northern Areas of Pakistan with the western world".

The Parthians were in turn usurped by the **Kushans**, a group who themselves had been forced southwards by the continued expansion of the Chinese Han Dynasty. The Kushans controlled a large empire across much of Central Asia, Afghanistan and the upper reaches of the Indus and Ganges valleys for almost a century. At the northern margins of the Kushan empire, professional studies have drawn attention to a marked shift in the geographical distribution of rock art between the Scytho-Parthian eras and the period of Kushan rule, suggesting a shift in the centre of activity from the Chilas area towards Gilgit and Hunza (eg Alam Bridge petroglyphs, see page 234, and the Sacred Rocks of Hunza, see page 297). Their conclusion is that the Indus basin area around Chilas became uninhabitable for most of the Kushan era, perhaps linking the change in river level with the catastrophic earthquake that struck Taxila in AD 30. Under the patronage of the Kushans' great Buddhist ruler **Kanishka** (around AD 120, although this date is strongly contested), a famous art and cultural school referred to as **Gandharan** flourished in the Vale of Peshawar and the surrounding valleys. Peshawar became the king's new winter capital and a third city was established at Taxila. It was from the Peshawar Valley, and via the routes north now described in this guide, that Buddhism spread into Central Asia and China, passing along the now well-established Silk Road.

The decline of the Kushan Empire was precipitated by the **Sassanian** invasion (c. AD 224), their route via the trans-Pamir region being responsible for the *Sogdian* and *Bactrian cursive* styles of rock inscriptions that are found today. The nature of these inscriptions (by pilgrims, travellers and businessmen) suggest close links between China and Central Asia through this region. Indeed, it is remarkable just how much rock art can tell us about the history of the region. Calling cards in the form of rock inscriptions point towards the growing phenomenon of Chinese Buddhist pilgrims penetrating the lands covered by this guide, on their way to Gandhara and India in search of knowledge and manuscripts. Perhaps the best known of these was **Fa Hsien**, who left us with a graphic account of his epic journey through this region (c. AD 399-414). Furthermore, the appearance of *Gupta Brahmi* inscriptions in the fifth century AD suggest that Indian influences were gradually pushing their way north, in time leading to the establishment of *Brahmi* as the system of writing and *Sanskrit* as the medium of literary communication. Meanwhile, the appearance of contemporary Gandharan art (eg at Chilas and Thalpan) suggests the resurgence of Buddhism in the region.

The arrival of a diverse group (of indeterminable origin) known as the **Huns** (or 'Hunas') in the fifth century AD spelt the end of Sassanian rule, and also precipitated the demise of Taxila. They established their capital at Peshawar, although their tentacles spread as far as the Kabul Valley and much of the upper Indus Valley, with the image of their warriors on horseback adorning many of the major petroglyph sites in the Northern Areas and beyond (Indus Kohistan, Shatial, Chilas, Gilgit, Hunza, Baltistan, plus Tibet and Ladakh). The Huns are credited with introducing a new socio-economic pattern to the region, with the majority share of land and produce placed within the hands of the *raja*, or holder of local authority. In the context of the Northern Areas, it was at this period that the various linguistic groups (eg Burashaski, Shina) established themselves in their particular regions, coninciding with the evolution of distinct ethnic groups (eg the Shin) that tend to be defined predominantly by language. The fifth century AD also sees reference to a distinct area known as Po-lu-lu or Great Bolor, ie **Baltistan**. Indeed, the *raja* system soon led to the development of numerous semi-independent kingdoms, notably in Baltistan, Gilgit, Chilas and Hunza.

Further information on some of the lands covered by this guide can be gleaned from the writings of another intrepid Chinese Buddhist traveller, **Xuanzang** (Hiuen Tsiang), who passed this way between AD 629 and 645. Another contemporary event of significance was the life of the **Prophet Mohammed** (AD 570-632) in far away Arabia.

Medieval history

More empire building

Professor Dani identified four key developments that brought about the medieval period in the region's general history: i) the movement of the **'Turks'** from the north; ii) the rise of the **T'ang Dynasty** in China (AD 618-907, during which time the Silk Road was arguably at its peak); iii) the penetration of the **Arabs** into Central Asia and the Pamir region; and iv) the **Tibetan** advance through Ladakh, Baltistan, Gilgit and Yasin into Wakhan. The latter is of particular significance, leading to military alliances between the T'angs and the various tribal leaders in regions through which the Tibetans were advancing. The Tibetans were eventually defeated by the Chinese in AD 750, who were in turn defeated by the Arabs the following year. Other powers battling for supremacy in the region included the Kashmiris, the Buddhist **Shahi** rulers of Gilgit and the resurgent Turks. The upshot of all this jockeying for supremacy, at least in the context of the Northern Areas, was the weakening of Chinese power at its western margins, a consolidation of Islamic power in Central Asia (but unable to advance due to the change in the power structure of the Khilafat), Tibetan advance stalled in Baltistan, and the bid for power in the Gilgit region of the non-Muslim 'Turks' so recently dispossesed in the trans-Pamir region. It is generally believed that it is from this latter source that the **Trakhan Dynasty**, which ruled Gilgit through eight distinct dynasties, evolved.

If truth be told, the medieval period for many of the regions covered by this guide is not well documented, in what is now the Northern Areas of Pakistan at least. Part of the problem is that the period relies heavily on the oral tradition, in addition to the difficulty in deciphering the interconnecting dynasties where marriages of alliance compete with patricide and fraternicide in determining succession.

The **first period of the Trakhan Dynasty** (c. AD 643-977) ruled the Gilgit region at the start of the medieval period, while the **Makpons** held sway in Baltistan. It was during this period that **Islam** first begun to penetrate the region. Although Mohammed bin Qasim, on behalf of the Umayyads, had conquered much of Sind and Punjab in AD 711, his mission had not been one of evangelism (although undoubtedly converts were made). Likewise, the arrival of Sayyid Shah Afzal into the Gilgit region from Badakhshan c. AD 725 may have led to the ruling family embracing Islam, but there were no wide-scale popular conversions. In fact, this did not occur until the 11th century AD, when **Mahmud of Ghazni**, ruler of the **Ghaznavid Empire** (977-1186) centred on modern-day Afghanistan, made regular raids on the Punjab between 1000 and 1026. Although his initial motif was plunder (to finance his extensive central Asian empire), he was also a great patron of the arts and learning, and in the wake of the invading armies came many Islamic scholars, notably from the *Sufi* order. Meanwhile, the demise of the T'ang Dynasty in China (c. AD 907) marked the passing of the peak of importance of the Silk Road, while the emergence of the **Qarakhan Dynasty** (999-1211) in the Tarim Basin saw the dawning of Islam there.

The successor to the Ghaznazid Empire was the **Delhi Sultanate** (c. 1192-1526), which held sway over a vast tract of North India, from Afghanistan to Bengal, while to the north the **second period of the Trakhan Dynasty** (977-1241) was emerging. Again, this period is marked by more successional disputes, and bids for independence by an assortment of princes set up in their own regional power base, and the emergence of the **Raisia Dynasty** in Chitral that was to hold sway there for some 300 years.

This period also saw the emergence in Central Asia of the **Mongols**, led for a period by the legendary **Genghis Khan** (c. 1206-27). Ironically, following his capture of Kashgar in 1219, such was the fear generated by the 'Horde' that relative stability was brought to the region, allowing the Silk Road a new lease of life. However, the plundering raids of Genghis Khan through Central Asia all but cut the Delhi Sultanate off from its cultural, religious and political heritage. As a result, Islam itself underwent major modifications in response to its new social and religious environment, accounting partly for the distinctive form of Islam found in South Asia today.

Likewise, the repeated invasion of the Gilgit and Kashmir regions meant that new alliances and bonds were being formed, particularly in response to the 1326 invasion, and this is one of the key features of the **third period of the Trakhan Dynasty** in Gilgit (1241-1449). This era is also notable for the emergence of the ruling **Maglot** family in **Nagar** (c. 1440) and **Ayash** family in **Hunza** (slightly later).

The Delhi Sultanate suffered a major blow when Delhi was sacked by **Timur** (Tamerlane) in 1398, although things seemed rosier in the north, where the **fourth period of the Trakhan Dynasty** (1449-1561) saw a further closening of ties between Gilgit and Kashmir, plus a measure of cooperation between the various branches of the same family now ruling Gilgit, Hunza, Nagar, Punial, Yasin and Chitral. Of course, it was only a matter of time before the various queens and princes of the smaller vassal states sought greater independence from the Gilgit throne. It is also suggested that it was during this period that the people of Nagar accepted Islam, through the teachings of Sayyid Burya Wali (a holy man from Isfahan who arrived via Kashmir). Local legend in Baltistan, however, dates the spread of the Shia faith there to 1379, following the teachings of another Persian who had arrived via Iran.

In 1526, following his victory at Panipat over the armies of the last ruler of the Delhi Sultanate, **Babur** ('The Tiger') founded the **Mughal Dynasty**. In less than 100 years, Babur and his successors (**Humayun** and **Akbar**) established an empire ruling the greater part of what is modern-day Pakistan, as well as a huge swathe of modern-day India and Bangladesh, while their successors (**Jahangir**, **Shah Jahan** and **Aurangzeb**) left a lasting impression on the cultural landscape, not least in the form of some of the magnificent Mughal monuments in Lahore, Delhi and Agra. Meantime in the north, Makpon power in Baltistan was at its zenith under **Ali Sher Khan Anchem** (1595-1633). The assorted fathers, sons, brothers, uncles, cousins ruling the various branches of the **fifth period of the Trakhan Dynasty** (1561-1635), in their little fiefdoms of Gilgit in Hunza, Nagar, Punial, Yasin, Chitral, Mastuj etc, were intent upon murdering each other in order to expand their power bases.

Modern history

Sikh rule and the rise of British power

While the **sixth period of the Trakhan Dynasty** (1635-1800) saw a continuation of rivalry among the royal houses for the possession of power in Gilgit, further south the Afghan warlord **Ahmad Shah Durani** had succeeded in usurping Mughal power across much of what is now NWFP and the Punjab, and by 1752 his fiefdom also included Hazara. His defeat at the hands of the **Sikhs** in 1764 heralded the arrival of a new regional power and, following **Ranjit Singh's** victory over the Afghans in 1799, this new force now ruled all of the Punjab and Peshawar Valley. Meanwhile, the Tarim Basin was falling under the control of the **Qing Dynasty** ('**Manchu**') as they took Kashgar in 1755 (eventually creating the new province of **Xinjiang** – 'New Dominions'– in 1878).

Of course the most significant act of the region's early modern history was taking place several thousand kilometres away, in Bengal. Although the **British** had been trading in India for almost two hundred years (the British East India Company received its charter in 1600), it was the defeat of the Mughals by the Company's troops at Plassey in 1757 that really established the British as the new power on the subcontinent. Their subsequent expansion inland from the coast was effectively empire-building dressed in the guise of trade. Nevertheless, it was not until the middle of the 19th century that the British began to exercise any form of control over the northwest area of the subcontinent covered by this guide. The reason for this was

> **❝❞ Thus is verified, wrote a civilian captive who was later rescued, what we were told before leaving Kabul; that Mohammad Akbar would annihilate the whole army except one man, who should reach Jalalabad to tell the tale...**

simple: whereas almost all the previous invasions of South Asia had come through the passes to the west and northwest, the British had come by sea, and most of these ports were some considerable distance from this northwest frontier region. Meantime, true to form, the **seventh period** (1800-1825) and **eighth period** (1825-1840) of the **Trakhan Dynasty** in Gilgit were again marked by continuing internecinal wars (for an account of exactly which uncle killed his brother's cousin's wife's sister's grandson in order to assume the throne, see Dani's 1991 'History of Northern Areas of Pakistan').

British policy in what was to become NWFP was largely a result of their actions in Afghanistan, and their relations with the Sikhs. Afghan pride had been seriously wounded over the loss of Peshawar to the Sikhs, and **Dost Mohammad**, who was on the throne in Kabul, was keen to regain the city. In 1836, **Alexander Burnes** led a mission to Kabul, hoping to gain the allegiance of Dost Mohammad. His task was, however, complicated by the fact that the British were undecided on the question of Peshawar; on the one hand they could hardly afford to antagonize the Sikhs by handing Peshawar back to him, but on the other hand nothing less would satisfy Dost Mohammad. Sir Olaf Caroe said that "It has never been sufficiently stressed that the desire to possess Peshawar ... was the real cause of the First Afghan War."

In the event, Burnes was outmanoeuvred by the Russians, who offered to support Dost if he were to attack the Sikhs. At the same time, Herat to the west (at that time an independent kingdom opposed to Kabul) came under siege from a Persian force supported by the Russians. Burnes's mission had failed and he was forced to return to India. The British opted to install a sympathetic ruler, acceptable to the Sikhs, on the throne of Kabul. In 1838, the **Tripartite Treaty** was signed between the British, Ranjit Singh and **Shah Shuja**, a Durrani and former ruler of Kabul. The British despatched their **Army of the Indus**, invading Afghanistan and installing Shah Shuja on the throne. In 1841 the Afghans got their revenge, killing Shah Shuja and the two British envoys, Burnes and Macnaghten, and triggering a general uprising. The Army of the Indus, still in occupation of Kabul, started its retreat. They were shown no mercy by the Afghans. In what was later described as the worst ever defeat of the British army in Asia, just one man, Dr William Brydon, reached Jalalabad alive. "Thus is verified" wrote a civilian captive who was later rescued, "what we were told before leaving Kabul; that Mohammad Akbar would annihilate the whole army except one man, who should reach Jalalabad to tell the tale." A year later the British returned with a second army to seek revenge in Kabul, before marching "as swiftly as terrain and dignity permitted" back to British India.

In 1819, after a series of campaigns, the Sikh ruler **Ranjit Singh** eventually succeeded in annexing Kashmir. For the next 25 years or so Kashmir was ruled quietly, if oppressively by a Sikh Governor appointed by the court at Lahore. This situation continued until the outbreak of the First Sikh War between the British and the Sikhs in 1845-46. The Dogra Maharaja of the mainly Hindu state of Jammu, **Gulab**

Singh, was a very shrewd ruler, and managed to avoid getting embroiled in the war. Had his great ally Ranjit Singh (d. 1839) been the man fighting the British there is little doubt that Gulab Singh would have entered the war on the Sikh side. Having less respect for Ranjit Singh's successors, however, and having consolidated his own power-base in Jammu, Gulab Singh remained aloof from the conflict. He was a great opportunist though and, at the conclusion of the war, he acted as a mediator between the British and the defeated Sikhs.

In 1846, a treaty was signed in Lahore that handed over all Sikh territory, including Kashmir, to the British. When Gulab Singh offered to pay the Sikh war reparations (a sum in the region of Rs750,000 which he in fact looted from the Sikh treasury), a second treaty was signed at Amritsar one week later. The **Treaty of Amritsar** stated that "The British Government transfers and makes over for ever, in independent possession, to Maharaja Gulab Singh and the heirs male of his body, all the hilly or mountainous country, situated to the eastward of the River Indus and westward of the River Ravi." Thus Jammu and Kashmir came under Hindu Dogra rule. The name 'Jammu and Kashmir' refers to this administrative district assembled by the British that included not only the Muslim-dominated Vale of Kashmir, but the largely Hindu region of Jammu to the south, and Ladakh, the predominantly Buddhist eastern highlands of the great Himalayan axis. It is interesting to note that, in hindsight, the British believed that they had made a gross error in separating Kashmir from the Punjab, for, had it remained part of the Sikh Empire, it would have fallen into British hands following victory in the Second Sikh War in 1849. Britain formally annexed Punjab and NWFP, with the whole region being controlled from Lahore via a system of frontier forts and military roads connecting them. Outside the settled areas, agreements were made with the tribes in an attempt to maintain peaceful relations in return for subsidies and allowances.

While this was happening, the Trakhan Dynasty in Gilgit was coming to an end, as **Gohar Aman**, ruler of Yasin and Mastuj, was taking control of Gilgit. He was driven out of Gilgit in 1842 with Sikh assistance sent from Kashmir, although to the chagrin of the local ruler the Sikh contingent decided to stay (Gulab Singh had already annexed Skardu in 1840). Under the terms of the 1846 Treaty of Amritsar, it was understood that Gilgit and Baltistan were to come under the suzerainty of Gulab Singh. In practice, however, his control over the Northern Areas remained entirely nominal. The various small kingdoms in what is now the Northern Areas feuded repeatedly among themselves, but periodically succeeded in repelling the Dogras and the Sikhs (for example, Gohar Aman recaptured Gilgit in 1852).

When studying the history of the British in India, it has to be said that the turning point was the **Mutiny** in 1857 (or 'War of Independence' depending upon your viewpoint). The Mutiny effected the end of Company rule in India and in 1858 the Government of India Act transferred the empire of the Company to the British Crown. Having now acquired this resource-rich new colony, the British were keen to hang on to it, and the most pressing concern was to secure the vulnerable and ill-defined northwest frontier. Although Sind and Punjab had already been annexed, the unpredictable frontier tribes of modern NWFP and the Northern Areas proved to be a major source of anxiety to the British administration. When they weren't raiding into British territory, they were flirting with Britain's imperial rivals across the frontier (such 'flirtations' were one of the causes of the **Second Anglo-Afghan War**, 1878-1880), and towards the end of the 19th century the British became obsessed with Russian expansion in Central Asia.

The 'Great Game' between the two regional powers followed. In 1877, the first **British Agency** was established in Gilgit, only to be abandoned in 1881 after a major revolt of Kohistani tribes. In 1889, a second British Agency was established, this time with improved road and telegraph links as well as a permanent British military presence. Throughout the 1890s, a tenuous control was maintained. Later the Gilgit

Scouts were established as a well-trained force which could keep internal order and respond to any external aggression. The British also had an eye open over the border, where Russia had opened a consulate in Kashgar (1882). The British were unable to open theirs for a further eight years, no doubt as a punishment for supporting **Yaqub Beg** in his Muslim rebellion in Kashgaria (1867-1877). This era of the 'Great Game' also led to the British annexation of territories such as Hunza and Nagar (1891-1892) and the establishment of the **Durand Line** (1893) that remains today as the international border between Pakistan and Afghanistan. The border cut through the tribal areas of the Pathans. This fact, together with the fear that Britain's *Forward Policy* advocating more direct control of the region would compromise their freedom and independence, prompted them to rise up in a series of revolts in 1897. As many as 70,000 troops were mobilized in seven military operations to put down the rebellion, and eventually, in 1901, **Lord Curzon** established the North West Frontier as a separate province administered from Peshawar. The British never really attempted to rule the province directly. Instead they allowed the small chiefs of the tribal areas to govern themselves under the watchful eye of a Political Agent. Force was continually necessary to maintain the status quo. As late as 1937, 40,000 British troops took part in a series of campaigns that ultimately left the tribes of Waziristan 'masters of their own house'. Other rebellions against British control were also eventually dealt with (eg the **Indus Valley Rising** of 1893 and the **Siege of Chitral** in 1895).

Britain and Russia eventually resolved their 'sphere of influence' dispute following the 1897 and 1907 agreements on Pamir boundaries. Changes were also afoot in China, where revolution in 1911 precipitated the end of the 'dynasty' system. Likewise, the Bolshevik Revolution in Russia (1917) would change the world forever.

Independence and Partition

Within 30 years of the Mutiny, the new western educated elite of Indian society were again articulating a demand for greater political rights and, ultimately, self-government. The main vehicle for these demands was the **Indian National Congress**, formed in 1885. Although founded as a secular organization, the Congress was viewed with suspicion by the educated Muslim elite of north India, who saw it as a tool of Hindu nationalism. The Muslims sensed a threat to their political rights, even their own identity, with the emergence of a democratic system that would give the Hindus of India, with their greater population and in-built natural majority, significant advantages. Thus, the Muslim elite thought it wise to form an organization that could act as a platform for their views and aspirations. In December 1906, the **All-India Muslim League** was founded and seven years later it defined its goal for the first time as self-government for the subcontinent. Although the Secretary of State for India announced in Parliament in 1917 that the British goal in India was the gradual development of self-government institutions within the British Empire, this fell far short of Congress and League expectations. By 1930, the Muslim League's then President, **Dr ('Allama') Mohammad Iqbal**, was articulating a demand for a separate state for South Asia's Muslims (the **'two-nation theory'**).

Given impetus by its charismatic new leader **Mohammad Ali Jinnah**, the Muslim League were able to reject the **Government of India Act**, 1935, as not going far enough down the road to true independence, instead issuing their own **Lahore Resolution** in 1940 (23 March, now 'Pakistan Day') that suggested that "geographically contiguous units are demarcated into regions which should be so constituted, with such territorial readjustments as may be necessary, that the areas in which the Muslims are numerically in the majority as in the Northwestern and Eastern zones of India, should be grouped to constitute 'Independent States' in which the constituent units should be autonomous and sovereign". Some seven years earlier, a Punjabi 'student' at Cambridge, **Chaudhuri Rahmat Ali**, had coined a name for a new Muslim state in South Asia – PAKISTAN. This acronym referred to *P*unjab, *A*fghania, *K*ashmir, *S*ind with the suffix *stan*, Persian for country (although the 'stan' is said by some to stand for Baluchistan). By coincidence, Pakistan also means 'land of the pure'. Across the border in China, an uprising was occurring in Xinjiang (1931-34) as the Tungans (Chinese Muslims) sought greater autonomy. They were defeated by a Soviet-backed warlord who reigned as Governor until pensioned off by the Chinese in 1944. The subsequent semi-independent Republic of East Turkestan (Xinjiang) lasted only until Mao Zedong declared the foundation of the People's Republic of China in 1949.

With Britain virtually bankrupt following the Second World War and a new socialist government in power in London, the writing was on the wall for the British colonial empire in India. By 1947, the gulf between the Hindu and Muslim political leaders over the future of India was as wide as ever, and thus British Prime Minister Atlee declared that power would be transferred to 'responsible Indians' by June 1948 at the latest. **Lord Mountbatten** was appointed Viceroy charged with overseeing the transfer of power and, once both Congress and the Muslim league had voted a resounding 'yes' to partition, the date of transfer of power was brought forward to 14/15 August 1947.

When Independence arrived, many questions remained unanswered. Several key Princely States had still not decided firmly to which country they would accede; the most notable being Kashmir, a situation still unresolved today. The question of the borders, most notably in Punjab and Bengal, was to be resolved by a Boundary Commission headed by the distinguished British barrister, **Sir Cyril Radcliffe**. His main qualification for the job was, according to sources, that he "had never even visited India and expressed no known opinions on its problems." To further complicate a task that was to decide the destiny of millions of Muslims, Hindus and Sikhs, he was given just five weeks to complete the task. When the boundary 'awards' were announced on 17 August 1947, the Punjab and Bengal descended into chaos as millions of Muslims, Hindus and Sikhs fled across the respective borders. It is estimated that between a quarter and one million people died in the massacres that accompanied Partition.

This state was given concrete form by the Radcliffe Commission, which drew the boundary between India and Pakistan according to the distribution of the Muslim and non-Muslim populations. The main variation from that principle was made in the case of Princely States, where, as a result of pressure from Jinnah and the Muslim League, the Princes themselves were allowed to choose which country they would accede to. This caused a number of problems, the most difficult being that of Kashmir. On 14 August 1947, the Dogra **Maharaja of Kashmir** had not decided whether to accede to India or Pakistan, and hoped that Kashmir could remain fully independent.

There are two versions of events in Kashmir at Partition; one supported by Pakistan and the other by India. In fact, indigenous accounts of this period of South Asia's history are generally so skewed in their bias that they are almost unreadable. What actually happened immediately after independence is vehemently contested by India and Pakistan to this day. According to Indian historians, Pathan tribesmen from NWFP, supported and encouraged by Pakistan, invaded Jammu and Kashmir, attempting to annex the state for Pakistan. Those writing from a Pakistani viewpoint suggest that there was an insurgency among the Maharaja's own people, demanding accession to Muslim Pakistan, and the Kashmiris were joined in their struggle by civilian volunteers from across the border. Either way, with the 'rebels' only a few miles from the capital at Srinagar, the Maharaja asked for Indian help, which Lord Mountbatten insisted should only be given if Kashmir first acceded to the Indian Union. Thus, on 25 October 1947, Hari Singh signed an instrument of accession to India, and Indian troops were flown into the state. In the meantime, in Gilgit and Baltistan to the far northwest of the state of Jammu and Kashmir, the local people rebelled against the decision, declared their independence from Kashmir and vowed to join Pakistan (the 'Gilgit Uprising').

The war in Kashmir between India and Pakistan was one of the first major crises to be discussed at the **United Nations**, and remains its longest unresolved dispute. India charged that Pakistan had sent "armed raiders" into the state, and called upon the UN to demand their withdrawal. Pakistan countered that India had used "fraud and violence" to manoeuvre Hari Singh's accession, and demanded that a plebiscite be held under the supervision of the UN in order to settle the dispute. Hostilities between the two countries continued until 30 December 1948 when a UN sponsored **ceasefire** was agreed upon. The ceasefire line, or **'Line of Control'**, has been the de facto border between the Indian State of Jammu and Kashmir and Pakistani- administered Azad Kashmir ever since.

After the war, a **plebiscite** was agreed to by India on condition that the armies of both parties withdraw from all the territories of the former state and that peace and normalcy be restored first. These conditions, not surprisingly, have never been met and the plebiscite is yet to be held. In 1957, a bill was passed in the Indian parliament integrating the State of Jammu and Kashmir within the Indian Union. In 1965, Pakistan and India began another brief war over the status of Kashmir, although the war rapidly ground to a stalemate. Following Pakistan's crushing defeat in the 1971 war over Bangladesh, Prime Minister Zulfikar Ali Bhutto was of the opinion that Pakistan could not resolve the issue by military force. In 1972, he signed the **Simla Agreement** with Indian Prime Minister Indira Gandhi, recognizing the Line of Control and seeking to resolve the issue through bilateral negotiations.

With no sign of a resolution to the dispute, the **'Kashmir question'** still dominates relations between India and Pakistan. In fact, following the uprising, or 'jihad', that began in the Indian-occupied part of Kashmir in 1989, there has been a hardening of stances between the two sides. India charges Pakistan with arming, training and funding the 'terrorists', while Pakistan insists that it offers just moral support to the 'freedom fighters'. Pakistan further charges India with acts of state terrorism in occupied Kashmir, a charge seemingly substantiated by the reports of independent human rights organizations. Pakistan fought a further war with India over Kashmir in 1965, while much 'Kashmir' rhetoric was expounded during the war fought between the two sides over West Pakistan/Bangladesh in 1971. The 'Kargil War' of 1999 was over the same issue, and tensions between India and Pakistan over Kashmir have been seemingly heightened after the two states both became declared **nuclear powers** (the latter following underground tests at Chagai in the Baluchistan desert in May 1998).

Post independence

Pakistan's experience post independence has been one of missed opportunities. The country has been under **Martial Law** four times (October 1958-March 1969 under **General Ayub Khan**, then March 1969-December 1971 under **General Yahya Khan**; July 1977-August 1988 under **General Zia ul-Haq**; October 1999 to present day under **General Pervez Musharraf**), although each time the Commander-in-Chief of the armed forces has sought to bring an air of respectability to the state of affairs by calling himself 'President'. Furthermore, these periods of military rule have been interspersed with civilian governments who have been remembered notably for their staggering levels of corruption and incompetence. Notable among these have been **Zulfikar Ali Bhutto**, December 1971-July 1977; **Benazir Bhutto**, December 1988-August 1990 and – even worse – October 1993- November 1996; **Mian Mohammad Nawaz Sharif**, October 1990-April 1993 and another calamitous turn February 1997-October 1999. Considering the manner in which the country has been run, it's quite some miracle that the Karakoram Highway was built at all.

Recent events

The military coup of October 1999 removed the incumbent Prime Minister, suspended the constitution and took control of the senate and assemblies, with General Musharraf assuming the title of Chief Exectutive. Legitimacy was given to the coup by Pakistan's Supreme Court in May 2000, and a month later Musharraf declared himself President and Head of State and dissolved the suspended assemblies. The subsequent provincial and national elections that took place in October 2002 (in which the religious parties performed much better than expected) resulted in a hung parliament, with much party haggling over the make-up of the ruling coalition. In November 2002, the National Assembly chose Musharraf loyalist Mir Zafarullah Jamali as the new civilian prime minister.

President Musharraf held a referendum on 30 April 2002, asking the question 'do you want to elect President General Pervez Musharraf as President of Pakistan for the next five years for: survival of local government system; restoration of democracy; continuity and stability of reforms; eradication of extremism and sectarianism and for the accomplishment of Quaid-i-Azam's concept?' Official figures reported a 71% turn-out and 98% 'yes' vote, while opposition figures dispute this. In February 2003, the ruling party won most seats in voting for the upper house, completing what Musharraf calls "transition to democracy".

However, perhaps the most significant recent development has been the US-led 'War on Terrorism' military campaign in Afghanistan that followed the 11 September terrorist attacks on the USA. Of course, the immediate impact of this was to wipe out the resurgent tourist industry in Pakistan. Musharraf was seen as being very much pro-tourism, introducing a number of measures (visas on arrival, upgrading roads in the north, promotion of 2002 as the 'International Year of the Mountains', perhaps even a new university in Gilgit with a 'Department of Tourism' that would train those involved in the industry) designed to boost visitor numbers to the country. In fact, until September, 2001 looked like being the best year on record for tourism with the consistent flow of backpackers joined by all the tour groups that had invariably cancelled in previous years (eg due to the Kargil war, nuclear testing etc).

As this guide goes to press, the long- and short-term future of Pakistan is difficult to predict, although Musharraf appears set to remain as President for several years in order to see the smooth return to civilian rule.

Culture

People and language

From the earliest beginnings of history, this part of the subcontinent has been a zone of contact. As such, it is not surprising that today there is an enormous diversity of peoples, the result of centuries of new settlement that came with the repeated waves of migrations and invasions, and the intermingling of these new arrivals with indigenous populations. Most of the ethnic groups found in Pakistan are descendants of the Aryans, who spread into the region from the northwest. This is reflected also in the languages spoken in the country, the majority of which belong to the Aryan branch Indo-European group. These are divided into three further groupings under the Aryan branch; Iranian (Baluchi, Pashto, Wakhi), Dardic (Khowar, Kalasha, Shina, Kohistani, Kashmiri) and Indo-Aryan (Punjabi, Seraiki, Sindhi, Urdu).

It is important to make the distinction between linguistic and ethnic classifications when speaking of the various groups that inhabit this region. For example, Wakhi is part of the 'Iranian' branch of Indo-European Aryan language grouping, yet the Wakhi people are not Iranians from the present-day Iran. The term 'Iranian' implies that there is a linguistic link, rather than an ethnological one. Likewise, there is much confusion over the term 'Dard' or 'Dardic' when describing both linguistic and ethnic groups. Although some fourth and fifth century rock inscriptions mention a 'king of the Dards', no group in this region refer to themselves by such a name, and there has never been a 'Dardistan' as such. It was probably Dr GW Leitner who first popularized the name (in his 1877 work *The Languages and Races of Dardistan*, see under Chilas), although the most common usage of the expression today is with regard to a branch of the Indo-European language group, rather than any ethnic, racial or historical affiliation. Indeed, there has been a move to abandon the term 'Dardic' altogether, with this language group now commonly referred to as 'Indic'.

A number of languages, notably **Urdu**, **Punjabi** and **English**, are spoken by people sent to the regions covered by this guide as officials and administrators, while for the purposes of business these languages are also spoken by many shopkeepers and traders. It should also be noted that many parts of the Northern Areas (most notably Hunza and Gojal) have some of the highest literacy rates in Pakistan (particularly among women), and more and more children are being taught in English and Urdu medium schools.

There are four main languages that are classified under the 'Dardic' branch. **Khowar** is spoken by the Kho, who comprise the majority of the population in the Chitral Valley. The real heartland of this group is the Turikho and Mulkho Valley areas in the Upper Chitral Valley, although marriage ties have seen the language spread throughout the Upper Ghizr Valley area (eg Yasin). There are few dialectical differences between the Khowar spoken in these separate areas, although it should be noted that the Kho comprise both Sunni Muslims and Ismailis. **Kalasha** is spoken by some 3,000 people living in a series of connecting valleys (Kalash Valleys) in Lower Chitral, and, although the language comes under the 'Dardic' branch, its speakers are the region's only significant non-Muslim group (see page 132). Kalasha has a number of dialects, the main division being between Urtsun and the dialect spoken in the valleys covered in this guide (Birir, Bumburet, Rumbur), but it is related to Khowar. **Shina** is another language that is used across a wide geographical area and by disparate groups. Shina speakers can be found as far apart as the Gilgit Valley, the Ishkoman Valley, Lower Hunza, Baltistan, Astor Valley plus many valleys off the Indus Valley (eg Darel, Tangir, Jalkot, Palas). This language group is so widespread, with many of the regions in which it is spoken having been separated both by physical geography and factional fighting, so it is little wonder that the language has split into so many dialects (eg Gilgit, Palas, Tangir, Phalura, Savi etc). Indeed, the latter two of these dialects (Phalura and Savi) are often termed languages in their own right, with many Shina speakers unable to understand other Shina speakers from distant regions. Likewise, different groups of Shina speakers across different regions worship as Sunni Muslims, Shia Muslims or as Ismailis. **Maiyan** is another branch of the 'Dardic' linguistic group, sometimes referred to as **Kohistani** since it is the Indus Kohistan region where it is spoken. There are two further main dialects of Maiyan, namely Mani and Manzari, although only limited research has been done on them. Most Maiyan speakers are Sunni Muslims.

Of the 'Iranian' linguistic grouping, **Pashto** is perhaps the best known and is in fact spoken by around 13% of the population of Pakistan. It is the language of the **Pathans**, who comprise the majority of the population in NWFP. Fiercely independent and more obviously Aryan in descent with their often fair complexions and green or blue eyes, the Pathans are a formidable people whose social structure is deeply tribal in nature. As an ethnic group, they extend beyond the political boundaries of Pakistan, accounting for around half of the population of Afghanistan (the present border between the two countries was a highly artificial one created by the British and based on strategic rather than cultural considerations). Pashto has numerous dialects, reflecting the fragmented nature of Pathan tribal society. **Wakhi** belongs to

> *Other languages spoken in regions covered by this guide include Punjabi, Hindko (related to Punjabi and spoken in Hazara), plus a variety of languages spoken across the international border in China (Mandarin Chinese, Uiygur, Tibetan etc). There is a very brief language glossary in Footnotes, page 381.*

the 'Pamirian' branch of 'Iranian' languages, and is spoken in the Upper Yarkhun Valley above Chitral, in the Upper Ishkoman Valley and in Gojal (Upper Hunza). The origins of these Wakhi speaking communities are with their kinsfolk in the Upper Oxus Valley (Pamirs) and Wakhan corridor regions, with the version of the language spoken in the Wakhi areas covered by this guide marginally more archaic in its vocabulary. The Wakhi people are almost exclusively Ismailis, with the men being renowned guides and porters and the women being charged with tending the livestock up at the high summer pastures.

Another interesting group are the **Balti-pa**, or Balti people of Baltistan whose language is strongly reminiscent of Tibetan (a spoken version of classical literary Tibetan). Indeed, their whole way of life demonstrates their Tibetan roots, and the men are regarded as some of the finest examples of mountain men, famed for their work as guides and porters. In contrast to their Buddhist neighbours in Ladakh, most Baltis are Shia Muslims, but there are a minority who belong to the **Nurbakski** 'sect' (see Religion below).

Finally, there are several languages spoken in the lands covered by this guide that are difficult to classify. For example, **Burushaski**, the main language of the Hunza Valley, is unrelated to any other linguistic group. The Burusho, or people who speak this language, are found in Hunza, Nagar and Yasin, with the latter having a dialect ('Werchikwar') that is markedly more archaic than the versions spoken in Hunza and Nagar. Those living in Hunza and Yasin tend to be Ismailis, while those in Nagar are almost exclusively Shia Muslims. **Domiki** is the language of the Doms, or Berichos, the hereditary lower caste members of Hunza society who occupy the 'lower' professions, such as those of blacksmiths, cobblers and musicians (see page 293). Another 'lower caste' group are the **Gujars**, a nomadic group of pasturalists travelling in the southern Chitral and Ghizr districts, as well as between the Kaghan Valley, Indus Kohistan and Swat. The latter group tend to speak their own language, Gojri; those in Chitral/Ghizr speak Khowar and/or Shina.

Religion

The land that now constitutes Pakistan has a rich history of religions. It gave birth to Brahmanism, which later developed into Hinduism. It saw the flourishing of Buddhism in Gandhara and the establishment of the *Mahayana* school. Prior to the arrival of the British, the Sikhs established their powerful empire which centred on the Punjab.

Today, Pakistan is an Islamic state and 97% of the population are Muslim. Despite its monotheism, Islam displays a remarkable diversity within Pakistan, as well as having its own 'Asian' feel to it, distinctive in many ways from Islam in other parts of the world. This is a reflection of its diverse origins in the region, as well as the many different influences which acted on it.

The Sufis, responsible for spreading the faith in much of the country, have left their unique mark, particularly in Sind and southern Punjab. While the Arabs brought the first Islamic contact, it was the Ghaznavids who were responsible for establishing Islamic political power in the region. They came from the northwest and were Turks of slave extraction. From the middle of the 13th century, when the Mongols crushed the Arab Caliphate, the Delhi Sultans were left on their own to exercise Islamic authority in the subcontinent, and the main influence came from Persia. Meanwhile, there was a constant process of assimilation and accommodation between the Muslim rulers and local peoples. While the Islamic elites who arrived from Iran or Turkey maintained 'pure' forms of Islam, isolated and less literate communities developed devotional and pietistic forms, incorporating many of their pre-Islamic beliefs, customs and practices. The caste system for example, completely at variance with Muslim injunctions regarding discrimination, remains a fact of life even today in much of the country.

A number of other religions are also represented in Pakistan, albeit as small minorities: Christian, Hindu, Sikh and Parsee (Zoroastrian) communities are all found in different parts of the country. There is also the Kalasha in the lower Chitral region.

Islam

Mohammad, the founder of the Islamic faith, was born around AD 570 in the city of **Mecca** in present-day Saudi Arabia. His family were of noble descent, members of the house of **Hashim**, belonging to the **Abd Manaf** clan and part of the **Quraish** tribal confederacy of Mecca. The Abd Manaf clan had a semi-priestly status, being responsible for certain functions during the annual pilgrimage to the *Ka'ba* in Mecca (the Ka'ba, the cube-shaped building to which Muslims face when praying, pre-dates Islam; Muslims believe that it was established by Adam and revere it as a sanctuary where closeness to God can be achieved).

At the age of 40, Mohammad received his first revelations of the Qur'an and began preaching his message. He encountered stiff opposition from the powerful Quraish leaders, the temple guardians and the rich traders, and was eventually forced to flee to **Medina**, known then as Yathrib (the famous *Hijra* which marks the beginning of the Islamic calendar). There he established himself and achieved a position of power, fighting three major battles with the Meccans before finally returning to Mecca in triumph two years before his death in AD 632.

In his lifetime, he had become recognized as a prophet and founded the Islamic faith. Part of his success was in fusing many aspects of the ancient Arabian religions, such as the pilgrimage to Ka'ba, as well as aspects of Judaism and Christianity. But his success was not purely in religious terms. He was also an accomplished statesman who laid the foundations for what would become a great Islamic Empire.

Islamic Sects

In the century following Mohammad's death, Islam divided into two major sects. Mohammad left no sons and therefore no obvious heir, and gave no instructions as to who should succeed him. There were two main contenders; **Abu Bakr**, the father of Mohammad's wife, and **Ali**, the husband of Mohammad's daughter Fatimah (and his cousin). In the event, Abu Bakr assumed the title of *Caliph* (vice-regent). He died two years later in AD 634 and was succeeded by **Omar** who was killed in 644. **Uthman**, a member of the powerful **Umayyad** family, was chosen to succeed him, but proved to be a weak leader and was murdered in 656.

At this point, the aggrieved Ali managed to assume the title of Caliph, thus ousting the Umayyads. However, **Muawiya**, the governor of Syria and a member of the Umayyad family, soon rose up in revolt. He managed to gain the upper hand; in 661 Ali was murdered (by one of his own supporters) and Muawiya proclaimed himself Caliph. Ali's eldest son **Hassan** set up a rival Caliph in Iraq, but was soon persuaded to abdicate. However, the seeds of the schism in Islam had already been sown; between the Sunnis (those who accepted the legitimacy of the first three Caliphs) and the Shias (those who recognized only Ali as the first legitimate Caliph). Later, when Muawiya died in 680, Ali's second son **Hussain** attempted to revolt against the Umayyads, but was defeated and killed in 681 at Karbala, providing the Shias with their greatest martyr.

Followers of the **Sunni** sect, generally termed 'Orthodox', account for around 80% of Muslims in Pakistan (globally they represent a similar majority), although the percentage is less for the areas covered by this guide. They base their *Sunna* (path, or practice) on the 'Six Books' of traditions. They are organized into four orthodox schools or rites named after their founders, each having equal standing. The *Hanafi* is the most common in Pakistan, and the most moderate. The others are the *Shafii*, *Maliki* and *Hanbali*, the latter being the strictest. Many Muslims today prefer to avoid identification with a particular school, preferring to call themselves simply Sunni.

> **Heaven is portrayed in Muslim belief as a Paradise filled with sensuous delights and pleasures. Hell, on the other hand, is portrayed as a place of eternal terror and torture...**

Followers of the **Shia** sect account for most of the remainder of Muslims in Pakistan. Those that can trace their descent from Hassan bear the title *Sharif*, and those that trace their descent from Hussain, the title *Sayyid*. However, there are also many Sharif and Sayyid families in Pakistan who are Sunni. Both lineages hold a position of religious aristocracy in Islam. Aside from the dispute over the succession of Mohammad, Sunnis and Shias do not generally differ on fundamental issues since they draw from the same ultimate sources. However, there are important differences of interpretation which partly derive from the practice of *ijtihad* ('the exercise of independent judgement') amongst Shias, as oppose to *taqlid* ('the following of ancient models') as adhered to by Sunnis. Thus Shias divest far more power in their *Imams*, accepting their role as an intermediary between God and man and basing their law and practice on the teachings of the Imams. **NB** The term Imam is also used more generally by both Shias and Sunnis to refer to the prayer leader of a mosque.

The majority of Shias are known as *Ithna asharis* or 'Twelvers', since they recognize a succession of 12 Imams. They believe that the last Imam, who disappeared in AD 878, is still alive and will reappear soon before the Day of Judgement as the *Mahdi* (One who is rightly guided) who will rule by divine right.

An offshoot of the Shias, and an important minority in Northern Pakistan, are the **Ismailis**. The Ismailis reject the seventh Imam acknowledged by the Twelvers, recognizing instead Ismail, the elder son of the sixth Imam. They are also sometimes referred to as *Sab iya* or 'Seveners'. There was, however, much dispute among themselves as to who was in fact the seventh Imam. The Fatamid Ismailis of Egypt recognized a grandson of the sixth Imam and in turn gave rise to several schismatic offshoots, including the Nizari Ismailis found in Pakistan. The latter recognize the **Aga Khan** as their spiritual head and trace his descent directly to the Prophet Mohammad through his daughter Fatimah. The philosophy of the Ismailis is a largely esoteric one; their theology is based on a cyclical theory of history centred around the number seven, which is considered to be of enormous significance. They are less restrictive in their customs and practice, allowing much greater freedom to women. Likewise, prayers are not linked to a specific formula. The mosque is replaced by a *jamat khana* which also serves as a community centre. Within Pakistan they are found mostly in the Northern Areas and Chitral region, where the Aga Khan is very active in development work. Various other Muslim minorities are found in Pakistan. The **Nurbakshi** are a small minority found only in parts of Baltistan. They are closely linked with the Shias Sufis. The Sufis do not represent a separate sect of Islam; rather they aspire to transcend sect and suffer none of the persecution to which the Ahmadis and Zikris are subjected.

Sufism is the mystical aspect of Islam, often described as the "science of the heart". The word *Sufi* is most probably derived from the Arabic word *suf* meaning 'wool', a reference to the woollen garments worn by the early adherents, emphasizing the importance of personal spiritual development to be found only through the Qur'an. The Sufis were instrumental in spreading the Islamic faith in

Pakistan, and numerous shrines dedicated to Sufi saints are to be found scattered throughout the country. These shrines still draw large numbers of pilgrims during the annual Urs, or death anniversary of the saint, a testimony to their popularity among the people.

Islamic beliefs and practices

The word Islam translates roughly as 'submission to God'. The two central tenets of Islam are embodied in the creed "There is no god but Allah and Mohammad is his Prophet", which affirms the belief in the oneness of God and recognizes Mohammad as the divinely appointed messenger of God.

The **Qur'an** (generally referred to as the Koran in English) is Islam's holiest book. The word translates literally as 'recitation' and, unlike the Bible, is considered to be the *uncreated* (that is, direct) word of God, as revealed to Mohammad through *Jibril* (the angel Gabriel). The text consists of 114 chapters, each known as a *sura*. Each sura is classified as Meccan or Medinan, according to whether it was revealed to Mohammad in Mecca or in Medina. Most of the text is written in a kind of rhymed prose known as *saj*, and is considered by Muslims to be inimitable. Each chapter of the Qur'an begins with the words "Bismillah al-Rahman al-Rahim" ("In the name of Allah, the Merciful, the Compassionate"), an invocation which can also be heard being uttered by Muslims in numerous everyday situations; when boarding a bus or before eating food for example.

> *For full details of the Islamic calendar and the significance behind Islamic festivals, see Festivals and Events, page 39.*

In addition to the Qur'an, there is the *Hadith* body of literature, a record of the sayings and doings of Mohammad and his followers, which forms the basis of Islamic laws (*Shariat*) and precepts. Unlike the Qur'an, the Hadiths are recognized to have been written by men, and are therefore potentially flawed and open to interpretation. Thus they are commonly classified into four major categories according to their trustworthiness; *Sahih* (sound, true, authentic), *Hasan* (fair, good), *Da'if* (weak) and *Saqim* (infirm). The two most revered compilations of Hadiths are those of *al-Bukhari* and *Muslim*. It is in the interpretation of the Hadiths that most of the controversy surrounding certain Islamic laws and their application originates.

While Mohammad is recognized as the founder of the Islamic faith and the principal messenger of God, Muslims also regard him as having been the last in a long line of Prophets, starting with Adam and including both Moses and Jesus. They do not accept Jesus as the son of God, but simply another of God's Prophets. Both Jews and Christians are considered *Ahl-e-Kitab* ('People of the Book'), the Torah and the Gospels being completed in Islamic belief by the Qur'an.

Nearly all Muslims accept six basic articles of the Islamic faith; belief in one God; in his angels; in his revealed books; in his Apostles; in the Resurrection and Day of Judgement; and in his predestination of good and evil. Heaven is portrayed in Muslim belief as a Paradise filled with sensuous delights and pleasures. The idea of heaven as paradise pre-dates Islam. Alexander the Great is believed to have brought the word into Greek from Persia, where he used it to describe the walled Persian gardens that were found even before the birth of Christ. Hell, on the other hand, is portrayed as a place of eternal terror and torture, the certain fate of all who deny the unity of God.

Islam has no ordained priesthood or clergy. The authority of religious scholars, learned men, Imams, judges etc (referred to collectively as the *Ulema* and individually as *Mullahs* in Pakistan), derives from their authority to interpret the scriptures, rather than from any defined status within the Islamic community. Many Muslims in Pakistan complain that the growing influence of Mullahs interferes with the direct, personal relationship between man and God which Mohammad originally espoused (and was indeed one of the reasons he was driven from Mecca, as it threatened the privileged position of the temple priests).

Non-Muslim minorities

Although **Christians**, **Hindus** and **Parsees** are to be found in Pakistan, there are no significant communities in the regions covered by this guide. For details of the **Kalasha**, see page 132.

Land and environment

Geography

The physical geography of Pakistan falls into two major regions, each formed by distinct geomorphic processes: i) the extensive flat plains of the Indus and its tributaries resulting from the deposition of sediments washed down from the Himalaya; ii) the mountains to the north and west produced by the action of the Indian plate that carries the ancient rocks of the subcontinent subducting beneath the Eurasian landmass. This guide is primarily concerned with the latter, a region that features the greatest concentration of high peaks in the world and the longest glaciers outside the polar regions.

Mountains and glaciers

Large areas of Pakistan comprise of mountain systems and plateaux and, despite great variations in height and extent, the origins of the building process are common to all: the dramatic slow-motion collision between the Indian plate and the Eurasian landmass (a process which continues today). The process of mountain building has been a relatively recent phenomenon on the geological timescale. Although the Karakoram range may have begun to form 100 million years ago, the core of the Himalayas date to about 35 million years ago, with two further major movements between five and 25 million years ago. Sub-Himalayan ranges such as the Siwaliks are even more recent. The rocks at the core of the Himalayas were formed under the intense pressure and heat of the mountain building process.

The mountainous north of Pakistan extends across the whole of the Northern Areas, much of NWFP, and into parts of Punjab. The geological region extends across the international borders into Afghanistan, Tajikistan, China (including Tibet), India and Nepal, and includes most of the world's great mountain ranges. The westernmost extension of the **Greater Himalayas** is marked by the massive Nanga Parbat (8,126 m), in the Northern Areas. The chain is dominated by high peaks, many over 4,500 m. To the south are the **Lesser Himalayas**, a highly folded and faulted chain that includes Murree and the Galis, the **Pir Panjal** range in Kashmir, and much of Hazara District. Heights vary from 1,800 m to over 4,500 m. Finally, the southernmost ranges of the Himalayas are the **Siwaliks**, or **Sub-Himalayas**. Rising to only 1,200 m, they are deeply folded and faulted.

The dominant chain in the mountainous north is the **Karakoram**, an awesome blend of high peaks, glaciers, plateaux, lakes and river valleys. The Karakoram range, and the various sub-ranges that bifurcate from the main chain, rise to an average height of 6,100 m, and include some of the world's highest peaks. The Northern Areas are home to 12 of the world's top 30 peaks, with five over 8,000 m, 25 over 7,500 m and almost 100 over 7,000 m. In **K2** (8,611 m), Pakistan can boast a mountain second only to Everest in height. The Karakoram chain contains some of the longest glaciers outside of the polar regions, including **Siachen** (72 km), **Biafo** (62 km), **Hispar** (61 km), **Batura** (58 km), **Baltoro** (58 km), **Gasherbrum** and **Chogo Lungma** (both 38 km). Ice cover in the Karakoram is estimated at 23-25% as opposed to 8-10% in the Himalaya and 2.2% in the Alps. The region's glaciers provide both a creative and destructive force, being responsible for loss of agricultural land and damage to road networks through encroachment, but also providing the source for irrigation in a region where rain-fed agriculture is not possible.

To the west of the Karakorams are the rugged and heavily glaciated **Hindu Kush** range (literally 'Hindu killer'), which raise a formidable barrier along the western and northern border with Afghanistan. Averaging over 6,000 m, the highest mountain **Tirich Mir** reaches 7,708 m. Further north, the **Pamir** mountains with their high plateaux reach over into the Wakhan Corridor and the Central Asian states of the former Soviet Union. The lower **Shandur** range (referred to during colonial times as the Hindu Raj) separates the Gilgit River basin to the north from the hills and mountains of Dir, Swat and Indus Kohistan.

Rivers

Although the Indus appears to be the dominant river in the north of Pakistan, the significance of its many and varied tributaries cannot be overstated. Indeed, it can be generally observed that the pattern of human settlement is one of occupation of the 'gentler', more manageable side streams, rather than the Indus valley itself. Such tributaries include the Shigar (and Braldu), Shyok (and Hushe) in Baltistan, the Gilgit, Ghizr (and Karambar and Yasin), Hunza (and Khunjerab, Chapursan and Shimshal) in Gilgit, Hunza and Gojal, plus the numerous other rivers that join the Indus on its journey through Diamar and Kohistan. The Indus is one of the world's great rivers, stretching 2,880 km from its source at 5,180 m in Manasarovar Lake in Tibet, to its mouth in the Arabian Sea. From its source, the river runs east-west, cutting a deep gorge through the Himalaya and Karakoram ranges, before turning sharply south at Sazli. It then makes a tortuous journey through the dramatic gorges of Kohistan before emerging onto the Punjab plains at Attock, still 1,600 km from the sea. The Indus Plains include most of the provinces of Punjab and Sind, which have been formed by the alluvium laid down by the Indus and its major tributaries.

Climate

Pakistan can be divided into three main climatic zones, only two of which are relevant to the regions covered in this guide. Of these, there's the narrow east-west belt of land stretching from Lahore (via Rawalpindi/Islamabad) to Peshawar that experiences a **humid subtropical climate**, where rainfall exceeds 800 mm. To the north of here the moderating effect of altitude produces a **Highland** climate, with little rainfall, fairly mild summers, cool and cold winters and positively arctic temperatures which are produced at great heights.

Spring (March-May) can be very pleasant, particularly in cultivated areas such as Hunza, although most of the passes are still closed. **Summer** (June to mid-September) sees livestock taken up to high altitude pastures, with most passes being open between April and July as the snow line recedes to over 5000 m. This is the main trekking season, but it should be noted that places below 2,500 m can get very hot. The end of summer sees the livestock brought back down from their summer pastures. Around mid- to late September, **Autumn** arrives, bringing with it the splendid 'riot of colour' that makes Hunza so appealing at this time of the year. It can be pleasantly warm during the day, but night time temperatures drop markedly, and many of the higher passes are already snow-bound. By the onset of winter (November-March), nights are long and bleak, days are short and in many steep-sided valleys there may only be several hours of sunshine. Skies are often overcast, although most precipitation falls only on the higher altitudes, as snow. River flows decrease, so hydro-generated electricity is in short supply. Gilgit is particularly bleak at this time of year, with severe water and power shortages. However, this is an ideal time to visit the rest of Pakistan, as pleasant daytime temperatures make sightseeing less of an ordeal.

Flora and fauna

Vegetation

There are around 5,700 different plant species in Pakistan, 500 of them listed as endangered. Many are of great value in medicinal terms. However, since the greater part of the country experiences a dry climate, vegetation cover is for the most part scarce. There are also three large desert areas in Pakistan (Thar-Cholistan, Thal, Kharan), in addition to vast regions of the mountainous north that are under snow and ice, or above the tree-line (approximately 3,800 m).

Although parts of Azad Kashmir, Kohistan, Swat Valley, Murree and the Galis, Chitral, Kaghan Valley and Hazara are heavily forested, less than 4 % of the land area of Pakistan is under forest (this figure excludes the Northern Areas). As in many other parts of the world, figures on forest cover, afforestation and regeneration are highly sensitive and subject to manipulation. Current figures suggest that forest cover in Pakistan has actually doubled since Partition, despite the fact that deforestation is seen as a major threat in many areas.

There are seven forest types recognizable in Pakistan, of which three are found in areas covered by this guide. **Alpine forests** occur above the tree-line in parts of NWFP and the Northern Areas, although the severity of the environment means that they are not extensive. **Coniferous forests** extend across parts of NWFP, including Swat, Dir, Malakand, Kohistan and Hazara, plus Rawalpindi District of Punjab, and parts of the Northern Areas. They occur between 1,000 and 4,000 m and are dominated by fir (*Abies spp*), spruce (*Piceaminda*), deodar (*Cedrus deodara*), kail (*Pinus excelsa*) and chir (*Pinusroxburghii*). Coniferous forests are often mixed with **deciduous** trees, including oaks (*Quercus*), maple (*Acer*), birch (*Betula*), poplar (*Populas*), walnut (*Juglans*) and juniper (*Juniperus*). Such forests are generally key sources of timber. **Subtropical dry forests** occur in many of the foothill regions of Punjab and NWFP up to 1,000 m, and provide mainly a supply of firewood. The key trees are phula (*Acacia modesta*), kao (*Olea cuspidata*) and the main deciduous trees mentioned.

Wildlife

Despite its often harsh environment, Pakistan is home to a surprisingly rich diversity of wildlife. Five out of six of the **Markhor** species (a type of goat) found in the world occur in Pakistan. **Wild sheep** species include the Afghan, Punjab and Ladakh Urial (*Ovis orientalis*), as well as the famous Marco Polo (Great Pamir, *Ovis ammon polii*) Sheep and Blue Sheep (or Bharal, *Pseudois nayaur*), although the latter seem to have contracted a virulent and deadly malaise. **Himalayan ibex** (*Capra ibex sibirica*) are also found, but many animals and birds found in Pakistan, including the **Himalayan brown bears** (*Ursus arctos*), **snow leopard** (*Panthera uncia*), and seven different species of **pheasant**, are either rare, seriously endangered or on the point of extinction. Indeed, it is rare to spot any of the country's large mammals, with perhaps the exception of Himalayan ibex and golden marmots (*Marmota caudata aurea*).

Many migratory birds pass through Pakistan, flying along what is known as the **Indus Flyway** as they migrate from Central Asia to South Asia and East Africa. One of the most important of these is the **Houbara Bustard**, which breeds in Central Asia, mainly in the Kizil Kum Desert region southeast of the Aral Sea, before migrating to Pakistan, Afghanistan, Iran and India for the winter. In Pakistan its main habitats are in Baluchistan, Punjab and Sind. Due to excessive hunting, the Houbara Bustard is now under serious threat in Pakistan. Ironically **Sakar Falcons**, captured in Chitral (and themselves a threatened species) are used by visitors from the oil-rich Gulf States to hunt the bird. Many endangered duck species, including the **Marble Teal** and **White Headed Duck** also pass through. In the Chitral area, migrating ducks have been hunted for centuries, with local people going to great lengths to build artificial ponds alongside rivers in order to encourage the birds to land there.

Conservation

Pakistan is a signatory to the Convention on Trade in Endangered Species (CITES), the Convention on Wetlands of International Importance (Ramsar) and the Convention on the Conservation of Migratory Species of Wild Animals (Bonn). It is also a member of the World Conservation Union (IUCN), World Wide Fund for Nature (WWF), and International Waterfowl and Wetland Research Bureau (WRB), all of which are active in Pakistan.

Listed here are some of the national parks and protected areas that fall within the scope of this guide, but it should be noted that some exist on paper only or do not have full legal status. **Khunjerab National Park** covers over 2,000 sq km of Gojal (see page 331), although few areas are readily accessible to visitors, due partly to remoteness and partly to proximity to the border with China, and you will still be charged for the privilege of travelling through the park when taking the bus from Sust to China. Effectively, only the area adjacent to the KKH is being managed, although the region is home to Marco Polo sheep, Tibetan wild ass (*Equus hemionus kyiang*), snow leopard (in theory), Tibetan red fox (*Vulpes vulpes montana*) and the ubiquitous golden marmots. Contact WWF in Gilgit for details.

Central Karakoram National Park covers the dense knot of high peaks (including K2), glaciers (including Baltoro, Biafo and Hispar), rock and ice at the heart of the Karakoram range. Currently awaiting World Heritage status, most of the treks and climbs in this region require permits from the Tourism Division of the Ministry of Culture, Sports and Tourism in Islamabad (see page 83).

Shandur-Handrap National Park (see page 151) covers the area around the Shandur Pass and the Handrap River, although it's largely a 'paper' national park. It remains a beautiful area, but you are unlikely to see much wildlife.

Fairy Meadows National Park was almost a case of shutting the stable door after the horse had bolted (see page 198). The owner of the *Raikot Serai* camp here is a good person to talk about this conservation project (office in Islamabad also).

Chitral Gol National Park (see page 127), a former hunting reserve, now provides a refuge for snow leopards and black bears. Permits and guides from Chitral. **Deosai National Park**, in Baltistan, is home to the Himalayan brown bear, and visits can be arranged through the Himalayan Wildlife Project office in Skardu or Islamabad (see page 246). There are also a number of wildlife sanctuaries and game reserves, visits to which are best arranged locally. One that is of particular note is in the **Bar Valley** (see page 264), where the Siberian ibex forms part of a successful sustainable wildlife project based on the concept of trophy hunting!

However, the establishment of national parks and other protected areas often leads to a conflict of interests with local populations. The Khunjerab National Park in particular has been the focus of bitter disputes between park authorities and local people, who resented the outright ban placed on their traditional grazing and hunting rights in the area. Initially the park was a failure, with people continuing to graze their livestock and hunt in the area. Indeed the population of Marco Polo sheep fell from over 1,000 when the park was established in 1975 to less than 50 by the early 1990s. This experience has demonstrated the importance of first gaining the active support

● *Over 1,000 different species, comprising 666 bird species, 178 mammal species, 176 reptile species and 16 amphibian species, are found in the Pakistan.*

and participation of local people with regard to the establishment of national parks in the country. Central to this is the need to raise public awareness and to demonstrate the tangible benefits of conservation strategies. The Western concept of protecting wildlife and its environments for largely aesthetic reasons has little relevance in a country where many people, particularly those most affected, are living close to subsistence level.

Books

Bookshops in Islamabad, Rawalpindi and Gilgit are excellent places to buy books. Not only are they comparatively cheap (many are locally produced reprints), it is also possible to find recently published versions of books that have been out of print for years. Many are also available through companies such as amazon.com. Dates refer to the most recently published version. The books listed below comprise a highly selective and subjective list, although reading just a small selection will help give an insight into the regions covered by this guide, and Pakistan in general.

History and politics

Caroe, O, reprints, *The Pathans*; first published in 1958 and widely regarded as the definitive study.
Collins, L and Lapierre, D, reprints, *Freedom at Midnight*; easily digestible history, although distinctly pro-Gandhi and sadly underestimating Jinnah's role in partition.
Dani, AH, 1991,*The History of the Northern Areas*; the definitive study.
Dani, AH, 1995, *Peshawar: Historic city of the Frontier*; a detailed history of Peshawar and its environs.
Duncan, E, 1989, *Breaking the Curfew: A Political Journey Through Pakistan*; one of the best books on Pakistan available, compulsory reading for anyone interested in modern Pakistan, rather dated now but lessons haven't been learned.
Lamb, C, 1991, *Waiting for Allah: Pakistan's Struggle for Democracy*; similar to Emma Duncan's book. Ms Lamb is regularly chucked out of the country!
Robertson, GS, reprints, *The Kafirs of the Hindu Kush*; written at the turn of the century and now dated in many respects, but this book is still considered to be among the most authoritative works on the Kalasha people.
Wolpert, S, 1984, *Jinnah of Pakistan*; the definitive biography of Jinnah, though for a long time versions sold in Pakistan excluded details of Jinnah's penchant for pork sausages.
Wolpert, S, reprints, *Zulfi Bhutto of Pakistan*; authorized biography that papers over some of the cracks, but nevertheless fascinating.
Yousaf, M and Adkin, M, 1992, *The Bear Trap: Afghanistan's Untold Story*; fascinating insight into Pakistan's involvement in the Afghan war from the former head of the Afghan Bureau of the Inter Services Intelligence (ISI). Includes an interesting summary of the various theories surrounding Zia's death.

'Great Game' and colonial exploits

Biddulph, J, reprints, *Tribes of the Hindoo Koosh*.
Durand, A, 1899, *The Making of a Frontier*.
French, P, 1995, *Younghusband*; excellent biography of this fascinating character.
Hopkirk, P, 1990, *Great Game: On Secret Service in High Asia*; readable account of the Great Game and the history of Central Asia.
Keay, J,1977, *When Men and Mountains Meet*; excellent historical companion to travelling in this area.
Keay, J, 1979, *The Gilgit Game*; ditto above.
Knight, EF, 1894, *Where Three Empires Meet*; classic colonial writing, often unintentionally hilarious.
Schomberg, RCF, 1935, *Between the Oxus and the Indus*; entertaining, but terribly bigoted, colonial writing.

Religion

Ahmed, Akbar, 1996, *Living Islam*; based on the BBC series of the same name, this is an excellent introduction.
Baldick, J, 1989, *Mystical Islam: An Introduction to Sufism*.
Chaudhry, Mhd Sharif, 1991, *Women's Rights in Islam*.
Holt, Lambton, Lewis (eds), 1970, *The Cambridge History of Islam* (two volumes).

Travel writing

Bealy, J, 1999, *For a Pagan Song*; not just travel in India, Pakistan and Afghanistan, but fight to overcome dyslexia.
Danzinger, N, 1987, *Danzinger's Travels: Beyond Forbidden Frontiers*; highly readable account of travel through Turkey, Iran, Afghanistan, Pakistan, China and Tibet, but rather self-important.
Denker, D, *Sisters on the Bridge of Fire*; familiar theme (woman travels in Northern Pakistan), reasonably well executed.
Fa Hsien, reprints, *A Record of Buddhist Kingdoms*; account of this monk's 5th century journey through the region.
Fairley, J, 1975, *Lion River: The Indus*.
Hopkirk, P, *Quest for Kim*; search for the story behind Kipling's classic.
Hovey Wriggins, S, 1996, *Xuanzang: A Buddhist Pilgrim on the Silk Road*; readable account of 7th century Buddhist monk Xuanzang's (Hiuen Tsiang) remarkable journey through the region.
Jamie, K, 1990, *The Golden Peak: Travels in Northern Pakistan*; uneventful, but beautifully written account of a young woman's journey as she travels through Northern Pakistan.
Moorhouse, G, *To The Frontier*; well-written account of a journey through the region.
Murphy, D, 1965, *Full Tilt: Ireland to India on a bicycle*; a great fun read and inspirational too.
Murphy, D, 1977, *Where The Indus Is Young: a winter in Baltistan*; account of a winter spent in Baltistan by the author and her young daughter, but rather self-important.
Newby, E, 1958, *A Short Walk in the Hindu Kush*; one of the best travel books ever written, details a hilarious expedition to Nuristan (in Afghanistan).
Workman, FB & WH, 1900, *In the Ice-world of Himalaya*; 1910, *The Call of the Snowy Hispar*; 1917, *Two Summers in the Ice-Wilds of Eastern Karakoram*; understated, British stiff-upper-lip travels.
Younghusband, F, 1884, *Wonders of the Himalaya*; 1896, *The Heart of a Continent*; one of the all-time great explorers.

Climbing

Bechtold, F (translation by Tyndale, HEG), 1935, *Nanga Parbat Adventure*; very moving account of the tragic 1934 expedition.
Brown, J, 2001, *The Hard Years*; the 'Manchester Climbing Plumber' includes some Karakoram attempts in this anthology.
Buhl, H, 1998, *Nanga Parbat Pilgrimage*; account of the classic 1953 ascent.
Clinch, N, 1983, *Walk in the Sky*; first successful ascent of Gasherbrum I.
Curran, J, 1989, *K2: Triumph and Tragedy*; tale of the dramatic 1986 season;
Curran, J, 1996, *K2: The Story of the Savage Mountain*; good records of various attempts on K2.
Houston, CS, & Bates, R, *K2, the Savage Mountain*; account of 1953 expedition.
Howkins, H, 2001, *K2: One Woman's Quest for the Summit*; single mum mountaineer Heidi Howkins was, in 2000, one of only 2 women who have climbed K2.
Kaufman, AJ & Putnam, WL, 1993, *K2: The 1939 Tragedy*.
Messner, R, *All 14 Eight-Thousanders*; did the lot between 1970-86.
Willis, C (ed), 1999, *High: Stories of Survival from Everest and K2 (Extreme Adventure)*.

Fiction

Kipling, R, 1901, *Kim*; the classic novel that created the expression 'the Great Game'.
Kipling, R, reprints, *The Man Who Would Be King*; fantastic adventure story of two deserters from the British Indian army who find themselves revered as royalty in a remote valley of the Northwest Frontier.
Rushdie, S, 1983, *Shame*; bitterly sharp critique of South Asian life.
Singh, K, 1956 (reprints), *Train to Pakistan*; Khushwant Singh gives a moving insight into the trauma that accompanied partition.

Specialist texts

Ali, S & Dillon Ripley, S, *Handbook of the Birds of India and Pakistan*; available in compact edition, or five volumes.
Dani, AH, *Chilas: City of Nanga Parbat*; excellent guide to petroglyphs in Chilas.
Jettmar, K, *Rock Carvings and Inscriptions in the Northern Areas of Pakistan*; another excellent guide to petroglyphs.
Dani, Messerli, B & Ives, J, 1989, *Himalayan Crisis: Reconciling Development and Conservation*; excellent review of the controversial debate over environmental change in the Himalayas.

Footnotes

Useful words and phrases	**382**
Urdu	382
Burushaski	385
Wakhi	385
Shina	386
Balti	386
Khowar	387
Kalasha	387
Food glossary	388
Index	**390**
Map index	**394**
Map symbols	**395**
Complete title listing	**396**
Credits	**398**
Acknowledgements	**399**

Useful words and phrases

If you're going to learn one language for travel in this region, then learn Urdu. While travelling in northern Pakistan you will come across numerous other languages and dialects. It's rare not to find someone who can speak at least some English, and rarer still to find a non-Urdu speaker. However, it is always good to be able to address someone in their own language, so a few very basic words and phrases are below.

Pronunciation ā as in 'ah' ī as in 'ee'
ō as in 'oh' u as in 'oo' in book
nasalized vowels shown as an, un etc

Note These marks to help with pronunciation do not appear in the main text.

Urdu words and phrases

Hello, good morning	alsālam aleikum
Goodbye	hudā hāfiz
Thank you/no thank you	shukriyā/nahīn shukriyā
Excuse me, sorry	mihrbānī
Yes/no	jī hān/jī nahīn
Nevermind/that's alright	koi bāt nahīn
Very well/I see/OK	āccha
What is your name?	āpkā nām kyā hai
My name is...	merā nām...hai
Do you speak English?	āp kō angrezī āti hai?
a little	thorī-sī
How are you?	kyā āp kaise hain?
I am well, thanks, and you?	main thīk hun, aur āp?
I am not well	main thīk nahīn hun
Where is the...?	...kahān hai?
Who is...?	...kaun hai?
What is this?	yeh kyā hai?
I like/I don't like	mujhe pasand hai/mujhe pasand nah
What time is it?	yeh kitnī baaje hai?
God willing	inshallah
How much is this?	kitnā/iskā kitnā paisa hai?
That is very expensive!	yeh bahut mahangā hai!
Make it a bit cheaper!	thorā kam kījiye!

Sleeping

What is the room charge?	ek din kā kirāyā kitnā hai?
Please show me the room	zarā mujhe kamrā dekhāiye
Is there an air-conditioned room?	kyā a/c kamrā hai?
Is there hot water?	kya kamre men garam pānī hai?
bathroom/fan/mosquito net	ghusal khana/pankhā/machara
The room is not clean	yeh kamrā sāf nahīn hai
Please clean the room	yeh kamrā sāf karwā dījiye
Are there clean sheets/blankets?	sāf chādaren/kambal hain?
This is OK	yah thīk hai
Please give me the bill	mihrbānī, bill dījiye

Transport

Where's the railway station?	railway station kahān hai?
How much is a ticket to Gilgit?	Gilgit kā ticket kitnā paisa hai?
When does the Gilgit bus leave?	Gilgit bus keb jāegī?
Is it far?	kyā yeh dur hai?
left/right	bāien/ dāhinā
go straight on	sīdhā chaliye
Is it near the station?	station ke nazdīk hai?
stop	rukiye
train	rel gari
north	shimal
south	junub
east	mashriq
west	mahgreb

Restaurants

Please show the menu	menu dekhāiye
No chillis please	mirch nahīn dālnā
sugar/milk/ice	chīnī/doodh/baraf
I do not like meat	mujhe gosht pasand nahīn
I do not want chicken	mujhe murghi chāhiye nahīn
spoon/fork/knife	chamach/kāntā/chhurī
fruit	phal

Days

right now	abhī
morning/early morning	suba/suba saveray
midday	dopahar
afternoon/evening	shām
night	rāt
today	āj
tomorrow/yesterday	kal/kal
day	din
week	haftā
month	mahīnā
year	sāl
Sunday	itvār
Monday	pir
Tuesday	mangal
Wednesday	budh
Thursday	jum'erāt
Friday	jum'ā
Saturday	haftā

Numbers

1	ek	*7*	sāt
1½	derh	*8*	āth
2	dō	*9*	nau
2½	dhāi	*10*	das
3	tīn	*11*	gyāra
3½	sārhe tin (etc)	*12*	bārah
4	chār	*13*	terāh
5	pānch	*14*	chaudāh
6	chhai	*15*	pandrāh

16	solāh	40	chalīs
17	satrāh	45	paintālis
18	athārāh	50	pachās
19	unnīs	55	pachpan
20	bīs	60	sāth
21	ikkīs	65	painsāth
22	baīs	70	sattar
23	teīs	75	pachattar
24	chaubīs	80	assī
25	paccīs	85	pachasī
26	chabbīs	90	navve
27	sataīs	95	pachanve
28	athaīs	100/200	sau/do sau
29	untīs	1,000/2,000	hazār/do hazār
30	tīs	100,000	ek lākh
35	paintīs		

Basic vocabulary

Airport, bank, bathroom, bus, doctor, embassy, ferry, hotel, hospital, juice, police, restaurant, station, stamp, taxi, ticket, train – these English words are used locally and often pronounced differently eg *daktar*, *haspatal*.

bathroom	ghusl khāna
beautiful	hūbsūrat
big	barā
brother	bhai
chemist	dawāi kī dukān
Christian	isai
cold	thanda
day	din
delicious	lazeez
difficult	mushkil
dirty	gandā
English	angrezi
excellent	bahut achhā
food/to eat	khāna
hot (spicy)	jhāl
hot (temperature)	garam
hunger	bhūk
luggage	samān
medicine	dawāi
Muslim	musalman
pen	qalam
post (office)	dāk khāna
road/route	rāsta
room	kamrā
sick (ill)	bīmār
sister	bahin
small	chhotā
tea	chai
thirst	pyas
tourist	sayyah
water	pānī

what	kyā
when	kab
where	kahān/kidhar
which/who	kaun
why	kiun
wife	bivi

Burushaski words and phrases

Numbers

1	han	7	thalo
2	ālta	8	altāmbo
3	ūsko	9	hūncho
4	wālto	10	tūrūmo
5	tshūndo	20	āltar
6	mishindo	100	thā

Phrases

How are you?	besan hāl bilā?
I'm well	shūa bā
How much?	bearūm
When?	beshal?
Where?	āmūlo?
good	shūa
bad	gūnekish
near	āsir
far	māthan

Food and drink

water	tshil
soup	daudho
milk	māmū
rice	bras
bread	shapik
meat	chap
cheese	burūs
salt	bāyū
apricot	jū
dried apricot	batering
mulberry	biranch

Wakhi words and phrases

Numbers

1	yīu	7	hub
2	būi	8	hāth
3	throi	9	naō
4	sabur	10	thas
5	pānz	20	wist
6	shāth	100	yīsad

Phrases

How are you?	toot sīyeta/chiz hol he ?
I am fine	vidurt em/woozem siyet
What is your name?	ti nunge chīst
My name is...	jhu nunge ...
good	baf
bad	shak

Food and drink

water	yuphkh
milk	zharzh
bread	xich
rice	grinj
vegetables	xazk/sauzi
cheese	qurūt
meat	gusht

Shina words and phrases

Numbers

1	ek	*7*	sat
2	dū	*8*	ānsh
3	che	*9*	naū
4	chār	*10*	daī
5	posh	*11*	bī
6	shā	*12*	shal

Phrases

How are you?	jhek hāl hain ?
Where?	kon ?
How much?	kachāk ?
good	mishto
bad	khacho

Food and drink

water	weī
milk	dūth
bread	roti
rice	briūn
vegetables	sabzī
meat	mos

Balti words and phrases

Numbers

1	chīk	*7*	bdūn
2	ngīs	*8*	bgyet
3	khsūm	*9*	rgū
4	bjī	*10*	phchū
5	gā	*11*	ngī shū
6	trūk	*100*	bgya

Phrases
How are you?	yāng chĭ hālyo?
I'm fine/good	lyākhmo
What is your name?	yari ming tākpo chĭin?
My name is...	nge ming tākpo...yin
good	lyākhmo
bad	changmen

Food and drink
tea	chā
salted tea	payū chā
milk	ongā
bread	khurbā
rice	blas
meat	shā
chicken	byango
Chicken McNuggets	byango McNuggets
food	zāchas
apricots	chūlĭ

Khowar words and phrases

Numbers
1	ĭ	7	sot
2	jū	8	usht
3	troĭ	9	nĭu
4	chor	10	jush
5	ponch	11	bishir
6	chhoĭ	100	ĭ shor

Phrases
How are you?	tū kichā āsūs?
I am fine	bo jam
What's your name?	ta kĭāgh nām?
My name is...?	ma nām ...

Food and drink
milk	chĭr
bread	shāpĭk
rice	grinj
meat	phūshūr
apricot	palogh

Kalasha words and phrases

Phrases
Hello	ishpāda
How are you?	tabiyet prūsht?
good	prūsht
bad	shūm
Where is...?	kawa...

Food and drink

water	ūkh
tea	chīr chai
milk	chīr
wine	dā
bread/food	aū
meat	mos

Food glossary

Pronunciation guide ā as in 'ah' ī as in 'ee'
ō as in 'oh' ū as in 'oo' in book

Nasalized vowels are shown as a<u>n</u>, u<u>n</u> etc

Basic food and vocabulary (Urdu)

khana	food, to eat (verb)
anda	egg
chāwal	rice
chini	sugar
gosht	meat, usually mutton
macchli	fish
murghi	chicken
panīr	drained curds
phal	fruit
roti	bread
sabzī	vegetables

Vegetables

āloo	potato
bai<u>n</u>gan	aubergine
band gōbi	cabbage
bhindi	okra, ladies' fingers
dāl	lentils
matar	peas
piāz	onion
sāg	spinach

Pulses (beans and lentils)

masoor dāl	pink, round split lentils
moong dāl	most common lentils
chanā dāl	chick peas
rājmā	red kidney beans
urhad dāl	small black beans

Roti – breads

chapāti	thin, plain, unleavened bread cooked on a griddle, usually made from wheat flour
makkai-ki-roti	same with maize flour
nān	oven-baked (traditionally in a tandoor) white flour leavened bread often large and triangular
parāthā	fried bread layered with ghī, sometimes cooked with egg or stuffed with vegetables
poori	thin deep-fried, puffed rounds of flour (in Punjabi bhaturā)

Rice

chāwal	plain boiled rice
biriyani	partially cooked rice layered over meat, baked with saffron
pulao/pilau	fried (and then boiled) rice with spices and vegetables

Accompaniments

achār	pickles (usually spicy and preserved in oil)
chutnī	fruit or tomato, freshly prepared, sweet, mildly spicy
dahī	plain yoghurt
mirch	chilli
numuk	salt
raita	yoghurt with shredded cucumber
salat	salad, usually onions, tomato or cucumber

Methods of preparation

bhoona	a thick, fairly spicy sauce
chargha	similar to tandoori (see below)
chops	minced meat, fish or vegetables, covered in mashed potato, crumbed and fried
cutlet	minced meat, fish, vegetables formed into flat rounds or ovals, crumbed and fried
jhāl frāzi	spicy, hot sauce with tomatoes and chillies
karahi (balti)	cooked and served in a metal wok, with onions, tomatoes and spices
Kashmiri	cooked with mild spices, ground almonds and yoghurt
kebab	skewered (or minced and shaped) meat or fish
kīma	minced meat (usually mutton)
kofta	minced meat or vegetable balls
korma	in fairly mild rich sauce using cream/yoghurt
Mughlai	rich north Indian style
Peshwari	rich with dried fruit and nuts
tandoori	baked in a tandoor (special clay oven) or one imitating it
tikka	marinated meat pieces, baked quite dry

Some typical dishes

aloo gosht	potato and mutton stew
aloo gobi	dry potato and cauliflower with cumin
aloo matar	potato and peas in a dryish mildly spicy sauce
bhaji, pakora	vegetable fritters (onions, potatoes, cauliflower etc) deep-fried in batter
bhindi bhaji	okra fried with onions and mild spices
boti kebab	marinated pieces of meat, skewered and cooked over a fire
chana choor	Bombay mix: lentil and flattened rice snacks mixed with nuts and dried fruit
chapli kebab	spicy burger made with mince, eggs and tomato and served with nān
keema matar	minced meat with peas
matar panīr	curd cheese cubes with peas and spices (and often tomatoes)
rogan josh	rich, mutton/beef pieces in creamy, red sauce
sāg aloo	potato and spinach
sāg gosht	mutton and spinach
samosa	cooked vegetable or meat wrapped in pastry circle into triangles and deep-fried

Sweets

barfi	fudge-like, rectangles/diamonds often with nuts
gulāb jāmun	dark fried spongy balls, soaked in syrup
halwa	dry sweet made with thickened milk, carrots and spice
kulfi	cone-shaped Indian ice cream with pistachios/almonds

Drinks

chai	tea boiled with milk and sugar
doodh	milk
lassi	cool drink made with yoghurt and water, salted or sweetened
pāni	water

Index

A

Abbottabad 168
  directory 174
  eating 173
  sights 168
  sleeping 172
  transport 174
Abdullah Khan Maidan 318
Abgerch 318
accommodation 36
  See also under individual towns
Afiyatabad 329
Agurtsab Dar 220
Ahmedabad 292
air
  international links 24
  flying into the northern areas 70
  internal flights 31
Aksur Das 281
Alai Valley 186
Aliabad 280
  sleeping 281-282
  transport 282
Aling Glacier 263
Altit 290
  sights 291
  sleeping 298
  transport 299
  walks 292
Ambush Point 205
Andan Dehri Stupa 119
Andare Fort 306
Anish 138
Arriving at night 80
Askole 252
Askordas 304
Astor 203, 247
Astor Valley 202
  sleeping 207
Astor village 203
  sleeping 207
  transport 208
Asumbar Pass 157
Asumbar Pass trek 157
Atabad 298
Attock 93
  eating 94
  sleeping 94
  transport 94
Ayeenabad/Aienabad 298

B

Baba Ghundi 322
  sleeping 324
  treks 323
Baba Ghundi Ziarat 322
Baba Wali's Shrine 93
Babusar Pass 178, 180
  sleeping 183
  warning 180
  background 357
Bagrot Valley 219
  sleeping 223
  treks 220
Baisakhi Festival 93
Bala Hisar 102
Balakot 175
Balambat 120
Baltar 272
Balti words and phrases 386
Baltistan 229, 232
  background 233
  religion, culture and society 234
Baltoro Glacier 252
Bar Valley 270
  background 270
  eating 278
  sleeping 277
  transport 278
  treks 272
Bar-daru-kush Lake 272
Bargo 160
Barit 218
Barkhun 333
Barkulti 154
Barpu Glacier 303
Barpugram 303
Barsat 150, 151
  sleeping 160
Barseen 189
Bat Khela 119
Bathraiz River 152
Batrik 139
Battagram 172
Battakundi 178
Battal 172
Batura Glacier 309, 311
Batura Muztagh 312
Bekitchang Woton 277
Ber 220
Bericho Kor 303
Beriski 293
Besal 179
Besham 186
  directory 191
  sleeping 190
  transport 191
Beyal 201
  sleeping 206
Biafo Glacier 253
Biafo-Hispar trek 253
Bibaware 120
bike travel 33
  See also under Cycling
Birir Valley 137
  sleeping 140
Birmugh Lasht 127
Biyabari 220
Boesam Pass 318
Boiber Valley 318
books 378
Borit Lake 306, 310
  sleeping 313
Borit Sar 310, 311
Boroghil Pass 143
Bras 1 279
Brep 143
Brun 139
Bualtar Glacier 303
Bubulimating 285
Buldiat Valley 298
Bulunkul 342
Bumburet Valley 137
  sleeping 138
Bunar 197
Bungidas 275
Buni 142
Burawai 178, 179
Burawai to Besal trek 179
Burche Glacier 220
bureau de change 23
Burji La 248
Burrum Char 302
Burushaski words and phrases 385
bus travel 32
buses
  See under individual towns

C

car hire 33
Central Hunza 279
Chakdara 119
  sleeping 121
  transport 122
Chalinj 157
Chalt 271
  eating 278
  sleeping 277
  transport 278
Chamarkhan Pass 151
  trek 151
changing money 23
Chapali 143
Chapchingol Pass 318
Chaprot 271
Chaprot Valley 270
  background 270
  eating 278
  short walks 271
  sleeping 277
  transport 278
Chapursan Valley 319
  festivals and events 324
  trekking 324
Charsadda 118
Chashi 152
Chatorkhand 157
  sleeping 161, 162
Chattar Plain 172
Chaudhuri Rahmat Ali 365
Chaupi Ol 251
Chhurka Khanqah 251
Chidin Harai 303
Chilas 180, 195
  directory 208
  history 195
  sights 196
  sleeping 205
  transport 207
children 16
Chilinji 323
Chilinji An 323
Chilinji Pass 323
China 336
  travel tips 337
  border with 328, 333, 338
Chirah 219
Chitral Gol National Park 127
Chitral town 126
  activities and tours 129
  directory 131
  eating 129
  shopping 130
  sights 126
  sleeping 128
  transport 130
Chitral Town 126
Chitral Valley 123
  background 123
Chogolisa and Charaksar Glaciers 263
Chowk Yadgar 105
Chu Tron 252
Chuchuanotik 157
Chuinj 143
Chukutans 303
Chuman Bakhur 304
Churchill's Picket 119
Chutiatan 120
climate 375
Colombo 65
communication 61
Concordia 252
conservation 377
culture 368
customs and etiquette 28

Cycling 33
  Pakistan to China 330

D

Dachigan 303
Dadarili Pass 151
Daddar 172
Dahimal 152
Daintar Base Camp 217
Daintar Pass 217
Dalnati 159
Dalsan Pa 263
Daman-e-Koh 73
Damas 159
Danyore Valley 217
  sleeping 277
  trek 218
Dar 220
Darchan 220
Darkot 155, 156
  sleeping 161
Darora 120
Darra 108
Darra Adam Khel 108
Darshal 146
Dassu 252
Dasu 187
  sleeping 190
  transport 191
Davdar 338
Deosai National Park 246
Deosai Plateau 244
  land and environment 245
  treks 247
departure tax 21
Dhodial 171
Diamar District 189, 192, 193
Dilisangsar base camp 321
Dir town 120
  activities and tours 122
  directory 123
  eating 122
  sleeping 121
  transport 122
Diran Base Camp 220, 274, 276
  sleeping 278
disabled travellers 15
Doghani 256
Dom 293
Domiki 293
Dorkhan 281
drink 37, 38
Drosh 121
  sleeping 122
drugs 31
Dudupat Lake 179
Duikar 292
  sights 293
  sleeping 299
Durand Line 365

Dut 316
duty free allowance 20
Dzig 143

E

eating 37
  See also food and under individual towns
Edara 340
embassies 19
entertainment 39
essentials 11
export restrictions 20

F

Fairy Meadows 198, 200
  sleeping 206
  treks and walks 201
Faisal Masjid 71
Fatmahil 312
festivals and events 39
flora and fauna 376
food and drink 37
  glossary 388
  See also under individual towns

G

Gahkuch 159
  sleeping 161
  transport 162
Ganesh 281, 295
  background 295
  sights 295
  sleeping 299
  transport 299
Garam Chashma 127
  sleeping 129
Garelht 281
Gargoh 220
Garhi Habibullah Khan 176
gay and lesbian 16
Gaymaling 280
geography 374
geology 188
Ghalapin 318
Ghashumaling River 271
Ghez 342
Ghez River 342
Ghoulti 158
Ghujerab River 331
Ghujerab Valley 318
Ghulam Ali Pass 323
Ghulkin 306
  sleeping 313
Ghulkin Glacier 306
Ghulmet 272
  sleeping 278
Gich 159
Gilgit 159, 208
  activities and tours 225
  directory 228

eating 223
festivals and events 224
history 210
shopping 224
sights 211
sleeping 221
transport 226
Gilgit District 208
Gilgit uprising 214
Gini 197
Gircha 319
Girindil 303
Gittidas 179 180
glossary 382
Goherabad 159
Gojal (Upper Hunza) 305
Gondogoro La trek 261
Gondogoro Pass 253
Great Game 348
Grum 137
Gulapur 160
Gulmit 305
  directory 315
  shopping 314
  short walks around 306
  sights 306
  sleeping 313
  transport 314
Gulmit Glacier 306
Gulmuti 159
Gunar Farm 197
Gupis 149, 152, 155
  directory 162
  sleeping 161, 162
Gupis Bridge 152
Gurikot 203
Guru 137
Gutshim 312

H

Ha Noi 350
Haiderabad 281
Haji Beg's Camp 323
Hamdar 303
Handrap Lake 151
Hapakun 275
Haramosh La (Pass) 221
Haramosh Valley 219
  sleeping 223
  treks 220
Harkeesh 312, 323
Hasan Abdal 93
  sleeping 94
  transport 94
Hasanabad 277, 279
Hasis 157
Havelian 168
Hayatabad 106
Hayward, George 156
Hayward's Rock 154
Hazara 16
health 55
Herligkoffer Base Camp 204

hiking 45
Hinarche Glacier 220
Hinarche Harai 220
Hispar Pass 253
history 358
hitch-hiking 34
holidays 39
Hon 285
Honboro Glacier 263
Hoopkerch 323
Hoper
  sleeping 304
  transport 304
  treks 303
Hosht 293
Hunza Peak 285
Hushe Valley 259
Hushe village 259
  sleeping 264
  transport 264
  trekking 262
Hussaini Bridge 306, 309

I

Iatar Pass 158
Imit 159
  sleeping 161, 162
immunization 55
Indian National Congress 365
Indus Kohistan 184
innoculations 20, 55
insurance 21
internet 61
Irshad Pass 323
Isekere 221
Ishkoman 'proper' 157
Ishkoman Valley 155
Islam 371, 373
Islamabad 66, 69
  accommodation 74
  activities and tours 78
  directory 81
  eating 76
  entertainment 77
  essentials 74
  history 71
  shopping 78
  sights 71
  transport 79
Islamic holy days 41
Ispenji 321
Isperu Dok 145

J

Jafarabad 273
Jaglot 202, 270
Jaglot Goor 270
Jaglot to Gilgit 205
  sleeping 207
Jalipur 197
Jalkhand 179

Jamal Khan Istan shrine 321
Jamrud Fort 108
Japuky 159
Jareed 177
Jehangira 94
Jiji Shawaran 157
Jinnah
   Mohammad Ali 365
Jurjur 316
Jut/Utz 217
Jutal 270

K

K2 252
Kacheili Lake 276
Kachikani Pass 149
Kachura lake 238
   sleeping 240
Kaghan 177
Kalash Valleys 132, 175
   exploring valleys 137
   festivals and events 140
   history 133
   religion 133
   role of women 136
   sleeping 138
   social structure 134
   treks 137
Kalasha words and
   phrases 387
Kamaris 306
Kampir Dior 321
Kanchey Bridge 159
Kande 261
Kandia Valley 189
Kara Kuli 341
   activities and tours 344
   eating 344
   sleeping 343
   transport 345
Karakoram Highway 167
Karambar Pass 144
Karambar Valley 155
Kargah 213
Kargah Buddha 213
Kargah nala trek 214
Karimabad 282
   background 282
   directory 289
   eating 287
   festivals and events 287
   history 283
   pubs, bars and clubs 287
   shopping 287, 288
   sights 283
   sleeping 285
   tour operators 288
   transport 289
Karun Pir Pass 318
Kashgar 345
   activities and tours 354

directory 356
eating 352
entertainment 353
history 347
shopping 353
sights 349
sleeping 352
transport 354
Kat Kala 119
Kekor 340
Kermin 320
Kermin Pass 320
Khaibar 318
Khal 120
Khaltar Harai 279
Khaltaro 220
Khalti lake 152
   sleeping 161
   transport 162
Khanian 177
Khapulu 255, 257
   history 255
   sleeping 258
Khapulu village 257
   eating 258
   sights 257
   sleeping 258
   transport 258
Kharamabad 312
Khowar words and
   phrases 387
Khunjerab National Park 331
Khunjerab Pass 328, 331, 333, 336
Khunjerab River 331
Khyber Pass 107
   eating 112
   sleeping 111
Khyber Railway 108
Killik Pass 331
Kirgas Washik 312
Kohistan 184
Kohistan island arc 188
Koksil 333
Komila/Dasu 187
   sleeping 190
   transport 191
Krakal 139
Krui Bokht 217
Kuk 317
Kukhil 312
Kuragh 142
Kutwal Lake 221
Kuz sar base camp 323
Kyrghizstan 351
   transport 356

L

Laila Camp 221
Lake Saiful Malik 177
Lal Patthar 217
Lalazar Plateau 178
Landi Kotal 108

Langar 150
language 15, 293, 368, 382
Lawrencepur 93
Liachar Nala 202
liquor permits 77
Lok Virsa 73
Lowari Pass 120
Lower Hunza 268
   history 269
Lower Shani 217
Lower Shishkin 303
Lujhdur 313
Lulusar Lake 179
Lupdor 312
Lupgar Pir Pass 323
Lupgar Valley trek 323

M

Machilu 260
Madur Kushi 304
magazines 63
Mahandri 177
Maidun 318
Malakand Pass 118
Mamubar 304
Mani Camp 221
Mansehra 170
   directory 174
   eating 173
   sights 170
   sleeping 173
   transport 174
Maqbara Hakiman 93
Mardan 118
Margalla Hills 73
Margalla Pass 92
Masherbrum Base Camp 263
Massaga 119
Mastuj 143, 149
   sleeping 147, 160
Mastuj Village 143
Mazeno Base Camp 204
Mazeno High Camp 204
Mazeno La (Pass) 204
media 63
Melishkar 292
Miar Glacier 303
Minapin 273
   sleeping 278
   transport 279
   walks 276
Minapin Glacier 276
Mintaka Pass 331
Misgar 331
Moghlong 146
Moghulmirir 145
Mominabad 293
money 22
Mor Pagoda 350
Morkhon 318
Mount Kongur 340
mountains 374

Muchutshil Glacier trek 280
Muduri 154
Mulungutti Glacier 317
Murtazabad 277
Muslim League 365
Muztagh Ata 341

N

Nagar 1 300
   background 301
   sleeping 304
Nagar 2 268
   history 269
Nagar Khas 302
Nagar 121
   sleeping 122
Naltar 215
   sleeping 223
   transport 227
Naltar Pass 217
Naltar Valley 215
   treks 216
Naltar/Pakor Pass 217
Nanga Parbat 198, 199, 201, 204
Naran 177
   activities and tours 183
   directory 183
   shopping 183
   sleeping 181
   transport 183
Nasirabad 277
national parks 377
Nazimabad 297, 298
Nazir Sabir 320
New Sust 329
newspapers 63
Nicholson, John, Brig-Maj 92
Nilt 273
   battle of 275
Noh 153
Nowshera 94
   sleeping 94
Nuri Nar Gali 179
Nurpur Shahan 72

O

Old Sust 329
Oshikandas 219
Owir Pass Trek 141

P

Pabbi 94
Pakistan Museum of Natural History 74
Pakistani embassies 19
Pakor Pass 217
Pakora 157
Palas Valley 187
Pamiri 321

Panja Sahib Gurudwara 93
Panja Shah Ziarat 320
Paras 176
Pari 205
Partition 214
Passu 307
  short walks 309
  treks 311
Passu Gar 310, 311
Passu Glacier 308
Passu village 307
  eating 314
  sleeping 313
  transport 314
Pathans 98
Pattan 187
  sleeping 190
  transport 191
Patundas 313
permits 18, 19, 77
Peshawar 99
  activities and tours 113
  directory 116
  eating 111
  entertainment 112
  history 101
  Old City 102
  sights 106
  shopping 113
  sleeping 109
  tourist information 101
  transport 113
Peshawar Valley 95
  background 98
  people 98
Phandur 151, 152
  sleeping 160
Phandur Lake 152
Phari Phari 303
Pingul 152
Pirali 337
Pisin 277
plants 376
police 30
polo 149
post 62
Punial 159
Punji Pass trek 158
Purien-e-Ben 317

Q
Qasimabad 273
Qissa Khwani Bazaar 104

R
Radcliffe, Sir Cyril 366
radio 63
Rahimabad 270
Raikot Bridge 197 202
  sleeping 206
Rakaposhi south face trek 218

Rakaposhi/Diran base camp trek 274
  sleeping 278
Rakhan Gali (Pass) 220
Rama Lake
  sleeping 207
Ramadan 41
Raminj 320
Ratti Gali 179
Ravai Lake 321, 322
Rawal Lake 74
Rawalpindi 65, 83
  activities and tours 89
  directory 92
  eating 87
  entertainment 88
  history 85
  shopping 88
  sights 85
  sleeping 85
  transport 90
  reading 378
  religion 370
Reshit 321
Reshun 142
  sleeping 147
responsible tourism 30
restaurants 37
  See also under individual towns
Rewak 145
Rezgeen-e-Ben 317
rivers 375
road travel 32
rock art 197
Rumbur Valley 137
  sleeping 138
Rupal Valley trek 204
Rush Phari 303

S
Sacred Rocks of Hunza 297
Sadpara Lake and buddha 238
  sleeping 240
safety 29
Sahibabad 120
Saidpur Village 73
Saiful Malik Lake 177
Saio-daru-kush 272
Salmanabad 298
San Xian Caves 351
Sangemarmar Sar 276
Saral Gali 179
Saral Lake 179
Sarat 298
Sazin 189
Sekr Jerab 323
Shabbat 293
Shachmirk Pass 317
Shagai Fort 108
Shah Ghari 146
Shah Jinali Pass Trek 144

Shah Kamal Mosque 302
Shaikhanandeh 140
Shakarparian 73
Shalkuch 145
Shandar 280
Shandur Pass 149
  polo 149
  sleeping 160
Sharan 177
Shatial 193
  sleeping 205
  transport 207
Shayar 304
Shelmin 312
Shenote 160
Sher Qila 159
Sher-e-Sabz 321
Shewert 318
Shigar River Valley 248
  background 248
  treks 252
Shigar village 249, 254
Shigarthang Valley 248
Shimshal Pamir trek 317
Shimshal Valley 315
Shimshal village
  sleeping 319
  treks 317
Shina words and phrases 386
Shinkiari 171
  sleeping 173
Shinu 177
Shishkut 297, 298
Shishpar Glacier trek 279
  shopping 43
Shujerab 317
Shutmerg 321
Shuwe 272
Silpi 159
Singal 159
Skardu 235
  activities and tours 241
  directory 243
  eating 240
  shopping 241
  sights 237
  sleeping 239
  transport 242
Smugglers' Bazaar 106
Snow Lake 253
Sor Laspur 149
Sor Rich 146
South Jalipur Peak 201
Spandrinj 320
Spantik 293
Spantik Base Camp 303
sports and activities 44
student travellers 16
Subash Plateau 340
Sultanabad 292
Sumar Nala 189
Sumayar 304
Sumayar Bar 303

Sumayar Bar Glacier 303
Sust 320, 328, 329
  directory 336
  eating 335
  sleeping 334
  transport 335

T
Tagaphari 276
Tagh Arma Basin 340
Takht-e-Bhai 118
Taling 217
Tarashing 204
Tarbela 94
Tarbela Dam 94
Targeen 317
Tashkurgan 336, 339
  directory 345
  eating 343
  sights 340
  sleeping 343
  transport 344
Tatta Pani 197
Teru 151
Teru Bahach 160
Thakot Bridge 172, 186
  sleeping 173
Thal 120
Thalichi 202
Thalle la trek 256
Thaous 154
  sleeping 161
Thing Das 159
Thingai 152
Thole 273
Thore 194
Three Immortals Caves 351
Thui Pass 154
Tibet 351
Timargarha 120
  sleeping 121
  transport 122
Tirich Mir Base Camp 146
Tolibari 217
Toltar 272
Torboto Das 272
Torkham 108
Tourgat Pass 351
tourist offices 15
tour operators 14
train travel 31
transport 24, 31
  buses 32
  hitch-hiking 34
  jeeps 33
  trains 31
trekking 45
  See also under individual regions
trekking maps 49
Tupopdan 309
Turikho Valley 146

393

Twin suspension bridges 309

U
Uiygurs 345
Ultar 285
Ultar Glacier hike/trek 285
Ulugrabat Pass 340
University Town 106
Upper Chitral 140
Upper Hunza 305
Upper Naltar 215
Upper Shani 217
Urdu words and phrases 382
Urumqi 351

Uween-a-Ben 316
Uzantal 342

V
vaccinations 20, 55
vegetation 376
visas 17
Vween-e-Sar Pass 317

W
Wah Mogul Gardens 93
Wakhi words and phrases 385
walking permits 19
Wara 120
Werthum Pass 312
wildlife 45, 376

women travellers 16
  trekking 49
Wyeen Glacier 323

Y
Yagistan 193
Yangal 155
Yarkhun Valley 143
  sleeping 147
Yarzrich 320
Yashkist 145
Yashpirt 312
Yasin 153
  sleeping 161, 162
Yasin Fort 153
Yasin Valley 153
Yishkuk 323

Younghusband 315
Yunz Valley 311
Yunzbin 312
Yusup Khass Hajib 349

Z
Zagaro Pass 151
Zani Pass 146
Zarabad 309
Zardgarben 318
Ziarat 316
Zood Khun 320, 321
  sleeping 324
  trekking

Map index

A
Abbottabad 169
Altit 291

B
Baltistan 232, 233
Besham 186
Biafo-Hispar traverse 253

C
Central Hunza (including Hasanabad Nala &Ultar Nala treks) 280, 281
Chalt 271
Chalt, Chaprot Valley and Bar Valley 272
Chilas 194
Chitral to Gilgit 150, 151
Chitral town 125

D
Danyore, Bagrot & Haramosh Valleys 218, 219
Deosai Plateau 245
Diamar district and Gilgit sub-district 192, 193

F
Fairy Meadows, Nanga Parbat & the Astor Valley 198

G
Ganesh 294
Gilgit 210, 211
Gilgit centre 212, 213
Gojal (Upper Hunza) 305
Gulmit 307

H
Hazara 167
Hushe Valley 260

I
Indus Kohistan 185
Islamabad 72
Islamabad, Blue Area 74, 75
Islamabad-Rawalpindi overview 69

K
Kaghan Valley 176
Kalash Valleys 135
Karimabad 284
Kashgar 346, 347
Khapulu 257
Komila/Dasu 189

L
Lower Hunza, Nagar 2, Central Hunza & Nagar 1 268, 269
Lower Kaghan Valley 175

M
Mansehra 171

N
Nagar 1 300
Naltar Valley (including Daintar Pass and Naltar Pass treks) 216
Naran 178

O
Old Sust and New Sust (Afiyatabad) 329

P
Passu 308
Peshawar- Old City 102, 103
Peshawar overview 100, 101
Peshawar- Saddar Bazaar & Cantonment 104
Peshawar to Chitral (showing Swat Valley) 118
Peshawar- University Town 107

R
Rawalpindi, Cantonment 89
Rawalpindi, Rajah Bazaar/ Murree Road 84
Rawalpindi, Saddar 86
Rawalpindi/Islamabad to Peshawar 93

S
Shigar 249
Shimshal Valley & Shimshal Pamir 316, 317
Skardu 236, 237
Sust to Kashgar 332

T
Tashkurgan 339
Turikho Valley, Upper Yarkhun Valley, Karambar Valley (including treks from Yarkhun Valley to Yasin Valley and from Yasin Valley to Ishkoman Valley) 144, 145

U
Upper Chitral 142, 143
Upper Shigar Valley, Braldu Valley, Baltoro Glacier and Concordia 250, 251

W
Walks and treks around Passu and Sust (including Chapursan Valley) 310

Map symbols

Administration
- ▫ Capital city
- ○ Other city/town
- International border
- Regional border
- Disputed border

Roads and travel
- Motorway
- Main road
- Minor road
- 4WD track
- Footpath
- Railway with station
- ✈ Airport
- 🚌 Bus station
- Ⓜ Metro station
- Cable car
- Funicular
- Ferry

Water features
- River, canal
- Lake, ocean
- Seasonal marshland
- Beach, sand bank
- Waterfall

Topographical features
- Contours (approx)
- Mountain
- Volcano
- Mountain pass
- Escarpment
- Gorge
- Glacier
- Salt flat
- Rocks

Cities and towns
- Main through route
- Main street
- Minor street
- Pedestrianized street
- Tunnel
- → One way street

- Steps
- Bridge
- Fortified wall
- Park, garden, stadium
- Sleeping
- Eating
- Bars & clubs
- Entertainment
- Building
- Sight
- Cathedral, church
- Chinese temple
- Hindu temple
- Meru
- Mosque
- Stupa
- Synagogue
- Tourist office
- Museum
- Post office
- Police
- Bank
- Internet
- Telephone
- Market
- Hospital
- Parking
- Petrol
- Golf
- Detail map
- Related map

Other symbols
- Archaeological site
- National park, wildlife reserve
- Viewing point
- Campsite
- Refuge, lodge
- Castle
- Diving
- Deciduous/coniferous/palm trees
- Hide
- Vineyard
- Distillery
- Shipwreck
- Historic battlefield

Complete title listing

Footprint publishes travel guides to over 150 destinations worldwide. Each guide is packed with practical, concise and colourful information for everybody from first-time travellers to travel aficionados. The list is growing fast and current titles are noted below.
Available from all good bookshops and online at www.footprintbooks.com

(P) denotes pocket guide

Latin America and Caribbean
Argentina
Barbados (P)
Bolivia
Brazil
Caribbean Islands
Central America & Mexico
Chile
Colombia
Costa Rica
Cuba
Cusco & the Inca Trail
Dominican Republic
Ecuador & Galápagos
Guatemala
Havana (P)
Mexico
Nicaragua
Peru
Rio de Janeiro
South American Handbook
Venezuela

North America
Vancouver (P)
New York (P)
Western Canada

Africa
Cape Town (P)
East Africa
Libya
Marrakech (P)
Morocco
Namibia
South Africa
Tunisia
Uganda

Middle East
Dubai (P)
Egypt
Israel
Jordan
Syria & Lebanon

Australasia
Australia
East Coast Australia
New Zealand
Sydney (P)
West Coast Australia

Asia
Bali
Bangkok & the Beaches
Cambodia
Goa
Hong Kong (P)
India
Indian Himalaya
Indonesia
Laos
Malaysia
Nepal
Northern Pakistan
Pakistan
Rajasthan & Gujarat
Singapore
South India
Sri Lanka
Sumatra
Thailand
Tibet
Vietnam

Europe
Andalucía
Barcelona (P)
Berlin (P)
Bilbao (P)
Bologna (P)
Britain
Copenhagen (P)
Cardiff (P)
Croatia
Dublin
Dublin (P)
Edinburgh
Edinburgh (P)
England
Glasgow (P)
Ireland
Lisbon (P)
London
London (P)
Madrid (P)
Naples (P)
Northern Spain
Paris (P)
Reykjavík (P)
Scotland
Scotland Highlands & Islands
Seville (P)
Spain
Tallinn (P)
Turin (P)
Turkey
Valencia (P)
Verona (P)

Lifestyle guides
Surfing Europe

Also available:
Traveller's Handbook (WEXAS)
Traveller's Healthbook (WEXAS)
Traveller's Internet Guide (WEXAS)

Credits

Footprint credits
Text editor: Laura Dixon
Map editors: Sarah Sorensen, Jane Bevan
Picture editor: Kevin Feeney
Proofreader: Sarah Chatwin

Publisher: Patrick Dawson
Editorial: Alan Murphy, Sophie Blacksell, Sarah Thorowgood, Claire Boobbyer, Felicity Laughton, Davina Rungasamy
Cartography: Robert Lunn, Claire Benison, Kevin Feeney, Melissa Lin, Peter Cracknell.
Series development: Rachel Fielding
Design: Mytton Williams and Rosemary Dawson (brand)
Advertising: Debbie Wylde
Finance and administration: Sharon Hughes, Elizabeth Taylor

Photography credits
Front cover: Sheep herding, Matthieu Paley
Back cover: Gircha carving, Matthieu Paley
Inside: Matthieu Paley, Dave Winter (image 3, page 7)

Print
Manufactured in Italy by LegoPrint
Pulp from sustainable forests

Footprint feedback
We try as hard as we can to make each Footprint guide as up to date as possible but, of course, things always change. If you want to let us know about your experiences – good, bad or ugly – then don't delay, go to **www.footprintbooks.com** and send in your comments.

Publishing information
Footprint Northern Pakistan
1st edition
© Footprint Handbooks Ltd
July 2004
ISBN 1 904777 06 6

CIP DATA: A catalogue record for this book is available from the British Library

® Footprint Handbooks and the Footprint mark are a registered trademark of Footprint Handbooks Ltd

Published by Footprint
6 Riverside Court
Lower Bristol Road
Bath BA2 3DZ, UK
T +44 (0)1225 469141
F +44 (0)1225 469461
discover@footprintbooks.com
www.footprintbooks.com

Distributed in the USA by
Publishers Group West

All rights reserved. No part of this publication may be reproduced, stored in a retrieval system, or transmitted, in any form or by any means, electronic, mechanical, photocopying, recording, or otherwise without the prior permission of Footprint Handbooks Ltd.

Neither the black and white nor colour maps are intended to have any political significance.

Every effort has been made to ensure that the facts in this guidebook are accurate. However, travellers should still obtain advice from consulates, airlines etc about travel and visa requirements before travelling. The authors and publishers cannot accept responsibility for any loss, injury or inconvenience however caused.

Acknowledgements

First of all I would like to thank Ian Large for sharing the research workload, and for bringing such humour to NWFP and Baltistan. A special word must also go to my Pakistan Handbook colleague Ivan Mannheim, who was unable to work on this particular project (though I'm sure that the arrival of Joseph was more than ample compensation for you and Klair).

The researchers of this guide do not accept freebies in exchange for positive recommendations. That said, there are a number of hotel owners in the north of Pakistan who have become such good friends over the years, it's always a real hassle to get them to accept payment for my stay. This is particularly the case at the Madina Hotel in Gilgit, the Diran Guesthouse in Minapin, and the Kisar Inn/Eagle's Nest in Altit/Duicar. All three do receive good reviews in this Handbook, though I have no doubt that these are honestly earnt.

Praise too, for Mohammed Yaqoob of Gilgit, who has been such a good friend all these years; keep at it Yaqoob, there are a lot of travellers out there who appreciate all your hard work. Hospitality and entertainment beyond the call of duty was provided by Israr Hussein of Minapin, Ali Madad of Altit and Rehmat Nabi at Fairy Meadows. I'm also grateful to Mirza Baig, Altaf Hussain and Karim Mutrib, who between them always had a funny story to tell or an answer to my queries, whilst Ifti Hussain and Rowena Newberry opened my eyes to all things Ganesh.

Researching this Handbook presented me with one of my best ever trips to Pakistan, and I'd particularly like to mention some of the people that I met along the way. Brian Sommerville (star of the 1974 FA Cup Final); Mareile Obersteiner and Matthieu Paley (the latter having taken the best photos of Pakistan I've ever seen, and used in this guide); Simone Carignani, polo expert and Chapursan Valley fan; Max, the Polish TV star; Tom, Sandy, Jacob and Richard, for the introduction to the Qi Par Disco Bar in Kashgar; Jordan Levy, undercover Israeli in Pakistan; Jordan Van Voast, for such a moving Tibet travelogue; Akhtar Hussain, for being such a laugh. I'd also like to thank all those who wrote or emailed suggestions and recommendations about the Pakistan Handbook, although special credit must go to Christine and Malcolm Clark (www.kiwisonbikes.com) and Tim Tucker ('the Coventry proof-reader'). I'd also like to pay tribute to my long-term travelling companion, my eight year old copy of French In Three Months, which has now made five visits with me to Pakistan without ever getting out of my backpack.

Finally, this Handbook would not have been possible without the love and consideration of my wife Laurence, who proved such a fantastic single-parent to our daughters Amélie and Chloé whilst I was away on Handbook duty.

Ian Large would like to thank:

Ian Large would like to thank the following for their help, friendship and advice: Abbas Ali, AKCSP, for helpful and detailed information about AKCSP renovation projects in Baltistan; Salah-ud-Din, Assistant Tourism Officer, PTDC, Peshawar, for providing honest and accurate information about the city and its environs; Craig Dunlop, Adelaide, for his dodgy altimeter, Ozzy wit, for being 'doctor on call' and for not mentioning The Ashes!; Ali Haider Sadpara, Skardu, for information on trekking routes in Baltistan; Gareth Howard, Bristol, for his advice on the geology of the Chitral to Gilgit route, for trekking notes and for being an excellent travelling companion; S.F. Rauf Jan, Dir, for helpful hints and advice; Mumtaz Hussein, PTDC, Chitral, for doing his job; Agha Muhammad, Tourism Officer, PTDC, Skardu, for doing much of my research in advance and for sharing it with me; Ghulam Murtaza, Skardu, for background information regarding the Deosai Plateau ; Hamid-ur-Rahman & friend,

Mastuj, for giving me a quick-fire tour of Mastuj in fading light, despite the long walk which nearly killed me!; Haidar Ali Shah, Chitral, for useful background information; Syed Harir Shah, Chitral, for being a good friend and guide, and for providing his services when he must have had many more important things to do!; Mohabat Shefi Bhai, Gilgit, for being an excellent driver and for returning my life intact having entrusted it to him for 4 days across the Shandur Pass; Siraj & Ghazala ul-Mulk, Chitral, for being the perfect hosts and for imparting good background information about the Chitral area; Dave Winter & Ivan Mannheim, Europe, for 'metalling the road'! Last, but not least, to Anna Kartalski, Antwerp for putting up with another long absence and for watching me toil for hours at the computer, playing pinball when I should have been writing!

Northern Pakistan

Altitude in metres
Glacier
8000
5000
4000
3000
2000
1000
0
Sand dune
Neighbouring Country

- International road
- Major road
- Minor road
- Other road
- Unsurfaced road
- – – – International boundary
- – · – Disputed boundary
- ······ Provincial boundary
- ▲ Mountain

④ Kashgar (Kashi), Taklamakan Desert, Shufu, Upal, XINJIANG UYGHUR AUTONOMOUS REGION, Pamir Range, Ghez, KKH, Kara Kuli Lake, CHINA, Karasul, Tashkurgan

② TAJIKISTAN

③ CHINA

AFGHANISTAN

Afiyatabad, Zhunza, Karimabad, Minapin, Sikanderabad, Chalt, Rakaposhi (7,789m), Karakoram Range, Mt Goodwin Austen (K2) (8,611m), Baltoro Glacier, Area claimed by Pakistan

Gakuch, Gupis, Gilgit, Shigar, Skardu, Baltistan, GILGIT AGENCY, Chilas, Nanga Parbat (8,125m), Deosai Plateau

Shandur Pass

① NORTH WEST FRONTIER PROVINCE

Komila/Dasu, Besham

INDIA, JAMMU AND KASHMIR

Dir, Khanju, Mansehra, Muzaffarabad, AZZAD KASHMIR, Abbottabad, Haripur, Murree, Khaur, Malakand, Hasan Abdal, ISLAMABAD, Mardan, Attock Khurd, Wah, Rawalpindi, Charsadda, Nowshera, Attock City, Grand Trunk Road, Jhelum, Khyber Pass, Peshawar, PUNJAB, Jhelum River, Landi Kotal, Indus River

0 km 30
0 miles 30

The Government of Pakistan state that "the accession of Jammu & Kashmir to Pakistan or India remains to be decided by U.N. plebiscite"

The Government of India state that "the external boundaries of India are neither correct nor authenticated"

Map 1

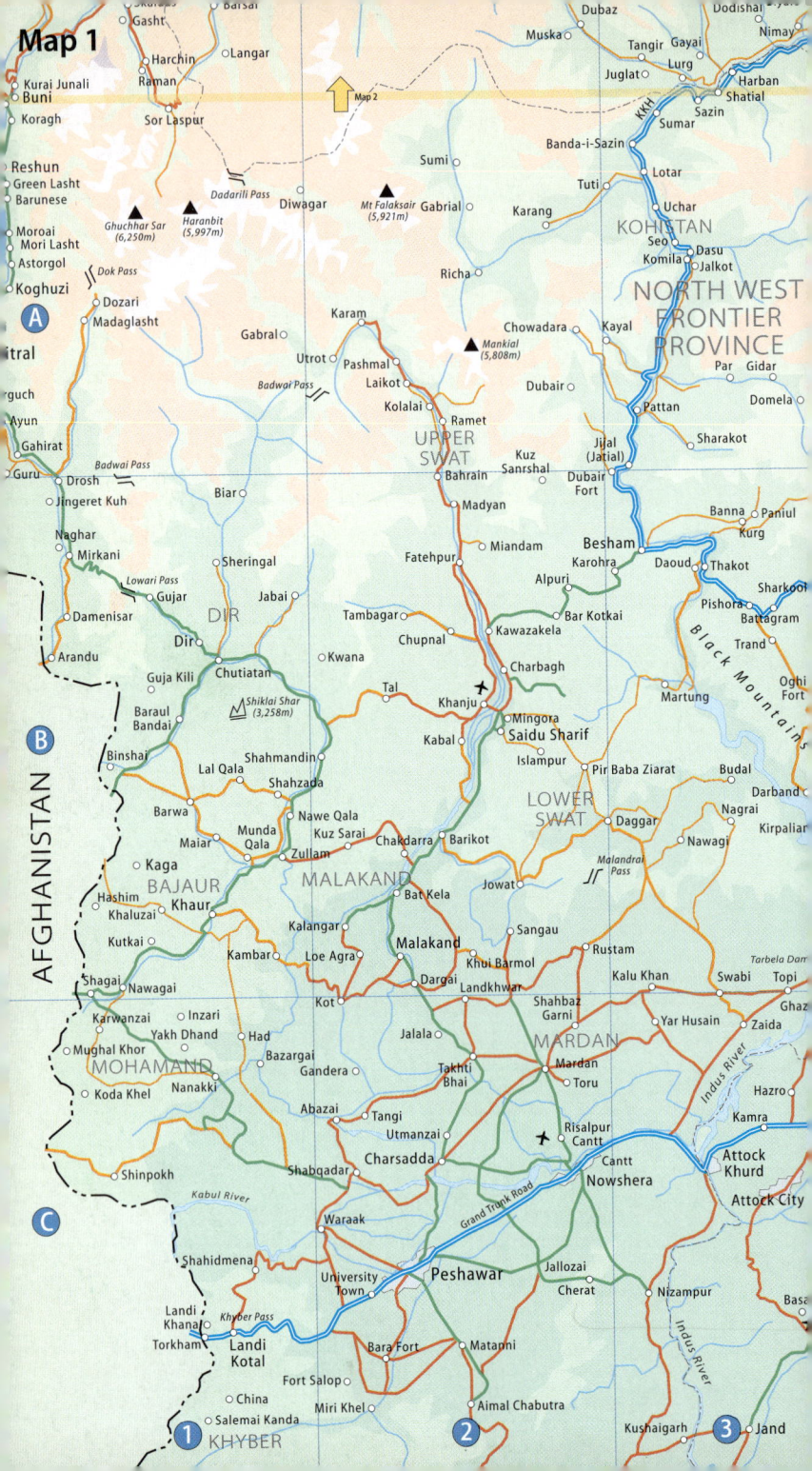

Thak Wat
Bunar
DIAMIR
Chilas
Thore
Thak
Niat
Chochargah
Babusar
Babusar Pass
Burzil
Minimarg
Kamri
Gittidas
Lake Lulusar
Besal
Gumot
Kel
Great Himalaya
A
Samgam
Jhalkhand
Shardi
Burawai
Battakundi
Lalazar Plateau
Doarian
INDIA
0 km 10
0 miles 10
Naran
Lake Saiful Muluk
Thod Gali Pass
Sukai Peak (4,761m)
Malika Parbat (5,290m)
Kaghan
Jared
Khanian
Patian
JAMMU AND KASHMIR
Shinu
Sharan
Paras
Kawai
Shogran
MANSEHRA
Dadar
Balakot
AZZAD KASHMIR
Maharaj Gund
Chattar Plain
Dasiabad
Shinkiara
Ahl
Dhodial
Muzaffarabad
Chakothi
Baffa
Garhi Habibullah
Halian
Garhi
Kahuta
B
Mansehra
Asoka Rocks
Phulra
KKH
Thandiana
Konala
The Government of Pakistan state that "the accession of Jammu & Kashmir to Pakistan or India remains to be decided by U.N. plebiscite"
The Government of India state that "the external boundaries of India are neither correct nor authenticated"
Nawan Sheher
Nathia Gali
Rawala Kot
Hajira
Sherwan
Dungagali
Ayubia
Abbottabad
Bhurban
Sehra
Murree
Havelian
ABBOTTABAD
Patriala
Tarbela Reservoir
Bagra
Lora
Kotli
Charrapani
Haripur
Sensa
Bhagpur Dheri
Chattar
Sambli Lake
Khanpur Lake
Nar
Chhochh
Margalla Hills
Hasan Abdal
Faizabad
Islamabad Airport
Kahuta
ISLAMABAD
Rawalpindi
Chauk Pandon
Hil
Wah
Mangla Reservoir
Margalla Pass
Riwat
Mankiala
New Mirpur
Mandra
Mangla
Pandori
Gujar Khan
GT Road
C
Fatahjang
Gobindput
Jhelum
Dina
PUNJAB
Jhelum River
Dudyal
Rasul
4
5
6

Map 2

TAGDUMBASH
(SARIKOL) PAMIR

CHINA

○ Davdar

○ Beyik ○ Pirali

Kunlun Shan Range

Khunjerab Pass
(4,934m)

○ Koksil ○ Pidakkesh
KKH
Chapchingal Pass

Khunjerab National Park

○ Chindrikit

Shimsal Pass
(4,620m)

Chat Purt
(5,569m) ○ Shujerab

Needle Peak

○ Uchiloo
High Needle
(5,995m)

Little Karakoram Range

Baraldu Glacier

▲ Karun Koh
(6,977m)

○ Afiyatabad
○ Sust
○ Gulsha
Karun Pir Pass
○ Morkhon ○ Ziarat ○ Shimshal
○ Dut
○ Khaibur
Tupopdan
(6,106m)

▲ Little K2

Yazghil
(5,993m)

○ Yashpirt
Batura Glacier
Passu P
(7,284m) ○ Passu
▲ Shisper ○ Hussaini
(7,611m) ○ Ghulkin
6000 Ultar ○ Gulmit
Atabad (5,185m)
Babulingmating
○ Karimabad ○ Nazimabad
○ Ganesh ○ Ahmedabad
○ Haiderabad ○ Hispar
○ Aliabad ○ Nagar ○ Hoper ○ Huru
○ Murtazabad Barpu Glacier Rush Lake
○ Nasirabad
○ Jafarabad ○ Minapin ▲ Spantik
○ Gulmet (7,024m)
○ Sikanderabad
GILGIT
▲ Rakaposhi ▲ Myar
(7,789m) (6,824m)

Lupghar Sar
(7,199m)
Distaghil Sar
(7,885m)
Khanjut Sar
(7,760m)
Trivor Yukshin Sar
(7,783m) (7,530m)
Khinyang
Chhish
(7,852m)
Makhrong
Chhish
(6,607m)

Choktoi Glacier

Hispar Pass
Biafo Glacier

Karakoram Range

▲ Trango Towers

○ Arandu

Chogolungma Glacier

▲ Malubiting
(7,454m)
Haramosh Pass
Haramosh II
(7,405m)

○ Hurimal

○ Dassu ○ Gor
○ Mango ○ Kashumal
○ Tissar ○ Alchori
○ Baricha ○ Soro
○ Bagicka SKARDU
○ Marsha Kala ○ Shigar
(5,569m)
○ Kachura

○ Dorchan ○ Barche ○ Goor
○ Chirah ○ Isekere
○ Balla Rahimabad ○ Farpu ○ Dassu
○ Nomal ○ Hunuchal ○ Sassi ○ Stak
○ Jutal ○ Sinakkar ○ Yulbo ○ Tinko ○ Tuar
○ Sultanabad ○ Jalatabad ○ Gangi ○ Tuar Paeen
○ Danyore ○ Shangus ○ Bilamik ○ Ronde
○ Jutial ○ Sakwar ○ Buachi (Mendi) ○ Basho
○ Baseen ○ Gilgit
Khomar Pass ○ Damot ○ Jaglot
○ Pahot ○ Hurkus ○ Bunji Cantt ○ Buni
○ Gashu ○ Thalichi ○ Muskhir
KKH ○ Harchu

○ Skardu
○ Sadpara ○ Dechingpa
○ Shigarthang
Dari Pass
○ Katisho Pass

GILGIT AGENCY

○ Gor ○ Jalipur ○ Tato
○ Gomas Fairy Meadows □ ○ Chorit
○ Duro ○ Dusi ○ Beyal Chongra Peak ○ Gurikot ○ Gudai
○ Seri ○ Gunar Farm (6,829m) ○ Rampur
○ Thalpan ○ Bunar Das Tarashing ○ Chilam
○ Hudor ○ Gass ▲ Nanga Parbat ○ Rupal ○ Rattu Gantt
○ Thak Wat (8,125m)
○ Thore ○ Chilas ○ Bunar
DIAMIR
○ Thak
○ Niat

○ Astor
○ Rama

Trango Pir Pass

Deosai Plateau

Chhachor Pass

Burzil Pass
○ Burzil

Map 3

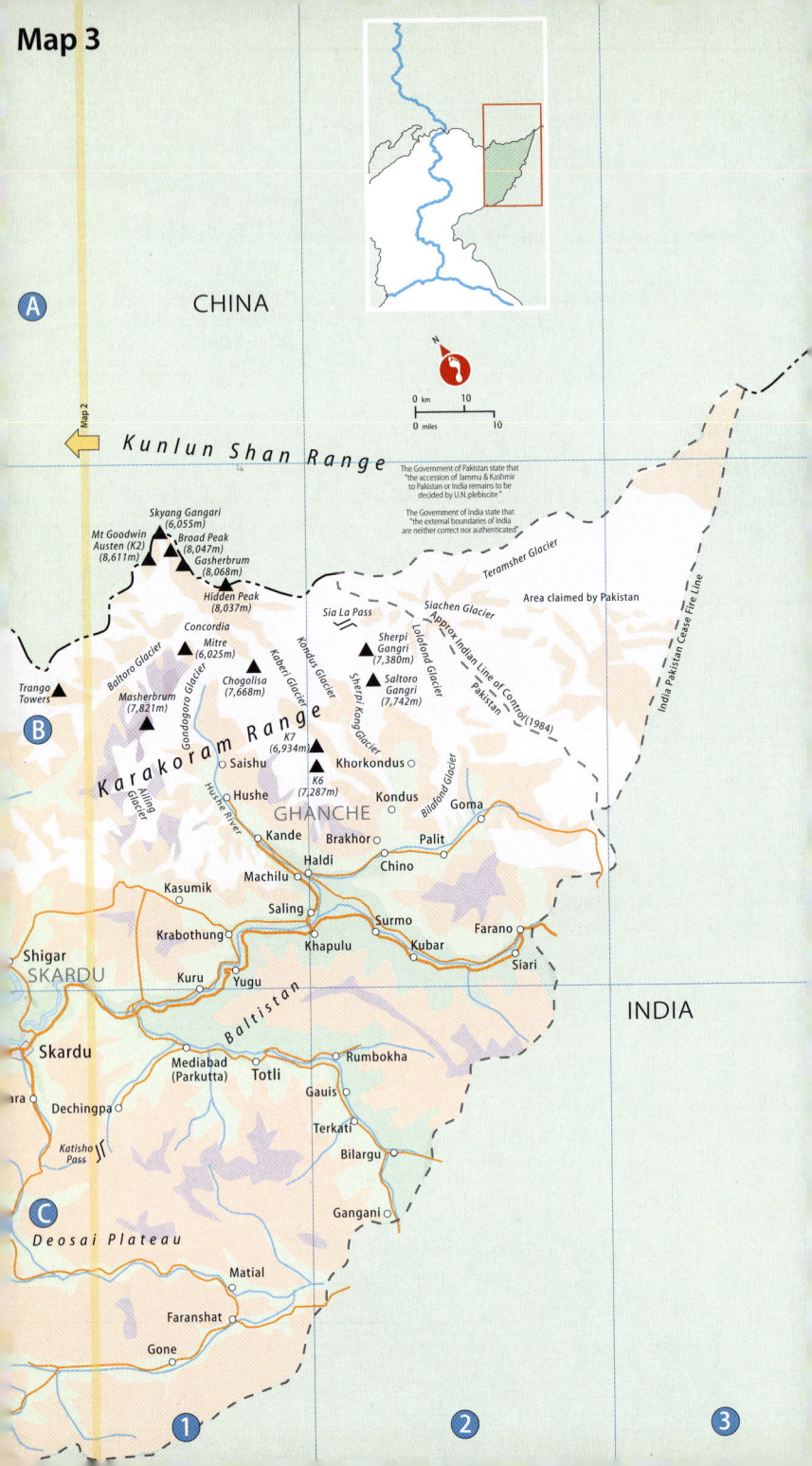

CHINA

Kunlun Shan Range

← Map 2

"The Government of Pakistan state that 'the accession of Jammu & Kashmir to Pakistan or India remains to be decided by U.N. plebiscite'"

"The Government of India state that 'the external boundaries of India are neither correct nor authenticated'"

Skyang Gangari (6,055m)
Mt Goodwin Austen (K2) (8,611m)
Broad Peak (8,047m)
Gasherbrum (8,068m)
Hidden Peak (8,037m)

Teramsher Glacier

Sia La Pass
Siachen Glacier
Area claimed by Pakistan
Approx Indian Line of Control (1984)
Pakistan

Concordia
Mitre (6,025m)
Sherpi Gangri (7,380m)
Saltoro Gangri (7,742m)

Baltoro Glacier
Kondus Glacier
Lolofond Glacier

Trango Towers
Chogolisa (7,668m)
Koberi Glacier
Sherpi Kong Glacier

India Pakistan Cease Fire Line

Masherbrum (7,821m)

Karakoram Range

Gondogoro Glacier

K7 (6,934m)
K6 (7,287m)

Saishu
Khorkondus

Aling Glacier
Hushe
Kondus
Bilafond Glacier
Goma

Hushe River
Kande
Brakhor
Palit
Haldi
Chino
Machilu
GHANCHE

Kasumik
Saling
Surmo
Farano
Krabothung
Khapulu
Kubar
Siari

Shigar
Kuru
Yugu
SKARDU

Skardu
Baltistan

Mediabad (Parkutta)
Totli
Rumbokha

Dechingpa
Gauis

Katisho Pass
Terkati
Bilargu

Gangani

Deosai Plateau

INDIA

Matial

Faranshat

Gone

Map 4

For a different view of Europe, take a Footprint

Superstylish travel guides – perfect for short break addicts.
Harvey Nichols magazine

Discover so much more...
Listings driven, forward looking and up to date. Focuses on what's going on right now.
Contemporary, stylish, and innovative approach, providing quality travel information.